2.1 May 1983

Dear Harry,

This is Just a small token of my love to you

DYNASTY
The New York Yankees 1949–1964

& Since you See to be the only one in my life Connected with the Big League's I thought maybe you might enjoy it Some day you Just might be Playing in the World Series

Best Luck always

Your Housekeeper
Pearl

DYNASTY

The New York Yankees 1949–1964

by

PETER GOLENBOCK

Prentice-Hall, Inc., *Englewood Cliffs, N.J.*

Printed in the United States of America
Prentice-Hall International, Inc., London
Prentice-Hall of Australia, Pty. Ltd., Sydney
Prentice-Hall of Canada, Ltd., Toronto
Prentice-Hall of India Private Ltd., New Delhi
Prentice-Hall of Japan, Inc., Tokyo

10 9 8 7 6 5 4 3

Library of Congress Cataloging in Publication Data

Golenbock, Peter
Dynasty: the New York Yankees, 1949-1964.

1. New York (City). Baseball club (American League)
—History. 2. Baseball. I. Title.
GV875.N4G64   796.357'64'097471   75-4705
ISBN 0-13-222208-6 pbk.

To my wonderful family, Mom and Dad and Rob and Wen,
inspirations all; and to Puppa, wherever you
and your magical dreams may be.

CONTENTS

INTRODUCTION

Many baseball fans around the country are bitter about the New York Yankees purchasing free agents Catfish Hunter, Don Gullett, and Reggie Jackson, three of the top performers in the game, for a king's ransom. I, however, am not one of those fans. I think it's great. And if the Yankees could buy Joe Morgan, Cesar Cedeno, and Vida Blue, well, shell out the money George Steinbrenner, because we diehard Yankee fans don't care how we win games and pennants so long as we win them.

It has been this way since Jacob Ruppert owned the club in the 1920s. That was the period when Boston Red Sox owner Harry Frazee was in financial difficulty. Frazee produced plays, and his productions were losing bundles of money, so Ruppert, bless his heart, to keep Frazee afloat purchased Frazee's greatest stars including Hall of Fame pitchers Waite Hoyt and Herb Pennock, pitching stars Carl Mays, and Joe Bush, catcher Wally Schang, shortstop Everett Scott, and a pitcher-outfielder named Ruth, George Herman. Also, when Red Sox general manager Ed Barrow realized his ship was sinking under him, he jumped to the Yankees. Pennants followed in abundance. Do you think Ruppert cared that he had stripped the Red Sox?

Ruppert, the owner of the Knickerbocker Brewery, was a rich man, and he was a competitor. It was he who so perfectly exemplified the Yankees' arrogance of power. Ruppert once described his idea of a perfect afternoon at Yankee Stadium: "It's when the Yankees score eight runs in the first inning, and slowly pull away."

For millions of Yankee fans since the 1920s such a game was likewise their perfect afternoon. From my earliest remembrances in the early 1950s to 1964, it was mine as well. In the sixteen-season span from 1949 to 1964 the New York Yankees won fourteen pennants, a victorious dynasty unparalleled in the history of baseball.

Casey Stengel won ten pennants in twelve years. His successor, Ralph Houk, won three out of three. And Houk's successor, Yogi Berra, won a pennant the one year he managed. Rooting for the Yankees was indeed like rooting for U. S. Steel. This book is about those Stengel-Houk-Berra years and what I discovered about the people who made the dynasty what it was.

And now, after more than a decade of famine, thanks to owner George Steinbrenner's extravagance and to general manager Gabe Paul's shrewd trading, the Yankees are back on top. And for some irrational reason, this makes me deliriously happy.

Steinbrenner runs his business the same way Barrow used to, with a single-mindedness toward one objective—to win. For some owners, their baseball team is a tax loss. It's been said that some owners are loath to finish above .500, for if their teams should improve, then the fans would come to expect excellence, and owners would be forced to pay higher salaries. To Steinbrenner, and to me, this makes no sense. Steinbrenner was smart enough to understand how quickly a winning Yankee team could generate big dollars, so he spent the money, and I with thousands of others will come flocking to the Stadium opening day and on many other days during the season to come.

Do you think we can win ten years in a row, George?

When I was growing up in upper-middle-class suburbia, I attended private school, belonged to a country club, all my friends were white, and I rooted for the Yankees. Which only figured. I felt that the Dodgers and Giants were supported by a different kind of person—the blue-collar masses of the Bronx, Queens, and Brooklyn—and that somehow they were different from the Yankees and me. Later I found out that bank presidents rooted for the Dodgers and Bowery derelicts wore Yankee caps. But in many minds the powerful Yankees were seen to be the embodiment of the Establishment—a fantastically successful corporation with everyone from the owners down to the batboys working together for the good of the firm. If you weren't willing to submerge your individuality and conform to the aristocratic Yankee mold, unless you had the talent of a Mickey Mantle, you were not welcome into the Yankee family. Thus when I was growing up, no Yankee player was as publicly outspoken as Jackie Robinson of the Dodgers, and no Yankee player appeared to be a flake in the class of Billy Loes of the Dodgers, a pitcher who before a Yankee-Dodger world series predicted that the Yankees would win.

General manager George Weiss and his predecessor, Ed Barrow, two aristocrats themselves, set the tone for the Yankee image. Weiss and Barrow were serious and solemn, and they wanted their Yankee players to be as undemonstrative and conservative as they were themselves. To Dodger and Giant fans, who hated the Yankees and bitterly resented their success, the Yankees appeared methodical and impersonal. Except for Babe Ruth, a legend whose personality transcended even the strict Yankee image, and not until the final years of Mickey Mantle's career, was a Yankee player loved for his personality as much as he was respected for his individual excellence. Lou Gehrig and Joe DiMaggio, flawless performers, were not players the fans could ever warm up to, but they were certainly people who were proficient at winning, and winning, and winning again.

And I guess, to be honest, all that winning made some of us Yankee fans not only complacent, but perhaps arrogant at times. I can remember so vividly a game in the mid-1960s in which Joe Pepitone hit a grand-slam home run in the first inning against the Boston Red Sox in the Stadium. I gleefully turned to my college roommate, a Beantowner, and said, "I really hope your relief pitchers are better than the bum who started." They weren't though, and the fans in the park reveled through a thoroughly delightful afternoon as the Yankee base runners mercilessly circled the bases.

Between 1964 and 1976, the fortunes of the New York club plummetted badly. And though the team won a pennant in 1976, nevertheless many Yankee fans still speak fondly of their old stars as the "real Yankees," players like DiMaggio and Mantle, Yogi Berra and Allie Reynolds, Whitey Ford, Billy Martin, Roger Maris, Bobby Richardson and Tony Kubek, Phil Rizzuto and Gil McDougald. These men still live, and thrive, in the minds and hearts of millions of Yankee fans. I go to the Stadium and wonder why number 1 isn't at second base, why number 7 isn't batting fourth and playing centerfield, and why number 16, that cagey left-hander with the wicked move to first, isn't on the mound. I ache for the success of the old Yankees. So, I suspect, do millions of others, both in Yankee Stadium suburbia and thousands of miles away from it: people who in their youth traded away ten Rocky Colavito baseball cards or the entire St. Louis Browns team for one card of "the Mick," or who sat in the enervating heat of a July afternoon to watch Roger Maris pursue Babe Ruth's unbreakable record, or others who, around a hearth during the dead of winter, plotted trades with the Kansas City Athletics which would further solidify the Yankee position for the coming spring.

I can remember the thrill of taking the New Haven Railroad from Stamford to Grand Central Station, racing for the Woodlawn-Jerome subway on the Lexington Avenue line, and then making my way to the front car where I stood enthralled as the dimly lit tracks and pillars rushed toward me until finally the train emerged from the darkness onto the elevated tracks, the majestic Yankee Stadium suddenly appearing bigger than life beside the station at 161st Street.

Outside the Stadium thousands of people milled about, many waiting on line to buy tickets from gruff ticket sellers standing inside ornate red kiosks with vertical bars across a small opening. As I grew older I learned that if I tipped the ticket man a buck, I could even get box seats near the field. It was worth the extra dollar. Inside, I would watch batting practice, and I would wait in expectation for Bob Sheppard, the St. John's professor, to orate the line up over the echoing loudspeaker. "Now batting in the first position," Sheppard would begin, and no matter how often I went it was still a magical moment, and I would cheer lustily for each Yankee performer as Sheppard continued through the order, his voice an integral part of the special Yankee Stadium atmosphere.

And once the team took the field, no team ever played baseball as superbly as those Yankees.

This book is my attempt to describe the circumstances which produced the 1949-1964 dynasty and the players who performed then—as it really was and as they really were. I have interviewed around ninety ex-players, former executives, and present executives, traveling 27,000 miles over two years to garner material in order to be able to tell this story. I have interviewed in depth almost all of the players involved, and from their accounts I have been able to learn of the events of the period and the personalities of the players. Interviewing a player and twenty-five or more of his teammates gives one an excellent idea of what that player was really like.

I looked up to and emulated these athletes when I was a boy, and nothing I have discovered has or ever will change my attitude toward them, for it is one that has enriched my life and allowed me to transcend the realities of everyday existence. This, then, is not an exposé, but rather a tribute to these Yankees as they really were—and are. What I have attempted to do is separate the baseball-card fantasy from the reality, trying to couch those personal frailties which I have encountered with compassion, not rationalizations.

I was happy to find that unlike many of the Dodger players in Roger Kahn's *The Boys of Summer*, there is very little sense of personal sadness among the ex-Yankees, except for the retired athlete's natural longing for lost youth and wasted opportunity. Playing baseball was something most of these men loved as much as anything else in their lives, and when their careers ended, each of them left a little piece of themselves on the Stadium diamond and on diamonds across the country, a piece that no amount of civilian success could ever replace. Some have left a little piece. Most have left more. This book, then, is the sum total of all those pieces left behind.

Peter Golenbock
Englewood, N.J.

In Memoriam

Dan Topping
Del Webb
George Weiss
Casey Stengel
Red Rolfe
George Stirnweiss
Fritz Brickell
Jim Konstanty
Duke Maas
Jimmy Cannon
Arthur Daley
Milton Gross
Lenny Shecter
Ed Sohn
Rudy Guliani
Dr. Oscar Carp

"Happiness is the full use of your powers along the lines of excellence."
—President John F. Kennedy quoting from the Greek.

"The only real game in the world, I think, is baseball. You've got to start from way down, at the bottom, when you're six or seven years old. You've got to let it grow up with you."
—Babe Ruth, Yankee Stadium Farewell Speech,
June 13, 1948.

PROLOGUE

The Hiring of Casey Stengel

The New York Yankees were completing the final week of the 1948 season in pennant contention despite the retirements of pitchers Spud Chandler and Bill Bevens and even though outfield star Joe DiMaggio was playing with painful bone spurs on his heels and had developed constricting bursitis. Manager Bucky Harris had done a masterful job of manipulating his players and keeping the team's morale high all season. But Harris and general manager George Weiss were not seeing eye to eye, and their differences had become more pronounced, their icy conversations more acrimonious as the season wore on.

Manager Harris held a loose rein over his players, who were relaxed and enjoying the season. A few of the gayer blades were partying until the late hours, but Bucky felt that their free time was not his concern, though it did perturb Weiss who secretly put private detectives on the players to keep a record of their late-night activities. Frank Shea and Joe Page, stars in '47 but undependables this year, particularly offended Weiss who felt that their lack of success was a result of their disregard for curfew and Harris's laxity.

When Ed Sullivan reported in his *Little Old New York* column that detectives, including females, had been following the Yankees and that one of the players had become ''close'' friends with a female detective, Weiss was chagrined. Harris and many of his players were furious with Weiss. Later, when Weiss showed Harris the reports and ordered him to read them to the players in the clubhouse, Harris did so, but in a light vein. The esteem in which Harris was held by his players rose, but the chasm between him and Weiss grew wider.

Another disagreement arose between the two men when Harris kept insisting that Weiss elevate Newark pitching star Bob Porterfield to bolster the Yankee staff. Weiss didn't think the kid was ready for the majors, and he also didn't want to weaken his successful Newark franchise by bringing Porterfield up. After two months of Harris's badgering, Weiss finally capitulated against his better judgment. Bolstered by the early excellence of Porterfield, the Yankees played flawless ball in late August and early September. They raced toward the top and finally caught Cleveland and onrushing Boston during the final week of the season. The three teams battled for the pennant right down to the final two games. When the Sox defeated the Yankees twice in those two games, they tied Cleveland for the pennant and knocked New York out. Porterfield lost the second game.

Weiss was already planning for '49 before the season was over, and Harris did not enter into those plans. He would have been out even if the Yankees had won the pennant. Former general manager Ed Barrow had chosen Joe McCarthy, a compatible manager; Larry MacPhail had chosen Harris, a man with whom he worked well; and now new general manager Weiss wanted a manager to suit his own specifications. Weiss wanted a manager who would come to the ball park early and work with the young kids who were coming up. Harris had always had an unlisted telephone number, and away from the ball park, no one could reach him. Weiss wanted a manager who would be available at all times.

On October 6, the day Cleveland defeated the Red Sox in their one-game play-off to win the 1948 American League pennant, Weiss and Yankee owners Dan Topping and Del Webb held a press conference to announce that Harris's contract had not been renewed. This surprised the Yankee players who had been fond of Bucky, and shocked Harris who thought he had done an excellent job under the circumstances, which he had. "It was like being socked in the head with a steel pipe," Harris told the sympathetic press. Some writers felt that Harris had been fired because he still remained friends with Larry Mac-Phail after MacPhail had been ousted as Yankee general manager. He had been, but that was not the reason he was fired. Harris later went on to manage Washington for five years, and Detroit for two—his teams never finishing higher than fifth. With Harris gone, the MacPhail influence was now completely eradicated.

Less than a week after Harris was fired, the Yankees held another press conference and named their new manager. He was an old man, with deep lines crisscrossing his pliable face, and on his cheeks, pronounced creases which flowed toward a jutting jaw. He had palm-leaf ears and a broad nose, and his legs angled oddly, and when he talked he waved his arms and made exaggerated gestures. He looked comical, like an elderly gnome, though the New York sportswriters were not amused. He had been a National League manager since 1934, and never a very successful one in the nine years he managed Brooklyn and the Boston Braves. His reputation was one of a clown, not that of an astute handler of men. The old man was Casey Stengel.

Weiss had known Stengel for many years, going back to the Eastern League in the mid-1920s. Webb and Stengel, both West Coast residents, had also been acquainted for years, with Webb hiring Stengel to manage the Yankees' Kansas City farm team in 1945. Kansas City didn't finish very high that year, because while the majors were weak from wartime attrition, the minors were even weaker, and with Stengel leading a team so woefully thin that the second-baseman was a left-hander, Webb had nevertheless been impressed with Stengel's interest in teaching his players and working with them as well as his ability to maneuver his limited forces. A year later Milwaukee hired Stengel, and he led the team to the American Association pennant, and when he was fired after the Milwaukee management changed hands, Webb and Weiss helped him land the manager's job at Oakland in the Pacific Coast League. At Oakland in 1948 Stengel led "Nine Old Men" to the club's first Pacific Coast League pennant since 1921. Webb and Weiss then hired him to manage the Yankees.

Charles Dillon Stengel was born in Kansas City in 1890, or maybe 1889, or possibly even earlier, though no one knows for sure. After graduating from high school he enrolled in Western Dental College in Kansas City for two and a half years, but an Aurora, Illinois, professional team scouted and signed him, and he never did complete his studies. While playing for Aurora, Stengel was discovered by a Brooklyn Dodger scout, and after the Dodgers bought him, he joined the team a year later in 1912. He was a regular Dodger outfielder for the next five years.

While still a Dodger, Stengel injured his arm in spring training of 1914, and while incapacitated, agreed to coach baseball at the University of Mississippi for a few weeks when his old high-school coach, who had become the UMiss athletic director, asked him to help out. Stengel was appointed a full professor for his short stay at UMiss. Casey returned to his Dodger team just as spring training ended, but his nickname, the Professor, remained with him the rest of his career. In later years he became known as the Old Professor, or Perfessor.

Stengel, however, did not have the demeanor of a professor. He was a hard-nosed brawler who loved his likker. After one late-night bar brawl engaged in by Stengel and a half-dozen other Dodgers, Brooklyn owner Charlie Ebbets asked, "What kind of hoodlums do we have on this club?" But though Stengel preferred to spend his evenings on the town rather than keeping minister's hours, the rowdy outfielder always hustled and showed great desire on the field, developing an excellent reputation as an entertaining player. Some of his performances are now legendary. After he was traded from Brooklyn to Pittsburgh in 1917, he returned to Ebbets Field with the Pirates to play the Dodgers. Just before his first at bat, as the formerly Brooklyn faithful booed him as vociferously as they had once cheered him, Casey bowed low to the crowd and removed his cap, where underneath, perched on Stengel's head, was a sparrow, which flew away. Stengel had found the small bird dazed in the outfield during batting practice. He knew the Brooklyn fans were going to boo him, so he figured that if they were going to give him the bird, he would give them one in return.

Before another game with the Pirates, Stengel stood in center field, so rigid and stock-still that his manager ran out to find out what was wrong. Stengel told him that he was too weak to move because he wasn't getting paid enough to eat.

On to the Philadelphia Phillies in 1920, he was traded early in 1921 to the New York Giants, where he played under the legendary John McGraw. Under McGraw, Stengel was platooned in the outfield with Bill Cunningham, the left-handed Stengel usually batting against right-handed pitchers and the right-handed Cunningham batting against left-handed pitchers. Stengel, a lifetime .284 hitter during his fourteen-year playing career, batted .368 in 1922 and .339 in 1923 under McGraw's platoon system, and in the 1923 world series Stengel hit two home runs to defeat the Yankees. Rounding the bases after hitting one of them, Stengel is remembered for giving the Yankee bench the finger, enraging Yankee owner Jake Ruppert. After the series McGraw traded Stengel to the Boston Braves for the younger and heavier-hitting Billy Southworth. Stengel finished his major league career in 1925 and retired to become the president, manager, and right fielder of the Worcester, Massachusetts, team in the Eastern League. At the end of 1925 Stengel, unhappy there, made history by giving himself his release as a player, firing himself as manager, and then quitting as president. He continued to manage in the minors until 1932 when he was hired as a Brooklyn coach, and in 1934 he was hired by the Dodgers to manage, inheriting a squad of mediocre bumblers. Stengel managed there for three seasons, finishing sixth, fifth, and seventh, and at the end of the third season, though he had another year left on a two-year contract, the Dodgers fired him, thus paying him in 1937 for *not* managing.

While with the Dodgers, Stengel made himself visible on the third-base coaching lines, delivering impromptu orations, conversing with the opposition, performing an occasional soft-shoe, and badgering the umpires, thus providing more entertainment than his players did. Stengel drove his players hard and tried to instruct them, but most of them had neither the talent nor the intellect to take advantage of his guidance. It is said that Stengel invented a pick-off play that he taught his team, a play to be used in a situation when there was a runner on third and a right-handed batter up. Stengel instructed his pitcher to throw at the head of the batter and then yell, "Look out," as he released the pitch. Stengel figured that the runner on third would take his lead and then be so concerned about the welfare of his fallen teammate that he would freeze, allowing the catcher to pick him off third. Stengel finally had to discard the play, however, because his third-baseman froze along with the base runner, and the left fielder always ended up chasing the throw which sailed by third base into the left field bullpen!

"Managing the team back then," Stengel would say years afterward, "was a tough business. Whenever I decided to release a guy, I always had his room searched first for a gun. You couldn't take any chances with some of them birds."

While managing Brooklyn, Stengel's most important personal gains were monetary. A teammate from Texas, Randy Moore, convinced him and three other teammates, Al Lopez, Van Lingo Mungo, and Johnny Cooney, to invest money in an east Texas oil field. Stengel's wells began gushing in 1941 and continued to do so for many lucrative years afterward. A Dodger stockholder also touted Stengel on a firm that was beginning to produce the new miracle drug called penicillin. He made a killing. He was becoming almost as wealthy as his wife, Edna, whose father was a successful banker. Edna herself was an astute business woman, a manager of apartment buildings before her marriage. "As a girl," Stengel said, "Edna worked all night in motion-picture theaters for two dollars and fifty cents. And," he said, "she still has that same two dollars and fifty cents."

After sitting out the '37 season while getting paid by the Dodgers, Stengel in 1938 signed a contract to manage the Boston Braves, another collection of ragtags and has-beens. Again he became the center of attraction in order to divert the minds of the fans from the poor quality of the baseball being played. One dreary, rainy afternoon Stengel appeared on the field to exchange the lineup cards with the umpires wearing a raincoat and holding an umbrella in one hand and a lantern in the other. It was classic Stengel, and most of the writers loved him for his antics, his colorful stories, and his congeniality. Once Stengel was relating to a group of writers an incident concerning a catcher who had once played against him back in the twenties. The catcher's nickname was Horseface. "When Casey showed how the catcher used to look," said a writer who was there, "he not only looked more like a horse than a catcher, he looked more like a horse than Whirlaway."

"For us," wrote Boston sportswriter Harold Kaese, "it was more fun losing with Stengel than winning with a hundred other managers. Unfortunately the Boston fans did not have the benefit of Stengel's company." In his six years in Beantown, Stengel's Braves finished fifth, seventh, seventh, seventh, seventh, and sixth. When he was accidentally struck down by a cab in the spring of '43, breaking his leg and missing the first two months of the season, Boston *Record* writer Dave Egan voted the cabdriver "the man who did the most for Boston in 1943." At the end of the year Stengel was released, traveling to Milwaukee where he won the American Association pennant in '44, to Kansas City, where he impressed Yankee owner Del Webb, and to Oakland where he won the pennant in '48. Weiss's first and only choice as a replacement for Harris was Stengel. This was a man Weiss trusted, a man he could work with, a man who would work with the younger players, and the perfect buffer to keep the press from the shy and private general manager.

When the announcement of his appointment was made at a press conference, Stengel was unusually serious and close-mouthed. He knew he was on the spot because of the firing of the popular Harris and because of his own tarnished reputation. "I didn't get this job," he said in a low, gravelly voice, "through friendship. The Yankees represent an investment of millions of dollars. They don't hand out jobs like this just because they like your company. I got the job because the people here think I can produce for them."

1949

*Old Reliable . . . DiMaggio's remarkable comeback
. . . The strange, indifferent Joe Paige . . . John
Lindell, team prankster . . . Mean Vic Raschi . . . A
pennant on the last day . . . The start of the Dynasty.*

When the Yankee players reported to their St. Petersburg, Florida, training camp in the spring of 1949, they were expecting Casey Stengel to release birds from his hat, but instead he greeted them with a strenuous, unprecedented two-workouts-a-day training regimen which Stengel and his coaches organized with cold efficiency. It was the new manager's belief that too few major league performers were properly trained in the fundamentals of the game, and for hours he drilled his men in the basics, stressing bunting, hitting behind the runner, and base stealing. "It will look new and baffling," Stengel predicted. He permitted his veteran stars, Joe DiMaggio, Tommy Henrich, Charlie Keller, and Phil Rizzuto, to work out according to their own training schedule.

When Stengel held his first team meeting, he addressed a squad primarily consisting of mature, experienced, hard-bitten servicemen. He sensed that they were skeptical, and he was keenly aware of their strong loyalties to both Joe McCarthy and Bucky Harris, his predecessors. Rather than rush to impose his will on the players and perhaps plant seeds of dissension, Stengel instead played down his role.

"I know nothing about the American League," Stengel said softly. "You guys are big league ballplayers, and this year you will be on your own. I'm not even going to give you signs. You just play. This is my year just to observe and find out what the American League is all about."

What he immediately observed was that the team seemed to have many weaknesses, and that its strengths were concentrated in the pitching staff and the outfield corps. Except for Joe DiMaggio in center field and Phil Rizzuto at shortstop, Stengel had little idea who would be starting at the other positions on opening day.

George McQuinn, the regular first-baseman, had retired, leaving Stengel to choose among untried rookies, and at second base there was Snuffy Stirnweiss, once the fastest runner in the league during the wartime years, but now slowed perceptibly by age and injury. Rizzuto, the starting shortstop since 1941, was still as quick and agile as ever, but he only hit .252 the previous year and a sore arm was hampering his throwing. At third base Stengel could choose between brawny Billy Johnson, the regular since 1946, a top fielder but a slow runner who hit into too many double plays, and Bobby Brown, the medical student who was a legitimate three hundred hitter and to whom Larry MacPhail paid a large bonus, but who was a poor fielder. A rookie, 25-year-old Jerry Coleman, was competing for a spot on the roster as a utility infielder.

At catcher there were Charlie Silvera and Gus Niarhos, two excellent defensive players who were both singles hitters. A third candidate was outfielder-catcher Yogi Berra, a powerful left-handed batter, but one who had been so intimidated during the 1947 season and world series by opposing base runners that Bucky Harris caught him in only seventy games in '48. The Yankee pitchers did not enjoy pitching to him, because when there were men on base, he would always signal for a fast ball so it would be easier for him to throw out a base runner. Stengel expressly asked Bill Dickey, who for seventeen years had been the Yankees' all-star catcher, to teach Berra the fundamentals of catching; though few who had seen Berra behind the plate really believed he would ever improve enough to become a regular there.

The Yankee outfield talent was considerable. In center field was Joe Di-Maggio, the greatest living ball player, a lifetime .325 hitter, a home-run slugger, and a matchless fielder. In right was Tommy Henrich, Old Reliable, an excellent fielder who, while not so charismatic a figure as DiMaggio, was to DiMaggio what Gehrig was to Ruth, a dangerous batter overshadowed by a star. In the late innings in clutch situations Henrich, too, could kill you. John Lindell, a strong aggressive player, hit .317 as the team's regular left fielder in '48. Berra, a potential home run champion, hit .305 in '48, and there was also Charlie Keller, another powerful left-handed batter, a nine-year veteran who had been recovering from a serious spinal operation. In addition, there were three highly touted rookie outfielders: Hank Bauer, a 26-year-old ex-Marine who had hit .305 for Kansas City in '48; 27-year-old Gene Woodling, the Player of the Year in the Pacific Coast League where he hit .385 for San Francisco; and Cliff Mapes, an Oklahoma strong boy touted by scouts as the second coming of Babe Ruth.

Pitching was also a strong suit. Allie Reynolds had won thirty-five games in the last two years since he was traded to New York from Cleveland. Vic Raschi was a nineteen-game winner as a rookie in '48, and Eddie Lopat, a heady athlete with a clever assortment of pitches, won seventeen the previous year, his first as a Yankee since he was acquired from the White Sox. Tommy Byrne, one of the fastest throwers in the league, would be a fourth starter, and Bob Porterfield, the man Harris had demanded from Weiss, would also be back. Another acquisition, pitcher Fred Sanford, had been obtained from the St. Louis Browns for over $100,000. Though Sanford had lost twenty games for the Browns, he had defeated the Yankees twice in the final days of the '48 season, and he seemed a good bet to be a big winner with New York. Joe Page, the best relief pitcher in baseball in 1947, but an erratic disappointment in '48, was also on the staff.

Throughout the spring Stengel juggled and experimented and maneuvered, compensating for a rash of injuries which struck his players. Berra drove his car into a palm tree and suffered facial lacerations. Keller tore muscles in his side,

Porterfield developed a sore arm, and, most seriously, DiMaggio came to camp after a winter operation on his right heel expecting no further trouble from his bone spur tortures, but after several days of light workouts the stabbing pain started to afflict him as badly as it had before the operation. DiMaggio spent sleepless nights aimlessly wandering the beaches of St. Petersburg, fearful that his baseball career was reaching a premature end.

The condition of DiMaggio's heel also kept his manager awake. Stengel sat on his bed until the early hours trying to figure the various DiMaggio-less combinations which might result in a respectable starting team, but without him the team displayed a lack of consistency during the exhibition season, defeating a strong opponent one day and losing to Greenville, Texas, a B League team, the next. At first base Stengel played a couple of rookies, then tried Bill Johnson, and also Henrich. He tried Coleman, a shortstop in the minors, at short and second and third, played Berra at third, behind the plate, and in the outfield, as he continued to seek his best combination.

Less than a week before opening day, Stengel called his players together for a clubhouse meeting. "Fellas," he said, "Joe won't be with us for a while." DiMaggio was flying to Johns Hopkins Medical Center for another operation on his heel. He would be out indefinitely.

Without DiMaggio, the Yankees seemed to have no more chance of winning the pennant than the lowly St. Louis Browns or the Washington Senators. The esteemed *New York Times* columnist Arthur Daley wrote, "Stengel never had a first-division team. It could very well be that his record in that respect will remain unbroken." When one writer picked the Yankees for third, Stengel joked, "Third ain't so bad. I never finished third before. That's pretty high up."

In a final three-game exhibition series against the Dodgers, Jackie Robinson stole four bases on Berra as Stengel looked on in disbelief, and Dodger sluggers Duke Snider and Gil Hodges homered to sweep the Yankees. Standing in the dugout, hands in his back pockets, Stengel was muttering to himself, "What's going on here? What's going on here?"

Reporters were beginning to analogize this 1949 team to the 1925 Yankees. In 1923 the Yankees won the pennant and in 1924 they were nosed out for the pennant. In 1925 they collapsed and finished seventh. In 1947 the Yankees won the pennant and in 1948 they were nosed out for the pennant. This was 1949.

When the season finally opened in early April, there were pleasant surprises. After Stirnweiss was spiked and severed a nerve in his left hand during the opening week, Stengel tried the unknown Jerry Coleman at second base though Coleman had never played the position in the minors. With Coleman teaming with shortstop Rizzuto, Stengel stumbled upon what fast developed into a flashy double-play combination, two fleet acrobatic operators who whirred the ball around the diamond like sleight-of-hand magicians. Coleman was also confounding the experts by hitting well over .300. Yogi Berra began absorbing what coach Bill Dickey had been drilling into his head during his extensive crash course on learning to catch, and a few weeks into the season, base runners who took liberties with the kid catcher's strong arm were getting thrown out.

Stengel, meanwhile, solved his first-base problems by settling on Tommy Henrich after a process of elimination. Henrich, who had played some first base in earlier years, became the regular there, a switch that also allowed Stengel to keep another of the many talented outfielders in the lineup.

Only at third was Stengel uncertain as to who should start. To get the maximum out of men he felt to be limited in talent, he revived the practice of platooning players subscribed to by his New York Giant manager, John McGraw. At third Stengel started right-handed batter Billy Johnson against left-handed pitchers and played left-handed batter Bobby Brown against right-handers. Both men hated to be platooned, each thinking he should be playing regularly.

Their careers were a study in contrasts. Billy (The Bull) Johnson was a strong and silent player from the old school. He had signed in 1937 for the munificent sum of $100, and after spending six years struggling through the bush leagues, he reached the Yankees in 1943, starring as a rookie at third. The military then claimed his services for the next two years, and when he returned George Stirnweiss had his job. Stirnweiss was switched to second base in 1947, and that year Johnson found himself sharing third with rookie Brown.

Brown, the Golden Boy, was a fair-haired, fuzzy-cheeked medical student, a player to whom Larry MacPhail paid a bonus of $52,000 to sign. After only one year in the top minors, here was Brown, playing third on the orders of MacPhail. The Yankee veterans who were partial to Johnson were resentful, and only when Brown broke his finger during the summer of 1948 did Johnson return to third where he played excellently, hitting .294. In 1948, with Mac-Phail gone from the Yankees, manager Bucky Harris played Johnson more than he did Brown, prompting Brown to threaten to quit. Brown's bat was called the Magic Wand because he was a professional hitter, but he was wooden afield, despite endless hours of diligent practice.

Johnson was an excellent fielder and a steady hitter, but Stengel felt he was too slow a runner, often hitting into double plays. Stengel, not happy about playing either of these men regularly, platooned them.

With DiMaggio out, there was less leeway to platoon in the outfield, but Stengel, when choosing his three starters among righties Hank Bauer and John Lindell and lefties Gene Woodling and Cliff Mapes, often chose according to whether the pitcher was a lefty or a righty.

By the end of April the totally unexpected transformation from early-season misfits to a smooth, polished team was the talk of professional sports. The Yankees raced out in front immediately, beginning their season 16–5, and with only a few days remaining in June, they were leading the second-place Philadelphia Athletics by a full four and a half games. Vic Raschi was 11–2. Reynolds was 8–1, and Tommy Henrich, who won the opening game of the season with a home run with two outs in the bottom of the ninth, filled the leadership void created by DiMaggio's absence. Twelve of Henrich's sixteen spring home runs were the key hits in ball games. Of the Yankees' forty wins, he had driven in the winning run in almost half of them.

With DiMaggio still in the hospital after his operation, Keller incapacitated with back pain, and Lindell on the bench with a sprained ankle, Henrich was the big man on the team, pairing with Berra to supply most of the offense. Beset with injuries, Stengel before a June game cornered Henrich. "Tommy," Stengel said, "I don't want you to sit in a draft. Don't slip and fall in the shower. And under no circumstances are you to eat fish, because them bones could be murder. Drive carefully and stay in the slow lane, and sit quietly in the clubhouse until the game begins. I can't let anything happen to you."

Tommy Henrich was a fiercely independent individual who jealously guarded his private life. He made a conscious effort to appear to live as clean and virtuous a life as Babe Ruth led a rowdy and hell-raising one. For Henrich letting his hair down meant having a few drinks, smoking a big black cigar, or organizing his teammates to harmonize "When Irish Eyes Are Smiling," "Take Me Out to the Ball Game," and "Down by the Old Mill Stream" in the shower of the clubhouse after a Yankee victory.

Mostly what Henrich was was serious. He was a bad loser, and he worked hard at becoming a success. He drove his teammates to be successes too, and if he thought another player was taking money out of his pocket by not hustling or by making a stupid mistake, Henrich would lash into him with a biting criticism, causing hard feelings. The young players on the team feared Henrich's tongue-lashing even more than they did Stengel's.

Henrich was the living embodiment of Frank Merriwell and Chip Hilton. In a storybook romance he married a nurse who came to visit him in the hospital just to see what "the star" was like. On the field of play he performed Merriwellian game-winning feats. To the press he said things like, "I get a thrill every time I put on my Yankee uniform. It sounds corny, but it's the gospel truth," and it was the gospel truth. A respected, respectful, and patriotic citizen, with all the Christian virtues, Henrich displayed a restraint and moderation and a lack of flair which too often has blurred the memory of his skillful ability to hit a baseball, especially with a runner in scoring position in the late innings.

Mel Allen, the Yankee broadcaster, nicknamed him Old Reliable, and it is this reliability to deliver key hits in crucial situations for which he is best remembered. His lifetime batting average reads .282, a respectable figure, but he was one of the best .282 hitters in the game, and in the outfield he was admired for his guile and intelligence.

Henrich was always considering the wind currents and the position of the sun and the habits of each batter, and he practiced for hours fielding rebounds off the tricky Yankee Stadium fences. His favorite trick was to wait under a fly ball with a speedy runner on first and a slower one at bat, pretending to set himself to catch it. At the last second he would let it drop, trapping the ball and throwing out the speedier runner at second, sometimes getting a double play if an inattentive batter, lulled into believing Henrich was going to catch the ball, did not hustle down to first.

Henrich first signed with the Cleveland Indians in 1934. After performing spectacularly in the minors for three years, but getting bounced from one farm team to another, he was beginning to feel that the Indians were deliberately trying to impede his progress to the majors. Though Cleveland general manager Cy Slapnicka had told him that he had received offers to buy him from a couple of major league clubs, Slapnicka himself kept Henrich from coming to Cleveland, leaving him in the minors. Henrich, an intelligent thinking man, and a force to be reckoned with when angered, daringly wrote to baseball commissioner Judge Landis, asking him to investigate, knowing that if Landis saw no wrongdoing, Cleveland might let him languish in the minors forever. Landis did investigate, and he declared Henrich a free agent. Eight major league teams, including the Yankees, rushed to sign him. The Yankees offered him $25,000, outbidding everyone else. Henrich was sent to Newark, the Yankees' top farm club where he played one week. In April of 1937 Yankee manager Joe McCarthy became angry with the attitude of outfielder Roy Johnson. After ordering general manager Ed Barrow to "trade, sell, or release Johnson," he told Barrow, "bring up that kid at Newark." Henrich became a Yankee fixture in right field for ten seasons, joining Joe DiMaggio and Charlie Keller to form one of the all-time classic outfield combinations. Despite a three-year Coast Guard hitch during World War II, for eleven seasons Henrich starred for the Yankees. He retired in 1950 because of 37-year-old arthritic knees.

For the past twenty years Tommy Henrich has lived in home-town Massillon, Ohio, with his wife and children in an unassuming two-story frame dwelling just up a little hill from Route 30, which runs through the heart of the city. Across the street from his home a Grant's department store covers the field where Rockne and the Massillon Tigers once played brutal football against the Bulldogs from nearby Canton and other early professional football teams. When I arrived at Henrich's home, it was mid-April. His coveralls and work shirt were dirt-stained from the labored attention he was giving the spring planting of his backyard vegetable garden, and he apologized for his informality. He stopped what he was doing and greeted me warmly.

Inside, the furnishings reflected an unexpected sophistication, and the strains of a Beethoven sonata wafted through the house from the living-room stereo. Henrich, now in his early sixties, was still lean and sinewy, and he stared intently from behind a hawklike nose, his eyes piercing, alert, and aggressive in an attempt to learn something of the visitor. When he spoke, it was with force and authority; there was a conviction, almost a defiance, in his speech.

He enjoyed arguing a point and tenaciously trying to prove his position. Some of his teammates had dubbed him the Great Debater because of his relish for a good argument.

"What facet of major league baseball is hurting the most today?" Henrich asked. I thought for a second, but before I could answer, he said, "Hitting. You know why?" And again before I could answer, he said, "Because of Little League, another manifestation of America's way of going at everything." Henrich's eyes were starting to squint a little, and he was thrusting his chin forward, looking very much like I had always imagined Daniel Webster during one of his orations. "Everything," said Henrich, "has to be so blooming organized. They've lost the concept of having fun. Today kids nine, ten, eleven years old go down to the ball field and the manager is the boss and he says, 'This is what we're going to do,' and it might get so ridiculous that they're going to practice relays and cutoffs instead of putting the ball bat in their hands and letting them hit. I once said to Joe Gordon, 'Joe, did you ever get fifty hits in one day?' And he thought about three seconds and said, 'Certainly.' I said, 'So have I, but you don't have any of these kids on the ball field today who ever got fifty hits in one day. They don't have the ball bat in their hands. They don't know how to operate a ball bat.' Let the kids play. When they play, they're practicing. I don't think DiMaggio practiced very much, if ever. He played.

"Joe DiMaggio," Henrich went on, "I watched him day in and day out, and I never saw such perfection in all my life. I would say that he did everything closer to perfection than anybody else I ever saw. He may not have been the greatest base runner, but he was as great as anybody I ever saw. May not have been the greatest hitter, but he had absolutely no fear of anyone he ever went up against. I never heard him say, 'That doggone clown, I can't hit him nohow.' He wouldn't say that. If he felt that, which I doubt, he wouldn't allow anybody to know. Take Bob Feller, for instance, wild man Feller. Tremendous speed and the tremendous curve, against him right-handers by the dozen shied from home plate. They don't want any part of Feller. Out of fear. You could get killed. And I don't blame them. But not DiMaggio. Feller is the greatest, but DiMaggio inside says, 'Not in my book he's not. I'll show you who's the greatest.' "

I mentioned to Henrich that he was considered one of the smartest outfielders in baseball history.

"Who said that?" growled Henrich testily.

"Joe DiMaggio said it for one," I said.

Henrich thought a second. "I believe it," he said, breaking into raucous laughter, drowning the classical music in the background. Then, more subdued, "I hope he said it."

"Let me give you a good quote," Henrich said. "Did you ever hear of a guy named Benny Epstein? Benny and I were good friends. He was a sportswriter from Little Rock, and later he went to the New York *Daily Mirror,* and one spring he says, 'Tom, I want to talk with you. You're the right fielder, and I'm writing a series of articles, picking one position each day.' He says, 'I want to talk to you about playing right field.' So we get in depth on this thing. I'll never forget it. He didn't even know that a ball will curve going out into the outfield. When a right-hander twists one to the right field line, he didn't even know the ball curves! So he's asking me about some of the problems of playing the outfield and about catching the ball, and I said, 'Catching the ball is a pleasure, knowing what to do with it is a business.' And you know who used that expression? Ring Lardner. He used it about our affluent society. He said, 'Making money is easy, knowing what to do with it becomes a problem.' But what I said about catching a ball is true. If you are a major leaguer, you know how to catch a ball. But after you catch the ball there are several alternatives where you can throw it, and to throw it there is footwork you've got to get down before the ball comes down.

"You talk about practicing," Henrich said. "In my opinion that's not work, that's fun. Baseball's the only thing I have ever gotten into where practice wasn't work. I love to shoot pool. I practice, practice, practice, and the first thing you know I go stale. I don't want any more of the pool table. Never got to where I got very good at pool. I go stale. The only thing in my life that wasn't boring after a time was baseball. And that goes back to what I was saying about Little League. When you drill, drill, drill, and force them to play, the kids say, 'Get out of here. Who needs this.' You don't drill them. You *allow* them to come out and play. Why should an eight-year-old kid play ball? To have fun. What the heck else is there? For a young boy to go out and say, 'I'm going to go out and play like a professional,' you've got to be out of your mind.

"I had a lot of fun playing baseball. For me it was a dream come true. Playing the game I loved for a living."

It was 1949, a bright summer morning late in June, and in his room at the Edison Hotel in Manhattan, Joe DiMaggio rolled out of bed. When he gingerly lowered his right foot to the floor, the incessant, stabbing pain in his heel that had dogged him for the past couple of years had miraculously vanished in the night. He lifted the foot off the floor, and lowered it back down slowly. Still no pain, and when he felt the heel with his hand, it was no longer hot and burning. He rose and in his pajamas cautiously walked about the room, both puzzled and elated by the sudden disappearance of the soreness.

An operation had been performed to correct the condition over the winter, and the doctors had told him the problem had been cured. Yet when he had tried to practice during spring training, there were days when the heel pained him so badly that his lips flowed blood, he was biting them so hard. While his teammates were getting into shape for the coming season, he would sit for hours on the beach of his bungalow home on the Gulf of Mexico, staring at the horizon and at the lapping waves, wondering if and when the pain would ever go away. Before spring camp broke, he finally agreed to return to Johns Hopkins Medical Center in Baltimore for another operation.

DiMaggio, always a distant person, became morose and especially ill-tempered from the discomfort he was in, and when he arrived at Baltimore after a long plane ride, the reporters greeted him with the same haunting questions he had been hearing all spring. "How's the heel, Joe?" or "You think you're through, Joe?" As he limped from the plane, when another reporter asked him if he thought he was finished, DiMaggio snarled, "Go fly a kite," and walked by. DiMaggio's illness was the biggest sports item of the day, a front-page story, and even in the hospital he was afforded little peace or quiet. Toward the end of his recuperation after the operation, he agreed to meet with reporters for a final interview.

"Look," he said. "Don't you guys think you've gone far enough? You guys are driving me batty. Can't you leave me alone? This affects me mentally, you know."

When he moved to New York his whereabouts was kept from the public and the press better than the atom bomb secrets had been kept from the Rosenbergs. DiMaggio disconnected his phone in the Edison Hotel and tried to hide.

In his hotel room he lay in bed and watched the Yankees on television, the new electronic marvel of the day, and he would umpire the pitches on the screen trying to retain his batting eye. But the angle of the camera was misleading, and when DiMaggio saw he was consistently calling the pitches incorrectly, he began to fear that he was losing his batting eye. Lying in bed, the muscles of his long, lean body were softening from lack of exercise, and nagging thoughts of an untimely retirement were making his ulcers burn inside him. He began to lose weight from not eating, and he wasn't sleeping well at night.

DiMaggio didn't want people to see him in this condition, and only Toots Shor and one or two other close friends visited Joe with any regularity. The other players didn't know where he was, and they only saw him when occasionally during a game he would stand in the dugout runway and watch the game in his street clothes.

Through the months of April and May and much of June, DiMaggio remained in seclusion, waiting for the pain in his heel to subside as the doctors had promised it would. He really didn't believe them as he lay in bed day after day after day until the sunny morning in late June when he arose to find that the pain had finally disappeared.

June 28 was a sunny afternoon in Boston, and though the heat had eased for the past couple of days, still there was no rain to bring relief to the parched Massachusetts Bay city. On street corners newsboys hawking the *Herald* and the *Globe* and the *Record* were announcing that Joe DiMaggio would be playing in the upcoming three-game series beginning here tonight, his initial appearance of the season after having missed the first sixty-five games. In front of the windows at Fenway Park, long lines of Boston baseball fans and DiMaggio *paisanos* queued up to buy tickets for the games.

The day before, DiMaggio had asked to start his first game, an exhibition played for charity against the cross-borough New York Giants in the Stadium. He had been working out lightly for about a week, and this exhibition gave him a chance to face some live pitching. Though he did not hit the ball out of the infield in four tries and was gasping for breath after long runs, he was nevertheless moving without pain. He would play himself into shape.

There were bad feelings between the Yankees and the Red Sox, and more than thirty-six thousand people, the largest crowd ever to attend a night game in Fenway Park history, were crunched into the little antiquated Boston bandbox to see the matched skills of the two teams.

The bad feeling was heightened by Yankee general manager George Weiss's inflammatory statements that the Red Sox's recent purchase of several St. Louis Browns' players, including Jack Kramer, Ellis Kinder, and Vern Stephans, was making the St. Louis team a joke and hurting the league. Weiss himself had traded for St. Louis pitcher Fred Sanford during the winter, and the Boston fans, many of whom had never forgiven the Yankees for raping their team in the twenties by purchasing so many of their star players including Babe Ruth, were calling Weiss a villainous hypocrite. There was also a natural rivalry between the two teams because of their history, the rivalry between Joe DiMaggio and Ted Williams, and the fraternal battle between DiMaggio and his little brother Dom, who played center field for the Sox. Had there been room, a hundred thousand would have been there that night.

Inside the Yankee clubhouse, in the bowels of the park beneath the stands, there was an uncharacteristic revelry. DiMaggio, a man who rarely joined in the pranks or the joking, preferring instead to remain aloof, wrestled with Charlie Keller and clowned with Phil Rizzuto. He displayed an unconcealed joy just to be playing again, and his teammates could feel a lightening of their load by his mere presence. Without DiMaggio they would not have been able to survive over the long, protracted schedule, but with him back, they now had a real chance. They were experiencing a surge of confidence, like that felt by a long-distance runner when he suddenly finds his second wind and loses all feeling of fatigue.

The Yankees jumped out to a quick three-nothing lead in the second inning on a home run. In the third inning Phil Rizzuto singled, and then DiMaggio, standing at the plate with his feet spread wide and parallel, his bat held back and stock still, snapped his wrists at a fast ball and pulled it on a high arc into the screen which tops the six-story high, left-field wall for two more runs. Rizzuto, on first, started jumping up and down as he raced around the bases, shouting, "Holy cow, holy cow," and after DiMaggio rounded third and loped toward the plate, the rest of the Yankees met him and escorted him back to the dugout. DiMaggio's home run gave the Yankees a total of five runs, one more than the Red Sox, who put the tying run on third with two outs in the ninth only to see relief star Joe Page retire Ted Williams on a fly ball to DiMaggio to end the game.

DiMaggio had less dramatically demonstrated his leadership in other ways. Early in the game Johnny Pesky, the combative Red Sox second-baseman, raced from first to second base trying to break up a double play on a ground ball hit to second-baseman Coleman. Yankee shortstop Phil Rizzuto raced to second to take the pivot, fearlessly firing to first to complete the play. As he did, Pesky slid into him with a hard rolling block, tumbling the little shortstop to the ground, kneeing him in the face, and knocking him unconscious for several minutes. The shaken Rizzuto was able to continue, and by the eighth inning most of the spectators had forgotten the incident when DiMaggio led off the inning for the Yankees with a walk. The next batter hit a ground ball to the infield, and Red Sox shortstop Vern Stephans glided over toward second to take the throw. As he did so DiMaggio threw a vicious block at Stephans, hurtling him to the ground and separating him from the ball and most of his senses. The Boston fans booed the play, but DiMaggio was only retaliating, giving notice to Pesky and any of the others that if there was going to be any funny business, they would have to answer to him personally.

Another large crowd arrived for the second contest of the series and there was much more whooping and hollering when the Red Sox opened a 7–1 lead after only four innings. DiMaggio, who awoke stiff and swollen legged, was having a more difficult time in the field, getting a poor jump on one ball which he would have reached on stronger legs and allowing a runner to take an extra base on one ball he didn't charge quickly enough. In the fifth inning two men reached base before DiMaggio came to bat, and for the second time in two days he snapped a fast ball for a home run making the score 7–4 and drawing a nice hand from the Boston crowd. The Yankees scratched out three more runs to tie the score at 7–7. There were two outs in the eighth inning when DiMaggio dragged himself to the plate. After taking the first pitch, he pulled a high curve ball and lined the ball a good ten feet above the Fenway Park wall and screen for a third home run and the ball game. Stengel bounded up the steps of the dugout at the crack of the bat, and as DiMaggio unemotionally glided around the bases, the Yankee manager raised his arms high and began bowing like a Moslem praising Allah. In the stands the deafening ovation for DiMaggio transcended all partisan lines. They were still cheering him after reliever Joe Page had retired the Sox in order in the ninth to end the game.

Afterward in the crowded, sweaty visitors' locker room, the reporters mobbed around DiMaggio's locker. Many of these men had predicted that DiMaggio would never play again, and they were staring at him in unprofessional awe. One asked, ''Joe, you only had eight workouts before you came here. You've hit three home runs in two games. What's the secret?''

DiMaggio, exhausted, sitting back in his locker sipping beer, considered the question and somberly answered between sips, ''You merely swing the bat and hit the ball.''

Before the third and final game of the set, a single-engine biplane circled the park, streaming a large banner that read ''The Great DiMaggio,'' and late in the game with the Yankees leading and two men on base, The Great DiMaggio deposited a fourth baseball over the left-field wall. This one was the longest of them all, the baseball soaring out against the unlit light-tower far above the left-field screen. Again the crowd rose to applaud and to marvel at this remarkable athlete. Three games. Three victories. Four home runs. Nine runs batted in. Five runs scored. The Yankees were now leading the league by five and a half games and leading Boston by eight and a half. The rest of the Yankees' summer would be spent trying to keep the powerful Boston team behind them.

Most of the Yankee players were still loyal to either McCarthy or to Harris, and though Stengel had the Yankees in first place, they were nevertheless skeptical of his ability and would be skeptical long after he had proved himself many times over. Some of the McCarthy-Harris veterans resented being addressed by their uniform number, as was Stengel's practice, and some of them resented being platooned. Behind his back they called him ''the Broken-Legged Manager,'' a reference to his being run over by a taxi in Boston. They also referred to him as ''Casey Stinkle.''

But though the players may not have liked him, they couldn't help but be astonished by his enthusiasm and vigor. Stengel had a unique way of keeping his players awake and alert during a ball game. In the dugout he would walk up and down the aisle in front of the players, throwing left hooks and right crosses, trying to keep everyone apprised as to what was happening. He'd constantly yell encouragement out onto the field, his gravelly voice carrying into the outfield above the crowd's din. During a rally, he'd shout, ''Town hall tonight. Let's go get 'em.'' While Stengel was releasing energy, at the same time he was keeping his players and his bench alive. A live bench, he felt, had a disturbing effect on the opposition, especially on a hot, humid day when the other team's reserves were tired and lazy and lacking the energy to provide their own team with encouragement.

Furthermore, Stengel's strategies were winning ball games, and grudgingly his players were forced to respect him as he brilliantly platooned and manipulated them both offensively and defensively in the face of a rash of serious injuries to key players. Stengel quickly learned everyone's capabilities, and his ability to choose pinch hitters was uncanny. He knew, it seemed, when there was a hit in a player's bat.

In one game the Yankees trailed by three runs in the ninth inning, and with the bases loaded and a left-handed pitcher on the mound, Stengel pinch hit the right-handed Hank Bauer for the left-handed Gene Woodling, and Bauer singled in a run. The opposing manager immediately brought in a right-handed pitcher to face righty batter Charlie Silvera, and Stengel pinch hit left-handed Berra for Silvera. Berra singled in another run. Stengel then pinch hit Charlie Keller for the pitcher, and Keller lined a triple to center field for the lead. In the bottom of the ninth the Yankee manager called in Joe Page from the bullpen, and Page was one, two, three in the ninth, striking out two of the three batters who faced him to save the win.

In yet another game New York led 3–2 with one out in the ninth. With opposing base runners on first and second, Stengel substituted Page, his superb relief pitcher, and sent rookie outfielder Cliff Mapes to right field to replace Gene Woodling, who was still recovering from a knee injury. Mapes had a powerful throwing arm and Stengel wanted him out there in the event that the runners attempted to tag up on a fly ball or to score on a ground single. Sure enough, the batter hit a long fly ball, the runner on second tagged and raced for third, and Mapes threw him out. The next batter ground out, and the Yankees were out of the inning with another victory.

In mid-August Boston began a late surge that seriously threatened the Yankees' hold on first place, but because of Stengel's uncanny foresight and his players' excellent execution, the team was somehow hanging onto the lead despite widespread injuries to key players. The pitching staff was holding up satisfactorily, and Joe Page, the controversial relief pitcher, was at the top of his form, sneering at the hitters, and throwing bullets by them.

When everything was going right for Page, he was awesome. To remember him in his prime is to see the tall, lanky pitcher stare down at Ted Williams and taunt him with a rising fast ball which sailed in toward the lefty Williams. Page took a special pleasure in beating the Red Sox, partly because Joe McCarthy, the ex-Yankee manager who was always giving Page hell, was managing the Red Sox, but mostly because of the heated discussions which concerned the relative merits of Williams and DiMaggio, his roommate. Page was DiMaggio's stoutest defender, and his strongest argument was blazing his fast ball past Williams, a hitter Page retired with uncanny regularity.

Joe Page was Henry Fielding's Tom Jones in a baseball uniform, a tall, handsome celebrity with jet-black hair and a toothpaste smile, a rounder who enjoyed being noticed in public, a night owl who greeted the rosy-fingered sunrise through bloodshot eyes after a lusty night's play.

For two years of his checkered career Joe Page was the most valuable pitcher in the American League, a left-handed relief specialist who would insolently saunter to the mound from the right-field bullpen, his jacket saucily slung over his shoulder partially covering the number 11 on the back of his pinstriped uniform. When he got there he took the ball from the manager and nonchalantly fired a half-dozen warm-up pitches of medium velocity. Then after the batter stepped in, Page would survey the runners dancing off the bases, sneer defiantly at the batter, and then streak exploding, rising fastballs past the usually overmatched batsman.

To his teammates positioned behind him as he stood on that hill in the late innings of a close ball game, with the shadows lengthening and the game hanging in the balance, when Page had his control he was as important a member of the Yankees as any one of them—a fact which they grudgingly admitted. When the game was over, though, most of them had little to do with him socially. Page, a coalminer son of a coalminer, possessed attitudes that were very different from theirs.

Page came from the coal country of the Allegheny valley where human life was cheap. During the depths of the Depression the life of a miner wasn't worth much more than the cost of a good headstone. A little after sunrise the miner was lowered straight down to the depths of the confining hole, with black dust swirling through his nostrils and lungs, in order to pick away at the sooty anthracite and start it on its journey to the steel mills of Pittsburgh. When the six P.M. whistle sounded, the men left their picks and shovels and rode the elevator in silence back up to the mouth of the shaft where for the first time since the morning they could breath fresh, cool air and count another day of survival from a cave-in or a gas explosion. At the end of the day there was no substitute for a little beer to quench the thirst and smooth the way for a little hell raisin'. It was eat, drink, and be merry for tomorrow you may die, and for those miners who contracted the fearsome black lung disease, tomorrow often came much sooner than even they expected. In mining society the threat of death was really the way of life, something which had to be stoically accepted because its likelihood was so immediate. Few miners put money in the bank for a rainy day. Instead they took that money and lived life day by day. This was Joe Page's milieu, a lifestyle most of his teammates could never understand. They thought him to be irresponsible, out for himself, and an attention-seeker who loved public adulation whereas they wanted to be left alone. They even mocked Page's close friendship with Joe DiMaggio, because they felt that Page was merely trying to bask in DiMaggio's limelight, copying his dress and adopting his tastes, while in exchange he caddied for DiMaggio, acting as his go-for. Page's reaction to this rejection was a veneer of indifference, as he traveled his side of the tracks while they traveled theirs.

It was this veneer that also drove his managers into fits of rage when they would chastise him, only to see him shrug his shoulders. Few could understand how a man could be so excellent one year and so mediocre the next, yet seem so indifferent to his change in fortune.

Page reached the Yankees in 1944, but tragedy overshadowed his first personal triumph when his oldest sister, Georgeanne, was struck and killed by a car back home near Pittsburgh while he was at spring training. Page started the season winning five of his first six starts and was named to the 1944 All-Star team by manager McCarthy. There was a tremendous amount of pride in his local community when he was named to play in the game, being held in Pittsburgh that year. But on the day that was to be his triumphant homecoming, his father suffered a stroke, and Page, instead of playing, sped to the local hospital where his father died before he could see his son pitch in the majors.

Abruptly Page stopped winning, and for the first time McCarthy took notice of Page's extracurricular activities. After six straight losses, Page was returned to Newark, which was okay with him, and where Page was named to pitch on the International League All-Star team. When he returned to the Yankees in 1945 his relationship with McCarthy had not improved. Page continued to lead his own life style, and though the occasional fines and tongue-lashings hurt his feelings, his outward reaction continued to be one of total indifference to McCarthy's martinet influence, and it was this indifference which so agitated the gruff Yankee manager. McCarthy was strict, but he was concerned, and he righteously contended that Page was throwing his career away and wasn't considering his future. What McCarthy couldn't accept was that Page was only interested in the adventures of the next game or the next evening.

In 1946 McCarthy's frustrations with managing the losing wartime Yankee teams and with fighting a seemingly losing battle to reform Page finally surfaced on a plane trip from Cleveland to Detroit in May. The Yankees had just lost to the Indians at League Park in Cleveland on a ninth inning home run, and after the game, manager McCarthy remained in the dugout fuming, raging uncontrollably, his Irish temper boiling over long after all the fans had left the ball park. After so many years of managing winners, he had become such a perfectionist that he was unable to abide anything less than a first-place finish. His nerves were becoming taut, the tension was driving him to drink, and he was so irritable that the players were making a concerted effort to avoid him whenever possible.

After the game the Yankees were flying from Cleveland to Detroit. At this time, the Yankees were the only team which flew from town to town because Larry MacPhail believed in the airplane and it was his policy that the team should fly. While the plane was en route, Page was sitting in a window seat alone, staring out the window of the DC-3. Manager McCarthy slipped into the aisle seat next to Page and propped up his right leg, pushing the sole of his right shoe firmly against the back of the seat in front of him to lock Page in. He tapped Page on the arm to get his attention. "You're going to sit and listen to what I have to say," McCarthy said.

"Sure," said Page breezily.

"What the devil's the matter with you?" McCarthy asked.

"Nothing," Page said.

"When are you gonna settle down and start pitching? How long do you think you can get away with this?" McCarthy's voice level was beginning to rise.

"Get away with what?" Page asked annoyedly. "I'm not trying to get away with anything. I'm doing the best I can. What do you want outta me?"

McCarthy began shouting, so that he was audible throughout the entire plane. The other players and the press, embarrassed, tried to act like they weren't listening and like nothing unusual was happening. "Who the hell do you think you're kidding?" McCarthy shouted, his Irish temper at the boiling point. "I'll tell you what I'm going to do. I'm going to send you back to Newark, and you can make your four hundred dollars a month for all I care."

Page, unruffled, shrugged his shoulders. "That's okay with me," he said. "You wanna send me to Newark, send me to Newark. Maybe I'll be happier there."

Had McCarthy remained with the Yankees, Page would have been banished, much as Roy Johnson had been after displeasing McCarthy. But that afternoon when the plane landed in Detroit, McCarthy did not go to the ball park. He was too hypertense to manage. After a rest in his hotel room, he flew directly home to his Tonawanda, New York, farm. The next day he telephoned his resignation as Yankee manager, a job he had held since 1931.

Page didn't become a big winner until 1947 under the much more live-and-let-live Bucky Harris, who switched him to the bullpen. In '47 Page appeared in fifty-six games, winning fourteen and saving twenty others. He was fourth in the voting for Most Valuable Player. In the world series he saved the first and third games. In the seventh and deciding game Page entered in the top of the fourth inning, and over the final five innings, he blew his fast ball past the Dodgers, allowing one hit and no runs. After the final game, the entire team toasted Joe Page and his live fast ball, including owner Larry MacPhail who earlier in the year had dispatched a female private detective to follow Page around. Columnist Ed Sullivan wrote about Page and the female detective, and before long there were stories that she had fallen in love with Page and was sending MacPhail the most glowing reports.

After Page's 1947 triumphs, he spent the entire winter celebrating, and the following year he arrived in camp thirty pounds overweight, and after crash-dieting to lose the weight, he was weak all season. He also suffered from a tired arm after Harris used him with mixed success in fifty-five games. Again, stories and rumors of Page's extracurricular escapades surfaced. Primarily there were stories of his drinking bouts, and reporter Benny Epstein wrote, "If Joe Page is seen in a dairy store at nine o'clock at night, the next morning it's ninety-nine proof." Nevertheless, when the Yankees lost the '48 pennant by two games, Page was accused of being the major factor in Harris's dismissal. If Page's failure that year was the reason, Harris didn't hold him at fault. Toward the end of the season the team was in Penn Station, ready to board a train to take them to Washington, D.C., when the mild-mannered Harris took Page aside. "Joe," Harris said, "whatever happens in the future, if I get let go, which is probably going to happen, it's not on account of you."

When Stengel became manager in '49, Page, rested and fit, regained his 1947 form and pitched in a record sixty games, winning thirteen, saving twenty, and holding the opposition in fourteen other games without getting credited in the records. It was another incredible, magical year—the last such season he would ever have.

In 1950 he again suffered from a tired arm, pitching with mixed success, and then in 1951, in spring training, Page was on the mound when his right leg, the striding leg, slipped after his windup, and releasing the ball off-balance, he tore the bursar muscle in his pitching arm. His career was over. Before the end of the

'51 spring training, Stengel released him, and he was gone with a shrug. For a couple of years he pitched minor league ball and in 1954 was asked by the lowly Pirates to try a comeback and perhaps draw some local interest, but Page's effectiveness was minimal after that arm injury.

With only a dozen games remaining, the Yankees were barely maintaining their slim lead over the Red Sox, when on September 18 Joe DiMaggio again left the team. He was suffering from a viral infection and pneumonia, and he was confined to his hotel room. In the three months he had played since his incredible inaugural performance in Boston, DiMaggio had hit .345 and in the seventy-four games he had driven in sixty-seven runs, third on the team despite having missed almost half the season.

With DiMaggio in the hospital, the recently-acquired slugger John Mize out with a sprained shoulder, Yogi Berra out with a broken thumb, and Tommy Henrich playing in a bulky corset after cracking a couple of ribs, the decimated Yankees were finally passed by the Red Sox with only four games remaining in the season. When the season came down to the final two-game series between the Yankees and the Red Sox, the Sox were still leading by one game. It looked like 1948 all over again, but this year the crucial series was being played in Yankee Stadium.

Yankee Stadium was shaped like a horseshoe with three tiers of grandstands stretching in foul territory from the left-field line around behind home plate out to the right-field line. Rows and rows of wooden bleachers sat behind the outfield. Because the Stadium was designed to take advantage of the left-handed power of Babe Ruth, the architect made it easier to hit home runs to right-field and right center than to left and left center, thus removing all symmetry but at the same time giving the Stadium its unique dimensions. Down the lines home runs were easy if a pitcher was foolish enough to allow the batter to pull the ball. It was 296 feet in right and 301 in left, and from both foul lines the stands dropped back deeply toward straightaway center field, and hitting home runs into the power alleys, 407 feet from the plate over a fourteen-foot wall in right and 457 feet over a thirteen-foot wall in left, took strength of a Ruthian nature. Dead center was 461 feet, called Death Valley because 425-foot towering blasts became routine outs, ruining many batting averages.

Without standees the seating capacity of the Stadium was 65,000, and because there were no fire regulations, as many as 15,000 standees could be jammed into the park in addition to the seated customers. In 1949 baseball was America's pastime, the national sport, the premier sporting entertainment in a sports-hungry nation still recovering from the trauma of World War II, and the two-game season finale between the Yankees and the Red Sox created such excitement that more than 68,000 tickets were sold for both the Saturday and Sunday afternoon games.

The morning of the Saturday game, owner Del Webb called on Casey Stengel at the manager's midtown Manhattan hotel room to meet him for breakfast. It was nine-thirty, and when Stengel answered the knock on the door, he was still in his pajamas. On the floor beside his bed were dozens of little balls of crinkled-up paper.

"What in the hell is that mess?" asked Webb.

"Lineups," said Stengel. "Spent the whole night trying to decide on a lineup." Stengel hadn't slept the entire night. This was his tenth season as a major league manager. He had never come this close before.

Joe DiMaggio hadn't slept much either. It was Joe DiMaggio Day at the Stadium, and that was making him more nervous than the game itself, though he was still weak from a siege of pneumonia and that, too, was upsetting him. DiMaggio with sunken cheeks looked drawn and very tired. He'd dropped fifteen pounds in two weeks, and his loosely hanging clothes made him look like a scarecrow. The day before Joe had told Stengel that he was well enough to play, though he wasn't sure if he could last the entire nine innings, and for the first time in two weeks Stengel could write the name "DiMaggio, J." into the fourth spot on the lineup card.

The other invalids seemed to be recuperating at least enough for them to play. Henrich still had a very painful back, but he was getting through the pain and playing an excellent first base. Berra, the other important invalid, was finally convinced by Stengel and the other players—who had become impatient with his protestations that his thumb pained him too much to play—that he could play despite the pain. The doctors had given Yogi permission to catch again, but through the last few weeks of the season he had been reluctant to get back behind the plate while his thumb was still sore. Stengel and the veteran players kept goading him.

"Grab his hand," Stengel would say to another player, "and shake it good and hard." One of the players said to Yogi, "You know what we might do? We might stand up in a team meeting and suggest that you don't deserve a full share of the series money on account of not being in enough games when it mattered." Berra had been appearing as a pinch hitter, but for these final two games Berra told Casey he was prepared to catch.

After much deliberation Stengel decided to start right-hander Allie Reynolds in the first game on Saturday and pitch his other right-handed ace, Vic Raschi, on Sunday. Boston needed just one win for the pennant. The Yankees needed them both. Early Saturday morning the people started streaming into the park, and even after the noon starting time, they were still flowing through the ramps leading to the seats. There was a holiday mood on this crisp, clear final day of September. Reynolds, the Yankee starter, was the type of pitcher who occasionally needed an inning or two to find his pitching rhythm, and as the partisan Yankee throng watched in dismay, this was one of those days. Boston, batting first, scored a run on two singles, a wild pitch, and a long sacrifice fly before everyone was seated, and then in the third inning Reynolds completely lost the plate, walked the first three batters to face him, and then allowed a blooping single for a second run.

Stengel quickly called time-out and slowly walked out to the mound to talk with his pitcher while relief star Joe Page heated up in the bullpen. Calling on

Page so early seemed to be a brazen, desperate move, since he rarely worked more than an inning or two, but before Stengel walked to the mound he had spoken to Page on the phone and asked him how far he could go.

"A long way," said Page.

"Get ready," Stengel said.

After Page peremptorily lobbed a few throws to loosen his arm, he informed bullpen catcher Houk that he was ready, and on Stengel's signal, in came the arrogant, insolent Page. With the bases still loaded, Page ran the count on the first batter he faced to 3–2 and lost him high to force in the third Boston run. Then he walked the next batter on four straight pitches, to make the score 4–0, as Stengel paced the concrete floor of the Yankee dugout, shouting out onto the field, swearing over the din. Page, raging inside, recovered his control, reared back and threw, striking out the next two batters on rising fast balls to end the inning. After his initial spell of wildness, Page pitched overpowering baseball. In the final six and two-thirds innings he pitched, Page only allowed one harmless single and not one Boston batter reached second base. Of the three base runners he allowed, two of them were erased on double plays.

The Yankees, meanwhile, scored two runs in the fourth and two in the fifth, and with two outs in the bottom of the eighth and the score tied 4–4, John Lindell came to bat against reliever Joe Dobson. The right-handed hitting Lindell had spent most of the season on the bench, platooning with Gene Woodling, a young favorite of Stengel's. Because Dobson was a right-hander, Lindell was surprised that Stengel was letting him bat. Dobson, a crafty veteran, had had success in the past against Lindell, pitching him high and tight, but after throwing a ball, Dobson threw a pitch waist-high instead of letter-high, and the powerful Lindell lined the ball down the left-field line high and deep. With on-deck hitter Jerry Coleman giving the descending ball as much body English toward the right side of the pole as he could muster, the ball crashed fair into the lower stands, ten feet to the right of the pole for a home run and a 5–4 Yankee victory. It was only Lindell's sixth home run of the season, his first since July, a drop in performance from '48 which he freely blamed on Stengel's platoon system.

After the game, photographers were clamoring in the Yankee locker room for close-ups of Page and Lindell together. Garry Schumacher, a reporter watching the two men embrace before the cameras, said, "What I liked about this game is that the rogues won it."

John Lindell was a veteran on a team composed mostly of veterans. He was an agitator and free spirit who loved to haze rookies, growling at them not to speak unless spoken to, calling them "bushers," demanding that when they were in the dugout they root to earn their money. After manager McCarthy left in 1946, the somberness of the Yankee clubhouse disappeared, and Lindell's sense of humor descended on many of his teammates. He was a prankster, a practical joker, and often he selected one player as the target of his inspiration as the rest of the team looked on. Lindell was off-color, ribald, and probably gross, but in the rude clubhouse atmosphere of pro athletes, he was hilariously funny, and his irreverence was thoroughly enjoyed by all his teammates, even the victims. One time he put a soggy prophylactic between two pieces of bread of a teammate's ham sandwich as everyone sat around the clubhouse waiting for the teammate to take a big bite into it. Lindell would command peals of laughter as he stood in the shower room innocently urinating on the leg of an unsuspecting teammate or slobbering spit on his finger and sticking it into his teammate's ear, whinnying loudly like a palomino in heat. Lindell, whom they called Big Meat, particularly enjoyed playing pranks on Phil Rizzuto, the little shortstop. He would put snakes, spiders, or mice in Rizzuto's belongings, knowing how much the little guy hated anything that crawled. Often his jokes were spontaneous and unpredictable. On one airplane flight Lindell and Billy Johnson combined their talents to scare the phobia-laden Rizzuto out of his wits. The team was flying at night, and outside the window sparks from the propellers were easily visible. Johnson looked out the window and said, ''Phil, look at those sparks. I think the plane is on fire.''

The gullible and innocent Rizzuto turned white when he looked out and saw the sparks, so Johnson, to ''calm'' him, told Phil that the two of them would go speak to the pilot in the cockpit. Lindell, of course, was waiting in the cockpit. Before Johnson went inside, he suggested that Phil wait outside the door for him. Rizzuto, airsick, agreed.

Inside the cockpit Johnson and ''Captain'' Lindell discussed the dangerous situation in loud voices.

''Captain,'' shouted Johnson, ''I think the plane is on fire. What should we do?''

''I don't really know what to do,'' Lindell shouted back. ''It looks bad. I think we're going to have to ditch in the ocean.'' Outside the cockpit, Rizzuto, a non-swimmer, was becoming petrified. The rest of the team, meanwhile, was watching Phil's discomfort, biting their lips and tongues, trying to keep from breaking up.

Lindell on other flights would innocently pull out the airsick bag and say, ''You know what these are for, Phil?'' causing Rizzuto to turn all shades of green. To outsiders some of the things Lindell did certainly seemed malicious, but he only chose targets who enjoyed being targets, and never did anyone become angry at him because of his hijinks.

There was another side of Lindell's personality which emerged in the dugout or on the field. He was a deadly serious competitor. On the bench Lindell was a biting, effective bench jockey, and when he was playing, he was a battling mountain of muscle, a 6-foot 5-inch, 210-pound athlete who would chase an opposing infielder into left field to run him over if the situation called for him to break up a double play. Lindell, in fact, once pursued Chicago White Sox infielder Nellie Fox so far into left field before flattening him with a crushing block that league officials passed a rule that a base runner could only knock over the fielder making the double-play relay if he was within close proximity to the base.

Lindell signed a Yankee contract in 1936 for, as he described his bonus, ''a handshake, a comb, and a bar of Lifebuoy.'' After he spent six years in the organization learning how to pitch, in 1942 he finally made the Yankee pitching staff. Lindell spent his rookie year in the bullpen, watching and learning under manager Joe McCarthy's tutelage. But when the war came, and the Yankee team was decimated, McCarthy felt that Lindell could help the team more as an outfielder than as a pitcher. After all those years of learning to be a pitcher, Johnny Lindell became the Yankee center fielder in 1943, replacing DiMaggio and becoming an integral member of the '43 world champions. In 1944 Lindell became an American League star, batting .300 and finishing third in the league in RBI's. He was the key man in the war-time Yankee attack, the offensive leader among kids, old men, and 4-F's who disappeared as soon as the players in the service returned. At war were Bill Dickey, Joe Gordon, Phil Rizzuto, and Billy Johnson, and by mid-1944 Charlie Keller, Joe DiMaggio, and Tommy Henrich had enlisted, too. Lindell, who had a pre-Pearl Harbor son, wasn't drafted until 1945. In '44, the makeshift cast of Yankees finished third to the St. Louis Browns.

When Lindell returned to the Yankees from the service in 1946, so had DiMaggio, Keller, and Henrich, and it was too late for Lindell to resume his pitching career. For the rest of his Yankee career he filled in as a utility ballplayer, bench jockeying, staying in shape, ready when needed. Always Lindell hustled. He hustled to put his uniform on until the day it was taken away from him. In 1947 when Charlie Keller slipped a disk and missed most of the season, Lindell played left field, going nine for eighteen in the 1947 world series. "After that series the Dodgers asked me to take a saliva test," Lindell said. In '48, still in a utility role for Bucky Harris, he batted .317 and played excellently when called upon. In 1949, under Stengel, Lindell slumped badly, hitting only .242. Unhappy under Stengel, in 1950 he held out, almost begging to be traded. Stengel, who was building his team with youth, and Weiss, never enamored of John's irreverence, sold Lindell to the St. Louis Cardinals. Much of the craziness departed from the Yankee clubhouse when Lindell was traded away, and even Rizzuto missed him after he was gone. He went back to the minors to become a pitcher again, winning twenty-four games for the home-town Hollywood team in the Pacific Coast League, and in '53 he pitched for the Phillies and the Pirates in the National League with little distinction.

Jarrin' John Lindell, a wartime star, a big fish in a little pond who never got the opportunity to be the big fish in the big pond, nevertheless left an imprint on his teammates on the field, and left some fond memories off it. He taught opposing fielders to get out of his way when he was barreling into a base, and he taught his teammates to inspect their sandwiches before biting into them.

Nobody said it out loud, but when the Yankees won the Saturday game, they felt they were going to win the Sunday game, too, and before that final ball game there was a foreboding tenseness in the Red Sox locker room, a deadened spirit, while across the diamond under the Stadium stands Lindell, Page, Stirnweiss, and several of the other Yankees rushed to the sinks to fill their water pistols to continue a year-long shoot out. In another part of the locker Rizzuto and Henrich were discussing yesterday's game, and in another cubbyhole Joe DiMaggio sat quietly, still very weak. In another locker sat Vic Raschi, the starting pitcher for the day, silent and unsmiling. Raschi was normally a mild man with a humorless quality that kept strangers at a distance, but before a ball game he was starting his face would harden perceptibly, and his deliberately unshaven and bristly beard would surround a mean scowl as he pondered the enemy batters he would be facing shortly. To Raschi the business of pitching required the killer instincts of war and the frame of mind that went with them. It required complete concentration that demanded no one speak to him before a game he was to pitch. The others knew this and left him alone.

Into the packed Stadium came an endless procession of people, and by game time the tension in the air was almost visible. It was a hot autumn afternoon, the first day of October, and as the cigarette smoke was rising from the stands, it looked like a shimmering screen as it wafted upward and was kissed by the bright western sun. Players took several short gulps of the smoky air to retain the needed oxygen. Everyone was nervous, sweating heavily in the heat as the first Red Sox batter stepped into the box to face Raschi, who at over six feet tall and weighing two hundred and twenty pounds appeared as big as a house. He had a silky smooth, effortless overhand motion that was deceptive, for the ball he threw was alive and frighteningly fast.

Raschi's repertoire of pitches included a quick-breaking slider which darted away from a right-handed batter and an unimpressive curve ball, called "Aunt Susie" by his teammates, which he used for a change-up. But like Page, Raschi's bread and butter was the rising fast ball, nothing fancy, and he would simply rear back and fire. When he had to throw the ball just a little harder, he would take a deep breath and from a hidden reserve, muscle up and throw still harder.

For the Yankees in the first, Rizzuto led off with a drive into left field that Ted Williams lost in the fierce fireball sun which hung just above the Stadium's roof façade. When the ball finally fell, it was twenty feet from where the blinded outfielder was standing, and by the time Williams could recover, the speedy Rizzuto was standing on third.

It was early in the ball game, so manager McCarthy of Boston instructed his infielders to play back on the grass and concede the run in the event of a ground ball. At the plate Tommy Henrich, seeing McCarthy's strategy, was intent upon taking advantage of it. Rather than try for a base hit, Henrich purposely choked up and chopped a slow-bounding ground ball toward second base, enabling Rizzuto to score. New York led 1–0.

For eight torturous, breathtaking innings, it was the only run of the ball game, as Raschi and Ellis Kinder pitched brilliantly against exceptional batsmen. Fingernails were bitten to the quick, cigarettes burned furiously, nobody moving from his seat as the game and the pennant hung in the balance.

The Yankees scored four times in the bottom of the eighth, three of them scoring on a bases-loaded bloop single by Jerry Coleman, a rookie revelation all season long. The Yankees led 5–0, and the Red Sox, who had managed only two insignificant singles against Raschi, had only one at bat remaining.

If Raschi had a fault, it was his tendency to relax with a big lead, and Boston, aided by a triple by Bobby Doerr that rolled past Joe DiMaggio when his legs knotted, constricting his movement like he was caught in a vise and causing him to fall heavily, scored three runs in the ninth inning. With a runner on first, the tying run at the plate, and two outs, first baseman Tommy Henrich started to walk from first to the mound to say something encouraging to the tiring Raschi. Catcher Berra also waddled out to give the big pitcher a few words of encouragement. Raschi, hands on hips, defiant and angry, was spitting tobacco juice from the large chaw in his mouth. He wasn't interested in any pep talk. "Gimme the goddamn ball," Raschi said to his catcher, "and get the hell out of here." Berra, accustomed to Raschi's rages, flipped him the ball and returned to his crouch behind the plate. Henrich, taking the hint, also turned quickly and returned to his position at first.

Birdie Tebbetts, the next batter, lifted a high foul just behind first base. Henrich drifted back under it, loudly called off second-baseman Coleman, and as the ball smacked into his glove, the first-baseman squeezed it securely for the final out and the pennant. Coach Bill Dickey jumped in the air in jubilation and crashed his head against the roof of the dugout, knocking himself unconscious and adding to the total of more than seventy assorted Yankee injuries over the course of the season. After the players raced to the mound to deluge Raschi, they whooped and hollered into the locker room, stopping at DiMaggio's locker to ask how he was feeling and to shake his hand.

Manager Stengel, humble, grateful, and above all, numb, stood in the middle of the throng of dazed players, reporters, and photographers. After ten years of trying he had fulfilled a career ambition to win a pennant, and there were tears in his baggy eyes.

"I want to thank all these players for giving me the greatest thrill of my life," Stengel said. "And to think that they pay me for managing so great a bunch of boys."

For Vic Raschi, an earnest, intelligent, no-nonsense individual, another product of a Depression childhood, life had always been serious. When Raschi became a professional athlete, he understood and appreciated the importance of success, and he dedicated himself to that success with a solemn passion. Even at the end of his career he was one of the hardest workers. During spring training he could always be seen running wind sprints and doing sit-ups, working behind gritted teeth long after everyone else had packed it in for the day.

Raschi was a quiet, conservative person, a religious family man who outside of his intimate friends remained closed and introverted. He made a special effort to avoid publicity. When a reporter insisted upon interviewing him, Raschi would be evasive and unresponsive to the questions, and there were times when a particularly annoying reporter would discover his shoes covered with tobacco juice after an interview. Inevitably the press began to seek less recalcitrant athletes to interview, which was fine with Raschi. A cold, humorless quality kept him at arm's length from strangers.

When Raschi crossed the white foul line to the mound, his latent hostility actively simmered. He was grim and ornery, a frightening man to face, and when he pitched even his teammates behind him left him alone. Once when Raschi was in a jam with runners on base, Stengel wanted Yogi Berra, early in his catching career, to tell Raschi to pitch with more deliberation. While Stengel shouted out to Berra to call time and go out to the mound, Berra kept looking over to the dugout and shaking his head no. Finally, Stengel took some money out of his wallet and shook the bills in the air, a warning that Berra would be fined if he didn't go out there. Reluctantly Yogi called time-out and started to the mound. Getting about halfway, he was met by a brown stream of tobacco juice. "Not another step," barked Raschi, standing imperiously at the top of the mound. "Get the hell out of here now." Berra, without a word, returned to his position behind the plate as Raschi pitched out of the jam.

As Berra began to mature as a catcher, there were many times when he would play on Raschi's temperament. If Raschi was having trouble with his control, Berra would tease the pitcher about his receding hairline. "Come on, Onionhead," Berra would say, "you've been pitching all these years and you still can't throw a strike," and Raschi would call Berra every name in the book and bear down harder.

On occasion, when he had a big lead, his infielders enjoyed teasing him, though gently. Raschi had one superstition to which he adamantly adhered. After the Yankees threw the ball around the infield following an out, Raschi insisted that he be positioned with his right foot on the rubber before he would accept the ball from the third-baseman. Most of the time third-basemen Billy Johnson and Bobby Brown respected Raschi's idiosyncrasy, but sometimes they would deliberately throw the ball a couple of feet behind Raschi so he had to reach back, losing his balance and removing his right foot from the rubber to catch it. Raschi would glare menacingly at the offender as the rest of the infielders laughed behind their gloves.

Vic Raschi was one of the best of the modern-day pitchers, for seven years the most dependable pitcher on the Yankee staff, an uncomplaining man who never mentioned the bone chips in his pitching arm and who successfully hid a painful ligament condition in his right knee. "I only have so many years in the game," Raschi once said, "and any time they ask me to pitch, I'm going to pitch."

Between his rookie year in 1947 and his final year as a Yankee in 1953 when Yankee general manager George Weiss coldheartedly traded him after a salary dispute, Victor Angelo John Raschi started 207 games, completed 99 of them, winning 120 and losing only 50: Hall-of-Fame quality pitching. Raschi was 7–2 for New York his rookie year in 1947, and for the next six years he compiled won-lost records of 19–8, 21–10, 21–8, 21–10, 16–6, and 13–6. With Raschi starring, the Yankees won pennants in '47, '49, '50, '51, '52, and '53, also winning the world series each of those years.

When the Yankees needed to win one game, Raschi was the man usually called on, despite his pitching the last few years with torn cartilages in his right knee. After a game, Raschi's knee would pain him so that he would hide in the trainer's room to keep the extent of his injury secret from the press. Even some of his teammates didn't realize how much pain he endured when he was pitching. But Raschi had learned to live with the pain, compensating by taking three strikes and staying off the base paths when a hit by him would have been meaningless.

At the end of each of his superb seasons Raschi exacted a healthy salary from George Weiss, who found Raschi to be as stubborn as he was. Because Raschi was the backbone of the staff and because the Yankees needed him so badly, Raschi usually had the advantage in the negotiations. Every year there would be salary battles. Weiss would say, "Didn't you get your world series money? Didn't I have something to do with our winning when I brought so-and-so up from the minors?" And Raschi would always talk of his value to the club. Not how many strikeouts he had or what his earned run average was or even the number of ball games he won. His value to the ball club. He never allowed Weiss to pick out, "Why was your earned run average over four?" because Raschi knew that for him ERA was meaningless. If he had a one-nothing lead, he would win one-nothing. If he was ten runs ahead, so what if he gave up four or five runs? Raschi merely argued his value to the Yankee team, and what was Weiss going to say, that Raschi wasn't valuable? For years Raschi tied Weiss's hands.

In 1952 Raschi had won sixteen games, but in spring training of 1953 his knee problems were worsening, and Weiss knew it. Despite the knee, after another prolonged salary fight Raschi again got what he was asking with the aid of Casey Stengel's prodding. As Raschi rose to leave Weiss's office after signing his contract, Weiss looked at his big pitcher and said, "Raschi, don't you *ever* have a bad year."

In '53 Raschi won only thirteen games—for the big money he was getting, a bad year. When Raschi received his '54 contract calling for a twenty-five percent pay cut, Raschi said to his wife, "Mom, we're gone." Raschi returned the unsigned contract. "Mr. Weiss," he wrote, "I have made a cripple of myself."

That year Raschi was one of a dozen holdouts. After five consecutive world championships, the Yankee payroll was swelling beyond Weiss's penurious budget. When Raschi arrived in St. Petersburg, Florida, to continue negotiations he learned that Weiss had sold him to the St. Louis Cardinals, creating a furor among his teammates, but also sufficiently scaring the other holdouts so that they quickly lined up to sign their contracts. A newspaperman informed Raschi of the sale. Weiss hadn't even bothered to call to tell him. Raschi went to see Weiss and said simply, "Mr. Weiss, you have a very short memory."

1954 was the first year since 1948 the Yankees did not win the pennant. The Raschi sale had made some of the other veterans leery and cynical, hurting the morale of the team. With Raschi, the Yankees could have won in '54. They needed him to win the big one, and he wasn't there.

The 1949 pennant race in the National League had been as exciting as that in the American League. The Brooklyn Dodgers and the St. Louis Cardinals were tied on the last day of the season, but the Cardinals, who folded in the final week, completed their collapse by losing the final game while the Dodgers squeaked by the Philadelphia Phillies, the third-place club, in extra innings. Both the Yankees and the Dodgers were mentally and physically exhausted. In comparison to the magnificent pennant races, the series, which the Yankees won in five games, was an anticlimax. At the Stadium Tommy Henrich homered in the ninth inning to give Allie Reynolds a 1–0 win in the first game. The Dodgers beat Raschi 1–0 in the second, and when the series shifted to

Ebbets Field the Yankees swept, Johnny Mize winning the third game in the ninth, 4–1, with a bases-loaded pinch single; Bobby Brown tripling with the bases loaded to give the Yankees a 6–4 win in the fifth game, and the Yankees racing to a 10–0 lead against Rex Barney and coasting to a 10–6 victory for Raschi in the finale.

In the locker room after the cakewalk the photographers grouped around the players, surrounding DiMaggio who had batted .111 in the series and about whom rumors were swirling that his retirement was imminent. The Yankees were happy, but too fatigued to be demonstrative, and the cameramen had to force the players to give a victory yell. Stengel, asked to lead the posed victory cheer, bellowed at the top of his lungs hoarsely, "Happy New Year!"

1950

The Scooter . . . Wild Tommy Byrne . . . Johnny Mize,
the angry Big Cat . . . A brash youngster, Eddie Ford,
arrives . . . The destruction of the Whiz Kids . . .

Joe DiMaggio had intended to retire after the 1949 season, but Dan Topping personally asked Joe to return. Joe reluctantly agreed, repaying a debt he felt he owed the Yankee owner.

During the 1947 season Larry MacPhail had orally promised DiMaggio a $10,000 raise as the starting point for the following year's negotiations, but MacPhail had sold his interests in the team before he got around to negotiating with DiMaggio, and so DiMaggio figured he was going to get the "you made that agreement with him" runaround when he went to talk contract for '48. Instead, Topping had said, "If that's what you and MacPhail agreed, then that's it," and Topping raised Joe's salary from $32,500 to almost $75,000 for the '48 season. In '49 DiMaggio asked for $100,000, the first baseball player to demand that magic figure, and Topping, a tremendous fan of DiMaggio's and cognizant of his box-office value, agreed to his price amid much fanfare. Now, when DiMaggio came to tell Topping he was quitting, Topping did all he could to talk him out of it.

"You mean too much to the Yankees to quit, Joe," Topping said. "Please play another year. Pick your spots. Play when you want, and the money will be the same."

"It would be taking your money under false pretenses," DiMaggio said.

"I can assure you," Topping said, "that it wouldn't be."

Stengel was opening his second spring training on much surer footing than in 1949. He had undergone his baptism and was learning his way around the American League. All insecurity was gone. He was no longer Stengel, clown. He was Stengel, Manager of the Year. It made his job easier, though the older McCarthy-men never did warm up to him.

When camp opened, problems developed. Rizzuto's arm was sore, and the best he could do was lob the ball over to first. Mize's arm was still out of order from his injury from the year before. Henrich's left knee did not permit him to walk, and Bobby Brown had to miss the entire spring training period because of his medical studies at Tulane University. Stengel had to evaluate a growing collection of excellent minor league prospects: Joe Collins, a first-baseman, infielder Billy Martin and outfielder Jackie Jensen, two players Stengel had managed at Oakland in '48, plus a bevy of young pitchers.

But DiMaggio's legs seemed all right, some of the younger players like Coleman, Bauer, and Woodling had a year of experience under their belts, again Raschi, Reynolds, Lopat, and Byrne were strong, and Stengel felt confident, though the experts were picking the Red Sox to win in 1950.

"What nobody seems to realize," Stengel said, "is that I've been rebuilding the ball club and still winning. At this time a year ago I figgers I ain't got enough outfielders. Now this year I'm beginning to figger that I got too many, and they're the same fellers."

The Yankees didn't win many of their exhibition games because Stengel was preoccupied with experimenting with his minor league prospects and second-line arms. He wasn't worried about Raschi, Reynolds, Lopat, Byrne, and Page. He knew they would be ready, and he knew his offense would be sound. There was an air of confidence in the Yankee camp, and with the players having experienced a year under Stengel, they too could relax a little.

One afternoon when Stengel gave the veterans the afternoon off, Joe Page, George Stirnweiss, John Lindell, and a couple of others decided to rent a charter boat and fish for marlin and sailfish. It was a powerboat with long poles and swivel chairs, and after traveling ten or eleven miles out to sea, the men rocked gently with the waves and fished. Joe Page, in a chair for over an hour under the hot, enervating tropical sun without success, became weary. He put his pole into the holder beside the chair and started below.

"If I get a strike," Page shouted back over the roar of the motors, "call me."

While Page was resting below, John Lindell began to work. He whispered something to George Stirnweiss, who immediately rushed to speak to the skipper of the boat. Meanwhile Lindell was reeling in Page's line. After Lindell reeled it in, he emptied a wooden bucket that was being used to hold bait, tied it to the end of Page's line and reeled out the line. Then he ran to awaken Page.

"Joe, Joe," Lindell hollered, shaking Page awake on his bunk, "you've got a strike. Hurry!"

Page rushed from the cabin, bounded up the steps onto the deck, and quickly strapped himself into the chair. For close to four hours Page fought to land his quarry. Whenever the Great Catch would seem to be getting close, the captain would speed up the boat, making it impossible to reel in, and wearily Page would have to let the line out. Then the captain slowed the boat, and the ritual would begin again. Finally, with Page on the edge of exhaustion as the sun was sinking, Lindell signaled for the captain to allow Page to reel in the line. Page began his final battle as the monster fish seemed to be losing its strength. Finally he managed to reel his catch right beside the gently rocking boat. Page leaned over the side to gaff it, and when he saw the gaping round perimeter of the bucket a foot below the waves, he joyfully exclaimed, "Look at the mouth on that son of a bitch!" When he discovered the bucket at the end of the line, Lindell and Stirnweiss and the others laughed until their guts ached.

For the rest of the season Page was continually asked, "Wanna go bucket fishing, Joe?"

Days before the opening of the regular 1950 season, Page took advantage of another wildlife adventure to gain his revenge. Several of the Yankees traveled to Presque Isle, Maine, near the Canadian border. They were playing an exhibition game in Portland, and since Page, Lindell, Stirnweiss, Rizzuto, and a couple of teammates had bought shares in a cabin up in Presque Isle, this was the perfect chance for them to get in a day's hunting.

Snuffy Stirnweiss had always wanted to shoot a bear, so the day before their arrival at the cabin Page phoned a hunting-guide friend to arrange for Stirnweiss to "get" his bear. The guide knew of a large, fearsome but crippled brown bear prowling the area, and by arrangement he tracked it down and shot it.

It was evening when the tired players arrived at the cabin, and while everyone else was bedding down for the night, Page excused himself to go to the outhouse a hundred feet from the cabin. The hunting guide was waiting for Page with the carcass of the dead bear in the back of his pickup. Page and the guide removed the cumbersome bear from the truck and hauled it into the outhouse, where they propped it onto the toilet seat, it's large toothy head leaning against the outward-opening outhouse door. Page and friend then joined the rest of the tired party inside the cabin to get a good night's sleep in preparation for the next day's hunt.

It was still pitch black when Page awoke at five in the morning, and the first thing he did was awaken Stirnweiss. The first thing Stirnweiss did was what every person does when he wakes up in the morning: he made a beeline for the john. As Stirnweiss groggily left the cabin, Page quickly awakened everyone else and told them about the bear. Outside, meanwhile, Stirnweiss was groping his way toward the outhouse in the darkness, and when he yanked open the creaky wooden door with the half-moon on it, the large hairy bear carcass fell heavily on top of him. Reflexively Stirnweiss wrapped his arms around the bear to keep from falling down. The petrified Stirnweiss screamed a noiseless scream. He fought to push the ponderous bear carcass away and then raced back to the cabin, his feet barely touching the ground. Stirnweiss was so frightened that he blasted through the cabin door without opening it, shattering it into splinters. Once inside the cabin Stirnweiss tried unsuccessfully to explain to the others about the bear. His mouth was moving but no words were coming out as he kept pointing to the outhouse.

"Spit it out, Snuff. What are you trying to tell us?" they asked him, before finally shrieking hysterically.

Later Page got even again. Several of the players had bought the cabin in equal shares with Page holding the deed. When Page found himself in financial difficulty, without telling the others, he sold the cabin.

Stengel returned all his rookie pitchers to the minors several days before the start of the season, so the 1950 Yankees differed very little from the team of the year before. Stengel kept 28-year-old rookie Joe Collins to alternate with Henrich at first and sent Johnny Mize to the Kansas City Blues farm team so he could get treatment for his bad shoulder and work himself into shape. He kept both Martin and Jensen, though neither figured to play much. Henrich, Coleman, Rizzuto, and either Johnson or Brown, who was back from his medical studies, were again in the infield, with the much improved Berra behind the plate. DiMaggio was back in center, and Bauer, Woodling, Mapes, and Lindell on the flanks. Charlie Keller had been sold to the Detroit Tigers. Stirnweiss would soon be on his way to the St. Louis Browns.

The season opened in Fenway Park against Boston, and the Yankee-Red Sox rivalry intensified when the Red Sox mauled Reynolds and his replacements for a 9–0 lead only to see the Yankees score nine runs in the eighth inning and go on to win the game, 15–10. Stengel danced around like he had just won another pennant, and the Yankee players hugged each other in glee.

By late spring every regular was hitting close to .300 with the exception of DiMaggio, whose timing was off but who was driving in a sufficient number of runs to remain in the lineup. Rizzuto and Coleman were developing into the finest double play combination in the league. Raschi and Lopat were winning. Reynolds, though he was losing a slew of close ball games, was pitching well, and though Page was hot and cold, Tommy Byrne after losing his opening game posted eight straight victories, a major reason why the Yankees were sitting atop the league in mid-June.

Tommy Bryne was a left-hander who signed with the Yankee organization in 1940 for $10,000, till then the highest bonus ever paid to an untried prospect. Byrne pitched a few games for the Yankees in '43, but when he returned after three years in the service, manager McCarthy asked Byrne to switch to first base to take advantage of his excellent hitting ability. Byrne, however, refused, and in 1946 he pitched exactly nine innings in four ball games, and in 1947 was sent back to the minors. Not until 1948 did Byrne finally get a chance to pitch regularly for the Yankees, finishing 8–5, in 134 innings striking out 93 and walking 101. In 1949 Byrne was 15–7, a top pitcher, but his 179 walks led the league. In 1950 and again in 1951 Byrne led the league in walks.

Off the field Tommy Byrne looked like the quiet, unassuming doctor he once had planned to become. On the mound he displayed so many nervous idiosyncrasies that he drove anyone watching him pitch mad. He would stand on the pitching rubber for an eternity before delivering the pitch, making the batter jumpy, distracting his own fielders who had difficulty staying alert between pitches, and driving spectators in the stands absolutely insane with impatience as he tugged at his clothing, straightened his hat, wiped his brow, hitched up his pants, turned around to look at the outfielders, and tied his shoelaces before finally, with great reluctance, throwing the little white ball at high speed toward its uncertain destination in the vicinity of home plate. Inevitably his first pitch would be a ball, and he would then repeat a variation of the pre-pitch tug, wipe, hitch, turnaround routine until the batter either walked or struck out. Byrne rarely allowed more than five or six hits in a game, but often he would have ten walks and ten strikeouts, and the nerves of everyone involved became so raw that only a person with the greatest self-control could prevent himself from either pulling out his hair by the roots or attempting mayhem upon Byrne.

Because Byrne won more than he lost, his many walks didn't concern or bother him, though they surely bothered everyone else. Byrne felt that if a batter did walk, chances were that he was not going to score because rarely did he allow enough hits for the walked batters to score. From the end of 1949 to the middle of 1950 Byrne was 17–2, ending '49 with a 9–1 record and starting '50 8–1. Though Byrne didn't start as many games as Raschi, Reynolds, and Lopat, he was doing exceptionally well at winning. Nevertheless, everyone who watched Byrne carped about his great number of base on balls.

The eccentric Byrne drove manager Stengel to distraction. Every time Byrne found himself with men on base, which was often, Stengel would get on the phone to the bullpen to warm up a relief pitcher, and a couple of pitchers would heat up. Then Byrne would get out of the jam, and the reliefers would sit down again, so that even if Byrne did pitch a complete game and win, the arms of the relief pitchers would be shot for the next couple of days.

Once Byrne was standing on the mound during the middle of an inning, with runners dancing off first and third, when rookie first-baseman Joe Collins came over to settle him down. Before Collins could say anything, Byrne nodded in the direction of the bench and said, "Look at 'em in there, Joe. They're going crazy. Watch. In a second they'll be on the phone to the bullpen." As Collins stood with Byrne and watched, pitching coach Jim Turner picked up the phone to the bullpen. "See, Joe," Byrne said. "There he goes. There he goes. I told you." Byrne was laughing ecstatically. Mumbling, Collins walked back to first, and Byrne retired the side without allowing a score.

In those games when Byrne's lack of control forced Stengel to remove him, Byrne would plead with the manager to let him stay in. "Give me one more chance. Just one more batter," Byrne would say. Stengel would shake his head no and put out his hand for the ball, but Byrne would refuse to give it up until Stengel almost had to wrest it from his grasp.

Sometimes before Byrne delivered the pitch, he would stand on the rubber with men on base and playfully toss the ball up and down, up and down, while Stengel held his breath hoping Byrne wouldn't drop it for a balk. Byrne also loved to talk to the batters before pitching to them. Sometimes when his pitches were just missing the plate and he wanted the batter to swing, he would tell the batter whether he was going to throw a fast ball or a curve. Byrne figured that by telling the batter, the batter would take it as an insult and try to show Byrne up by trying to clobber the pitch. Byrne figured the percentages were with him because rarely was he hit solidly, even when he advertised the pitch. And if the batter swung, there was less likelihood of his walking.

Byrne sometimes tried to make a batter overanxious by agitating him in other ways.

"Hey Runnels," he would yell to Red Sox Pete Runnels. "You from Texas?"

"Yeah," Runnels would say. "What of it?"

"Thought so," Byrne would say. "I could tell because you're bowlegged."

Or Byrne would talk to Ted Williams, asking Ted about his wife, from whom Williams was separated, causing Yogi Berra behind the plate to break up laughing. While Byrne held the ball and held the ball, Williams would grind the bat into sawdust with his hands. One time Williams became so frustrated he growled at Berra, "I don't have to hit against that left-handed son of a bitch to make a living." All the while Byrne would stand out on the mound smiling —and holding the ball.

Byrne finished 1950 only 15–9 overall after his 8–1 start, and in the spring of 1951, Yankee owner Dan Topping ordered him off the club. Topping's nerves finally couldn't take it any longer either. After one of Byrne's walk one, strike-out one games, Topping went to general manager George Weiss, one of the few times Topping interfered with Weiss, and said, "George, we've got to get rid of this guy. I absolutely refuse to come to the ball park when he's working. He drives me crazy." That week Weiss traded Byrne to the St. Louis Browns, angering manager Stengel who had not been consulted. "Sure he's wild," Stengel screamed, "but he won fifteen games for us last year and the year before. Who's gonna do that for us now?"

At the end of June 1950 the darkening clouds of war settled over the country when the Russians successfully exploded a nuclear bomb and the Chinese communist forces invaded South Korea. At home Wisconsin Senator Joseph McCarthy announced before a Senate subcommittee that the communists were infiltrating the State Department, and there was much fear that the Russians would support the Chinese and engage the U.S. in a nuclear war.

In baseball, pitchers throughout both leagues were complaining that the ball had been given a new liveliness, that it traveled longer distances when hit, and one pitching pundit whispered that "the atom bomb secrets had been sold to Spaulding, not to the Russians."

The Detroit Tigers, managed by ex-Yankee third-base star Red Rolfe, and led by ex-Yankees Jerry Priddy and Aaron Robinson, had moved ahead of New York into first place. The Yankees, playing well, were clinging close to the lead, though manager Stengel was concerned about his first-base situation with Henrich ailing badly and rookie Collins's batting average dropping steadily. He was also concerned that Joe DiMaggio's weary legs were hampering him in the outfield. On July 3, Stengel tried to solve both problems. He shocked the team by shifting DiMaggio to first base against the lowly Washington Senators, and starting an outfield of Woodling, Mapes, and Bauer. It was the only game of DiMaggio's major league career that he did not play the outfield, and the move proved to be a mistake: DiMaggio became annoyed that Stengel had asked Topping to request the switch instead of the manager's coming to ask, and during the game he was so unsure of himself at the strange position that though he made all the plays, he dripped sweat as if he were going through the tortures of hell. He was petrified that he would embarrass himself in public.

In the latter part of the game Bauer seriously injured his ankle, and DiMaggio returned to center field, the experiment never again to be repeated, though it continued to leave a bad taste in DiMaggio's mouth. The Yankees brought Johnny Mize back from the Kansas City Blues to play first base, and DiMaggio remained in center field.

DiMaggio, though never talkative, was usually congenial, but during the summer he was becoming more and more despondent. He brooded, submerged in his thoughts, unwilling to confide in his teammates, who could sense that there was something much deeper troubling him than his mediocre batting average. True, he hadn't been hitting well, and Stengel had dropped him to fifth in the order behind Berra and Mize, a further blow to Joe's fierce pride, but for a stretch of over two weeks DiMaggio had remained absolutely silent, staring mutely out the train window as the rest of his teammates played cards and swapped stories. Because Joe did not discuss his private life with anyone, including his roommate Joe Page, they could only speculate as to what was troubling him.

In the fall of 1939 DiMaggio had been introduced to actress Dorothy Arnold while she was filming the movie "Manhattan Merry-Go-Round," and during their three years of marriage (that ultimately ended in divorce when Joe entered the service), they had a son, Joe Jr. Now during the summer of '50 DiMaggio had learned that Miss Arnold was in the process of divorcing her second husband and that there was a possibility of another marriage and hence another "father" in the life of Joe Jr. It was something DiMaggio feared but was helpless to control.

The disruption in DiMaggio's life was likewise troubling Stengel. Joe had registered his 2,000th hit, only the third active player—Luke Appling and Wally Moses were the other two—to reach that mark, but it was clear that DiMaggio was no longer even a shadow of his old self. "I haven't got that feeling that I used to have," he said, "that I can walk up there and hit any pitcher who ever lived." Stengel knew that his teammates might resent a move to bench him and that DiMaggio surely would, yet on the other hand the Yankee manager feared that the team would suffer if he did *not* make the move. It was a most difficult decision. On August 12, Stengel made front-page headlines by announcing that DiMaggio was going to take a week's rest.

"I know some people say I am through," DiMaggio said bitterly, "but those are the same people who said the same thing in 1946."

After resting a week DiMaggio returned to the lineup on August 18, back in his customary number-four spot in the lineup. Raschi had battled the Philadelphia A's to a 2–2 tie going into the ninth inning, when DiMaggio, who had failed to hit the ball out of the infield all day long, came to bat. The A's pitcher threw a ball a little too good, and DiMaggio powered a long drive into the upper left-field seats of the Philadelphia ball park. There were only 6,054 fans in the park for the game, but each one rose and cheered the man as he rounded the bases, despite the realization that his home run had beaten them. As DiMaggio passed third base, a grin crossed his face, and at home plate he was mobbed by all his teammates who felt joy for DiMag, a hero to them as well as to millions of baseball fans. Out of the next eleven games, New York won ten and DiMaggio batted around .450. The Yankees sat three games out of first, patiently waiting for the upstart Tigers to fold.

Through the end of August and the first half of September the Yankees played excellently, catching the Tigers as Rizzuto continued to perform his miracles at short, and DiMaggio, Berra, and the rejuvenated John Mize supplied the brunt of the home-run power. Mize, back with the team since returning from Kansas City in June, had hit nineteen home runs, and he won the first-base job from Collins.

When the Yankees traveled to Detroit to meet the contending Tigers for a three-game series on September 14, 15, and 16, the Yankees led the Tigers by half a game.

Few predicted the Tigers would be in contention so late in the season, but pitchers Art Houtteman, Fred Hutchinson, and Hal Newhouser were winning consistently. George Kell was leading the league in hitting, outfielders Vic Wertz, Hoot Evers, and Johnny Groth all were hitting over .300, and in the infield Jerry Priddy and Johnny Lipon were leading even Coleman and Rizzuto in double plays. The Tigers were certainly a surprise, and manager Red Rolfe knew his team would have a real shot at the pennant if they could win at least two out of three from the Yankees and climb back into first place.

The two teams split the first two games. Raschi won the first one, as DiMaggio, Cliff Mapes, and Johnny Mize all homered, but in the second game Art Houtteman beat Reynolds in relief of Byrne, 9–7. It was a loss that certainly could not be attributed to Mize. The powerful first-baseman hit three of the longest drives ever hit in Briggs Stadium, high-arching home runs for six of the seven Yankee runs. It was the sixth time in his illustrious career that he had hit three home runs in one game.

During Johnny Mize's eleven-season career with the St. Louis Cardinals and the New York Giants, he was THE slugger in the National League, leading it in home runs in 1939, '40, '47, and '48, and in RBI's in 1940, '42, and '47. In 1939 he hit 28 home runs to win the home-run title, and in 1940 Mize set a Cardinal team record for home runs with 43. That year Mize might have had a chance to break Babe Ruth's season record of 60 home runs, but a temporary wire mesh fence was erected above the low right-field wall, and many of the 31 doubles and 13 triples he hit banged off the screen instead of going into the stands for home runs. In 1942 his 137 RBI's led the league, and after he spent three years in the Navy, he hit 51 home runs for the Giants in 1947, becoming only the second left-handed batter in baseball history to hit more than 50 home runs in a season. That year his 138 runs batted in also led the league. He hit 40 home runs to lead the league in 1948, and his 125 RBI's made it the eighth season that he batted in over 100 runs.

Mize was 36 years old when the Yankees bought him from the Giants toward the end of the 1949 season. Mize played first base for manager Stengel and during his five-year Yankee stay, he became Stengel's number one pinch hitter, leading the league in pinch hits in 1951, '52, and '53.

When Mize finally retired at the end of the '53 season, he had hit more home runs than any other active player. His 359 career home runs placed him sixth on the all-time home-run list behind an exclusive group of Hall-of-Famers: Babe Ruth (714), Jimmy Foxx (534), Mel Ott (511), Lou Gehrig (493), and Joe DiMaggio, two ahead at 361. Behind Mize were two more Hall-of-Famers, Ted Williams, at 337 the only active player close to him, and Hank Greenberg (331).

He was 40 years old when he retired, a member of the exclusive 2000-hit club, and one of three men in the history of the game to have hit a home run in each of the American League *and* National League parks in which he played. Do not, however, look for his plaque in the Hall of Fame. For some mysterious reason, Mize was never voted into the hall, a terrible injustice to this man who starred for sixteen seasons as one of the great power hitters in the game.

The Yankees were fortunate to acquire Mize in August of '49. He had led the National League in homers for the past two years and had been named to the All-Star team in '49, but the Giants had hired a new manager, Leo Durocher, in mid-'48, and Durocher preferred players with speed and finesse who could steal bases and hit-and-run, and he began to bench some of the older, less mobile veterans including Mize. In midsummer of 1949 the Yankees were playing the Giants in the annual Mayor's Trophy game for charity, and Stengel, knowing that Mize was not playing regularly, approached him before the game. "How you doing?" Stengel asked the big first-baseman. "I'm not playing much," Mize responded. "Over here you'd be playing," Stengel said. Stengel then urged George Weiss to acquire him. Mize had a .324 lifetime batting average, he had been a league All-Star for nine years, and he would be a perfect batsman to challenge Yankee Stadium's short right-field porch. For the Yankees there were also disturbing rumors that the rival Red Sox were trying to get him.

Weiss called Dan Topping, a personal friend of Horace Stoneham, the owner of the Giants. Stoneham was having money troubles, and it was hoped that he would be willing to sell his high-priced slugger. In August Topping, Weiss, Del Webb, and Stoneham met secretly in Topping's apartment. After a few drinks and some chitchat, Topping got to the point. "Horace," he said, "we would like to buy Mize from you."

Stoneham was skeptical. "I can't do that," he said. "If I sell him to you and he becomes a star, it'll make the Giants look bad."

They had a few more drinks. "Tell you what I'll do," Topping said. "I'll give you $50,000 for Mize, cash. And if he does end up helping us this year, we'll give you an added $25,000 for a total of $75,000."

"Hell," added Webb, "Mize isn't helping you any. Durocher won't play him."

"Who's going to decide whether I get the extra twenty-five thousand?" Stoneham asked.

"We'll let George decide," Topping said, nodding in Weiss's direction. Stoneham agreed, and Mize became a Yankee.

Immediately Mize won two games with his bat in a year that saw the Yankees win the pennant by one game, and then he severely injured his shoulder. Mize didn't do much the rest of the season, but in the series he won an important game with a pinch hit. After the series Weiss approached Topping and Webb. "I don't think Mize helped us that much," Weiss said. "Stoneham doesn't deserve the extra money."

"For Christ's sake, George," Webb said, shaking his head. "How can you be that way?"

When Mize came to the Yankees, he and Stengel got along famously. For many years Mize had been a one-man destruction gang against Stengel's Dodger and Brave teams, and Casey highly respected Mize's knowledge of the mechanics of hitting. When he wasn't starting, Mize would sit on the bench next to Stengel and act as the unofficial batting coach, making suggestions and annoying some players who didn't particularly desire his criticism, especially right after they had made an out and were returning to the dugout. But Mize could help, because he knew how to analyze what they were doing wrong and could tell what the batter should expect from a particular pitcher. Often he gave his teammates clues as to what they should be looking for at the plate.

If he was on the bench, as the later innings of a ball game approached, Mize would anticipate a possible pinch-hitting situation and grab a bat from the rack, leave the dugout, and go under the stands into the locker room. There he would practice his swing, pretending to bat against the opposing pitcher of the day, and after five or ten minutes of practice swings, he would return to the dugout, mentally prepared to hit. As a pinch hitter he batted close to .300.

In early June of 1950, Weiss was intending to send Mize down again because his shoulder still had not healed, but when he was put on waivers, rival Detroit claimed him, and Weiss was forced to keep him. Mize then proceeded to hit twenty-five home runs at the age of 37, prompting Dan Parker of the New York *Daily Mirror* to write:

> *Your arm is gone; your legs likewise,*
> *But not your eyes, Mize, not your eyes.*

What is immediately discernible about Mize on first glance is that he is a huge figure, carrying more than two hundred and fifty pounds over a six foot two frame. Mize speaks in a deep, slow cadence, and with strangers he is reserved, not at all chatty, displaying a southerner's suspicion of them. About many facets of his baseball career he is a very bitter man.

"In 1950 I only had 76 hits for the entire season, and I drove in 72 runs," Mize said. "Average didn't mean much for the simple reason that if we played a club like the Browns, I would get taken out early. The games I played the full nine innings were the real tough ball games or the games where we were getting beat. As soon as we got the lead, Casey would say, 'Well, let somebody else play.' I remember during contract time, Weiss would always say, 'You don't play regularly,' and I'd tell him, 'Every time they put my name in the lineup, I play.'"

On the subject of the Hall of Fame Mize is actively resentful. He is more than 60 years old now, and he has seen almost every one of his illustrious contemporaries inducted, men like Ted Williams, Joe DiMaggio, Mel Ott, and Hank Greenberg, and as the years have passed young sluggers have obscured his place in baseball history. Sluggers like Hank Aaron, Willie Mays, Mickey Mantle, Frank Robinson, and Harmon Killebrew have passed him on the home-run list, but they were playing in a different era when the world was home-run crazy. Baseball had been Mize's entire life, and the one honor he wants more than any other has been kept from him, and he does not know why.

"Rabbit Maranville was working with kids for the *Journal-American* when I was doing a radio show with WMCA, and he died in January of '54," Mize said. "The next summer he was voted into the Hall. Why did his record get so much better after he died?"

We had talked for a couple of hours, and it was getting dark. I had to start a long drive from the west coast of Florida where Mize was vacationing to cold

New York City, but before I left I felt like telling this giant, hard-bitten old pro that he shouldn't be bitter and that the real fans would always remember his ability to hit a curve ball. But it would have sounded stupid, so I didn't.

He thanked me for coming, and as we shook hands he said, "Next time you drop by we'll have a few beers, and I could really tell you some stories." Just before I left, he asked me if I had heard how Frankie Frisch, a Cardinal teammate of his, a Hall-of-Fame infielder, was doing. Frisch had been involved in a serious auto accident the day before and had been listed in serious condition. I wasn't sure how Frisch was, but trying to leave the Big Cat in a better mood, I impulsively told him Frisch was going to be all right.

The next morning I had just passed Orlando on Route 4 on my way across the state, when there was a short bulletin on the radio. Frankie Frisch had died.

Going into the final September 16 game of their three-game series, the Yankees still led the Tigers by a half-game. In New York baseball fans were discussing a cherubic, blond youngster the Yankees had brought up from their Kansas City farm. His name was Eddie Ford, and though at age 21 he looked more like he was fourteen, he had defeated six straight second-division opponents without a loss. The veterans teased him about his youthful appearance, making cracks that suggested he hadn't yet reached puberty, but Ford always had a quick comeback. He was a cocky kid, and when he got out on the pitcher's mound, he impressed everyone with his poise and savvy.

The year before while the Yankees were fighting the Red Sox for the 1949 pennant, Ford had telephoned Stengel, volunteering to pitch the Yankees to the pennant. At the time Ford was pitching for Binghamton, Class A. "You may think I'm cocky," Ford said, "but I can win for you. I've learned everything I can learn in the minor leagues." Stengel rejected Ford's offer, but many years later he confided that he should have listened to the kid. "I'll bet he would have done just what he said he would do," Stengel said.

During the 1950 spring training Ford told a reporter, "I've won every place else the Yankees have tried me, so it's only human nature for me to believe that I can keep winning if they give me a chance in the majors."

When Ford first came up in June, manager Stengel started him against the lowly Senators. "It's up to you, kid," Stengel said. "Maybe you can go out and beat somebody and put some life into our guys."

"Okay, Case," Ford said. "You just sit back and watch. You've got nothing to worry about." He was so cocky, but by September he was 6–0, and he had saved the Yankees, throwing a fast ball that was faster than it looked and throwing sharp-breaking curve balls for strikes on 3–1 and 2–0 with the poise of a veteran.

Off the field Ford chose Joe Page to be his buddy, and their friendship was the subject of talk by the players and especially the management. It soon became evident that though Ford had fuzzy cheeks, he was no babe in the woods. He was a kid who could down his Scotch with the best of them.

Stengel decided to gamble and pitch Ford in the third game of the Detroit series. It was probably the most important game of the season to this point for both the Yankees and Tigers, and in Detroit an overflow gathering of more than

56,000 stuffed themselves into antiquated Briggs Stadium to see if Red Rolfe's Cinderella Tigers could struggle past the Yankees. The Tigers needed this one desperately to keep their carriage and coachmen from turning into a pumpkin and a flock of mice. The Yankees needed it to stay in first.

After the anthem, veteran shortstop Rizzuto visited with the young pitcher, figuring it would be a good idea to go to the mound and give him a little pep talk. Solicitously Rizzuto put his arm around Ford's neck and said, "Eddie, just take it slow and easy, and you'll beat these guys. Just go out and pitch your game." The words didn't mean anything, but Rizzuto was trying to calm Ford's nerves. They didn't need soothing.

"Scooter," Ford said. "All I gotta do is throw my glove out there, and I can beat these guys. Don't be worrying about me." Ford allowed one run in a game that was tied 1–1 until the ninth when the Yankees exploded to win, 8–1, as Joe DiMaggio hit his thirtieth home run.

Several days later Ford won his eighth straight without a loss, and with surprisingly tenacious Detroit continuing to win and ten games left in the season, New York and Detroit were still tied for the lead.

For the third season in a row it was the Boston Red Sox who were the major obstacles to the pennant for the Yankees. After Red Sox manager Steve O'Neill had replaced Joe McCarthy during the summer, he led the team to a 23–5 fall finish, and with the days left in the season numbered, the Red Sox found themselves only two games behind the Yankees and the Tigers. Boston had lost the pennant on the final day in both 1948 and 1949, and again the Sox were within range. The Red Sox were visiting Yankee Stadium for a two-game series. The Tigers, meanwhile, were facing a strong Cleveland Indian team in a four-game series. If the Indians could win a few of those games, then either New York or Boston had an excellent chance of going on to the pennant.

On September 23, a cloudless afternoon, 63,998 filled Yankee Stadium close to capacity for what had become the most intense rivalry in baseball next to the one between the Dodgers and the Giants in the National League. At stake was the American League pennant.

In the bottom of the first with a runner on first base, Joe DiMaggio, continuing to discount the rumors that he was washed up, swung at a Mel Parnell pitch. Though he swung late, he hit the ball with enough power to carry it down the right-field line into the front row of box seats for a two-run homer. In the third a walk, a Rizzuto double, an intentional walk to DiMaggio, and a two-run single by Mize put the game out of reach as Lopat continued his shutout. When Coleman tripled with the bases loaded over the head of Ted Williams in the eighth, the Yankees completed an 8–0 rout.

The next day an even larger crowd of 66,924 packed the Stadium as everyone could begin to smell a second straight pennant. The Indians had beaten the Tigers in the first two games of their series to give the Yankees a one and a half game lead. Snarling Vic Raschi was pitching for the Yankees, and though the Red Sox scored first on a home run by Ted Williams, by the fourth inning the Yankees had scored six runs. Yogi Berra hit three singles and a triple and little Phil Rizzuto hit a single, a double, and a home run and was brilliant defensively as the Yankees won, 9–5. In the ninth the fans stood for a long ovation when the scoreboard announced that the Indians had defeated Detroit for the third straight game.

After the Yankees disposed of the Red Sox, they breezed home with the pennant. DiMaggio extended his hitting streak to nineteen games, hitting a gaudy .373 in the final month and a half of the season to end the year with a .301 average. With two days left in the season Phil Rizzuto capped a brilliant 200-hit season with four hits and the game-winning single in the tenth inning against the Philadelphia A's to clinch a tie for the pennant. The following day the Tigers were defeated, and for the second year in a row the Yankees were the champions.

Joe Williams, writing in the New York *Telegram*, called this pennant a "baseball miracle." It was the second unexpected pennant in a row under Stengel.

Phil Rizzuto made the impossible plays look easy for so many years that by the end of his career his unique talents were being taken for granted, but for over ten seasons Rizzuto was the finest shortstop in the major leagues, a defensive genius who won more games with his glove than any of the big hitters won with their bats. He was speedy *and* quick, a rare combination, and no one was better at ranging to his left or right for ground balls or racing at full speed into left field with his back to the plate to catch a pop-up. He was expert at the close-in play around second, the shovel for the double play, the backhand flip, and on tags never did he give ground to the runner. Defensively Rizzuto was the Rock of Gibraltar of the Yankee infield.

On offense the five-foot six-inch Rizzuto realized early in his career that his size would be a handicap to hitting the long ball, so instead he concentrated on reaching first base, getting a base on balls, or bunting for a hit, and he learned to hit to all fields, hit behind the runner, and sacrifice.

On base Rizzuto was a daring and intelligent base runner. Once he was on first when the batter tried to bunt him to second and popped the ball in the air. The third-baseman rushed in and caught the ball at his shoe tops, and as the fielder was congratulating himself on the catch, Rizzuto tagged up and raced safely into second. Another time he was on third when the batter grounded to first base. Rizzuto bluffed a break for the plate, and when the first-baseman fielded the ball, he immediately looked to see whether Rizzuto was going home. Halfway down the line to home Rizzuto stopped, the first-baseman faked a throw home and then raced to first to retire the batter, too late. As soon as Rizzuto saw him running toward first, he sped home safely ahead of the belated throw. So quickly could he stop and then start again that he and Jackie Robinson were acknowledged as the two finest base runners in the majors during their era.

A little guy who was accused of being a hypochondriac and a worrier, a guy who off the field was deathly afraid of insects and mice and flying in planes and bad luck and his own shadow, Rizzuto on the field was fearless, holding his ground at second base to make a relay or a tag in the face of a hard-charging runner. He was a remarkably durable ball player who, when hit, always acted like he had been mortally wounded, lying on the ground motionless for a while before gingerly picking himself off the ground and continuing. Through two grueling 154-game seasons in 1949 and 1950, Rizzuto missed exactly four games.

During his era no other major league shortstop (except perhaps Pee Wee Reese of the Dodgers) was in his class, and yet like Mize, Rizzuto has not yet been voted into the Hall of Fame.

Manager Casey Stengel, a baseball observer since he broke in with Brooklyn in 1912, once said of Rizzuto, "He is the greatest shortstop I have ever seen in my entire baseball career, and I have watched some beauties. He can do anything anybody ever did with a baseball. He beats you in so many different ways. Honus Wagner was a better hitter, sure, but I've seen this kid make plays Wagner never did. If I were a retired gentleman I would follow the Yankees around just to see Rizzuto work those miracles every day."

It is a credit to Rizzuto's determination and grittiness that he ever became a professional athlete at all. He encountered so many obstacles as a result of discrimination against his short stature that his road to the majors was as tough as Pilgrim's trip to the City of God. When he graduated from high school four teams turned him away because of his height. He earned a contract with the Yankees largely because their manager and their head scout weren't much taller than he was. His major problems always revolved around getting the *chance*, though once he did get that chance, his superior skills always won over his detractors.

Conversely, his size occasionally worked to his advantage. Despite the initial cynicism which always dogged him, the cynics ultimately loved him wherever he went. He became the underdog, and combined with his bubbling childlike innocence, he became a favorite of the fans, who constantly lavished their affection on him, sending him gifts, baking him Italian food, and inviting him into their homes.

The players loved him too, and on the field they fiercely protected him. They, too, sent him gift-wrapped presents—like a box of worms or a dead mouse. They knew Rizzuto was incredibly gullible, and they also knew he was laden with phobias. He had fears. The fear of flying, the fear of bugs and insects and things that go bump in the night. The fear of failure. The fear of rejection. And they took advantage of all these fears, playing one against the other. When they played tricks on him, he was glad, because it meant that the guys still liked him. When his teammates stopped playing their tricks, Phil would worry about why they had stopped. On the Yankees, as in the minors, Rizzuto was the "professional victim," and the most docile, quiet people would change like Jekyll to Hyde when it came to playing tricks on Phil.

Even when Rizzuto was the elder statesman of the Yankees toward the end of his career, the younger players would ruffle his hair, chase him around, and pull practical jokes on him. Most of the jokes related to his fear of crawling things. The most popular pranks were pulled on the ball field between innings of a game, because during Rizzuto's early career the infielders left their gloves on the field between innings, giving the rival left fielder (and often the Yankee left fielder when Lindell was playing left), the opportunity to slip a foreign object into the fingers of Rizzuto's glove as it lay there on the grass. After

Rizzuto returned from the bench to the field and put his glove on to play defense, he would feel a worm, a soggy chaw of tobacco, or a dead mouse inside, and he would let out a blood-curdling scream and throw that glove just as high in the air as he could while all the Yankees howled in glee in front of a totally perplexed audience. And until one of the other Yankees removed that object, he refused to put his glove back on. Once he found an eel in his glove and almost fainted dead away. After a number of years of this, Rizzuto began to bring his glove into the dugout with him after the inning, and before long everyone was bringing them in.

In the clubhouse the players would hang a dead bird or a rubber spider or a red fuzzy ball of gauze covered with Merthiolate above his locker from a string. After a game Phil would be taking off his uniform, and one of the players would slowly let out the string to lower it closer and closer to Rizzuto until it was at eye level. Ultimately Rizzuto would look up and see this thing, and again he would scream in terror and run away. Once they put a mouse in the valuables box that had been holding his car keys and his wallet. For three days he refused to drive home, until finally the pranksters removed the mouse so he could get his keys. "It's a funny thing about his fear of mice," said his wife Cora. "I've seen him stand there and get knocked six feet in the air by some big guy in a play at second base, but as for those mice, he's deathly afraid of them."

After a while the players could just walk up to him with their hands closed, and chase him all over the ball park.

Phil Rizzuto lives in a large two-story gray-brick mansion in Hillside, New Jersey, only a stone's throw from Newark Airport. Like his compadres Di-Maggio, Crosetti, Berra, and Raschi, he has invested his money wisely and has become a man of means. Yet despite his exalted position as a star athlete and a TV and radio personality as the Voice of the Yankees, Phil Rizzuto is a private person who enjoys his family life and who has never really considered himself a star. He remains the honest, unassuming person he always was, an extremely intelligent, articulate, and outspoken man who will unabashedly scream, "Holy cow!" or "Did you see that?" while describing a play, or who during a ball game will tell the audience, "There's my buddy down there. I can hear him yelling, 'Rizzuto, ya bum.' " Rizzuto has become the finest baseball announcer in New York City.

We sat in his cozy living room watching the Rangers play hockey on his color TV set with the sound off as we talked. Rizzuto is a sports nut, enjoying pro sports all year round.

He was a kid from Brooklyn, an excellent athlete at Richmond Hill High School despite his 4-foot 11-inch (lack of) height. By the end of his senior year in 1936 the major league teams from New York, the Dodgers, the Giants, and the Yankees, all had been touted about Rizzuto, and all invited him to tryout camps. His first tryout was with the Dodgers.

"You'd run from the left-field foul pole to the right-field foul pole," said Rizzuto, "and the first twenty-five guys who made it stayed regardless. I was very fast so I always was one of the twenty-five. Then you got five swings. I got up and the first pitch that batting-practice pitcher threw hit me right in the back. I kind of stiffened up, and I didn't hit the ball out of the infield. I remember that workout with the Dodgers. A one-day affair. Casey Stengel was the manager of the Dodgers. At the end of the day, he said, 'Kid, you're too small. You ought to go out and shine shoes.' Oh gad. He said, 'You'll never be a big-league ball player.' I never let Casey live that down, and he didn't like it one bit because I would always tell the reporters about that.''

He didn't have any better success with the Giants, and the Yankees, a team in the hated rival American League, were his last chance. During the Yankee tryouts, head scout Paul Krichell, a little guy himself who knew baseball talent, looked past Rizzuto's size and saw his lightning reflexes, his quick hands, his speed, and his ability to hit with authority. On the third day Krichell invited Yankee manager Joe McCarthy to watch the tryouts. McCarthy was also impressed by Rizzuto.

"Best I saw the whole day," said McCarthy, also a short man, to Krichell, "was the little fella at shortstop, but he's too small to play in Yankee Stadium."

"You'd be surprised," Krichell said. "He's almost as big as you are."

After the tryouts Krichell told Rizzuto to wait for his call, that the Yankees would be offering him a contract. For several days Rizzuto waited as instructed, but when the call came, it was from the Boston Red Sox, not the Yankees, prompting Rizzuto to believe that the Red Sox must have had a spy in the stands the day he tried out at the Stadium. The Red Sox scout told Rizzuto that they were interested in signing him and that a contract would be coming soon. First, though, Boston wanted to check on the signing of another shortstop, Harold Reese, before they signed Phil. The scout had to go down to Kentucky to check on this fellow Reese, and then he would be back to sign Phil. Before the Red Sox scout returned from Kentucky, however, Krichell called Rizzuto back, and with Rizzuto anxious to sign with the first team who offered him a contract, he signed to become a Yankee for $75 a month. He was to report to Bassett, Virginia, Class D. He received no bonus, and he had to pay his own way to Bassett. When the Sox scout returned from Kentucky after signing Reese, he was too late. Several years later the Red Sox sold Reese to the Dodgers, and Pee Wee Reese starred for Brooklyn for sixteen seasons.

"It wasn't difficult living on $75 a month," Rizzuto said. "In those days, in fact, I thought that was a lot of money, because the previous two summers I had worked in Brooklyn for a company called S. Gumpert. They paid me $17 a week, and I had thought *that* was a lot of money. In those days nothing was taken out for income taxes, and you could get steak and potatoes for sixty cents. When I was making $75 dollars a month with the Yankees, you paid board of like $6 a week. Oh, it was unbe*liev*able.''

When Rizzuto left for Bassett in the summer of 1936, he was eighteen years old and had never been away from home in his entire life.

"It was tough," Rizzuto said. "I mean a fellow from Brooklyn who had never been out of Brooklyn. He suddenly finds himself on a train going to Virginia. Virginia was like Europe then. I'll never forget that train trip either. My father gave me a ten-dollar bill. He pinned it to the inside of my undershirt. He was from Calabria, in Italy, and he had never been away either. So he was afraid of my traveling. He was afraid the Black Hand would steal my money. So he pinned it to the inside of my undershirt.

"When I got to Virginia," Rizzuto said, "it was like a whole new world. I didn't understand them, and they didn't understand me. I really had a Brooklyn accent, and those southerners, holy cow, I just didn't know what they were saying! I'm telling you, I was frightened. I got to Bassett, got off the train, and I couldn't see anything but hills. No town. Absolutely nothing. And then when the train pulled away, there was the town on the other side of the tracks! It was a drug store, a theater, a little hotel, and a diner. And I couldn't believe it! You can imagine with all the hustle and bustle of Brooklyn and then coming down to something like this!

"But I was lucky," he said. "Ray White, who had been my manager in semi-pro ball in Brooklyn was my manager at Bassett, so he knew my capabilities at the time, and even though there were several shortstops trying out, he kept me." It hadn't been total luck. George Weiss purposely sent Rizzuto to play under White.

"And then I almost ended my career right there at Bassett," Rizzuto said. "I stepped in what they call a gopher hole running down to first base, and I played for about three weeks after that, and every night I was in agony. It was unbe*liev*able. When you're playing in Class D you don't have a trainer. The manager is the trainer, the bus driver, the secretary, everything, and Ray used to rub my leg every night, really pound it, because he thought massaging it would be the best thing for it. Finally it got so bad, an old umpire at Bassett said, 'Kid, you better get that thing looked at. I've never seen anything like that.' So the next day Ray White took me to Roanoke, which was the only big town with a hospital anywhere near. The doctor examined me and in one minute he said, 'We've got to operate on you immediately. Gangrene has set in.' Holy cow! I mean here I'm eighteen years old, and I'm scared to death, and they had to call my mother and tell her, and they operated on me immediately. In those days, don't forget, they didn't have penicillin or sodium pentothol. They had to give you ether or gas, and when I woke up, I was throwing up, sick as a dog. The doctor told me, 'Another week and you'd have lost the leg.' The gangrene had eaten away so much of the muscle that they had to cut away all the dead muscle and sew each end to another muscle. I still have a scar on my leg from my knee to my thigh. Awful. Ugh! An ugly-looking thing. I'd been playing only about a month and a half, and then I missed two and a half months. But I finished the year, batted over .300, and we won the playoffs. I was very, very lucky.

"Then the next year I played for Norfolk, Virginia, in the Piedmont League," Rizzuto went on. "That's an interesting story, too. Ray White was promoted to Norfolk and he took me along with him. That spring Norfolk had a kid by the name of Claude Corbitt, a local southern boy, and he and I were battling for shortstop. In the minors you're only allowed to keep sixteen men, and they had to get rid of one infielder, and Ray kept me. Geez, they almost threw us both out of town. In minor league ball being a local player means an awful lot. They were up in arms, two New Yorkers coming down there and trying to take over. The booing! Oh, I never heard such booing in my life. They tried to boycott the team. The papers, the radio were against us. Ray was quite worried for his job, and of course, so was I." Rizzuto shook his head at the memory. "But as it turned out," he said, "I had one of my best years." It took the Norfolk fans about two weeks to fully accept him. At the end of the year he had batted .336, was an all-star, and became one of the most popular players ever to perform there.

Rizzuto's next step up the minor league ladder was Kansas City, Triple-A, the top of the minors, and for two years, 1939 and 1940, Phil starred at short. In 1940, after batting .347, he was named the Minor League Player of the Year.

"That's where I really learned about life," Rizzuto said. "I was so naive. I believed everything. I can remember when I was working at S. Gumpert's factory in Brooklyn, they'd say to me, 'Get me a can of striped paint' or 'Get me the key to the pitcher's box' or 'Find me the skyhook,' and I'd fall for everything. Once they got a suitcase and filled it with bricks and had me carry it up to the fourth floor. Gad. And I never got mad. I remember at Kansas City they took me on two snipe hunts. It was spring training, my first year there, and we were in Florida. They took me way out in the middle of an orange grove, like five or six miles out, and they gave me a flashlight, a loaf of bread, and a paper bag, and they said, 'We'll go and hide, and then we'll come out whistling and yelling and we'll scare the snipe and the snipe'll run towards you. And all you have to do is flash the light in the bag and throw in a piece of bread, and the snipe will run in.' That sounded easy enough. So I said, 'Okay', and they came out screaming and yelling, and they would say, 'There goes one,' and I'm throwing the bread in the bag and putting the flashlight on, and nothing. Nothing. Not one snipe. So they said, 'Okay, we'll try it again. We'll hide again and come out and see if this time you'll catch one.' So they hid, and they left me there alone, and it's dark as hell in the orange grove, and I'm out there half an hour, an hour, flashing the light in the bag and throwing the goddamn bread in there, and what they did was go back to town. And I'm all alone, and I'm really getting scared. Finally I ended up walking all the way back to the town, and they're sitting there waiting for me, laughing like hell." Kansas City teammate Johnny Lindell was laughing as hard as anyone.

"So anyway," he continues, "the next year they say to me, 'Remember that snipe hunt we pulled on you last year? This year we want to pull it on a rookie, and we want you to show him how to do it.' And me like a dummy. Again I'm in the orange grove in the dark and everyone takes off including the rookie, and this time they called the sheriff and told him there was a prowler in the orange grove." The sheriff, in on the caper, raced to the orange grove, his siren wailing, arrested Rizzuto, handcuffed him, and threw him in jail for a couple of hours. "And don't think I wasn't scared to death," Phil said. "I tell you. Some of the tricks they played on me there were unbe*liev*able. Frogs in my bed. They would nail my spikes to the floor. Ripped my underwear to shreds. Ripped my letters so badly I couldn't read them. And Jerry Priddy, our second baseman, he would get so mad. He wanted to fight the others for me. But it never made me mad. I have no temper. To me it was funny. I figured they played tricks on me because they liked me."

Between 1941 and 1946 when Rizzuto played on the Yankees under Joe McCarthy, most of the practical joking on Rizzuto ceased, but after McCarthy left the Yankees in May of 1946 they resumed full blast. Between 1941 and 1946 Rizzuto had other problems: making the Yankees, fighting in the war, and deciding whether or not to jump to the outlaw Mexican League.

Rizzuto earned his spot on the Yankee roster in 1941 after four outstanding years in the minors, but he did not gain acceptance without a struggle. When he reported to training camp at St. Petersburg, he had difficulty entering the clubhouse to get his uniform. "Beat it, kid," said the clubhouse man. "You can see the players when they come out on the field. Out." Rizzuto, having grown to about 5 feet 5 inches, had to convince the guy that he belonged. It was much more difficult convincing the Yankee veterans that he belonged. They resented the presence of both him and second-baseman Jerry Priddy who were attempting to wrest the starting second-base and shortstop jobs from veterans Joe Gordon and Frank Crosetti. Priddy and Rizzuto were only 22 years old, and because Gordon and Crosetti were so well-liked, Priddy and Rizzuto were ostracized by the veterans. Rizzuto's locker was between those of Red Ruffing and Bill Dickey, two large imposing men, and for the entire spring neither man said one word to Rizzuto. The rest of the players also gave him the silent treatment, and during batting practice rarely did Rizzuto get up to hit because just before it was his turn to bat, a veteran would step in front of him, and Rizzuto was not the type of person to stand up for his rights and argue. Priddy, on the other hand, was more aggressive—he talked back and refused to be pushed around, and was actively disliked for it.

After a number of weeks of this torture for Rizzuto, Joe DiMaggio, a team leader and an apolitical person, spoke up. "Listen guys," he said, "if this kid is going to play short for us this year, we'd better give him a chance." And then Crosetti made it easier by reiterating what DiMaggio had said.

Except for the war years, Rizzuto was the Yankee shortstop from May 1941 until August 1956 when he was released.

In 1941 and '42 Rizzuto started for the Yankees and played excellently, batting .307 and .284 under McCarthy's tutelage. Then in '43 Rizzuto enlisted in the Navy. For the first year he starred on the Navy baseball team, playing exhibitions for servicemen on all the Pacific Islands and Australia, and playing in the armed services world series in Honolulu, Hawaii, in October 1943. It was in the Navy that his buddies concocted one of their more sadistic pranks.

It was the day before Rizzuto's wedding. Rizzuto had been asking his girl friend, Cora, to marry him for over two years. Finally she agreed, and they decided to hold the wedding in Norfolk where he was stationed. On this day Rizzuto played a game for the base, and after the game he and the rest of his team including Eddie Robinson, Dom DiMaggio, and Benny McCoy, all professional ball players, went in to take their showers.

While Rizzuto was showering, Robinson, a huge brute, grabbed the naked Rizzuto and pinned him down as he hollered and squirmed. The others painted his genitals with gentian violet, an ugly purple dye that even sandpaper won't remove. For the rest of the day Rizzuto tried to scrape the stain off his body. He wasn't sure if he would be able to explain the purple blotch to his wife-to-be. Fortunately for Rizzuto, though, the night of his wedding there was a blackout alert along Virginia Beach where he was spending the night, an event which made explanations unnecessary. The newlyweds spent the entire evening in the dark.

For Phil the war was a holiday until the Gold Star mothers protested that their sons were getting killed in the Pacific and in Germany while the professional athletes were getting preferential treatment, and in February 1944 there was a blanket order that special service personnel, including all athletes, be shipped overseas for fighting duty. Rizzuto's career as a fighting man closely resembled that of the Marx Brothers fighting for the honor of Fredonia in *Duck Soup*.

"I'll never forget the day they told me I was going overseas," Rizzuto said. "All I had done in the Navy was play ball. I wasn't prepared to go into any battle, and they put me in charge of a 20-millimeter gun crew! On a ship! When they shipped us overseas, they gave us a camouflage bag with a rifle in it. A rifle. I didn't know the first thing about shooting a gun. I never even had a fight in my life. Imagine, being from Brooklyn and never having a fight! My brother was a hell of a fighter. Every time someone picked on me, my brother would fight him. Even in baseball someone else always did my fighting, Priddy or Billy Martin. I just wasn't a fighter. So they sent me to New Guinea, and I'll tell you, I was miserable. Got fungus infections. Came down with shingles, a nerve condition. Got malaria. I was supposed to take atabrine pills to keep me from getting it, but when you first start taking them it turns your skin yellow, and I didn't like the way I looked, so I stopped taking them and I got malaria. And also, on top of all that, I had chronic seasickness! As soon as I would stand up on that boat, I got seasick. Violently ill. So I would lay down. The captain of the ship would come over and he'd say, 'Rizzuto, get your gun crew out.' And I would just lay there. They were going to court-martial me! Planes would fly over the ship, and me the leader of the gun crew, I was supposed to spot the planes, identify them, whether they were American or Canadian or Japanese, but they came over so fast. They flew so low you didn't know who they were. Sometimes we actually shot at our own planes! You know, if we had had more men like me, we'd have lost the war." Fortunately the war ended before Rizzuto could do any further damage.

Bucky Harris became the Yankee manager in '47, when the major leagues returned to normalcy after the war.

"And he was a fine manager, too," Rizzuto said. "I think he got a raw deal. He could have had that big Yankee dynasty that Stengel inherited. He was a great guy like McCarthy—never overmanaged, never took any bows. And he was tough. Tough as nails. And like McCarthy he treated everybody differently. You got to know how to treat them. And Bucky could. So could McCarthy. And then George Weiss fired Bucky and brought in Stengel. Prior to that Casey was just regarded as a nice man, very funny, but a clown. You know he never won anything with the Dodgers or the Braves. He inherited a great team of players coming up. You or I could have managed and gone away for the summer and still won those pennants. I mean it. That's how good we were. Of course Casey and I never got along that well anyway. I was the last of the old guard. Henrich was gone, Keller and Dickey were gone, and I was the last. Stengel wanted all the old-timers out so he could get all these young kids in and really let them know who was boss." Stengel, remember, had been the Dodger manager who had told Rizzuto he would never become a major league ball player.

"So Casey was responsible for Lindell, Johnson, and Stirnweiss being traded away, too," I said.

"Oh yes," said Rizzuto. "Sure. He wanted his own men in there. He and DiMag never got along either. Oh geez, one time Casey tried to play him at first and he got spiked. Then Casey took him out of cleanup, batted him fifth, and Joe got so angry. But he never said anything. Joe would never complain. He'd just go out and do whatever he had to do to help win. Everybody who played for McCarthy or Harris, Stengel wanted out. He couldn't wait till DiMag retired. Joe used to say, 'How can this guy win?' But we would win because we had the talent. I was the last one left. And then around '53 he started platooning me. I didn't like it, and I told him so many times, and after that he and I never hit it off." The Yankees ultimately cut Rizzuto adrift in the summer of 1956.

Ironically, it was under manager Stengel that Rizzuto had his finest years. In 1949 he was named the Major League Player of the Year by the writers, leading the team in games played, hits, runs, doubles, triples, and total bases, as well as leading the league in fielding percentage. He finished third to Ted Williams and Joe Page for MVP. In 1950 he was named the Most Valuable Player in the American League, batting .324 with 200 hits, winning the Hickok Belt for the Pro Athlete of the Year. In 1949, '50, '51, and '52 he was chosen as the best major league shortstop.

"You know," said Rizzuto, "I never felt that I was doing anything extraordinary. I figured that I was doing my job. If I made a good play, I never expected to get written up. My teammates appreciated me, and that's all that really mattered."

The '50 Philadelphia Phillies, known as the Whiz Kids, were the Yankees' opponents in the world series. A collection of hustling youngsters, led by Robin Roberts and Curt Simmons, and reliever Jim Konstanty, they hadn't expected to finish in the first division. In the series they were no match for the Yankees, even though the New Yorkers were not exactly balls of fire themselves.

The first two games were played in antiquated Shibe Park in Philadelphia, and in the first one Vic Raschi allowed the Whiz Kids exactly two hits and no runs, as the Yankees won, 1–0. The most serious trouble Raschi experienced all day was when he returned to his hotel room before the game to discover that thieves had stolen 140 box-seat tickets he had collected for relatives and friends.

After Raschi's powerful performance manager Stengel was bubbling in praise of the great pitcher, expounding on how impressive Raschi had been, citing his perseverance to go to college for eight years in the off-season to earn his degree. "He wins," Stengel said, "because he pitches here, here, and here," and the manager touched his finger to his head, his arm, and his heart.

The second game was tense like the first, with Reynolds pitching against

Roberts. Stengel purposely had saved Reynolds for the game in which Roberts was to pitch. Reynolds was working on a streak of twenty-two consecutive shutout innings in world series competition and needed just eight more to break the record held by Babe Ruth. He missed the record by two innings.

At the end of the ninth inning, with the score 1–1, Reynolds was sneaking a cigarette in the Yankee locker room when he heard a loud roar coming from the stands. Roberts had tried to rear back and throw a fast ball past Joe DiMaggio, the best fast-ball hitter in baseball, and DiMaggio lost the ball in the seats. Reynolds finished his cigarette, strolled out to the mound, and after walking the lead-off batter, finished the inning with little difficulty for his 2–1 victory. New York had scored three runs in two ball games and was leading the Phillies two games to none.

The third game was played in the Stadium, and the Phillies kicked it away. The Yankees were losing 2–1 going into the eighth inning when they were handed an unearned run. Then in the bottom of the ninth, disaster again struck Philadelphia: two cheap infield singles and a Coleman bloop scored the winning run. Coleman now had personally won two games, this one and the first game in which he drove in the only run of the game with a sacrifice fly.

Eddie Ford was chosen to pitch the fourth game, both because the kid had been drafted into the Army and would probably spend his next two years in khaki, and because he deserved the start after his 9–1 regular season record which brought the Yankees into the series.

Ford was a lock. The Phils couldn't touch him, and the kid took a 5–0 shutout into the ninth and final inning. Ford had two men on and two outs in the ninth, when the batter lifted an easy fly ball toward Gene Woodling in left. Ford pounded his glove and started to walk off the field, secure in his triumph. Unfortunately, the ball rose high into the direct rays of the blazing fall sun which combined with the haze created by the smoking of cigarettes. Woodling saw the ball all the way until the final descent, when it struck the blinded fielder on the leg as a run scored. Ford, unsettled, allowed another hit for a second Phillie run, and Stengel called time and waved in Allie Reynolds from the bullpen to pitch the final out. The Big Indian was pitching into the fall shadows, and he knew few batters alive could hit his fast ball when it was thrown from the light into the shadows. He busted three fast balls by the final batter before he could take the bat off his shoulder. The Yankees swept the series in four straight, and the biggest benefactors were Woodling and Coleman. Before the series few people knew who Woodling was, but after he dropped that ball in left field, people felt sorry for him and invited him to every banquet in New England. Sweet are the uses of adversity. Coleman was named as the outstanding player in the series and was given the Babe Ruth Award for his performance.

In the roughneck world of professional baseball, Jerry Coleman was a gentleman athlete. Mild of manner, he was an exemplary model of decorum and modesty, a Mr. Niceguy who never seemed to get his uniform dirty. He was so meticulous that he tied the tails of his shirt down with string to keep it from blousing. Good-looking, observant, and intelligent, Coleman was one of many Yankees to come from the San Francisco Bay area.

Coleman signed as a shortstop in 1942, but in spring training of 1949 Yankee manager Stengel converted him into a second-baseman, and the switch was one of Stengel's most successful experiments. Coleman played second with grace and style, and on the double play relay he had the unique ability to catch the ball, jump high to avoid the onrushing base runner, and throw to first without looking where he was throwing. He was acrobatic and accurate with his method, and after long practice he became so proficient that it almost seemed the ball would ricochet in and out of his glove without actually touching it. His flair earned him the nickname of Fancy Dan.

In 1949 he was named Rookie of the Year, and in 1950 he was awarded the Babe Ruth award, prompting Hall of Famer Frankie Frisch to predict that Coleman himself would ultimately be voted into the Hall. Unfortunately, though, 1950 would be the apex of Coleman's career, and after slumping in 1951 because of a serious injury, Coleman was drafted back into the Army for two years. Never again did he regain his former skills, and during his final few years before his 1957 retirement, Stengel platooned him. Coleman's mediocre hitting in his last few years made the fans forget how excellent he had once been.

1951

A child prodigy named Mantle . . . The Indian, Allie Reynolds, and two no-hitters . . . Another pennant . . . and a subway series victory over the Giants . . . Joe DiMaggio says, "I have played my last game."

The Korean War began as an innocuous skirmish, but the fighting now was entering its eighth month, and for the men stationed in the barren wastelands and the rice paddies, it had been an eternity between June 1950 and February 1951. Inside the United States the relentless witch-hunt for subversives was making the nation jumpy and suspicious.

The Yankees had lost rookie star Eddie Ford to the Army, and it seemed certain that other players like Jerry Coleman and Bobby Brown were soon to be drafted. Replacements would have to be found. Also, the Yankee management, looking to the future, realized that some of the veterans were aging and would have to be replaced before long. Joe DiMaggio was 37 and would soon retire, and Rizzuto at 33 was suffering from spring arm miseries. For protection Stengel was seeking a back-up shortstop, and because of his dissatisfaction with both Bill Johnson and Bobby Brown, he was looking for a third-baseman as well.

To facilitate the search for replacements, in February 1951 Del Webb arranged for Stengel to conduct a special instructional camp for promising minor leaguers, bonus prospects, and some of his younger Yankees. The camp would be held for three weeks before the regular training period was to begin. The eighteen Yankee farm clubs had produced sixty all-star minor leaguers during the 1950 season, or one all-star for every four minor leaguers under contract, and Webb and Stengel felt that it would be beneficial for the brightest of these prospects to be exposed to manager Stengel and also get a chance to meet the coaches and some of the Yankee ball players. Webb as a youth had been a professional ball player, and he had experienced terrible loneliness and anxiety when at the age of 17 he tried out for the Salt Lake City team in 1917. During the entire training period with Salt Lake City the only player who would speak to him was his assigned roommate, Bill (Raw Meat) Rogers. Rogers—a grizzled veteran who ate raw beefsteak and raw eggs, shells and all—was not one to really understand a rookie's feelings of loneliness. The manager and coaches ignored Webb, and burdened by the added pressures of depression and insecurity, he was cut from the squad before he had an opportunity to display his pitching talents. The Yankee owner didn't want his young players to suffer the way he had nor be given a short shrift in training camp. Manager Stengel, also partial to the idea of an instructional camp, felt that in three weeks of intensive training and instruction he could advance some prospects more quickly through the minor league chain.

General manager George Weiss and his scouting staff handpicked forty minor leaguers and bonus babies to attend the camp; Stengel invited Billy Martin, Jackie Jensen, Hank Bauer, Gene Woodling, and a couple of other Yankees. The rules forbade a major leaguer from coming to camp before March 1, so Stengel designated these young Yankees as "instructors" to try to circumvent the rule.

Webb arranged for the instructional camp and the regular training camp to be held in Phoenix, Arizona, in 1951. The Yankee owner wanted his West Coast friends and associates to see his team, so he and New York Giant owner, Horace Stoneham, traded camps in '51, with the Giants training in St. Petersburg, Florida.

In early February Stengel opened his instructional camp. It was a baseball innovation, and it proved so beneficial that several other teams copied the idea over the years. Among the youngsters at the camp were Andy Carey, a 20-year-old bonus baby infielder, Tom Sturdivant, a 21-year-old infielder with blazing speed, Gil McDougald, an impressive 23-year-old minor league infielder, Mickey Mantle, a 19-year-old shortstop who hit with unusual power, Bill Skowron, a 21-year-old outfielder who was signed to a large bonus off the campus of Purdue University, Bob Cerv, another young outfield muscleman, and pitcher Tom Morgan, a 21-year-old with exceptional poise and control. Topping and Webb had spent several million dollars on these youngsters, and Stengel was highly impressed with the quality of the talent.

The instructional camp began with footraces, and one kid, Mantle, the 19-year-old shortstop from Class C, was winning each race with such ease that the coaches were certain he was jumping the starting gun. The skeptics watched him intensely, and when they saw he was winning legitimately, they couldn't believe his acceleration and stamina.

Originally Mantle had not even been invited to the camp because general manager George Weiss didn't want him there. Weiss felt that rushing such a young prospect was not in his best interests. Tom Greenwade, however, the man who had signed Mantle, kept badgering minor league director Lee Mac-Phail to invite him, and Stengel, who had seen Mantle play at the end of the 1950 season, insisted as well that Mantle attend the camp. Camp, however, opened without Mantle. Weiss had not sent the kid expense money to make the trip from his Oklahoma home out to Phoenix. The meticulous Weiss had not *forgotten* to send it—he just didn't send it.

Stengel, awaiting Mantle's arrival, was irate when he didn't report, and immediately the manager made certain that Mantle was sent his expense money.

When Mantle finally did show, a few days late, his prodigious hitting and sprinting speed became the talk of the camp. Mantles, as Stengel called him, was a switch-hitter who hit long home runs from either side of the plate, and though very husky, could run from home to first in just over three seconds.

Through the rookie camp Stengel allowed the baby-faced Mantle to play both shortstop and third base. He had a strong arm and the speed to reach ground balls quickly, but little finesse. No one knew where he would throw the ball after he fielded it. On one play he fielded a grounder in the shortstop hole and then fired a throw into the mezzanine press section in the second deck of the Phoenix stadium. He was unpolished, but so obviously talented that the publicity which surrounded Mantle alerted commissioner Happy Chandler to the fact that the Yankees were working out early with some of their roster players. Chandler closed the instructional camp one week early as a result.

Despite the premature termination, Stengel had accomplished several objectives. He had instructed the prospects in every phase of the game, imparting his vast knowledge and wisdom about the intricacies and details of major league play. Stengel and his coaching staff of Frank Crosetti, Bill Dickey, and Jim Turner, assisted by minor league managers, Bill Skiff, Johnny Neun, and Harry Craft, were professional instructors of the highest quality, chosen for their teaching skills. Stressing fundamentals was another lesson Stengel learned from John McGraw, and every spring he stressed them over and over, even to the veterans. ''Most ball games,'' Stengel asserted, ''are lost, not won.''

In addition to his teaching goals, the camp enabled Stengel to get to know the minor leaguers for future reference. When the regulars arrived on March 1, waiting for them were three of the highly touted minor leaguers: Tom Morgan, a pitching star at Binghamton in the Eastern League in 1950, Gil McDougald, the Most Valuable Player in the Texas League with Beaumont, and Mantle, the MVP in the Western Association with Joplin. McDougald had shown ability at both shortstop and third base, and Morgan impressed Stengel with his pitching know-how. Though Mantle was raw and erratic in the infield, Casey Stengel saw in him the makings of another Casey Stengel, and to prevent Mantle from having to return to the minors to learn the complexities of infield play, Stengel switched the youngster to the outfield and decided to teach the boy how to play the position himself. He also retained Tommy Henrich as a coach to help Mantle learn to play the outfield. All along George Weiss kept insisting that Mantle would be optioned to Kansas City, but manager Stengel, equally resolute, wasn't allowing Weiss to send the boy anywhere, much as John McGraw had not allowed rookie Mel Ott to be sent to the minors in 1926. Ott starred for the Giants for twenty-two years without spending one day in the minors.

Mantle was so green. In one of the early exhibition games a batter hit a fly ball directly into the bright Arizona sun toward Mantle, who had never used flip-down sunglasses before. Mantle tried desperately to flip down the shaded glass over his blinded eyes, but the invisible ball struck him on the side of the head and bounced high off his forehead as the runner streaked for three bases. Mantle wasn't seriously hurt, but he lay on the ground in embarrassment for a long while.

Mantle, a shy, introverted, and vulnerable youngster, cared deeply about what others thought of him. He came from a small Oklahoma town where five hundred people was a huge crowd, and at the Yankee training camp, as Weiss had feared, the overflow crowds and the attention were overwhelming him. He was awkward and spoke with a slow western twang that increased his self-consciousness. He was also scared—of people and of failure. Before his first exhibition game Mantle was so frightened he could barely raise his arms high enough to catch a baseball.

Throughout the training period, Stengel and Henrich worked with and encouraged him. Henrich taught him the correct way to catch a ball, how to set his feet before making the long throw to the infield, and how to get rid of the ball quickly after catching it. For hours Mantle eagerly practiced with Henrich as the old perfectionist taught the young one the fundamentals of outfield play.

But Mantle's hitting overshadowed any lack of refinement in his fielding. Mantle, who stood about 5 foot 10 and weighed about 165, was not a large person, but he had the shoulders and arms of a blacksmith. When it was his turn to bat during training, the veterans would stop to watch him hit. They just couldn't believe the long, arching drives which clattered against the distant outfield bleachers.

When the team broke camp in Phoenix, it traveled up the West Coast to play exhibitions against Pacific Coast League teams, and at each stop the combination of California-bred DiMaggio and super-rookie Mantle packed the stadium to capacity. The tour of California became a showcase of Yankee power with Mantle, DiMaggio, Mize, Hank Bauer, and Gene Woodling all hitting excellently. In San Francisco, in a game against the Seals, Stengel paid tribute to the California influence being exerted on the Yankees. A Californian himself, Stengel started a team composed entirely of Californians. Fenton Mole, a strapping rookie, started at first, with Coleman on second, Martin at short, and McDougald at third; and in the outfield were DiMaggio, Jackie Jensen, and Woodling. Charlie Silvera caught, and Tom Morgan pitched. Substitutes Lindell and Brown were also from California.

But it was Mantle who drew most of the attention. Against the Coast League teams he was hitting majestic home runs—long, towering drives that made everyone who saw them marvel. Mantle, who hit .402 in exhibition play, was being touted as the most exciting young player since Jackie Robinson.

People were also becoming impressed with his fielding. In one game with a man on third and one out, he waited under a fly ball in medium-right field and in one motion caught the ball and threw to the plate on the fly, hitting the catcher's glove just to the third-base side of the plate. The runner, speedy Bobby Avila of Cleveland, was out by five feet. Personal instructor Henrich called it the greatest throw he had ever seen in his life. "There isn't any more that I can teach him," Henrich said. Stengel, equally impressed, confirmed his belief that though the kid was only 19, he would remain on the Yankee roster, George Weiss notwithstanding. "If he can't play regularly after the season starts," Stengel said, "I gotta farm him out. But if he's good enough, I got room on this ball club for him. It doesn't matter to me if he's a rookie or a thousand years old. If he can play, he stays."

As Mantle's batting average climbed and the publicity surrounding his feats mounted, a small but vocal group of "patriots" were wondering aloud how the 19-year-old *wunderkind* was healthy enough to play baseball but not healthy enough to serve his country. As a schoolboy in Commerce, Oklahoma, Mantle had been kicked in the left ankle during a football game, and shortly thereafter developed osteomyelitis, a serious, sometimes deadly, bone disease. He was hospitalized for treatment in 1947 and again in 1948, and the disease had been arrested. It was apt, however, to reappear after the slightest jar, and as a result the service doctors who examined him found his condition serious enough to merit a 4-F classification.

For some people, unfortunately, this medical explanation was not sufficient. "What does osteomyelitis have to do with being 4-F?" one columnist wrote. "There's no rule that says he has to kick somebody in the war."

Mantle began to receive vituperative hate mail, and as the debate raged around him, the shy, uncommunicative boy shrunk deeper and deeper into his shell of silence. In private Mantle would ask, "Would they rather have a son in the Army or a son with osteomyelitis?" Cries of "draft dodger," "coward," and "commie" were often shouted at him from the stands when he batted.

In an attempt to stem the public clamor over Mantle's physical eligibility, general manager George Weiss asked the state board of Oklahoma to reexamine his young prospect. One week before the season opened Mantle flew to Miami, Oklahoma, for a reexamination while, holding their breaths, his teammates played the Brooklyn Dodgers in a couple of exhibitions. Meanwhile, Mantle was bewildered by all the negative attention. He was playing by the rules. It had not been his fault that the draft board rejected him. When asked by newspapermen about his feelings toward serving in the Army, Mantle told them that he would be glad to fight for the Army, or play ball in the Army, but that if he didn't go into the Army, he wanted to play major league baseball. Despite another rejection, this time by the state board, the hate mail continued.

With Allie Reynolds missing the entire training period because of painful bone chips in his elbow, Vic Raschi getting shelled, and Ed Lopat only mediocre, the Yankees had another poor spring exhibition record. But once the season started Raschi pitched a shutout and Lopat began a streak of eight straight wins.

Dan Daniel, a reporter for the New York *Mirror,* came into the clubhouse after one of Lopat's easy wins and said, "Eddie, what gives with you guys? You look so bad all spring and then you look like this now."

"Daniel," Lopat said, "the bell rang."

When the season opened Mantle, McDougald, and Morgan were still on the roster and challenging for regular jobs, and Jackie Jensen, a 24-year-old bonus prospect was also challenging for an outfield berth. On opening day all four started. Mize was at first, Coleman at second, Rizzuto at short, and McDougald at third, with Berra behind the plate. In the outfield Joe DiMaggio was flanked by Jensen in left and Mantle in right. Morgan, a rookie, was the scheduled opening-day pitcher. He had pitched twenty-five consecutive scoreless innings in exhibition play, and Stengel inserted him into the rotation.

"I wish I didn't have so many green peas," Stengel said, "but I can't win with my old men. We have to rebuild."

As May blossomed into June, Mickey Mantle continued to impress with his speed and power, but his batting average slowly but steadily began to fall as the veteran pitchers learned his weaknesses. He hit his first home run in May off

Randy Gumpert of the White Sox, a 450-foot shot over the head of center-fielder Jim Busby and into the Chicago bullpen. The fan who caught the ball exchanged it for twelve autographed balls from Mantle. It wouldn't be the last time someone got the best of Mantle. He was hitting a handful of long homers, second only to Yogi Berra in runs batted in, but he was striking out too much.

Pitchers like Walt Masterson of Washington and Satchel Paige of St. Louis were throwing him high, hard ones just above the letters, pitches that Mantle could not refrain from chasing. Masterson would throw his pitches just a little bit higher each time until Mantle was swinging at balls he couldn't reach, and Paige, the ageless Negro League veteran, would throw a rising fast ball that Mantle *never* was able to hit. Ole Satch would stand on the mound and laugh out loud at the youngster's frustration. Against the Red Sox in one doubleheader Mantle struck out five times and burst into tears on the bench. Cleveland's Bob Lemon struck him out three times in one game. After the third strikeout he smashed two of his bats against the dugout wall. Other times it was his fist that he smashed against the wall, and Stengel threatened to fine him for acting so petulantly. Mantle, like DiMaggio, was a perfectionist, and he was so anxious to succeed that as his slump deepened, he became overanxious and began to swing at anything thrown in his direction, even pitches in the dirt. By mid-June his average had dropped to .269.

Mantle's other problem was that after he struck out, in several situations he lost his concentration in the outfield and made crucial mistakes, so concerned was he about his hitting. In one game he failed to get a proper jump on a fly ball because he was still thinking about striking out, and a ball that he should have caught eluded him. After the inning Lopat cornered him in the dugout. "You want to play?" Lopat yelled at him. "If not, get your ass the hell out of here. We don't need guys like you. We want to win."

Mantle began platooning with Jackie Jensen, and finally in mid-July Stengel sent the kid down to Kansas City. Despite his forty-five runs batted in, Mantle had 52 strikeouts in less than 250 at-bats. He was confused and his confidence badly shaken. Stengel figured that at Kansas City he would not be under such intense pressure to succeed.

On July 12, Allie Reynolds pitched a no-hitter against the Cleveland Indians. Though he had missed the entire spring training session with bone chips in his elbow, the no-hitter was his tenth win and his fifth shutout. It was the first no-hitter by a Yankee since Monte Pearson no-hit the Indians in 1938.

The night before Reynolds pitched his masterpiece, a Cleveland reporter asked manager Stengel why he refused to allow the Yankee relief pitchers to ride in from the bullpen on the motorized carts that the Cleveland management was providing. Stengel told him that the Yankees only ride in Cadillacs. For the game Cleveland general manager Hank Greenberg rented a large black Cadillac and had it waiting in the Yankee bullpen before the game.

Reynolds' opponent was Bob Feller, who only weeks before had thrown a no-hitter against the Detroit Tigers, and for six quick innings, Reynolds and Feller battled to a 0–0 tie. In the seventh Gene Woodling pulled a ball into the right-field stands for a 1–0 Yankee lead.

Reynolds still had his no-hitter with two outs in the ninth, and the batter was

Bobby Avila, the leading hitter in the American League. With Avila, an excellent bunter, at bat, Stengel motioned for Gil McDougald, the third-baseman, to move in so Avila could not lay one down. Casey was trying to protect Reynolds' no-hitter. Reynolds, on the other hand, was more interested in winning his 1-0 game, and he ordered McDougald to move back to the bag and protect the line against a double. Avila kept fouling off pitches, and before each pitch Stengel kept waving McDougald closer and Reynolds kept shouting for him to move back. Rookie McDougald, feeling very much like a yo-yo, finally called time and walked out to the mound.

"Hey Indian," said the brash rookie to Reynolds, "what's your number?" Reynolds, taken aback, said, "What the hell are you talking about?" "If your number don't read 37," said McDougald, "don't tell me where to play." On the next pitch Reynolds settled the controversy and struck Avila out on a high fast ball. Catcher Yogi Berra leaped in the air and in three bounds landed on Reynolds' back. Allie had retired the last seventeen batters in a row for his no-hitter.

The next night the Cadillac was gone from the Yankee bullpen.

On July 20 Boston surged to tie the White Sox for the lead with the Yankees and the Cleveland Indians only one and a half games out of first. Stengel, still unsatisfied with his offense, made another of his important and decisive moves when he benched slumping Jerry Coleman at second base, moved rookie Gil McDougald from third base to second base and inserted Bobby Brown into the lineup at third. Brown, the Golden Boy, was platooned his entire career because his fielding, wooden and uncertain, was inadequate. No one, though, questioned his ability to hit. "Bobby reminds me of a fellow who's been hitting for twelve years and fielding one," was Stengel's analysis. But Stengel needed another bat, and the young doctor launched a hitting barrage which saw him hit safely in eighteen of his first twenty games, raising his average fifty points to .280 and sparking the Yankees to a 17-3 streak as the team passed both Chicago and Boston.

The year 1951 had begun with great promise for Joe DiMaggio. He was again courting his ex-wife, Dorothy Arnold, and at every stop along the coast during spring training, she was with him. Even after the season started, Dorothy would meet him on the road. But their budding romance wilted somewhere along the way, and in the spring his throwing arm lost its power to the ravages of arthritis. As his various nagging injuries accumulated, he slowed markedly in the field, and at bat, balls that he once would have pulled into the left-field seats were now looping weakly into right field. His athletic deterioration was creating tension in the clubhouse again. In the first week of July it reached a head when manager Stengel removed DiMaggio from a ball game at the start of the second inning after he had misplayed a hit the inning before. Joe had already taken his position in center field, and when Jackie Jensen trotted out to inform him that he had been replaced, DiMaggio had to trot off the field in full view of the Stadium spectators. He became sullen and morose. "There is nothing wrong with my legs or anything else," Joe snapped after the game. "I was taken out, and if you want to know any more about it, ask Stengel." DiMaggio stopped communicating with anyone and pulled himself into a shell of pride and loneliness, unable to reconcile his incredibly high standards with the reality of his performance. Through August he was hitting in the .260's, with only flashes of his former self, and even after such triumphs, DiMaggio still seemed to rue his inevitable losing battle against time and nature. He struck a home run and a triple to win a ball game against Washington, and after the game one of the reporters jokingly asked him whether he was trying to make the writers' epitaphs look premature. "You're darn right I wanted you writers to look bad," he snarled. "I'll always try to make you look bad. Just because I have a bad day, you guys try to fire me. Some of you guys are the ones who washed me up in 1946. But here I am, five years later. I don't want your pity," he said. "I have not asked anything from anybody."

Toward the end of the summer, the Cleveland Indians and the Yankees played leapfrog with each other in the standings as the White Sox faded badly. Rookie Gil McDougald was leading the team in hitting, and with DiMaggio sub-par, catcher Berra was supplying most of the punch with Woodling and Bauer also playing excellently.

To bolster the pitching staff Weiss obtained veteran Johnny Sain from the Boston Braves for $50,000 and minor league pitcher Lew Burdette. Stengel had managed Sain back in 1942, and when the Braves let it be known that Sain was available, Stengel asked Weiss to get him.

With the Indians leading the Yankees by only one game, on September 16 and 17 Cleveland was scheduled for its final visit of the season to the Stadium. To face the right-handed aces of the Cleveland staff, Bob Feller and Bob Lemon, Stengel chose Allie Reynolds and Eddie Lopat.

For the opener of the two-game set, more than 68,700 people, the largest crowd of the 1951 season, jammed into the Stadium to see if the defending champion Yankees could stay in the race. Reynolds, the Oklahoma Indian, was pitching the best baseball of his career, and though Feller, one of the great pitching stars in the history of the game, was 22–7 going into the game, historically the Yankees defeated him as often as he defeated them. DiMaggio, especially, had had greater success against Feller than any other hitter, and Yogi Berra, a superior fast-ball hitter, also looked forward to facing the Iowan pitcher. The youngest of the Yankees, Mickey Mantle, was back on the team after a two-month stay in Triple-A with the Kansas City Blues, where he hit .361, and he too was in the lineup.

On this gleaming late-summer afternoon Reynolds pitched brilliantly, allowing only five hits, two in the fifth for a run. But the Yankees had scored three runs, and in the bottom of the fifth Mantle, batting third in the lineup, doubled, and Berra, batting fourth, was intentionally walked by Feller who preferred to pitch to DiMaggio. DiMaggio, burning inside because Stengel had dropped him to fifth in the order, lined a ball into the cavernous depths of left-center field, gliding into third with a two-run triple and a 5–1 Yankee lead, finishing Feller and the Indians for the day.

After the game a pile of yellow Western Union telegrams rested in DiMaggio's locker, congratulating him on his clutch hit. "Now when I get a hit," said DiMaggio with contempt, "they send me telegrams." The Yankees were back in first place by .003 percentage points.

The second Yankee-Indian game pitted Eddie Lopat, trying for his twentieth win of the year, against Indian sinker-ball pitcher Bob Lemon, who already had posted seventeen wins for the year and was expected to give the Yankees difficulty.

This was another pitchers' battle, a 1–1 game that going into the ninth looked like it would not end. Then Phil Rizzuto came up in the ninth with DiMaggio at third and called a favorite play—the suicide squeeze bunt—and executed it perfectly as DiMaggio raced home with the winning run and a sweep of the two-game series. Pitcher Lemon threw the ball and his glove into the stands and stormed off the mound.

With twelve games to go, New York led by one full game.

In 1950 the Indians had knocked off the Tigers to enable the Yankees to win the pennant, and in '51 it was the Tigers who reciprocated and beat the Indians three straight in late September to help the Yankees. Feller, Lemon, and Garcia, overworked and arm-weary, folded down the stretch. A cartoon in the Cleveland *News* had depicted the Cleveland Pennant Train, the Lopez Limited. "We'll be back on September 20 ON TOP—we hope. Al Lopez," read a banner draped over the picture of the train. After the Indians folded, a derailed train was drawn, and the banner read, "We'll be back September 29—we hope. Al Lopez."

With five games left in the season the Yankees needed only one more victory to clinch their third straight American League pennant, and Stengel selected Allie Reynolds and Vic Raschi to pitch against the Red Sox in a doubleheader at the Stadium. It was September 28, and coincidentally it was American Indian Day across the country.

Reynolds, part Creek Indian, son of an Oklahoma minister, seemed upset. His wife had been ill, and until she took her seat near the Yankee dugout he kept looking anxiously into the stands. Despite the distraction, Reynolds was pitching well, and though he had walked a batter in the first and one in the fourth, the Red Sox were experiencing great difficulty hitting his tremendous fast ball. The ball left the mound in bright sunlight, but as it reached the plate it entered the shadows of the autumn afternoon, making the batters temporarily lose sight of it as it hurtled toward them. The Yankee batters were having no such trouble with Mel Parnell or his replacements, as Joe Collins and Woodling hit home runs, and the Yankees built an 8–0 lead going into the seventh inning. Reynolds allowed another walk in the seventh, but he continued to throw his smoke, and as yet the Red Sox were unable to register a hit against him. It was an important game because the pennant was at stake, but as Reynolds retired Boston easily in the eighth, with the game securely won, the focus of the fans' attention riveted on the Yankee pitcher. Under the Boston hit column there was a big goose egg as the drama of another Reynolds no-hitter was unfolding.

With two outs in the ninth Terrible Ted Williams was the batter. Behind the plate, catcher Yogi Berra greeted the Boston slugger, trying to distract him by making small talk as Reynolds threw Williams a strike. On the next pitch Williams lofted a high pop behind the plate. Berra threw his mask and circled under the ball, popped ten stories high between the plate and the Yankee dugout. As the ball began its descent the wind gave it a little kiss for which Berra failed to compensate, and at the last second he made a desperate lunge backwards at the ball. Reynolds, noticing that his catcher might be in trouble, raced to back Yogi up, and in one terrible moment the ball hit the edge of Berra's glove as Yogi and the ball fell to the ground. Reynolds stepped across Berra's hand in his futile attempt to save the out. Williams was still alive.

Carmine Berra, Yogi's wife, was in the hospital—eight months and several weeks pregnant—where she was listening to the game on the radio. When Mel Allen shouted across the airwaves that the ball had fallen safely and Williams was alive, Mrs. Berra, lying in bed, let out a piercing scream. Orderlies came rushing to her aid. "What's the matter? What's the matter?" they asked. "It's my husband," she said. "He dropped the ball."

On the field the sprawled Yankee catcher was examining his right hand where Reynolds had just barely spiked him. "Hey Indian," said Berra, "you stepped on my hand." Yogi grinned. Reynolds grinned back. The two men returned to their positions, still faced with having to again retire the dangerous Williams.

Standing beside the plate, Williams said to Berra, "You son of a bitch. You've put me in one hell of a fix. Even though your man has a no-hitter, I've got to bear down even more than before. You had your chance. But you blew it."

The umpire called time-in, Reynolds set himself on the mound, and Berra squatted behind the plate. Reynolds threw, and again it was a fast ball, and once again Williams lofted a mile-high foul pop behind home plate. The ball again drifted toward the Yankee dugout, where first-baseman Joe Collins and Reynolds and Berra all converged under it, but Yogi was not about to allow any other fielder near that ball. After an eternity of waiting he caught this one securely for the final out. Reynolds bear-hugged Yogi, and the rest of the Yankees converged on the two men in conjunction. Owner Del Webb came down to the clubhouse after the game to congratulate the two men. "Yogi," Webb said to Berra, "when I die I hope They give me a second chance the way They did you."

In the second game of the afternoon Vic Raschi blew the ball past the Red Sox for his twenty-first win as the Yankees scored seven runs in the second inning. Later Joe DiMaggio hit a three-run home run, the final regular season home run of his glorious career. The Yankees won 11–3 and Stengel became the first manager to win three pennants in his first three years in a league since Hugh Jennings did it with the Detroit Tigers in 1907, '08, and '09.

Allie Reynolds began his career in the chain of the Cleveland Indians in 1939. After four desultory seasons in the minors, he was promoted to the Indians in 1943. The great Bob Feller was in the Army, and the Indians called up Reynolds to replace him. Reynolds was not another Feller. He lacked control and walked a lot of batters—he would pitch five or six impressive innings and then walk batters and get into a jam, and inevitably make a bad pitch that someone would hit for a home run to beat him. The other Cleveland pitchers began to grumble behind his back, saying he lacked courage and was the type of guy who wanted the credit for the win but wanted out of the game when there was pressure. In baseball there is no worse reputation than being branded a coward. Reynolds responded to their insinuations by carrying himself with a haughtiness that made the situation worse.

In 1946 the Indians traded him to the Yankees for Joe Gordon in a swap of malcontents. Gordon had been loudly criticizing interim Yankee manager Bill Dickey, and as a result the Yankee management sought to trade him away.

It was a trade that greatly benefitted both teams. Gordon led the Indians to the 1948 pennant. Reynolds helped the Yankees to pennants in 1947 and from 1949 through '53. In his eight Yankee seasons Reynolds won 131 games and lost only 60.

It took Reynolds several seasons before he was accepted as the outstanding pitcher that he was. His reputation for choking followed him to the Yankees, and for the first couple of years, though he won regularly, he continued to walk too many batters and throw gophers in critical situations. His teammates fortunately were supplying him with comfortable cushions, and they would become irritated when he would seem to fritter them away. In 1948 DiMaggio became so infuriated by Reynolds' inability to hold a big lead that he challenged him to a fight in a rare display of temper. It was broken up before it could start.

It wasn't until Casey Stengel and his pitching coach Jim Turner came to the Yankees that Reynolds finally stopped being a thrower and learned the art of pitching. He began rooming with Eddie Lopat, who also helped him. Lopat taught Reynolds to *slow down* his pitches to give the batter a better chance to swing and miss, and taught him how to change speeds.

By 1951 Reynolds's reputation as a coward had vanished. By coincidence, so had his lack of control.

"They told me, 'Don't count on this guy when the chips are down,' " Stengel said in 1951, "but all I can see is this fellow keeps getting tougher and tougher and better and better. He don't run to the bullpen for the weak ones. But when it's the Red Sox, Indians, Tigers, or White Sox, even when he started the day before you look beside you and the guy ain't there any more. He's in the bullpen. There's no use kidding about it. That big guy comes close to being the most valuable pitcher in baseball right now." In 1951 Reynolds finished third behind Berra and St. Louis pitcher Ned Garver in the Most Valuable Player voting, and won the Hickok Belt award for the Pro Athlete of the Year after compiling a 17–8 record, two no-hitters, seven shutouts, and seven saves in fourteen relief appearances. In 1952 he was 20–8, leading the league in ERA and strikeouts. He finished second to Bobby Shantz in the MVP voting.

It wasn't until Reynolds was in his mid-thirties that he became a great pitcher. "That's the hell of it," Reynolds said. "You get smart only when you begin getting old."

In his prime Allie Reynolds threw a baseball as fast as Bob Feller. He also had a sharp-breaking curve ball, and he could be as mean as any of them. When a batter tried to get a toehold up at the plate, Reynolds would fire that fast ball by the batter's ear, and on the next pitch the batter would be standing several inches farther from the plate. Once Reynolds learned to control his pitches, he was very difficult to hit. Stengel usually spotted him against the opposition's best pitcher, and he still won consistently.

He had been a track and football star in high school, and for a large man Reynolds possessed excellent running speed and always kept himself in peak condition. At spring training he would be the one who ran the most and worked himself into the best shape. All three star pitchers, Reynolds, Raschi, and Lopat, worked hard at conditioning.

In 1951, 21-year-old Tom Morgan joined the Yankees. Early in the season before a game against the Browns, the three veteran pitchers asked the rookie if he would like to run wind sprints in the outfield with them.

"Sure," said the youngster, "if you old guys can keep up with me."

It was 105 degrees in the hot St. Louis sun, and for five minutes the pitchers ran sprints from foul line to foul line, back and forth without stopping. When they were finished the three "old men" were barely winded. The 21-year-old Morgan was on the verge of throwing up.

Off the mound Reynolds always remained a congenial guy—win, lose, or draw. He did not smolder the way Raschi did, and after the game there was always room for a smile.

I visited Reynolds, who is an easy person to like, at his office at the Atlas Mud Company in Oklahoma City. He is the president. I discovered a keen baseball mind that combined with his exceptional speed and toughness to effect a brilliant career.

"Lopat taught me how to pitch to a batter's enthusiasm," Reynolds said. "I always talked with the hitters. I would ask them about anything. I just wanted to find out how they think. And I'd take it from there. You don't ask them about hitting, because they say to themselves, 'This guy is trying to find something out,' and then they decoy you. But if you just carry on a normal conversation, then you can find out if a man is possessive or selfish, and if you know this about a man, you know if he gets overanxious or whether he is patient, and you know how to work to him. You pitch to their enthusiasm. When I first started in the minors playing in the outfield, I was told to study the first pitch and get a handle on the pitcher. When I first started pitching there weren't many college boys in baseball. These college boys when they came in learned real quick, and the first good pitch was the one that they'd swing at. And if they couldn't hit you one way, they changed. This was the tough guy to pitch to. The one who continually changed. So I had to learn how to change, too.

"I recall one hitter, I won't bring up his name, who was a big strong right-handed guy with St. Louis. If you'd throw the ball on the inside part of the plate, he'd hit the nicest 200-foot fly to left field that you ever saw. This one time he wasn't standing in the batter's box where he always stood. He was standing at the back and he was choking up. So I said to myself, 'You have to do something different.' So I threw a ball outside three times, and he took three strikes with the bat on his shoulder and walked away. And again the next time: one, two, three, and again a called third strike. And a third time. I've thrown him nine fast balls and haven't missed a strike. I was very accurate even though I threw hard. The fourth time, he was right back where he always was, and I threw him inside, and he hit a nice little fly to left. Hah. I always felt the pitcher had the advantage—it's like serving in tennis.

"Stengel began working me against contenders and against certain pitchers,'' Reynolds said, ''something a lot of ball clubs don't do. There aren't many one-run pitchers, or two-run, or three-run pitchers, but I usually pitched against them. For instance, on a road trip, in Boston I'd face Parnell. Well, you know you're not going to get many runs to work with. Then you come to Cleveland and get Lemon or Wynn or Garcia or Feller, and you're not going to get many runs again. Then to Chicago to face Billy Pierce, and when they start pitching you against people like that, you're up against the tightrope. But I enjoyed it, because it was a highly competitive thing. Lopat would say to me, 'They don't treat you fair, pitching you against certain pitchers.' I would say, 'Eddie, I'd rather have it that way.' He'd say, 'Why?' I'd say, 'When you play a contender, that son of a gun has to be orthodox. You never know what's going to happen with a second line club.' A lot of people say that if they wanted me to look lousy, just pitch me against the Browns or the Senators. It seemed that against contenders it was easier for me to get up. At least I always felt this was so.

''A lot of people also said that if they wanted me to look lousy, just get me a four- or five-run lead and I would start to be an Einstein and experiment—let up and fool around. I didn't really feel I did that, but evidently I did from the way they talked about it. So after coming to the Yankees with a lousy record and with a reputation of being a nonfinisher, then I became a tough pitcher. I only pitched against the best.

''I thought Casey understood his personnel as well as anyone I've ever seen. He knew when his pitcher was tired. He was excellent. He always had two men warming up. He'd jump off that bench and ask Turner, 'Who have you got?' The reliefers had to be ready for any situation. Casey always had one rule: don't walk off the mound after he took you out until he was ready to go back to the dugout with you. If you did he would really blast you. I heard what he told one fellow. 'You son of a bitch. You screwed up. Now you stand out there and take it right with me until we get out of there.' And that's the time you want to go and hide.''

During the first few years with the Yanks, Reynolds was strictly a starting pitcher, but after he relieved Whitey Ford in the final game of the 1950 world series, Stengel became intrigued at the possibility of his Big Chief entering a ball game in the late innings with the shadows of Yankee Stadium making it difficult for the batters to see his fast ball. Stengel began using Reynolds in short-stint relief more and more. Double duty seemed like a guaranteed way of shortening one's career.

''Many pitchers didn't believe in this,'' said Reynolds. ''But I wasn't afraid of it. I even pitched a couple of relief jobs after I had started and pitched the day before. Vic Raschi told me I was crazy, but what the hell. You have to live with yourself, and as long as I could help I figured I would. I had a lot of confidence in myself. It was always easier for me to pitch than it was to sit on the bench. You never have quite the confidence in the other fellow that you do in yourself. In fact, after the 1952 world series Casey told me he wanted me to be a relief pitcher, but I said, 'No.' He said, 'Why not?' and I told him, 'Because you can't make the money.' He said, 'Every time you climb over that fence, half those hitters faint.' I said, 'Well, I wasn't aware of that. It's nice of you to say it.' He asked, 'Would you do it if you could make the same money or get a raise?' I said, 'If you could do that, at least I'd talk about it.' So he gets Topping and Webb together with me, and I say I can't make the same money as a reliefer, and Webb says, 'What do you mean you can't?' I say, 'I relieve all year, and let's say I have six saves and seven wins, and I go to Weiss. In two years I'd be paying the club to let me pitch.' Mr. Webb says, 'You'll make the same money with a nice raise each year.' So I said, 'Okay.' And it was a hell of a lot easier for me. I had the type of arm that allowed me to relieve more than others. But Stengel also had me starting, and that starting and relieving, that was like pulling teeth. The muscles in my arm drew so tight that I couldn't put my hand in my pocket. But they didn't have that many starters, so I had to go back to that dual role."

"Do you remember the second no-hitter you pitched against the Red Sox to clinch the 1951 pennant?" I asked.

"There is an element of luck when you throw a no-hitter," Reynolds said. "I pitched ball games where I had better stuff and lost. Some balls are going to be hit hard, but they have to be at somebody. The right things have to happen at the right times. Let me put it this way: a player understands that an element of luck has to be with you, and the good Lord has to smile on you. I don't quite believe in Murphy's Law. Maybe I can quote it for you. 'What can go wrong will go wrong.' But I accept things. You're going to have good days, and you're going to have bad days. That was one of the good ones."

"Can you recall the Boston ninth inning of that game?" I asked.

"Yup. I was aware of all of it. There were two outs and Ted Williams was up. Usually I tried to walk that damn Williams if I could, because I'll tell you, I couldn't pitch to him, and to me it was stupid to let the outstanding hitter get a hit and beat you. It just wasn't worth it. When I pitched to him, usually I walked him. But I walked a lot of people, because it didn't make any difference to me. If they didn't hit what I wanted them to hit, why I'd put him on and start with the next guy. I was the pitcher. I felt I had the advantage. Some days when I was taking a shower I had a little trouble convincing myself of that, but that was the thinking that I put into the game. I can remember all the home runs Williams hit off me, what the pitches were, and where they were in the strike zone. When I first came up with Cleveland, he yelled at me, 'You throw me your fast ball, and I'll pull it.' And I said, 'Where does it have to be?' And he said, 'In the strike zone.' Well, I thought, that guy is a big pop-off, and the wind was blowing in from right field anyway, so I said to myself, 'I'll throw him one.' He hit it up in the bleachers. And yet in that no-hit ball game, it never occurred to me once to walk him when I had religiously walked him all those years. And I did something that I hadn't done in thirteen years to Mr. Williams. I threw him all the same pitches at the same speed and in the same place. And with the same results."

"In 1951 Mickey Mantle was a Yankee rookie," I said. "Were you impressed by him?"

"Tremendously," Reynolds said. "He was a nice kid. A country boy. He had a tough road to hoe though, coming from a C league. And I was complaining about coming from an A league. He had another thing working against him—Mickey didn't have the advantage of a formal education. His father was a miner, and nothing had really been easy in their life. That's one reason it was so hard for him to go from the C league at $200 a month to the major leagues. He was making more money than he ever dreamed of and he had leisure time. How to use your leisure time is the biggest problem of a ball player. I once heard Branch Rickey say that, so I know I'm not far wrong. For a ball player in New York City there just isn't anything that you can't get if you want it. And we had some other kids there, Whitey Ford and Billy Martin. They weren't too helpful to him. Really. Also, because Mickey was a country boy, people would take advantage of him. Mickey finally got in with a very good businessman in Joplin, but unfortunately he made it look too easy. The next few things he got into were not successful.

"Both of us being from Oklahoma, I tried to help him as much as I could. I think one time I hurt the boy, and I didn't do it intentionally. I was just trying to jar him. He said to me, this was early in the season of '51, 'Do you know that I'm leading the league in average, RBI's, and home runs?' and I said, 'Did you ever stop to think what that can mean to you economically?' And I think after that he lost twenty-five points off his batting average. I created the pressure. Each trip I'd spend impressing on him, 'What does the pitcher think about you? The hell with what you think about the pitcher. What does he think about you?' This is what I was trying to get across to him. He used to get so mad at himself. Casey let some of the veterans hit with the count two and oh. And for a while he wouldn't let Mickey. He'd get two and oh and start swinging at bad pitches, and he wasn't helping anybody. He was just hurting himself, so Casey put the take sign on him. And I told him why. I said, 'If you can stand up there and swing at good pitches, hitting them isn't the point. You're going to miss some because you swing so hard, and you go for the long ball. But you have to swing at good pitches, and if the count is two and oh and you swing at a pitch over your head, the pitcher has an advantage, and Casey has to take the advantage away from him.' You know, problems of life are not hard. They are pretty simple. It's accepting them that is the tough part. Mickey fought himself very hard.

"I'd say to him, 'Who's the toughest pitcher for you to hit?' and every time he'd name an old pitcher. He'd say, 'He never gives me anything to hit.' I'd say, 'Mickey, that's what it's all about. Why should I let you knock the ball out of the park when the next guy is only half as tough? It just doesn't make any sense.' When Kiner or Greenberg was over at Pittsburgh, they didn't have a good ball club, but they had that one big guy, and when some pitcher gets in in the late innings and gets runners on base, and then lets the big guy hit one out of the park, he's got to be the stupidest son of a gun that ever walked down the pike. Walk him. If they beat me with three singles, I can accept that. I was outdone. But just to say, 'Here it is. Hit it out of here.' You have to think."

After winning twenty games in '52, Reynolds won thirteen in '53 and '54 and then retired. In the first week of July 1953 the bus the Yankees were riding to the railroad station from the Philadelphia ball park struck an overhead abutment, and in the crash Reynolds severely injured his back. Mechanically he could still throw the ball, but he had difficulty with his control, and when he felt he could not produce to his potential, he quit, after a 13–4 season in '54.

"Because of my back I couldn't condition," said Reynolds, "and if I couldn't condition, I knew I couldn't last as a pitcher. I had a nice record, but with that record I couldn't expect not to get a cut in salary, and this would have hurt me. I got out of baseball and drilled some wells for a while and raised money to finance drilling, but I didn't like having to tell people this might happen or this might not happen, and after two years I came out here to Oklahoma City and was asked to join the Atlas Mud Company by one of the five stockholders, and the next year I became president. About 1964 I bought them all out. It's a tough business—we're on call twenty-four hours a day. Once a well is started they need us. We have a nice big phone bill." Reynolds leaned back in his executive chair behind his mahogany executive desk. He had sued the bus company and won a settlement of about $30,000, a nest egg to start him on his way to business success. He was the son of a preacher and at one time threw a mean fast ball on a dusty New York diamond. Now he is the Mud King of Oklahoma City, and he's sitting pretty.

With the American League pennant clinched and three days remaining in the season, all eyes were riveted on the pursuit of the fast-fading Brooklyn Dodgers by the stampeding New York Giants. Brooklyn had had a seemingly insurmountable lead of thirteen and a half games as late as mid-August, but the Giants were winning thirty-seven and losing only seven down the stretch, and the lead dwindled until the two teams finished the season in a tie. A two-out-of-three play-off was needed. The Giants won the first game 3–1, when a youngster named Bobby Thomson cracked a two-run home run off Dodger starter Ralph Branca, but the Dodgers avenged that defeat by emphatically winning the second game 10–0. When outfielder Bobby Thomson hit a three-run home run in the bottom of the ninth off Ralph Branca to win the third play-off game for the Giants, over at Yankee Stadium, where a number of the American League champs were watching the game on TV, a loud roar went up from the Yankee players. They weren't Giant fans per se, but there were 35,000 more seats in the Polo Grounds than in Ebbets Field, and that difference, they knew, would greatly increase their players' share of the gate receipts. Enlightened self-interest.

The first two games of the 1951 world series were played in Yankee Stadium, with the Yankee players certain that the series would be a sweep, as it had been the year before against the Phillies. Allie Reynolds started the first game against the Giants' Dave Koslo, a journeyman veteran of little distinction. But Monte Irvin stole home against Reynolds in the first inning, Al Dark hit a three-run home run, and Koslo shocked the Yankees with a 5–1 win. It was the first opening-game series loss for the Yankees since 1936, ten series ago. Monte Irvin connected for four hits against Reynolds in the first game and had three of the Giants' five hits in the second game against Eddie Lopat. In this game, however, Irvin's heroics were not enough. Joe Collins golfed a low and inside curve ball from Larry Jansen into the second row of the box seats, just inside the right-field foul line, for all the runs Lopat needed in a 3–1 Yankee win. It was an uneventful game other than an incident in the fifth inning when Giant rookie Willie Mays lifted a routine fly ball out toward center field. As

DiMaggio waited under the soft fly, beside him right fielder Mantle, racing over to back him up, unexpectedly fell in a heap and lay motionless on the green lawn of the Stadium outfield. Mantle had been watching the downward flight of the ball, but when DiMaggio hollered, "I got it," Mantle stopped suddenly and caught the back cleat of his right shoe on a rubber drain cover in right center. Mantle had to be carried off on a stretcher, much to the horror of his mother and father who had traveled from Commerce, Oklahoma, to New York City to see him play professionally for the first time. Mantle did not play again in the series.

The series shifted to the Polo Grounds for the next three games. In the fifth inning of the third game, the Giants were leading Vic Raschi 1–0 when Giant shortstop Eddie Stanky walked. Stanky then tried to steal second, and Berra had him out easily on a perfect peg, but the nefarious Stanky flicked up his foot and kicked the ball out of Phil Rizzuto's glove as he slid into second. As the ball rolled into center field, Stanky continued to third. Two hits, an error, and a Whitey Lockman three-run home run later, the Giants had enough runs to win 6–2. To the fans, Stanky's clever act of kicking the ball out of Rizzuto's glove didn't seem so provocative, but to the Yankees Stanky was a dirty player who had galled them deeply by outfoxing them. Then when he bragged about it in the press for the next two days while rain delayed the series, he compounded the crime. For the first time the Yankee players realized that their complacency was costing them the series. Before the fourth game manager Stengel held a clubhouse meeting behind closed doors and appealed to the Yankees' pride. "Fellas," he said, in a moderate, unemotional tone, "I just want to mention one thing to you. You are not playing these guys twenty-two games. You only have four or five to play. What the hell are you going to do, let them run you out of the ball park?" He looked around the locker room, eyeing his players grouped around him. "Okay," Stengel said, "let's go."

Because of a rain delay, Reynolds was moved up in the rotation to replace rookie Tom Morgan. The Giants scored a run in the first against Reynolds, but Brown drove in a run in the second inning on a long sacrifice fly, Brown singled and scored in the fourth on a single by Reynolds, and in the fifth Joe DiMaggio, in a dreadful slump, golfed a Maglie pitch deep into the upper deck of the left-field Polo Ground grandstands, the final runs in a 6–2 victory.

In the ninth with a man on and one out, Reynolds faced Giant rookie Willie Mays who had already hit into two double plays. Manager Stengel walked toward his pitcher from the dugout, but before he crossed the first-base line Stengel stopped, and at the top of his growly voice he yelled, "Hey Indian. You haven't thrown him a curve all day. Try one, but keep it down."

Reynolds threw the thoroughly intimidated rookie a high curve. Mays bounced it to the infield for another double play. The series was tied at two games each.

The fifth game was a 13–1 Yankee rout. Lopat only allowed five hits, tantalizing the Giants with his slow stuff, and against Larry Jansen, rookie Gil McDougald hit a grand slam home run in the third inning. DiMaggio drove in three runs, and Rizzuto hit a two-run home run. Despite a tight left arm during the final innings on this cold and windy afternoon, Lopat was in complete control. After the game he talked with reporters and drank a few beers, and when he went to take off his uniform, his left arm was so stiff he couldn't lift it high enough to remove his soaked sweatshirt. The injury limited his productivity for the rest of his career.

With the Yankees leading three games to two, Giant manager Leo Durocher picked Koslo to start again. This time the pitcher didn't approach his first-game excellence. He dueled Vic Raschi 1–1 into the sixth, when with one out the Yankees loaded the bases. Koslo ran the count to 3–2 against Hank Bauer, and on the payoff pitch Bauer jumped on a fast ball, hitting it deep over the head of left fielder Monte Irvin. Irvin turned to his left when he should have turned right, and after the ball sailed over his head, it struck a metal railing in front of the lower box seats and bounced away with Irvin in desperate pursuit. Three Yankee base runners scored, and they led 4–1. Newly acquired John Sain shut out the Giants in the seventh and eighth, but in the ninth he faltered. Stanky singled, Al Dark bunted safely, and Whitey Lockman blooped a single to center to load the bases with no outs. Again Stengel went to his bullpen. He called on another recent acquisition, left-hander Bob Kuzava, the better-than-average Senator who had won eight games for the Yankees in relief. Kuzava had only allowed three runs in twenty-six innings of relief pitching down the pennant stretch. Stengel knew that Kuzava, though a left-handed pitcher with right-handed batters coming up, was a control pitcher who wouldn't walk anyone.

The first batter, Irvin, hit a 400-foot fly ball deep to Woodling in left as the runner at third tagged and scored and the runner on second raced to third. Hero Bobby Thomson, the next batter, hit an almost identical fly ball, a shot more than 400 feet deep that Woodling again caught near the fence. Again the runner on third tagged and scored. It was 4–3 Yankees in the ninth, with two outs and a man on first. With Giant reserve catcher Sal Yvars pinch hitting, Stengel called time and went out to talk with his pitcher. "You know this guy?" Stengel asked. "Yeah," said Kuzava. "I know him from the minors." Stengel, satisfied, returned to the dugout. Kuzava looked into his outfield and motioned his fielders to play Yvars straightaway. Kuzava threw an outside fast ball, and on the pitch, Lockman, the base runner, took off around the bases. The ball was hit sharply to right field, and as Hank Bauer pursued it, the ball began to fade away from him. Momentarily he lost it in the shadows. With Lockman streaking around the bases, 70,000 Stadium fans rose in unison and gasped as Bauer relocated the ball. After seven or eight long strides he lunged forward, sliding on his knees, and caught the ball only inches off the ground for the final out. On three pitches Kuzava had allowed three drives that traveled a total of more than 1,200 feet! All were caught, and the Yankees won the series.

There was very little celebrating after it was over. Stengel kept yelling, "We did it. We did it. We did it," and Joe DiMaggio kept repeating over and over, "We won. We won," but there were rumors that DiMaggio had indicated to reporters he was retiring, and one by one his teammates approached him, almost reverently, asking him to sign autographs on balls, bats, gloves, and photographs. "I no longer have it," said DiMaggio, "and when baseball is no longer fun, it is no longer a game." Before the series *Life* magazine had printed a scouting report by Andy High, a top scout of the Dodgers, who didn't make the series. The report was brutally forthright in its judgment of DiMaggio. "He can't stop quickly and throw real hard," it said. "You can take an extra base on him if he is in motion away from the line of throw. He won't throw on questionable plays, and I would challenge him even if he did throw a man or so out. He can't run, and he can't pull the ball at all."

While DiMaggio was sitting at his locker, he peeled off his shirt, opened a cold beer for the last time in the clubhouse and said, "I have played my final game." Even hours of subsequent pleading by his friend Topping could not make him change his mind.

Joe DiMaggio was born in 1914, the eighth of nine children. His father, Joseph Paul, Sr., was a Sicilian fisherman from Palermo, Italy, who left the old country around the turn of the century to resettle in America. San Francisco's climate was the same as what he was used to in Palermo, and with skills as a crabber and a fisherman, he knew he could eventually find work. For five long years the elder DiMaggio worked on building the Northern Pacific railroad at ten cents an hour before he was able to send for his wife and small family to join him in the New World. He then settled northeast of San Francisco on San Pablo Bay in Martinez, a community of fishermen. The elder DiMaggio bought a fishing boat, expecting to raise a family of fishermen. Brothers Tom and Mike remained with their father, mending nets, cleaning the boat, and catching fish, but the next son, Vince, was the first to rebel, and he began playing the unintelligible game of baseball, much to the chagrin and initial frustration of Papa DiMaggio.

Little is known of Joe (Giuseppe) DiMaggio's childhood, but those who remember him say he did not like school and that his strongest interests were baseball and tennis. Tennis champion Bill Johnston was from San Francisco and was said to have influenced DiMaggio, who did become one of the better junior players in the area.

DiMaggio, however, began his professional career in baseball, playing with his brother Vince on the San Francisco Seals. The final three days of the '32 season Joe played shortstop for the Seals. The next year, 1933, Joe was shifted to right field, and in his rookie season he hit .340, batted in 169 runs, and hit in 61 consecutive games. In '34 he batted .341, but because he ripped a cartilage in his left knee and was out six weeks, most of the major league scouts lost interest in him. In those days when a leg was placed in a cast, often it would become rigid and a player could easily lose most of his mobility and speed. Scouts feared that this would happen to DiMaggio. Only Yankee scout Bill Essick felt otherwise. Essick was sold on the boy, and he convinced George Weiss to make a deal for him whatever the cost. Ed Barrow, the general manager, was suspicious of DiMaggio's physical condition, but Weiss, on Essick's say-so, went over Barrow's head to owner Jake Ruppert, and Barrow was authorized to meet the demands of San Francisco Seals owner Charlie Graham. Graham wanted five minor leaguers, $25,000, and insisted that

DiMaggio spend one more year with the Seals. Ruppert accepted, gambling on Weiss's judgment. Weiss was gambling on Essicks'.

The next year DiMaggio amassed 270 hits, drove in 154 runs and batted .398 for the Seals. End of gamble.

In the first seven years that DiMaggio played for the Yankees, beginning in 1936, they won the pennant six times. Between 1936 and 1942 DiMaggio's batting averages were .323, .346, .324, .381, .352, .357, and .305. His RBI totals were 125, 167, 140, 126, 133, 125, and 114.

Manager Joe McCarthy normally had forced all of his exceptional rookies to sit on the bench for a period of adjustment. The lone exception had been DiMaggio. McCarthy was a man who gave advice every day of his life, but he never once instructed or advised DiMaggio in any way. All he said to him was, "You're playing center field today." When a reporter once asked McCarthy if DiMaggio knew how to bunt, McCarthy replied: "I will never find out." Long after McCarthy retired, he swore that never once did he lose a ball game when he had DiMaggio hit away instead of sacrifice.

Among the restaurants on bustling Fisherman's Wharf in San Francisco is a modern two-story dining spot called DiMaggio's. It is a seafood and Italian restaurant run by Thomas DiMaggio, the oldest brother of Joe. I arrived at the restaurant at a little past eleven in the morning expecting Joe to be seated for breakfast in his special corner of the bar, as is his custom. He was not there, or rather I was told he was not there. He was said to be out of town on a golf trip. I asked a waiter if Joe's brother Tom was around, and after a few minutes a short, mustachioed man, husky and dressed in work clothes, introduced himself as Tom and unsmilingly asked me my business. I told him I had been working at Yankee Stadium for the past two years, hoping that my association with the Yankees might impress him at least enough to smile, and I told him about the book I was writing. My friend Vince Natrella was the director of season ticket sales for the Yankees and had asked me to find out if Joe would be willing to allow the Sons of Italy to throw a Joe DiMaggio Day at the Stadium. I gave Tom Vinnie's card and told him of the honor they wished to pay Joe. Tom took the card, looked at it and at me, and said brusquely, "I no know where Joe is." He started to walk away.

"B-b-b-but, would you mind just talking to me about Joe's childhood for a few minutes?" I said. Tom looked at me disdainfully. "I am sorry," he said. "I am no authorized to talk about Joe without his permission." He left the room, leaving me with my mouth open.

Even while Joe DiMaggio was a Yankee star in the late thirties, the forties, and the early fifties, there was always an air of mystery surrounding him. Like Rizzuto and Berra, he came from a sheltered Italian upbringing and did not feel comfortable in conversation. He shied from interviews. "I can remember a reporter asking for a quote," DiMaggio once said, "and I didn't know what a quote was. I thought it was some kind of soft drink." DiMaggio's terse, one-sentence answers to reporters' questions forced them to write entire columns around that one sentence but helped prevent him from being misquoted. DiMaggio took pride in avoiding controversy at all costs. He knew instinctively when he was becoming involved in a conversation or a situation that would reflect negatively upon him, and his guard would always be up. He was suspicious of strangers, aloof, closemouthed, and standoffish. This was his best protection against a prying outside world.

DiMaggio was always an extremely shy man. He traveled to his first Yankee spring training camp in Florida by car in 1936 with two Yankee veterans from the San Francisco Bay area, Frank Crosetti and Tony Lazzeri. During the entire four-day trip DiMaggio was too reticent to engage them in conversation. Only one time during a stop in Texas was there any conversation. The two veterans ordered DiMaggio to drive, knowing that he didn't know how. "Then you'll have to walk the rest of the way," they said. After they told him that they were only joking, the trip continued in silence.

The constant attention paid DiMaggio by the public coupled with his shyness made him, during the latter years of his career, practically a recluse. The incessant demands for autographs wherever he went, the shoving, the pushing, and the occasional abuse made it extremely difficult for DiMaggio to make an appearance in the outside world. It would have been difficult for a gregarious individual, but for DiMaggio, the son of a Sicilian fisherman bred in a provincial culture where the street block was the entire world, the adjustment was impossible. Suddenly this man was the toast of New York City and every stranger who had anything to sell wanted him to buy a piece of it and everyone who was running a banquet wanted him to be a guest. He was as big as the biggest movie star.

All Joe DiMaggio really wanted was to be left alone.

Joe DiMaggio was to his era what Babe Ruth had been to his. He was the best baseball player in the game, a cool and serious performer who made the game seem basic and effortless. DiMaggio carried 200 pounds on his 6-foot 2-inch frame, but when he moved to catch a baseball on the field, he was like a fish in water, gliding toward the ball with grace, without the furious motions normally associated with running at full speed. He was an uncanny judge of fly balls. Wherever the ball was hit, it always seemed that DiMaggio would be waiting there under it, pounding his fist into his glove as the ball descended to him. One time DiMaggio was standing behind the batting cage during batting practice, and John Lindell hit a towering drive. "Over the fence," several of the players shouted. Without emotion DiMaggio said, "Hit the fence." It hit the fence. "I can judge a ball within five feet," DiMaggio said matter-of-factly.

He was a lifetime .325 hitter who hit 361 home runs, only the eighth player to have hit more than 300 career home runs. Voted the greatest living ball player several years ago, DiMaggio has been in the Hall of Fame since 1955.

Yet despite his athletic greatness, his expressionless, unsmiling demeanor on the field gave many the impression that he was sullen and cold. He chose to keep his feelings to himself. The night his fifty-six game hitting streak was stopped by Cleveland pitchers Jim Bagby and Al Smith, DiMaggio and rookie Phil Rizzuto were the last players to leave the clubhouse after the game. They were in Cleveland, and the two were walking back to the Cleveland Hotel in silence when after a couple of blocks Joe discovered he had left his wallet in the clubhouse. "Phil," said DiMaggio, "let me have all the money you've got." The rookie dutifully gave him what he had, about fifteen dollars. DiMaggio took it and started to walk into a tavern. Rizzuto started to follow. "No," said DiMaggio, "you go back to the hotel. I have to go in here to be alone and relax." That was the only demonstration of DiMaggio's feeling about the end of the streak.

Rarely in his long career did DiMaggio show any emotion on the field. The first time was during Bill Dickey's short stay as Yankee manager in the summer of 1946. Dickey confounded everyone by ordering DiMaggio to sacrifice-bunt a runner to second base. Joe saw the sign, stepped out of the box, and stared—since his rookie year in '36 he had never been ordered to bunt. Dickey gave him the sign again. DiMaggio successfully bunted the runner over, returned to the dugout, and gave the water cooler a vicious kick. No one ever asked him to bunt again.

Another time was when DiMaggio hit a ball 450 feet in the 1947 world series that was sailing for the Stadium left-center field bleacher wall. Al Gionfriddo, a Brooklyn reserve outfielder, ran for an eternity, reached the wall on a dead run, and pulled the ball out of the seats. DiMaggio rounded first and was halfway to second when he saw Gionfriddo holding up the ball in triumph. DiMaggio in a rage continued to second and gave the bag a violent kick before running back to the dugout.

Once he was asked why he was so insistent upon not displaying his emotions. In his deadpan ultra-serious manner, he said, "I am a ball player, not an actor."

During most of his career there was an undercurrent of hostility toward him by many fans because he was so impersonal and so well-paid. It began as far back as 1938 when DiMaggio held out for a salary of $25,000 during the depths of the Depression. He even refused to play the first few games until general manager Ed Barrow met his demands. Then in 1942 after DiMaggio had hit in fifty-six straight games and won the Most Valuable Player award, Barrow forced DiMaggio to hold out again. Barrow made a statement about DiMaggio being greedy when so many Americans were serving in the Army for a pittance. Again there was a public outcry against Joe. For the big money DiMaggio was making, the fans expected him to perform glorious deeds every day, and whenever he failed to live up to their expectations, he heard the boos. The bad feeling reached its peak in 1946 after DiMaggio returned from three years in the service. Reporter Jimmy Powers wrote a scathing, libelous piece saying that DiMaggio had used an ulcer condition to avoid combat, and though many reporters jumped to Joe's aid, he stood convicted by those who couldn't understand why so many baseball players had managed to avoid combat during the war. During that year, 1946, DiMaggio "only" hit. 290, by far the lowest mark since the start of his career, and those who felt he was arrogant and overpaid began to boo him unmercifully.

During DiMaggio's entire baseball career he bore an even bigger self-imposed cross. He was an uncompromising perfectionist. If the Yankees lost a ball game and he went oh for four, DiMaggio felt that he had let the club down and it was his fault that the Yankees had lost. DiMaggio knew that the success of the team mirrored his personal success, and every game he played became an intense, bitter personal struggle. For seventeen years DiMaggio worked under this internal pressure.

It took its toll. There was a bad case of ulcers. Furthermore, though he was a lifetime .325 batter, that meant 675 times out of a thousand he failed to get a base hit, and every one of those outs affected him. He was a moody man whose moods mirrored his performance, and this affected his relationships with all around him. He would go for a week without talking—to anyone. His moodiness ultimately affected his marriage, which broke up in 1942 after lasting three years. It also made it difficult for DiMaggio to have meaningful relationships with his teammates. Because he was such a perfect ball player, his teammates respected him tremendously—some even worshiped him—but only Lefty Gomez, an outstanding Yankee pitcher under Joe McCarthy, ever developed a relationship of mutual trust with DiMaggio. Gomez was a natural comedian, a loose, easygoing man who knew how to keep DiMaggio as relaxed as he could ever be. Gomez knew how to needle DiMaggio and was the only one DiMaggio allowed this privilege.

Once while the Yankees were waiting to board a train in Detroit, the players were milling around a newsstand when Gomez picked a couple of comic books off the rack. DiMaggio was leafing through some magazines at the other end of the newsstand; Lefty held up the comics and in a loud voice hollered across to DiMaggio, "Hey, Joe, do you want these? Aren't these the ones you wanted?" DiMaggio, embarrassed because all the people at the newsstand might think he read comic books, growled, "No, I don't want any of those things." Others, not wanting to laugh for fear of angering Joe, grinned broadly at Gomez's unsubtle wit, but only Lefty laughed uproariously at DiMaggio's discomfort. "Aaaaaah," said DiMaggio to Gomez, "go on with you." Gomez left the Yankees in 1943, the same year DiMaggio left to enter the service. When DiMaggio returned in 1946, he became friends and roommates with Joe Page, the young pitcher who was one of his worshipers. DiMaggio recognized that young Page idolized him, and he allowed Page to keep him company. Page did DiMaggio's bidding—buying his tickets, acting as his go-for, accompanying DiMaggio to movies and plays and dinner when DiMaggio felt like going. The two men got along very well because Page never let his own desires interfere with DiMaggio's. Whatever was asked of him, Page was more than willing to do. Also, Page did not mind DiMaggio's spells of silence. If Joe didn't wish to talk, Page respected his privacy. When Page left the Yankees in 1951, Billy Martin spent the remainder of that year fulfilling Page's role.

DiMaggio was curiously insecure, particularly about how he looked while at the plate. Returning to the bench after hitting, he'd say to one of his teammates, "How . . . how . . . how did I lo-lo-look up there? Did I look okay?" His teammates would always assure him that he looked fine. Several, like third-baseman Billy Johnson, understood this insecurity and would go over to his locker after a game to tell him how well he hit or how good he looked. DiMaggio also enjoyed little pep talks before he hit. "You've got to really bear down and knock in these runs," Johnson or Lindell would say to DiMaggio. "What do you think I'm doing?" DiMaggio would reply. "You think I'm not trying?" Yet he would bear down harder because of the challenge they put to him.

Though some were confidence-boosters, all were aware that DiMaggio was *the* leader, *the* ball player, for many reasons. He led by example, with a characteristic grace and almost royal demeanor. The others knew if they could get a couple of runners on and give DiMaggio the chance to bat, he would come through. Because he produced so often, many believed he knew all the answers to the mysterious secrets of the game. Consequently, when he said something, they listened. All DiMaggio ever had to say before a game was "let's go," and everyone could feel the surge of adrenaline.

Every so often DiMaggio did lead actively, too. During the summer of 1949 Vic Raschi had been losing a string of close ball games, the tough, gritty pitcher putting in a lot of effort and getting very little to show for it, and he was discouraged, angry, and tired. After a close defeat by the Indians, Raschi was sitting in his locker when DiMaggio came over and asked him to come up to his room and have dinner. They had a couple of drinks and talked about how things were going, and DiMaggio encouraged Raschi enough to help him through the rough spot of a long, hot summer. To Raschi, DiMaggio's encouragement had been very important. Instinctively DiMaggio had the knack of doing and saying the right thing at the right time.

DiMaggio's career was at its peak before the war. In 1941 he performed his renowned feat of batting in fifty-six straight games, one of only three records that most experts agree are beyond the reach of today's ball player, the others being Lou Gehrig's iron-man record of 2,130 consecutive games played and Cy Young's incredible record of 509 lifetime victories. DiMaggio batted .357 that year.

But in 1946 when he returned after three years in the service, doctors discovered bone chips in both heels. That year he also tore cartilage in his left knee, a recurrence of the injury that had plagued him with the San Francisco Seals. In 1946 he hit .290, and reporters were predicting the end of his career.

In January of 1947 he had a bone spur removed, but the operation had been done improperly. Instead of cutting the back of the heel, the doctors went through the cushion, the fatty part of the bottom of the heel. DiMaggio could always feel the pressure on it, occasionally forcing him to miss games. The excruciating pain he suffered during the 1947 and '48 seasons made many of his teammates wonder why he continued. In 1948 he also suffered from a painful bone spur in the other heel, the right heel, and by the middle of '48 he wasn't sure which leg to limp on. Nevertheless, in 1948 DiMaggio hit .320 and led the league with 39 home runs and 155 runs batted in, prompting columnist Red Smith to write, "The Yankees have a guy named DiMaggio. Sometimes a fellow gets a little tired writing about DiMaggio. A fellow thinks, 'There must be some other ball player in the world worth mentioning.' But there isn't really, not worth mentioning in the same breath with DiMaggio."

On the final day of the 1948 season the Red Sox and Indians each needed victories to stay in contention. The eliminated Yankees were playing the Red Sox, and though DiMaggio suffered from stabbing pain in his heels, he refused to bench himself. His brother, center fielder Dom DiMaggio, was playing for the Red Sox, and Joe didn't want anyone accusing him of nepotism. On that final day, literally dragging himself around the bases whenever he moved, DiMaggio went four for four, including two doubles and three runs batted in.

When manager Bucky Harris replaced him with a pinch runner after his final hit in the ninth, more than 30,000 people in Fenway Park rose in unison to applaud the valiant Yankee star as he unsmilingly glided into the dugout. In defeat DiMaggio had been magnificent.

In 1949 DiMaggio missed the first sixty-five games of the season and on his return hit four home runs in three victories against the Red Sox. For the very first time in his career DiMaggio was hearing cries of adoration without accompanying boos. His pain made him more human and more sympathetic, and his greatness was even more universally admired. In 1950, after Stengel benched him for a week, he responded by hitting close to .400 during late August and September, and again he was the catalyst to victory. Finally in 1951 when his aching legs and arthritic right shoulder combined with aging reflexes, DiMaggio retired.

The Yankees brought him back as a color commentator during the pre- and postgame Yankee broadcasts in 1952, but DiMaggio felt uncomfortable reading idiot cards and feared the live audiences, so he meticulously wrote his script in longhand before each telecast. He was wooden and unspontaneous, and as uncomfortable as on the day Stengel played him at first base. After one year he quit the job, again spurning a $100,000 offer from Topping.

In January 1954 DiMaggio resurfaced with the announcement of his marriage to film goddess Marilyn Monroe. He was asked, "Is this marriage going to be good for you?" Deadpanned, he answered, "It's got to be better than rooming with Joe Page." But the marriage to Marilyn did not last the year. Though Joe loved her, Marilyn's extroverted manner and her publicly exposed cleavage embarrassed him. He was such an introvert and she the opposite, that a compromise in their life styles was impossible. He did not like the way men looked at her, and he was uncomfortable around her show-business friends and acquaintances.

From the beginning the marriage was destined to failure. Before they were married Joe had promised to join Lefty O'Doul to give a series of baseball clinics in Japan. After the marriage Joe tried to get Marilyn to go along, but she had been asked to tour Army bases in Korea to entertain the troops, an important engagement for her career, and she felt it was important that she go. On returning, Marilyn tried to tell Joe of the ecstatic reception the GI's had accorded her, but Joe was sullen and unhappy that her career was interfering with their marriage.

"You've never heard cheering like that," she said to Joe.

Quiet, unemotionally, but with a devastating bluntness, Joe replied, "Yes, I have."

By the end of October the marriage was terminated, a nine-month press agent's dream at an end. At the divorce hearing Marilyn testified, "My husband would get into moods where he wouldn't speak to me for days at a time. If I tried to coax him to talk to me, he wouldn't answer at all or he would say, 'Leave me alone.'

"I don't believe," she continued, "I asked anyone to our home more than three times during the nine months we were married. I offered to give up my work in hopes that would solve our problems. But it didn't change his attitude at all. I had hoped to have love, warmth, affection, and understanding in our marriage. But instead he gave me coolness and indifference."

DiMaggio, shaken by the divorce, had said, "I just can't understand what happened, but I hope she'll see the light and come back." She never did. Marilyn married Arthur Miller in 1956. After that divorce in 1960, Joe and Marilyn began to date again. When the Yankees invited DiMaggio to spring training in 1961, Marilyn was there, too. They remained close friends until the day she died in August 1962.

In 1954 Topping asked DiMaggio to return to the club as a coach, hang around for a couple of years, and replace Casey Stengel when he stepped down. DiMaggio declined the offer. He didn't want the pressure of managing or the task of disciplining players. He was a coach with Charlie Finley's Oakland A's, but after one season he quit. In the early 1970s he made inquiries of commissioner Bowie Kuhn about the possibility of purchasing the Yankees. When he did not receive a response, DiMaggio ended his interest in professional baseball.

Except for his yearly appearances at Yankee old timers' games and playing golf privately with his many friends, acquaintances, and hangers-on, DiMaggio has remained in seclusion. His face has become synonymous with a savings bank in New York City, and he has begun to do other commercials, but while making public commercial appearances he has remained a private person. DiMaggio has become an American institution like Frank Sinatra, Jack Benny, and Bob Hope. Mystery and mystique still surround the man. A song written by Simon and Garfunkel suggests his elusiveness and continued power of attraction twenty years after his retirement:

> *What's that you say, Mrs. Robinson,*
> *Joltin' Joe has left and gone away.*

1952

Mantle and Martin produce . . . The Peripatetic Gil McDougald . . . Tough Eddie Lopat . . . Another pennant . . . A classic Yankee-Dodger world series

In December 1951 Joe DiMaggio made it official and retired, leaving manager Stengel with a position to fill and a legend to replace. With the Jolter gone and Ted Williams flying Corsairs in Korea, Yogi Berra, Eddie Robinson of Chicago, and Luke Easter of Cleveland became the top home-run attractions in the league. To replace DiMaggio, Stengel had a trio of kids vying for the center-field job: Bob Cerv, Jackie Jensen, and a still-gimpy Mickey Mantle. "Who's gonna hit the fence this year?" Stengel asked. "Who's gonna make home runs now that Joe DiMaggio is gone?"

In mid-March during spring training, Billy Martin broke his right ankle in two places while he was filming a demonstration on proper sliding techniques for Joe DiMaggio's television show. Martin's spikes caught in the ground during a slow-motion demonstration, and as the young infielder lay on the ground grimacing in pain, both Martin and DiMaggio were privately wondering how the hell they were going to explain this to Stengel. The next day Yogi Berra, the Most Valuable Player in the American League in 1951, sprained ligaments in his right foot running out a grounder in an exhibition game. Mantle, still recuperating from his world series accident, was limping badly and couldn't play at all.

After ten exhibition games, Bob Cerv, the mountainous Nebraskan Stengel was starting in center field, had hit three home runs. The rest of the team had hit two others. With Collins, Berra, Martin, and Mantle on the sidelines and Brown and Coleman scheduled to be inducted into the service, there was little levity in camp. Only Phil Rizzuto's new sports car provided humor. Rizzuto had been presented a tiny Austin Healey by New Jersey admirers, and he drove it down to St. Petersburg for spring training. During one exhibition game Stengel allowed Lopat, Woodling, and a couple of other veterans to leave early. As they were walking across the parking lot, they noticed the tiny car. None of them had to say a word.

Three days later the car was found. It had been wedged sideways between two old buildings in a narrow, deserted alley.

The Yankees played five-hundred ball during the exhibition season. Raschi,

Reynolds, and Lopat pitched well, Rizzuto starred at short, and Woodling and Bauer continued to impress and improve in the outfield, but the rest of the team was unsettled. Collins and Mize were at first, Carey fielded well at third but didn't show enough hitting ability, and Coleman and McDougald played both third and second. In center field Cerv, though he hit with power, did not display enough speed in the field to suit Stengel, and when the season started Jackie Jensen opened the year there. Mantle began playing, but he was not running with the same speed and fluidity as the year before.

Collins, Berra, and Martin were still out when the season started. Coleman was scheduled to return to the service at the end of April. Stengel decided to play Coleman at second until he had to report, and started Gil McDougald at third. When McDougald had arrived in rookie camp in 1951, he was an unknown, minor league second-baseman, and as the spring training period passed, he began to catch the eye of manager Stengel, though he did not receive the press that the flashier Mantle was getting.

In the early part of that '51 training session, Stengel had approached McDougald with the idea of learning to play every one of the infield positions to make himself more valuable to the team. "Will you try it at third?" Stengel asked. "I never played there before," McDougald said, "but I'll try. They can't do no more than knock my teeth out."

The cocky rookie played third, and he played it better than anyone else. By the start of the 1951 season Stengel had enough confidence in the skinny, awkward rookie to trade away veteran third-baseman Billy Johnson and start McDougald. "I figured," said Stengel, "a kid as cocky as that has got to get a chance to lose a few teeth."

In 1951 McDougald played both second and third for Stengel, and was named the Rookie of the Year in the American League. He batted .306 despite one of the strangest batting stances in the game. McDougald spread his feet wide apart, his front left foot pointing at the pitcher, his back foot at a right angle, much like a fencer's stance in the ready position, and his body turned toward the mound so the pitcher could read all of the lettering on the front of his uniform shirt. Holding the bat high, McDougald would allow the end to droop toward the ground instead of point to the sky. "He's the lousiest looking ball player in the world," Stengel said, "but he gets things done." For ten unheralded seasons McDougald starred at second, shortstop, and third base —one of the most versatile athletes the Yankees ever had. In 1952 he led American League third-basemen in double plays, in 1955 he led all A. L. second-basemen in double plays, and in 1957 he led all A. L. shortstops in double plays! During the 1950s McDougald was probably the third most valuable player in the American League behind Mickey Mantle and Yogi Berra.

On the field he was hard-nosed, combative, and consistent rather than spectacular. "It's easy to have a good day when you feel good," he once said, "and easy to have a horseshit day when you feel horseshit. The question is, when you feel horseshit, can you still have a good day?" McDougald could, and did.

He was fearless, and the worst mistake a pitcher could make was to throw at him. All that would do was make him angry and more determined. When the league first required batting helmets, McDougald said, "With these, if I want to get on, all I have to do is stick my head in front of the pitch."

But considering his superior ability, he rarely received the public recognition he deserved, for he was always overshadowed by his more home-run oriented teammates. In 1956 President Eisenhower threw out the first ball of the season and McDougald caught it. Gil brought the ball to the President for his autograph. Ike wrote, "To Joe McDougald, Best wishes."

Off the field McDougald was friendly and gregarious. He loved the fans and their attention and would sign autographs until the last fan had been satisfied. Among his teammates, he was called Smash or Old Red-neck because he was stubborn and argumentative, and they enjoyed goading him into arguments just to see him become animated and excited. On the Yankees the foursome of McDougald, Hank Bauer, Gene Woodling, and Ralph Houk were very close friends. When they would go to dinner, McDougald often would be engaged in an argument with the other three, who banded together against him in the debate. They would stuff their food down, taking turns arguing while McDougald fought them all, and when they finished their meals, they'd get up and leave him, McDougald's cold food still on his plate. Barnstorming together at the end of the season, they would hurriedly dress while Gil remained behind signing autographs and talking. On several occasions McDougald, in full uniform, had to hitchhike back from the ball field.

At the end of the 1960 season McDougald retired despite a huge offer from the expansion Los Angeles Angels, who had drafted him off the Yankee roster. He had started a business maintenance company in New Jersey and didn't want to leave the New York metropolitan area. Today he continues to run his business and is also the baseball coach at Fordham University in New York City.

In 1955 Stengel changed McDougald's strange batting stance. McDougald batted excellently his rookie year, but the next year the pitchers discovered they could get him out on called strikes on the outside corner of the plate. Stengel and Lopat and Reynolds kept telling him that the opposing pitchers would learn how to pitch to him, but he had always had success in the minors and he refused to change to a more orthodox stance. McDougald had been a dead-pull hitter like DiMaggio. He did not, however, have DiMaggio's strength. The next few years Gil's average bounced up and down—.263, .285, .259—and finally early in 1955 when he was hitting around .240, Stengel ordered him to adjust his stance or face dire consequences. Reluctantly McDougald moved his front foot closer to the plate and pointed his bat up instead of down. His ego was bruised, but his average soon rose fifty points.

With the adjusted stance that Stengel had demanded, McDougald batted over .300 in 1956 for the first time since his rookie year, hitting vicious line drives to all fields and running second to Mantle in Most Valuable Player recognition. In 1957 he was hitting just as well when a line drive off his bat struck Cleveland pitcher Herb Score in the face. The accident affected McDougald deeply, and he never again was the aggressive, offensive threat that he had been.

"That took a lot of starch out of me," Gil said in the cozy warmth of his Tenafly, New Jersey, home. "If he had lost his eye, I would have quit. I began to look at baseball in the right light, and the game didn't mean that much to me anymore. I had accomplished what I had set out to do, to be a major leaguer, and after that happened a lot of other things, like winning, didn't mean anything to me. This young man, who a month before Boston had offered a million dollars for, in the next breath wasn't worth a cent. Herb was a hell of a nice guy, and his mother felt worse for me than she did for her own son, I think. She called me and we talked. 'You've played baseball for a long time,' she said, 'and you have no control over where you hit the ball, and there's nothing you can do.' It was true. But let's face it, it doesn't change what happened, and you can't erase it.

"And at the time I was never hitting the ball so good. I was beginning to read in the papers that they were saying I was dangerous with a bat in my hands. So I started jerking everything. It's funny, but when you are hitting everything up the middle, your timing is close to perfect, but after that I just couldn't shake it. It took some of the starch out of me. I guess a lot of guys may be harder than I am on the inside. I had had enough. That's when you know you're losing a little bit of the quality that is needed to play. That ingredient was important, but in my gut I just couldn't do it anymore." The next three years Gil hit in the .250's, and he retired at the end of the 1960 season.

"In 1960 you lost your job," I said.

"Nah," he said. "I don't think I lost it. See, Stengel knew that I was going to quit anyway. After '59 I told him, and in '60 he pinch hit me some, and I had a hell of a year pinch hitting (9–20), and I hit the shit out of the ball. I had never pinch hit before, but it was fun. What I liked about it, there was always somebody on. It was a challenge. Clete Boyer was a good ball player, but I don't think he beat me out. I was retiring at the end of the year and Stengel knew it. I wanted to play ten years. Period. I had made up my mind that was what I wanted to do. Expansion was coming, and no way I wanted to pack up and move roots to another location."

"The Los Angeles Angels wanted you to be their player-manager," I said.

"I didn't want it," McDougald answered. "They enticed me with dollars, which burned my ass because I couldn't get them when I thought I was at the peak of my career, and my partners in my maintenance business thought I was nuts, too, but as it turned out it was definitely the right decision, because my feeling is that people remember you as you go out. If you go out pretty good, they remember you as pretty good. If you go out horseshit, they remember you as horseshit. You know. Three or four more fights and I'll be champ again. You can't do that. I had made up my mind and nobody was going to change it." McDougald retired at the young age of 32. "I figured with time and effort, in a year with my maintenance company I would be able to bring my salary close to baseball levels, and I wasn't far off. In a couple of years I got it up there and passed it. If a guy is a competitor, all he has to do is apply himself in his work with the same zest and he's a winner. It really bugs me that people feel that athletes can only make money in their sport. It's just a matter of application."

McDougald is a grandfather. His oldest daughter, Christine, has a child. His two oldest sons have graduated from college, and his daughter Denise is a senior in high school. A family man, McDougald has adopted three more children.

"I have a good wife, Lucy, who loves children and is a good cook," Gil said. "We adopted Courtney Ann, she's eight, and my two young sons, we adopted them. They're both biracial babies. One guy black and Irish, the other black and Slavic. Hell raisers and real boys, and probably the most enjoyment of anything that I have." Gil was bouncing one of his young sons on his lap, and the toddler put his thumb in his mouth and snuggled his curly head against McDougald. Gil leaned back in his cushioned chair and beamed at the little boy. From the kitchen the smell of fresh cake drifted through the warm home.

Only Hank Bauer and Gene Woodling were playing up to their potential in the early spring of 1952. Though Reynolds pitched fifteen complete games in a row to open brilliantly, Raschi was unable to complete games because of the deteriorating condition of his knee, and Lopat's arm pained him, so the Yankees floundered badly, winning one, losing one. Both Boston and Cleveland had a four-game lead over the Yankees into mid-May. Jackie Jensen did not suit Stengel's needs in center, and in Yankee Stadium the young right-hander's long drives into left field were merely long outs. Jensen was a hotheaded kid, and some of the older players thought him to be a collegiate know-it-all. Tommy Henrich said about Jensen, "His greatest problem is he must forget he was an all-American football player at California. Once he gets his head out of the clouds and his feet on the ground, he'll be great." To Stengel all Jensen lacked was experience. "If we weren't going anywhere," Stengel said, "I'd give that kid a steady job and let him learn while he was playing. That way he'd develop into the damnedest outfielder in baseball." But the Yankees *were* going someplace, and because Mantle's right leg still had not recovered from surgery, Stengel and Weiss decided that the Yankees desperately needed a veteran outfielder to fill DiMaggio's shoes. Weiss traded Jensen and pitcher Frank Shea to Washington for Senator outfield star Irv Noren. Jensen went on to fulfill his promise, but for the Boston Red Sox who acquired him from Washington.

Before long Stengel became dissatisfied with Noren in center, too. In the final week in May he decided that Mickey Mantle's knee was strong enough for him to play, and Stengel stationed the powerful youngster in center even though he had never played the position before. Stengel also inserted Billy Martin into the lineup after the little infielder demonstrated that his ankle had mended sufficiently. Stengel played Martin at second and shifted McDougald back over to third. He continued to shuffle the lineup, looking for a power hitter, and a team leader to replace DiMaggio. "We would be all right if we had DiMaggio back," Stengel said.

Against the Red Sox in Fenway Park before one game, Boston rookie Jimmy Piersall started agitating Billy Martin. "Hey, Pinocchio," Piersall kept shouting at Martin, calling attention to Martin's Roman nose, "I dare you to fight me."

Martin, as hotheaded as the Red Sox rookie, readily agreed to fight. "I'll meet you under the stands, big shot,'' Martin shouted back. The emotionally unstable Piersall agreed. Each went into their respective dugouts and circled under the stands to their rendezvous behind the home-plate stands, with Yankee coach Bill Dickey in hot pursuit of Martin. Before Dickey could catch Martin, however, Billy got to Piersall. With two short, vicious rights to Piersall's face, Martin slugged the Boston shortstop to his knees, leaving him bloodied. Ellis Kinder of the Sox and Dickey broke up the fight before Martin could inflict further damage.

Stengel, who had managed Martin back at Oakland, could not hide his approval of Billy's fierce combative nature. "It should wake my other tigers up," Stengel said, beaming. "It's about time they realize they gotta fight harder this year. I just hope that some of the kid's fire spreads to some of the others.

"Another thing," Stengel said, still crowing, bragging like the kid was his own son, "I'll have to ask him to confine the fighting to his opponents. He knocked Dickey's cap off and damned near spiked him trying to get at Piersall again. I don't want to lose any of my coaches." Stengel gave a broad, all-encompassing wink. Stengel had found his leader.

In a June awakening, Yogi Berra began to fill the role of power hitter. In a dozen June games Berra hit ten home runs, pulling the Yankees even with Cleveland as the Indians slumped momentarily. Woodling, Bauer, and Mantle were all hitting over .300, and with Berra beginning to drive in runs, the Yankees grabbed the lead on June 14, holding onto it dearly.

Gene Woodling was hitting .330, battling Ferris Fain of the Philadelphia Athletics and Dale Mitchell of the Indians for the batting title. A short, husky outfielder his teammates called Porkie, Woodling batted in a low, pronounced crouch, rarely striking out and rarely hitting into double plays, two Stengel prerequisites. He was a good fielder who got an excellent jump on the ball. Woodling applied himself with a burning singleness of purpose, always alert, always fighting for the advantage, always looking for a way to beat you.

Woodling was outspoken, and he was rated near the top of Bobby Brown's list of RA's (Red-Ass), a baseball term for a player who becomes angry at himself when things do not go perfectly. An RA has a violent, observable temper, swears a blue streak, and is constantly seething—at himself. Brown's favorite gag was his RA list. He was always threatening that he was going to put the heads of the most violent Yankee RA's into jars of formaldehyde. Brown, a doctor, was the keeper of the RA list, and he ranked the players in the order of their RA-ness, though he never would reveal who the number-one RA was. Woodling was rated very high on that list along with Raschi, Reynolds, Lopat, McDougald, and young Mantle. Brown would often needle Woodling that he was moving up even higher on the list. "Brownie," Woodling would respond, "if I ever get sick, don't you dare show up. You have such bad hands I never want you operating on me."

Woodling was high on the RA list because of his battles with manager Stengel. Stengel platooned Woodling with right-hand hitting outfielders, and there were times when Woodling would confront the ornery Yankee manager and berate him to his face for not playing him, much to the amazement and delight of his less audacious teammates. Woodling would walk out to the dugout to see if his name was posted in the lineup, and when it wasn't, he would shout at the top of his lungs, "You son of a bitch. You son of a bitch," and there were times when Woodling would stand right up to the manager face to face and call him that and worse. The two men fought like alleycats, swearing at each other, but at the same time retaining an abiding respect for each other. During one clubhouse meeting Stengel said, "There is one guy in this room who don't talk behind my back." All the Yankees turned and looked toward Woodling.

In 1948 Woodling hit .385 for the San Francisco Seals. An opposing manager, Casey Stengel, liked his ability and forcefulness, and when he was named Yankee manager in 1949, he urged Weiss to acquire Woodling. Once with the Yankees, Stengel platooned him during most of his Yankee career which ended in 1954 when he was traded to Baltimore. Ball players thought that Stengel and Woodling hated each other—nothing could be further from the truth. When Stengel was the manager of the New York Mets, he acquired the 40-year-old fast ball hitter in 1962. "I'm having a tough time getting hitters into my lineup," Stengel said at the time, "but I just traded for a guy who won't say one damn word because he can't. He gave me hell all those years about wanting to play. Now he can play all he wants." At age 40 Woodling finally was getting to play both games of doubleheaders under Stengel.

After Cerv, Jensen, and Noren had failed to fill DiMaggio's shoes, it was Mantle who finally satisfied the Yankee manager. The Yankees had not forgotten DiMaggio, but they did not really miss him and rarely talked about him. By July 1952 they were talking about Mantle, and how the 20-year-old kid could hit a baseball—high arching drives that seemed beyond human capability.

One day the Yankees were playing a ball game in Cleveland, and in the seventh inning first-baseman Joe Collins hit a long drive into the upper deck in right-center field. The ball traveled about 475 feet, his best shot. Mantle was on deck, and as Collins trotted home, he said to the youngster, "Go chase that."

The next pitch Mantle hit about twenty-five feet to the left of where Collins had hit his homer and about fourteen feet farther back. Mantle circled the bases, came into the dugout, and went over to the drinking fountain where Collins was standing. Mickey took a drink, and without looking up, said, "What did you say, Joe?"

"Go shit in your hat," Collins replied, walking away from the grinning Mantle.

Mickey Mantle was only in his second season of major league play, but already Stengel was calling him the greatest switch-hitter in the history of the game, and with his timely hitting and improved fielding, people were already calling the kid the most exciting player in the American League.

Not that it was easy for him. Early in the 1952 season Mantle suffered the death of his father, a man who had meant the world to him, and with his father's death, Mickey became the sole support of his new bride, Merlyn, a high school sweetheart he had married before the season, plus his mother, two brothers, and a sister. Also, to add to the pressure, the self-styled patriots of the country continued to boo him wherever he went. Often drunken sailors and soldiers leaned into the Yankee dugout and shouted "coward" and "draft dodger" at him. In July of '52 the Army passed a new regulation designed to make Mantle draft-eligible. The regulation permitted induction for "men with osteomyelitis who have been treated successfully for the last two years." It was the Mickey Mantle regulation, and one week after it was passed, he was recalled for yet another physical. One of the members of his local board, however, suffered a coronary, and the examination was postponed until the first week in October.

Pinky Lee was a new talent on television, and Warren Hull donated thousands of dollars of merchandise to the needy across his "Heartline." Tom Corbett, Space Cadet, rivalled Flash Gordon. In the race for the presidency, General Dwight Eisenhower, the Republican candidate, seemed to have the attention of the public and the press despite the obvious quality of Democratic nominee Adlai Stevenson.

Billy Martin continued to make his presence felt on the Yankees. He became involved in another fist fight, this one on the field, when St. Louis Brown catcher and bully, Clint Courtney, brazenly slid into Billy with spikes high. Martin, enraged, forcefully tagged the bespectacled Courtney right between the eyes to end the inning. The dust cleared, and as Martin walked back to his dugout, Courtney followed on his heels. Discerning the unfriendly footsteps, Martin stopped brusquely, wheeled around, and landed a couple of sharp rights to Courtney's jaw, also knocking over two umpires who tried to intervene. To add insult to Courtney's injured jaw, the umpires threw Courtney out of the game and allowed Martin to continue.

The Yanks held the lead into August, but three straight losses to the White Sox and a fourth loss to the Indians dropped them into a tie with the Indians on August 22. The Indians were a team with three 20-game winners: Bob Lemon, Mike Garcia, and Early Wynn. All three had earned run averages under three. The pitching staff of the Red Sox was falling apart, and it was Cleveland who would be challenging the Yankees for the pennant for the next few years. Leading the Indians on offense were a Jew, two Negroes, and a Latin. Al Rosen starred at third, with Luke Easter and Larry Doby supplying most of the power. Bobby Avila, their second-baseman, was the batting champion in the American League in 1954.

When the two teams met for the final time on September 14, the Yankee lead was only one and a half games despite a 14–5 Yankee September. The Indians had won their last nine in a row.

Cleveland manager Al Lopez announced he was pitching his ace, Mike Garcia, against the Yankees with only two days rest. A few days earlier Lopez told reporters that he was only going to pitch his Big Three, Garcia, Wynn, and Lemon, during the remaining dozen games, starting and relieving with them.

"What do you think of Lopez's plan?" Stengel was asked.

"I always heard it couldn't be done," Stengel said, "but sometimes it don't always work."

Manager Stengel chose Eddie Lopat to face Garcia before the largest crowd of the season, 73,609, in cavernous Municipal Stadium. The Cleveland faith-

ful were turning out, convinced this was finally their year. Garcia, 20–9, went
into the game having pitched twenty-eight consecutive scoreless innings. This
year he was 4–0 against the Yankees. Lopat himself had pitched three complete
games in a row after a summer of arm miseries and inactivity. He was going
into the game with a lifetime record of 34–9 against Cleveland, one of the
reasons Stengel was starting him. Like Gene Woodling, Lopat seemed to have
the measure of the powerful Indians, and he would tantalize their power hitters
with breaking pitches, continually outguessing the free swingers.

Garcia, tired and struggling, extended his scoreless streak two more innings
to thirty before the Yankees clubbed him for four runs in the third inning, two of
them on a bases-loaded single by Yogi Berra. Later Hank Bauer drove in two
runs, and Mantle hit a long home run and a double for two more runs. The
Yankees jumped out to a large lead as Lopat continued to throw his junk
effectively.

Eddie was not an overpowering pitcher. His off-speed pitches resulted in
many ground balls, and the airtight Yankee infield again and again turned over
double plays to prevent trouble. Lopat always looked so easy to hit, and the
Indians' impotence against him made each defeat all the more galling. In the
sixth, with men on first and second, Stengel walked out to the mound, asking
his pitcher how he was.

"I'm getting tired," Lopat, always the professional, said to his manager.

"I can bring in the Indian," Stengel said. Lopat and Stengel both knew that
Reynolds' fast ball would be very effective in the late afternoon haze.

"Bring him in," Lopat said. For the final innings Reynolds threw his
overpowering smoke to give Lopat and the Yankees their 7–1 victory. Minutes
after the game ended, the skies opened, and it poured through the night. The
Yankee lead was two and a half games over the Indians with eleven to play.

Eddie Lopat was acquired by George Weiss from the Chicago White Sox in
1948, in his first trade as Yankee general manager. Lopat had never been a
great fast-ball pitcher, but Weiss liked his combativeness, his intelligence, his
control, and also his ability to defeat the Yankees, often a Weiss prerequisite to
acquisition.

The press called him "The Junkman" because his fast ball neither hummed
nor whistled, but Lopat was a highly successful pitcher because his off-speed
pitches did a mean boogaloo before reaching the plate. He threw a curve ball
that broke to the right, a screwball that broke to the left, a slider, and a fast ball,
all of which he threw with exactly the same motion. He could also throw his
breaking pitches at different speeds, usually slooooooooooooow. When a
batter was least expecting it, Lopat would mix in his fast ball which everyone
insisted he didn't have, but because the other pitches were so slow, he could zip
it past an unsuspecting batter. A quiet, burning competitor, Lopat baffled 'em
with science, outguessing the batters and laughing at their frustrations.

Often Stengel would open a series with Reynolds and Raschi, who would
throw fast ball after fast ball, and then he would follow with Lopat, and Lopat
would throw off their timing with his junk.

It was a hot, humid afternoon before one of the many important games Lopat was to pitch against the contending Cleveland Indians, and Eddie decided to leave his sweltering hotel room and wander down to the Cleveland ball park. A night game was scheduled, but Lopat thought that perhaps the Indians might be practicing. He sneaked into Municipal Stadium and for twenty minutes watched Indian pitcher Sam Zoldak pitch batting practice, imitating Lopat's slow off-speed pattern of pitching while the Indian regulars practiced hitting it. So apprised, Lopat returned to the hotel.

Just before the evening game, Lopat told manager Stengel and catcher Berra what he had seen. "We might have some fun tonight," Eddie said. The first time through the batting order with the Indian batters choking up and expecting slow off-speed pitches, Lopat threw nothing but fast balls and fast sliders, breaking four or five bats and leaving the Cleveland batters open-mouthed in amazement. The second time through the lineup the batters returned to their free-swinging ways, and Lopat switched back to his off-speed pattern of pitching. Cleveland never scored a run.

The next day Lopat came out early to the Cleveland ball park and ran into Indian manager Al Lopez and coach Tony Cuccinello. "Hey Al, Tony," Lopat said, "next time you hold batting practice, hold it early in the morning so I don't see it."

Lopez looked at the Yankee pitcher in amazement and sputtered, "You Polack son of a bitch."

Lopat pitched seven seasons for the Yankees, nearly always against top contenders, and compiled an outstanding winning percentage with a 113–59 record. He was an extremely intelligent pitcher and a steadying influence on the young pitchers while working closely with pitching coach Jim Turner. He had great confidence in his ability to control all of his pitches and took great delight in making hulking sluggers look foolish.

When dinosaurian Walt Dropo played first base for the Red Sox and the Tigers in the early fifties, Lopat would laugh at him when the big slugger came up to the plate.

"They going to actually let you hit?" Lopat would taunt.

"Don't you worry about it," Dropo would say, "you just pitch."

Dropo would swing with all his power, inevitably hit a little dribbler to the infield, and curse all the way down to first. After several seasons of frustration, Dropo finally admitted defeat. "You son of a bitch," he said, "whatever you're throwing, I can't hit it to save my life."

Lopat, lacking magnanimity, replied, "Dropo, you're just a lousy hitter."

Ed Lopat is now a scout and troubleshooter for the Montreal Expos. He has had a long career in baseball, becoming a Yankee coach in 1960 after he retired, and then manager of the Kansas City Athletics in 1963 under Charlie Finley, a man with whom he, like many others, could not get along. When I met him, Lopat talked easily about his career, his teammates, his pitching, and though he was comparatively short at 5 foot 9 and wore glasses, his manner and hard-nosed attitude toward his job left little doubt why he had been successful.

"We were a twenty-five man unit," Lopat said. "Hell, I didn't give a damn if Raschi won forty games or Reynolds won fifty. I didn't give a damn *who* won, just as long as New York won. We had an esprit de corps on that ball club.

There wasn't one jealous bone on that whole ball club. That's what amazed Stengel, too. He never saw that before. Also, the older players used to reprimand the younger ones for lack of hustle. If they didn't put out, we'd say, 'Hey, you're playing on this club, and you'd better put out because that's the way we play ball here.' You know a player can fool a manager or even a coach, and a lot of guys burn the candle at both ends six nights a week, especially the younger ones, but you can't fool your teammates. We'd corral them and say, 'Hey, we're going into Cleveland or Chicago, and you'd better get your ass in bed because you're taking money out of my pocket.' Mickey Mantle and Whitey Ford used to say that they thought we were the meanest men they ever knew.

"I can remember one incident in 1948," Lopat said, "when we were playing Detroit in the Stadium. It's the seventh inning and we're behind 3–2, and Yogi Berra, he's the first man up, hits a short pop fly to right center between the second-baseman and the right fielder, and the ball drops in. Well, Yogi thought the ball was going to be caught, and he trotted down to first, and had he been running, it would have been a double. The next man hits a grounder that forced him at second, but if he had been at second, he would have been able to run to third, and then there was a fly ball that would have scored him with the tying run. We lost the game, 3–2. When he came in, and this is what shocked me, he's sitting there putting on his catching stuff, and Charlie Keller walks up, not vicious or malicious, and Charlie says, 'You feeling all right, Yoge?' He says, 'Yeah. Fine.' And Keller says, 'Then why the hell didn't you run the ball out? You cost us a run.' Well, he couldn't argue, because before Keller got through, the other guys, Lindell, Henrich, Billy Johnson, jumped on him too. They all told him, 'Bust your ass when you're in there buddy. That's the way we play.' DiMag never said anything. He just looked at him with a stern look. But he was steaming. So anyway, from then on, when Yogi hit a pop fly, oh boy, he ran.

"Now the other incident I remember," said Lopat, "was the same year, 1948, and we were in Washington, a doubleheader on Sunday, and it was hot. So we won the first game, and I'm pitching the second one, and Yoge begs out of the second game. He was tired. And he was a youngster, and this is no disrespect to the guy who replaced him, Charlie Silvera, but Silvera come up four times with men on base and didn't drive in any runs, and we wind up 3–3 called on account of darkness. So when the game was over, DiMag, who had played both games, was totally out on his feet and had to be helped into the clubhouse, he flopped himself down, took off his wet shirt, put it down in front of him, and started to take a beer. We had won the first game, and some of the guys were happy, bopping around, and Yoge was sitting about three lockers from DiMag, cracking jokes. This was the first time I had ever heard DiMag say anything, and he says to Yoge, 'What the hell's wrong with you?' So Yoge says, 'What do you mean?' DiMag says, 'You're 23 years old, and you can't catch a doubleheader? My ass.' And boy, you could have heard a pin drop in that clubhouse. He chewed his ass out for twenty minutes. Then Lindell hopped on him and three or four other guys. After that Yogi caught more games than any other catcher. They made him realize that he cost us the game. When you compare his bat to Silvera's, it's like comparing a battleship to a canoe. Until 1955 Yoge never begged out, and even when Case asked him, he'd say, 'No. I'm catching.'

"We had a smart club," Lopat said. "Rizzuto was an intelligent infielder. Coleman was great. They knew your pattern of pitching. A good infielder at the tail end of a game will play a batter differently than at the beginning of the game. Where he was playing a guy straightaway, in the seventh or eighth he'll move a step or two into the hole because the pitcher figures to be a little tired and the batter is more apt to pull the ball if he gets it in the right spot. A good example of that was DiMaggio. I'm pitching against Cleveland, and this is about June in the Stadium, and we're winning 3–2. They had a man on first and second with two outs and Lou Boudreau up, and I got two balls and no strikes on him. I looked at my outfield the first two pitches, and Joe was playing Boudreau in dead center, and when I got to 2–0 I didn't look around again. It's about the fifth inning, and I was mad because I got myself in a tough spot against a good hitter, and I came in with the pitch, and he hit one right over Rizzuto's head at shortstop, and the ball was hit into the left-center field alley. I said to myself, 'Oh, no. A sure triple.' But when I looked up, there was Joe, waiting under the ball. He never even moved for it! If he isn't there, the ball goes to the 457 marker in left center. When the game was over, I walked up to Joe and said, 'What made you come over from dead center? I saw you there in dead center the first two pitches.' He said, 'I've seen you pitch enough, and normally you don't let them pull the ball, but I know that when you are behind on the count, you can't pitch that way and you have to come in with it, and you're at the batter's mercy, so I figured I'd make up the difference.' That's what made the guy great. He knew what was happening out there.

"Pitching was so great," Lopat said. "It's a battle of wits, but you have the advantage because you know what you're throwing and the batter doesn't. Later on I found out through long experience that the reflexes of the batter will often tell you what he is ready for if he's an intelligent hitter. A dummy up there just swings, and you can give him good stuff to his weakness and forget about him, see, but an intelligent hitter like Al Rosen, Ted Williams, George Kell, Lou Boudreau, or DiMag, they remember what you throw them just the way you remember what they hit. And I could remember just what I pitched to a hitter, what he hit me when he beat me a month ago, where the pitch was. Even when I coached, with certain pitchers on the club I would remember exactly which pitches beat them, say a month or five weeks ago, and I'd tell them, 'What did this guy hit last time?' and they used to look at me like I was crazy. I tried to tell them, 'You've got to start remembering, and if you can't remember, make notes of each player, and before the game review your notes. It's part of the business.' I was fortunate because I could remember those things, and if a batter changed his stance from one time to the next, though it could be a month later, I knew, and I used to say, 'Now he changed his stance for a reason. What's he looking for?' Then I would have to find out."

"How do the reflexes of a batter tell you what he's ready for?" I asked.

"Say I got Ted Williams out with a fast ball the first time he was up," Lopat said, "and the second time I got him out on a curve. Now he comes up the third time. Well, I know he's looking for either a fast ball or a curve, and if it's in the strike zone, and he's guessing right, he's going to lose it. So I don't want to gamble. I want to find out definitely what he's looking for. So the first pitch I throw, I will throw just a little bit outside, because I know he won't swing at a ball, but at the same time a hitter will usually give you a response to the pitch, and I watch his reactions, watch the hands on the bat. If I threw a fast ball, did he show me that he was a little late? If so, he was probably looking for a slower, breaking pitch or something off-speed. So the next pitch should be a fast ball. You say, was he ahead of the pitch or was he ready for the pitch, and you can tell from that what he is expecting. Now here's what happens sometimes with a good hitter like Williams. You throw that fast ball outside, and he purposely commits himself, commits himself as a decoy. And you say to yourself, 'You dirty so-and-so, you're thinking the same way I am.' And if that first pitch you threw him was a ball, now you have to try to make the next pitch a strike and try to hit a spot where he won't lose it. Also, the good hitters will fall away from the pitch and won't show you anything. It was a battle of wits. That's why I enjoyed it so.''

Ahead by two and a half games over the Indians with eleven to play, the Yankees won eight of their next nine games, losing only to 24-game winner Bobby Shantz of the Philadelphia Athletics. Every victory was important because the Indians won nine of their next ten games, keeping the pressure on until the end. The Yankees, however, didn't fold, and retained their lead until they were able to clinch the pennant in the final few days of the season. In the final six weeks Mickey Mantle batted .362 to finish the year at .311, and Raschi, Reynolds, and Lopat were unbeatable. Stengel won his fourth straight pennant with what the critics called his worst team since his arrival in 1949.

"They said we couldn't win in 1949," said Yogi Berra, the Yankee catcher. "They said we weren't good enough in 1950. They gave us a chance in 1951. In 1952 all the experts said Cleveland was going to win. We won again. And we will keep winning. With the kids we got playing down at Kansas City, we not only could win in 1953, but in 1954, and again in 1955, too."

In the National League the Brooklyn Dodgers made amends for their disastrous 1951 collapse and won the pennant in a cakewalk. Jackie Robinson had appeared on the television program "Youth Wants to Know," and was asked whether he thought the Yankees deliberately excluded black athletes from their team. He answered, "Yes," though emphasizing that he was talking about George Weiss and not the players. Weiss, meanwhile, steadfastly insisted that the Yankees had been looking for a Negro ball player "good enough to make the Yankees" while Larry Doby, Satchel Paige, Al Smith, Minnie Minoso, and Luke Easter were starring in the American League and Robinson, Roy Campanella, Joe Black, Don Newcombe, Henry Thompson, Willie Mays, and Sam Jethroe starred in the National. The entire Yankee organization sported two black minor leaguers, Ruben Gomez and Vic Power. "We will not be exploited," said Weiss. Robinson's rejoinder to Weiss was, "Bullshit."

The series opened in Ebbets Field where Stengel had played several years as a Dodger. The Yankee manager personally took young Mantle out to the tricky right center-field wall to teach him how to play the intricate caroms.

"You mean *you* once played here?" Mantle asked. Stengel commented later, "The kid thinks I was sixty years old when I was born."

In the first game Dodger manager Charlie Dressen gambled and started reliefer Joe Black. Black, a 28-year-old Negro rookie who had pitched for the Negro League's Baltimore Elite Giants, was making the third start of his major league career. Allie Reynolds, arm-weary and lacking the proper rest, opposed him and gave up home runs to Jackie Robinson and Duke Snider. Dodger captain Pee Wee Reese sealed the 4–2 Dodger win by homering against reliefer Ray Scarborough. Black used his fast ball and his intelligence to shackle the Yankees, allowing only a home run by McDougald. After the game the Yankee clubhouse was filled with anger. "How could he beat us?" they kept repeating over and over, their attitude one of utter contempt. "How could he beat us? He had nothing!"

The Yankees came back in the second game as Vic Raschi allowed only three hits. Against Carl Erskine and Billy Loes in the sixth, the New Yorkers vented their frustrations with five runs. With the bases loaded and no outs, Joe Collins grounded to second-baseman Robinson, who tagged the runner coming from first and then threw on to first-baseman Gil Hodges, who dropped the ball, allowing a run. After McDougald successfully bunted to drive in another run, pesky Billy Martin homered into the left-field stands for an insurmountable 7–1 Yankee lead. Ed Lopat pitched the third game, as the series crossed town, and with Brooklyn leading 3–2 in the ninth, one out, and Reese on second and Robinson on first, the two base runners surprised Yankee reliefer Tom Gorman and completed a double steal. Gorman, pitching carefully to outfielder Andy Pafko, fired an inside fast ball that eluded catcher Berra and allowed Reese to score and Robinson to race home from second for another run before Berra could retrieve the bounding baseball. Preacher Roe only allowed six hits, and a ninth inning pinch-hit home run by Johnny Mize was not sufficient to catch the Dodgers, the 5–3 victors.

The fourth game pitted Reynolds against Black, a rerun of the first contest, and though the Yankees once again scored only two runs against Black, on this day Reynolds was virtually unhittable, allowing four harmless hits. Jackie Robinson struck out three times on nine straight fast balls, prompting manager Stengel to comment, "Before that black son of a bitch accuses us of being prejudiced, he should learn how to hit an Indian." Mize hit a home run into the lower right-field seats in the fourth for a 1–0 lead. That was all the Yankees needed. John Drebinger of *The New York Times* wrote, "The situation passes from Black to bleak." After the game reporters asked Robinson whether the called strikes that he took were in the strike zone. "How could I argue," said Robinson, "when I couldn't even see the ball. I didn't strike out. I looked out." Reynolds revealed that the first time Robinson batted he threw him four curves, and in the next three at-bats he threw him nothing but fast balls. "I could almost see his mind work," said Reynolds. "He was saying to himself, 'He won't do that again.' "

The final Stadium contest, one of the most exciting games in series history, was an eleven-inning heart stopper that the Dodgers finally won 6–5. Erskine pitched against Ewell Blackwell, a veteran of the Cincinnati Reds who had been most successful against the Dodgers in his long National League career. Blackwell, "the Whip," a late-season Yankee acquisition, was a tall right-hander with a long, elastic sidearm motion, the kind of mean, ornery pitcher who fired high inside fast balls close to the heads of right-handed hitters, and then snapped vicious sidearm curves thereafter. But the Dodgers jumped on Blackwell for four runs in the fifth. The Yankees rebounded with five of their own against Erskine, the final three of the inning scoring on another home run by the 40-year-old Georgia Cat, Johnny Mize. The Dodgers tied the game in the seventh against Johnny Sain, on an infield hit by Bill Cox, a Reese sacrifice bunt, and a single by Snider, and with the score 5–5, Sain and Erskine threw goose eggs into extra innings. No one scored in the eighth, and ninth, and tenth, but in the eleventh Cox singled off third-baseman McDougald's glove. Reese singled Cox to third, and Snider delivered again, the Duke of Flatbush doubling off the right-field bullpen railing, inches from a home run, and scoring Cox. Sain walked Robinson intentionally to load the bases and then induced Carl Furillo to ground into an inning-ending double play. In the Yankee ninth Mantle grounded out harmlessly to Erskine for the first out. Then Mize, his chaw of tobacco shoved back in his cheek, measured an Erskine fast ball and sent it on a low line deep toward the lower right-field stands. Furillo turned quickly in pursuit, and when he got to the low wall, he braced himself with his bare left hand, using the wall as a springboard to jump as high as he could. Mize didn't run far when he hit the ball, because he knew it was all or nothing. As he watched, the number 6 on the back of the Dodger right fielder rose higher and higher, and at the last second the gloved hand opened and enveloped the disappearing baseball. Furillo landed, his glove held high with the valuable trophy inside. Erskine struck out Berra looking to end the game. The Dodgers, one victory from their first world championship after losing to the Yankees in '41, '47, and '49, were anticipating the gala celebration.

At Ebbets Field for the sixth game it was 22-year-old Billy Loes against veteran Vic Raschi, the guy Stengel usually pitched in the visitors' ball parks during the world series. Loes and Raschi traded zeroes for five and a half innings until Snider added to his burgeoning reputation by homering over the left-field screen for the lead, but in the Yankee seventh, Berra pulled a Loes pitch over the right-field wall to tie. After Woodling singled, the rattled Loes dropped the ball as he stood on the rubber, a balk that allowed the Yankee outfielder to go to second. Loes retired Irv Noren and Billy Martin, but Raschi bounced a grounder off Loes's kneecap which allowed Woodling to score another run for a 2–1 Yankee lead. Mickey Mantle, playing excellently throughout the series, delivered his first series home run in the eighth to give New York a 3–1 margin, but in the bottom of the inning Snider again delivered his magic for four bases to close it to 3–2. Reynolds entered the game and threw his smoke to hold the lead.

After the game Loes, a cocky guy, spoke in awe of Mantle's power. "He fell away from the pitch when he hit it out," Loes said. "Imagine if he had taken a full swing."

The final game of the 1952 world series was played under a crisp, clear autumn sky. Thirty-four thousand fans crowded inside the picturesque, anti-quated Ebbets Field as Hilda Chester and her cowbell led the Brooklyn faithful from her wooden outfield bleacher post. After a sleepless night, Stengel had a light breakfast and over coffee decided to start Lopat despite the realization that starting a left-hander in Ebbets Field was usually disastrous. Dressen chose Joe Black once again.

In the Yankee fourth Rizzuto drove a hard-hit ball between the third-base line and third-baseman Billy Cox for a double, and Mize, after sending shock waves through the crowd with a foul "home run" near the right-field pole, singled sharply into right field for the first run of the game. The Dodgers replied in kind. Snider singled in the bottom of the fourth, and with Jackie Robinson up, Lopat called his third-baseman, McDougald, to the mound to discuss strategy, agreeing not to play the mercurial infielder for the bunt, but Robinson crossed them up with a drag bunt that neither of them could handle. Lopat again called McDougald to the mound for a conference. "Campy's gonna bunt, too," said Lopat. "Nope," said McDougald. "Play in," said Lopat. "Nope," said McDougald, and he played back on the grass again. Campanella then dragged the ball past Lopat and in front of the surprised third-baseman to load the bases with no outs. "Son of a bitch should have listened to me," said Lopat as Stengel walked slowly to the mound, left hand in hip pocket, right hand wagging for a new pitcher. Reynolds sauntered in from the pen to pitch to Hodges, the prodigious Dodger first-baseman who had not yet delivered a base hit in his seventeen at-bats in the series. The bases were loaded. Nobody out. Reynolds fired and Hodges hit a line drive at Woodling in left, scoring Snider with the first Dodger run. Reynolds then threw three strikes past George "Shotgun" Shuba and induced Furillo to bounce out to McDougald to end the inning with the score tied 1–1. Woodling, a haunting, personal tormentor of pitcher Black, whether in spring training or in the world series, lofted a home run into Bedford Avenue over the right-field fence to give the Yankees a 2–1 lead in the fifth. Again the Dodgers duplicated on a one-out Cox double and a run-scoring Reese single.

In the top of the sixth young Mantle stroked his second home run on consecutive days, jerking a Black slider deep over the right-field scoreboard onto the far sidewalk of Bedford Avenue. Reynolds retired the Dodgers in order in the sixth, and the Yankees added their final run in the seventh against crafty Preacher Roe as McDougald singled, Rizzuto sacrifice-bunted him to second, and Mantle singled to drive in his second run of the afternoon. Reynolds, protecting the 4–2 lead, looked arm-weary in the sixth, so Stengel relieved him with Raschi at the start of the seventh even though Vic had thrown seven and two-thirds innings the afternoon before. Raschi's arm, however, was physically unable to respond to the challenge, and when Furillo walked, Rocky Nelson popped out, Cox singled, and Reese walked, Stengel hustled out to remove him from further indignity. Again the bases were F.O.B., "Filled with Brooklyn," in the lexicon of Dodger announcer Red Barber, with only one out.

The partisan Dodger crowd scanned its programs to see who the pitcher to relieve Raschi would be. Blond-headed. A lefty. Number 21. "Is Stengel bringing in a lefty to relieve in Ebbets Field? He must be crazy," knowledge-able fans thought. It was Bob Kuzava, the same Kuzava who had saved the final game of the Giants' series the year before. Kuzava had to face Snider and Robinson, two heavy-weights, the power of the Dodgers lineup. As he made the long stroll to the mound, he said to himself, "This guy has got to be crazy to bring me in here." Kuzava turned his head to look back at the frighteningly short left-field porch. With Snider up, Kuzava felt confident, though, because as International League opponents, Kuzava had had little trouble with the Dodger slugger. Kuzava made The Duke pop out to the infield. Two outs.

Robinson was the next hitter, and he too popped the ball straight up just to the first-base side of the pitcher's mound. With two outs, Furillo, Cox, and Reese started running for home as soon as the ball started skyward, and as Kuzava got himself as far from the play as he could, catcher Berra yelled for the first-baseman to make the catch. Collins, however, never for a moment saw where the ball was hit as it went into the afternoon sun, and he didn't move an inch. As it started its downward path, Furillo and Cox had crossed the plate, and Reese was rounding third with the potential winning run. Billy Martin at second saw the glare on Collins's sunglasses and realized he was blinded and that none of the other fielders was going after the ball either. As the wind carried the ball away from him, Martin raced beside the mound where he caught the ball belt-high and fell to his knees with the game-saving catch. Stengel, his heart palpitating in the dugout, showed no sympathy for Collins. "Wake up out there," he yelled. In the Yankee box general manager George Weiss showed no appreciation for Martin's heroics. "Little show-off," said Weiss. Martin had not thought very much of the catch until he saw it on film and realized how far he had run.

With the shadows making it even more difficult to see a pitched ball, Kuzava held the Dodgers safely at bay and preserved the world series victory. In the Yankee dressing room Dressen came over to congratulate his old friend Stengel. Stengel had recommended Dressen for the Boston Braves manager job when Casey had been run over by the taxicab, and after the Yankees hired Stengel from the Oakland Oaks, he had recommended Dressen to replace him.

Outside as the gloom descended on all of Brooklyn, Dodger organist Gladys Gooding said goodbye to 1952 with a medley of songs including "Blues in the Night," "What Can I Say, Dear, After I Say I'm Sorry," "This Nearly Was Mine," "What a Difference a Day Makes," and finally "Auld Lang Syne." "Wait till next year," consoled one Brooklyn fan. "Next year?" said another. "They should only choke next year." Stengel had won his fourth world series in a row, duplicating the feat of Joe McCarthy in 1936, '37, '38, and '39.

Fifteen years later Robinson would call Stengel a "lousy manager, over-rated," and when asked by columnist Jim Murray to comment on Jackie's evaluation, Stengel responded, "I would have to say Mr. Robason shouldn't think he was the only man who was brought in the big leagues who was a wizard. Why, he hit the lousiest pop-up I ever seen in a world series. I brought in this left-hander and they say, 'My goodness, you shouldn't bring in a left-hander as Brooklyn was built with left-handers in mind,' and this left-hander, Gazzara [Kuzava], I said to him, 'Why wouldn't you change speeds on this amazing wizard?' and this wizard Mr. Robason hit the ball clear to the pitcher's mound and Mr. Billy Martin catches it and we beat Mr. Robason's team for the fourth time in five, and the time they beat us [1955] he wasn't in the lineup, he took the day off in the seventh game, you could look it up, so it's possible a college education doesn't always help you if you can't hit a left-handed change-up as far as the shortstop, but I'm not bragging you understand, as I don't have a clear notion myself about atomics or physics or a clear idea where China is in relation to Mobile.'' Stengel's pride had been pierced, and as always he used his steel-edged tongue to protect his reputation. Stengel and Robinson were two fierce, unyielding competitors, both in their own way scourges of their respective leagues.

1953

Hank Bauer—with a face like a clenched fist . . . The Chairman of the Board—Whitey Ford . . . The "little bastard," brawlin' Billy Martin . . . Another pennant . . . The Dodgers lose again

Through the winter of 1952 the Korean War continued to rage, and into the spring of 1953 there were reports of peace talks, but these reports had been alluded to since the middle of 1951, and the people at home were getting tired of ballooned hopes and then disillusionment. Twenty-three thousand Americans were dead and 70,000 wounded. At the U.N. Dag Hammerskjöld replaced Trygve Lie. McCarthyism was peaking as the Justice Department refused to allow comedian Charlie Chaplin's return to the country without investigating him for subversion and moral turpitude. Chaplin stayed in Switzerland. Eddie Fisher sang at the Paramount Theater, cofeatured with Vincent Price's *House of Wax*. Patti Page was singing "How Much Is That Doggie in the Window?"

The Yankees were having an excellent spring training, with young Eddie Ford returning from the service to rejoin the triumvirate of Raschi, Reynolds, and Lopat. For the first time manager Stengel was starting with a pat hand. He had Joe Collins at first, Billy Martin at second, Phil Rizzuto at short, and Gil McDougald at third. Bauer, Mantle, Woodling, and Noren were the outfielders, and Yogi Berra was the catcher. John Mize supplied the bench power.

"They better catch us this year," Stengel said, "because with the rookies we have coming up, it may be difficult for quite some time."

Mantle, who again failed his draft physical, this time because of the ligament damage he had suffered in the 1951 world series, batted .412 during spring training. The 21-year-old, who had finished third in the Most Valuable Player voting in '52, only his second year in the majors, culminated an awesome spring with a left-handed home run that traveled over the one-hundred-foot-high doubledeck grandstand in the distant right field of Forbes Field in Pittsburgh. Only Babe Ruth and minor leaguer Ted Beard had ever cleared that grandstand before. Lopat and Reynolds were chatting on the bench when the Pirate pitcher threw Mantle a slow curve ball. "I'd like to see him throw that again," Lopat said. The pitcher did just that and Mantle put it over the roof.

A few days into the season Mantle fired the imagination of the sporting public by hitting the second-longest home run in the history of baseball. It was a windy night in Washington's old Griffith Stadium and against left-handed pitcher Chuck Stobbs, Mantle, batting right-handed, drove a pitch a measured 565 feet over the tall left-field bleachers and into the backyard of a neighboring home. The ball was hit so hard that the Washington outfielders did not move an inch to chase it. They just turned and followed the rocketing ball, carrying higher and higher into the teeth of the wind, until it disappeared far behind them. Mantle first swore harshly when he hit the ball, because he didn't think he had hit it solidly. As the young performer circled the bases, there was silence in the Yankee dugout with players looking at each other, shaking their heads and shrugging their shoulders in amazement. His other hit of the day was a bunt that sailed on a line over the pitcher's head, over second base, and into center field. "I've never seen that before either," Stengel said.

Of fourteen April games, the Yankees won eleven, and behind solid pitching and timely hitting, they forged to a lead they would not relinquish all season. This team had it all: pitching, hitting, defense, and the ability to fight.

In a game in St. Louis in the top of the tenth inning, Gil McDougald tried to score from second on an infield single, and the throw home had him beaten by ten feet, but the aggressive McDougald bowled over Browns' catcher Clint Courtney, his ex-minor league roommate, separating Courtney and the ball as Gil scored the go-ahead run.

In the bottom of the tenth Courtney was the lead-off batter, and when he came to the plate he bragged to catcher Berra that "someone is going to pay." After he singled sharply to right, Courtney, swearing loudly, made the turn at first and continued toward Rizzuto at second—with no chance of arriving there safely. As Courtney approached second, Reynolds, Collins, Martin, McDougald, and right fielder Hank Bauer all charged toward the bag, anticipating the mayhem in Courtney's mind. Courtney jumped feet-first at Rizzuto and caught Little Phil's right leg, gashing it bloody in two places.

After both Collins and McDougald swung at him, Reynolds pinned Courtney's arms and Billy Martin wound up and cold-cocked him, bloodying his face and knocking off his glasses. Big Bob Cerv got to the glasses first and stomped the lenses into slivered pieces. From the stands in Sportman Park it rained bottles and garbage at the Yankee players. There were three cops in the entire stadium, and the Yankee outfielders were forced to take cover from the bottle wielders. Yankee left fielder Woodling complained to umpire John Rice. "Oh, just ignore them," Rice said. Woodling returned to the outfield. When another pop bottle hit the ground beside him, Woodling picked it up, walked toward the infield, and hurled the bottle at umpire Rice's legs. "You son of a bee," Woodling said, "now we can ignore them together."

Coming into June, New York was winning consistently and each day a different player seemed to be winning the game. First-baseman Joe Collins, batting over .300, beat the White Sox with a home run in the last inning, Bauer made a sensational diving catch to stop the Tigers in the bottom of the ninth, Mantle hit in sixteen straight games to lead the league with a .353 average, Mize was 9–13 as a pinch hitter, and in a Cleveland doubleheader before 74,700 people, Yogi Berra homered to win the first game and tripled in the winning run of the second. Ford and Lopat each had 7–0 records and Reynolds was credited with seven saves in seven relief appearances. The Yankees won their last four games in May and their first fourteen in June to streak to a ten-and-a-half game lead over the second-place Indians.

During their eighteen-game winning streak, a three-week period, manager Stengel became the meanest, toughest, most critical slave driver, calling team meetings and chewing out his players for the smallest imperfections on the field. The longer the streak, the rougher he became, partly because he badly wanted to break the major league record of twenty-six straight wins set by the New York Giants under Casey's former manager, John McGraw. More important, as long as the team was winning, Casey knew that his players could take the rough treatment and benefit by it.

In the streak the Yankees outscored the opposition 129 runs to 44. Many critics were praising this team as the finest to be assembled since the end of the Second World War. By the final game of the streak the entire Yankee outfield was batting well over three hundred and playing excellent defense. No outfield in the American League could match it. Mantle in center was leading the league with a .340 average, Woodling in left was hitting .327, and Hank Bauer in right was at .321.

Bauer, like Woodling, was often platooned by manager Stengel, and like Woodling, he chose to avoid publicity. Bauer, an ex-Marine who had fought on Okinawa, was a tough, hard-nosed player who hustled from dawn to dusk. Unlike Woodling, he was not an RA. He was a competitor, but rarely did he lose his temper at himself or the umpires the way Woodling, McDougald, Ralph Houk, Raschi, Reynolds, Lopat, and Martin did. But Bauer *looked* fearsome. Columnist Jim Murray once wrote that Bauer's face looked like a closed fist. But Bauer was an easygoing man compared to the others.

Bauer possessed one of the hardest swings in the league and could hit the home-run ball, but his main attribute was his consistency. Often he would get one hit on the day, and more often than not, it would be a key one. In the outfield he was fast, and he got a quick jump on the ball, and his strong and accurate arm swayed runners from taking an extra base.

Always Bauer hustled. Pete Rose of the Cincinnati Reds is the Hank Bauer of this era. When Bauer drew a base on balls, he *ran* to first. When he traveled from the dugout to his right-field position and back, he *ran*. He slid headfirst into bases when he had to, and he would break up the double play by knocking the relay man on second into left field with thunderous slides. Bauer immersed his total being into the game and made it his entire life. He was one of the first to arrive at the ball park and one of the last to leave it.

As a 12-year-old kid in St. Louis, he grew up a fan of the Cardinals' fabled Gas House Gang. He followed Pepper Martin, Ducky Medwick, Leo Durocher, Frankie Frisch, and the Dean brothers as they hustled and fought to the 1934 pennant. They were Bauer's prototypes, and during his career he continued to emulate their daring, hell-bent-for-destruction style.

Had Bauer not been a Yankee, his .277 batting average and his home-run total of 164 would have been considerably higher. He was a right-handed batter, a dead-pull hitter who hit many a 400-foot drive into the deep chasm of Yankee Stadium only to see them hauled down by fielders playing on the warning track. When he played in parks with short left-field fences like Fenway Park in Boston, Bauer was a terror at the plate.

Bauer starred for the Yankees from 1949 until 1958, averaging just over .300 for his first six years in the majors. From 1950 through 1954 he hit .320, .296, .293, .304, and .294 as Stengel platooned him, benching him against particular sidearm right-handers who gave him difficulty. During the final years with the Yankees his batting average dropped considerably, but his value never lessened because it was Bauer who continued to come up with the spectacular catch, the crucial relay, or the timely hit. He was one of the very best clutch hitters, and in world-series play hit safely in an incredible seventeen consecutive games. Stengel said of Bauer, "Too many people judge ball players solely by a hundred runs batted in or a three hundred batting average. I like to judge my players in other ways. Like the guy who happens to do everything right in a tough situation."

After a twelve-year career with the Yankees Bauer's productivity fell off, and at age 37 he was traded to the Kansas City Athletics. In 1961 he was named the player-manager of the A's team. In 1966 Bauer managed the Baltimore Orioles to the world championship against the Los Angeles Dodgers.

Prairie View, Kansas, in the cold midwest winter, is just a fifteen-minute slip and slide south from downtown Kansas City, and in February, the dry, freezing winds send a frosty chill through sweater, jacket, and over them, even overcoat. I called Bauer to tell him I had arrived at the airport and was on my way to see him, and from the other end of the phone he sounded angry. "Goddamn it, I waited here at home all day for you to come last Tuesday and you never showed up," he growled.

"This Tuesday, Hank," I said defensively. "Not last Tuesday. I told you *this* Tuesday."

"All I know," he said, "was that I waited for you all day. All damn day."

Now the last person in the world I wanted mad at me was Bauer, so instead of trying to deny guilt, I figured it best just to apologize. "I'm sorry, Hank," I said. "I'm really sorry. Really I am."

His voice softened in a quantum jump. "Get the hell over here," he said, a hint of humor creeping through the phone lines. "I'll be waiting for you."

"Why, you old phony," I thought to myself, chuckling softly.

Bauer greeted me at the door of his ranch-style home with a big smile and a firm handshake, and after I stripped my outer covering, Hank's wife, Charlene, came in and poured us some coffee.

"Okay," he said, growling the way he had on the phone. "Let's get on with those goddamn questions you got. How many of them you got, anyway?"

I showed him the list. "I got a bunch of them," I said. "You played a long time."

"Twelve and a half years," he said. "I was fortunate. I had good legs. I only had one pulled muscle in twelve years. Baseball was real good to me—wound up being manager. I never had any aspirations of being manager while I was playing. Wound up getting a hell of a pension. I think I got 20 years and 123 days in the big leagues. I can't kick.'' Hank had been the manager of Tidewater, the Mets' top farm club in 1972. In 1973 his contract was not renewed, and for the first time in thirty-two years it looked like Bauer would be out of a baseball job.

"I grew up in East St. Louis, across the Mississippi in Illinois,'' Bauer said. "It's all colored now. I grew up during the Depression. My Dad made sixty bucks every two weeks. My oldest sisters used to bring home support. We all lived at home and bought our own clothes. I remember I had to be home at nine o'clock until I was 16 years old. They had a whistle in town that blew at nine o'clock. When that thing started blowing, I started running.

"You know," Bauer said, "my parents were born in the old country, and they didn't understand my playing baseball. They'd say, 'How the hell can you get paid for playing?' My Dad saw me play one time. It was 1949 and he went to see me play a game in St. Louis against the Browns. I had had two singles and a triple, and it was hotter than hell. I came home after the game, and he's sitting on the screened-in porch, and he says to me, 'Tell me something. Don't they ever let you walk? Do you always have to run?' I had to laugh. I said, 'Poppa. If I start walking, they'll start getting rid of me.' Much later on, after we had won a lot of pennants, he told me, 'You better let someone else win once in a while, because the people are getting mad at you for winning all the time.' I told him, 'I'm married and got some kids, and I got to put some groceries on the table.' ''

Bauer's baseball career began in 1941 with Oshkosh, Wisconsin—he was 18. At the end of the year he enlisted in the Marines.

"Why the Marines?" I asked.

"Hell, I don't know," he said. "I really wasn't gung-ho or anything like that until I got over there, but they told me I could take up a good trade, and you know the old German dad of mine, he was trade-minded. You know—if you have a good trade, you're all right. So I was going to take up a trade. Pipe fitting. But I never saw a pipe for four years. I just carried that damn old rifle. We landed on New Georgia, Guadalcanal, Guam, and on Easter Sunday morning, 1944, I landed on Okinawa.

"You remember the landing?" I asked.

"Yeah," he said. "They gave us seventy-two hours to take the airfield on the island. We landed eight o'clock Easter morning with no opposition at all. We walked across that damn thing in fifteen minutes. And that night we set up our defense around that airfield, and I remember about four o'clock in the afternoon here comes a Jap airplane. She landed on that airfield, and the pilot tried to get out. I don't know what he was thinking. We had about fifteen hundred ships out in that harbor. He tried to get out of that goddamn airplane, and everybody hit him at once. He looked like Swiss cheese. Then we started heading north, and we didn't get much opposition until a few nights later. Then all hell broke loose. They was up there waiting for us, and they hit us with everything they had.''

Of the sixty-four men in Bauer's platoon, all but six were killed. Bauer, hit on the thigh by shrapnel, helped evacuate some of the other wounded. He received a Purple Heart for his bravery, the second he won.

"Was Okinawa frightening?" I asked.

"No," he said. "That was my fourth landing. It wasn't frightening. I just prayed to the good Lord that I'd get a nick and get the hell out of there." His wound was far more severe than a nick. He carried pieces of shrapnel in his leg during his entire playing career. In January of 1946 Bauer was discharged from the service and soon thereafter was signed by Frank Lane, the general manager of the Kansas City Blues, the Yankees' Triple-A farm club. After an excellent year with Quincy and two with the Blues, the day before Labor Day, 1948, Bauer was promoted to the Yankees.

"My first game there were sixty thousand people in the Yankee Stadium, and shit, I didn't think there were that many people in the whole country," Bauer said. "I remember the first inning. Snuffy Stirnweiss led off with a double, and Henrich popped up to the infield. I was hitting third, and I had one and one on me, and Snuffy was stealing third, so I was going to protect him, and I lined a base hit to center field. The first three times up I got three singles. I said, 'Shit, this is easy.' That month I hit .180.

"And I hit one home run that year. In Philadelphia off Dick Fowler. When I got back to the dugout, there was Bucky Harris, smoking them cigarettes, and he says, 'Well, you German son of a bitch, it's about time.' "

"What were your first impressions of Casey Stengel?" I asked.

"He started that platoon system, and at the time I thought he was wrong, and so did Woodling, and he used psychology on both of us. He kept us mad, and when we did get into a game, we'd bust our ass to stay in there. But then at the end of my career—I was 39—I said, 'Maybe he helped me play two years longer.' Gene played until he was 40. The Old Man knew baseball. He knew how to handle men. That's what I think his secret was, plus he had some pretty good ball players around."

"Didn't he once pinch hit for you in a game after you hit a home run the first two times you got up?"

"In Detroit. I had a home run and a double, and it was the eighth inning or the top of the ninth, the score was tied, and he sent Woodling up. I had gone three for three, and Woodling came out of the dugout, and I almost sawed his leg off with the bat. I threw the goddamn bat, I threw the goddamn helmet, and I walked right out of there. I didn't say nothin'. Jensen had a home run and a double in that game, and Stengel pinch hit for him, too. Stengel knew I was mad, but I never called him a son of a bitch to his face." Hank chuckled, picturing his buddy Woodling doing just that. "I remember one day we had already won the pennant, I was sitting on the bench before the game, and Stengel had all these newspapermen around him, and I wasn't playing. And he said, 'Yeah, Henry is pissed off at me again. He's not playin'.' Stengel says, 'He always says he can hit right-handers.' So I get up and walk over to him, and I said, 'Why don't you stop that shit. We're going to play those goddamn Dodgers in the series, and that Maglie, he's going to open up, and I'm going to be leading off.' And he says, 'That's riiiiiight.' "

Bauer's constant hustle and desire made him a favorite of Stengel's during the eleven years they were together. In the 1952 world series Bauer had only one hit in eighteen at-bats, and after the final game he slinked over to Stengel and extended his hand. "I wish I could play for you a few more years," Bauer said quietly, assuming that his poor series hitting meant the end of his Yankee career. Stengel, who had let go of Bauer's hand, grabbed it again, held it tightly, and yelled at the tough Marine, "Look, you son of a bitch. You can play for me. I *want* guys like you. So do a lot of other managers in this league, but they're not going to get you. You are one of the reasons we got here. You got strawberries on both sides of your ass. Now get the hell out of here and don't do anything this winter but ask for more money."

"I wasn't blessed with natural ability like a lot of ball players," Bauer said. "I had to work like hell. I was blessed with a good arm and a good pair of legs. I could run. But for the other skills in baseball I worked my butt off. I wasn't a real good hitter. I had to work at it. I wasn't a real good outfielder. But a lot of other ball players have natural ability which just goes down the drain.

"I remember one game we played in New Orleans during spring training. I played four or five innings, and Dick Wakefield pinch hit for me with a man on and hit one downtown for two runs. The next inning he went to right field, and I think the bases were loaded, and a guy hits a ground ball to right field that went through his legs, and he kind of walked after it. I remember the Old Man saying in the dugout, 'I don't like them fellows who drive in two runs and let in three. That starts me minus one. I can't win too many games that way.'

"It's like the Old Man used to say about some of them guys who couldn't run, but who could hit the hell out of the ball. They'd come up and he'd yell, 'Put that donkey on and let him clutter up the base paths.'

"One thing that helped everyone stay close," Bauer said, "was that we used to ride the trains from city to city. I think the ball players talked a hell of a lot more baseball than the guys do today. We took the Pullman all the time, and what the hell were you going to do on a Pullman? You couldn't hardly sleep on those damn things, and the Old Man would open up the private dining room, and we'd go back there and eat. He'd allow us a couple of drinks. Or we'd play cards. And we'd B.S. baseball. Today they get on the airplane, and they're two and a half hours from any place they have to go, and they disperse when they get there. Everybody goes in different directions. Today the athlete, the ball player, has lost a little of his pride. He goes to the ball park, and he can't wait for the goddamn game to be over with to go someplace else. Hell, we used to sit in our clubhouse in Yankee Stadium two, three, four hours in our shorts and talk about the game and drink a couple of beers while we were there. Always there were about four or five of us. I was one. You know, the beer drinkers. We drank a few beers and talked about the game."

"How did you get the managing job at Kansas City?" I asked.

"I was traded to the A's in 1959 for Maris," Hank said, "and I had lived in Kansas City all the time I was with the Yankees, so it was coming back home really. I played a year and a half, off and on, and that was it, and then in 1961, July, Finley asked me if I wanted to manage. He fired Joe Gordon. I said, 'Yeah. I'll give it a crack.' So I lasted until '62, September, and I told him I was quittin' as manager. He wasn't going to get the chance to fire me. So in '63 Lee MacPhail hired me as a Baltimore coach. In '64 he hired me as manager over there. Yogi was managing the Yankees that year, and he beat me out by two games. They had a hell of a September that year. Baltimore had no power, and in the winter of '65 we got Frank Robinson and in '66 we won the pennant. Frank was the big guy, the inspiration, the leader. He was the difference. Then in '67 all the kid pitchers got sore arms, and in '68 I got fired. In '69 I went with Finley again, and he fired me in September. I had a contract for two years, and I sat out all of '70 and got paid. In '71 Whitey Herzog wanted to know if I would manager Triple-A for the Mets. I said, 'Yeah, I'll go down and give it a crack,' with the intention of getting another chance at the big leagues. In '71 we got beat in the final game of the play-offs by Rochester who had Grich and Baylor and those guys. In '72 we wound up third but won the play-offs against Louisville. And that was my career. I wasn't rehired. I was in it thirty-one years. I didn't get any phone calls last winter or anything. I said, 'Shit. There's nothing available so I guess I'll run my liquor store here in K. C.' ''

Bauer sat silently for a few long seconds. He was expressionless. The sharpness, the competitiveness had left his voice. ''I imagine I'll have a hell of an adjustment to make. I'm not saying I wouldn't like to be in the big leagues again. I'd be crazy not to like to, because I would like to. But,'' he said, ''the phone didn't ring.''

The 1953 pennant could have been clinched soon after the eighteen-game winning streak, but in the last week of June the Yankees lost nine home games in a row as the large lead dwindled to five games. Stengel became physically ill as a result of his anxiety. He openly feuded with the press who chastised him for playing Mickey Mantle, who had a swollen and painful right knee. They accused him of punishing the young outfield star. After the eighth consecutive loss Stengel barred all reporters from the clubhouse after the game. After the ninth straight loss the reporters boycotted Stengel.

Toward the players, however, Stengel was uncharacteristically forgiving while the team was losing. After the first few losses they just could not believe how patient and unconcerned the manager was. By the sixth straight loss they were expecting a clubhouse meeting, certain Stengel would really rip into them. But there was no meeting. They lost the seventh and eighth and ninth straight, and still no meeting. Finally the Yankees broke the spell, beating the Red Sox in the ninth inning on a run-scoring pinch hit double by Johnny Mize and a single by Billy Martin that drove him in. The next day Stengel held his meeting. He chewed into the players for forty minutes, accusing them of lax play and complacency, talking in generalities but at the same time conveying stern, personal messages. The team again began to win with regularity, and the Yankees held their five-game lead over the Chicago White Sox into August.

Apart from the long losing skein, the closest the Yankees came to disaster occurred on the night of July 7. The team had just finished a night contest against the Philadelphia A's at Connie Mack Stadium in Philadelphia and the team bus was racing from the Stadium to catch a train. As the bus driver sighted the train station, he pulled into the right-hand lane of traffic, failing to notice the ''Taxis Only'' warning posted on the oncoming trestle above. When the players spotted the station they began to shift in their seats, gathering their belongings, preparing to get off. Reynolds had just started to get up, as had Stengel and Jim Turner, when the bus violently slammed into the low overhanging abutment, shearing off most of the roof of the bus. The sudden halt sent passengers flying helter-skelter. Reynolds fell awkwardly against the railing of the seat behind him and Gene Woodling, seated in the last row of the bus, was thrown forward until he came to rest by the front-door steps. Berra, also sitting in the back, was thrown forward behind Woodling. Stengel, Turner, and some of the players were tossed about but not seriously injured. Trainer Gus Mauch was hit on the head by flying baggage. There was a great deal of broken glass, and several of the players were cut.

The driver hit his head on the windshield and lay unconscious, slumped over the door handle. With the smell of escaping gasoline in the air, Red Patterson, the traveling secretary, shoved the inert driver off the handle, forced open the bus door, and hastened everyone out of the vehicle. Only when they were safely out were the players able to joke about their near disaster. The bus had crashed within sight of the station and the team was even able to catch its train.

The next day Reynolds, a prime candidate for Most Valuable Player, awoke with severe pains in the back. In two years of relief pitching he had not lost a game, and in his twenty-two relief appearances over that period he had figured in eighteen victories. After the crash, he was able to appear only occasionally. He could still throw hard, but he no longer could pitch to spots, and Stengel only pitched him against the second-division teams. He was used the same way in '54, and at the end of that year retired at the age of 37. In 1957 Reynolds collected $30,000 from the bus company in an out-of-court settlement. After paying his lawyer, it didn't amount to half a year's salary.

The United States had set off the largest atomic bomb in history, a huge holocaust high over the Nevada desert, and when Russian Premier Malenkov announced that his country had successfully tested the hydrogen bomb, suddenly the world situation became even more frightening. In August 1953 the Supreme Court refused to stay the execution of Ethel and Julius Rosenberg, originally scheduled to die in May of 1951, and despite pleas from the Pope and Albert Einstein, President Eisenhower refused to grant them clemency. On June 19, 1953, twenty-six months after they were first sentenced, they were fried in the electric chair at Sing Sing, two more victims of the cold war.

It was the Golden Age of Television as the American public embraced the TV screen passionately. TV was a welcome escape from the troubled world around them, so were the Yankees. Radio personalities were making the transition to the screen. Burns and Allen. Amos and Andy. Ozzie and Harriet. There was "Our Miss Brooks" with Eve Arden, "The Original Amateur Hour," "I've Got a Secret," "I Love Lucy," Dinah Shore, "Dragnet," "The Cisco Kid," "The Lone Ranger," and "Wild Bill Hickok." "Your Show of Shows" with Sid Caesar and Imogene Coca was the top-rated show on the air.

The Korean War finally ended. The first exchange of ill and injured prisoners was completed between the Allies and the North Koreans, and returning prisoners brought home stories of communist brainwashing and atrocities. It was August 1953.

On August 7, 8, and 9, the second-place White Sox visited the Stadium for a four-game series. Cleveland had been favored to win the pennant, but the Indians had fallen more than ten games behind, and the White Sox, five games out, were now the only team with a chance of catching the Yankees. Chicago had an excellent starting lineup with outfielders Minnie Minoso, Jim Rivera, and Sam Mele providing most of the offense, and its infield was strong defensively with Nellie Fox and Chico Carrasquel in the middle and sluggers Ferris Fain and Bob Elliott at the corners. Ex-Yankee Sherm Lollar caught and Billy Pierce and Virgil Trucks headed a decent pitching staff. If the Sox could sweep this four-game series, they would only be one game behind.

The New York-Chicago rivalry was a bitter one. In the Windy City the powerful Yankees were hated for their success and their arrogance. In June, after one game which the Yankees won 18–2 in Comiskey Park, manager Stengel went to a local restaurant for dinner. The waiter, a White Sox fan, refused to serve him. After that same game Yogi Berra, Joe Collins, and Charlie Silvera hailed a cab for a ride back to their hotel. When the cabdriver realized who they were, he threatened to self-destruct his vehicle into a tree with the three ball players in it.

The Yankees were not seen to be gracious about their success. Unlike some teams and organizations, every time the Yankees were criticized, general manager George Weiss or manager Casey Stengel would defensively respond to the criticism rather than remain silent. Stengel especially enjoyed answering the critics with some well-honed barbs of his own.

Before this August series, Chicago manager Paul Richards had smugly announced that he had discovered a flaw in the Yankee team and that he was going to exploit it. He then refused to elaborate. When the reporters rushed to Stengel to get a response from him, he was ready with sarcasm. "If he's so smart," Stengel snorted, "why can't he beat the Philadelphia A's?" a weak team that gave Chicago fits. The gnashing of teeth in Chicago could be heard for miles. Most baseball feuds are rigged by the participants. This one was not.

In the opening game of the series Mantle, Berra, and Martin hit home runs, and the Yankees won 6–1 behind Eddie Lopat. In one of Reynolds' infrequent appearances, the Chief pitched shutout ball for the final two innings.

A doubleheader was scheduled on Saturday, and Stengel decided to pitch two more left-handers, Whitey Ford and Bob Kuzava, the world series relief hero. Ford had returned from the Army in '53, and he proved that his 9–1 rookie season in 1950 was no fluke. Ford, in the starting rotation in '53, won his first seven games before Satchel Paige and the St. Louis Browns beat him to end the Yankees' eighteen-game winning streak. He was 12–4 going into this game against the White Sox.

Sixty-eight thousand Ladies' Day fans mobbed the Stadium. They were treated to one of the finest one-two pitching performances in Yankee annals. Ford, displaying a complete lack of pressure-jitters, battled Chicago right-hander Sandy Consuegra to a 0–0 tie going into the ninth inning. In the bottom of the ninth Woodling walked and went to second on a sacrifice bunt. For Ford Stengel then pinch hit Big Jawn Mize who singled sharply to the opposite field to win the game 1–0. The 40-year-old wonder still knew how to swing a dangerous bat. It was Ford's third shutout of the season and his third '53 defeat of Chicago. Against the White Sox he finished the year perfectly, with five wins and no losses. In the second game Kuzava, a hero in each of the last two world series, pitched a no-hitter going into the ninth inning, and he retired the first batter in the ninth before substitute outfielder Bob Boyd lined a clean hit up the left center-field alley to spoil Kuzava's no-hit try. Boyd's hit was the only one Kuzava allowed in the 3–0 victory, and though the White Sox won the final game of the series behind Billy Pierce, they left New York City seven games back. Chicago, and the rest of the American League, were finished for 1953.

1953 was only Edward "Whitey" Ford's second season with the Yankees, and he had already become their big winner. Vic Raschi, fighting an arthritic knee, won thirteen games, Reynolds, who also won thirteen, was limited in his effectiveness by his back injury, and Eddie Lopat, finishing with a 16–4 record and a 2.42 ERA was completing his last season in the regular rotation. John Sain, 14–7, pitched brilliantly in his final year as a starter. Ford, 9–1 as a rookie in 1950, finished the '53 season with an 18–6 record and a 3.00 ERA. By mid-1954 Paul Richards, one of the Yankees' severest critics, grudgingly conceded that Ford was the best pitcher in the American League. When his career finally ended in May of 1967 after elbow miseries made it impossible for him to continue, Whitey Ford was generally acknowledged to have been the best pitcher of his era.

Historically the Yankees have boasted a small, select roster of strong, durable, successful pitchers. Before Ford, only ten pitchers in Yankee history had won more than 100 games in New York pinstripes. In the first decade of the 1900s Hall-of-Famer Jack Chesbro (126–92 as a Yankee) was the pitching star. Then came Bob Shawkey (158–131) in the 1910s–1920s, and in the 1920s–1930s came Hall-of-Famer Waite Hoyt (153–84) and Hall-of-Famer Herb Pennock (164–90), both bought from the Red Sox. In the 1930s–1940s pitching leaders were Hall-of-Famer Red Ruffing (231–129), Lefty Gomez (189–101), and Spud Chandler (109–43), and after World War II in the 1940s–1950s Allie Reynolds (131–60), Vic Raschi (120–50), and Eddie Lopat (113–59) were outstanding. In the 1950s–1960s Whitey Ford (236–106) was the Yankee pitching leader. He was elected into the Hall of Fame in 1974.

Ford's 236 wins are the most ever recorded by a Yankee, and his .690 winning percentage the second highest ever achieved by a major league pitcher behind Chandler's .717 record. When Ford retired he was leading all active pitchers and all Yankee pitchers, past and present, in wins, shutouts (45), and strikeouts (1,956). Despite manager Stengel's philosophy of spotting Ford against the contending teams during his first nine seasons, his lifetime earned run average was 2.74. He was one of the smartest, classiest, most succesful pitchers in the history of the game.

In many ways Ford was the symbol of Yankee success. Though he was a witty man off the field, on it he was serious and almost arrogant, exuding a confidence in himself that suggested infallibility. For sixteen years happiness was rooting for the New York Yankees when Whitey Ford was the starting pitcher.

Ford, a hard-boiled competitor, was guileful and slick, and had outstanding control over his varied assortment of pitches and over his emotions. Ford took both his victories and his losses with equal casualness. If he lost 1–0 in the ninth inning on an error by a teammate, he would calmly shove his glove under his arm, walk to the clubhouse, grab a beer, and chat amiably with the teammate who cost him the game. Anger was never a part of his makeup.

Off the field Ford enjoyed going out and having fun, and though his best friends were Mickey Mantle and Billy Martin, he never cared who joined him in his hijinks, whether a big-name teammate, a member of the ground crew, or a time-on-his-hands reporter. Ford was free, easy-going, happy-go-lucky, and simply a good guy to be around.

"Why didn't you start out as a pitcher?" I asked.

"Because I thought I was a pretty good hitter," he said. "I was a good fielder. I just never grew. I was 5 foot 9, 150 pounds in high school and never got any bigger. I couldn't hit the ball that far, and when I went to the Stadium for a tyrout in April 1946 as a first-baseman, Paul Krichell, the top scout there, told me I ought to try pitching." Again Whitey grinned. "This was after he saw me hit. I had never pitched in organized baseball, but we used to play a lot of pitching a tennis ball against a wall with a stick-ball bat. I think I learned to throw a curve with a tennis ball. Toward the end of my senior year in high school Johnny Martin, the manager at Manhattan Aviation, said, 'Why don't you try pitching?' So I pitched a few games, and when high school finished and we went into sandlot, I would pitch every Sunday. Don Derle and I. He was the first-baseman when I pitched, and I was the first-baseman when he pitched. It was always doubleheaders. I think we each won eighteen games. We didn't lose a game. Then when we got into the *Journal-American* play-off, I did all the pitching because we only had to play one game a week. So we won two to nothing to get into the finals, and we won one to nothing in that game. I really came on in August and September. I wasn't fast, but I had a good curve ball and I could get it over the plate."

"Why did you sign with the Yankees?" I asked.

" 'Cause they offered me $7,000," Whitey said. He laughed at the obviousness of the answer. "The Giants only offered me six."

"So if the Giants had offered you eight, you would have been a Giant?" I said.

"Exactly," he said.

The Dodgers had also had a chance to sign him. Ford had called Fresco Thompson, the farm director of the Dodgers and told him of the $7,000 Yankee offer, giving Thompson a chance to better it.

"Seven thousand dollars," said Thompson. "You'd better take it." Ford was a small athlete, and for the same reasoning that both the Dodgers and Giants rejected Phil Rizzuto and Eddie Lopat, they also chose not to sign Ford. As Krichell had with Rizzuto, the Yankee scout saw the potential of Ford despite his size, and in October of 1946 Krichell signed the youngster to a Yankee contract.

In the spring of 1947 Ford was sent to Binghamton for spring training. He was only there a month before Binghamton manager Lefty Gomez shipped him to Butler in the Mid-Atlantic League, but during that short stay Gomez tagged Ford with the nickname "Whitey."

"What kind of manager was Gomez?" I asked.

"Terrible," Whitey said. "But I liked him. We had a ten o'clock curfew, and one night about twenty to ten, Ray Passapanka and I walked to a nearby amusement park and got on the ferris wheel. We figured five minutes to get to the ferris wheel, five minutes on it, and five to get back. Plenty of time. So we got on the ferris wheel, and the guy who was operating it wouldn't let us get off. It kept going, and finally at five after ten it stopped. Well, we gave him hell, and ran back to the hotel which was about four or five blocks away. We get in there, and Gomez is waiting in the lobby, and he says, 'Where have you been?' We said, 'You ain't going to believe this, but we got on this ferris wheel, and the guy wouldn't let us off.' So Lefty says, 'Oh, bullshit,' and he fined us five dollars each.

"So," Whitey continues, "many years later Dizzy Dean is doing his after-game show at the Stadium, and he's got Gomez on as a guest. We're sitting in the clubhouse watching on TV, and Gomez tells this story which I had never heard before. Gomez says to Dizzy, 'When these two kids got on the ferris wheel,' and he mentions me and Ray Passapanka, 'I give the kid working it two bucks and told him to keep them on it a half hour. And I went back to the hotel and waited for them, and when they came in, Ford said, ''Skip, you ain't going to believe this. . . .''' Well Dizz, I could hardly keep from laughing. But I fined them.' So after the show Gomez comes back in the locker room, and I says, 'You son of a bitch. All these years.' Christ. Nine years must have gone by. I says, 'Why didn't you tell me this before? Give me my ten bucks back.' So he gave me the ten dollars." Whitey laughed heartily. "And he had only fined me five."

Ford spent three years in the minors, pitching impressively and moving up the minor league ladder each year, completing a 16–5 record with a 1.61 ERA for Binghamton in the Class A Eastern League in 1949. Toward the end of that season, while the Yankees were struggling to defeat Boston for the pennant, Ford telephoned manager Stengel to inform him that he was available to help the Yankees in their pennant drive. He was 22 years old, cocky and brash.

"He didn't bring me up," Ford said, "but he got me to spring training the next year. When I called him he told me he was looking for hitters who could help him. It was only Class A that I was pitching in, and they didn't think I could help them."

The next year, 1950, Ford went to spring training with the Yankees, and he was such a cocky, chesty guy that the veterans called him "The Fresh Young Busher." Pitching coach Jim Turner asked Eddie Lopat to work with Ford, to take him under his wing, but when Lopat tried to show the kid something, Ford's response often was, "I did it this way at Binghamton, and it worked for me there." After a short while Lopat said to himself, "What the hell am I breaking my ass for?" He told Turner, "Take him back. He's too much for me."

"I was in awe when I first came up in spring training in '50," Ford said. "In spring training Dick Wakefield was my roommate. He was the first big bonus boy. I had one suit and one sports jacket and two pairs of shoes, and I remember it took the bellhop three trips to bring all of Wakefield's clothes up to the room. He had thirty sports jackets. Twenty suits. But he didn't stay long with the Yankees.''

Neither did Whitey. He was shipped to Kansas City, but he pitched impressively there, and when he returned in June, he had developed some maturity and he began listening closely to Turner and Lopat. Quickly he developed into a serious student of the game, and in 1950 the rookie was 9–1, leading the Yankees to the pennant.

"You and Yogi got along pretty well on that field," I said.

"I'd say I probably threw more of what Yogi wanted than any other pitcher," Ford said. "I very seldom shook him off. I think he knew the batters probably better than I did. He could almost outguess them. He'd call two fast balls for strikes, and the batter would say, 'Geez, he'll never throw me another fast ball,' and he'd be looking for a curve, and Yogi would call for a third fast ball. Yogi did everything crazy. A batter couldn't believe the combination of pitches he would call for. I'll tell you, he outguessed a lot of good hitters. He had a natural instinct. He *knew* what the batters were looking for. Yogi made you bear down.

"Mickey was always teasing Yogi about calling a horseshit game, so one game in Cleveland Yogi says, 'If you're so smart, why don't you call the game?' And I'm pitching, and I don't know about it, but I found out later that Mickey was calling the game from the outfield. If he was standing up straight, it was a fast ball, and if he bent over it was a curve. So whatever he did, Yogi called. We went six innings that way. We were winning five to nothing or so, and Mickey gave it back to Yogi. He said, 'Shit, Yogi. It's easy to call a game.' ''

"Do you remember the first time you met Mickey?" I asked.

"Yeah," he said. "It was the end of the 1950 season. He and Bob Weisler came up from Joplin to sit on the bench with the Yankees for a week. Moose Skowron also joined us. They were giving him a workout. He wasn't signed with us yet. Between Moose and Mickey they put on quite a show. In fact, DiMaggio let them each take an extra round of batting practice. The whole time I don't think I talked to Mickey. He was a very quiet guy. He was sort of thin. I remember he could run fast. Then the next year the whole team came over to my wedding in 1951 when I was in the Army, and I met him again at the wedding. They had just come from Ebbets Field in spring training, and only had like one or two drinks. I just talked to Mickey for a minute. He was very shy. He wouldn't say a word. Then in '53 I got to know him in spring training. He was still quiet, a real bashful guy. Then we started going out together. We did a lot of fishing and took up golf. We were both very bad golfers. We drank a lot of beer. He was a very uncomplicated guy. A lousy dresser. In fact Joe Trimble of the *News* called him that, ask Trimble, and two years later Mickey was one of the best-dressed ball players, $300 suits, and Trimble was still wearing $50 suits, and oh did Mickey get on him about that.''

Ford and Billy Martin had played together at Kansas City in 1950 and they had become close friends, and while Whitey was in the Army, Mickey and Billy were becoming friendly. When Ford rejoined the team in '53, the Yankee version of the Three Musketeers was formed.

"What were some of the crazy things that you and Billy and Mickey did together?" I asked.

Ford grinned and laughed. "Oh, shit," he said, "I can't tell you all of them. Some of them are funny, but I couldn't tell them to you."

"Can you give me an idea?" I asked.

Whitey laughed. "One time we were in Chicago, and we went to a Polynesian restaurant. The waiter said he would only give us two zombies each, so naturally we decided to have three. And we convinced him to give us the third one. I think there were seven ounces of rum in each one of them. And after we finished the third one, we looked at our watches, and it was late, and we had to catch the train to the next city. We must have run about five blocks to the train station. It was a real hot night, and when we got there we were soaking wet. And then Mickey and Billy got into a wrestling match. The two of them, they used to wrestle all the time. And we got on the train, and the next thing you know the two of them are throwing up all over the train." Ford shook his head and smiled, remembering three, footloose young kids who happened to be three of the best athletes in the world, kids who played professional baseball with the certainty that the fun and games would never end. Their fun was the fun of comparably aged fraternity brothers at any university except that their names were household words across the country.

"Mickey and I used to tease Billy that he was leading us astray," Whitey said, again laughing with exuberance, "but that wasn't the case 'cause Billy really didn't drink that much. He wasn't what you call a real big drinker. But he'd go out with us. I don't believe any one of us led the others astray. The three of us just got along real good together."

"But George Weiss really didn't appreciate your off-the-field activities, did he?" I said.

"He didn't believe in any fooling around," Ford said. "He didn't go in for that night life that we went in for. He didn't believe in any fooling around. But I think our night life was overrated. We went out, sure. But you just can't sit in your room night after night. We picked our spots, like if there was a day off the next day, especially them two because they had to play every day. I pitched every fourth or fifth day." A big hands-in-the-cookie-jar grin crossed Ford's face. "I *really* could pick my spots."

Weiss didn't think it was so funny. During one of Ford's rare less-than-productive seasons Weiss was going to fine Whitey $5,000 because of his activities. Ford refused to pay the fine and threatened to quit the team if Weiss ordered him to pay. After Dan Topping intervened, Weiss's demands for the money ceased, and Ford pitched another eight years for the Yankees.

"Weiss fined me once in Chicago for being out late," Whitey said, "and I hadn't even gone out that night. He fined me $200. He later gave it back to me, though. It was a case of mistaken identity. I told him I wasn't even out that night. I said, 'I'll bring Mickey up here if you'll take his word. He'll tell you I wasn't out.' So he gave me the money back."

"But we sure had fun," Whitey said. "I remember once we three went on a hunting trip. We were in Kerrville, Texas, and we had an old 1930 Model-T convertible which is good in rocky territory, and we were chugging along when we spotted a deer. And I was sitting in the rumble seat on top, and they were sitting in the front seat, and we saw the deer, and they both jumped out in front of me, and they were about five feet apart, Billy on my left, Mickey on my right, and I stayed in my seat, and I fired right between them. Pow. I aimed and shot right between their heads. They hit the dirt, face first in opposite directions, like you see the guys do in war movies. They turned sheet-white. Every time I think of that, I shudder." Whitey grinned. "I almost wiped out the Yankee team."

It was getting late, and Ford had to go to a dinner thrown by the Sports Cartoonists Association. He finished another drink, shook hands, and went outside to hail a cab for the dinner. Never once did he mention the Hall of Fame election results being announced that afternoon. Ford had missed by only a few votes. In 1974 he was elected, along with his pal, Mantle.

Whitey Ford is a wealthy man. He has invested his money wisely in stocks and real estate, and is now doing commercials on Long Island where he lives. He is also the proprietor of a fancy restaurant. Despite his financial success, he has returned to baseball as the Yankee pitching coach. When he stands out in the bullpen instructing one of his young pitchers, he still looks like he should be pitching himself.

In the off-season one of the first names mentioned in connection with fund-raising for charities or youth organizations is Whitey Ford. Rarely is he too busy to comply.

Ford came up to the Yankees a cocky kid, and when he retired, he went out content. He was a great pitcher with a tremendous curve ball and the guts of a burglar. Ford was a winner; but above all, he was and is likeable and unassuming, a regular guy.

"I don't like to be made a big thing of," Ford once said. "I just like to go someplace, and you buy one and I buy one."

Only the reinjury of Mickey Mantle's right knee during the early August series with the White Sox marred the Yankees' summer. Before that series his left knee was sprained and weak and he had water on the kneecap, and because he had to put added pressure on his good knee, it weakened too. When Mickey raced to his right to cut off a bouncing White Sox base hit, he planted his right foot to pivot and throw the ball back into second, and his right knee, the one he injured in the 1951 world series, buckled from under him. Ligaments were torn. It was an injury that hounded him throughout his long career. For the remainder of the season Mantle wore a bulky knee brace to protect it, and played despite manager Stengel's protests.

After the Yankees built such a commanding lead through August, the pennant race became a matter of how early the Yankees would clinch their fifth consecutive league championship, a new record of continued excellence.

In late August the Yankees received a letter from a Boston fan addressed to

HELLO..MICKEY
        Tom Umphletts got you 50 to 1.Don't show you
    face in ~~Roksberry~~ Boston again or you're baseball
    carrer will come to and end with a 32....

        Remember I make almost every RED SOX-and
    cheater yankees game and Iéll be sure to be there
    September 7.Ive got a good gang that don't like
    the yankess and you'll find out if you play the
    series starting Septtember 7.
        Thàs ain't no joke if you think it is.

                    yours untruly,

                A loyal RED SOX fan

    you may take this
    is a joke or not
     think any thing
    of it but you'll wish you had~~nit~~ thought of it you better
    tell casey to keép you out of the game it would be better
    if you didn't bring your damned team to boston.

    MICKEY MANTLE
    YANKEE STADIUM
Bronx   NewYork

Mickey Mantle, threatening Mantle with death "at the end of a .32" if he showed his face for a Yankee-Red Sox doubleheader in Fenway in early September. The Boston police infiltrated the crowd for the game. Mantle played and hit a home run, and the threat turned out to be an empty one. A few days later Mantle found himself in controversy when an Associated Press photographer ran a picture of the 22-year-old Yankee center fielder blowing large chewing gum bubbles in center field. Stengel chastised him publicly for his unprofessional conduct. Mickey promised he wouldn't do it again.

Jerry Coleman returned to the Yankees from the service, and on September 13 the Yankees clinched a tie for the pennant when John Mize golfed a Mike Garcia sinker into the right-field bleachers to win the game. The next day Billy Martin drove in four runs against Early Wynn and two Indian reliefers to clinch the pennant for the Yankees, ahead of second-place Cleveland by thirteen games. The pennant clinching had been expected and was taken with an air of nonchalance.

That night the Yankee management threw a victory dinner for the players at the Stadium Club, and afterwards a large player contingent drove to the posh Latin Quarter nightclub to continue the festivities.

Hank Bauer, Gil McDougald, Whitey Ford, Billy Martin, Mickey Mantle, and rookies Andy Carey and Gus Triandos were there, and all ordered large dinners and a few drinks. The bill mounted to more than $250. When the evening ended and the waiter brought the bill, Billy Martin, who was carrying cash, offered to pay for it. After several drinks, Whitey Ford, his mind at work as usual, thought it would be a clever idea to sign Yankee owner Dan Topping's name to the bill and charge it to him. "He's got a million bucks," Whitey said.

It was supposed to be a joke, but unknown to the players, Topping was seated at another table around the corner and out of their sight, and he did not find the large bill with his name on it at all funny. He fined all the players, except Carey and Triandos, who he didn't know were there, $500! Billy Martin was wrongly accused of perpetrating the misdeed.

At the victory party after the Yankees beat the Dodgers in the world series Topping returned the fines. Martin and Mantle got their money and told Ford that he should see Topping and get his money back.

Ford, however, was annoyed that he had been fined in the first place. "Tell him," Whitey said, "to shove it up his ass."

In the National League the Dodgers won the pennant for the second year in a row, winning their championship the day before the Yankees. Under manager Chuck Dressen the Dodgers swept through their league with Jackie Robinson, Duke Snider, Gil Hodges, Roy Campanella, Carl Furillo, Pee Wee Reese, Billy Cox, and newcomer Junior Gilliam, each regular a star in his own right. Two of the finest teams in the history of baseball were playing for the world championship.

In the first game at Yankee Stadium Carl Erskine faced an injured but rested Allie Reynolds. Neither did well. In the first inning Yankee first-baseman Joe Collins walked and Bauer tripled him home as the ball skipped by center fielder Duke Snider. After Erskine then retired Yogi Berra on strikes, he walked both

Mantle and Woodling, and second-baseman Martin, an excellent curve-ball hitter, hit a sharp-breaking pitch over the head of left fielder Jackie Robinson, who lost the ball looking into the bright fall sun. It fell for a triple, and all three runners scored for a 4–0 Yankee lead. Before the series Robinson had boasted, "If Woodling can play left field, I shouldn't have any trouble."

Later Jim Gilliam homered, and Berra matched it for a 5–1 Yankee lead. But Reynolds allowed three more runs on home runs by Hodges and George Shuba. Against reliefer John Sain in the seventh, Campanella, Hodges, and Furillo singled to tie the score at 5–5, but in the bottom of the inning against sinker-ball reliefer Clem Labine, Collins worked the magic he consistently performed against low-ball pitchers, and lofted the game-winning home run into the right-field seats for the ball game. Three insurance runs later, the Yankees won 9–5.

The second game was a duel of crafty lefties, Ed Lopat against Preacher Roe, and Roe held the upper hand, 2–1, until the seventh inning when the ubiquitous Martin walked up on a screw ball and hit a line drive home run into the left-field seats just out of the reach of left fielder Robinson to tie the score. In the eighth Bauer singled and Mantle, still playing on weak legs, swung off-stride at a Roe change-up and flat-footedly pulled the ball ten rows deep into the left-field stands for two runs and the ball game. It was a bad pitch, low and outside, but at the loud thwack of the bat it was evident that no one was going to catch it. Lopat pitched cunningly to complete the 4–2 victory.

When the scene shifted to cozy Ebbets Field for the next three games, the Brooklyn team fared better. Dressen started Erskine against Vic Raschi, and though the Dodgers were only able to scratch two runs against Raschi going into the eighth, the Yankees were being held to only one run by the curve-balling Erskine. Erskine's curve ball was particularly sharp, starting out at eye level and then dropping suddenly until it almost struck the plate. Erskine struck out Mantle and Collins four times each and was on the way to a series strikeout record.

In the top of the eighth as the Yankees were scoring the tying run, manager Stengel conferred with Raschi. Pointing to his scorecard, Stengel reminded the big Yankee pitcher that Roy Campanella would be the lead-off hitter and that Campy liked to swing at the first pitch. "Don't forget," warned Stengel, "watch out for that first pitch." "Yeah, I know," said Raschi. Just before the team grouped to take the field, Stengel again reminded Raschi. "The first pitch," he said. "Remember."

At the plate Campy set his feet, the stubby, muscular, black catcher hefting his heavy bat like it was a toothpick. On Raschi's first pitch Campanella jerked a cannon-shot home run into the lower left-field stands to give the Dodgers a 3–2 lead. When the bat met the ball, Stengel angrily jumped up from his seat and solidly cracked his head on the concrete roof of the dugout. Raschi kicked the mound with his spikes, wondering more how he was going to face Stengel than how he was going to finish the inning.

In the top of the ninth 35,000 Brooklyn fans were waiting to see whether Erskine could retire the final three Yankees and set a new world series one-game strikeout record. He had registered twelve strikeouts, one short of the record set by a Philadelphia Athletic pitcher, Howard Ehmke, who established it against the Chicago Cubs in 1929. In the ninth Yankee Don Bollweg, pinch hitting for Rizzuto, struck out on a fast-dropping curve to tie the record. Stengel then sent up John Mize to pinch hit for the pitcher. All game long Mize had been sitting next to Stengel grumbling that the batters should lay off the sharp-breaking pitch for a ball instead of swinging at it. "Hit a good pitch, for Christ's sake," Mize kept saying as the batters struck out on pitches in the dirt. To Mize three times Erskine threw his fast-dropping specialty, and three times Mize swung lustily and missed completely at pitches dipping around his ankles. He became the thirteenth strikeout victim, and Erskine had his record. When Mize got back to the dugout, Martin cornered him. "What happened, John," said the sharp-tongued infielder, "that low curve take a bad hop?" Collins grounded out to end the game.

The fourth game pitted Whitey Ford against Billy Loes, two youngsters who grew up only ten blocks from each other in Astoria, New York. Ford was the perfectionist, Loes the character. Before the series Loes had predicted that the Yankees would win! Once when Loes was asked why he had fumbled a ground ball, he replied seriously, "I lost it in the sun." But on this day the character outpitched the perfectionist. The Dodgers scored three runs in the first inning, the last two on a double by Duke Snider, who later hit a home run. Despite a triple by Billy Martin and a home run by McDougald, the Dodgers tied the series at two games each with a 7–3 win. In the ninth the Yankees had the bases loaded with two outs when Mantle singled to left field for the final Yankee run, but when Martin tried to score from second on the hit, left fielder Robinson pegged home perfectly on one bounce, and catcher Campanella registered the final out of the game with a crashing tag against young Martin's forehead.

If either team had a weakness it was lack of pitching depth, and the fifth-game starters reflected that problem. Dressen chose 20-year-old John Podres, and Stengel chose Jim McDonald, a free-spirited race-car fanatic who put a Cadillac engine in his Mercury and who constantly put smoke bombs, sirens, and other paraphernalia in Phil Rizzuto's car, scaring the life out of the poor shortstop. Left-hander Gene Woodling made McDonald's task easier by leading off the game with a home run against Podres, and it was Woodling in the bottom of the second who saved him with a line throw from left field to catcher Berra who tagged out Hodges trying to score. In the top of the third with two outs Collins bounced a bad hop past the erring Hodges at first to score Rizzuto with the second Yankee run, and after Podres hit Bauer on the wrist and walked Berra to load the bases, with Mantle coming up Dressen decided that Podres had had enough. The Dodger manager brought in another of his eccentrics, Russ (Monk) Meyer. Mantle, playing on legs that often would buckle when he batted left-handed, ran in almost constant pain, but still he insisted on playing. Mantle had struck out his last five at-bats, but on the first pitch from Meyer, he lofted a high fly ball that fell into the left-field stands for a grand slam home run.

In the eighth McDonald finally cracked and Reynolds was ineffective in relief, but pesky Martin hit another home run for two insurance runs, and the Yankees won 11–7.

With New York leading in games, 3–2, the series returned to the Stadium for the sixth game, one of the classic contests in series history. In a game played in a cold and biting wind before 62,000 fans, Stengel chose Ford; Dressen, Erskine. With Ford holding a 3–1 lead into the eighth, manager Stengel brought in Reynolds to pitch the final two innings. Before Stengel sent his relief star into the game, he asked him how he felt. Reynolds told him he had speed but poor control, but Stengel went with him anyway. The Indian did fine in the eighth, but in the top of the ninth he walked Snider, and then Carl Furillo pulled a fast ball over the left-field fence to tie the game 3–3, staving off a Dodger defeat.

Dodger relief specialist Clem Labine was pitching in the bottom of the ninth, and the Brooklyn righty opened the inning by walking Hank Bauer. Mantle bounced a high chopper between third and the mound that third-baseman Billy Cox charged in for but was unable to handle cleanly. Both runners were safe. With one out Billy Martin was the batter. The cocky Yankee infielder, the series hero the year before, followed a fast ball and stroked a one-one pitch on a line over second base to score Bauer with the winning hit in the 4–3 triumph. It was his twelfth hit of the six-game series, a record. The Yankees had registered their fifth straight world series championship and their sixteenth series win in twenty years of competition. For the Dodgers it was their seventh series loss in a row without a victory. One disgruntled Dodger reporter expressed his extreme frustration. "Rooting against the Yankees," he said, "is like rooting against United States Steel."

After the final game the reporters surrounded hero Martin. "The Dodgers are the Dodgers," Billy said. "If they had eight Babe Ruths they couldn't beat us." Martin had batted 12–24, the second most productive batting performance in series history behind Babe Ruth's 10–16, .625 in 1928. Martin struck a double, two triples, and two home runs and drove in eight runs, second only to the nine runs driven in by Lou Gehrig in 1928. Martin won the Babe Ruth Award, for the first time given to the outstanding world series performer. "That's the worst thing that coulda happened to Martin," Stengel said. "I ain't gonna be able to live with that little son of a bitch next year."

In contrast Mantle, playing on weakened underpinning, batted only .208 against the Dodgers. It seemed that no matter how well Mantle performed or under what handicaps, Stengel always demanded more from his young star. "We kept telling him to cut down on his swing and hit down on the ball," Stengel criticized after the series. "The kid's got power enough to hit it in the seats just punching it like he did for the big one he hit. You tell him to stop trying to kill the ball, and he won't do it. That's the difference. You tell the fresh kid," referring to Martin, "something, and he listens and does it. You tell the other fellow something," referring to Mantle, "and he acts like you tell him nothing."

Billy Martin was an outstanding ball player with the Yankees in 1952 and 1953, but like Jerry Coleman before him, Martin was drafted into the Army after his second year of steady play, serving for two years and never again showing the form which brought him his early fame. It seemed that Martin was being crucified by the selective service system. He had been drafted in 1950, and after serving for five months, the Army discharged him on a dependency deferment because he was the sole support of his parents, wife, and daughter. By the end of '53 Martin's wife had divorced him, and at the age of 25, only four months before he would have been ineligible for the draft, the Army ruled that his parents were no longer in need of his support, and he was reclassified 1-A and drafted. Bitterly Martin fought the ruling and lost. "I'll fight willingly if they can figure some way to support my dependents," he said. However, his Berkeley, California, draft board showed no sympathy. In April '54 when Martin again applied for a hardship deferment, Billy drove to the hearing in his late model baby blue Cadillac. "How broke can he be?" the Army brass reasoned in turning down his application. At the same time the Army forbade Martin from playing on the Fort Ord baseball team, refused to give him credit for the five months he served earlier, and gave him fewer passes than his fellow GI's. Martin had won his fame, and in the Army he paid for it dearly.

Billy Martin was a bona fide star in 1952 and 1953, and when he returned to the Yankees in September of '55, he sparked the team to the pennant. By 1957, however, Martin was deep in general manager George Weiss's doghouse, and though Stengel fought with Weiss for years to keep Martin on the team, after the Copacabana nightclub fracas in May 1957, Stengel no longer could prevent Weiss from trading Martin. Bitter and disillusioned, Martin lost much of his desire and exuberance, bouncing from one team to another until he finally retired at the end of 1961. Because of his reputation as a troublemaker and his mediocre final few years, Billy Martin will always be remembered as an average ball player. Nothing could be further from the truth. He looked awkward at bat and in the field, but in critical situations Billy Martin could carry the team on his shoulders. In his prime Martin was every bit the star that his buddies Mantle and Ford were.

"There has been a tendency to underrate Martin," said manager Stengel, "because he is scrawny, is no beauty with that big schnozz of his, and looks like he was underfed and weighs only 135 pounds. But he has been a strong factor in every club for which he has played since he asked me for a chance in that Oakland park in 1946. I defy anyone to knock Martin down as a great ball player. Can he make double plays? Will he fight, especially against big odds? Will he come through when coming through means most? You have to say 'yes' to all three questions. They say I have been biased in favor of Martin because I gave him his first chance and nursed him along to be sold to the Yankees. Well, if liking a kid who will never let you down in the clutch is favoritism, then I plead guilty."

U.S. 1, the federal highway, travels from the potato country of Maine all the way south to the islands of the Florida Keys. Traveling south into the city of Pompano Beach, Florida, if you make a right after the local driving range on U.S. 1, the road will wind its way to the training camp of the Texas Ranger baseball team, once the cellar-dwelling ex-Washington Senators, but given a lift and a transfusion by new money and a new manager. It was early morning in March, and the tropical Florida sun was not yet at full intensity. While groups of players ran sprints in the outfield and played pepper, husky batters practiced their home run derby swing in the cage. Martin, the Ranger manager in 1974, sat on an outfield bench, watching his men and getting a suntan.

When Martin saw that I had arrived, he joined me on the green-flaked wooden grandstand down the left-field line. Martin is a great believer in delegating authority, so while his coaches put the players through their paces, he was able to sit and talk and watch over things at the same time. Martin had always had the reputation of being a street fighter and somewhat of a hoodlum because of the numerous players he had beaten up during his career, including a couple of his own players while managing. I was very much surprised to find that Martin, away from a situation where he was being challenged or provoked, was actually a congenial, softspoken, humble man. Martin answered everything I asked, including several sensitive questions, with honesty and feeling. When we finished I had gained tremendous respect for the "little bugger," as Casey Stengel called him. His life has been a difficult one, and rather than fold up his tent, he chose instead to fight for his self-respect and for whatever he felt was owed him. To that end Martin is still fighting, because his self-doubts are deep-seated and his fears of poverty and rejection still lurk just below the surface.

Alfred Manuel Martin grew up on the street. His father, a crop-hand, ran out on his mother when Billy was young, and until the day he began playing professional baseball he was poor. His mother remarried, but his stepfather, an asthmatic, was in the WPA during the thirties because he was never able to find steady employment. The situation was so bad that Billy often swept out the local church in exchange for food donations to his family. It was a solemn, life-and-death struggle. For Martin it was even more difficult because in addition to his large nose which was the butt of constant joking, compounding the normal adolescent fears of being ugly and unattractive, he was also short and small. It's tough enough for a kid to be poor, but the combination of poor *and* ugly *and* short made Martin feel like a total misfit. When the kids would call him Pinocchio, Banana Nose, or Shrimp, Martin would fly into uncontrollable rages and strike out at his tormentors.

"I had plenty of street fights when I was a kid," Martin said without any expression of pride. "I grew up in a tough neighborhood in Berkeley where you had to either fight or run. I never wanted to be a fighter. But I'm like I was when I was a kid. If the other guy wants to fight, I'll fight him. You can't show 'em that you're afraid. No matter how big they are.

"My childhood was different for me," he said, "than for most kids because it taught me how to handle life. I mean I learned it when I was young. Guys learn it now when they're 25. It was an area where it was the survival of the fittest. Every day there'd be a new guy to challenge you in a fight. Fifty to a hundred kids would be sitting in a circle in Jenxton Park, and you come along, and a new guy came along and challenged you. They did it to everybody. That's just the way they lived. Like a jungle. And after you whip so many, they leave you alone, but before that you had to whip a bunch of them."

By the time Martin was 15 he was an experienced, proficient street fighter, a juvenile delinquent, and a school problem. He excelled in football, baseball, and basketball, leading his school to the county basketball championship three years in a row, but his violent, unpredictable antisocial behavior got him into serious trouble. His opponents would taunt him about his nose, and Martin would start swinging. Several times he charged into the stands and beat up spectators who were riding him. He was suspended more than once. He always returned to play sports. Sports kept him in school—and out of jail.

"I fell in love with baseball when I was very young," Martin said. "Jenxton Park was about a half a block from my home, and when school was over I was there from morning to late at night. At night they turned the lights on. We played capture-the-flag, football. I played every game they played. You know, I excelled in football and basketball, too. I won a basketball scholarship to Santa Clara. But my first love was baseball."

While Martin was still in high school he played semi-pro baseball for the Oakland Junior Oaks, a team sponsored by the Oakland team of the Pacific Coast League. In August 1946 he began playing in the Oakland farm system.

In his first full season as a pro, Martin played for Phoenix in the Arizona-Texas League in 1947. Batting in the eighth position in the lineup, he hit .392 and drove in 174 runs! He was named the Most Valuable Player in the league. For Martin, though, gaudy statistics were a poor mask for lingering insecurities. At the dinner where he was awarded his MVP trophy, he got up to speak, looked at his statistics engraved on the bowl, and the first thing he said was, "Hey, somebody made a mistake. I didn't hit .390, I hit .392."

"I joined the Oakland Oaks the last month of the '47 season," Martin said. "Casey Stengel was the manager. And I played with him in '48 and we won the pennant. Then in '49 he got the job with the Yankees. I joined him on the Yankees in 1950."

Casey Stengel and Billy Martin became like father and son. Stengel himself had always been a fighting brawler and a no-holds-barred competitor, and he recognized and encouraged those traits in Martin. Stengel would pay Martin $25 to get hit by a pitched ball. Stengel would encourage him to defend himself and his teammates from opposing bullies. "He's got it here in the heart where it counts," Stengel would often say of his protégé. Even before Martin arrived on the Yankees, Stengel was telling the Yankee players about him. When Martin finally did join Stengel, the affection the Old Man held for Billy was public and obvious. The other Yankees called the kid Billy Stengel.

"You and Casey hit it off immediately," I said.

"Yeah," said Martin. "He was just sensational. He was just great with kids. He tried to wear me out with the fungo stick, and he could never do that. I'd tell him, 'Hit me some more.' He'd say, 'Don't you ever get tired?' He was just great. Really."

"Was Casey a character at Oakland?" I asked.

"I think that was just newspaper talk," he said. "He could be anything he wanted to be. He knew how to bring people to the ball park. He knew how to hold a ball club together. He was a master psychologist. I thought he was a very brilliant man in many ways. He'd leave one player alone. He'd get one mad. Like Yogi he'd leave alone, and me he'd get mad all the time. He'd ride me all the time. I remember one day he took me out for making a couple of errors. I was yelling. I took my glove and went down to the end of the bench. I was pouting. 'Cause he's one of those guys, you yell back at him, and he'd yell at you, and it was forgotten the next day. It was about the seventh inning, and I was waiting to say something smart to him like, 'You old Dutch son of a . . . ,' you know, whatever. So he came walking down there, and I'm really ready to pop off, and he looks at me and says, 'Is wittle Biwwy mad at me?' I didn't say a word, I just walked away. He knew I was going to say something before I said it. He was that smart. A wonderful guy. I just wrote him a letter about two weeks ago, telling him how great it was playing under him, and what a great manager I thought he was.''

When Martin came up to the Yankees in 1950, he made it clear that he wanted to start. In spring training he got angry when any of the veterans came near second base. He acted like he himself was a veteran, refusing to observe the code of silence traditionally imposed on rookies. In his first spring training he was assigned an upper berth on train trips. He complained to road secretary Bill McCorry, who told him the lowers were for the regulars.

Martin retorted, ''And what the hell makes you think I'm not a regular?'' During that same spring training Billy went out to the mound to throw batting practice. He wasn't getting much work at second because of Jerry Coleman, and he was restless. Pitching coach Jim Turner ordered him to get off the mound.

''Who the hell are you?'' Martin said to Turner. ''When you're managing this club then you can tell me what to do.''

Martin even talked back to some of the veterans. Johnny Mize had a habit of being late for the bus on road trips, and often the bus would sit idling in the parking lot for ten minutes while everyone waited for Mize. Big Jawn finally arrived, and as Mize walked up the steps, from the back of the bus Martin yelled out, ''Now Big John, give us a few thousand words.'' Mize's face lit up cherry-red. ''Why you bush little bastard,'' Mize said. Nevertheless, everyone liked Martin, despite his cockiness. He was fresh, insulting, and insolent. The last Yankee like him was Leo Durocher who played in 1928 and '29.

Martin didn't play much his first two years on the Yankees in 1950 and 1951 because Coleman was playing so well, and for those two years Martin unceasingly harangued Stengel to let him play. Stengel even sent Martin to Kansas City for a couple months in 1950 to get him off his back. When Martin returned he was just as insistent about starting ahead of Coleman. ''He's a nice guy and all that,'' Martin kept telling Stengel, ''but I can play second better than he can.''

When Stengel finally benched Coleman in the middle of the 1951 season and started Martin, Casey batted Martin eighth in the batting order.

''Why am I batting eighth?'' Martin literally screamed at Stengel. ''Why the hell don't you play the bat boy over me?''

''Where do you think you should be hitting, Mr. Martin,'' Stengel answered, ''fourth?''

''And why not?'' Martin screamed back.

In 1952 Billy Martin finally became the regular second-baseman for the Yankees, and though he only batted around .265, his value far transcended his batting average. Martin thrived on the competitive atmosphere with the Yankees and was an inspiration to his teammates. When Stengel needed someone to break up a double play, Martin was there. When Stengel needed a batter to hit behind the runner and get him into scoring position, Martin did it. When an opposing bully knocked over Phil Rizzuto and Stengel needed a policeman to retaliate, Martin struck the answering blow. Once Rizzuto received a death threat from a Boston Red Sox fan. This was not long after Martin had slugged Jimmy Piersall of the Sox in their pregame battle. To ease Rizzuto's fright, Stengel told Martin to switch uniforms with Rizzuto. During the infield drill before the game Martin, wearing Phil's number 10, didn't once stop moving. He was a man in perpetual motion, darting this way and that, listening for the whine of the bullet. They wore each other's uniforms during the entire game. After the game Rizzuto demanded his uniform back. When he had gone up to the plate wearing Martin's number 1, he was booed so loudly that he decided the booing was worse than the threat of getting shot.

Billy was totally fearless, and when the bench jockeying from the opposition became fierce, Stengel would shout, "You SOB's better watch out. That Martin will get you." Martin himself was an intimidating bench jockey. In the world series against the Dodgers he would ride the hulking Don Newcombe until Big Newk was ready to tear Martin apart. During batting practice before one of the series games, Martin went over to Newcombe and said, "Hey Newk, ain't no way you're going to get out of this park until we rip you. We have all the exits blocked."

"Why you little kid," said Newk, "come over here and I'll take you over my knee and spank you."

"And after that," said Martin to the 225-pound Dodger pitcher, "I'm going to beat the living shit out of you."

Martin's most famous on-field fights were against Clint Courtney of the St. Louis Browns.

"He didn't know how to fight," Billy said. "He don't know how to fight right now. You know what he was? He was just a crude player. He looked like he was doing things dirty, but he really wasn't. Like he wouldn't slide properly. He'd jump at somebody. It started a long time ago when we were in Phoenix. He spiked a kid by the name of Eddie Lenee. Eddie was a neighbor of mine in Berkeley. He got killed in Korea. We played high-school baseball together. All that year I only missed one game, and that was the game. Eddie was playing third base, and he's got Courtney out by twenty feet, and Courtney jumps up and rips his right leg open. That day I couldn't get him. I was in the stands. But from that day on, every time I got a chance I punched him. Every time."

His two fights with Courtney and the one with Piersall were the only significant fisticuffs he engaged in for many years, yet those few fights made his reputation as a fighter. It was a well-deserved reputation according to pitcher Bob Grim who played with Martin at Cincinnati in 1960. "Off to one side of the dressing room," Grim said, "they had a little gymnasium, and there were a few weights and a punching bag there. That Billy had to have had a little fighting experience. You don't learn what he could do in a week. He could make that baby talk. Not just left and right, but he could hit it with his elbows or hit it with his head. I really don't think he wanted people to know what he could do with his fists. He used to come down to Key West occasionally, and I used to know a couple of the bartenders that he knew, and they told me that he once got into some trouble with some Navy guys down there. Three of them, and they were supposed to be a pretty good size. Billy says, 'I'll take on all of youse.' And he did. He was the only one that came back into that bar. I wouldn't put it past little Billy.''

By 1952 Martin had become a world series hero after the game-saving catch he made of Jackie Robinson's pop-up to end the series, but as his fame grew so did his personal problems. Martin had married in October of 1950, but rarely were he and his wife together. For five months he was in the Army. During the summer he was with the Yankees. During the off-season he was playing on barnstorming teams or attending banquets. Two weeks after his daughter was born in the latter part of 1952, his wife filed for a divorce. She had been home from the hospital for about a week when there was a knock on the door of the Martins' Berkeley home. ''Here,'' a man said, presenting Martin with a summons and complaint for divorce. It was the first Billy knew of his wife's plans.

''What's this?'' Billy said to his wife.

''I don't love you anymore,'' she answered.

Throughout the 1953 season Martin was close to a nervous breakdown. He had difficulty eating and sleeping, and he was on tranquilizers. Each day when the Yankees played at home Martin would go to St. Patrick's Cathedral to ask for strength. His only relief from his personal hell was his ball playing. On the field during 1953 he played the best baseball of his career, though only his friendship with Mickey Mantle saved him from mentally going over the edge.

''He'd see me call and try to talk to my wife and daughter on the phone,'' Billy said, ''and she'd hang up on me, and I'd be upset, and he thought one day that I was going to tear up the whole hotel room. But,'' said Billy, ''I got over it. It took a while, though.''

''Mickey,'' Martin said, ''is like a brother to me. He calls me all the time. I remember I was living in Kansas City and he was living in Dallas, and I was supposed to take out my present wife, and Mickey called. He had an abscessed tooth, and he was sicker'n hell, and he says, 'I have to go to the hospital to get it pulled.' I said, 'Okay, I'll be there.' I flew down there to take him to the hospital.''

''How'd you two become friends, the city slicker and the country boy?'' I asked.

''It was strange,'' Martin said. ''He kind of thought that I was a smart aleck kid.''

''You were,'' I said.

''Not really that much,'' he said. ''Only when I was pushed.''

''You must have been pushed a lot,'' I said.

''Yeah,'' he said. ''Because I was small. When you're small, they always test you. And when they find out that you push back just like a big guy, it upsets them.''

In 1953 for the second series in a row Martin led the Yankees to victory over the Dodgers. Again he was spectacular.

"We had a helluva ball club in 1953," Martin said. "Just a great ball club. Everybody was contributing. And the Dodgers had the greatest team that they ever had. But once you took the Dodgers out of Brooklyn and put them in Yankee Stadium, they were just another ball club. Those guys were hitting forty, fifty home runs, but that Ebbets Field left-field fence . . . hell, they wouldn't have hit eight home runs in Yankee Stadium. DiMaggio one year should have had seventy, eighty, but that left field just eats you up in the Stadium. The Dodgers would hit their best shots 400 feet in left center, and it was just a big can of corn. Our park would just kill the Dodgers. In '53 I hit fifteen home runs and drove in seventy-five runs with the Yankees. If I had been playing in Brooklyn, I think I could have hit thirty-five or forty because that ball park was such a bandbox.

"I always enjoyed those series because of Jackie Robinson," Martin said. "See, there was a black lawyer by the name of Walter Gordon out in California that helped my mother when I was a kid, and he also helped Jackie, so when we played against Jackie in the series, I always wanted to show that I was a better second-baseman. That was my real challenge. And I always outhit him, and I always outplayed him. Every series we played in.

"You know," Billy said, "I didn't have the average, but I always got the winning hits that clinched the pennant. My one for four would kill ya. And it would always make everyone mad. If Mickey or Yogi hits a home run, it's, 'a nice guy,' but if I hit one, it's, 'that little bastard.' They didn't give me credit for all the plays I made out there. I was 'the Little Brat.' " Billy shook his head, because what he was saying was true. His personality and fighting nature made the critics concentrate on his eccentricities and overlook his real contributions as a ball player.

When Martin returned from the Army to the Yankees in September 1955 in the midst of a pennant fight, Stengel immediately inserted him into the lineup. He was an inspiration, batting .300 and providing a missing spark. Mentally he continued to suffer from melancholia, depression, and hypertension. "I was never able to get a handle on myself in this game," Martin said. In May 1956 he rushed off the bench to take a swing at Kansas City pitcher Tom Lasorda, and later that year he had to be restrained from going after some hostile fans who were baiting him. Billy was not playing with confidence, he could see that he was slipping, and he was afraid. Adding to his insecurity was the promise shown by youngster Bobby Richardson. Richardson was not yet 20, yet Billy recognized the excellence in the kid. Martin enjoyed teasing him. "What are you doing here?" Billy would ask with a straight face. "What do you mean?" Richardson would respond naively. "It's just that I put something in your milk last night, and you shouldn't be here today. Didn't you drink it?" Or Martin would say: "I wrote your draft board today. You'll be hearing from them soon." Martin was joking, of course, but the youngster was a real threat, and to keep ahead of him Martin scrapped even harder than before, working himself into a frenzy, hoping that general manager George Weiss, a man who never appreciated Martin's talents, was not going to trade him.

Weiss had always disliked Martin, ever since he had come up to the Yankees in 1950. He called Martin "Casey's pet" to his face, and it seemed that no matter how friendly Billy tried to act, Weiss would act that much more distant and aloof. Weiss and Stengel were both brilliant men who worked together in harmony, but on occasion evidences of jealousy surfaced, and the fact that Martin was Stengel's protégé never sat well with the Yankee general manager.

"The trouble," Billy said, "started in 1950. I got two hits in the first game I played. I didn't play for a month, but then I got to play and hit a home run. Next time I pinch hit in the tenth inning, I drove in the winning run, and before you know it, I'm sent down to Kansas City. I was disgusted, naturally, because I had had a good spring. Casey said, 'Wait a minute, aren't you going to say something to Weiss?' I said, 'I don't know if I should.' Casey said, 'Tell him you don't like it.' So I went up to Weiss, gave him hell. I was crying, feeling real bad. 'You'll be sorry,' I said. 'You shouldn't be sending me out.' And then we got into a shouting argument that should never have happened. And from that day on he never did like me. I never should have gone up to his office that day. It all started from way back when Stengel first came up. Being I was Stengel's boy, I think Weiss kind of took it out on me. Used me. And Stengel kind of used me against Weiss also. It was unfortunate. Weiss made my contracts so difficult and everything. He was very difficult when I was with the Yankees."

Weiss was difficult because to him Martin the streetfighter, the two-fisted brawler, was not genteel enough, whatever his other positive qualities may have been. Weiss liked his players to have his own aristocratic gentility. Weiss was chagrined when he received a letter from the mother of a girl Martin was dating saying that Martin had taken her to a nightclub. "I didn't know big league players were allowed to go to nightclubs," she wrote in the letter. When Weiss read the letter to Martin, Billy laughed in his face. "You've got to be kidding," Martin said. "I'm single. Divorced. I like girls. What's wrong with a single guy liking girls?"

Nothing was wrong with it, but Weiss continued to look for reasons to trade Martin and would jump down Billy's throat at the least excuse. What especially bothered the Yankee general manager was that Mickey Mantle's name was beginning to appear in gossip columns, and for this Weiss blamed Martin. Weiss did not give Mickey enough credit for getting into his own trouble. Martin and Mantle had missed a couple of trains and buses, and a couple of times Mickey had injured himself as a result of their fooling around. The final blow before Weiss traded Martin was when federal investigators came snooping around looking into Billy's finances. To Weiss Billy had become *persona non grata*. In Weiss's eyes he could do no right. In May of 1957 a half-dozen Yankees threw a birthday party for Billy at the Copacabana in New York City. At the party there was an altercation that made front-page headlines in the papers the next day. Weiss blamed Martin. One month later Billy was gone. To Weiss the Copa incident was further proof that Martin was a bad influence on the club.

When Martin learned of the trade, he said, "How can you be a bad influence on six pennant winners? In three seasons I roomed with Rizzuto (1950), Berra (1951), and Mantle (1956), and at the end of the three years each won the MVP. If I ever led anyone astray, it was myself. I'm no drinker. I can nurse one drink so long that bartenders have said to me, 'Do you want me to put that in a container so you can take it home?' I roomed with Mantle and he won everything that year. How bad,'' he said between tears, "an influence could I have been? I busted my ass for that team, and Weiss acted like I didn't care.''

Seventeen years after he was traded, Billy still does not fully understand the reasoning behind Weiss's trading him. All Billy knows was that Weiss had it in for him.

"Getting traded was like a nightmare,'' Billy said. "It was very sad. But I knew it when that Copa incident happened. I knew that I was going to be gone. I had all my stuff packed the next day when I went to the ball park. Mickey and all them guys said, 'Hell, they can't blame you for that.' I said, 'They will. I'm gone.' They said, 'Aw, no.' I said, 'You watch.' My birthday was May 16, and June 15 I was gone. One month later. I had all my stuff packed. I was ready for it. The day before was the trading deadline, and Coleman was scared to death. He thought he was gone. So I said to Jerry, 'There is only one way to find out. Go and look at the lineup. If your name is on it, you're not gone, I'm gone. If my name is on it, you're gone.' And he went and looked and came back and said, 'You're not on it.' It was the first time I ever sat in the bullpen. I sat in the bullpen. In the middle of the game the Old Man called me. He said, 'We want to talk to you.' I went to the clubhouse. He said, 'We traded you to Kansas City and I told them guys that you're the greatest player.' I said to Casey, 'I don't want you to tell them nothin'.' He said, 'What?' I said, 'You heard me.' So the owner of the A's, Arnold Johnson, came over, and Casey started to tell him about me. I said, 'You don't have to tell him nothin'. I'll play for you, Mr. Johnson. You don't have to worry.' And I didn't talk to Casey for seven years after that. I felt he let me down. But I liked him so much, I was afraid he was going to die without me getting a chance to talk to him, so I finally went up to him. It was breaking his heart and mine too. Mantle'd say, 'Jesus Christ, the Old Man wants to talk to you so bad, and you won't talk to him.' It was worse than just a manager doing that. It was like a father letting me down. 'Cause the one person I never thought would let me go was him. I always knew Weiss was trying to get rid of me, but I figured Casey'd hold on to me and tell Weiss that I wasn't that bad.''

"After you left the Yankees,'' I said, "you played for six clubs in five years.''

"It took something out of me,'' Martin said. "I wasn't the same ball player that I had been. I didn't have that push or that drive or that pride or whatever it was. And I'd lost a couple of steps. Then when I was with Cleveland in 1959, Tex Clevenger hit me in the head, I had seven broken bones, cracked my eye. Knocked the cheekbone loose, and I was fed from my arms. The next year I was with Cincinnati, and my heart said yes, but there was that inner fear. I had to have guys throw at me and hit me with pitches. Then just as I started to become a good hitter again with Minnesota in '61, they released me.''

Billy remained in the Twins' organization as a scout and a coach through 1968 when Cal Ermer was fired as Twins manager and Billy replaced him. Billy then became the manager of Detroit, and he would have been the Yankee manager in 1972, but the Tiger general manager Jim Campbell refused to release him. In 1974, after Campbell got tired of Martin's feistiness and fired him, Martin became the manager of the Rangers. Martin was named Manager of the Year in '74. In July '75 he was fired again, when the Texas management got sick of his quarrelsome nature.

Thirteen days later Martin became the Yankee manager, replacing Bill Virdon who had been named Manager of the Year in 1975. It was Old-Timers' Day at Shea Stadium (the Yankees played at Shea for two years while Yankee Stadium underwent a $100 million face-lifting), and said old-timer Hank Bauer about Virdon: "How could a guy [Virdon] be manager of the year and then supposedly get so bad over the winter?"

But Bauer knew why, having been fired as manager a couple times himself. It was front office politics. Lee MacPhail had hired Virdon, and after MacPhail left the Yankees to become president of the American League, Gabe Paul took over as general manager, and Paul and Steinbrenner wanted Martin. On Old-Timers' Day, Billy the Kid upstaged all the old-timers, including DiMaggio and his buddies Ford and Mantle. Martin was the last of the long list of old-timers to be introduced, his first introduction as Manager of the Yankees. He ran onto the field to a standing ovation, with some light booing, indicating that some fans either didn't like him or didn't like the abrupt manner in which Virdon was dumped. Billy was back in pin stripes, 18 years and six weeks after that June day when George Weiss traded him to Kansas City.

At the beginning of the 1976 season, Martin wrote a letter to each of his players. It read: "The days of the Yankees being just another ball club are over. We are going to have pride. We are going to have desire. We're going to have the will to win. I have never been with a loser, and I'm not going to start now."

During spring training Martin said, "I'm dedicating the 1976 season to Casey Stengel," and the Yankees won the pennant, the team's first since 1964.

Said Frank Lane, a general manager for many years, about Martin, "He is a feisty little son of a bitch. He's the type of guy you'd like to kill if he's on the other side, but you'd like to have ten of him if he's on your side. The little bastard."

Yankees finished a dismal sixth.

asey Stengel with Vic Raschi (left) and Allie Reynolds. (*New York Times photo*)

Umpire John Flaherty and Yankee manager Casey Stengel
cool-headedly discuss public affairs. (*N.Y. Daily News photo*)

Two millionaires, a genius general manager and a brilliant manager. Weiss, Topping, Stengel, and Webb—architects of fourteen pennants in sixteen years. (*N.Y. Daily News photo*)

Fuzzy-cheeked youngsters Yogi Berra and Joe Garagiola —August 1947. (*N.Y. Daily News photo*)

A young Yogi Berra congratulates rookie Whitey Ford after Whitey's ninth straight win in 1950. (*United Press International photo*)

Rookie Mantle starts his first season; veteran DiMaggio begins his final year. Spring training 1951. (*Wide World photo*)

The 1952 Yankees—
Mize, Collins, Woodling,
McDougald, Bauer, Rizzuto,
Martin, Noren, Berra, and
Mantle. (*New York Times
photo*)

Mickey Mantle in the outfield
—September 1953. Mantle
was 22. (*N.Y. Daily News
photo*)

Berra (8), Collins (15), and Bauer (9) greet Mickey Mantle after grand slam home run during the 1953 world series. (*New York Times photo*)

Tom Byrne fires to Yogi Berra during the second game of the
1955 world series. (*New York Times photo*)

Casey Stengel introduces the 1956 Yankee All-Stars: Mantle,
Berra, Ford, Kucks, McDougald, and Martin. (*N.Y. Daily
News photo*)

Acrobatic Phil Rizzuto completes double play against Dodgers in the 1955 world series. Junior Gilliam slides too late. (*Wide World photo*)

Second-baseman Jerry Coleman watches shortstop Gil McDougald complete a double play during the 1957 world series. Johnny Logan is out at second. (*New York Times* photo)

The final pitch of Don Larsen's perfect game in the 1956 world series. Billy Martin is at second. The photo won a Pulitzer Prize. (*United Press International photo*)

A familiar sight—catcher Y
Berra crosses the plate afte
slugging a 1957 home run
Bill Skowron and the bat bo
greet him. (*N.Y. Daily New
photo*)

1954

*Moose and Andy Carey arrive . . . The sad story of Bob
Grim . . . Cleveland's revenge*

The Korean conflict had ended in the summer of '53, but though most of the
boys had come home, the spectre of world conflict was worsening. The U. S.
detonated a horrifying hydrogen bomb on the South Pacific isle of Eniwetok,
and "The Morning Show" on CBS carried the first films of the terrifying
mushroom cloud. The Russians responded with the comment that atomic war
might mean the destruction of civilization. The U. S. later announced that
through the research gained from previous explosions, a new type of bomb, a
cobalt bomb, was now possible, transforming the vapor of an explosion into a
deadly radioactive cloud that was capable of traveling thousands of miles with
the prevailing winds, destroying all life in its path. President Eisenhower
declared that communism could not prevail against the spiritual and material
might of the U. S.

Meanwhile, in the remoteness of Southeast Asia, the Vietminh communists
launched a massive attack against the French defenses at Dien Bien Phu in
Vietnam. Eisenhower warned that a communist takeover of Indochina would
set off a chain reaction throughout Asia resulting in disaster for the free world.

The Arabs and the Israelis continued a struggle without end, and inside the
United States New Jersey's Governor Meyner risked the wrath of Senator Joe
McCarthy, branding the Wisconsin senator a "modern Robespierre" who had
set out to create a "reign of terror in America." CBS commentator Edward R.
Murrow devoted his award-winning "See It Now" program to films of McCarthy in action, charging the senator with using half-truths, innuendos, and deceit
and with giving comfort to the enemy. In a reply McCarthy sought to link
Murrow with the communist party. President Eisenhower, asked to comment
on the dispute between the two men, said, "I regard Mr. Murrow as a friend."
The faculty of Duke University voted against inviting Vice President Nixon to
speak at graduation. Nixon, who had accepted before the surprising vote, in
turn decided that his business commitments in Washington the coming June
would not have allowed him to speak anyhow.

The Yankees, after an unprecedented five straight world championships,
were themselves in turmoil. In February general manager Weiss sent pitching

star Vic Raschi his 1954 contract, and when Raschi did not respond, as was his custom, Weiss peremptorily sold him to the St. Louis Cardinals. Weiss decried the debilitating air of complacency among the players. Many of the players had held out for higher salaries, and it was Weiss's intention to jolt his warriors by making an example of one of them. Raschi, a month shy of his thirty-fifth birthday and only a spot starter the year before, was the scapegoat. And because the Yankees did not receive a player in return at the time, it was assumed Weiss had given the star pitcher away, an added insult to the man who had averaged seventeen victories a year over his seven-year Yankee career. Weiss's cold-hearted tactic was successful, though. The rest of the holdouts rushed to sign.

Mickey Mantle's two postseason operations on his right knee were successful in 1953, but because the Yankee center fielder did not heed the doctors' orders to exercise the knee, when he arrived for spring training the surrounding muscles were weak. It was not until the final days of the training period that he was able to run. Hampered by a bulky leather and metal brace, Mantle was unable to bat left-handed, and Stengel platooned him with the left-handed hitting Irv Noren. Throughout the spring months Stengel expressed his frustration and disgust with Mantle's physical condition. That Mickey had failed to do his leg-strengthening exercises clearly upset the Yankee manager.

"If he did what he was told after the first operation," Stengel said when he saw that Mickey would be unable to play in the exhibition games, "he would be playing now. This kid—you can't ever teach him nothing in the spring because he's always hurt. You want to work on him batting left-handed and you can't. You want to do something for him and he don't let you. What's the good of telling him what to do?" he said angrily. "No matter what you tell him, he'll do what he wants." Casey touched his arm and his body. "He's got it here and here." Stengel then tapped himself on the side of the head. "But he ain't got it here."

Three farm-system youngsters about whom Stengel had been bragging were showing great promise. Bob Grim, a strong right-handed pitcher, displayed a live fast ball and a crackling slider. Grim had been 16–5 at Class A Binghamton in 1952 and then spent two years in the service, and after impressing Stengel throughout the instructional period and the exhibition season, Stengel was inclined to keep the serious and silent youngster on the roster.

Stengel also decided to keep Bill Skowron, a powerfully built right-handed first-baseman who had signed off the campus of Purdue University for $25,000 in 1950, angering the Purdue football coach, Stu Holcombe, now the general manager of the Chicago White Sox, because Skowron was the starting halfback on the team. When Skowron signed with the Yankees Stengel promised him that after a three-year apprenticeship in the minors, he would become a Yankee. Skowron's exceptional three years completed, Stengel added him to the team.

For a man so large, the muscular Skowron was unusually diffident. He didn't speak unless spoken to, and he was in such total awe of the veterans that when catcher Yogi Berra asked Skowron to room with him, Skowron politely declined, fearing the other players might think he was trying to be a social climber. Skowron didn't realize that no one else particularly wanted to room with Yogi, a man of peculiar habits. Skowron had been very nervous in his battle to win a spot on the roster, but early in spring training Joe Collins, his competition, took him aside and said, "Bill, we'll work together. I'll pray for you when you're playing. And when I'm playing, I hope you'll pray for me." Skowron was grateful, his trepidation faded, and he fit easily into the framework of the team.

The other rookie, Andy Carey, was a third-baseman who had signed a $60,000 bonus in 1951. In a short period of time Carey had built a reputation not for playing ball, but for eating large quantities of food. During one sitting he would eat a dozen eggs, five pounds of steak, a quart of milk, and top if off with a double shrimp salad while the other players sitting around him grew more nauseous by the minute. Because of Carey the Yankees discontinued their practice of allowing the players to sign their meal checks. Instead the Yankees gave the players a set amount of money per meal. Carey was bankrupting them. Carey was unlike the usual rookie in another respect. Manager Stengel had planned on switching him from third base to shortstop, hoping that the talented youngster would become Phil Rizzuto's successor, but when Stengel asked Carey to make the switch, Carey told the disbelieving manager that he had always been a third-baseman and that he refused to switch. At the beginning of spring training Carey drew a line between third and short with his spikes and cockily told Rizzuto and Gil McDougald and the other infielders that the third-base territory was his and that everyone else should stay away. Scout Joe Devine, who had signed Carey, predicted that Carey would be the best third-baseman in the majors someday. After two seasons with the Kansas City Blues, and a part-time chance when he hit .321 in '53, Carey was getting his first opportunity to play regularly.

As usual the team did not fare particularly well in the exhibition games as Stengel juggled his lineups, but in addition there was an undefinable lassitude that ran through the Yankee camp without the steadying influence of firebrands Raschi, who was traded, John Mize, who retired, and the khaki-clad Martin.

The Army traded Martin for Jerry Coleman and Bobby Brown, neither of whom had played in a while. They lacked confidence, and Phil Rizzuto, at age 36, was getting old as were pitchers Allie Reynolds and Eddie Lopat. The Yankees won one and lost two, won one and lost two throughout the grapefruit-league season, and though manager Stengel did not show any out-ward alarm, Mantle's absence and the lack of consistency shown by the pitching staff kept the Old Man awake at night. On the trip north from St. Petersburg the team showed some spark against a half-dozen minor league teams, but when it played the Dodgers two games back in New York City, the Yankees lost both to finish 8–19 for the exhibition season.

The day before the opening game Weiss announced that the Yankees had acquired St. Louis Cardinal star Enos (Country) Slaughter for three minor league prospects, Mel Wright, Emil Terwilliger, and Bill Virdon. Slaughter was 38 years old, but he had been picked for every all-star game since 1941, and of all active major league players, only Stan Musial had achieved more lifetime hits, and only Ted Williams had batted in more runs. In the spring Slaughter had boldly told the press, "From what I've seen in them young outfielders in camp, they ain't none of them gonna take my job away," but he was wrong, and when Wally Moon won the starting job, Slaughter became expendable. The Vic Raschi sale to the Cards, it turned out, was only the first half of a larger transaction. The acquisition of Slaughter was the second part.

The Yankees played five-hundred ball in April, and May saw the team three games out in sixth place. Jerry Coleman, platooning with McDougald at second, was not hitting, and he did not show his old ability in the field, and Phil Rizzuto did not have his former range. Bobby Brown was playing third because Andy Carey had suffered a muscle tear. Brown was scheduled to retire July 1 to begin his hospital internship, and just before he left the team, he finally revealed who the Number One RA on his list was. It was Stengel.

After Brown retired, Carey finally got his chance to play regularly, and when Stengel inserted the rookie into the lineup, the youngster immediately injected a needed spark into the Yankees, homering to beat Cleveland in one May contest and driving in almost a run a game for the month of May, trailing only Yogi Berra in that department. The Yankees won fourteen of their next seventeen May games with Carey playing third base, and only because Cleveland won sixteen out of twenty, behind the pitching of Early Wynn, Mike Garcia, and Bob Lemon, were the Yankees off the lead, and then only by one game.

Through the spring and the summer of '54 the Yankees were winning more games than they had ever won before under Stengel. But the Cleveland Indians were also winning big, ripping off streaks of seven and eight games in a row, playing at a pace that if sustained would break the major league record for games won in a season, 110, a record set by the 1906 Chicago Cubs.

By June, Mickey Mantle had fully recovered from his knee surgery, and by midsummer he was the most productive hitter in the league, a threat to win the Triple Crown. He was leading the league in home runs with twenty and was tied for the RBI lead at seventy-four with Minnie Minoso of the White Sox. His .323 batting average was third behind Yankee teammate Irv Noren and Cleveland second-baseman Bobby Avila.

Irv Noren, originally a Branch Rickey wonder-boy in the Brooklyn organization, didn't drink, smoke, or swear, and his conscientiousness was an asset to the Yankee ball club. Congenial and sincere, everyone who played with Noren was a "great fella" and most thought the same of him. Noren was platooned, but he was content to do his share and respected the judgment of his manager, whatever it should be. In 1954 Noren was hitting around .350 until September, when he slumped about thirty points to lose the batting title to Avila. In addition to Mantle and Noren, catcher Yogi Berra was hitting over .300, and he was driving in runs at a personal-record pace. Berra had been the MVP in 1951 and a runner-up and third-place vote-getter in '52 and '53. He was in the running for the award again in '54. Hank Bauer, hitting lead-off, was also having another excellent year, hitting around .300. Third-baseman Carey was around .300 too. At first base Stengel platooned Joe Collins, Eddie Robinson, a left-handed slugger acquired from the Philadelphia A's for Vic Power, one of the two Negro players in the Yankees' minor league system, and Moose Skowron, the rookie home-run threat. Among the three first-basemen, the position supplied twenty-two home runs and 114 RBI's. Skowron batted .340 as a part-time player and looked very impressive.

General manager Weiss traded Bob Kuzava to Baltimore, and to shore up the staff he purchased veteran reliefer Jim Konstanty from the Phillies and a former employee, Tommy Byrne, from the Seattle team in the Pacific Coast League. In the minors Byrne had developed a slow curve and a slider because at 35 years old his fast ball no longer had its former zip. In five months with Seattle Byrne won twenty games and finally realized that all along Eddie Lopat had been right. It was not necessary to throw the ball by the batter to win. In his first start for the Yankees Byrne defeated the Orioles 8–2. "He won ten straight at Seattle," said manager Stengel, very pleased to have Byrne back on his team. "He played first base and the outfield, pinch hit, and did everything but collect tickets."

On Sunday, September 12, the Yankees arrived in Cleveland for a show-down, trailing the Indians by six and a half games and needing a doubleheader victory in their final meeting with the Indians to still have a chance for the pennant. In this industrial community on Lake Erie, the Indian faithful were whispering that finally, after five years of unsuccessfully chasing New York, this would be The Year. Into Municipal Stadium flocked 86,000 fans, including 12,000 standees. They came to watch the downfall of the Yankee empire. It was the largest crowd in the history of professional baseball, a circus and a quick afternoon of baseball. Cleveland's Bob Lemon won the first game 4–1 on a six-hitter, and Early Wynn won the second game 3–2 despite a Yogi Berra home run. The Yankees fell to eight and a half games with only a couple of weeks left to play. The Yankees won 103 games, the most games they had ever won under manager Stengel, yet the Indians finished 111–43, a .721 percentage and a major league record, and finished eight games in front.

Stengel blamed himself as much as anyone for not winning the pennant despite Cleveland's awesome winning percentage. "I was surprised that I lost it," Casey said. "Until after those last two games in Cleveland I didn't expect to lose it. The fault was carelessness in all parts including myself. I kept saying, 'We'll catch 'em next week.' "

Stengel, looking to the future, was considering moving Mantle into the infield in '55. "If I'm still around," Casey, who was 65 years old, said. He would have to decide if he would return. Also he would have to confer with Weiss to see if the general manager wanted him back. Under Stengel his players always felt an uncertainty. Would they be playing the next game? Would they be traded? Weiss used the same psychology with his employees. Stengel had won five pennants in five years and had lost a sixth while winning 103 games. Yet Casey nevertheless had to wait and see if Weiss was going to ask him to return.

Despite a second-place finish, there were positive developments, the most promising one being the unexpected blossoming of pitcher Bob Grim.

Grim had not even been on the spring roster, but the young flame-throwing right-hander had pitched brilliantly in rookie school and in spring training, and against Weiss's objections Stengel kept him on the club. When Grim was finally given the opportunity to pitch, the 24-year-old rookie won with ease and consistency, splitting his time between starting and relieving. After he lost his first two starts, he won eleven of his next thirteen decisions, and after a brilliant relief stint against the Indians, Bob won nine of his next eleven decisions to finish with twenty wins against only six losses. He pitched like a young Vic Raschi, the man whose spot in the rotation he had taken. It was the first time a Yankee rookie had won twenty games since Russell Ford won twenty-six games in 1910.

Grim was an uncomplicated pitcher. He threw a fast ball and a quick-breaking slider, and just reared back and threw, hoping the batter would not guess which pitch he was throwing. The fast ball often tailed in to a right-handed batter. The slider broke in the opposite direction. He was extremely difficult to hit when he was right, and in 1954 the Yankees felt that Grim would be a great one, taking his place with Raschi, Reynolds, Chandler, and Ruffing as right-handed pitching stars. He was Rookie of the Year in a landslide.

But after that rookie year, Grim never fulfilled his promise. He injured his arm the following year, and the injury forced Stengel to move him to the bullpen where he became the Yankees' top relief specialist for the next few years. Then when Grim's slider no longer slid, Grim rode the rails to the Yankees' dumping ground at Kansas City. When the euphoric roller coaster ride hit its headlong finale to the bottom, it was a melancholy, dismal ending. If Grim had not been an early sensation with unlimited potential, the fall might have been easier. But for one year Grim knew what it meant to be a star pitching for the Yankees, with all the extracurricular ramifications. Everything else in his life had paled in comparison. When he retired from baseball in 1962 at the age of 32, Grim moved to Florida to enter the charter-boat business and pursue his love of fishing. He couldn't make a success of it there. He then moved to Kansas City where he sold newspapers door-to-door before he was hired as a liquor salesman. It has been a hard road since 1954.

When I called Bob on the telephone to tell him about my book, he said that he would be more than happy to talk to me, but offered that he didn't really belong with the others because he felt he really "hadn't done too much" as a Yankee. I tried to assure this total stranger that the records indicated otherwise and that there were still Yankee fans who remembered the big pitcher with the easy motion. Grim seemed pleased to hear that.

Like most of the pitchers, Grim was a big man, over 6 feet and around 200 pounds. His hairline had receded, the reason his teammates had called him Jarhead, and he looked to be in good shape. He offered me a ham sandwich and a Coke, and at the kitchen table of his one-bedroom apartment we talked about his career.

"I was just tickled to death that they thought well enough of me to invite me to instructional school in 1954," Grim said. "I didn't set any goals. I was just a young punk kid. Well, I was 24, but I didn't have any ideas to make the Yankees. I figured I'd go down there and the least I could get out of it was to go to A or maybe Double-A, maybe jump a notch. Never in my wildest dreams did I think that I could make the Yankees. And when the school was over, and the regular spring training started and I was still there, I said to myself, 'What the hell am I doing here?' There was Mantle and all those guys you read about. I just felt I didn't belong."

"It must have been frustrating trying to catch Cleveland that year," I said.

"Hell," Grim said. "I didn't have any idea about catching anyone. I was on cloud nine. I was just doing my job. Not in a million years did I ever figure I'd play with the Yankees."

Grim was a bona fide star. Led by his twenty wins in '54, the Yankees won more games in a season than any Yankee team since Joe McCarthy's 1942 team won 103 games. Grim's accomplishments, however, went largely unnoticed because Cleveland won 111 games and raced past the Yankees for the pennant, and without a world series appearance, Grim was not seen on coast-to-coast television and his pitching excellence was not seen by the entire baseball public. He was Rookie of the Year, but there was no world series check in the mail, and for most, awards meant nothing compared to the world series cut. Nevertheless, for that one glorious year, Grim was a star.

"When did your arm trouble develop?" I asked.

"I don't even remember hurting it," Bob said. "It was in '55 against Detroit, and I was pitching a pretty good ball game until about the sixth or seventh inning, and the next three guys up singled, doubled, home run, boom, boom, boom, and I just didn't have anything. I wasn't tired. I don't remember hurting it. But they knocked me out of the box, and from that time on it seemed I could go three or four innings and my arm would start to go." Grim finished 7–5 in 1955. "They finally diagnosed it. Tendons pulled from the bone. All through the rest of my career I had trouble. That's one of the reasons I quit at age 32. I could throw hard just for a little while. I told Casey and Jim Turner, and that's the only time I ever had words with Mr. Turner. He said it was all in my head. I said, 'If it's in my head, it's hurting my arm, too.' Then in June of 1956 I was pitching a two-hitter against Washington, and that's the only time I ever remember hurting my arm. I had real good stuff," Grim said, "and I threw a fast ball, and as soon as I threw it, I felt something snap or pop. It just tore. In my mind I knew something just exploded in there. It hurt real bad. So they put me on the disabled list." Grim finished with a 6–1 record in 1956. He was 12–8 in '57. Both years he was the relief star of the team when his arm was healthy, usually in the opening months of the season. For the second half he was virtually useless.

"I was relieved to be traded," Grim said. "No one *likes* to be traded. But I was relieved to get it over with and try to get a fresh start. If I had stayed with New York, I would have been sent to the minors. So in 1958 they sent me to the Kansas City Athletics. I wasn't unhappy leaving New York, either.

"I knew that at Kansas City I wouldn't be bothered. A more relaxed situation. You knew the A's weren't going anywhere, but you didn't care. I was making a halfway decent salary then. I had money in my pocket and two dollars in the bank, and I had a few girl friends, which always helps. Kansas City is a swinging town.

"I remember I had played against the Yankees," he said, "and Ralph Houk was still a Yankee coach, and he caught me in the runway after the game. I was going out to the street and he said, 'How would you like to come back to New York?' I said, 'Ralph, no thanks.' I was happy at Kansas City. And I just walked right by him. 'No thank you.'

"I didn't like New York," Grim said. "I hated New York. People always bugging me for tickets. I liked to think of myself as a person like Mantle was. You mind your own business, and I'll mind mine. And you can't do that in New York.

"I don't know what the hell it was with my makeup, but I just didn't like to be noticed. I just wanted to crawl out, get the hell in my car and go home. If someone stopped me, it just embarrassed me. I don't know why I was that way. A psychiatrist might tell me why. But I just didn't want to be noticed. Once I got to the ball park, I was okay. I've seen Mickey brush by kids, and I kind of feel sorry about it now, because if I had kids I would kind of be put off if my kid was waiting all day and then was refused an autograph. I feel sorry about it now. But that's the way I was then. I signed plenty of autographs, but there was a lot that I didn't sign which I'm truly sorry for right now."

Grim didn't stay in Kansas City very long. He became a baseball nomad after he left the Yankees in June of 1958. Kansas City for a year and a half, then Cleveland, Cincinnati, St. Louis, and then the minor leagues, San Juan, Portland, and a cup of coffee back at Kansas City in 1962. Bob was afraid to pitch and afraid to quit. He hung on as long as he possibly could.

"When I hurt my arm and lost my slider," Grim said, "it was all downhill from there. And then I just lost my confidence, and you don't know what a feeling it is to go out on that mound without any confidence. I used to sit in the bullpen and pray, 'Please don't call me.' You're done before you start."

"Why didn't you just quit?" I asked.

"You are always looking for miracles or grasping at straws," he said. "You hope something in your arm will change. It's a hell of a feeling to go to a ball park knowing you're not the pitcher you used to be, knowing you're getting along on nothing. And actually you are afraid of not doing well. And when you're not doing well you have a tendency not to like anybody including yourself, so when you're not doing well, you're just mad at the world. And when I was released by Kansas City in 1962, that was the end of the line. That was the end of the world. Hey," Grim stopped momentarily. He had to regroup his thoughts. "Don't get me wrong," he said. "I love baseball. I wouldn't knock it. I never would knock it. But you're 32 years old, and that's all there is. They have no use for you because you can't get anyone out. I would have liked to play longer, that's all. I was only 32 when I finished. It was a hell of a love story while it lasted. How can anyone have any regrets even if he just participated in one game? So many kids played in the minors eight, nine, ten years and never saw a major league city. I was one of the fortunate ones." Bob smiled wanly. He knew he wasn't really fooling himself. If only his slider had not deserted him. If only.

The Middle Years: 1955–1960

1955

Prejudice and the N.Y. Yankees . . . The Gentleman—
Elston Howard . . . Yogi . . . A pennant . . . Brook-
lyn's first world series victory . . . A trip to Japan

Though the Yankees won 103 games in 1954, general manager George Weiss was dissatisfied because the team had not finished first, and after a detailed analysis of his team, he determined that a trade for a couple of young, strong-armed pitchers was imperative. Vic Raschi was gone, and Allie Reynolds, hampered by a bad back, decided to retire. Of the Yankees' big three only the 36-year-old Ed Lopat remained, and it was questionable how long he could continue. John Sain, at age 38, was nearing retirement age as was 36-year-old Tommy Byrne. Whitey Ford and Bob Grim would have to carry the team under the status quo, and Weiss, not wishing to be caught short of pitching, thus traded for help.

He and Baltimore Oriole (née St. Louis Browns) general manager Paul Richards engineered a seventeen-player swap. Weiss traded pitchers Harry Byrd, Jim McDonald, and Bill Miller; veteran outfielder Gene Woodling; catchers Gus Triandos and Hal Smith; utility infielder Willie Miranda; and minor league prospects Don Leppert and Kal Segrist in exchange for 25-year-old Bob Turley and 26-year-old Don Larsen, two strong-armed right-handed pitchers; Billy Hunter, an excellent shortstop to spell 37-year-old Phil Rizzuto; and five other minor leaguers who never made the Yankees.

Turley had been an instant Baltimore hero, a star of the team in the first year after its transfer from St. Louis. The Orioles still played like the Browns, of course, finishing seventh in front of the pathetic Philadelphia A's, but Turley compiled a 14–15 record and pitched well despite the lack of support. Turley was reputed to have the liveliest fast ball in the American League, and whenever he was scheduled to pitch in Baltimore the local citizens packed their crabcakes and came out to the park in droves.

Larsen, the other pitcher, was a horrendous 3–21 in '54 for the Orioles, but general manager Weiss felt that Larsen had even more potential than Turley. Weiss's only reservation was that Larsen greatly enjoyed the night life. When Larsen broke in with the Browns in '53, he drove manager Marty Marion to distraction because of his many curfew violations. And after a season in Baltimore under Jimmy Dykes, the patient Dykes said of Larsen, "The only thing Don fears is sleep.'' The players called him Gooneybird, which is how he addressed everyone else. His favorite expression was, ''Let the good times roll, baby doll,'' but the big kid could throw a baseball with tremendous velocity, and after Larsen impressed Stengel by beating the Yankees twice in 1954, Weiss acquired him from the Orioles.

Overnight the Yankees boasted one of the youngest staffs in the league. In addition to 26-year-old Ford and 25-year-olds Grim, Turley, and Larsen, when Stengel opened the spring training camp in St. Petersburg he brought from the instructional school a 22-year-old pitcher named John Kucks, who threw a fast ball and a sinker ball with professional control. Kucks, 19–6 at Binghamton in 1952, had spent the last two years in the service. Like Grim the year before, he was inexperienced, but seemed to have the ability to make the big jump from Class A to the Yankees. Grim and Kucks roomed together during spring training.

When Kucks first checked in at the Soreno Hotel in St. Pete, it was with a sense of awe that he knocked on Rookie of the Year Grim's door. Kucks heard a voice from within call, ''Come in,'' but when he entered the room and looked around, he saw twin beds and some bags, but no Grim. ''Anybody here?'' Kucks asked. ''Yeah,'' said Grim. ''I'm in the bathroom. Come on in.''

In the bathroom, with the bathtub filled three-quarters full of water, Kucks was amazed to see this sports celebrity balancing with one foot on the toilet bowl, the other foot on the edge of the bathtub, trying to take a photograph of a live sea bass swimming in the tub. Kucks, from Jersey City, could only stare at Grim with his mouth wide open. Grim, seeing Kucks's look of incredulity, explained that he was taking a picture of the fish to prove to the rest of his teammates that the stories of his fishing prowess were not fish stories. For the rest of the exhibition season Grim and Kucks would go down to the end of the Soreno Hotel pier and fish to relax and pass the time.

There were three other rookies on the team. Two of them were teen-age bonus babies who under the new league rules had to remain with the parent club. Tommy Carroll was a 19-year-old shortstop from Notre Dame, and Frank Leja was an 18-year-old slugging first-baseman Paul Krichell predicted would be the second coming of Lou Gehrig.

The other rookie, a quiet, reserved, and polite gentleman, was the center of controversy wherever he went in St. Petersburg. His name was Elston Howard, a tall, broad-shouldered catcher-outfielder who was readily identifiable even among his more illustrious teammates. Howard stood out because he was black, the first Negro ever to be invited to a Yankee spring training camp.

Jackie Robinson had broken the racial barrier in baseball in 1947, but despite Jackie's courage and ability, and despite the abilities of his Negro teammates Don Newcombe, Roy Campanella, Joe Black, and Jim Gilliam, only a handful of general managers rushed to sign outstanding Negro prospects.

The New York Giants signed and started Willie Mays, Hank Thompson, and Monte Irvin; the Boston Braves started Sam Jethroe, Billy Bruton, Jim Pendleton, and Henry Aaron. In the American League the Cleveland Indians, owned by Bill Veeck, acquired Luke Easter, Harry Simpson, Larry Doby, and Al Smith while the Chicago White Sox signed Minnie Minoso, and searched for talent in Latin and South America. Chicago signed Chico Carrasquel, Luis Aparicio, Jim Rivera, Hector Rodriguez, Sandy Consuegra, and Luis Aloma.

Teams owned by the millionaires Tom Yawkey of the Red Sox, Briggs of the Tigers, Dan Topping and Del Webb of the Yankees, Gussie Busch of the Cardinals, Bob Carpenter of the Phillies, and Phil Wrigley of the Cubs were the last to bring black players to their clubs.

On the Yankees the fault did not lie so much with Topping and Webb. When Topping owned the football Dodgers, a number of black athletes played on the team. But neither Topping nor Webb interfered with George Weiss's affairs, and it was Weiss who systematically excluded black players from the Yankees.

When Larry MacPhail owned the Yankees and acted as general manager, he was quick to see the value of signing the best black talent, and as soon as Jackie Robinson arrived in the major leagues, MacPhail organized a scouting system for the Negro Leagues. When he resigned from the Yankees at the end of the '47 season, his organization remained. His successor, Weiss, however, made it clear that he had no intention of signing black players. For all his genius, Weiss was a conservative man, and since he entered baseball in the 1920s, there were no blacks in organized baseball. Weiss didn't see any reason for baseball to change. He didn't feel that the Yankee fans wanted a change either. He looked at the "colored problem" in terms of economics.

"I will never allow a black man to wear a Yankee uniform," Weiss once proclaimed at a cocktail party after one drink too many. "Boxholders from Westchester don't want that sort of crowd. They would be offended to have to sit with niggers."

When MacPhail had set up the scouting organization for the Negro Leagues in 1947, Joe Press was one of the scouts. Press ran the Bushwick semi-pro baseball team that Paul Krichell subsidized to test prospects. Press and Krichell worked together very closely. In July of 1949, after two years of scouting the Negro Leagues, Press wrote Krichell asking why the Yankees were not signing the players he was recommending.

"Dear Paul," he wrote, "It is quite hard for me to understand your complete turn-about as far as the Negro Baseball players are concerned.

"Within the past two years, I have given you reports on practically every player, with the exception of a very few, that have been signed to contracts by other teams, in organized baseball.

"At that time, you mentioned that the Organization was not interested in these players. You could have had practically all of them, just for the asking.

"A few of those that I mentioned to you, were Luther Easter, Art Wilson, Oreste Minoso, and many others. There are still more of these players, whom in my opinion would fit in Organized Baseball, without any trouble. They are Piper Davis, Infielder, and Mays, Outfielder, both of the Birmingham Black Barons.

"I will be happy to sit down with you and go over this entire situation again, whenever you find it convenient.

"If there is any further information that you want, please don't hesitate to get in touch with me.

"Very truly yours, Joseph Press."

"Mays, Outfielder," of the Birmingham Black Barons, was, of course, Willie, and as the letter said, the Yankees could have signed him. The reason they didn't was that Bill McCorry, the Yankees' traveling secretary, an old-time southern ball player, had also scouted Mays, and when McCorry reported back to Krichell, he told the Yankee head scout that the 18-year-old Mays couldn't hit a curve ball and was not a prospect. Later McCorry let on that Mays's inability to hit a curve ball was not the *sole* reason he had not recommended him.

After Mays joined the New York Giants and began to burn up the National League, John Drebinger of *The New York Times,* always a Giant fan at heart, enjoyed teasing the crotchety McCorry about Mays. Mays had just hit two home runs to win a game for the Giants when Drebinger saw McCorry and chortled, "Hey McCorry, two more today for Willie."

There was venom in McCorry's reply. "I don't care what he did today or any other day," McCorry said. "I got no use for him or any of them. I wouldn't want any of them on the club I was with. I wouldn't arrange a berth on the train for any of them."

In his letter Press indicated to Krichell that he could not understand the Yankees' complete turnaround with regard to Negro players. It was not really that difficult to understand. Larry MacPhail had wanted to sign the best players he could find. Weiss wanted to sign the best white players he could find.

Weiss, however, was unable to live in a vacuum much as he would have liked, and by the early 1950s external pressures began to force his hand. Weiss hated to be pushed into doing anything against his will, but the Yankee management began to feel the stinging attacks by the local press. By 1952 pickets appeared in front of the Stadium decrying the discriminatory practices of the Yankee organization. With the Korean War at a close, the black men who were drafted to fight were beginning to examine their position in American society, a society which allowed them to get killed fighting for their country, but which prevented them from voting or getting a hot cup of coffee at a segregated, whites-only lunch counter. The civil rights movement was beginning in the early fifties, and one impetus was coming from the New York City liberal establishment. Weiss was beginning to feel the pressure.

To postpone the inevitable as long as possible, he did what a number of other clubs did. He signed a handful of black players to minor league contracts. Tokenism was having a Negro playing in the farm system. In the early 1950s the Yankees signed Artie Wilson (recommended by Press), Ruben Gomez, Vic Power, Frank Barnes, and Elston Howard. Then, whenever Weiss was criticized for being a racist, he would arrogantly reply that "the Yankees will bring up a Negro as soon as one that fits the high Yankee standards is found."

Ernie Banks and Gene Baker were similarly treated in the Chicago Cub organization. "They are a year away," the Cub management would say year after year. Sam Lacey, a black writer for the Baltimore *Afro-American* wrote, "Banks will be a year away when he is 60."

Barnes, Wilson, and Gomez all were traded to other organizations, and in December 1953 Vic Power, a slick-fielding first-baseman who hit .349 with the Kansas City Blues to lead the International League in batting, was traded to the Philadelphia Athletics for Eddie Robinson and Harry Byrd. A media blitz by the Yankees accused Power of being stupid, hot-tempered, and a showboat. There was also talk that he liked white women. Nothing, however, could convince many people that Power was not traded solely because his excellent record made him eligible for a shot at the Yankee varsity, a charge that Weiss, Topping, Webb, Stengel, Lee MacPhail, and publicity director Arthur Patterson all vehemently denied, though it seemed that everyone was protesting much too much.

In the spring of 1954 Elston Howard, the one Negro left in the Yankee organization, was converted from an outfielder to a catcher, a position played by the indestructible Yogi Berra. There were screams that Howard was switched in order to keep him from making the Yankees. By 1955 the crescendo of criticism had become a din, and that year it was almost impossible for Howard *not* to make the Yankees after the tremendous season he had had at Toronto in the International League in '54. He had batted .330, hit twenty-two home runs, drove in 109 runs and was named the Most Valuable Player of the league, the top echelon of minor league competition. Paul Richards of the Orioles offered Weiss $100,000 and a top minor league pitcher for Howard, but reluctantly Weiss rejected the offer. It would have been a trade simply too difficult for him to explain, because Elston Howard was both an exceptional baseball player and a gentleman. He was quiet, pleasant, noncontroversial, the son of educated parents. Howard seemed the perfect Yankee—even if he was black. He didn't make headlines. He kept his nose clean and he could hit a fast ball a long way.

During the spring of 1955 Howard was in the clubhouse in St. Pete, and head scout Krichell came over to introduce himself. "How do you do, Mr. Krichell," Howard said. "I've heard so much about you." Later Krichell said to Weiss, "I like that young man. Even though he's black, he has manners."

"The Yankees," Krichell said, "have been criticized by racial agitators as anti-Negro because they got rid of several Negro players. The fact is any player turned loose by the Yankees was released because he didn't measure up to requirements, and that has nothing to do with color, creed, or race. Both as a man and a ball player, this boy Howard looks every inch a Yankee." Krichell was not exactly telling the truth as he knew it. The Yankees had signed very few Negro players, and of that handful only Ellie Howard measured up to Weiss's standards, and only because of the pressure brought to bear was Howard even then promoted. During Weiss's reign as general manager of the Yankees, not one other black player would work his way through the Yankee farm system and become a Yankee. If Weiss had to have a Negro on the Yankees, he would have one. But only one, and he wasn't going to have an aggressive, crusading, loudmouthed Negro like Jackie Robinson or Vic Power. He would be a Negro who would accept the conditions under which he had to play and not make trouble or headlines. He would live in segregated quarters during spring training and in the southern cities and accept it, and he would be grateful just for the opportunity to play on the Yankees. Ellie Howard fit George Weiss's requisites perfectly. In 1955 Howard became a Yankee.

Most of the clamor directed at Weiss ended when Howard made the team, but there were still a couple of small hurdles before the storm ended entirely. James Hicks, a writer for the Amsterdam *News*, berated Howard in his column for accepting his position as a second-class citizen on the Yankees when Ellie found he was not allowed to live with the other white Yankees at the Soreno Hotel in St. Petersburg. And then on the annual trip north after spring training the Yankees were scheduled to play an exhibition game in Birmingham, Alabama, against their Birmingham farm team, when Weiss was informed that an Alabama ordinance prohibited white players from competing against blacks. Weiss ordered Howard to skip the game rather than cancel it. "Because of their preeminence in the game," wrote Red Smith, "the Yankees should be the last to conform to any segregationist policy." A few days before, the Brooklyn Dodgers had been scheduled to play the Milwaukee Braves in Birmingham, and when Buzzy Bavasi, Brooklyn's general manager, was apprised of the ordinance, he cancelled the game. "If they don't want us all, the hell with them," Bavasi said. Weiss, however, was concerned more with the public-relations value of the contest with their southern farm club and with the money to be made from 15,000 sold out seats than with the propriety of playing the game.

Weiss felt that Howard was fortunate to be on the team at all, and if Weiss wanted him to miss a game, he would miss a game. The bigger issue was not important to the running of his team. The game was played. Howard was sent on ahead.

The final hassle for Weiss arose on the Yankees' first western trip. Howard was barred from staying with the Yankees at the Emerson Hotel in Baltimore, the Del Prado Hotel in Chicago, and the Hotel Muehlbach in Kansas City, and though neither Howard nor the white players were concerned with the arrangement because it was the accepted custom of the land, there was outrage expressed in the press. The New York *Post* assigned black civil-rights reporter Ted Poston to travel with the Yankees on their second trip west to room with Howard and report on where he went in the cities in which he was not allowed to stay with the rest of the team. Poston, who won many journalism awards for his stories on desegregation and civil rights, was one man Weiss absolutely did not want covering the Yankees, and Weiss told the *Post* that Poston could not travel with the team because he was not an accredited baseball writer. Poston quickly applied for and received his accreditation, and Weiss then told the paper Poston could not come because he did not allow any writer to room with a ball player. When Weiss was informed that Poston would be going regardless of his objections, just hours before the Yankees were to head west again it was announced that Howard would be allowed to stay with the team in both Chicago and Kansas City. Poston never accompanied the team on the road, but he had accomplished his goal: to force Weiss to apply pressure on the hotels to allow Howard to stay with the team.

The remainder of Ellie Howard's ordeal would be private. Manager Stengel, 65 years old, was not accustomed to Negroes playing in the major leagues, and he had attitudes and a vocabulary which were offensive to blacks, though in no way was Stengel prejudiced against Howard. When Casey first saw Howard play, he said, "When I finally get a nigger, I get the only one who can't run," a remark that Jackie Robinson always referred to whenever Stengel was discussed. Stengel, a man who rarely called his players by their Christian names, addressed Howard as "Eightball" to his face, a not-so-cryptic reference to the jet-black color of that ball in pool. Never, however, did Stengel decline to employ Howard's bat or his fielding skills when the situation called for it. Stengel's admiration for talent overcame all racial barriers, and after Howard proved his value to the Yankees, Stengel became a fervent admirer of Howard. "You can substitute," said Stengel, "but you rarely can replace. With Howard," he said, "I have a replacement, not a substitute." Stengel included Howard on every all-star team beginning in 1957, and he never stopped praising Howard for his all-around ability and his strong desire. Still, like all the blacks who were pioneers, Ellie had to face a trial by epithet and to southern whites he was still a nigger even if he could hit a baseball over a roof.

Through it all Howard remained silent. He was not a person who enjoyed making waves. His primary goal was to play for the Yankees, even if his lack of action or reaction might cause him to be labeled an "Uncle Tom" or "the token nigger" on the Yankees. After one understands Howard's point of view these labels are patently unfair. Vic Power, a superbly talented athlete, handled the racial situation in his own way, fighting back and causing resentment even among his own teammates while with the Kansas City Blues, and Power never made it to the Yankees. Howard, a conservative man on an ultraconservative team, sought to become a Yankee, and he succeeded his way, playing on the team from 1955 to 1967, and in 1963 he became the first black in the American League to win the Most Valuable Player. After he retired, he was named as the first black Yankee coach, and he has aspirations to some day become the first black Yankee manager. If he accomplishes these goals, is it fair to criticize him for not cutting off his nose to spite his face? If he had said, "Burn, baby, burn," he would have set fire to his own house.

I waited for Howard outside the Yankee locker room, a room just down the corridor from the Yankee dugout, and when the Yankee first-base coach emerged, I was immediately surprised by both his heft and size and by his easy smile and warm greeting. It was a couple of hours before game time, and Howard suggested we sit in the dugout and talk before fielding and batting practice got under way.

"When you were a kid were there still racial barriers to playing in the major leagues?" I asked.

"There were racial barriers in everything right on up," Howard said, "and when I came to the Yankee organization there were still racial barriers. I couldn't live at the same hotel with the other ball players when I went down for spring training. I stayed with a private family in the black section of St. Petersburg. Bob Gibson, Sam Jones, and Bill White of the Cardinals used to stay with them. The Cardinals and the Yankees both trained at St. Petersburg, and at the time I was the only black training with the Yankees. Later on we had other fellows. [Later on was 1958. While Weiss was the general manager from 1947 to 1960, only one other Afro-American played on the Yankees, Harry Simpson, acquired in '58 and sold in '59. Hector Lopez, whom Weiss acquired in 1959, was a Latin from Panama.] I had a rough time in spring training,'' Ellie said. ''The camp would break at the end of the day, and you had to go back across the tracks to the black section to dress while the white boys would go back to the hotel to dress. They would all get on the bus, but I had to jump in a cab with my uniform and go back there to dress.''

After Howard played for the Kansas City Monarchs in the Negro Leagues for two years, hitting .375 in 1950, he was bought by the Yankees and assigned to Muskegon. Then he spent two years in the service running a gymnasium and playing baseball. At Kansas City in '53 Howard played the outfield and began to catch. Bill Skiff, the Kansas City manager, started him behind the plate, and in the spring training of '54 Bill Dickey worked with Howard as he had with Yogi Berra several years before. In '54 Howard caught for Toronto and was named the Most Valuable Player in the International League. In 1955 he came up to the Yankees to stay.

''I remember,'' Howard said, ''everybody tried to make everything pleasant for this black guy who was the first one with us. I remember Bill Skowron and his wife came to pick me up at the train station, which I'll never forget, and Phil Rizzuto, goddamn, he was great. I'll never forget him. I give Phil the most credit of anyone. He would call me up during the day and take me out to various places, go to the movies, meet people around the league. I would call him the Great White Father. He was the type of man I respected, and I give him a lot of credit. Also Hank Bauer. Another friend of mine was Andy Carey. The whole ball club was great. I remember one day the first year I was there I hit a triple that won a ball game. My biggest ball game. I won the ball game for the Yankees in the bottom of the ninth, and I was outside doing an interview. I came into the locker room, and they had towels lined up from the door to my locker. Joe Collins, Mickey Mantle. They lined the towels up. It was like a red carpet. Laid out for me. I was surprised. And when they did that, I figured I was accepted just like everyone else.''

Ellie Howard was a valuable man on the Yankees whether catching, playing first base, or the outfield. He was trained to be a catcher, but because Yogi Berra was ahead of him, he didn't become the Yankees' regular catcher until 1961, his seventh season with the Yankees. Howard was chosen for every all-star team between 1957 and 1964. Once Berra slowed down after 1961, Howard began to win the belated acclaim that he had deserved for so many years. On another team he would have been *the* star. On the Yankees he was one of several great players. As a catcher he ranked with the great ones, on an exalted plateau with Yogi Berra and Roy Campanella.

Yet some things didn't change. In 1963 Howard was the MVP in the American League. In spring training in '64 he was unable to rent an apartment in Fort Lauderdale. To Floridian landlords, he may have been the Most Valuable Nigger, but he was still a nigger. ''I remember when I received the Most Valuable Player Award, there was a picture in the newspaper of me and my wife. My wife is a light-skinned, black person. And I received a letter from a nut in Delaware saying that he didn't know I was married to a white woman. He said, 'You ought to go back to Africa.' '' The smile was gone. There was pain on his face, and his voice was noticeably softer and the words were heavier. But Elston Howard was uncomfortable making waves. Thus when he was barred from living with the Yankees during spring training in St. Petersburg, he told one writer, "I do not understand them, but I can't be the one that's gonna do the breaking down." Time, he felt, was on his side.

Howard, an intelligent baseball man with an ability to lead men, fervently desires an opportunity to manage in the major leagues, hopefully with the Yankees. He is a patient man. One day he will get his chance. In the background the thwack of bat on ball resounded through the cavernous, empty Stadium. Ellie got up for a second and grabbed a quick drink of water from the cooler beside us. "You know," he said, "I never would have gone through what Jackie Robinson went through. I don't think I could have taken it. I give Jackie a great deal of credit for opening the way up for me."

After a respectable spring training, manager Stengel felt that his 1955 starting eight would be better than anyone else's. The big question, however, was his pitching. The staff was young, but it had promise. Ford, Grim, and Turley were regulars in the rotation, but Larsen, out with a sore arm, was inactive. Stengel retained 22-year-old John Kucks, hoping the youngster would give the team some depth along with elder left-handers Lopat and Byrne. Tom Morgan, and Jim Konstanty, acquired from the Philadelphia Phillies the year before, were the bullpen. Stengel had remembered Konstanty from the 1950 world series, and when the opportunity arose to acquire him for the 1954 pennant run, the 38-year-old relief specialist was added to the club, another of the ex-National League castoffs like Mize, Sain, and Slaughter, who could give valuable experience to a Yankee pennant run.

Woodling would be missed, and Billy Martin still had several more months of military service, but Stengel had Skowron, Collins, and Ed Robinson at first, McDougald and Coleman at second, Rizzuto and Billy Hunter at shortstop, and Andy Carey at third. Yogi Berra and Ellie Howard were the catchers, and Mickey Mantle, Hank Bauer, Irv Noren, and Enos Slaughter were in the outfield with Howard and Collins also available to play there. The pitching would be the question.

Whitey Ford began the season excellently with three shutouts and six wins in his first seven games, and newly acquired Bob Turley gave Weiss something to gloat over as he won eight of his first nine games, consistently striking out ten batters a game with his blazing fast ball. Turley pitched a one-hitter against the White Sox and a two-hitter against the Red Sox; though he walked almost as many as he struck out, it was exciting to watch Turley walk the bases full and then strike out the side.

In addition, young Kucks pitched excellently in spurts, and Byrne chipped in with a couple of complete game victories. Konstanty and Morgan were strong in the bullpen. Larsen, however, was a disappointment. The big pitcher had arrived in camp with a sore shoulder and what the Yankee manager considered a lackadaisical attitude, and Larsen found himself in Denver early in the year. When he was sent down, Larsen told a couple of the other players, "I'm going to take my sweet time reporting, and I don't give a damn if I ever come back here." After spending a week with friends in St. Louis, Larsen finally reported to Denver, and under manager Ralph Houk, he was nine and one, playing in the American Association All-Star game and hitting a home run to win the game.

With Enos Slaughter and John Sain shipped to Kansas City (now a major league town after the Philadelphia A's moved there at the end of the '54 season) for A's pitcher Sonny Dixon in early May, and with Woodling gone, Hank Bauer was given the opportunity to play every day, and he starred. Carey became a fixture at third, and Berra and Mantle developed into the league's best one-two punch, with the elfin catcher and the rustic center fielder also giving the Yankees an unparalleled defense up the middle. By mid-May Mantle was exhibiting signs that he was finally beginning to lay off the high inside pitches, and as his strikeouts dropped his home-run total rose. In one game he hit three titanic homers at the Stadium against the Tigers, the first home run hit lefty, the second and third righty—only the third time in history a batter hit a home run from each side of the plate in one game. During one stretch in May Mantle reached base fifteen times in a row, hitting a home run, a triple, two doubles, a bunt single, and walking nine times!

Around this nucleus there was much shifting by Stengel. McDougald pulled a back muscle in early April, and then a week later Coleman fractured his left shoulder blade in a collision at home plate. When McDougald came back and replaced Coleman, he didn't hit well. Gil continued to employ his golf-swing stance, much to Stengel's displeasure, and finally at the end of one clubhouse meeting, the Old Man intemperately approached McDougald. "You," he screamed, "I want you to change that horseshit stance of yours. I don't care how you change it. Just change it, and I mean now." McDougald bolted out of the meeting with a beet-red neck, but that afternoon he took extra batting practice and concentrated on hitting with a normal stance, giving him a better opportunity to hit outside pitches, and though he was sure he was going to get hit in the head with the ball, he became a much improved hitter, lining solid drives to all parts of the field and raising his average to respectability.

Bill Skowron pulled a hamstring muscle in his leg stretching for a ground ball and missed a couple of weeks, and with Collins in Lenox Hill Hospital suffering from a viral infection, Eddie Robinson played first and struck fifteen home runs before it was summer. When Collins returned, Stengel played him in the outfield. The Yankee depth was making itself felt. Ellie Howard contributed a couple of game-winning hits and displayed a potent bat when he was given the opportunity. That Howard was black was unimportant to the other players. They accepted him immediately and took personally the insults directed at him. During one home game Hank Bauer crawled on top of the dugout to confront a fan who was shouting racial insults at the young rookie. Bauer, glaring, peered into the stands to see if he could identify the heckler. He searched a long while, hoping the man would incriminate himself by making another remark. Fortunately for the guy, he didn't. After the game a reporter, watching this scenario, asked Bauer about the incident. Bauer just shrugged his shoulders. "Ellie's my friend," he said.

Stengel fought for his rookies so long as they hustled for him and kept their noses clean. When Casey and rookies Ellie Howard and John Kucks were scheduled to appear on the Horace Heidt pregame show, Stengel was offered $1000, and the rookies $250 each. Stengel refused to appear unless the money was split evenly, each man receiving $500. Both Howard and Kucks, struggling first-year men, were grateful to their wealthy manager for his fairness.

Tommy Carroll, the teen-age shortstop, was not so tenderly treated by Stengel. It was about a hundred degrees in the shade before a ball game in Kansas City in midsummer, and Carroll was standing in the dugout boasting how fast he was. One of the veterans, unimpressed, bet Carroll that he couldn't even beat the 33-year-old Hank Bauer in a race. Carroll took the bet, $100 on the winner. Among the other Yankees the match suddenly created a commotion. They knew a pigeon when they saw one. Bauer and Carroll raced fifty yards, and the speedy Bauer won. For another $100 a race between Carroll and 35-year-old Joe Collins was arranged. This time Collins beat the youngster. Because Carroll was getting tired, the players bet Carroll another hundred that he couldn't beat Yogi Berra in a race. They shortened the race to forty yards. Carroll agreed, lessening his chances because Berra was lightning-fast over a short course. Berra and Carroll raced, and Carroll lost again. His ego and his wallet were being decimated. He had to win a race. A forty-yard dash between Carroll and Don Larsen, just recalled from Denver, was arranged. Carroll didn't realize that Larsen was probably the second-fastest runner on the team next to Mantle. Larsen beat Carroll decisively. When Carroll dragged himself back to the dugout, he collapsed from exhaustion on the floor of the dugout. Stengel, unsympathetic, stood over the prostrate Carroll and mumbled, "Get the stupid son of a bitch out of here."

It was apparent by the second week in June that Cleveland would be a much weaker team than it was in '54. Feller and Garcia had slumped drastically, and despite the excellent pitching of rookie Herb Score, it was clear that the Indians would not run away with the league again. The Yankees, sparked by Ford and Turley, were leading the American League by five and a half games.

When Turley lost five in a row in late June, the Yankees slipped a little, but Ford and Byrne were consistently excellent, and with Stengel platooning and substituting brilliantly, the team stayed ahead of the fast-closing White Sox and Indians.

Tommy Byrne no longer was the fireballing, rear back and throw pitcher he used to be. He learned to change speeds and throw a change-up and slider, and hitters could not believe the junk he was throwing and getting away with. He kept piling up wins through the summer, recording a 9–2 record after a brilliant 1–0 victory over the White Sox. One thing had not changed: his mound demeanor. He still was telling the batters what he was going to throw, though he lied more now. If he said he would throw a fast ball and then threw a curve, he would yell, "Oops, sorry. It slipped." Byrne kept his teammates in stitches, spitting at the batters before releasing the ball, and once again asking Ted Williams how he and his separated wife were getting along. In one game when manager Al Lopez of the Indians was riding him unmercifully, Byrne walked off the mound right in the middle of an inning and into the Cleveland dugout to confront the manager. Lopez apologized. Always unpredictable, Byrne won the Comeback Player of the Year Award in 1955, and his 16–5 record was a major factor in the Yankees' regaining the pennant.

Other players were not faring so well. On the last day of July Eddie Lopat was dropped from the team and claimed by the Baltimore Orioles. Mantle's legs were hurting again, and though not playing badly by anyone else's standards, when he was not superlative, the Yankee Stadium crowds booed him unmercifully.

Since 1951 the Yankee public-relations staff had been labeling Mickey the successor to the Great DiMaggio, and the fans were waiting for Mantle to approach DiMaggio's greatness. Mantle was the meal ticket, and thousands of seats were sold on his potential, but this was his fifth season with the Yankees, and the fans were becoming impatient with the young outfielder. The loud, intense chorus of boos perplexed and depressed the quiet man.

Part of the problem was certainly caused by Mantle's demeanor. Mickey never tipped his hat or in any other way acknowledged the fans' existence, even after he hit a home run. He crossed the plate with his head down, a reflection of his bashful nature, but the crowd saw this behavior as arrogant and boorish. Mantle was intense and rarely smiled, and the fans saw this absence of a show of emotion as the absence of a kinship with them. The fans wanted so badly for Mantle to love them, but Mickey never really knew how to respond to them. What he did was shy away, and as a result the fans reacted with a cascade of boos. Through his most productive years this state of affairs continued. Only in the latter part of his career when he loosened up and wooed the fans did the adoration begin.

By the end of August Mantle had thirty-five home runs, and he and Berra led a Yankee team that was only one step ahead of the White Sox, Indians, and the streaking Red Sox going into September. On September 1 Chicago took over first place. A few days later the Indians took the lead. Stengel was not optimistic about his chances of winning this year. Though Don Larsen was 6–1 since his recall from the minors, Turley had dropped to 13–13 after his tremendous 8–1 start. Third-baseman Andy Carey had fallen into a dreadful slump.

Earlier in the season Carey was hitting well, booming long drives into the Stadium's cavernous left-center field, which invariably, however, were just long outs. Stengel, harping at Carey to change his stance and spray the ball to all fields, would yell from the dugout, "Butcher boy, butcher boy" demanding Carey chop down at the ball. Stengel yelled this so often and so loudly it became a joke with the other players.

When Stengel finally did get the young third-baseman to hit to the opposite field, his average dropped precipitously. Furthermore, with Coleman and Rizzuto not hitting, the infield seemed to lack leadership and direction.

And then, unexpectedly, the Army returned Billy Martin to the floundering Yankees. As soon as Martin returned, Stengel benched Carey, moved McDougald to third, and started Billy at second. Martin, despite the long layoff, surprised everyone by hitting .300 and giving the team the spark and inspiration it had lacked.

"Until I arrived here in Chicago a few hours ago," sportswriter Bill Corum wrote, "I felt that, farfetched as it seemed, the perennial bridesmaids of the American League, the White Sox, might become bride. Now I know better.

Because I picked up the paper and the headline said that Billy Martin had rejoined the Yankees. That, of course, just about settled the pennant race in the junior league. The Indians have pitching, the local Sox have a pretty good club, and the Bo Sox of Boston are belligerent. But you don't beat Stengel when he's got Billy Martin.''

Stengel rejoiced when Martin came back. He was getting back an infielder, and also a son. "That fresh little bastard," Stengel would say. "How I love him." Upon his return, Martin said to Stengel, "Case, when we were bushers out in the Coast League and then when we came to New York, you and I never played on anything but winners. So take my word for it, there is nothing to worry about. We'll take the league apart before the end of the season."

It was a happy reunion as well for Billy's close buddies, Ford and Mantle. In Martin's first game, against Washington, with Billy at his vocal best, comrade Ford pitched a one-hitter and comrade Mantle stroked a three-run home run to win the game. It was September 2. New York trailed the White Sox by half a game.

Into the second week of September the Yankees continued to trail two games behind the Indians, as the White Sox suddenly and characteristically faded in the stretch. Martin was given the floor during one team meeting. He was angry. He told the others, "I had three cars when I went into the Army, and now I don't even have one. I'm broke, and you're playing as though you're trying to lose. We gotta get into the series. We gotta."

On September 16, with just eleven games remaining in the season, the Yankees trailed the Indians by half a game. The odds makers picked the Indians, because the Yankees had to play a three-game series against the tough Red Sox while Cleveland played the lowly Detroit Tigers three games.

The first game of the Yankee-Red Sox series drew 50,000 fans at Yankee Stadium, a particularly good turnout considering that the Yankees were now televising all their games. Stengel started Whitey Ford against Boston's bean-pole right-hander, 6-foot 6-inch Frank Sullivan. Yogi Berra hit a home run off Sullivan, and the Yankees raced to a 3–0 lead, but in the eighth inning Boston scored four runs against Ford and reliever Jim Konstanty. The day promised to be a complete disaster because during the game Bill Skowron struck out, returned to the dugout, and kicked the metal water cooler so violently that he broke the big toe of his right foot. Also, in the second inning Mickey Mantle dragged a bunt down the left-field line, and after he safely crossed the bag, he pulled up lame and limped to the clubhouse. Doctors diagnosed the injury as a muscle tear in the back of his right thigh. It seemed doubtful that Mantle, who had thirty-seven home runs and ninety-nine runs batted in, would play during the rest of the season. Trailing 4–3 in the bottom of the ninth, Stengel paced sullenly in the dugout pondering his rotten luck.

In the bottom of the ninth the Yankees were facing right-hander Ellis Kinder, once the ace of the Boston staff, but now its top reliever. Kinder retired the first batter, but threw Hank Bauer a fast ball which he lofted down the left-field line into the lower box seats for a home run to tie the score at 4–4. After the game the right-handed Bauer told reporters, "I've been trying to convince the Old Man for seven years that he has been wrong about my not being able to hit right-handers. Maybe this will convince him.'' Bauer had hit over .400 during the month of August, and his home run against Kinder was one of twenty he hit in '55.

Kinder retired the next batter for the second out, but the first pitch he threw to Yogi Berra was jerked far and deep into the lower right-field stands as the Yankees magically snatched a 5–4 victory from the Red Sox.

''It's like that,'' Jimmy Cannon wrote, ''rooting for the Yankees. Nice things will happen. I get the same feeling rooting for the Yankees like nice things I make up which never happen to me. It's a feeling of having something given to you for nothing which you couldn't grab any other way. I never have been on a yacht in my whole life. But I imagine rooting for the Yankees is like owning a yacht.''

Year after year Yogi Berra played a great part in producing those ''nice things.'' In 1951, '54, and '55 Berra was named the Most Valuable Player in the American League. In 1952 he finished fourth in the voting and in '53 and '56 he finished second as he established himself as one of the outstanding performers in baseball history. Berra led the Yankees in runs batted in for six years in a row beginning in 1950, and his 358 career home runs outdistance all catchers in that department by a long shot. No one else is even close.

Berra began his Yankee career in 1946 as the Ugly Duckling of the team, squat, gawky, unsophisticated, and in many ways truly comical, but with experience and patience from Yankee manager Casey Stengel, Berra developed into the team's elder statesman, iron man, and resident legend. Yogi Berra was a Liza Doolittle in shin guards.

When he first came up, some of his teammates hung from the dugout roof by one arm and made ape calls. When he retired as a player in 1963 after eighteen years of stardom, Berra was named manager of the Yankees and won a pennant in his first year as Yankee skipper. Events transpired against him and he was fired, but as manager of the New York Mets, he again won a pennant. Today nobody laughs at Mr. Berra. He is a millionaire sportsman with a lovely family and a palatial home. He is a unique, highly respected gentleman.

When I arrived at the Berra estate, the squire of Montclair, New Jersey, was not at home. It was early February, and snow covered the large oak trees in the front yard and the swimming pool in the back. It was freezing outside, so after knocking on the kitchen door and ringing the bell, I tried the door and was surprised to find that it wasn't locked. I went in. Inside, Italian opera was playing on the stereo system and Puccini wafted through the high-ceilinged house. In the living room stood an ebony grand piano. Little, delicate porcelain figures of birds lined the breakfront shelves. Casey Stengel once said, ''Berra's house is so big your kid'll get lost in the backyard if you don't watch him.''

It wasn't long before Yogi bounded in with a warm greeting and apologies for being a little late. He had been the guest at a youth organization breakfast, and the ceremonies had run a little long.

His hairline was receding some, but he was the same Yogi Berra whose baseball card was worth four Wes Westrums or six Clint Courtneys. His warmth took me by surprise. Of the stories I had been told about Yogi, many indicated that with strangers he could be close-mouthed and suspicious. Not in my experience. He was sincere, humble, and friendly. He had been one of the biggest names in the world of sports for over twenty-five years, and yet he was as modest and unassuming as he must have been when the Yankees first discovered him playing ball on the Hill in St. Louis. He lived in poverty then. He has spent his life making sure he will never live in poverty again.

"But the Hill wasn't tough," Berra said. "We never locked our doors. We didn't have to."

Lawrence Peter Berra, Lawdie to his family, Yogi to his friends, lived for sports and only very reluctantly attended school. Because he had difficulty with reading and math, he was forced to repeat the sixth grade. He was shy and self-conscious, and being older than the other kids made him even more withdrawn. By the eighth grade, Berra was spending most of his time in school staring out the window and wishing he were playing ball. Often he played hookey.

"The teachers treated me good," Yogi said. "I can say that. They didn't ever cause me any trouble. I guess I caused them some." He smiled shyly. "I just felt it was a waste of time—then. But I wish I was going now. I think it means a great deal."

Berra was 15 when he dropped out of school. For many years afterward his lack of formal education haunted him and contributed to his shyness. When he left school, he went to work. Every cent he made he gave to his parents. In turn they gave him two dollars a week to spend on himself. In his spare time Berra played baseball. He and Joe Garagiola starred for the Stockham American Legion Post team, and reached the finals of the Legion national tournament in 1939 and '40. Berra's lightning reflexes, strong arm, and powerful bat began to attract the notice of the scouts.

Continually, though, he had to fight his family to play ball. His father came to St. Louis from Milan, Italy. To him baseball was a waste of time. Lawdie should be working to make money. All of his older brothers worked, and only because older brother Tony promised his father that he would contribute a little extra if Lawdie were allowed to play ball was Berra permitted to continue.

"Tony was a better player than I was," Yogi said. "I always kidded my Dad. I'd say, 'See, if you had let all your sons play baseball, you would have been a millionaire.' And Dad would say, 'Awww, go blame your mother!' " Yogi's deep, rumbling laugh filled the room. "They believed in having a job and making money. What did they know about baseball?"

St. Louis had two professional teams, the Cardinals and the Browns. Neither signed Yogi Berra. Garagiola had signed a contract for $500 with the Cardinals, and the proud Berra therefore refused to sign for less than that. Bill DeWitt of the Browns wouldn't give him the money because he appeared so awkward. Branch Rickey of the Cardinals didn't want to give him the money because he was negotiating to move to the Brooklyn Dodgers. Rickey felt Berra was an excellent prospect, but couldn't tell Berra that he wanted him for the Dodgers. Instead he told Berra that he'd never become a professional. Rickey thought he could return with a Dodger contract later. It was one of the few times that Rickey outsmarted himself. Before he made his switch, the Yankees, owned by Rickey's enemy, Larry MacPhail, signed the eighteen-year-old Berra for a $500 bonus and $90 a month for the 1943 season.

"Right after I signed," Berra said, "Rickey invited me to come to Bear Mountain for the Dodgers' spring training. He said he had changed his mind and would give me the money I wanted." Berra chuckled. The Dodgers could have had Rizzuto, Lopat, and Berra. The Yankees had them all. "I was only making $90 a month playing for Norfolk," Berra said, "and after taxes that was $35 every two weeks. I sent it all home to my parents. My mother always sent me back $5 or $10. She always told me, 'Don't ever let your Dad find out I'm sending you this money or you're coming home.' The last time I sent money home was when I got married." Yogi was married in 1949 and was 24 years old. "And you know that $500 bonus?" Yogi said. "I thought I was going to get that right away, but Weiss put in the contract that I would only get it if I lasted the season. I had to wait until the end of the year!"

"And you sent *that* money home, too?" I said.

"Oh yeah," Berra said. "All of it."

After a .253 first year at Norfolk, in 1944 Berra enlisted in the Navy. On June 6, 1944, D-Day, he was a member of a crew on a rocket-launching landing craft, swaying and pitching with the seas off the coast of Omaha Beach. The craft was stationed 300 to 400 yards offshore, sending messages and searching for mines.

"You must have been pretty scared," I said.

"Naaaah," Yogi said. "I thought it was fun. It was like the Fourth of July. The battleship *Nevada* was bombarding the coast, firing over our heads, and we could see flashes, different colors, and the tracers were flying. I was looking up, watching, and our captain kept yelling at me, 'Keep your head down.' It was fun."

After World War II Berra returned to his base at New London, Connecticut, where he was the janitor and bouncer of the base movie house. Berra was a movie buff. He loved the Marx Brothers and all westerns. He also played on the base team against barnstorming pro teams and against neighboring college teams, so that when he was discharged from the service and reported to Newark in 1946, he had received some excellent game experience. Newark was the top team in the Yankee farm system, and in only his second year of minor league ball, Berra hit .314 and hit with power. When Larry MacPhail brought him up to the Yankees at the end of the 1946 season, he was 21 years old. Almost everyone else was a hard-bitten veteran who gave Berra an unmerciful ribbing. Yogi was bashful, so bashful that when he saw a girl he knew, he would walk to the other side of the street to avoid having to talk to her. He was self-conscious about his stocky build and Neanderthal features. His build was a cross between a gorilla and a bull penguin; he was inarticulate and rarely spoke, and when he did it sounded like a primitive grunt. Berra became the target of jokes by his Yankee teammates and cruel insults by the opposition. For years he suffered for his appearance and speech, keeping most of the hurt inside until the relentless harassment finally ended several years later.

"You were a bashful kid," I said to Yogi.

"Yeah," he said. "I still am."

Even his manager, Bucky Harris, made fun at his expense, calling him Nature Boy and the Ape, and his teammates would hang by one arm from the roof of the dugout, scratch their armpits, and grunt. Tarzan ape calls reverberated through the locker room. After Stengel came to the Yankees, the worst of his ordeal had ended. "No more of this stuff about him keeping house in a tree or swinging from limb to limb like those apes," Stengel ordered. "And stop feeding him peanuts."

The first time rookie Berra played the Red Sox in Boston, Red Sox coach Mike Ryba, one of the expert bench jockeys and agitators in the league, accosted Berra during batting practice.

"You all right, kid?" Ryba asked. "You must be sick. Nobody could look like you without being sick."

Berra, somewhat of a hypochondriac, thought that Ryba was being sympathetic. "Yeah," Yogi said. "I ain't feeling so good. My belly hurts."

"Not your belly," Ryba said. "I'm talking about your face. I never saw an uglier one." Ryba started to turn and walk away.

Berra, sensitive and usually defenseless in a battle of words, yelled at Ryba, "So I'm ugly. So what? I never saw anyone hit with his face."

The newspapermen also took swipes at him. One writer asked Bucky Harris, "You're not seriously considering keeping him, are you? He doesn't even look like a Yankee." Berra had an answer for him, too. "These guys who make fun of me in the papers," he said contemptuously, "how much money are they making?"

It wasn't only his appearance which made him a natural target. Because of his provincial background and lack of education, as a youngster he was rather crude. When he ate he would literally attack his food as if to get as much down as he could before someone came and took it away. A knife and fork were weapons, and when he finished what was on his plate, he would finish what was on everyone else's plate, too. He had a truly voracious appetite. Also he had funny tastes. He enjoyed banana and mustard sandwiches, for instance. His dress was rather peculiar, too. His unusual build with broad shoulders, a small waist, and short legs, made it difficult for him to find clothes that fit. His clothes never seemed to be tailored quite right, and getting dressed up to Berra meant wearing his most recent pair of sneakers. Jimmy Breslin said that when Berra first came to New York he was wearing a blue suit, a dark blue shirt, and sneakers.

On the field Yogi also looked comical. Bill Corum of the *Journal-American* said, "Nobody yet has come up with a pair of shin guards to fit that man. Watch him chase a few fouls. One or both of his shin guards come loose and start flapping. One winds up on the side of his leg or back of his leg. After catching the pop and watching any base runners, Yogi then must begin the chore of putting himself back together again. He puts on his shin guards like a fat lady trying to put on an undersized girdle. After that he goes and retrieves his cap, then his mask, and after straightening his chest protector, he is ready to go back to work. If the next pitch is fouled off where he has to chase it, he then starts all over again."

There were other quirks that everyone noticed. Berra loved to read comic books, and the Yankee fans would mail him hundreds and hundreds of comic books that would be piled up five and six feet high in his locker. Superman, Batman, Archie. Berra loved them all. At Newark in 1946 Berra was sitting in bed reading a comic book while his roommate, Bobby Brown, was studying one of his ponderous medical textbooks. It was late at night, and after Brown closed his anatomy text and readied for sleep, Berra got under the covers, threw his Superman comic on the floor, and said, "Say Bobby. How did yours come out?" The other players teased Berra about his love for comics. "Yeah," Berra once said, "but I notice when I put them down, there's always guys around ready to pick them up."

Once New York City Mayor Fiorello LaGuardia, a prolific comic-book reader himself, offered Berra a radio show so he could read his comics over the air. The Yankee front office, though, refused to allow him to do it. George Weiss said that it lacked dignity.

Berra had known Phil Rizzuto in the Navy, and when he came to the Yankees he asked to room with the little shortstop. In one respect they were excellent roommates. They each respected the other's ability, and neither had a malicious or playful nature. Rizzuto never kidded Berra about his appearance, and Berra never put spiders or bugs in Rizzuto's bed. There were, however, other causes that broke up the roommate pair several years later. The biggest problem was that Yogi hated to sleep. He also hated to be alone. Late into the night Yogi liked to talk and hated for Rizzuto to turn off the lights. If Rizzuto was asleep when Berra came into the room, Yogi would turn on the lights and wake him up. When Berra wanted to go to sleep himself, he would have Rizzuto tell him a bedtime story. Many nights the scrappy little shortstop could go to sleep only after telling Yogi the story of "The Three Little Pigs" or "Little Red Riding Hood" or "Snow White."

"Finally I couldn't take it any more," Rizzuto said. "I ran out of stories to tell him." For the rest of his career Yogi roomed with unsuspecting newcomers, with rookies, or alone.

During the world series of 1960, for instance, his roommate was Joe DeMaestri, a player who the year before had been traded to the Yankees from the Athletics. "We'd be in our room," DeMaestri said, "and if he wanted a pack of cigarettes, he'd want me to go with him. He'd say, 'Come on downstairs. I have to buy a pack of cigarettes.' He didn't want to go alone, and some nights he just wouldn't let me go to sleep. Every time I fell asleep he kept waking me up to watch television with him. We were playing the Pittsburgh Pirates in the world series. Finally it was two in the morning. When the national anthem came on, he wouldn't let me turn it off. There was the picture of the flag waving in the breeze, and he was watching it like it was *Ben-Hur*. Christ, I'm as patriotic as anybody, but I wanted to go to sleep so badly. 'Leave it on, Joe,' Yogi said, 'It's a good song.' "

"He was," Casey Stengel once said, "a peculiar fellow with amazing ability."

But what really gave Berra the reputation for being a character was his singular ability to garble an English sentence. Slips of syntax and the use of almost-correct words became known as Berraisms. His most famous occurred in 1947 when the citizens of St. Louis threw a day for him before a Yankee-Browns game. "I want to thank you," he said humbly, "for making this night necessary."

One time that same year Bucky Harris, trying to make Berra swing only at strikes, told him to think up at the plate. Berra struck out, and when he returned to the bench, he said to Harris, "How can a guy hit and think at the same time?" Another time Yogi was asked if he wanted to go to Toots Shor's to eat. "Nah," he said. "Let's don't go there. Nobody goes there any more. You can't hardly get a seat."

Before long gag writers and clever newspapermen were inventing their own Berraisms and attributing them to Yogi. "I went to see *Dr. Zhivago* last night," Yogi's wife was supposed to have said. "What's wrong with you now?" Yogi is supposed to have replied.

Longer stories evolved with Berraisms as the punch line. There was one story of Berra attending a banquet honoring a high school coach and his three most outstanding athletes. At the end of the banquet Yogi had to present them with trophies, and because he was afraid that he couldn't remember their names, he had written the name of the school on his left cuff, the name of the coach on the right cuff, and the names of the three players on the lapel inside the jacket. When it came time for Yogi to make the presentations, he looked at his left cuff. "I've enjoyed being with you here at So-and-So high school," and then looked at his right cuff, "and your coach, Mr. So-and-so, is really a fine man." Then Yogi looked inside his jacket. "And I want to congratulate your three outstanding athletes, Hart, Shaffner, and Marx!"

For the first few years of Berra's career, especially the two years he played under Bucky Harris in 1947 and '48, he suffered for his peculiarities. He also suffered because he was a terrible catcher. He crouched too far behind the batter, making it more difficult for his pitchers, and after a speedy batter reached first base, Yogi insisted on calling for high fast balls because they gave him a better chance to throw out the runner. He couldn't stop balls in the dirt, and if a runner did try to steal, he inevitably ended up on third because Yogi's throws either sailed over the shortstop's head or nose-dived and bounced in front of the shortstop and into center field. Also, Yogi didn't know how to call pitches. He preferred the fast ball, and he would call for fast balls until the pitcher would tire. Then when the pitcher had to rely on his curve ball, he couldn't control it because he hadn't used it all game long.

Berra had fared poorly in the 1947 world series, with Jackie Robinson stealing bases on him at will, and in the fourth game when Bill Bevens had a no-hitter going into the ninth inning with two outs, Al Gionfriddo stole second as Yogi's peg sailed high over the bag. Had Berra thrown the runner out, the game would have ended. The next batter walked, and then Cookie Lavaghetto doubled to beat Bevens, and Yogi was considered the goat. In 1948 his catching did not improve much, and he divided his time between catching and playing the outfield. Harris kept him in the lineup because in 1948 he drove in ninety-eight runs and hit .305, and a bat like that stays in the lineup, despite other inadequacies.

When Casey Stengel became manager after the 1948 season, one of his primary objectives was to teach Berra how to catch. Toward that end he hired Bill Dickey, who had been the Yankee manager only a couple years before. Berra was to be Dickey's pupil, a Plato teaching Aristotle. During spring training of 1949, for many long, hard hours, Berra slavishly followed Dickey's instructions. Dickey moved him closer to the plate, lessening the danger of his getting clipped by foul balls and improving his chances of throwing out base runners. Dickey taught him to step over the plate with his left foot as he threw to second. Berra learned how to fall down in front of balls thrown in the dirt. For hours Dickey bounced balls in the dirt in front of him and threw high pops behind him. Dickey showed Berra how to crouch and the right place to hold his fingers while giving the pitcher the signals. Dickey had Yogi wiggle his stubby fingers to better enable the pitchers to see his signs, and Dickey boosted his confidence by treating him kindly and paternally.

And while the Hall-of-Fame catcher worked on Berra's catching skills, manager Stengel boosted Berra's confidence at every opportunity. The manager would slide within hearing range of the kid and out of the blue start talking to a reporter. "The kid is going just great," Stengel would say. "Why has our pitching been so great? Berra, that's why. He handles the pitchers reeeeeal great. And the runners better not try and run on him." Berra, thinking he was eavesdropping, would beam. "He may not be built like a ball player," Stengel said, "but that's nothing. When I played for the Dodgers Uncle Robbie used to say that about me, too." Stengel was often criticized for being a push-button manager during his career, but it is doubtful that another manager would and could have undertaken the transformation of Yogi Berra from a woefully inadequate receiver to a Hall-of-Famer. Stengel saw the need for instructing young players—he enjoyed the challenge of developing them: Jerry Coleman, Gene Woodling, Hank Bauer, Gil McDougald, Mickey Mantle. With the help of Bill Dickey, Stengel made Berra a great catcher.

Stengel also had the guts to switch players around to improve their performances. He switched Coleman from the left side of the infield to second base. He converted Mantle from a shortstop to an outfielder. He moved Bill Skowron from the outfield to first base. On-the-field decisions were not the only reasons for Stengel's unparalleled success.

By May 1949 base runners had stopped taking liberties with Berra's arm, and in '49 he was named catcher on the American League All-Star team for the first of fourteen consecutive years. Berra starred through the 1950s while George Weiss developed and then traded away such minor league catchers as Sherm Lollar, Gus Triandos, Hal Smith, Hank Foiles, Lou Berberet, Cal Neeman, Moe Thacker, Ken Silvestri, Elvin Tappe, and Clint Courtney. Though Berra, like Rizzuto, was a hypochondriac who complained about his aches and pains, like Rizzuto, almost every day Berra was in the lineup. Because of Berra other Yankee catchers who rode the bench were Ralph Houk, Charlie Silvera, John Blanchard, and for many years Elston Howard.

Stengel was expert at handling his ever-aching catcher. "I ain't feeling so good today, Case," Berra would say.

"Neither am I," said Stengel. "It must be the New York climate."

"But Case," Berra would protest, "my legs are stiff."

"Yeah, I know," said Stengel, "but you ought to see who's pitching today."

Clearly Mr. Berra, as Stengel called him, was a favorite of the Yankee manager. As early as 1950 Stengel used Berra as an unofficial assistant coach, recognizing his ability to gauge the performances of the pitchers. Berra became a student of his craft, and his excellent memory helped him to learn the strengths and weaknesses of every opposing hitter.

Berra also knew how to work on a pitcher's emotions. "Come on, Onionhead," he would yell at Vic Raschi, "throw the ball." Raschi would swear at his catcher and bear down a little harder. When Berra felt he had to calm a pitcher, he could do that, too. Once when Joe Page was in a tight situation, Yogi went to the mound to settle him down. "Hey Joe," said Yogi, "you got any kids?"

Page was standing on the mound, runners all around him, and he couldn't figure out what Yogi was talking about. "No, I don't," said Page. "So what?"

"Ya gotta have kids, Joe," Yogi said. "Best thing in the world for a family." Yogi grinned, and Page began to laugh. Relaxed, Page retired the side without difficulty.

Fewer and fewer base runners tested his arm, and he became adept at catching tricky foul pop-ups, with the exception of the one he dropped which could have spoiled Allie Reynolds' second no-hitter in 1951. He became excellent at blocking balls in the dirt and was adept at corralling bunts in front of the plate. "Yogi looks cumbersome, like he can't run," Stengel once said, "but he's quick like a cat. He springs on a bunt like it was another dollar." Later he said, "To me he is a great man. I am lucky to have him and so are my pitchers."

Berra's transformation from caterpillar to butterfly was complete by 1950. After many had predicted that he would never even be an adequate catcher, one year later he was an all-star. "The metamorphosis of this young man from the worst catcher in baseball to perhaps the best," said Joe Williams, a New York writer, in 1950, "is an extraordinary thing, and those who continue to regard him as a clown or a freak not only do him an injustice, but stamp themselves as incompetent critics." People were comparing him to the great Roy Campanella of the Brooklyn Dodgers, and manager Stengel was insisting he was even better than the Dodger catcher. "There isn't anything," said Stengel, "that Campanella can do that my guy can't do better, except maybe dig the ball out of the dirt. And how many catchers has baseball had who were fast enough to bat third without hurting you on the bases? I mean real good catchers who could also hit. There was Bresnahan of the old Giants and Cochrane of the Athletics. They were the best, and I put my guy right up there with them. Campanella. Could you bat him third? Could you send him from first to third on a short hit? Could you?"

Yogi Berra was the batting leader of the Yankees before the emergence of

Mickey Mantle. He was a dead-pull left-handed hitter whose skills were perfectly suited to the cozy dimensions of Yankee Stadium's short right-field porch. He employed a lightning-fast swing, snapping his wrists at pitches over his head, below his knees, and sometimes even in the strike zone. Yogi's philosophy was, "If I can see it, I can hit it." His lifetime average was .285, but with men on base in critical situations he was a terror to the opposition. "When it gets around the seventh inning," said Paul Richards, "Berra is the most dangerous hitter in baseball."

Coinciding with Berra's rising athletic achievements was an accumulation of dollars. Though he had the disposition of a collie and looked like a person a confidence man would embrace with open arms, Berra was one of the sharpest businessmen on the Yankees. When his equally affluent teammates Mantle and Ford ran out of spending money on the road, they could always go to Yogi for a few bucks. His teammates kidded him about still having his first buck, but Yogi's acquisitive nature was only an extension of the lessons of his youth. When he had two dollars a week to spend, there was little room for frivolity. When he made thousands later, his frugal spending habits continued. Berra always insisted on paying his own way. He didn't believe in "you pay this time, I'll pay next time." He was an excellent contract negotiator. Like Raschi, he would argue his value to the team. "If you don't want to pay me," Yogi would say, "then trade me. Plenty of clubs will take me and pay me what I want." Weiss would harumph and squirm, but he usually gave Yogi what he wanted. One year Berra asked for a modest raise, and when Weiss was quick to give it to him, Yogi said, "He was so willing, I must have made a mistake." But when it came to money, Yogi made few mistakes. He didn't know how to write a check. Someone else had to fill it out and he would sign it, but he knew the world of investments, and he knew how to make his money grow. When he became the vice-president of the Yoo-Hoo soft drink company, he made his teammates pay for the Yoo-Hoo in the clubhouse, adding to his reputation for tightness. Berra never took a penny from his Yoo-Hoo endorsements. He took stock, stock, and more stock, and as the endorsements of Berra and his teammates helped sales rise dramatically, Yoo-Hoo, Yogi Berra's favorite drink, helped make him rich.

"Money is the last thing Yogi thinks about at night," Stengel once said, "before he goes to sleep."

Berra retired in 1963 after a brilliant eighteen-year career, and in 1964 the Yankees made him their manager. He was in the untenable position of having to replace Ralph Houk, a manager the players loved with religious fervor. He lacked experience and did not have Houk's support. Yet under Yogi the Yankees won the pennant in 1964. At the end of the year he was fired anyway. The next year he signed with the New York Mets as a coach under Stengel who also had been fired by the Yankees. In April 1970 Berra was named the Mets' manager after Gil Hodges died. In 1973 Berra again led his team to a pennant. His unemotional approach to the game, his unwillingness to overmanage and be the center of attention, and his kindly treatment of his players—all extensions of his personality—had in the past been seen as indications of his managerial weakness. After Berra won in 1973, his critics reevaluated his managerial attributes. They began to see the effect of his honesty and his unusual patience on his players. When his team fell far behind, he never panicked. In both years when he won pennants, key players had been injured, and all along he quietly insisted that when they recovered, his teams would win. Both years the players recovered. Both years the teams won. After the first pennant in 1964 they said he was lucky. After the second they better understood the shy, relaxed Mr. Berra, though he is still criticized for an inability to effectively tongue-lash a player or verbally puff him up.

On a kitchen cabinet door of Berra's home was Scotch-taped a saying by the Roman poet Horace. "Adversity has the effect of eliciting talents which in prosperous circumstances would have lain dormant." If anyone had to battle adversity, Berra did.

Many years after the night when Berra thanked the people for "making this night necessary" Yogi appeared at a sports banquet and made a speech. When Berra first joined the Yankees, Jackie Farrell, the head of the Yankees' speakers' bureau, would make the speech and Yogi would smile and sign autographs. Today Berra does his own talking, and in his own quiet way he has become the Mets' best PR man. On this occasion he harked back to his famous speech and then concluded, "I want to thank everyone here for making this night *unbearable*." Everyone laughed loudly, and Yogi stood before them, grinning at his malapropism.

"They say he's funny," Casey Stengel once said. "Well, he has a lovely wife and family, a beautiful home, money in the bank, and he plays golf with millionaires. What's funny about that?"

With Berra leading the way, the Yankees with ten games to go in the '55 season grabbed first place and never lost it. The Indians, confident of repeating, had printed world series tickets and mailed them out. When they were forced to return more than $3,000,000 in ticket orders, on the envelope of each refund was the doleful inscription, "We're sorry."

In the National League the Brooklyn Dodgers swept through their league, winning twenty of their first twenty-two games with husky right-hander Don Newcombe, back from the Army, 18–1 by July 31, and 20–5 for the season. Dodger stars Duke Snider, Roy Campanella, and Carl Furillo all hit over .300, with Gil Hodges only a few points below, and though Jackie Robinson was nearing retirement, he was still the most exciting performer in the National League. Snider, the Dodger center fielder, the batting star of the team, hit forty-two home runs and drove in 136 runs. One of the most provocative questions in professional sports was, "Who would you rather have on your team, Snider, Mantle, or Willie Mays?" Many a fight was started over that question.

Coming into the series, manager Stengel was realistically worried. The Yankees had stolen the pennant from the Indians on the strength of its young pitching, but only Whitey Ford and Tommy Byrne had ever pitched in a series before, and Stengel disliked playing inexperienced men in a series if he could avoid it. Turley, Larsen, and Grim were untested. Previous series' stalwarts Raschi, Reynolds, and Lopat were now all names from the past.

The other major problem Stengel faced was a shortage of experienced outfielders. Hank Bauer, who had had a brilliant year, was sound, but Mickey Mantle's torn thigh muscle had not allowed him to do much more than pinch hit during the last two weeks of the season. Stengel would have to rely on the inexperienced Ellie Howard and Bob Cerv, an unpalatable but unavoidable move for Stengel who strongly believed in the importance of playing veterans in pressure-packed games.

The infield picture was not much brighter. Bill Skowron, who platooned with Joe Collins, was favoring his broken toe and was untested in series play. At second Martin had hit well, but his fielding was uncertain, and at short both Rizzuto and Coleman had stopped hitting. Gil McDougald, at third, was a tower of strength, and catcher Berra, the MVP, was in a class by himself. Overall, though, because of injuries and inexperience, Stengel was not optimistic. Yet the Old Man, whose craggy face was gracing the cover of *Time* magazine, hadn't been optimistic about winning the pennant, either. The schedule for this subway series called for two games in the Stadium, three in Ebbets Field, and the final two back at the Stadium. After 63,000 Stadium spectators bowed their heads in silence for a minute to pray for the recovery of President Eisenhower from a heart attack, Whitey Ford and Don Newcombe opened the series for their respective teams.

Neither pitcher was sharp. The Dodgers took an early lead in the second inning on a short, opposite-field home run by Carl Furillo, a triple by Robinson, and a line single by second-baseman Don Zimmer. In the third Duke Snider hit a lead-off home run into the third deck of the right-field Stadium stands, but the Yankees came back on a walk to Collins and a long home run by rookie Ellie Howard in his first series at-bat. The Yankees tied the score 3–3 on a cheap run in the third, and against Newcombe in the fourth Joe Collins, unpublicized and rarely appreciated, led off with a pop fly home run for a 4–3 Yankee lead. A low-ball hitter, Collins had played against low-ball pitcher Newcombe in the International League, where the Yankee first-baseman had always had great success against him. In the sixth inning Collins faced Newcombe again and this time blasted a towering two-run shot into the right-center field bleachers to give the Yankees a 6–3 lead and the game. The Dodgers scored two more runs on a sacrifice fly and a steal of home by the electric Jackie Robinson, but Bob Grim relieved in the ninth to protect Ford's win.

The Yankees won the dull second game 4–2, but it was a disastrous victory. Hank Bauer singled in the first inning and when he tried to steal second, he suffered a severely pulled muscle in his right thigh. Bauer was forced to join Mantle on the bench. Stengel shifted the gimpy-kneed Noren from center to left, moved the strong-armed Howard from left to right, and started the inexperienced Bob Cerv in center.

Duke Snider drove Pee Wee Reese home from second for the first run of the game in the fourth, lining a hit into the right-field corner where Howard retrieved the ball and threw Snider out at second to end the threat. In the bottom of the fourth, after Noren limped into a double play, Howard singled, Collins walked, and Berra and Martin followed with run-producing singles to give the Yankees a 2–1 lead. Then when Dodger pitcher Billy Loes plunked pinch hitter

Eddie Robinson on the shoulder to load the bases, Yankee pitcher Tommy Byrne hammered a single over second base to score the third and fourth Yankee runs. On the mound Byrne limited the Dodgers to five hits and became the first left-hander to pitch a winning complete game against Brooklyn since September of the year before! Byrne garbaged the Dodgers to death, throwing change-ups and off-speed curve balls, keeping the Dodger power hitters off-stride.

When the series shifted to Ebbets Field, Dodger Manager Walter Alston predicted that the Dodgers would be a much tougher club, and he was right. Brooklyn won all three of its games in the little bandbox.

Dodger left-hander Johnny Podres started the third game against Bob Turley, but the Yankee righty was unable to survive the second inning, as Roy Campanella hit a towering two-run home run to spearhead a Dodger four-run outburst. Against Yankee relief pitching the Dodgers nickel-and-dimed the Yankees for four more runs for a total of eight. In the seventh Jackie Robinson again demonstrated his brilliant base-running ability, doubling to left and rounding second widely, challenging left-fielder Ellie Howard to throw him out. Howard threw back to second, and Robinson, grinning, steamed into third easily. He then scored when Sandy Amoros singled through a drawn-in infield.

For the Yankees Mantle, impatient and frustrated but still limping, asked manager Stengel if he could start the game in center, but after he had trouble catching a routine fly ball in the first inning, he moved to right field for the rest of the game rather than come out. In the second inning Mantle hit a towering home run that cleared the center-field wall in Ebbets Field, 400 feet from the plate, good for two runs. In the seventh Andy Carey, the forgotten Yankee, pinch hit an RBI triple, but Podres allowed no other damage and the Dodgers won 8-3.

The Yankees took a 3–1 lead in the fourth inning of the fourth game, but Campanella homered against Don Larsen, Furillo singled, and Hodges hit another home run to give Brooklyn a 4–3 lead. In the top of the fifth Larsen hit a high foul ball that struck Yankee owner Del Webb right on the top of the head, knocking him dizzy and sending him to the trainer's room for attention. In the bottom of the fifth Larsen joined Webb after he walked Junior Gilliam, who immediately stole second base. Stengel replaced Larsen with rookie John Kucks, and when Reese smashed a grounder wide of first, Joe Collins made the stop but had to eat the ball when the nervous Kucks forgot to cover first. Stengel clenched his fists in frustration. Kucks, shaken, made too fine a pitch to Snider, and the Duke hit a three-run home run into Bedford Avenue as the Dodgers won the game 8–5 behind the relief work of Clem Labine.

In the fifth game, with Mantle and Bauer still watching from the bench, Stengel started Bob Grim, a twenty-game winner last year, this year a 7–5 pitcher with one complete game and an ERA over four. Rookie Roger Craig started for the Dodgers. Grim pitched well, his slider sharp and effective, but the contours of Ebbets Field conspired to defeat him. In the second inning Gil Hodges singled and the Dodger left fielder, a Cuban national by the name of Edmundo Isasi Amoros, nicknamed Sandy by his teammates, lifted a short 300-foot pop fly down the right-field line that just barely cleared the right-field wall for a 2–0 Dodger lead. In the third Snider lofted a similar pop-up that dropped teasingly over the wall for a home run and a 3–0 lead. Snider batted again in the fifth, and this time hit a soaring home run that left few doubts about its destination, scattering passers-by ambling along Bedford Avenue far over the wall. Brooklyn led 5–0 and the Yankees were unable to catch up. Craig allowed a couple of late-inning home runs by Berra and Bob Cerv, and reliefer Labine allowed still another home run by Berra, but the Dodgers had scored enough runs against Grim to win 5–3, taking a 3–2 lead in the series. Reporters flocked to question Amoros about his home run but discovered that the native of Matanzas, Cuba, spoke only Spanish. Amoros knew only one or two words of English. One of those words was "curve." He pronounced it "coive."

Back at the Stadium, the Yankees needed both of the final two games to keep the Dodgers from winning their first world championship. Ford started the sixth game against a young left-handed phenom named Karl Spooner. Spooner, only 22, possessed a blazing fast ball, and when he could control it, he was devastating. In one regular season game he had struck out seventeen batters and pitched a one-hitter. In another game he struck out fifteen batters. Against the Yankees he struck out one batter. It was the only one he retired. In the first inning Spooner allowed two walks, two singles and a three-run home run by Bill Skowron for a 5–0 Yankee lead. Ford allowed only four hits in the 5–1 Yankee victory. Hank Bauer, back in right, connected for three hits in four at-bats. The seventh game would decide.

October 4 was a magnificent autumn day. The colorful bunting was draped around the Stadium, and under a deep-blue sky a shirt-sleeved crowd packed into the ball park. The managers chose left-handed pitchers to start, Tommy Byrne for the Yankees, John Podres for the Dodgers, and they produced an exciting pitchers' duel.

Podres was sailing beautifully through the sixth holding a 2–0 lead, throwing fast balls past the Yankees who were expecting him to throw his annoying change-up. All through the game the Yankee batters were saying, "We can beat this guy. He has nothing," but his nothing was keeping them shut out. In the sixth the Yankees still hadn't scored when Billy Martin led off and worked Podres for a walk and McDougald singled him to second. Yogi Berra was the batter. The overflow Stadium crowd began a rhythmic chant, "We want a hit," the words unclear as they rumbled from the reserve seats behind home plate and from the distant bleacher seats. Podres fed the Yankee catcher an outside fast ball. Yogi, looking for the change-up, swung late and lined the ball on a high-arching lob towards the left-field flagpole. It was a nine-iron shot headed toward the seats.

The large Stadium crowd stood and strained to see whether the ball was going to be a home run, a ground-rule double, or a long foul. That left fielder Sandy Amoros would catch the ball was not even considered. Inexplicably Amoros had not played Berra to pull, and instead was closer to the foul line than normal. Amoros, in pursuit of the ball on the dead run, was trying to follow the flight of the ball and at the same time prevent a collision with the fast-approaching low Stadium wall in left field. Just as his right foot reached the wall, Amoros stuck out his gloved right hand and caught the ball before it landed in front of the railing just fair of the foul pole. He wheeeled and fired a strike to Reese, still standing and waiting for the relay, and across the diamond Reese fired a long one-hop relay to first-baseman Hodges, who touched the bag just before the desperate McDougald slid back in. It was a double play, and when Hank Bauer grounded out to end the inning, a tremendous disappointment enveloped the Yankee dugout. "No way he catches that ball," all the Yankees were mumbling.

As all of Brooklyn held its breath in the ninth inning, Podres retired Skowron, Cerv, and Howard in order. When shortstop Reese gobbled up Howard's two-hopper and threw it easily to Hodges at first, the Dodgers' quest for their first series victory was over. After six tries, beginning in 1916, Brooklyn had finally won a championship. Podres allowed the Yankees eight hits in the 2–0 Dodger victory.

When the final out was completed, Billy Martin burst into uncontrollable sobbing, and when he entered the locker room pounded on the lockers with his fists, lacerating his hands. Martin hid in the trainer's room so his teammates wouldn't see his tears. An hour passed before he was able to control his emotions.

In the Dodger locker room none of the reporters were able to interview Amoros because of the language barrier, but his toothy grin was featured in every newspaper the next day. That winter Podres, the pitching hero, single and 1-A, was rewarded for his efforts by being drafted the same way a draft board had been pressured into drafting Billy Martin after his series heroics in 1953.

"Podres is paying the penalty for being a star," war hero Ted Williams said after he learned that the Dodger pitcher had been drafted. "If Podres had lost those series games, he would probably still be with the Dodgers. Gutless draft boards and gutless politicians get a few letters and panic. They make an object lesson out of a guy like Podres. They make me sick."

After the final game in the Brooklyn locker room a local politician, John Cashman, borough president of Brooklyn, exulted with the rest of the Dodgers. "The Dodgers," he proclaimed, "must never be allowed to leave Brooklyn."

The Yankees' season did not end with their defeat in the world series in 1955. Two weeks after the final series game the team embarked on a month-long goodwill tour of the Far East sponsored by the U. S. Government and Pepsi-Cola. The Yankees spent two weeks in Hawaii and then more than two weeks flying to Wake Island, the Philippines, Guam, and finally to Japan, playing twenty-four exhibition games before throngs of fanatical fans and admirers. Sixty or seventy thousand people attended each game, and wherever the Yankees went they were treated like visiting royalty, especially in baseball-crazy Japan, where two million people lined the streets of Tokyo to greet them.

Before they departed, most of the Yankees had not been enthusiastic about going. They had just completed a long, grueling season, but under Weiss's thinly veiled threats of punitive action, all the players agreed to go except Phil Rizzuto, who refused to leave his pregnant wife behind. Those who went were thankful for the unique experience. Weiss allowed the players' wives to go, and

John Kucks, Ed Robinson, and Andy Carey all got married the week before the trip so they could bring along their brides.

Before the team played its first exhibition game, Stengel assembled his players for a short talk. "Fellas," the Yankee manager said, "we're going on this trip to show the Japanese how to play this game. We're going to show them what this game is all about. And you fellows are going to perform 100 percent because your jobs next year will depend on how well you do. Your jobs are at stake. So you'll be hustling. You'll be winning. You'll be trying to earn a job for next year." The Yankees were playing the best professional talent in the Far East. When the tour ended, the Yankees returned with a 23–0–1 record. Though it was a pleasure trip, Stengel's primary consideration was nevertheless to win the ball games. That was the only way Stengel knew how to play.

The twenty-four game exhibition schedule enabled Stengel to prepare for 1956. He assessed the abilities of his rookies: Howard, Kucks, and another young pitcher, Tom Sturdivant. All played exceptionally well, and the slider that Kucks learned from Jim Turner in Japan made him the most effective pitcher on the tour. With Rizzuto back in the States, Gil McDougald kept kidding Stengel to let him play shortstop, and when Stengel finally relented, McDougald turned out to be as excellent a shortstop as he was a second- and third-baseman. In 1956 McDougald was named the All-Star American League shortstop, and Rizzuto was released. Andy Carey hit thirteen home runs to lead the Yankees and decided that he should be a home-run hitting pull-hitter, thus helping to ruin his career.

Along the way the Yankees visited the Imperial Palace in Tokyo. They visited Hiroshima, where only ten years before the U. S. had ended the second world war by dropping an atomic bomb. The ghost town looked like a movie set with pasteboard fronts and nothing behind them. The team was introduced to Japanese Prime Minister Hatoyama. He asked several of the players if they had ever been to the Far East before. Hank Bauer, the ex-Marine, nodded his head yes.

"When was that?" Prime Minister Hatoyama asked.

"When I landed on the beach at Iwo Jima," Bauer said. There was an uncomfortable silence as the prime minister quickly changed the subject.

Aside from the baseball aspects of the trip, it was a one-month happening for the players. Each player was given $500 in Japanese yen to spend, 180,000 yen, and the nightly poker games were played with Japanese money, the participants greatly enjoying a ten thousand yen minimum raise.

In Japan the players didn't have to worry about the eagle eye of the American press, and they let their hair down more than usual. Stengel and some of the players left their wives behind and visited the geisha houses for a massage. The liquor flowed freely. On the way from Tokyo to Sapporo, Billy Martin said to Mickey Mantle and Whitey Ford, "It's Wednesday, guys. How 'bout us planning to get some sleep by Friday?"

Martin was the life of the party. While the team was in Tokyo, Billy and Mickey were in the bar of the hotel at about three in the morning, when Billy decided that he wanted to have a party. In each of the players' rooms the phones jangled in their cradles, awakening the occupants. It was Billy on the other end of the line. "There's a big fight in the bar," Martin yelled, "and Mickey's getting hit. Hurry." Mantle, standing behind Martin, was banging two chairs together and screaming, "Help, help!" By the time Martin had called the troops, the entire team was in the bar laughing and drinking, some of the men in their undershorts, some in kimonos. Stengel was in attendance wearing screaming red pajamas. The party went on for hours, and when it ended Don Larsen fixed perpetrators Martin and Mantle. He signed their names to every one of the bar checks.

There were also lighter moments during the games. Before each game the Yankees were given a cocktail party, and every once in a while a player would have one Scotch and soda too many, and funny situations would result. Against the Tokyo Giants Whitey Ford was pitching, and there was a runner on second base. Ford signaled for a pick-off at second which neither McDougald at short or Martin at second saw him give. Ford spun around and fired the ball to second, and when no one covered, the ball sailed toward center field and struck the second-base umpire, who was standing right behind the bag, on the forehead and ricocheted past right-fielder Hank Bauer, who was trying to work off a hangover. Bauer, who had no idea how the ball got into the outfield in the first place, started weaving after it as the runner lit for home. Gil McDougald, meanwhile, walked over to see if the beaned umpire was all right. McDougald looked at him standing there, arms crossed, poker-faced like the inscrutable Buddha. He looked back at McDougald. The Oriental umpire never changed expressions, never moved a muscle. Gil then walked to the mound to talk with his pitcher. "Whitey," Gil said, trying not to laugh, "that's the fuckin' tip-off on you. When you can hit a guy dead center from sixty feet and you don't even leave a mark on him. Pal, can you imagine what it's like to have to play the infield behind you?" Meanwhile, by the time Bauer finally ran down the ball and threw it back into the infield, the runner could have circled the bases twice.

When the team finally returned from its travels, everybody needed a vacation from the vacation.

1956

An awesome season . . . The golden year of Mickey Mantle . . . Larsen's perfection . . . The last subway series

President Eisenhower recovered fully from his fall heart attack, and in the early spring of 1956 the powerful Republican incumbent ignored the upcoming presidential election, leaving Democratic aspirants Estes Kefauver and Adlai Stevenson to battle each other while he kept an eye on the dangerous Middle-East situation. Inside the U. S. a revolution was fomenting as a result of a Supreme Court ruling which held school segregation to be unconstitutional. There was dismay and fear among rural southern whites. In Birmingham several whites attacked Negro singer Nat King Cole during a performance in front of a white audience. The local White Citizen's Council in Birmingham had been campaigning to ban all Negro music because of its "decadent" nature.

The problems of the world did not concern Yankee manager Stengel, though. He had his own headaches. From the start of the spring training period in St. Petersburg, the Yankees were plagued by an alarming number of serious injuries. Early in camp Mickey Mantle again pulled the hamstring that had hampered him through the final weeks of the '55 season, and Gil McDougald, Stengel's first choice to be the starting shortstop, suffered a strained tendon in his left knee when he unaccountably slipped on oil-slick pavement in Miami and fell awkwardly. Bob Cerv pulled a muscle in his stomach and was unable to run. Ellie Howard fractured a finger, and Norm Siebern, a smooth rookie outfielder Stengel was counting on to play left, raced for a long fly ball and crashed heavily into the concrete outfield wall of Al Lang Field, fracturing his left kneecap. Compounding Stengel's woes were the weakened conditions of Irv Noren and Billy Hunter. Noren's knees were still too wobbly for him to be useful, even after two operations, and Hunter had not recovered from the broken ankle he suffered at Denver the year before. For much of spring training the Yankee team off the field was almost as strong as the one on the field.

There was a bevy of new faces in camp, talented farm prospects who greatly impressed manager Stengel. Siebern, 23 years old, had been a Birmingham outfield star in 1953, and after two years in the service, he was the most impressive newcomer until his collision with the outfield wall. There were three infield standouts: Tony Kubek, a tall 20-year-old infielder-outfielder who hit .334 at Quincy in the Three-I League; Bobby Richardson, a stocky 21-year-old infielder who hit .296 at Denver in the International League; and 23-year-old Jerry Lumpe, who after two years in the service had hit .301 at Binghamton, outpolling Luis Aparicio as the league's top shortstop. Lumpe was quick and agile and seemed the best bet of the three to stick with the Yankees.

To the pitching staff George Weiss promoted Rip Coleman, 25 years old, an eternal prospect with blinding speed and a poor sense of direction, and Maurice McDermott, once a young star with Boston, but now a hard-throwing veteran with time running out. From the beginning of spring training McDermott got off on the wrong foot with Stengel. At three in the morning McDermott strolled unsteadily into the Soreno Hotel lobby where Stengel was still holding court with reporters. They both got into the elevator, and Casey looked up at the big pitcher and said, "Drinking again?" And Maurie said, "Me too, Case."

Don Larsen, another pitcher with a growing reputation as a night owl, made headlines when he wrapped his rented car around a telephone pole at five o'clock in the morning. He was fined by the city of St. Petersburg for "assumed speeding," but Larsen explained to his manager that he had fallen asleep at the wheel. Larsen had been working hard during practice so Stengel did not fine him. Instead Stengel made him run wind sprints in the outfield. "He's tired," Stengel said, "but he ain't hurt."

When the season opened Stengel shipped Siebern, Kubek, and Richardson to Denver and named Lumpe the starting shortstop while McDougald recovered from his knee injury. Stengel had many talented bodies to play the other infield positions, but he wasn't impressed by any one set combination, and thus played musical infielders during most of the spring. Bill Skowron was beginning to push Joe Collins and Ed Robinson farther and farther into the background, and in May Robinson was sold to the A's. Coleman and Martin split the second-base duties, and Andy Carey started at third. At catcher Yogi Berra was starting his tenth season. In the outfield Hank Bauer was in right; Mantle, sufficiently recovered from his leg woes, was in center; and Ellie Howard was in left field. Outfield reserves Bob Cerv and Irv Noren were out with injuries. Stengel could not afford another outfielder to be injured.

Stengel was satisfied with his pitching staff. Ford was the best left-hander in the American League, and both Turley and Larsen were instrumental in the Yankees' 1955 pennant victory. Tom Byrne was still pitching well despite his 37 years, and Bob Grim, a bullpen star after his arm injury, Tom Morgan, and Jim Konstanty formed an excellent relief corps. Two youngsters, Johnny Kucks and Tom Sturdivant, pitched well during the exhibition season, though Stengel was not sure how much they were going to contribute.

After a successful opening set of games with the Washington Senators in the nation's capital, when the Yankees returned to the Stadium, shortstop Jerry Lumpe began having difficulty holding onto ground balls and throwing accurately. In the first nine games Lumpe was charged with eight errors. The combination of internal pressure, the fans' booing, and manager Stengel's lack of confidence in him made Lumpe press harder and harder, forcing Stengel to bench him. Gil McDougald returned as shortstop, and Martin played second.

Lumpe never received another chance. McDougald played so well that he was named the all-star shortstop in the American League, the third position he started in an all-star game. A week after Stengel benched Lumpe, he sent him down to Richmond, Virginia.

Everyone else was playing well, especially Mickey Mantle who for the first time was fulfilling his promise of super-stardom. In the opening game of the season against Washington in Griffith Stadium, a difficult home-run park, Mantle hit two towering home runs that were measured as traveling over 450 feet each. When the Yankees returned to the Stadium, Mantle showed that those eye-opening shots were not flukes, and during the Yankees' opening homestand a towering Mantle home run was a common occurrence. Feather-hungry sportswriters wrote reams and reams of columns about Mantle and his long home runs, and flocks of customers bought tickets to see the Yankees and Mantle. In one scoreless contest against the A's early in May at the Stadium, Mantle waited on a change-up thrown by a journeyman pitcher named Lou Kretlow, and jerked the ball high and deep more than 400 feet into the third deck of the right-field stands. Then when Kansas City tied the game, Mickey lined another shot that hit the facade hanging *above* the third deck just fair of the pole to win the game.

Through mid-May Mantle and Yogi Berra supplied most of the firepower to keep the Yankees in or close to the lead, with Cleveland again supplying the opposition. Berra, not normally a spring hitter, began the season with a rush, stroking twelve home runs and getting better pitches to hit because pitchers feared walking him to have to pitch to Mantle with a runner on base. Yogi was hitting around .350, and he and Mantle were being touted as the most explosive batting duo since Ruth and Gehrig.

On May 16 the Yankees defeated Cleveland and for the rest of the season they were never out of first place. In the fourth inning Tom Morgan entered the game and retired every one of the seventeen Indian batters he faced to win the game. Morgan, named the Ploughboy by Yankee announcer Mel Allen because he walked so slowly from the bullpen to the mound, appeared in forty-one games in 1956, won six and saved eleven others. He had come up to the Yankees in 1951 with Mantle and McDougald, but it wasn't until Stengel put him in the bullpen that he was at his best, throwing a hard sinker that caused batters to hit the ball on the ground, inducing rally-killing double plays.

Two bigger surprises, John Kucks and Tom Sturdivant, kept the Yankees on top.

In the spring of 1956 Kucks continued to be outstanding, throwing with a loose-jointed, easy three-quarter motion, imparting a heavy over-spin on the ball that caused batters to break their bats and sting their hands if they didn't meet the ball just right. The fielders enjoyed playing behind Kucks because he pitched quickly. He was the antithesis of Tom Byrne, who held the ball so long before pitching. The Yankees liked to see Kucks pitch on the road because the games went so quickly, and catching a train to the next town was assured. At Yankee Stadium Harry M. Stevens, the concessionaire, hated to see Kucks pitch because short games meant fewer hot dogs and less beer sold.

Off the field Kucks was very quiet and shy around the veterans, a rookie who knew his place, though on the mound he was fiercely competitive, continually swearing at himself for making bad pitches. Kucks got his chance in mid-May when he replaced Tommy Byrne who came down with the flu. Pitching regularly in 1956, Kucks compiled an 18–6 record, a crucial contribution from an unexpected source. By the end of the season Kucks' toothy grin would be renowned across the country after his victory in the final game of the world series. It would be his one year of glory.

Tom Sturdivant, 1–3 with the Yankees as a rookie in '55, had signed in 1948 as a pitcher-infielder. After several years of hitting .250 in the minors, Sturdivant was finally convinced that he had a better chance to make the Yankees as a pitcher. He had a live arm and a major league curve, and he was a tough competitor, a quality that Stengel liked in the kid. Stengel, though, had not pitched Sturdivant until mid-May, Tom doing nothing but throwing batting practice. Finally, several days before cut-down date, Sturdivant went to see Stengel. "Case," he said, "I've always known you to be fair. You give everyone a chance. But the sportswriters have all told me that I'm the unanimous choice to be let go, and I'd hate like hell to leave without getting a chance to pitch." A couple of days later between games of a doubleheader against Baltimore, pitching coach Jim Turner informed Sturdivant that he was the pitcher for the second game. Sturdivant became so tense that the trainer was unable to give him a rubdown. While warming up in the bullpen the relievers, especially Jim Konstanty, the elder statesman of the staff, were kidding Sturdivant about his being chosen by the writers to be the pitcher most likely to be shipped out.

After Sturdivant allowed a first-inning run, he shut out the Orioles the rest of the way until the ninth when Konstanty came in and allowed a couple of runs in relief. Sturdivant was in the clubhouse after the game, packing his bags, waiting for word that he was going to the minors, when Stengel called him into his office. Sturdivant was near tears. "We're keeping ya, young fella," Stengel told him. It was Konstanty Stengel released. Sturdivant remained in the rotation and finished the year 16–8, another crucial contribution from an unexpected source. Along with Ford, Turley, and Larsen, Kucks and Sturdivant gave the Yankees solid pitching.

By late May it was clear that the Yankees were the class of the league, but sports fans were focusing on Mantle's feats even more than on the team's. In one game against the White Sox Mickey had already hit one titanic home run, but the Yankees, when Mantle came up again in the ninth, were still trailing by a run. Mantle proceeded to hit another towering shot deep into the right-field stands to tie the score, and the Yankees went on to win in the tenth. Then after hitting his seventeenth and eighteenth home runs against Kansas City and Detroit on the road, Mantle struck a home run against the Washington Senators at the Stadium during a Memorial Day doubleheader that catapulted him to national fame, prompting cover stories on him in *Time, Newsweek*, and other major magazines.

Washington was leading by a run in the fifth, and the Yankees had two runners on base when Mantle came to the plate. Right-hander Pete Ramos, pitching for the Senators, tried to throw a fast ball by Mantle. Batting left-handed, Mantle took his usual vicious swing, and when the ball hit the bat, it rocketed towards the outfield so fast that the Yankees sitting on the bench almost got whiplash jerking their heads to the right. As the ball reached the apex of its flight, it looked like it was going to be the first fair ball ever hit out of Yankee Stadium. The soaring baseball appeared to be at a point higher than the Stadium roof, 120 feet from the ground. When it finally began descending near where the three-tiered grandstand stopped and the low one-story bullpen and bleachers began, it struck the grandstand's filigreed facade only eighteen inches from the top of the Stadium roof. The ball was going so fast when it struck the facade that it still had enough momentum to rebound more than 100 feet back onto the playing field. Had the facade not stopped it, the ball would have traveled more than 600 feet. It just didn't seem possible that a baseball could be hit that hard.

Mantle's Olympian home run won the game, and in the second game of the doubleheader, he hit another one against Camilo Pascual, this one landing more than 450 feet from home plate into the distant right-field bleachers as the Yankees won again. At the end of May, twenty of Mantle's sixty hits were home runs, and he was leading the majors in batting with a .414 average. With Berra batting .341 in front of him with twelve home runs, the Yankees were making a shambles of the league.

Gil McDougald, Bill Skowron, and Hank Bauer joined Mantle and Berra to give the Yankees a lineup of sluggers not seen in the American League since the Yankee teams of the 1930s with Lou Gehrig, Joe DiMaggio, Tony Lazzari, and Bill Dickey.

After the July 10 all-star break, the Yankees swept three games from Cleveland when Bauer hit a grand slam to win the first game for John Kucks; Tom Sturdivant then threw a two-hitter; and in the third game after Mantle hit his 30th home run, Billy Martin singled with the bases loaded to beat Bob Feller. At the same time, collapsing Chicago lost three straight to the Red Sox. The Yankees were leading the league by nine and a half games. John Drebinger wrote in *The New York Times*, ''If the National League could make up its mind as to the winner of the pennant in that circuit, the world series could start this week.''

The day after the Yankees' sweep of the Indians the starting lineup for the American Association All-Star team was announced. Of the ten starting players named to play against the International League All-Stars, eight of them were playing for Denver, the Yankees' top farm club. The entire American Association starting infield was composed of Yankee farmhands: Marv Throneberry at first, Bobby Richardson at second, Tony Kubek at shortstop, and Woodie Held at third. Denver's John Blanchard was the starting catcher, and Bob Martyn was a Denver outfielder. Both righty and lefty pitchers, Ralph Terry and Jim DePalo, were Denver pitchers. Another Denver player, Norm Siebern, would have been on the team had he not been called up by the Yankees. It was disheartening and depressing not to be a Yankee fan.

With the team so comfortably in the lead, Stengel responded by being as mean and ornery as he had been during the Yankee eighteen-game winning streak of 1953. He bitched to the press and screamed and yelled at Mantle,

Martin, and Ford. Once Stengel was riding Berra, second-guessing his pitch selection through most of the game, until Yogi came into the dugout after an inning was over and threw his mask, chest protector, and mitt right at the Old Man. "You old cocksucker," screamed the normally mild-mannered Berra, "if you want to call the pitches, do it yourself."

During one clubhouse meeting, Jim Turner was talking to the team about how to pitch to the Kansas City Athletic batters when Andy Carey began reading a comic book. While Casey was talking he had noticed Carey sitting in the back reading the comic. "Carey," Stengel screamed, "if it wasn't so fucking late in the season, I'd send you so goddamn far that nobody would ever find you."

Carey, despite Stengel's admonitions to "butcher boy," still tried to pull everything, and Stengel continued to be frustrated by his third-baseman's refusal to hit to the opposite field. Once in Boston, though, Stengel changed his orders to Carey who was batting in the eighth inning with two men on and the Yankees two runs behind. He had swung at two bad pitches, and Stengel, yelling for time-out, called Billy Martin, the on-deck hitter, back into the dugout. "Run out there," Stengel said to Martin, "and tell that guy to swing at a good pitch and hit a home run." "What did you say?" Martin asked. "I said," said Stengel, "to tell that son of a bitch to swing at a good pitch and hit a home run." Martin ran out to relay the message to Carey, and Red Sox catcher Sammy White, overhearing, said, "You guys have to be kidding." On the very next pitch Carey lashed out at a high, inside fast ball and pulled the ball over the left-field fence for the game-winning home run. As Carey rounded third, White said to Martin, "You know, that's the funniest thing I've ever seen in my life."

"When the Old Man tells us to do something," Martin said, "we do it."

It was August 25, Old-Timer's Day at the Stadium, and the old stars were out on the field cavorting before a packed house while some of the Yankees took their pictures. Phil Rizzuto, the 38-year-old all-star shortstop was one of those snapping photographs. Rizzuto didn't realize how soon it would be before he would become one of the old-timers.

This day Weiss and Stengel called Rizzuto from the field into Stengel's office in the clubhouse, and Weiss said, "We're going over the roster. Siebern and Noren are hurt, and we need another left-handed hitting outfielder for the world series. We want to go over this list with you and determine the most logical player we can let go." Rizzuto, flattered that Stengel and Weiss thought so highly of his opinion, readily agreed. Phil went down the list and suggested Charlie Silvera be released because the bullpen catcher never played. Weiss rejected that idea. Rizzuto suggested McDermott, who didn't pitch much. Weiss said no. He suggested Rip Coleman, and Weiss said no. Slowly it started to dawn on Phil. Weiss said, "Let's go over the list again." Again Rizzuto enumerated the players he thought expendable. Again Weiss said no to all of his suggestions. Finally Weiss summoned the nerve to tell Rizzuto what he had had in mind all along. It was Rizzuto who was going to be released. Stengel had McDougald, Coleman, and Billy Martin to play short, and Rizzuto was clearly over the hill. Rizzuto's career, which began in 1941, was over.

In tears, Rizzuto quickly left the Yankee clubhouse and drove home before the other players learned he was cut. Ex-Yankee George Stirnweiss, who had experienced the same rejection only a few years before, accompanied Rizzuto. George was afraid Phil was going to jump off the George Washington Bridge, he was so crushed. Rizzuto, though bitter, wisely did not publicly criticize the Yankee management. The next year he was hired as the team's third broadcaster joining Mel Allen and Red Barber.

In the first week of August the Yankees lost six games in a row, but despite a mediocre 16–15 August record, the team never led the league by fewer than seven games. Mickey Mantle, wearing a knee brace, hit only a handful of home runs in July, but then the pain in his gimpy right knee eased and he hit twelve more in August to give him forty-seven with the coming of September. Mickey needed fourteen homers to break Babe Ruth's hallowed record of sixty in one season. Mantle also had a good shot at the triple crown. He was leading *both leagues* in batting average (.366), home runs (47), and runs batted in (118). Only Rogers Hornsby in 1925, Lou Gehrig in 1934, and Ted Williams in 1942 had ever won the triple crown leading all players in both leagues.

During the first week in September Mantle's chance to catch Babe Ruth disappeared when he pulled a groin muscle running the bases, and in the first ten September games he failed to hit one home run or drive in one run as his batting average slipped a couple of points below Ted Williams' and his RBI lead over Tiger outfield star Al Kaline shrank. Mantle was mired in a 5–34 slump, and he made it more difficult by flying into rages at himself. Opposing pitchers stopped giving him strikes to hit, and in his strong desire to break Ruth's home run record, he reverted to his old habit of swinging at bad pitches, especially the high fast ball just out of the strike zone. When he struck out, the resounding metallic sound of the collision of Mantle's spikes and the dugout water cooler could be heard by fans sitting rows behind the Yankee bench.

Characteristically, it was the combination of buddies Mantle and Ford who won the game that clinched the pennant for the Yankees on September 17. Ford, who was 19–6 in 1956, battled Billy Pierce of the White Sox to a 2–2 tie through the eleventh inning in Comiskey Park when in the top of the eleventh Mantle came to bat right-handed against the left-handed Pierce and stroked his fiftieth home run, a towering line drive that traveled more than 400 feet into the upper stands in left field. It was Stengel's seventh pennant in eight years of managing the Yankees.

Mantle continued to slug the ball in the Yankees' next three games against the Red Sox, repassing Williams in batting average with a six for nine series including his fifty-first home run. Williams was held to two for eleven by the Yankee pitchers. In the final Fenway game Mantle again pulled his groin muscle running out a double, but his sudden hitting spurt enabled him to finish the season ahead of Williams in hitting (.353 to .345) and ahead of Kaline in runs batted in (130 to 128). In the final week Mantle managed one more home run to finish with fifty-two, twenty more than runner-up Vic Wertz of the Indians. In addition to leading every batter in both leagues in these three categories, he also led all major leaguers in total bases with 376, runs scored with 132, and slugging with a .705 percentage. Mantle was the unanimous choice as the Most Valuable Player in 1956, and he was given the Hickok Belt as the Professional Athlete of the Year. For the next ten years Mantle was the number-one athlete in all of professional sports, the best-loved and most widely lionized of all American athletes of his era by the time he retired in 1968. He had a career average of .298, and when he retired his 536 home runs placed him fourth on the all-time list behind Babe Ruth (714), Willie Mays (600), and Hank Aaron (554). In 1974 he was elected into the Hall of Fame in his first year of eligibility, only the seventh player to be so honored, joining Ted Williams, Stan Musial, Jackie Robinson, Bob Feller, Sandy Koufax, and Warren Spahn. During his era, Mantle was often compared to stars like Williams or Musial, and in New York City to Duke Snider and Willie Mays. But for Yankee fans, regardless of comparative statistics, none of these other players, as good as they were, could rival the Mick.

In June 1969 the Yankees held a day for Mantle, and 65,000 nostalgic Yankee fans flocked to the ball park to demonstrate their affection for the moody slugger. The Yankees had Mantle ride in a little cart that toured the perimeter of the large ball park, and as the cart slowly circled the Stadium, Mantle smiled self-consciously and waved to the thousands of fans who were waving back to him, clapping, screaming themselves hoarse, and thanking the man for eighteen years of thrills and excitement. As he rode by on that cart, wearing a brown suit instead of the Ajax whiter-than-white pin-stripe uniform with the royal blue number 7 on the back, Mickey waved his blue Yankee cap at the throng. There were tears in the eyes of many of the people there, because with his retirement, the Yankee dynasty came to an end. Mantle was the main reason it was so easy to be arrogant and smug while teasing those foolish enough to root for the cross-town Dodgers or Giants. Mantle brought with him to the ball park an expectation of success. For sore sports, poor losers, and perfectionists, there was only one baseball hero. And that hero was Mantle because he came through so often and failed so seldom. It was almost super-natural how often Mantle would hit one of his towering home runs when the Yankees needed a lift in the late innings. Forever indelibly imprinted in the minds of thousands of baseball fans is a picture of Mantle methodically, purposefully trotting around the bases, clenched fists slowly pumping at his sides, head and eyes down, unsmiling and seemingly unaware of the hysterical adulation swirling about him.

When Mickey Mantle burst into prominence in 1951, baseball experts were awed by his incredible talent. After many years of play the game had evolved into a natural balance with ninety-foot bases which enabled infielders to throw out even the fastest base runners, and distant fences which prevented the hitters from overpowering the pitchers. Mantle threatened the established framework of the game. He could run from home plate to first base in just over three seconds, and he could hit a baseball 500 feet, dwarfing even the largest parks. Had he not constantly suffered from a series of disabling injuries, it is possible that Mantle would have become the greatest baseball player in the entire history of the game. As it was, for fifteen years Mantle was clearly the biggest star, the most valuable player in the game. He was the heart and essence of the Yankee dynasty.

Commerce, Oklahoma, Mantle's home town, is located five miles north of Exit 6 on the Will Rogers Turnpike, not far from where the borders of Oklahoma and Kansas meet the western border of Missouri. Commerce used to be a mining town, though there are no indications of mining activity when you approach the town from Miami to the south. I stopped at a Phillips 66 station that sets along the seemingly deserted Main Street, and was told by an attendant that the Blue Goose Number Six Mine, where Mantle and his father and uncle and other relatives had toiled, had been played out years ago, and that rubber had replaced lead-zinc as Commerce's major industry.

The solitude of the barren town was eerie. It was the Main Street of *The Last Picture Show,* except that it was paved and I didn't see any tumbleweeds. The static, claustrophobic atmosphere was the same. The town sat under a vast sky, and long wisps of white, skinny clouds mixed with gray, puffy ones. All the buildings are one-story, and only the leafy green elm trees prevented one from seeing across the brown plain forever. A young boy in tattered blue jeans rode by on a too-small bicycle. He was carrying his fishing pole. No other cars passed by the gasoline station.

Mantle's childhood home is only a stone's throw from the hulking gray power plant that once surged energy into the Blue Goose Mine where the Mantle family had worked. The mine is closed up now, abandoned, but the awesome pyramids of waste materials stretch as far as the eye can see, giving the area a surrealistic quality. Deep cavernous wells, filled with rainwater, are dug as far into the ground as the mounds are high. Only an occasional hearty tree is interspersed among the barrenness. Mantle's home, also abandoned, still stands. The windows of the one-room shack are all broken. The white paint is peeling badly. It was built, it seems, for dwarves. You have to bend down to go into the kitchen. Inside there is only one bedroom, and in that room Mickey, his older brother, his half-brother, his younger twin brothers, and his sister, all slept. Mickey Mantle as a kid was poor. Really poor.

Because Mutt Mantle, Mickey's father, didn't want him to be a miner and live in this kind of poverty, he was determined that his boy was going to be a baseball player. Mutt Mantle worked for hours teaching his kid to play baseball, and at age 5 Mickey Mantle was learning a trade. Mutt Mantle threw to him right-handed, and Mutt's father threw to him left-handed, as the two older men taught Mickey to switch hit. When Mutt Mantle returned from a long day in the mines to work with Mickey, the young boy stopped playing and started practicing.

The practicing paid dividends. In his midteens Mantle played baseball and football for Commerce High, and barnstormed with a semi-pro outfit called the Baxter Whiz Kids. The manager of the Whiz Kids, Barney Barnett, was one of the men who touted Mickey to Yankee scout Tom Greenwade.

The St. Louis Cardinals had the best opportunity to sign Mantle, but after a Cardinal tryout, scout Runt Marr felt that he was too small to be a prospect.

Mickey was 16 at the time, and stood only 5 foot 7 and weighed barely 150 pounds. At the time he was known as Little Mickey Mantle. The other St. Louis team, the lowly Browns, never even scouted him. The entire Baxter club was supposed to drive the 150 miles across the state of Missouri to Sportsman's Park in St. Louis for tryouts, but on the night of the trip it rained heavily and the tryout was cancelled. Thus when Mantle graduated from Commerce High in the spring of 1949, only Yankee scout Tom Greenwade was interested in him. Mantle signed for a $1,000 bonus, and Greenwade became famous as the scout who signed Mickey Mantle. In truth, Greenwade, though an exceptional scout, was lucky. When he signed Mantle, he had no idea of his potential greatness. Not until Mickey completed two years of minor league ball with Independence in Class D and Joplin in Class C did Greenwade get an inkling of the magnitude of his find.

When Mantle first came up to the Yankees in 1951 he was a child, timid, self-conscious, and completely overwhelmed. Among his teammates he was well-liked from the start because he had a ready smile and was pleasant company. All the young kid wanted of life was to be liked—to be one of the guys.

When the Yankees broke camp and arrived in New York, Mantle, a hayseed from Commerce, Oklahoma, took one look at the Empire State Building and stood in open-mouthed shock. The image of a country rube gaping like a moron in his first face-to-face encounter with an urban society he never could have imagined seems trite, but in Mantle's case it's completely true. Mantle didn't fully comprehend what he was seeing. His world had always been poling for catfish on the Neosho River, working in a lead-zinc mine, or walking through a grassy field with a piece of straw between his teeth. When he was confronted by the hustle and commotion of New York City, he didn't know how to respond, so he instinctively withdrew into himself.

He was not a verbal person except when he felt at ease around his teammates. After Mantle won the Most Valuable Player award for the first time in 1956, teammate and friend Billy Martin badgered him into making an acceptance speech. Martin, a natural, outgoing ham, surely would have spoken an oration. Mantle had no such intentions. With Calvin Coolidge brevity Mickey told him, "I've got news for you, pal. I wrote a speech. Here it is! 'Thanks a lot.' "

Mantle had been a minor league shortstop at Joplin in Class C, and had led the league in errors with 55. He could reach ground balls with the best of them because of his blinding speed, but where he would throw the ball after he caught it no one, including Mickey, ever knew. Stengel moved him to the outfield to take better advantage of his speed, and though Tommy Henrich taught him well how to play the outfield he still was not an instinctive fielder like Willie Mays or Al Kaline. In the vast pastures of Yankee Stadium, Mantle would misjudge a fly ball and then use his tremendous speed to outrun his mistakes. He was stocky and didn't look like a sprinter, but he was the fastest base runner in the major leagues despite all his leg miseries. He was clocked going from home to first in 3 seconds flat batting left-handed and 3.1 seconds batting right-handed. No one has ever done it faster.

As a high school athlete Mantle had contracted osteomyelitis after he was kicked in the shin during a football game. While he was a Yankee the disease remained dormant, though Mantle and his teammates knew the potentially deadly affliction might be reactivated by any jarring shock to the affected area. Yet despite constant admonitions to slide gingerly, Mickey would run and slide just as hard as he could, crashing to the ground and blasting into the base with the brute strength of his 200 pounds. There were times when he would wait too long before sliding, starting only two or three feet from the bag, and when he hit the base opposing infielders claimed they could actually feel the ground shake. Meanwhile, in the Yankee dugout, his teammates would wonder whether the impact would reactivate the osteomyelitis. Nobody's legs were ever built for the strain Mantle placed on his.

His pride subjected his legs to added punishment because even when injured he forced himself to play. During most of his career Mantle was the Yankees' batting star, making the biggest money, and he always felt it was his responsibility to carry the club. When he didn't play, he felt he was letting his teammates down. There were many times when he would wrap himself from ankle to waist and go out to play when most men wouldn't have even dressed for the game.

Mantle, like DiMaggio, was a perfectionist. When he performed below his self-imposed standards, he could fly into fits of uncontrollable rage. Mantle would throw bats and helmets, punch the metal sign on the wall of the dugout that warned the players about socializing with fans, and kick the watercooler. He was some kind of RA! Stengel would become livid when he saw Mantle jeopardize his career by punching the wall or kicking the metal watercooler. "If you get hurt," Casey would say, "it's going to cost you plenty." After one such outburst Stengel went over to the bat rack and handed the kid a bat. "Here," the Yankee manager said. "Why don't you bang yourself on the head with this? If you're so intent on ending your career, you might as well do it quickly and get it over with."

In one game after Mantle struck out, he violently slammed his bat into the bat rack and threw his helmet down. Stengel went up to him and said, "Now Ignatz, this stuff costs money. The next time they strike you out and you get mad, think. Think." The next time Mantle batted, he struck out again. He came back to the dugout and gently laid his bat and helmet down, and walked to the end of the dugout where Stengel was sitting. Mantle put his face about three inches from Casey's and said, "Ha, ha, ha. I struck out again." Stengel and the rest of the Yankees roared.

Stengel, though he constantly criticized Mantle, loved him as a son much as he did Martin and Berra. From the beginning Stengel seemed to take special pleasure in Mantle's development, and though he was quick to criticize the young star, he usually did so for a reason.

"Know when he gets careless?" Stengel would say. "It's when some humpty-dumpty pitcher gets him out. Then he picks up his glove and trots out to center field—talkin' to hisself all the way. He keeps sayin', 'how did that bum get me out.' He keeps thinking about it. Then, all of a sudden, he says, 'Uh oh, there goes the ball,' and somebody on the other team has himself a triple. He gets careless, but he ain't dumb. Why, he's only 25, and he's smarter than I was when I was 30!''

Part of Stengel's genius was that on the Yankees everybody, from the bat boy to the biggest star, was treated alike. With Casey there were no stars on the Yankees, and as a result no one, including Mantle, ever overestimated his own importance. Even after Mantle won the triple crown in 1956, a season where he led the league in almost all batting categories, Stengel still found a way to tell Mantle that he better not become swell-headed. At the end of the season a reporter asked the Yankee manager, ''Who is the greater center fielder, Mantle or DiMaggio?'' Stengel responded, ''I'd have to say DiMaggio because he played right-handed and the park wasn't built for him and he didn't need a manager.'' Actually Stengel's reasons were fictitous, and it is doubtful whether he was really telling the truth when he chose DiMaggio over Mantle. Stengel merely wanted Mantle to know that there were still future goals to be sought. Stengel didn't want Mantle to become complacent. The kid had just won the triple crown. Stengel now wanted him to achieve the goal of becoming the greatest center fielder in the eyes of manager Stengel, a much tougher task. Stengel was challenging him and slapping him down at the same time.

Stengel knew Mantle's moods and understood him as a parent understands his own child. Stengel would deliberately agitate Mantle to make him angry, and when he knew Mantle's legs were killing him, he was always able to get Mickey to play. Before a game Stengel would write Mantle's name on the lineup card and then go into the clubhouse to talk to his star. ''Well, I guess I better keep you out today,'' Stengel would say. This, of course, would irritate Mantle, touching his pride. ''Goddamn it, Case, put me in,'' Mantle would say. ''You sure you want to play?'' Stengel would ask, knowing the answer. Mantle's name was already written on the card. Casey would walk away and give a little wink.

In other areas Stengel was not the best of influences. The Yankee manager had enjoyed his night life while he was a player, and even though George Weiss was always on him to curtail the evening exploits of Mantle, Ford, and Martin, Stengel never interfered with their merriment. Casey himself had always found it much easier to frequent the bars and have a few brews than stay in the hotel room and face the four walls. Stengel knew the loneliness of long road trips. Unfortunately for Mantle and Ford, and especially for Billy Martin, George Weiss was more concerned with the Yankee name than the psyche of his ball players. To Weiss the antics of his players were not amusing.

Another area in which Stengel and the Yankee management did not protect Mantle was that of investments. From the beginning Mantle was a country boy in the hands of city slickers. After the 1951 world series Mantle returned to his Commerce home with his winning share of the world series pot—a $7,000 check. A few days after his return, a man drove up to Mickey's home in a big, black Cadillac convertible with a busty blonde sitting in the passenger seat and two miniature poodles cavorting in the back seat. Mantle and his wife, Merlyn, had just been married. The man introduced himself as an officer in the Will Rogers Insurance Company. ''I want to let you in on a deal,'' the man said. ''You can't pass this by. I'm going to make you a half-owner in the company.''

Mickey listened as the man explained the merits of the company, and then went into the kitchen with Merlyn who suggested that Mickey call Harold Youngman, a trusted advisor. Youngman told Mickey to kick the guy out of the house. "Don't give the son of a bitch a penny," Youngman said. "Not a penny." But when Mickey returned to talk with the stranger, the man produced an ornate stock certificate with an eagle at the top and "Will Rogers Insurance Company" inscribed in flowery letters. Mantle was so impressed that he agreed to invest his world series money in the company. He endorsed his check and handed it over to the stranger, who presented him with the certificate and half-ownership of the company. And with his blonde and two poodles the stranger drove off, never to be seen again. According to Whitey Ford, Mickey still has the stock certificate.

Another inopportune financial move by Mantle was transacted during his second season, in 1952. A hustler contracted with Mantle to be his agent for the fee of 50 percent of all of Mantle's extra-baseball income during the rest of Mickey's life! The Yankee management was so incensed that anyone could be so unscrupulous that Arthur Friedlund, Dan Topping's attorney, stepped in and had the contract voided.

Harold Youngman did well for Mantle. He got Mantle and Whitey Ford to invest in a Holiday Inn in Joplin, Missouri, that did very well. Later Mickey on his own, invested in another motel—but this one had a lien of $60,000 in back taxes that he didn't discover until after he bought it.

During the height of the cold war in the early 1960s Bob Feller, the ex-Cleveland pitcher who himself was a wheeler-dealer, introduced Mantle and Ford and six or seven other Cleveland ball players to a promoter who convinced them to invest in the Canadian Survival Bomb Shelter Corporation. The company was going to build bomb shelters in Canada. It cost Mickey and Whitey $2,500 apiece. Between them they bought 100,000 shares. The stock turned out to be a bomb, not a shelter. Mantle and Ford still have the worthless stock of that company, too.

Later Mickey had an interest in a Dallas insurance company that went under, and in New York City, an employment agency, Mantle Men and Namath Girls, also failed. Mantle was making $100,000 a year, but between his investments and his expensive living habits, there wasn't that much left when he retired.

In order to interview Mantle one first has to catch up with him, not an easy task, because in addition to his public-relations duties for several Dallas, Texas, corporations, Mickey is a serious golfing fanatic, who travels from course to course searching for the perfect hole. With the help of Bob Fishel, formerly the Yankee vice-president in charge of public relations, I was able to catch up with Mantle, cornering him in the Yankee clubhouse after I had traveled to Dallas, his home town, only to learn that he had flown back to New York City to film a TV commercial at the Stadium. In those two days of travel, the common stock of Braniff Airlines went up more than a point.

After I arrived back at Kennedy Airport, my taxi driver, a Puerto Rican emulator of A. J. Foyt, delivered his quivering passenger to the Stadium, and with my luggage in one hand and my tape recorder in the other, I was informed that Mickey was still around and that he would be glad to talk with me.

I opened the heavy steel-gray door leading into the Yankee locker room, and I asked Pete Sheehey, the Yankees' clubhouse man since the days of Ruth and Gehrig, where Mantle was. He pointed to the far end of the locker-lined room, and sure enough, Mantle, dressed in buckskin, was standing by a wall mirror combing his blond hair. All that remained was for me to introduce myself and ask Mickey if he would consent to his fourteen trillionth interview.

I couldn't do it. I just could not approach Mantle and ask him to talk with me. As I stood there, scratching my head and wondering what to do next, I was madder'n hell at myself because I am hardly the shy type and this had never happened to me before. But to me Mickey Mantle was more than an old ball player. He was a legend. As a kid I wore a Mickey Mantle glove, and my uniform number on my Camp Winaukee uniform was 7, and when I went to the dentist, while the dentist was brutally drilling my teeth, I used to imagine that Mickey Mantle had hit a home run and was running around the bases. Usually by the time he crossed the plate, the drilling had been completed. It just was not easy for me to approach the man who had saved me from so much pain in that dentist's chair.

Ellie Howard was sitting at his locker reading his mail, and because I had already interviewed him, and he knew what I was doing, I asked Ellie if he would introduce me to his ex-teammate. Ellie said sure, and introduced me to Mantle and told him about the book. Mantle asked me about some of his other ex-teammates, wondering where they were and what they were doing, and then when I asked him if he would sit and talk with me for a few minutes, Mickey put his arm around my shoulder and with a straight face said "No."

I did a double take. I couldn't believe he had said no. I was stunned. As it turned out, I was another victim of Mantle's practical jokes, for his face then broke into a wide grin and he laughed at my incredulous reaction. "Where do you want to do this?" he asked as I breathed an audible sigh of relief and tried to laugh at his little joke. I told him we could sit right where we were, on a table at the far end of the Yankee locker room, and he agreed.

Stories of Mantle's hot and cold relations with the media people are legend. When he first came up and garrulous reporters asked him questions, he was self-conscious of his Oklahoma twang, and like DiMaggio, wary of the press. Rather than be controversial, he said little or nothing. For many years his relations with the press were either cool or hostile. Only a media blitz by the Yankee front office and Mantle's prodigious feats, which overshadowed all other facets of the kid's personality, kept the press from blasting Mantle with a vengeance. They described him as "spoiled" or "hotheaded" or "stupid" or "arrogant" at times, but they never fully revealed their deep feelings of resentment toward him in those early years. After Mantle was elected into the Hall of Fame by some of those same writers, Mantle expressed surprise that *anyone* voted for him. "We didn't get along too good the first few years," he said.

Mantle seemed to resent all intrusions into his private life, and he had no patience for interviews or photograph sessions. If a writer or photographer was taking too much time, Mickey would become impatient. "How much fucking longer is this going to take?" he would snarl. Mantle was one of the few athletes to get the best of Howard Cosell, because when Humble Howard would ask Mickey a question that Mickey thought to be too personal or controversial, Mickey would listen to the question and then stare into the camera without uttering a single word, ruining the taping and forcing Howard to rephrase or change his question until he asked a question that Mickey would answer. To other reporters Mantle would answer, "How do I know?" to a question he did not wish to answer. Other times his answers were simple, yes-no responses. Still other times his answers were not only unquotable, they were also unprintable.

But on this summery May afternoon Mickey Mantle was in a bubbly, effusive mood, and not once did he seem ill at ease or at a loss for words. On the contrary, he was articulate and honest, and when we finished I admired the guy more than ever.

As Mantle and I sat and talked there was a hum of activity in the Yankee locker room as the players prepared themselves for an afternoon game against Oakland. I asked him about his father and what his father did in the Blue Goose Number Six Mine in Commerce.

Mickey talked softly and slowly with that drawl that he never did lose. "He started out as a shoveler," Mantle said, "that's, you know, when they blast out the lead veins at night where everybody leaves them, and the next day they come up with big shovels, and hell, I don't know how big a can is, but it's a very big can. And he was able to shovel like fifty cans a day, which was great." There was pride in his voice as he spoke. "He was a shoveler when he first went into the mines, and when he died, he was the ground boss. He worked his way all the way up from shoveler to ground boss. He was about 22 or 23 when he started. Let's see. I was about 3 years old then. And he died when he was 39. He worked in the mines all his life.

"Dad was a real good semi-pro ballplayer. He was the one that said that someday there's going to be platooning, you know, two-platooning, and that's the reason he taught me how to be a switch-hitter. He said that someday to be a major league ball player, you're going to have to learn to hit both right-handed and left-handed pitchers, and he said, 'If you can hit both ways, you've got a better chance,' and sure 'nuff, when I joined the Yankees is when Casey Stengel started platooning everybody, so he knew what he was talking about."

"Did you work with your Dad in the mines?" I asked.

"Yeah. I worked in the mines the last two years of high school. In fact when I joined the Yankees in 1951 I was still working in the mines. I was a screen ape."

"A screen ape?" I asked.

"That's a guy that stands over the boulders, the boulders come by that go through a screen, and if they're too big you have to beat them up with a sledge hammer. Everybody thinks I lifted weights or something, you know, because when I first came up I was built good. I'm not built that good anymore."

Mantle looked up and he saw the retired *New York Times* reporter, octogenarian John Drebinger, approaching. Mantle's face broke into a wide grin. Mickey was where he belonged, in a baseball park, in *his* baseball park, and he was enjoying the reunions with his old buddies immensely. "Drebby, oh no," said Mantle. "Goddamn. I thought you'd be dead by now! Good to see you."

Mr. Drebinger, white-haired, crumpled suit, a hearing aid in his ear, shook hands with Mantle, and said, "I'm going into the press room. Might as well have a drink on you. That's what kept you so goddamned healthy!" and he was out the door.

"Did you ever hear about the first year I was supposed to go down to spring training with the Yankees?" Mickey asked. "About George Weiss wanting me to come down to spring training, and I never did show up, so they sent me a telegram saying, 'You know, you're supposed to be down in spring training,' so I had to call him back collect and tell him, 'Listen, you're going to have to send me the money. I don't have enough money to come down to spring training.' So they sent me a ticket to go to Phoenix. I was working in the mines then." Mantle was making a buck and a quarter an hour at the time. "That was my last year in the mines." Mickey continued. "When the baseball season was over at Independence in 1949, I went back to the mines, and when the baseball season at Joplin was over in 1950, I went back to the mines. I think I made $35 a week. My Dad was making about $100.

"You remember when I stepped on that drain in the 1951 world series?" he asked. "Most people don't know that it was Willie Mays that hit the ball," Mickey said. "I was playing right field, chasing a pop fly into center field, and I was getting ready to catch it, and Joe DiMaggio was standing under it and he hollered, 'I got it,' and you don't want to run into Joe DiMaggio," Mickey chuckled. "I slid on the brakes as hard as I could and my back spikes got caught on the drain, they had a rubber drain, and when they did, my knee just went right straight out. You know. It was stiff. Scared the shit out of me. I didn't know what happened.

"And then they took me to the hospital, and that's when I found out Dad was sick. My Dad was sitting on the side of me in the cab to the hospital," Mantle patted the table with his right hand, "and my knee had swelled up so bad I couldn't even move it. Dad got out of the cab first, and I put my arm around his shoulders to jump out of the cab, put my weight on him like this," and Mickey leaned on me, his strength weighing heavily on my left shoulder, "and he just collapsed on the sidewalk. They call it Hodgkin's Disease. It had eaten up his whole back. My mother told me later that he hadn't slept in bed for a year. But he never would tell me about it. That's the first I even knew he was sick. He still looked pretty good at the time. He had lost some weight. I noticed that he had lost a lot of weight. And when he crumpled to the ground, that's the first I even knew he was sick." Mickey screwed up his face and sighed.

"I got operated on," Mickey continued, "and then we went home, and he went back to work, and I could tell that he was really sick then. And I was told to take him to Mayo's Clinic, so when I got well I took him up there, and they cut him open and sewed him back up, and they said, 'Just let him do whatever he wants to. He doesn't have much longer to live.' And he went back to the mines. He worked until about a month before he died, in the spring of 1952."

Mutt Mantle was 39 years old when he died, and when he died a piece of Mickey died, too. Mantle at 20 was alone—without his closest friend. When the Yankees in mid-season 1951 sent Mantle to Kansas City for a couple of months, Mickey was so humiliated that he considered quitting and going home, but Mutt Mantle told him, "If that's all the guts you have, then come home." Mantle stayed, hit .361 at Kansas City, and returned to the Yankees before long.

I looked at Mantle sitting beside me. "Do you still miss him?" I said. "Do you still think about him?"

Mickey nodded. "Oh yes," he said. "I dream about him all the time."

When his father died, Mantle's burdens were compounded by a fear of early death. His two uncles and now his father, all were dead before they were forty. Mickey was convinced that he, too, would suffer an early demise. And from that year on, quite logically, he lived his life as though each day would be his last, and he did party a great deal, and he enjoyed his liquor, and he enjoyed his fun. To Mantle money was like Monopoly money. He was generous to a fault, lending money all the time to his less wealthy teammates. When he entered into a joint venture with other teammates, like the summer he and several others rented a house in the suburbs, Mantle would never allow the others to contribute a penny. He paid all the bills. In 1957, when Jerry Lumpe joined the Yankees, Mantle was moving out of his house. He gave the keys to Lumpe; Lumpe and his family lived there all season. Mantle did not allow Lumpe to pay rent. If Mickey rode in a cab with someone or ate at a restaurant with others, Mickey stubbornly insisted on picking up the tab. No matter how many others there were, Mantle footed the bill. He lived in the best hotels, ate in the most expensive restaurants, drank the best liquor, and lots of it, and spent money like he would be wealthy forever or dead at an early age, or both.

Mantle's fear of an early death haunted him despite assurances from his concerned teammates who argued that he was the picture of health. Once Hank Bauer saw that Mickey had arrived for a game rather hung over, and Bauer suggested that he wasn't serious enough, that he shouldn't be staying out so much and abusing his body.

Mantle looked at Hank through bloodshot eyes. "My father died young," Mickey said. "I'm not going to be cheated."

Mantle, born in 1930, has passed his fortieth birthday, and his fears of early death have subsided. But paradoxically, replacing those neuroses of an early death are neuroses arising from the aging process, that with his fortieth birthday his skills have been eroded, his reflexes slowed, and with his retirement from the Yankees he has been tormented by the realization that he would never again be able to play the game his father taught him, the game he loved so passionately for so long. Being voted into the Hall of Fame in 1974 was a welcome honor, but for Mantle, a man who never was impressed by his own accomplishments, he would trade all his awards, trophies, and honors to be able to play again, to be able to cavort with his teammates, to be able to hit long home runs and hear once again the adulation of the crowd. Today if Mickey drinks, it is not to cheat death, but to cheat reality.

"I never used to read scrapbooks," Mickey said softly. "Never. But I've gotten about fifty of them in the past few years from fans who saved them and sent them to me. I always keep one by my toilet. I read it every morning.

"I miss baseball," he said. "Since I've been away from it, I keep having nightmares. I always dream that I'm trying to make a comeback, you know, and I can't hit the fucking ball, and it pisses me off." Mickey was wringing his hands as he spoke. "Pitchers throw me fast balls, and I just can't hit them anymore. There's another nightmare. I'll be outside Yankee Stadium trying to get in, and I can hear them announcing my name on the loudspeaker, for me to hit, you know, and I'm outside and I can't get in. I hear Casey asking, 'Where's Mickey?' But I can't get in. Those are my two bad dreams."

"Did you ever think of coming back into baseball?" I asked.

"Not too much, no. I can do better outside of baseball than I can being coach. I do public-relations work in Dallas for the Metro Bank and the Reserve Life Insurance Company. I got to think of my family, too."

"Did you enjoy playing for Casey Stengel?"

"Yip," he said. "I really did. When my Dad died, and I was only 19 when my Dad died, I kinda looked toward Casey. Casey was like my Dad. Somewhere along the line my Dad talked to him and told him he'd appreciate it if he would look after me, and I think that Casey always remembered that, and took more of an interest in me than he would've otherwise.

"You know," said Mantle, "I always felt that I was really overpaid. Whitey and I figured out that I had 1,700 walks and 1,800 strikeouts. That's a total of 3,500. And if you get up 500 times a year, you figure I spent seven years where I never hit the ball!" Mickey laughed raucously.

"People think that I was always hurt," Mantle said with a sigh, "but I played for eighteen years. I played more games as a Yankee than anyone else who ever played for them." Surrounding the still-young Mantle was an overwhelming feeling of sadness. "You know," he said, "I miss playing very much."

The 1956 Yankee lineup, which included Mantle, Yogi Berra, Moose Skowron, Hank Bauer, and Gil McDougald, hit 190 home runs to break the one-season American League record of 182 set by the Gehrig, DiMaggio, Dickey Yankees of 1936.

Mantle, who hit fifty-two homers, led both leagues in home runs and won the Most Valuable Player of the American League, and Berra, after winning the MVP the past two seasons, finished second to Mantle after one of his finest years. Yogi batted .298 and slugged thirty home runs, the most hit by an American League catcher in one season. He drove in 105 runs. Bill Skowron, given a chance to play first base every day with Joe Collins suffering from phlebitis, consistently hit powerful opposite-field home runs and drove in ninety runs. Hank Bauer, though not hitting well for average, slugged twenty-six home runs, batting in the lead-off position in the lineup most of the season. McDougald batted .311 and performed brilliantly at shortstop all year long, and Gil and Billy Martin, who hit .293 until a September slump, were the hardest-hitting keystone combination in baseball.

Whitey Ford won nineteen games and was deprived of his twentieth win when, in Ford's final start, 22-year-old Charlie Beamon of the Baltimore Orioles pitched a four-hit shutout to defeat Ford and the Yankees 1–0. Ford had had two of the four Yankee hits and was on third base with one out in the ninth when Stengel pinch hit Mantle who popped out to the second-baseman deep on the grass. After the game Ford pretended anger toward Mantle for failing to drive him in. Mantle contended that Ford had robbed him of an RBI by not tagging up on the play and scoring.

Ford won ten of his last eleven decisions, and though Turley and Larsen both were plagued by wildness and did not complete many games, their winning percentages were high. Toward the end of the season they displayed better control after working with pitching coach Jim Turner on a strange-looking no-windup delivery. Though John Kucks did not win another game after September 3, he nevertheless finished with eighteen victories, and Tom Sturdivant was a pleasant surprise, coming through with sixteen wins. General manager George Weiss was asked where the Yankees would have been without youngsters Kucks and Sturdivant, had they not produced so spectacularly. "We would have come up with somebody else," Weiss answered. The Yankees finished nine full games ahead of Cleveland, twelve ahead of the White Sox.

In the National League the Brooklyn Dodgers won the pennant on the final day of the season by beating the Pittsburgh Pirates at Ebbets Field behind the pitching of 27-game winner Don Newcombe, the pillar of strength of the Dodger team. Milwaukee had led all year, but in mid-September the Dodgers caught the Braves and just held on to win.

The first two games of the 1956 series were played at Ebbets Field, and the Yankees didn't have any more success in their opening attempts in the Brooklyn ball park than they had had in their three Ebbets Field losses in 1955. In the first game, before an aristocratic gathering including the Duke of Windsor, President Eisenhower, J. Edgar Hoover, New York State Governor Harriman, and Mayor Wagner of New York City, Sal "the Barber" Maglie defeated New York 6–3. Maglie, acquired by Brooklyn in May from the Cleveland Indians, allowed Mantle a two-run home run and Billy Martin a solo homer; but in Ebbets Field, a graveyard for lefties, Whitey Ford was battered and lasted only three innings. Jackie Robinson, in the last series of his illustrious career, hit a long home run off Ford, and in the third inning Gil Hodges hit a three-run home run for the lead and the game.

Yankee pitching wasn't any better in the second game, and though the Yankees scored six runs against Newcombe in the first two innings, the final four on a Yogi Berra grand slam, the Dodgers routed Larsen, Kucks, Byrne, Sturdivant, Morgan, and McDermott in a 13–8 win, leaving the Yankee pitching staff in total disarray. Duke Snider hit a Tommy Byrne fast ball into Bedford Avenue for a three-run home run in the second inning to lead the Dodgers. Only Newcombe of the Brooklyn players didn't enjoy the afternoon. After his early exit a parking lot attendant said to Big Newk, "You never can win the big ones. You're a choke." Newcombe worked over the attendant who must have been sorry he opened his big mouth.

A providential rainstorm postponed the third game of the series an extra day, allowing Stengel to come back with Whitey Ford as the series moved to the Stadium. Ford, without the dangerously close Ebbets Field left-field wall behind him, won 5–3, allowing the powerful Dodgers only cheap runs, two on sacrifice flies and one on an error. Billy Martin, always at his best in the series, hit his second home run in two days against Roger Craig who ten years later became a New York Met folk hero after consecutive seasons of 10–24 and 5–22. In the sixth with the Yankees trailing 2–1 and another defeat becoming a possibility, 40-year-old Enos Slaughter, whom Weiss reacquired from Kansas City the day Phil Rizzuto was released, hit a high hanging Craig curve ball with two runners on base for a three-run home run and the victory. The home run was a personal triumph for the prideful Slaughter, because both he and Craig came from the same area of North Carolina, and all year long Slaughter had been annoyed that a Durham sportswriter had been writing stories about Craig without writing about him. Ford pitched a complete game, allowing the Dodgers eight hits.

In the fourth game Tom Sturdivant pitched the second complete game win in a row, a 6–2 win over Carl Erskine to tie the series. When Stengel told Sturdy that he was to be the fourth-game pitcher, the 26-year-old rookie immediately called his father to tell him to grab the next flight from his home in Oklahoma to watch him pitch. His father, a National League rooter all his life, told the kid, "There's no sense me flying all the way up there just to see you warm up." With that added incentive, Sturdivant kept the Dodgers at bay. Berra, Mantle, and McDougald drove in runs, and then Mantle put the game out of reach with a towering home run against reliefer Ed Roebuck, the ball literally disappearing in the low-hanging mist of the threatening afternoon before descending into the right-field bleachers over the wall behind the 407 sign. Hank Bauer hit a two-run home run for the final Yankee runs. Sturdivant was surrounded by reporters after the game, and he reveled in his day of glory. Sturdivant was called "Queen for a Day" by his teammates because the next day Yankee right-hander Don Larsen pitched the only perfect game in the history of the world series.

October 8, 1956, was a bright and clear day in New York City, literally a perfect afternoon for a ball game. Stengel chose Don Larsen, who had been knocked out in the second inning of the second game, to pitch this fifth game of the series. Dodger manager Alston picked Sal "the Barber" Maglie. Though neither team was able to manage a hit in the first three innings, nothing out of the ordinary seemed to be transpiring, as 64,519 spectators in attendance at the Stadium folded their arms and leaned back to watch a fast-moving pitchers' battle. In the second inning Jackie Robinson pulled a hard grounder between third-baseman Andy Carey and shortstop Gil McDougald, a bouncer that Carey touched with the edge of his glove, deflecting the ball at McDougald, who snared it and threw out the slowed, but still fleet Robinson at first.

Using his no-windup delivery, Larsen was pitching effortlessly. With his pitching hand in his glove, he would begin his delivery, hands together at chest height, leaning back on his left leg and then twirling the leg forward, using it as a whip before extending his right arm and delivering the pitch to the plate.

Maglie, as usual both unshaven and nasty, matched Larsen—and he himself had not allowed a hit when Mickey Mantle came to the plate with two outs in the fourth inning. Mantle, completing one of the magical seasons in sports history, broke the Barber's spell by depositing a pitch into the right-field lower stands. It was for Mantle a pedestrian home run, but it still counted for a run.

Mantle then displayed his sprinter speed in the next inning. With one out Gil Hodges lined a Larsen fast ball into the left-center field alley toward the long auxiliary scoreboard near where the numbers 457 marked the distance from home plate to the wall. Starting in straightaway center field, Mantle raced at top speed with his gloved left hand fully extended in front of him, eyes intently following the flight of the ball, and at the last second lunged to catch it just as he reached the dirt warning track. Mantle received a roar of appreciation from the crowd.

The Yankees returned to their dugout in the seventh inning, and Mantle sat down in the seat Billy Hunter had been occupying. Hunter, not normally superstitious, asked Mantle to move to another seat, and Mantle understood. Tom Morgan, seated out in the bullpen, badly had to urinate, but didn't want to upset the flow of the game, so he riveted himself to the bullpen bench, crossed his legs hard and didn't move. Larsen, feeling some tension, ducked into the runway leading out of the dugout to light up a Camel, and when Mantle came by Larsen asked his center fielder, "Do you think I'll make it?" Mantle walked away without answering. In the Yankee dugout it had become very quiet.

In the eighth Robinson led off against Larsen by grounding weakly to the mound. An unexpected roar swelled from the crowd. Hodges, who had hit that tremendous fly ball to Mantle the last time up, connected solidly again, lining the ball at third-baseman Carey's shoe-tops where the Yankee infielder caught it before it hit the ground. Carey threw to first just in case the third-base umpire had missed the catch. Sandy Amoros ended the inning by flying out weakly to Mantle in center field. Larsen received a standing ovation as he left the field, and when he came to bat to lead off the Yankee half of the eighth, the crowd rose en masse in tribute. Maglie then struck out Larsen, and also Bauer and Collins, the superb Brooklyn pitcher's outstanding performance accentuating the drama and giving added luster to what Larsen was doing. Maglie himself received a standing ovation when he walked off the mound. As Maglie walked off, second-baseman Martin called infielders Collins, McDougald, and Carey together. "Nothing gets through," said Martin.

When Larsen walked toward the mound and picked up the resin bag before pitching to the first batter in the ninth, suddenly there was an eerie silence in the Stadium. The Lexington Avenue IRT rumbled overhead and you could hear the wind as it lightly buffeted the flags atop the Stadium roof and on the center-field flagpole. Inside the Yankee dugout the aging Stengel and his henchman, Frank Crosetti, could be heard above the crowd yelling instructions to their men on the field—abnormal actions for them, especially Crosetti, who did not often place his emotions on display. The late afternoon shadows were lengthening and a haze, the result of many smokey cigarettes, hung heavily over the field.

The first batter was Carl Furillo, and Larsen worked purposefully and carefully. Furillo fouled off four pitches as the tension seemed to intensify. Furillo finally hit an easy fly toward Bauer in right, and the Yankee fielder's catch was accompanied by a boisterous roar. One out.

After the Yankees threw the ball around the infield, Larsen took the throw from third-baseman Carey. He took his cap off and shook the sweat off his brow with a sideways jerk of the head. Roy Campanella, the Most Valuable Player in the National League in 1951, '53, and '55, was the next hitter. On the first pitch Campanella pulled the ball far enough to be a home run, but it was foul, and the initial "Ooooooooh" of the crowd subsided quickly when it became apparent that the ball was in no danger of landing fair. On the next pitch Campy hit an easy bouncer to Martin at second base who routinely threw the Dodger catcher out at first. There were two outs, another deafening roar, and as much tension as any one human being could tolerate.

Maglie was scheduled to be the next batter, but everyone knew he wouldn't hit, and in the silence the fans checked their scorecards trying to anticipate the likely Dodger pinch batter. Manager Alston chose Dale Mitchell, just purchased from the Cleveland Indians in July. Mitchell had a lifetime average of .312 in eleven seasons with Cleveland, and in the stretch Mitchell had batted 6–14 as a Dodger pinch hitter. He had always been a dangerous hitter, a slap hitter who rarely struck out and who knew the strike zone well. Mitchell emerged from the Dodger dugout swinging a couple of bats.

While Alston was choosing a pinch hitter, on the mound Larsen began to react to the intense pressure. His knees were beginning to weaken, and though he retained his composure, his face looked gaunt and sallow. Larsen mumbled to himself, "Please help me get through this."

The first pitch to Mitchell was a ball. Larsen bent over, fondled the resin bag, and stared at the outfield. He was working very slowly. The next pitch was a called strike, and a cheer arose from the silence. Mitchell then swung at a hard fast ball and missed. Strike two. Again Larsen stepped off the mound and stared at the outfield. Stengel motioned Mantle and Bauer a few feet to their left. Larsen threw still another fast ball, and Mitchell fouled it back, hanging on tenaciously. Larsen was taking a deep breath between every unbearable pitch. A four-engine Constellation passed overhead, the roar of the engines competing with the wind for attention. Larsen toed the rubber, brought his two hands to his chest and fired a low and outside fast ball, a strike or a ball depending upon the inclination of the umpire. Home-plate umpire Babe Pinelli jerked up his right fist to signify a third strike and Mitchell turned to protest the call, but catcher Berra had already raised his fist triumphantly in the air, ball in hand, and as Larsen strode toward the dugout amidst a deafening, jubilant, ecstatic, throng, the round Yankee catcher jumped into Larsen's arms, bear-hugging the large pitcher as Larsen carried him toward the Yankee dugout.

Twenty-seven Dodgers had batted, and incredibly, not one of them reached first base. Larsen's control had been so superb that only one batter had been awarded three balls, and that was Pee Wee Reese, who subsequently struck out in the first inning on the very next pitch. All the Yankee officials rushed into the dugout to congratulate Larsen, and owner Webb was heard to exclaim, "This will set spring training back forever." Pinelli, umpiring his final game before retirement, returned to his dressing room and cried unashamedly. Many called it the greatest game in the history of professional baseball. After the game Larsen and his close friend, Art Richman, a sportswriter on the New York *Daily Mirror*, drove to Bill Taylor's bar on 57th Street, and with a pair of young ladies in tow, they celebrated late into the night. When Larsen won the Corvette presented by *Sport* magazine after the series, he said, "I shouldn't have any trouble picking up girls in this thing."

The world series reverted back to Ebbets Field for the final two games with the Yankees leading three wins to two. Bob Turley, also pitching with a no-windup delivery, battled Clem Labine of the Dodgers to a 0–0 tie for nine innings, and lost in the tenth. Turley walked Junior Gilliam to lead off the Dodger tenth, and Reese successfully sacrificed Gilliam to second. Stengel ordered Turley to intentionally pass Snider, but Jackie Robinson foiled the strategy by lining the ball deep toward left field, and left fielder Enos Slaughter, playing shallow to prevent a blooping single from driving in a run, took an initial step forward. The ball was over his head before he could recover. Slaughter, racing to the wall in desperation, watched the ball bounce behind him as Gilliam scored the winning run. Turley had pitched the finest game of his career, allowing the Dodgers only four hits, and he had lost. Throughout the game Turley and first-baseman Joe Collins, were engaged in a running commentary. "Kid," Collins had told him from the beginning, "just hold 'em for seven innings and you got it made, because the shadows will come in and you'll win." By the ninth inning Turley was shouting at Collins, "Hey, Joe, the damn shadows are out in right field. Where are my runs?"

After the game Stengel had great praise for Turley's pitching, but he lamented the loss. "I can't figger out that fella," Stengel said of Turley. "He don't smoke. He don't drink. He don't chase around none. But he can't win as good as that misbehavin' feller you know about who was perfect." Later Stengel told Turley, "I suffered more with you in this game than any game I've ever seen."

In the team bus going from Ebbets Field back to the Stadium after the game Billy Martin, in a foul mood, went up to the front and sat down beside Stengel. Most of the Yankees were deeply annoyed by Slaughter's fielding in left, but no one had the audacity to complain to Stengel. Except Martin. "If you're going to keep playing that fucking National League bobo out there," Billy said, "we're going to blow this series." Stengel asked Martin who he would play. "You better put Elston out there," Billy said, "and you better get Skowron's ass back on first base."

A writer who had overheard the conversation cornered Martin afterward. "You think you know the Old Man that well?" he asked the Yankee second-baseman. Martin said, "I'll pick the lineup for you for tomorrow." Martin's lineup included Howard in left and Skowron at first.

For the second year in a row a Yankee-Dodger series would be resolved in the seventh game. Brooklyn manager Alston chose Don Newcombe to start the final game, despite the adverse publicity Newcombe had brought upon himself by punching the parking attendant after the second game. Stengel, after staying up all night, chose Johnny Kucks, the forgotten man of the Yankee staff. Yogi

Berra had advised Stengel to start Kucks, a sinker-baller who would make the Dodgers hit ground balls in Ebbets Field instead of fly balls which could end up as cheap home runs. Stengel asked Sturdivant, the fourth-game winner, his advice. Sturdivant said that a fresh Kucks would be better than a tired Sturdivant. Whitey Ford was not considered because Stengel didn't want to chance starting a lefty again in Ebbets Field.

On the bus ride from Yankee Stadium, where the team dressed, to Ebbets Field, Jackie Farrell, the head of the Yankee speaker's bureau, a friendly little guy with a soothing manner, sat next to Kucks and entertained him with reminiscences of Jersey City politics and stories about the old days at Dickinson High School, Kucks' alma mater. Kucks still didn't know for certain whether he would be the starter. Not until he saw his name posted on the lineup card in the dugout did he know for sure.

Kucks gulped deeply and went out to warm up with Charlie Silvera, the bullpen catcher, as the capacity crowd filed into the Ebbets Field seats, the majority of the people Dodger fans hoping their team could win their second straight world championship. Kucks was nervous and tight warming up, and though he had finished the year 18–9, he hadn't won a game since September 3, and that worried him. When Kucks went out to the mound for the first inning, before he threw his first pitch he looked down the left-field line and saw Whitey Ford and Tom Sturdivant warming up on the sidelines. "Boy, big guy," Kucks said to himself, "they sure got faith in you."

It was his worst moment of the afternoon. After Yogi Berra slugged a two-run home run off Don Newcombe and then followed with another two-run home run off the big Dodger, the Yankees had a commanding 4–0 lead, and Kucks could relax. Newcombe, the Dodger fast-ball throwing ace, was once again overmatched by Berra, his personal tormentor. As Berra rounded the bases after the second home run, aware of the criticism directed at the big Dodger pitcher, Yogi yelled to him, "It was a good pitch, Newk." Newk nodded. Elston Howard, in the hospital with a strep throat during the first six games, but released to play in the finale, was in left field as Martin had predicted, and Ellie hit a solo home run in the fourth to finish Newcombe. Then in the seventh inning against Roger Craig, Bill Skowron, the other player Martin predicted would be in the game, hit a grand slam home run to make the score 9–0 and finish the Dodgers. In the dugout Jim Turner, sitting next to Kucks, pinched his pitcher's arm. "Are you for real?" Turner asked. "I just wanted to wake you up to see if you're alive." Till the game ended Turner kept pinching him.

Before the final game Martin approached Skowron, who had not played since the first game. "This is where we separate the men from the boys, Moose," Billy said. When he batted in the seventh inning, Moose was still angry because he had played most of the year at first base, and then without explanation Stengel had played the more experienced Joe Collins at first during most of the series. When Moose came up to bat in the seventh inning, Stengel whistled for him to come back to the dugout. The bases were loaded, and Moose was sure that Stengel was sending in a pinch hitter for him. His neck got beet-red as he called time to return to the bench. Roy Campanella, a gentle man, said to Skowron, "Don't worry, Moose. He's not going to take you out." "He is, too," Skowron said. "You'll see," Campy said. When Skowron returned to the dugout, Casey said to him, "I want you to try to hit the ball to right field. Stay out of the double play." Skowron returned to the batter's box. "I told you he wasn't taking you out, Moose," Campy said. The first pitch by Craig was on the outside corner of the plate, and Skowron swung early. With only one hand on the bat he pulled the ball over the left-field Ebbets Field wall for a grand slam home run. As Skowron crossed the plate, Campanella again spoke to Skowron. "See, Moose," Campy said. "You played, and you hit a home run." Moose and Campanella smiled at each other.

Kucks allowed two harmless fly balls all day, retiring the Dodgers on grounders, and his three-hit shutout was the fifth complete game in a row for the Yankee pitching staff in the series, a feat they hadn't accomplished during the entire regular 1956 season. There was a loud celebration in the Yankee clubhouse after the game. They had avenged their series loss of the year before. In the clubhouse Stengel sought out Martin, and noting the home runs by Howard and Skowron, Stengel said, "You're a smart little bastard, aren't you?" The two men hugged each other warmly.

Gladys Gooding played "Auld Lang Syne" on the organ as the disappointed Brooklyn fans departed the hallowed Dodger ball park. They didn't know it, but the Brooklyn faithful would never see another world series game in Ebbets Field. Dodger owner Walter O'Malley, while professing his great love for Brooklyn, was negotiating with the city of Los Angeles to build a modern, brand-new stadium 3,000 miles away.

It had been an exciting series, yet long after the results would be forgotten, the perfect performance in the fifth game by Don Larsen would be remembered. Though Yankee Stadium attendance for that game was 64,500, millions of people would later swear that they had been there.

Of all the Yankee pitchers, Larsen was the least-likely candidate for immortality. When he came to the Yankees in 1955 from the Baltimore Orioles, it was obvious that he possessed superior physical ability. A large man, he did everything with consummate skill and finesse. He had a strong arm, fielded his position well, hit better than some of the nonpitchers (and throughout his career was used extensively as a pinch hitter), and he was the second-fastest runner on the team behind Mantle. Had he not been a pitcher, he could have been a major league outfielder. All indications had been that Larsen would develop into one of the great pitchers in Yankee history.

However, Larsen never did fulfill that great promise. Why, no one, including Larsen, really knows. Like other young athletes before him, including Van Lingo Mungo of the Dodgers and Clint Hartung of the Giants, Larsen seemed to lack an essential ingredient necessary to greatness. Miller Huggins, the Hall-of-Famer who managed the great Yankee teams in the 1920s, called it disposition. Some called it ambition or desire or aggressiveness. Whatever that extra quality is called that makes the superior athlete something special, Larsen evidently did not have it. Through fourteen seasons of major league pitching, in Larsen's best season he won only eleven games. When he retired at the end of the 1965 season, his major league record was 81–91. "He should be good," said Stengel just before Don was traded from the Yankees in 1959, "but he ain't."

To further accentuate the difference between Larsen's potential and his mediocre won-lost record was that one game in the 1956 world series when he retired every Dodger he faced. Rarely in life does a person have the opportunity to achieve perfection. Very few things are even measured in terms of perfection. Even in statistically fanatical baseball, only certain aspects of the game can be so measured. For a pitcher to face twenty-seven men and retire them all, that is perfection, and in the thousands and thousands of major league games since the game was invented and recorded, only six men have pitched perfect games. Only one man, Don Larsen, has been so excellent and so fortunate on a given afternoon to pitch a perfect game in a world series.

1957

*McDougald and Herb Score . . . The Copacabana
fracas and the departure of Billy Martin . . . Old
Country . . . Tom Sturdivant, the laughter turned to
sadness . . . Mantle's mysterious "shin splints" . . .
Another pennant . . . Milwaukee and Lew Burdette
in the world series*

In Florida, at spring training, Casey Stengel presided over the most impressive contingent of talent since he arrived in 1949. After winning seven Yankee pennants, the normally pessimistic Stengel had to admit that the team would win again. "But," he said with prescience, "I don't think it's gonna be a runaway because that feller in center field can get hurt. And suppose something happens to Yogi Berra? It wouldn't be a runaway then."

But the oddsmakers in Las Vegas pooh-poohed the pessimism and made the Yankees prohibitive favorites to win again. To Stengel's dominating world champions were added pitchers Art Ditmar and Bobby Shantz, and in camp were eight Denver minor leaguers chosen for the 1956 American Association All-Star team.

Ditmar and Shantz were acquired from the Kansas City Athletics, a team once located in Philadelphia, but transplanted in 1955 when Chicago millionaire Arnold Johnson bought the team from Connie Mack and moved it. Johnson was a long-time friend of Yankee owner Dan Topping. Both men were officers in the American Canteen Company, traveling in the same circles of high society. Johnson was also a longtime friend of George Weiss, the man who suggested Johnson buy the A's from Mack. When Johnson bought the team and suggested to Topping and Weiss that he wished to move to Kansas City, Topping sold Johnson the Yankees' Kansas City Blues franchise and then transferred the minor league Blues to Denver. Anything for a friend.

The A's general manager, Parke Carroll, had been the business manager of the Newark Bears when Newark was a Yankee farm team. Carroll had worked for Weiss for over twenty years when Carroll became the A's general manager with Weiss's blessing. When the Yankees and A's began to trade with regularity, the relationship bordered on incest.

When Arnold Johnson, who didn't know very much about baseball, first set up shop at Kansas City in 1955, Weiss helped his old friend build by selling him Yankee minor leaguers and over-the hill veterans who, though they would not help the Yankees, would strengthen the struggling A's. Ewell Blackwell, Johnny Sain, Dick Kryhoski, Lou Sleater, Eddie Robinson, and Lou Skizas all were sold to the A's by Weiss. Later when the Yankees coveted a player on the A's, Weiss, like the Godfather, always had the surplus talent to make the A's an offer they couldn't refuse. The Yankees extracted quality for quantity, picking up one key individual here and there, filling a specific need, and filling it at a moment's notice. At the same time the A's, though never a contender, no longer were an embarrassment. Weiss sent them enough grade-B players to keep the Kansas City fans flocking to the ball park, making money for Johnson. Johnson and Weiss, business comrades, trusted each other. Their mutual back-scratching served each other's purposes well. The A's made money. The Yankees won pennants. The rest of the league general managers screamed foul. Beginning in the winter of 1956 Weiss began his wholesale player-swapping operation with the A's, and over the next four years Weiss made ten important deals with the A's, six of which were crucial to the Yankees' continued success.

In the first important trade of the New York-Kansas City series, Weiss acquired Ditmar, Shantz, and minor league infielder Clete Boyer. Ditmar in 1956 had been 12–22 for the A's, leading their staff in most of the positive and negative pitching categories, but he was consistent with Weiss's traditional practice of acquiring pitching talent without regard to won-lost record. In 1949 Weiss had acquired Fred Sanford (12–21) from the Browns, and in '54 Don Larsen (3–21) from Baltimore. Shantz, who had won twenty-four games and the Most Valuable Player award for the Philadelphia A's in 1952, was also an acquisition in the Weiss tradition. Shantz, because he had a sore arm, was a gamble, the throw-in of the deal, but he had always given the Yankees trouble. Young Boyer was much less of a gamble. Clete had been a high-school bonus prospect the Yankees had scouted intensively, but after signing bonus babies Frank Leja and Tommy Carroll, the Yankees had to pass up Boyer. The rules at that time forced bonus babies to remain on the major league roster, and Weiss couldn't afford to have three inexperienced rookies taking up valuable space on the Yankee bench. In 1955 Weiss told Carroll, the A's general manager, to sign Boyer. Finally Weiss succeeded in acquiring the young infielder, his intention from the start.

In exchange for these three men, Weiss gave up superfluous pitchers Tom Morgan, Rip Coleman, and Mickey McDermott, plus Jack Urban, a minor league pitching prospect, broken-ankled infielder Billy Hunter, and gimpy-kneed outfielder Irv Noren.

When the trade was announced, Cleveland general manager Hank Greenberg, aware that Weiss was amoral enough to take full advantage of his cozy relationship with Johnson and Carroll, was livid and fearful. "It must be great," he said sarcastically, "to have your own farm system in the same league."

With the addition of Ditmar and hopefully Shantz, Stengel had a staff of eleven quality pitchers, a mother lode of prosperity. "When I came to the Yankees in 1949," said Stengel, "I had three—Raschi, Reynolds, and Lopat. Now there's eleven. Who else has that many?" He had Ford, Kucks, Sturdivant, Turley, Larsen, and Ditmar to start, plus Grim, Byrne, and Shantz in the bullpen, plus two very highly touted rookies, Al Cicotte and Ralph Terry.

Other new young faces in camp were similarly intriguing. The rookie crop from Denver had been outstanding. The entire Denver infield of Marv Throneberry, Bobby Richardson, Tony Kubek, and Woodie Held was given a chance to remain on the Yankees. Jerry Lumpe, the Richmond shortstop who failed to make the team in 1956, was another infield prospect. In the outfield Norm Siebern and Bob Martyn of Denver looked excellent, as did Darrell Johnson, a strong, reliable reserve catcher.

Without the rookies, Casey had a nucleus of infielders: Bill Skowron, Joe Collins, Billy Martin, Jerry Coleman, Gil McDougald, and Andy Carey; with outfielders Ellie Howard, Mickey Mantle, Hank Bauer, and Enos Slaughter, with the indestructible Berra the catcher. The quality and depth of this array was awesome. Arthur Daley of *The New York Times* picked the Yankees to win the pennant by Labor Day.

Once again the Cleveland Indians were the team to beat. Bob Lemon, Early Wynn, and Mike Garcia were still around, but Cleveland's optimism centered around left-handed pitcher Herb Score, a blindingly-fast, 23-year-old pitcher who led the American League in strikeouts in 1955 and '56, and for whom the Boston Red Sox unsuccessfully offered a cool one million dollars. In 1956 Score struck out 263 batters and won twenty games. He had a long, successful career in front of him. Score by himself made the Indians contenders. The Chicago White Sox, led by second-baseman Nellie Fox and shortstop Luis Aparicio, had a strong starting team, but lacked depth. Stengel liked the chances of the Yankees this year.

He still worried, though. That was his nature. Mantle, despite the quality of the other athletes playing with him, was nevertheless the key to another Yankee pennant, and Stengel, realizing that Mantle and Billy Martin and, to a lesser extent, Ford were carefree, mischievous devils like he was, knew it was just a matter of time before he would be explaining away a potentially embarrassing scene or incident to George Weiss. In the spring of 1957 Mantle hadn't completed his March training before he injured himself fooling around. He sprained ligaments in his left foot and needed crutches for a short while after an accident during a round of golf with Billy Martin. Mickey and Billy each rented an electric golf cart to motor around the course. At first they were content merely to race each other from shot to shot, but after a while racing became too tame, and to make the round more interesting they played bumper cars like at amusement parks, ramming each other's cart at full speed, trying to tip each other over. Going toward the seventh green Martin faked a turn to the right and then abruptly zigzagged left, catching Mantle's cart broadside, rolling Mantle and the cart. When the Yankee center fielder and league MVP fell off, the cart fell on his leg.

It was explained to the press that Mantle had hurt himself stepping in a hole during fielding practice, and all spring his leg was weak and unsteady. When he finally did play in late April he limped when he ran the bases.

Billy Martin, too, seemed snakebit. Martin suffered from a stiff neck and shoulders, an injury which had resulted from a late-night wrestling match between himself and Mantle, and later in training Billy injured his foot, developed tonsilitis and a high fever, and then was struck on the head by a pitched ball. While Billy recuperated, 21-year-old Bobby Richardson played second base and played it spectacularly, displaying a quickness in the field that Martin didn't have.

Despite the physical woes of Mantle and Martin, baseball's Damon and Pythias still managed to find time to continue their golf, a new passion that they shared with their buddy, Ford. One morning late in April Stengel gave the pitchers and catchers the morning off, and Mantle, grasping the opportunity to get in a little tee time with the excused-from-practice Ford, called Stengel on the phone and told him that he had a stomachache. "I don't feel well," Mickey told the manager. "Can I have the day off?" Stengel gave it to him.

Mantle and Ford toured the local golf course for eighteen holes. On the eighteenth, as they approached the green Mantle noticed a short, paunchy man holding the flag stick. "Isn't that George Weiss?" Whitey said to Mick. "Sure looks like him," Mickey said.

It was Weiss. No one said a word as Mantle bent over his putt and holed out as Weiss lifted the stick for him. "How's your stomachache, Mickey?" Weiss growled. Mantle was nonplussed. "Eighteen holes are the best thing in the world for a stomachache," he said, giving the stern general manager a big shit-eating grin as he and Whitey trotted off for the clubhouse.

Spring training went well. Ditmar and Shantz blended into the staff and in addition to the excellent infield play of Richardson, Stengel was impressed by the versatility and excellence of another 21 year old, a tall kid named Tony Kubek who played both the infield and outfield with equal dexterity. Kubek, nominally a shortstop, had played center field while Mantle was nursing his various leg ailments, and though he had never played the outfield before training camp, he performed flawlessly and led the Yankee team in hitting. When Mantle returned, Stengel shifted Kubeck to left field where he still performed outstandingly. Kubek's father had played against Stengel when Casey was the player-manager for the Toledo Mud Hens in the American Association back in the twenties. One of the first comments that Stengel made to Kubek the first time they met was, "I knew your Dad. Ran well. Great base runner. Good hitter. Didn't have much power. Hit to the opposite field." Kubek nodded. "Yes sir," he said, "that's my Dad." It seemed that Stengel was taking a special liking to the cherubic youngster. Kubek received personal attention from the crusty manager that the other young players didn't seem to be getting.

Woodie Held, another versatile youngster, also performed well playing both the infield and outfield. After Stengel finished paring his squad, four of the Denver hopefuls remained on the Yankees: Richardson, Kubek, Held, and 21-year-old pitcher Ralph Terry. Only the 1951 rookie crop of Mantle, McDougald, and the recently traded Tom Morgan had been better.

In the season opener Ford, who had recorded seasons of 9–1, 18–6, 16–8, 18–7, and 19–6 in his first five years, beat the Washington Senators 2–1, and in his next start a few days later he was leading the Senators 11–2 when he took himself out in the seventh inning. The Yankees had scored a slew of runs in their half of the sixth inning, and while Ford waited on the bench in the April cold, his pitching arm tightened. In the seventh, he warmed up too quickly, and suddenly there was pain stabbing his left shoulder. Ford finished the inning, but the pain was there. In his next start Whitey held Boston scoreless for seven innings when the stabbing pain reappeared, and then on the fourth of May against the White Sox, the Yankee pitching star retired the first five White Sox batters, and with two outs in the second inning, called time-out and requested that Stengel remove him from the ball game. He could throw his off-speed pitches, but he was physically unable to throw overhand with speed, and he had to quit. Ford's ailment was diagnosed as tendonitis. For two months, with the exception of one premature start in mid-May, Ford remained on the bench nursing his ailing arm. Ford was unable to do more than lob the ball. Dr. Sidney Gaynor, the Yankee physician, prescribed a cure of patience and rest, but telling Ford to be either patient or restful was like telling Richard Nixon to stop running for public office. By June Ford was so depressed about his condition that he seriously considered a career outside of baseball.

To begin the month of May the Yankees swept six games in a row, the last three against the White Sox to give the Yankees the league lead. Andy Carey severely sprained an ankle early in the season, so Stengel moved Martin to third and played Bobby Richardson, the silent rookie, at second, and the team continued to function smoothly. The other rookie from Denver, Tony Kubek, platooned with Ellie Howard in left field. Mickey Mantle, recovering from his injuries, continued the spectacular hitting which won him the Most Valuable Player award the year before, and McDougald at short, Skowron at first, and Bauer in right were also playing at their peak of performance. Catcher Berra, normally a slow starter, was the only regular not hitting up to par.

On May 7 and 8 the Yankees traveled to Cleveland for a two-game series against the Indians, the opener a nighttime game pitting the Yankees' Tom Sturdivant, the surprise sixteen-game winner of the year before, against the Indians' boy wonder, Herb Score. Score was becoming one of the star attractions of the American League, a pitcher recognized for both his pitching skills and his engaging personality.

The Yankees batted first, and the Cleveland flame-thrower retired lead-off batter Hank Bauer on an easy grounder to the third-baseman. Fans continued to file into mammoth Municipal Stadium in Cleveland as Gil McDougald, the Yankee shortstop, stepped into the batter's box to face Score. Since the day manager Stengel ordered McDougald to discard his weird boyhood stance and bat more conventionally, McDougald's batting average had risen sharply: in 1955 Gil hit .285 and in 1956 he hit a career-high .311. Again this year Gil was proving himself to be one of the most valuable athletes in the major leagues, playing an outstanding shortstop and hitting stinging line drives to all fields. The Indian pitcher rocked into his windup, left arm reaching way back before he let loose a fast ball that crackled toward home plate. Score, who threw with every ounce of strength he had, was in the habit of turning his head away from the batter just after releasing the ball. McDougald wristed a level swing and lined the ball back up the middle of the diamond right at Score. Because Score had turned his head slightly, he lost sight of the ball as it rocketed through the box, and it struck the helpless pitcher squarely in the face near the right eye, knocking him to the ground semi-conscious. The ball caromed to third where Al Smith threw McDougald out before racing to the mound to aid the fallen pitcher.

Indian catcher Jim Hegan rushed to the mound, along with Smith, McDougald, Mantle, the on-deck hitter, and several other Indians. Score just lay there, hemorrhaging so badly that his right eye was not visible under the pool of blood flowing from his nose and mouth. His nose angled oddly. Players ran to the clubhouse for icepacks. Others ran for the stretcher. The PA announcer called for a doctor. Six rushed onto the field.

Score was placed on the stretcher, and on the long walk to the ambulance waiting outside the stricken pitcher sought humor amid his terrible anxiety. "I wonder if Gene Fullmer felt this way," he said. Only days earlier Sugar Ray Robinson had brutally KO'd Fullmer. No one smiled. Score was taken to Lakeside Hospital in Cleveland where the first reports were unspecific as to whether Score would lose the sight of his right eye. After the game McDougald rushed to the hospital, but Score's condition was guarded and no visitors were allowed. "If anything happens to his eye," McDougald said, "I will quit baseball." Gil's roommate, Hank Bauer, copped some sleeping pills from Gus Mauch, the Yankee trainer. Bauer knew that his roomie would need them. Stengel was meditative. He was worried about Score, but he was just as concerned about McDougald. Casey knew his ball players, and he feared a negative psychological reaction by his sensitive infielder. Stengel, as usual, was not wrong. Score was never the same player again, and neither was McDougald. That special zest Gil brought to baseball was lost, and until the day he retired in 1960, it never returned. It was worse for Score. On May 7 he was worth a million dollars. For him on May 8 the bottom fell out of the market.

A birthday celebration for Billy Martin had been planned for the night of May 15. Originally the next day was scheduled to be open, but even after a rain-out game was rescheduled for the next evening, because baby-sitting arrangements had been made and everyone was so looking forward to the evening out, the players decided to hold the party as planned. They would have the entire day to recuperate for the game.

It was Martin's twenty-ninth birthday, and Ford and Mantle had planned and arranged the party for Billy. The final party consisted of Martin, a bachelor, and Mantle, Ford, Hank Bauer, and Yogi Berra and their wives, and youngster Johnny Kucks and his wife. Kucks, the only "nonstar," at first was sorry that he had come because he felt uncomfortable and out of his class among the others. He had thought most of the team would be there. But because Berra had driven him into New York City from his home in New Jersey, he had no convenient way to return, and he and his wife decided to remain and enjoy the evening with his famous teammates.

The small band of Yankees first met at Danny's Hideaway, a classy mid-Manhattan restaurant where they had dinner. Afterward, Carmen Berra suggested they attend the show at the Waldorf Astoria which was featuring singer Johnny Ray, whose songs, "Just Walking in the Rain" and "Cry" were high on the hit parade. After they watched Ray, they then went to the famous

Copacabana to watch Sammy Davis, Jr. At the Copa the maitre d' set up a special table for his Yankee guests; the group ordered drinks and settled down to watch the show. Sammy Davis was singing and dancing and entertaining in his usual high-energy style, and all were enjoying the celebration for Martin, the scrappy little guy who was universally admired. It was a beautiful evening.

From a table adjacent to the one where the Yankees and their wives sat, a fat inebriate interrupted Sammy Davis in the middle of a song, yelling "You jungle bunny" at the entertainer. Davis, flustered, ordered the band to stop, walked toward the edge of the stage and said to the man, "I want to thank you very much for that remark. I'll remember it."

Hank Bauer, who was seated close to the drunk, a member of a plastered bowling party, had observed the racial prejudices that Ellie Howard had faced, and reacting immediately, told the guy to "shut the hell up." "Make me shut up," the drunk challenged. One of the other bowlers, equally drunk, recognized the well-known ball players and yelled over to Bauer, "Don't test your luck tonight, Yankee," and for the next half hour the bowlers heckled the Yankee players.

Finally Billy Martin, his beautiful evening being ruined, said to the tormentors, "We're here to enjoy ourselves. You've been spouting off all night. If you want to talk about this somewhere else, we can get away from the table and settle it outside so the rest of the people can enjoy themselves." "Let's go," the fat drunk said, and Martin, followed by Mantle, quickly left the table. The drunk and his friend also got up. Charlene Bauer told Hank, "It's none of your business, stay here," but Bauer also rose. When the bowlers and the Yankees started to leave their seats, a maze of tuxedo-clad people rushed to keep the two factions apart. Cooler heads started to prevail. Martin and the brother of the obnoxious fat drunk agreed to keep the guy away from the other Yankees, but when they entered the spacious men's room to break up any forthcoming slug-fests, they found Yogi Berra and Whitey Ford restraining Hank Bauer by the arms and the fat drunk out cold on the floor with a broken nose and other head injuries.

The scene incriminated Bauer who swore he never hit the guy. He had wanted to, but he never got the chance because two nasty Copa bouncers got to the troublemaker first and severely beat him like Mafia enforcers teaching a loanshark victim a lesson.

The first reaction of the players, fearing publicity, was to find the quickest route out of the nightclub. They were escorted out the back kitchen exit, a passageway leading to the lobby and the street, but before they were safely away, an entertainment columnist named Leonard Lyons from the New York *Post* saw them beating a hasty retreat, and like all good reporters, began asking questions. The Yankees disappeared from the scene, and Lyons was able to get only one side of the imbroglio, that of the drunk bowler who was accusing Bauer of punching him.

Their evening spoiled, the members of the Yankee party said good night to each other and tottered home, thinking their troubles were behind them.

At four-thirty in the morning Bauer's phone rang. It was a reporter from the *Daily News*. The crime reporter. He told Hank that there was a fat guy down at the police station swearing out a warrant for Bauer's arrest. "He says you beat the shit out of him," the reporter said. Bauer's first reaction was, "Whaaaaaaat?" His second reaction was more controlled. "I'm sorry," Bauer said, "but I didn't hit anybody." And he hung up the phone.

The next morning the *Daily News* had a front-page headline in the large-size type last used when the Japanese bombed Pearl Harbor. "Bauer in Brawl in Copa" it read.

When George Weiss awoke that morning and saw the headlines, he almost had apoplexy. Weiss's assistant, Roy Hamey, called Ford and Martin at Ford's home and instructed them to be in the Yankee Fifth Avenue office in a half hour or be fined $1,000. There was no way Ford was going to drive the thirty-five mile trip from Lake Success in a half hour, and he told Hamey so. Publicity director Bob Fishel called Kucks and told him that he and the others were being sued for a million dollars by the flattened drunk who had started the whole thing. Kucks had just bought his Jersey home the year before, and being young and unknowledgeable about the law, pictured himself behind bars for his alleged transgressions. When Kucks arrived at the Stadium for the meeting with Weiss, Dan Topping, and the Yankee lawyers, his knees were shaking uncontrollably. Berra and Bauer were also at the meeting, and for a couple of hours each of the party-goers described to the Yankee officials and lawyers what had happened.

George Weiss, livid, was convinced that Martin, the street fighter, had hit the man in the Copa. Weiss sat the players involved in his office and asked them what had happened, but no one admitted hitting the man. Not satisfied, Weiss took aside Yogi Berra, the Yankee catcher admired for his honesty, and said, "Now, Yogi. Please explain what happened that night." Yogi said to Weiss, "Nobody did nothin' to nobody." Weiss was still convinced that everyone was covering up to protect Martin.

Later the defendants were taken before the Manhattan Grand Jury in the Criminal Courts Building. Because Kucks looked young and collegiate, the all-American boy, the attorneys decided that he should testify first. As he sat in the witness chair looking up at forty or fifty grand jurors staring down at him with the district attorney asking tough questions and the stenographer sitting beside him taking it all down, Kucks patiently and courteously answered questions, all the while convinced that he was spending his final day of freedom before the slams closed behind him. After Kucks was finished, Martin took the stand and told his story, and then Berra went in and told his. Within an hour the district attorney threw the case out for insufficient evidence.

The matter should have ended right there, but it didn't. Weiss was still outraged that the players were even at the Copa, though on the face of it, a night out with one's wife the evening before a night game certainly seemed proper. But Weiss had always considered his Yankees something of an institution. Perhaps more importantly, unknown to the players, one of the TV networks was considering a highly complimentary documentary on the Yankees. Such publicity, Weiss felt, might have lured some high-school prospects into his camp. When the Copa fracas broke, the program was shelved. Manager Stengel was much less annoyed. The next day the cagey Casey announced that he was scratching Ford from his next start because of the affair, but in reality Stengel knew Ford had an aching arm and wouldn't be able to pitch regardless. He benched Berra, who was in the midst of a slump, and let Howard catch, and he continued to bench Martin, who had lost his infield job when the week before Andy Carey returned to health to play third while Bobby Richardson continued to play an exceptional second base. In reality, Stengel probably would have enjoyed being at the Copa with the rest of his men. Stengel's hilarious though somewhat mystifying comment on the evening was, "The reason they held the party there was that they didn't want to hold it in a hospital."

The real trouble came when owner Dan Topping insisted on fining Mantle, Martin, Bauer, Berra, and Ford $1,000 apiece and fining the less affluent Kucks $500. Gil McDougald, outraged, was more incensed than those who were fined, and Gil insisted his roommate Bauer ride right down to the commissioner's office and demand the fine be rescinded. "Nobody is going to tell me where I can or can't take my wife on an evening out," McDougald said. What also angered the hard-nosed McDougald was that the fine had been levied *before* the Grand Jury hearing, before the players had been given an opportunity to defend themselves. Topping played judge and jury without knowing the circumstances. The fines, serving little purpose, merely created resentment, and when Martin leaked to the press the amount of the fines, more animosity was created. At the end of the year Topping returned half the money, applying the other half to lawyers' fees, but the bad taste lingered for both players and management. Reporters and columnists assumed the Yankee players had actually done something at the Copa that night because of the fines and that the Yankees had used their political influence to cover it up. That the Yankee management might have pulled some strings for their dilettante players was more offensive to the public than if one of the players had actually punched out an obnoxious, bigoted drunk.

The Copa non-incident, furthermore, gave Weiss the opportunity, once-and-for-all, to trade Billy Martin, a player Weiss never liked or respected, even when he was contributing so magnificently in series after series.

When Bobby Richardson proved that he could successfully hit major league pitching, Billy Martin's days were numbered. During the final two weeks of May and into June the Yankees continued their mysterious batting slump as they played win-a-few, lose-a-few ball. At the same time the Chicago White Sox won nine straight, taking over a lead which swelled to six full games. The Yankees seemed flat, lethargic, and only Bobby Shantz, Weiss's throw-in from Kansas City who had taken Ford's spot in the rotation, was pitching well.

In early June the Yankees split two games in Chicago against the White Sox. The third game of the series—a crucial one for both teams—pitted Art Ditmar, the other Kansas City tradee, against Billy Pierce, Chicago's best pitcher. In the Chicago first Ditmar got off to a poor start, allowing a walk and an infield single. The seething Ditmar, never noted for his gentlemanly behavior on the mound, pitched two strikes to outfield star Larry Doby and then knocked him down with a dangerously close, head-hunting fast ball. As it was there was bad feeling between the two teams. The game before Yankee pitcher Al Cicotte had thrown a head-hunter at Minnie Minoso, and on the next pitch Minoso whipped his bat out toward the mound, making Cicotte skip rope. That Minoso and Doby were black and Cicotte and Ditmar white didn't help the situation any, either.

Doby sprawled to the dirt to avoid the lethal pitch, which eluded Yankee catcher Elston Howard and rolled to the backstop. Ditmar ran to cover home plate lest the runner on second make an attempt to score. When he reached the plate, Doby, dusting himself off, said to him, "If you ever do that again, I'll stick a knife in your back." "Go fuck yourself," Ditmar answered. Doby, himself hotheaded, and sensitive about white pitchers throwing at him, swung from the heels with a punch that breezed by Ditmar's face, knocking off his hat. Both benches emptied, and it took the umpires and the Chicago police thirty minutes to restore order. Yankee first-baseman Bill Skowron, once a halfback at Purdue, bear-hugged Doby to the ground, and Walt Dropo, the huge White Sox first-baseman, rushed at Skowron to get him off Doby. Enos Slaughter, once a member of the St. Louis Cardinals brawling Gashouse Gang, began wrestling Dropo, and when it was clear that Dropo was getting the better of Slaughter, Whitey Ford rushed to his aid. Even Casey Stengel limped into the middle of the melee to help Ford, and Jim Rivera, the Chicago center fielder, began a shouting match with him. When the crush of bodies was finally untangled, Skowron's pants had nearly been pulled off, and Slaughter's uniform shirt was ripped to shreds by Dropo. The umpires threw Doby, Dropo, and Slaughter out of the game inexplicably allowing Ditmar to remain, causing howls of protest from the White Sox bench.

As all the participants continued to mill around the field and the umpires discussed their punishments with the managers, Yankee second-baseman Billy Martin approached Ditmar to find out what Doby had said to him. "He said he was going to stick a knife in me," Ditmar told Martin. The enraged Martin ran toward Doby and pummeled him with blows before they were finally separated.

The Yankees ultimately won the game, and the melee was the impetus for a Yankee nine-game winning streak of their own. It was the beginning of the end for the White Sox.

Two days after the Doby brawl Billy Martin was traded. In the middle of the June 15 game with the A's in Kansas City Martin was called by Stengel from the bullpen where he was hiding. It was the day before the trading deadline, and Billy figured that if he could last until midnight, he would remain a Yankee. Midnight didn't come fast enough. Martin ran breathlessly to the clubhouse, fearing the worst but hoping against hope, and when he arrived, Stengel, his adopted father, said simply, "Well, you're gone." Billy, in tears, stopped listening and didn't hear the rest of what Casey was saying. "You were the smartest little player I ever had," Stengel was saying. "You got me the hit when I needed it. You did everything I ever asked."

Mantle and Ford, steadfastly unemotional, cried unashamedly when they learned that Martin, their blood brother, had been traded away. "It's like losing a brother," Mantle said. "He was the best friend I ever had."

The trade did not sit well with Stengel. The Yankee manager showed a pronounced resentment when the front office announced that Harry Simpson, acquired from the A's, was going to be the new Yankee left fielder. "I'll play who I want," Casey said.

After Martin left the Yankees his inner fire slowly faded. At Kansas City Martin and A's manager Joe Gordon didn't get along, and Martin drifted to Detroit, Cleveland, Cincinnati, Milwaukee, and finally to Minnesota, where he retired in 1961, his reputation sullied after too many years of mediocrity. Martin did get in a couple more fights, his most famous a one-punch KO of Cub pitcher Jim Brewer in 1960 when Billy was playing with the Reds. Martin broke Brewer's jaw, and when Brewer sued Martin for a million dollars, Billy said, "How would he like it, cash or check?" The joke, however, was on Martin who paid Brewer $20,000 in damages.

For many years the bitterness of his trade from the Yankees haunted Martin. "I needed Stengel only one time in my life," Martin said, "and he let me down." Stengel and Martin didn't talk for many years. "I'm not mad at him," Billy would say, "I just don't want to have anything to do with him."

Weiss's trade with the A's seemed like a one-sided one for Kansas City, but as usual the experts underestimated Weiss's acumen. Weiss sent Martin and three youthful prospects—Woodie Held, Bob Martyn, and Ralph Terry—to the A's in exchange for Harry Simpson, a powerful left-hand hitting outfielder, and a right-handed pitcher named Ryne Duren. Duren had faced the Yankees twice in the spring, and after one of those appearances in which he was blazingly fast and wildly dangerous, the Yankee veterans ordered Stengel to either buy the guy or have him banned from the league. Weiss couldn't ban him, so he bought him. Duren was sent to Denver, but he would return.

It was the second major transaction between the Yankees and the A's. The day after the trade Kansas City boasted eight ex-Yankees in the starting lineup. Vic Power was at first, Billy Martin at second, Lou Skizas at third, with Bob Martyn, Woodie Held, and Bob Cerv in the outfield and Hal Smith catching. Only shortstop Joe DeMaestri was a local A's product. Ex-Yankees on the Kansas City pitching staff included Mickey McDermott, Tom Morgan, Ralph Terry, Tom Gorman, Jack Urban, and Rip Coleman. On the KC bench were ex-Yankees Irv Noren and Billy Hunter. Whenever the Yankees played the A's it was like old home week. Sixteen of the twenty-five-man A's team had been Yankee property!

After the Yankees completed their nine-game winning streak, they regained the league lead. The Yankee depth kept the team on top. Even with Ford out, Stengel had men to take up the slack, with little Bobby Shantz a surprise, 9–1, to lead the staff. Shantz, whom Stengel called "Little Feller", stood only 5 foot 5, but without him the Yankees would have been in real trouble. Shantz was a left-hander with an excellent assortment of off-speed pitches who won eighteen games with the Philadelphia A's in 1951 and twenty-four games in '52. He was awarded the league's Most Valuable Player award in '52 despite being hit on his pitching arm and breaking his wrist in two places with three weeks left in the season. Most of that winter he wore a cast, and in the spring of 1953, he pulled tendons in his shoulder, and for the rest of his career severe pain limited his success. He started the season opener for the A's in 1954, tearing ligaments in his arm and missing the rest of that season. After his twenty-four-win season of '52 in the next four years he won five, one, five, and two games for the A's, and in the winter of 1956 Weiss acquired him from the A's in the Ditmar trade. He was the throw-in. He ended up the lifesaver in '57, and until the Yankees lost him in the expansion draft after the 1960 season, Shantz remained a valuable member of the Yankee pitching staff.

It was a team even greater than the one the year before. For an opposing pitcher to face the Yankees was the hardest task in baseball. The first five Yankee batters—Bauer, McDougald, Mantle, Skowron, and Berra—were the nucleus of an exciting hitting machine, one that often scored in the late innings of a game when the opposition weakened from the relentless pressure. In one game against the White Sox the Yankees were trailing 4–0 in the ninth inning when Bill Skowron hit a grand slam to tie and Yankee pitcher Tommy Byrne hit a pinch-hit home run to win. In another ninth inning victory over the White Sox Mantle tripled with the bases loaded to win the game. The game was played before a Stadium crowd of 50,000 people, and many of the fans had left before the ninth, certain that the Yankees were losers. The early exodus did not escape the watchful eyes of manager Stengel. In the papers the next day Stengel showed his displeasure. "I noticed that many fans took things for granted," he said. "They went home early. I don't like to see people get cheated out of the big thrills of our game which they did for themselves when they went home too soon. Please warn the fans that they are not to leave until the last man is out, not to sit there worrying about the traffic."

Mantle continued to be the key. He hit a home run in the eleventh inning to beat the Orioles in one game; hit for the cycle, a single, double, triple, and home run in another game; hit a 465-foot home run that landed in the next-to-last row of the center-field bleachers in Yankee Stadium to win yet another game. Mantle, batting .367 with twenty-six home runs and sixty-nine RBI's in mid-August, had a chance to become the first player ever to win the triple crown two years in a row, despite the pitchers' insistence on walking him, often intentionally, to keep him from destroying them. Wherever he went, the blond Oklahoman filled the ball parks with fans anxious to watch his prodigious batting feats.

Behind Mantle in the batting order was Bill (Moose) Skowron, emerging as a powerful slugger in his own right. Moose, who looked like the village blacksmith, enjoyed the affection of the fans, who bellowed a loud "Mooooooo, mooooooo, mooooooooo" when he came to bat. With his great strength Skowron sprayed long drives to every area of the ball park, driving in Mantle often and for a while leading the team in RBI's. Behind Skowron was Berra, suffering with a broken nose, but finally beginning to break out of his spring slump. Yogi, whose broken nose resulted in painful headaches and loss of sleep, nevertheless played every day, either behind the plate or in left field. At Stengel's request Yogi wore glasses for a while, but toward the end of August he discarded them, and went 11–20 to raise his average toward respectability.

In one game against Boston Yogi hit a three-run home run, two two-run singles, and a run-producing ground out, for an eight-RBI day. Stengel still wasn't convinced Yogi was doing right by discarding his glasses. "Maybe," the Yankee taskmaster said, "if he had worn them he would have been twenty for twenty." By mid-August the Yankees opened a seven-and-a-half game lead over the White Sox, and it looked like the prediction of a New York pennant by Labor Day would become a reality.

Then on August 18 Mantle was struck by a mysterious ailment. He suffered from a deep gash in his left leg, a jagged incision that went as deep as the bone, completely inhibiting his ability to run. The injury was diagnosed as shin splints, though it seemed very strange that shin splints would occur in the middle of the season. Mantle attributed the condition to the hard turf of the Kansas City ball park, and everyone accepted his explanation. Privately Mantle told Stengel that his car had been parked on a hill, and as he was getting into it he shifted the car out of park and when it started rolling, the sharp edge of the car door slammed against his shin.

On the day his shin splints were diagnosed, Mickey was hitting .385, trailing 39-year-old Ted Williams by a few points, and leading the league in both home runs and RBI's. Over the next few games, though, Mantle went two for sixteen, dropped ten points in batting average and finally admitted a need to rest his painful leg. With Mantle and Ford both out (Ford only appearing three times in August, losing twice) the Yankee lead dropped to three and a half games. A sweep by the pesky White Sox in their August 27, 28, and 29 series with the Yankees at Comiskey Park would put the Sox right back in contention.

The Sox didn't win a game. In the first game Yogi Berra drove in six runs, including the winning runs with a three-run home run. When Yogi had been at the depth of his summer slump, he kept saying, "The season ain't over yet, ya know," and he was right. He finished with twenty-four home runs and eighty-two runs batted in, not bad for a guy in a slump. Grim, the outstanding man in the bullpen for the last three years, won his eleventh game. In the second game Larsen and Turley combined to defeat Chicago with Bauer hitting a home run to win the game. The Yankees made it look easy. If they could win the third game, their lead would balloon to six and a half games, and Stengel could then safely rest his injured stars to prepare for the world series.

Forty thousand people, the largest weekday crowd in the history of Comiskey Park, attended the final game of the three-game series, fully realizing that this would be the last chance for the White Sox. Al Lopez started his right-handed ace, Dick Donovan, against the Yankees' Tom Sturdivant, winner of five of his last six decisions. Bauer continued his excellent hitting with a home run in the third inning, and a couple innings later Chicago scored a run against Sturdivant. With the score 1–1 in the sixth, Stengel unsuccessfully pinch hit for his young pitcher and relieved with Ford, still fighting shoulder miseries. Donovan and Ford battled into extra innings.

Mantle doubled in the tenth but was unable to score, and Ford kept the White Sox at bay as the game entered the eleventh inning. It had been agreed before the game that no inning could begin after four-thirty so the Yankees could catch a train back to New York City. The Yankees' traveling secretary, Bill

McCorry, hated to fly as did George Weiss, so the Yankees, unlike the other teams, didn't fly. Starting the eleventh inning the teams had only twenty minutes to go before the four-thirty deadline was reached. A 1–1 tie seemed inevitable.

Enos Slaughter was the first batter for the Yankees in the top of the eleventh. On the first pitch Slaughter, a left-handed batter now 41 years old, uncoiled a level swing and hit one of the longest home runs of his career, a deep drive into the right-field seats for a 2–1 Yankee lead, another Yankee reserve contributing to the team's success. The next two Yankees quickly retired themselves, and in the bottom of the eleventh Ford retired the first three White Sox with dispatch, beating the four-thirty deadline with minutes to spare.

"Ford was remarkable today," Stengel said after the game. "Yup, he was tremendous. And," he added, "so was the other guy who never stops running."

"Country" Slaughter was the "other guy" Stengel was referring to. A St. Louis Cardinal between 1938 and 1954, he averaged .305 over his illustrious Cardinal career. He was a swashbuckling, dynamic performer, and though the legendary Gashouse Gang was breaking up when he arrived in 1938, he continued to play in the image of the gang. He always hustled. He ran and never walked. He loved the game of baseball, and to him injuries were occupational hazards to be shrugged off whenever possible. Slaughter one time pulled a muscle in his side, and Stengel asked him how soon it would be before he could play again. "How soon?" said Enos. "Right now. Ain't nothin' but a little meat torn away from the rib cage that'll mend itself in no time." When he was hit by a pitched ball, even when he was in great pain, he refused to rub it to show the opposition that it hurt. He knew only one way to play—hard.

In 1942 Slaughter led the Cardinals to a world series victory against the Yankees. In the eighth inning of the seventh and final game of the 1946 world series against the Boston Red Sox he raced from first to home on a single to score the winning run and win the series. Ten times Slaughter was chosen to play on the National League All-Star team. In 1954, his final season with the Cards, Wally Moon took his job, and that April the 38-year-old Enos was traded to the Yankees for three minor leaguers, including Bill Virdon. Slaughter, who valued loyalty highly on his list of priorities, was shocked that after nineteen years the Cardinal organization would let him go. He felt betrayed, and in newspapers across the country there was a picture of this bald-headed, hard-bitten veteran crying uncontrollably into a handkerchief.

Slaughter's crying scene did not sit well with the Yankee players. The Yankees had just won five consecutive world championships, and they couldn't understand what he was so upset about. Slaughter didn't remain very long with the Yankees, though. George Weiss sent him and Johnny Sain to the Kansas City A's for pitcher Sonny Dixon, a prospective star who never pitched well in New York. Then in August of 1956, the Yankee outfield depleted by injuries, Slaughter returned to the Yankees amid controversy. George Weiss released Phil Rizzuto, the popular Yankee shortstop, in order to make room for him. Slaughter, at age 40, was two years older than Rizzuto. Slaughter remained with the Yankees for three stormy years until at the end of the 1959 season Weiss sold the 43-year-old War-horse on waivers to the Milwaukee Braves.

Slaughter was a loner, an outspoken individual who never was particularly popular with the other Yankee players. He was a rah-rah type on a team that was never especially rah-rah. He was opinionated, and if he wanted to say something, he said it, letting the chips fall where they might. He didn't believe in holding his tongue. Some of the Yankees resented him because he was a dyed-in-the-wool National Leaguer. He wore a Yankee uniform, but at heart he would always be a hustling Cardinal. Even though he was past 40 he continued to display hustle wherever he went, running to and from the outfield. When Hank Bauer did that, the players accepted it as Bauer's way of playing, but when Enos did it, they felt his show of hustle was unnecessary, an attempt to make them look bad. "Some of my players think he's a showoff," Stengel said about his aging warrior. "That's because every time they see him he's running."

The two old National League campaigners, Slaughter and Stengel, formed a mutual admiration society, and would usually sit together at the end of the bench. During Stengel's last few years as Yankee manager Stengel became very critical of the players, and he and Slaughter were especially critical of the young players. "What the hell did you do that for?" Enos would yell when a younger player made an error. Then Stengel would jump on him, too.

The kids resented Enos as much as he resented them. Slaughter felt he should be playing, that they couldn't play as well as he could. They felt that he was a hypochondriac who begged out of more games than he played. When Slaughter signed he didn't get a big bonus and he never made big money with the penurious Cardinals despite his outstanding career, and he felt cheated. Slaughter constantly teased bonus baby Clete Boyer, showing contempt by spitting tobacco juice on the kid's glove and spikes.

Yet Slaughter was a valuable outfield replacement and an excellent pinch hitter during his final three years with the Yankees. He hustled to the end. When he was sold to the Braves in early September 1959, he told the media that the Yankees lost the pennant that year because many of the veterans thought Stengel was in his second childhood and wouldn't listen to him. Howls of Yankee outrage resulted, and despite protestations by Slaughter that he was misquoted, he left the way he came, in controversy.

In September 1957 the Senate passed the first civil rights legislation since the Reconstruction eighty years earlier, a bill that gave the Department of Justice power to enforce citizens' civil rights—including that to attend an integrated school. When school integration began several days after the bill was passed, there was a riot in Charlotte, North Carolina, and Governor Faubus of Arkansas called the state National Guard to Central High School in Little Rock to prevent nine Negro students from entering the building. President Eisenhower, in response, federalized the Arkansas Guard, and sent 10,000 troops to the school to guarantee the admission of the nine children, calling on the people of the South to "preserve law and respect for the law even if they disagreed with them." Prices rose drastically, setting new records, and the price of food was at its highest level since 1952.

The Ford Company introduced its first new major automobile in nineteen years, called the Edsel, and critics said that it looked like a car that had swallowed a lemon. It turned out to be one, too. Rock and roll music began to develop from its Billy Haley, ''Rock Around the Clock'' inception, and Elvis Presley continued to be the biggest name in the industry.

The New York Giants' Board of Directors voted eight to one to move to San Francisco. Only board member Donald Grant voted against the move, saying, ''It just tears my heart out to see them go.'' It was also certain that the Brooklyn Dodgers were California-bound, their new home to be in Los Angeles.

Though the Yankees had defeated the White Sox three-straight and led by six and a half games, Stengel still did not feel that his team was assured the pennant, and his worries intensified when Hank Bauer broke his left thumb sliding and slugging first-baseman Bill Skowron severely injured his lower back while lifting a two-ton air-conditioning unit in his New Jersey home. Mantle continued to play with a painful left leg, and he missed fly balls that under normal conditions he would catch. Stengel kept Mantle out of his starting lineup for a week, pinch hitting his star, but as the pain of his shin increased, George Weiss finally stepped in and had Mantle hospitalized on September 7. On September 13 Mantle returned from the hospital, his triple crown hopes dashed because of his ''shin-splint'' injury. Mickey finished the season with a .365 average, but Ted Williams finished at .388. Mickey hit thirty-four home runs. Roy Sievers of Washington hit forty-two. Williams hit thirty-eight. Mantle finished with ninety-four RBI's. Five other players, led by Sievers with 114, finished with more.

After Mantle returned the Yankees won seven of their next eight games, with Tom Sturdivant defeating the Red Sox on September 21 to clinch a tie for the pennant. That night the Kansas City A's defeated the White Sox to give the Yankees the pennant. Some of the Yankees were in their clubhouse when they learned of the pennant clinching, but with so many key people injured or not up to par physically, there was little joy, more an expression of relief that they had somehow struggled through to win.

In 1957 the Yankees did not have one overpowering pitcher like Billy Pierce of the White Sox or Jim Bunning of the Tigers or Early Wynn of the Indians, but they had a staff of classy pitchers who led both leagues with a 3.00 ERA. Bobby Shantz led the league at 2.45, Tom Sturdivant was second at 2.54, and Bob Turley was fourth behind Bunning at 2.71. Whitey Ford's ERA was 2.57, but he didn't have enough innings pitched to qualify for the ERA title. Neither did Grim at 2.63.

Ford finished the season with an 11–5 record as did Shantz, his early-season replacement. Both little lefties were pitching in pain and performing well despite it. Reliefer Grim was 12–8 from the bullpen with nineteen saves, the most in the majors. Art Ditmar, 8–3, in August replaced Kucks in the rotation and made important contributions. Don Larsen won his last four games in a row to finish with ten wins, and Turley won three of four in September to finish 13–6.

Only John Kucks, 8–10, was disappointing. Sturdivant, who for the second year in a row won sixteen games, emerged as the top pitcher on the staff. Sturdy won eight of nine games in August and September including seven in a row to finish 16–6, the best winning percentage in the league. Sturdivant was a relatively anonymous player who rarely made headlines, but on the mound he was a tough, battling pitcher who had a great deal of confidence in his own ability and who pitched with intelligence and control. He threw a live fast ball, a sharp curve, and a fast-breaking slider, and mixed his pitches cleverly, keeping the batters off-stride.

Off the field Sturdivant kept everyone off-stride. He was a screwball in the grand tradition of John Lindell and George Stirnweiss, Yankees when Tom attended his first spring training in 1950. Tommy loved to laugh, to have a good time, to party, to play practical jokes. He was called Flakey by some of the others because he was so unpredictable. It was Sturdivant who took the cudgel from Lindell and Stirnweiss and put bugs and other crawling things into Rizzuto's glove, pants, and locker during the two years Sturdivant and Rizzuto played together before Phil was released in mid-1956. Sturdivant once put a lobster in Phil's trousers. Rizzuto put one leg in and when the other leg discovered the spiny lobster, he ripped his pants to shreds trying to get them off. Once in spring training Johnny Kucks was driving back to his apartment when he noticed Sturdivant's car coming toward him. The car whizzed past. No one was at the wheel. Sturdivant had ducked down under the dashboard to amuse his buddy, Kucks. "You could have killed us both," Kucks told Tommy later. Tom just laughed.

On the road the world was not safe from Sturdivant. From the top floor of the hotel room where he was staying, Sturdivant enjoyed playing the mad bomber. He tried to drown people by dropping water bombs on their heads. Sometimes he used wastebaskets of water to improve his chances of success. To Sturdivant it was fun. "Bombs away," Tommy would yell, as he and Kucks took turns matching their bombing marksmanship on unsuspecting hotel guests.

Sturdivant started as an infield prospect, but a hamstring injury ended that career. In 1952 he began his career as a pitcher, working his way through the Yankee farm system. After spending most of 1955 sitting on the Yankee bench and watching, Sturdivant broke into the starting rotation and in both 1956 and '57 won sixteen games. After the 1957 season he held out, missed a part of spring training, hurt his arm, had a poor year, and was traded in early 1959 to Kansas City. It didn't last long, but it was a gas while it lasted.

It was May, hot and muggy in Oklahoma City, when I arrived at Tom Sturdivant's home, which, I was fascinated to find, was fully equipped with a combination bomb-tornado shelter. On my way from Missouri through Oklahoma on the radio every ten minutes came dire warnings of tornadoes, and being an easterner, I spent as much time looking for twisters as I did watching the road. I much preferred getting hit by a car than a tornado. The people who live in tornado country, though, don't pay much attention to the warnings. It's not that they don't respect the awesome power of tornadoes; rather they know that there isn't much they can do about them. They ignore the constant warnings and go about their business.

Sturdivant's wife, Ryba, and I sat in the living room enjoying Tom's considerable story-telling ability.

"I expected to make the Yankees from the time I was 6 years old," Tom said. "I knew all along I was going to make the Yankees. Nobody else thought I was going to. But I *knew* I was. I had three goals in life: I wanted to be a Yankee, I wanted to pitch regular for the Yankees, and I wanted to win a world series game. Making the Yankees had been my whole life, my whole desire. I didn't have anything else to live for if I didn't make them."

"You broke into the starting rotation in 1956," I said.

"Around the middle of June Stengel started me in Cleveland," Sturdivant said. "I won that ball game, beat Herb Score, three to one, and Casey started to pitch me regularly. My wife says that the three most beautiful things that she's ever seen was, number one, Ted Williams swinging a baseball bat, number two, Mickey Mantle bunting and running to first base, and number three, Herb Score pitching. I never will forget later on we were in Cleveland, and I was pitching for the Yankees, and Herb was a-pumpin' one day, oh my gosh, and he was just mowing us down, and dadgum, it seemed like the longer the ball game would get, the harder he threw. And so I was hollering, 'Come on boys, let's get some runs,' and everything, so we started making bets. You know, if I get a base hit, I get a case of Yoo-Hoo from Yogi, and I'd get this from another one and that from another one, and I got up, and Score reached back and threw his hummer, and I just reached out and bunted at it, except I bunted it over the third-baseman's head. You know what I mean." Sturdivant let loose with a laugh that could have been heard down the block. "Hahahahahahahahahaha. Hell, I ran down to first base like I slugged him. You know what I mean! Hahahahahahahahahaha. I was cocky as hell. He was standing there shaking his head.

"1956 was nothing but happiness. That's the only thing I can think of. Was nothing but happiness. It was like a dream fulfilled. It just all happened, and I was there. I was doing what I wanted to do."

"So in 1956 after you beat Brooklyn in the series, you accomplished all your goals in one shot," I said.

"Well, that's right. And in '57 I had a better year, and I expected in '58 to have the same type year."

At the end of 1957, for the second year in a row Sturdivant was a sixteen-game winner, acknowledged to be the top right-hander on the staff. His 2.54 ERA was second only to teammate Bobby Shantz's. Nevertheless, despite this continued period of excellence, there was a scarcity of newspaper ink about Sturdivant. What people knew about him was that he wore number 47, an unusually high number for a regular, and that before he delivered a pitch he would bend over like a jack knife and shimmy his arms. They called him the Elvis Presley of baseball. He was a winner, but another anonymous Yankee winner.

"Did you have a particular pitching philosophy?"

"I don't know," Sturdivant said. "I just tried to keep the ball in the middle of the ball field, because Yogi was a great catcher, and shortstop and second were extremely strong, and in center field was probably the greatest athlete that ever lived, and if I could keep it in the middle of the field no matter how hard they hit it I had a great chance of getting somebody out. I didn't overpower anybody. I didn't blow it by anybody, but I had a place where I tried to pitch a lot of times. I liked to throw up and in on a lot of hitters. I had a little slider that I threw outside, and it didn't look like very much, and a lot of guys tried to pull it, and they'd hit it to center field, and Mickey would chase it down. Mantle once said to me, 'If you hadn't been pitching for the Yankees, I'd have played seven more years.' Hahahahahahahahahahahahahaha. I wouldn't say I was a particularly heady pitcher. I was an ordinary pitcher who happened to be with a great ball club at the time.

"What a team we had," Tom said. "Let me tell you a story about Yogi. I remember I was a rookie, and I was making $6,000 a year, and Ryba had two little kids, and I was struggling just to have her in New York with me. And Yogi said to me, 'Tom, you should get Ryba a maid.' He was so serious. I should get Ryba a maid.

"I'll tell you something about Yogi," he continued. "Everybody says a lot of things about Yogi. But Yogi had a lot of dry wit, and he joked a lot with the people that he knew, and you could tell when he liked you, because he would kind of tap around on you and punch you and kid with you. You could talk with Yogi, even when you were a rookie. He knew hitters, and he watched the way they moved around the plate, and Yogi would call you a tremendous ball game. But if you started shaking Yogi off a lot, and you got to thinking that you were a little smarter than he was, then he would set back there and let you throw anything that you wanted to, making it twice as hard for yourself, and he just let you know that he was a pretty fair country catcher. Yogi was a hell of a lot smarter behind the plate than a lot of people thought he was, and he could really help you, but you had to talk to Yogi and let him know that you needed his help. I never had any problems with Yogi. If he wanted a pitch, I threw it. He would have some reason for it."

"Did the Yankees miss Billy Martin after they traded him?" I asked.

"Now," Tommy said, "I'm going to be perfectly honest with you about the way I feel about Billy Martin. I felt that Billy Martin was an average major league ball player. But I believe that in ball games that you had to win, like in the series, that Billy could build hisself up to where Billy was a super-star during games that you had to have. But as an ordinary, everyday ball player, Billy was average. Like when we went into Chicago one series, and we had to win, and Billy had a hellacious series. He was unbelievable. And the next day we went to Kansas City, and they hit two ground balls to him, two mediocre ground balls, and he booted both of them. You know what I mean. But Billy could arouse a ball club. For a given number of games Billy could even carry a ball club. He could psych himself up. But when you're playing every day, you can't psych yourself up for that long.

"I used to get so mad at Billy I couldn't see straight," he continued. "I mean he would agitate me, and the more he would agitate me, the harder I'd throw. Some ball games I'd be out there, and I'd be struggling. You know what I mean? Just half-ass into it, and he'd come up and say, 'Why, you big pussy. Molly Putz could hit you. You could hit me right in my nose with your fast ball and it wouldn't hurt.' Boy, that next hitter, I'm telling you. That next hitter, I'd reach back and give him something—he'd know that I was out there! And if somebody knocked Billy down, he could agitate me, and I'd throw close to somebody, and I'd get my ass whipped.

"But I also remember another time when I had the bases loaded in the ninth inning and one out, and I was struggling, and Billy came over, and said, 'Look up over Yogi's right shoulder into the upper deck.' We were playing in Chicago. And I looked up there, and this little ole gal had her dress clear up to her ass. Hahahahahahahahahahahahaha. So I shot beaver for a little while, and I forgot what was happening. And I started waving to her. And I started saying, 'Poontang, poontang,' you know what I mean? And I turned around, and Martin was laughing, and I just zip, zip, zip, and got 'em out, and we went in. Hell. If he hadn't come over, mentally I was gone. I had battled it to a point of frenzy. And he just come in and got me out of it. But often Weiss traded to keep his front line players in line. It shook the super boys up a little bit. With no regard to sentiment. The individual meant nothing to Weiss. You were a number. I believe had Weiss not retired he would have traded Mantle if he could have gotten money for him. People forgit you real quick. Fans forgit you, especially if they get somebody to take your place. Weiss never took it into consideration that young men had this desire to be a Yankee. What being a Yankee meant. You know, after I left, I said that the Yankees were horseshit, but really, I was dying to go back.

"Mickey was such a big influence on the team," he said. "To me Mickey Mantle was the Yankees. I'm a kind of idolizer. First it was Lou Gehrig, then it was DiMaggio, and then it was Mantle. There was Ruth and Gehrig, but I was a Gehrig fan. I read the book *Pride of the Yankees* and I saw the movie seventeen times, and Gehrig, the pride of the Yankees, he was my ball player. And after I got to the Yankees and Billy Dickey was there, and he's from Arkansas, and all my folks are from Arkansas, and Bill and I became real close. When we rode trains at that time, we'd go to the dining car, and Bill, who was Gehrig's roommate, would tell me about Gehrig for hours and tell me what a great person Gehrig was.

"The greatest thing about Mickey is that I never heard him say anything detrimental about anybody," Tommy said. "My wife brought that to my attention. That was the one thing she admired most about Mantle. He just wouldn't say anything if he didn't like someone. Mickey was a quiet sort of person in a strange crowd, but in his group he was just a ball of fire and a lot of fun. He liked western music, and he just liked the good ole down-to-earth things. He'd give you anything. He'd loan you money and never ask you for it back. And I imagine that there was a lot of people that never did pay him back. And he'd never ask you for it. And I guess his theory was if they didn't pay him back after he was good enough to loan it, then they wouldn't get any more. And rookies, he was always tremendous with rookies, because he knew that they were broke, and he remembered how he was when he came to camp there, and if they didn't have the money to get their wives to New York, or things like that, well, Mickey would give them the money to do it. And of course, it might take them a year or two to pay him back. But they would be so grateful that they'd get the money back to him.

"He liked to have his fun," he continued. "I imagine that the pressure was more on Mantle than it was on anybody. You know the people came out to see the Yankees, but the people really came out to see Mantle, and it wasn't the Yankees that got booed, it was Mantle that got booed. Because Mantle was the greatest ball player walking.''

''That's why they booed him?'' I said.

''Yes. Why did they cheer the Mets? They were the worst ball players in America. I played with the Mets. When I first walked out there, they remembered me as a Yankee, and they gave me a booing ovation, but after I got killed and they saw how bad I was, they gave me a standing ovation. They thought that if I had guts enough to go out there with the junk I had left, I needed an ovation! Mickey once said to me after I was traded by the Yankees to Kansas City, 'My batting average is going to go up thirty points, and the Kansas City team average is going to drop ten points!'

''I remember one birthday party I had,'' Sturdivant said. ''It was my birthday over at our house, and Mickey was settin' there, and we got to talking about different drinks, and he was drinking Cutty Sark and water, and he was saying to us, 'There isn't any kind of a drink that I can't taste.' And all the time he was saying this, Ryba had the vodka bottle, and every time he would turn around, she would load his glass. And he was settin' there, and Larsen, Berra, and Kucks and everybody, we kept talking to him and agitatin' him, and he was getting more and more loaded, and he was saying, 'You're damn right. I can taste any kind of drink.' And Ryba said, 'Mickey, are you sure that you can taste vodka?' And he said, 'You're damn right I can taste vodka.' Well, by this time his drink was 100 percent vodka. No water. No anything. Vodka. So he started to get up to go to the bathroom, and he couldn't get up. He'd get up, and he'd fall back. He'd get up, and he'd fall back. And he said, 'Boy, my ass sure is getting heavy!'

''Did you remember Mickey's shin splints?'' Sturdivant asked me.

''Yeah,'' I said.

''Hahahahahahahahahahahahahahahahaha,'' Tom said. ''I'll tell you how that happened and how we explained it to Stengel. We were playing at the Englewood Golf and Country Club, Mickey and me, and Mickey had me one down going onto the ninth, and we were playing for something like $5,000. Not real money, but we'd go and mark it up on the board. It wasn't the idea of not losing money. It was the idea of not getting beat. And on the ninth hole, Mickey hit a beautiful drive up just to the right of the hole, and I hit my first shot and dribbled it down a ways, and he says, 'C'mon honey, pull up your skirt and don't let your bloomers fall around your ankles.' And he's agitatin' me all the way up the fairway. And he's giggling and everything. And my next shot I hit on the green, and he chips his up on the green, and we're both on in two, and I've got about a thirty-five-foot putt, and Mickey, he's got about a three-foot putt. And I sink mine. And he two-putts, and I win it. And when I was coming off the green, I went, 'Hehehehehehehehehehehehehehehehehe,' a high pitched laugh like that and it just killed him. It made him madder than hell. So as he was walking off, there was a tree limb hanging up there, and he had his putter, and he swung that thing at the tree limb over his head, and the putter wasn't quite long enough to hit the limb, and the club head came down and hit him right on the shin. He was bleeding like a stuck pig. And I said, 'Mick, we'd better go in.' And he said, 'Hell, no, we're not going in. We're playing the back nine.' And I couldn't talk him out of it, he was so mad. So all he does is wrap his handkerchief around it and as he was walking, you could hear the blood going, squish, squash, squish, squash. We continued to play, and as it turned out he won the back nine, and he was perfectly happy. And then we go in, and he said, 'What are we going to tell Gus Mauch [the trainer]? What are we going to tell the Yankees?' He put that putter into his leg right down to the bone. He didn't do *anything* halfway. He took the pain like a champion, and he played like a champion. So I said, 'Mickey, we're going to tell them that we were parked on a hill and you were getting into your car, and you pulled it out of park and the sharp point of the door hit you in the shin.' And that's what we told them. Hahahahahahahahahahahahahahahahahahahaha.''

Ryba spoke up. ''Mickey was on television, and I was watching him one day.''

''With Duke Snider and Willie Mays,'' Tom said. ''And one of the sportswriters asked Mickey exactly what shin splints are.''

''And,'' Ryba broke in, ''he started explaining, going err, ahhh, and he never did explain it, and he finished by saying, 'And that's what shin splints are.' ''

''And,'' said Tom, ''Willie says, 'Yes, suh, that's what ah calls shin splints, too, Mickey.' Hahahahahahahahahahahahahahahahahahaha. Man, I've seen him play with injuries worse than that. And George Weiss never found out about how he got those shin splints, either. Hahahahahahahahahahahahaha.''

''I'll tell you a funny story,'' said Tommy. ''It was in Yankee Stadium the first year after I had been traded to the Athletics. This was 1959. And we were playing the Yankees, and the night before the game Mickey and I go out for dinner, and he says, 'You know, Tom, you're the only right-handed pitcher who has enough control that I'd hit righty off of, and I believe off of you I could hit one completely out of Yankee Stadium.' You know. Hahahahahahaha. Actually that kind of got to me a little, putting it to me the way he was. So I said, 'I'll tell you what, Mickey. If the ball game's not at stake, now I'm not going to take anything off of it, but if you walk up there right-handed, I'll reach back and let you have the best fast ball I've got, letter-high and right down the middle. We'll just find out whether you're a better hitter or I'm a better pitcher.' And he said, 'You're on.'

''Well, the next day we get way behind and sure enough, here comes ole mop-up man Sturdivant in to pitch for the Athletics, and Mickey steps into the batter's box as a right-handed hitter. And our manager, Eddie Lopat, he whistles, which is the curve-ball sign. And Lopat at that time had an automatic fine if he called a pitch from the bench and you didn't throw it. And I was shaking my head trying to tell Lopat that my shoulder hurt, I can't throw a curve ball, you know. And he whistles again and sticks up some money in the air like he's going to fine me. So the first pitch I throw Mickey is a big ole roundhouse curve ball, and Mickey, he runs clear out of the batter's box. And he is some kind of mad somabitch. And he gets up there again, and Lopat whistles again. Well, instead of throwing a curve ball, I throw him a slider, which is a halfway fast ball." A slider, Tom failed to mention, is also a halfway curve ball. "And he hits a line drive, and our center fielder, Bobby Del Greco, runs out to the monuments and he catches it. Remember, he has to hit the ball clear out of the ball park to win the bet. But anyway, it's caught. And he runs to first and makes a circle and comes runnin' back at me. You know. I had already given him the mound. I wasn't going to stand on that mound and let that freight train run over me. And aw, he was mad, and everybody was giggling on our bench 'cause they knew what was going on. And later on, he said this was one of the funniest experiences of his career, me throwing him the big ole curve ball. Crossing him up, you know. Good ole Tom. Ole buddy Tom. But I want the truth to be known that I was told to throw the curve ball. Really, I didn't have enough curve ball that he couldn't hit it anyway. In fact after that first one, what he said to me was, 'Throw that goddamn curve again, and I'll kill you with it.' And he tried to. Only thing, he hit it too high. Hahahahahahahahahahahahahahaha-haha.''

"There were very few managers that could have managed the Yankee ball club," Tom said. "Stengel was an extremely good manager, a very good psychologist. I remember I had pitched thirty-six or thirty-seven consecutive scoreless innings one spring training, and Stengel came to me, called me over to the side, and he said, 'Mr. Sturdivant. I see here by the record that for the last two years your strikeouts were double your walks and almost as many as your innings pitched. To what do you attribute this kind of record?' I said, 'Mr. Stengel, I attribute this to my fast ball. It's my best pitch.' And he says, 'Son, when are you going to throw it?' He knew I was a competitive sort of individual. He just wanted me to throw a little bit harder. He would say something to me on that mound and walk back to the bench, and I'm liable to hit the next batter in the back."

"What would Casey call you?"

"Sometimes he would call me a dumb Dutchman. And sometime put somabitch on the end of it. And then he'd turn around, and that damn, gimpy, sawed off Dutch son of a bitch hisself would walk off, and I'd be so mad I'd want to kill him. Some people you have to build a fire under, and others you had to pamper and treat in a different way. This is where Stengel was great.

"It sure was funny," Sturdivant continued. "The sportswriters sure had a hard time understanding Mr. Stengel, but I never did. He never talked Stengelese to us. I mean we always understood just exactly what he meant.

"I look back at it," he continued. "I wasn't a super-star. And there wasn't any way that I ever was going to be a super-star. And if I had realized it early, then I might have had an entirely different career. But a lot of things affect people in different ways. Being with the Yankees, I guess I was cocky, and I guess I forgot that it takes continuous hard work, and that you're no better than your last ball game. You know, I started with Casey and ten years later I finished with Casey on the Mets. I don't know whether he liked it, but I did. Like you say, you have your idols, and I didn't find out how good he was until I started bouncing around and finding out how bad the rest of them were."

Sturdivant held out during most of the spring training of 1958, wasn't at full strength when the season started, and the second game of the season tore the ligaments in his shoulder on a cold and rainy day in Boston. After his disappointing 1958 season, 3–6, Sturdivant was traded to the Kansas City A's in May of 1959 along with John Kucks and Jerry Lumpe.

Waite Hoyt, the Hall-of-Fame Yankee pitcher of the 1920s, was the first to warn his fellow Yankee pitchers about the perils of holding out. "If you don't sign that contract," Hoyt said many years ago, "you might get traded, and then you'll have to pitch against the Yankees."

When Sturdivant left the Yankees he became a nomad, traveling to a new team each year, always hoping the Yankees would take him back. Sturdy was like a man whose wife leaves him for another man. He always hopes she'll come back, but he knows she never will. In 1964 Sturdivant ended his career playing with the Mets, and at age 34 he retired.

"I found out the Yankees could win without me. They had so much talent. Can't knock them, because they had so much success, but if I had to do it all over again, I'd do everything the same except I think I might change my mental attitude. Because still, I would still love to play." Sturdivant smiled sadly, "And even though when you are traded, when you say this one did me a dirty, and that one did me a dirty, that's not true. You're saying this because you want to come back. Anyone who says they didn't want to come back is a liar. 'Cause that was the only place to play."

"Why was that?" I asked.

"It was the Yankees," Tom said. "It was the Yankees."

I could see on Ryba's face that the life of the Sturdivants hadn't been any bed of roses since Tommy hurt his arm and was traded. Ryba fixed us dinner, and after dinner Tom showed me their combination tornado-bomb shelter. It was under the playroom, down a short flight of stairs, and it was filled with shelves and shelves of can goods and dry foods, enough supplies to last months. It was a pretty frightening concept to be hiding in a cramped hole whether as protection against an atomic bomb attack or a tornado. Somehow, both possibilities seemed remote.

The next morning I sat in the Oklahoma City airport watching the tornado warnings on the public television sets. It had turned suddenly very black outside, and it began raining in torrents, threatening the departure of the airplanes. On the television a reporter was warning residents in the area just west of the airport that there was a tornado alert. I ran to a large western window, and far on the horizon I could see a thin, undulating line of gray, looking like a piece of wavy string. That afternoon, after arriving in Dallas, Texas, in one of the heaviest downpours I have ever experienced, I read in the local paper that the tornado I had seen killed six people in Union City, just west of the Oklahoma City airport.

Milwaukee won the 1957 National League pennant by a wide margin, and after having blown it to the Dodgers the year before, the good burghers of the city that made beer famous really let loose, scattering confetti, ticker tape, and garbage in joyous celebration. The Braves had an excellent team, boasting a powerful lineup of hitters including outfielder Henry Aaron, third-baseman

Eddie Mathews, first-baseman Joe Adcock, and catcher Del Crandell. Short-stop Johnny Logan and second-baseman Red Schoendienst were an excellent double-play combination, and the pitching staff sported twenty-one-game winner Warren Spahn, eighteen-game winner Bob Buhl, and seventeen-game winner Lew Burdette. A solid team. Not as good as the Dodgers, the Yankees felt, because the Dodgers had so much more speed in the field and on the bases.

The Yankees, however, were going into the series at less than full strength themselves, and Stengel was worried. Mantle's "shin splints" hampered his hitting when he had to bat left-handed, and in the outfield he was slowed. Bill Skowron, wearing a bulky corset to protect his back, was having difficulty swinging a bat and was a doubtful participant. In fact, after Skowron batted in the first inning of the first game and grounded out, he immediately took himself out of the game, and during the entire series he batted only four times. The men who replaced him at first, Ellie Howard, Harry Simpson, and Joe Collins, only managed 3 for 23.

The first two games were played at Yankee Stadium, the next three in Milwaukee, and the final two back in the Stadium. The opening game was a crashing bore. Almost 70,000 fans packed the Stadium on a brilliant fall afternoon, and were given a chuckle when the Milwaukee fans, singing the national anthem, concluded with "The la-and of the freeeeeee, and the home of the Braves." It was the highlight of the day. Whitey Ford pitched a calculating, precise five-hitter to win 3–1 as Hank Bauer and Andy Carey drove in runs and Jerry Coleman squeezed home an insurance run against Spahn.

In the second game Lew Burdette, the ex-Yankee farmhand who had been traded to the Boston Braves in 1951 for John Sain, battled Bobby Shantz. After Shantz struck out Schoendienst, Logan, and Mathews in the first inning, he fell behind 1–0 when Hank Aaron blasted a towering fly ball to center field that Mantle misjudged. The ball bounced behind him and rolled to the 461-foot sign for a triple. Adcock singled Aaron home. In the bottom of the second Jerry Coleman hit a fifteen-foot single that neither pitcher Burdette nor catcher Crandall could reach, driving home Enos Slaughter to tie the score 1–1. With Coleman on first and Tony Kubek on second and two outs, pitcher Shantz pulled a drive deep down the left-field line, and with the runners moving, Braves left fielder Wes Covington, a highly touted rookie, raced toward the stands and at the last moment threw up his glove and backhanded the ball on the run to end the inning and save the game. Logan homered in the third to give the Braves a 2–1 lead, but Bauer matched it in the Yankee half of the inning to tie the score 2–2. In the fourth the Braves won the game on three consecutive singles by Adcock, Andy Pafko, and Covington, and on Covington's hit third-baseman Kubek allowed Slaughter's relay to get by him and bounce into the Braves dugout as Pafko scored from first to give Milwaukee the 4–2 win. In the final six innings the Yankees did very little against Burdette.

The teams were given a day off to travel back to Wisconsin for the next three games, and during the day, the Yankees bused to their living quarters at Browns Lake, a resort out in the countryside. The city itself was very noisy because of the continuing exuberance of the Braves rooters, so the Yankees stayed where they would be able to sleep in peace. Stengel called for a workout during the off-day, and after the drive from Browns Lake to the Milwaukee ball park, the team was surprised by the deluge of people who greeted the bus. When several of the local fanatics attempted to board the bus, Stengel called them "bush." The expression was picked up in the local newspapers, and for the next three days in Milwaukee, on the bus trip from Browns Lake to County Stadium and back, Milwaukee fans lined the route holding up placards reading "The Yankees Are Bush" and "Stengel Is Bush." There were hard feelings against the Big City slickers in Milwaukee.

The 45,000-seat County Stadium was filled to capacity, and the Braves officials had to return more than 200,000 requests for series tickets in this baseball-crazed part of the world. When Milwaukee pitcher Bob Buhl opened the game with a strike, a tumultuous roar thundered through the park. An even louder cascading of noise arose when lead-off Yankee Hank Bauer grounded out. But the next batter, Yankee rookie Tony Kubek, a 21-year-old youngster who had been born and raised in Milwaukee, swung at the first pitch and pulled the ball over the right-field fence. As Kubek sped around the bases, there was an eerie, deadening silence. There wasn't a boo or a whistle or a clap or a cheer. The Yankees led 1–0, and Buhl became so rattled by the home run that he walked Mantle and Berra. On a 3–2 count to Gil McDougald, Buhl spun and tried to pick Mantle off at second. The pick-off throw sailed to the wrong side of the bag, and as Mantle drove safely back to second, second-baseman Red Schoendienst leaped across him in a futile attempt to stop the ball from going into center field. Schoendienst fell heavily on top of the prostrate Mantle, who had to push Schoendienst off him before running to third. In the struggle to extricate himself, Mantle tore ligaments in his shoulder. The golf club injury had cost him the triple crown. This shoulder injury severely hampered his left-handed batting for the remainder of his career.

Mantle eventually scored on a long fly ball by McDougald, and Berra scored on a single by first-baseman Harry Simpson to give New York three first-inning runs. Stengel had started Turley, who was wild. In the second inning Milwaukee scored a run as Turley allowed a walk, two singles, and another walk. With the bases loaded Stengel lifted Turley and replaced him with Don Larsen, and in Larsen's first series appearance since his perfect game, he induced Hank Aaron to fly out to end the inning. Larsen neutralized the next six batters to run his perfect streak to an unbelievable thirty-four batters in a row. Meanwhile the Yankees pounded six more Braves pitchers for a total of twelve runs to give Larsen the easy win. Rookie Jerry Lumpe, whom Stengel started at third in a surprise move, singled in a couple of runs, Mantle hit a 410-foot home run off Gene Conley into the Braves bullpen, and Kubek, who had only hit three home runs all season long, hit his second home run of the game for three more runs. The deadly silence of the first inning continued throughout the game and only a two-run home run in the fifth by 23-year-old Henry Aaron, the National League leader in home runs with forty-four, broke the wake-like silence. The Yankees won 12–3. After the game Stengel cornered rookie Kubek in his locker stall. "Go home and thank your mother and father for me," he said.

The bad feeling between the teams worsened when local fans threw garbage on the lawn of Kubek's parents, who lived in the south side of Milwaukee. On the lawn someone posted a sign, "Get Out of Town, You Bush Traitor." In Milwaukee the Russian launching of the Sputnik satellite played second fiddle to the Braves world series.

The fourth game pitted Tom Sturdivant against Milwaukee's Bob Buhl. Sturdivant had a cold, and his discomfort was aggravated by a biting fall wind, though he led 1–0 through the fourth when Logan walked and Mathews doubled into the right-field corner to put men on second and third. Stengel came out to the mound, and he and his young pitcher decided that it would be better to pitch to the right-handed Hank Aaron than walk him. The wind was blowing in strongly from left field and Stengel reasoned that rather than pitch to the left-handed Covington with the bases loaded, it would be smarter to pitch to Aaron and make him hit the ball to left. "Make him pull it," Stengel advised his pitcher. "Babe Ruth couldn't hit one against that wind." Stengel left the mound, and on a 1–1 pitch Aaron hit the ball over the left-field wall just out of left fielder Kubek's reach for a three-run home run. Frank Torre, the first-baseman, then hit another home run to make the score 4–1. In the dugout Sturdivant said to Stengel, "I thought Babe Ruth couldn't hit one out against that wind?" Casey looked up at his pitcher. "He ain't Babe Ruth," Stengel said. "He's Henry Aaron." With the score 4–1 Spahn threw zeros till the ninth when with two outs Berra singled to keep New York's hopes alive. McDougald then singled, and with a 3–2 count on Ellie Howard who was playing first base, Spahn hung a curve ball and Howard hit it over the wire fence in left field for a 4–4 tie. As with Kubek the day before, the Milwaukee crowd responded with absolute silence. Howard ran the bases in solitude and his teammates mobbed him at the plate.

In the top of the tenth the Yankees took the lead. Again with two outs Spahn weakened, and after Kubek beat out an infield hit, Hank Bauer tripled over Aaron's head in center field for the tie-breaking run. Tommy Byrne, who had relieved in the eighth, was still on the mound in the bottom of the tenth. Nippy Jones, who was in the 1946 series as a St. Louis Cardinal rookie and had been a minor leaguer since 1952, pinch hit for the dejected Spahn. When Jones was announced, even the staunch Braves fans didn't know him. Byrne threw a sharp-breaking curve ball that darted low, glancing off Jones's right spiked shoe. The ball bounced quickly to the screen, where it hit the brick wall behind the plate and rebounded right behind the batter's box. Home plate umpire Augie Donatelli called the pitch a ball and ordered Jones who had started to run to first to return. Jones argued that the ball had hit his shoe. Connie Ryan, the Braves third-base coach, ran to the plate from his coaching box and joined the argument. Berra, the Yankee catcher, was arguing that the ball never hit Jones. Meanwhile Byrne, waiting on the mound, was trying desperately to get Yogi's attention. Byrne wanted Berra to reach behind him and throw the ball back to the mound where the sly pitcher would be able to scuff the ball and hide any incriminating evidence. Yogi never saw Byrne trying to signal to him. Finally it was Ryan who retrieved the ball, and he showed Donatelli a small black smudge on it, proof that the ball had hit Jones's shoe. As Jones trotted to first, Stengel rushed out of the dugout screaming.

Braves manager Fred Haney sent fleet Felix Mantilla to run for Jones, and Stengel, knowing that Schoendienst, the next batter, would bunt, brought in Bob Grim so that Grim could get his timing while pitching to Schoendienst before facing Johnny Logan. Schoendienst did bunt, sacrificing Mantilla to second. Stengel then called time and took Mantle out of the game, the first public indication of the extent of his shoulder injury, moving Kubek from left field to center and inserting Enos Slaughter in left. Mantle would have been unable to throw out a runner trying to score.

One out. Runner on second. Yankees ahead 5–4. Grim, Stengel's top reliefer in the game. By August Grim had peaked, 10–3 from the bullpen, but at the end of the season he had slumped and finished September with a 2–5 record. For four years Grim had produced for Stengel, and Stengel was going to go with his best. But Logan upset the strategy and banged a double down the left-field line to tie the score 5–5. Ed Mathews stepped in. Mathews had been a rookie in 1952 when the Braves were still in Boston, and in 1953 after the team moved to Milwaukee, he hit forty-seven home runs and Milwaukee fans picked him as the likely candidate to break Ruth's one-season home-run record. Mathews, born and raised in Milwaukee, was a fair-haired son. He fouled off several pitches, and then Grim threw a high slider that Mathews lofted over the right-field wire fence and into the distant bleachers to win the game 7–5 and tie the series at two games apiece. As the berserk Milwaukeeites screamed in delight, back in New York City Yankee fans watched the finish in stoney silence. First to lose Mantle and then the game when the world championship was all but theirs.

Whitey Ford faced Lew Burdette in the fifth game. Ford allowed only six singles and one run. Burdette allowed seven singles and no runs. Neither Mantle nor Skowron played for the Yankees. The closest the Yankees came to scoring was in the fourth inning when Gil McDougald drove a long, deep drive that looked to be headed over the left-field wall. Covington, reputed to be a poor fielder, raced to the fence, and just as the ball was clearing the barrier he leaped high, caught the ball, and bounced off the wire mesh to the ground, clutching the ball.

The two teams were given another day off as they returned for the final games at Yankee Stadium, and with Spahn under the weather with the flu bug that was severely hitting the country, Braves manager Fred Haney chose Buhl to start against Bob Turley.

It was a game of home runs, the type of game the Yankees usually won, and they won this one 3–2. Enos Slaughter walked in the third inning, and Yogi Berra, playing in his fifty-third series game (breaking by one Phil Rizzuto's record) pulled a Buhl fast ball into Yogi Berra-land in the Stadium right-field seats for two runs. For the Braves, Frank Torre, who had only hit five homers all season long, hit his second series homer, and Henry Aaron hit his third to tie the score 2–2. Then in the seventh Hank Bauer pulled an inside pitch on a line toward the foul pole in left where it hit the pole netting for a game-winning home run. Bob Turley, with a live fast ball, allowed only two hits in addition to the two home runs. For the third year in a row the series was extended to a seventh game. Across town in the borough of Brooklyn, Walter O'Malley officially announced that the Dodgers, a Brooklyn team in the National League since 1890, were moving to Los Angeles to join the Giants on the West Coast.

Fred Haney, influenced by Warren Spahn's weak condition, chose to start Burdette with two days rest in the seventh game. Stengel chose the unpredictable Larsen. A throwing error by third-baseman Tony Kubek on a sure double play helped the Braves to four runs in the third inning, and the Braves won going away 5–0. Burdette, completing his shutout, recorded the second greatest pitching performance in series history with his 4–2, 1–0, and 5–0 victories. Only the legendary Christy Mathewson ever pitched more effectively in a series, with three shutouts against the Philadelphia Athletics in 1905. After the game the unpredictable Burdette, a one-time Yankee farmhand, added salt to the wounds: "We'd like to play them again next year," he said. "I'm sure we're going to win the pennant, but I'm not sure about them." "The Yankees," said Warren Spahn, "couldn't finish fifth in the National League."

From Milwaukee office buildings and apartment houses, confetti and streamers covered the town in a celebration that has never been duplicated there since. People wept openly, and strangers hugged each other in the streets. Among the Yankees there was great ill will toward the Braves—particularly toward Burdette and Spahn.

In a little more than a month the city of New York lost two teams and a championship that one of its teams had held since 1949.

Home run number 61. Roger Maris breaks Babe Ruth's single-season home-run record on October 1, 1961, the last game of the regular season. (*N.Y. Daily News photo*)

The 1961 Yankees—the greatest team in baseball history. Front row left to right: Ford, Skowron, Reniff, coaches Hegan and Crosetti, manager Houk, coaches Sain, Moses, and Torgeson, Boyer, Berra, and Mantle. Second row left to right: trainer Mauch, Gardner, Hale, DeMaestri, Kubek, Clevenger, Terry, Lopez, Cerv, Howard, Maris, Turley, and trainer Soares. Third row left to right: Richardson, Downing, Arroyo, Blanchard, Stafford, Sheldon, Coates, Murray the batting practice pitcher, and Daley. Up front are bat boys Prudenti and Bengis. (*N.Y. Daily News photo*)

Clete Boyer performing his magic in the 1961 world series against Cincinnati. (*N.Y. Daily News photo*)

Final game, 1960 world series. Bad-hop grounder hits Tony Kubek in the throat, giving the Pirates life. (*Wide World photo*)

The classic Mantle home-run swing. (*Wide World photo*)

First pitch of the 1961 world series. Ford on the mound. Richardson at second base. (*Wide World* photo)

Ralph Houk during happier times. The Major celebrates 1962 pennant-clinching. (*New York Times photo*)

Four Yankee monuments—three in granite, one in the flesh.
Mantle fires home. (*New York Times photo*)

Manager Yogi Berra alone in a crowd during the 1964 world
series. (*New York Times photo*)

Two hall-of-famers and an 18-game winner—Mantle, Berra, and
Bouton celebrate in 1964. (*N.Y. Daily News photo*)

Joe Pep pondering. (*United Press International photo*)

Roger Maris, late in the 1961 season, a demonstration of both power and intensity. (Wide World photo)

Joe Page (*Courtesy N.Y. Yankees*)

Vic Raschi behind the counter of his liquor store. (*Peter Golenbock*)

Moose Skowron (*Peter Golenbock*)

Ryne Duren (*Courtesy N.Y. Yankees*)

Bobby Richardson (*Courtesy N.Y. Yankees*)

Roger Maris today (*Peter Golenbock*)

Clete Boyer (*Peter Golenbock*)

Mr. and Mrs. Joe Pepitone (*Peter Golenbock*)

The heart and soul of the Yankee dynasty—DiMaggio and Mantle. (*New York Times photo*)

1958

"Break Up the Yankees!" . . . Bullet Bob . . . Casey grows short-tempered . . . Weiss's private detectives . . . Another pennant . . . Revenge in a bitter series with Milwaukee

Springtime 1958 was an unsettled period for the world, the country, and the Yankees. Nikita Khrushchev became the Russians' new prime minister. After his appointment, he called for the end of nuclear testing, but President Eisenhower called the Russian plea a gimmick and a propaganda stunt. Secretary of State John Foster Dulles said, "Our duty to the American people and humanity requires continued testing to develop clean tactical bombs." In Cuba, rebel leader Fidel Castro called for all soldiers to desert and join him. Castro, entrenched in Oriente province, was not given much chance to succeed in his attempt to overthrow President Batista.

In the Yankee spring training camp at St. Petersburg, Casey Stengel was having trouble winning exhibition games. Winning these games normally was unimportant to him, but his pitching was so bad that he stayed up all night, walking the beaches until three in the morning and drinking too much. Larsen had a tender right shoulder. Turley had a bruised knee and was out for a while. Sturdivant was a holdout. Ford had been a victim of arm trouble the year before. Stengel knew that even the strongest team could not win without solid pitching.

Aside from the pitching, Stengel's nucleus of veterans and youngsters was the envy of the league. Bill Skowron, improving dramatically at first, drove in thirty runs and hit eleven home runs in spring training to lead the team. Gil McDougald and Bobby Richardson were available at second, McDougald and Tony Kubek at shortstop, McDougald, Andry Carey, and Jerry Lumpe at third. Also at first was Marv Throneberry, the 1956 Minor League Player of the Year with Denver. In the outfield was Mantle, who held out for $75,000 after his second straight super-star season. Mickey signed for close to that after some hard bargaining with Weiss. Flanking Mickey in center were Ellie Howard, Harry Simpson, Enos Slaughter, Hank Bauer, and Norm Siebern, the 1957 Minor League Player of the Year. Yogi Berra, at age 33 the oldest Yankee regular, was the catcher with Howard behind him. Two other rookies Darrell Johnson and John Blanchard, showed great potential behind the plate. Stengel had so many excellent ball players he didn't know who to start.

Three old faces were gone from the team. Thirty-eight-year-old Tommy Byrne, a rookie in 1943, a Yankee between 1943 and '51 and since '54, retired to devote his time to local businesses despite a lucrative offer from Weiss. Jerry Coleman, a rookie in 1949, retired to join the Yankee front office. Joe Collins, the Yankee first baseman who won so many games with his clutch hitting but whose injuries severely hampered his play the last couple of years, was sold to the Philadelphia Phillies during spring training. Rather than report, he retired. Joe like Coleman had been a Yankee since 1949.

As bad as the Yankees played during spring training, that's how good they were when the season finally started. Rarely did the Yankees lose a game. The pitching was uniformly excellent with Whitey Ford and Bob Turley doing most of the April throwing because so many games were rained out. Mantle and Berra started poorly, but Skowron continued his spring slugging, batting close to .400 and leading the team in homers and RBI's until mid-May, when he bent over for a ground ball and fell to the ground in a heap. Skowron was unable to get up, and was carried off the field on a stretcher. Doctors said the injury was a deep tear in one of his back muscles, one of a long series of nagging injuries which plagued the Moose during his career. Skowron spent several weeks in the hospital. "All there is to do here is read and watch TV," the gentle Moose said, "but this isn't so bad. Think of Campy." Several months earlier, Roy Campanella, the Hall-of-Fame Dodger catcher, had driven his car into a telephone pole, suffering a broken neck and permanent paralysis. Rookie Marv Throneberry substituted for Skowron during his absence. There were other injuries, but Stengel always had a first-rate replacement.

On May 26 the Yankee won-lost record was 25–6! The Yankees led the league by nine full games! Curiously, the team's success was accountable primarily to its superb pitching rather than its hitting. The earned run average of the Yankee staff was under two runs a game. Ford, Shantz, Kucks, and Larsen pitched excellently, and rookie Ryne Duren was excellent in the bullpen. Bob Turley, finally displaying the form and consistency that had been predicted of him when he was acquired by the Yankees at the end of the 1954 season, won his first seven games. Four of those wins were shutouts, and in the seven games he only allowed six earned runs for a 0.86 earned run average. Turley was threatening to become the first Yankee twenty-game winner since Bob Grim in 1954.

Turley was a pitcher with an exceptional fast ball. During his prime his game plan was to rear back and try to throw the ball past every hitter. He didn't pitch to spots. He just threw—hard. Usually the batter either swung and missed or he swung and foul-tipped the ball. Unlike control pitchers, Turley was unable to throw to a batter's weakness and make the batter hit out to a fielder. Instead Turley tried for strikeouts, making pitching more of a chore because he had to throw so many more pitches. When Turley pitched, it was a field day for the fans in the ball park because of the many foul balls hit into the stands.

Using a no-windup delivery, Turley was a power pitcher in the mold of Vic Raschi and Allie Reynolds, though Bullet Bob, as he was called, did not have the outer fire and pitching belligerence of the two ex-Yankee stars. Turley, a religious man, "a milk drinker" as Stengel called him, was too much of a gentleman to hit a batter. The batters knew this and fearlessly took advantage of him by crowding the plate and digging in. Nevertheless, when Turley's fast ball was at its crackling best and his curve was swishing in over the plate, he was overpowering. In 1958 he was the best pitcher in baseball, finishing with a 21–7 record to lead the American League in wins and winning percentage and finishing third to Early Wynn and Jim Bunning in strikeouts. On another team, pitching in a four-man rotation, Turley's record would have been even more impressive. On the Yankees, pitching in a five-man rotation, Turley only started thirty games in 1958, completing nineteen of them, winning twenty-one. On the Yankees a pitcher had to be almost perfect to win twenty games in a season. Turley had that kind of season in '58.

In 1959 Turley finished a dismal 8–11 as the entire ball club went sour. In '60 he was 9–3, though fourteen of the fifteen games he was taken out of early were won by the Yankees. In '61 he suffered his arm damage, finishing 3–5. The Yankees carried him in '62 and then sold him to the Angels at the end of the year. Two years with the Angels and the Red Sox finished his active career, and after a year as the Red Sox pitching coach in '64, he left baseball for good. He now lives in Atlanta, Georgia, and has become a respected entrepreneur and businessman in that community.

Turley, a quiet, serious man, was aloof from the practical jokes and the beer drinking, but he was respected by most of his teammates for his friendly nature and his passion for improving himself by reading books on finance, business, and real estate. For some of the hitters Turley became an integral aid, because he was probably the premier student of opposing pitchers, and he could tell the hitters whether a fast ball or a curve was coming.

"I simply had the ability to pick up signs from opposing pitchers," Turley said. "I picked up a tremendous amount of them and relayed them to Mickey, and I also picked up many of them where there was no relay. I would just tell Mickey, and Mickey would just see for himself what the pitcher was doing to give away what pitch he was going to throw. And very often, when he was up at the plate, he knew what pitch was coming. And he really loved to hit with signs. Usually there would be a tremendous amount of noise going on when Mickey came up to the plate, and it would be very difficult to hear voice commands, but I have a very shrill whistle that overcomes everything else, and I signalled Mickey that way. Everyone in the league knew what I was doing, but they didn't know the code Mickey and I had worked out. We had a system where we would start off where every pitch would be a curve ball unless I whistle. And then after my first whistle, he looks for all fast balls. The next time I whistle it's a curve ball and so on. They used to think they had us all confused. They'd say, 'He's whistling on the wrong pitches.' But we weren't confused. And any time Mickey would lose count, he would touch the top of his cap, and we would start all over again. There were a lot of pitchers in the league who tipped off their pitches. We had their signs all the years there. I called a tremendous amount of home runs for Mickey in the big leagues—just a tremendous amount.

"It got so that when I wasn't pitching and wasn't doing too well and wanted to go to the bullpen 'cause I wanted to get into the game, the hitters would go to

Stengel and say, 'Get him back here on the bench.' They wouldn't let me go to the bullpen. In fact there was one time when I had an injury, and they put me on the disabled list, and I had to sit in the stands, and they had a special seat for me so I could be close to home plate to call the signs.''

In June 1958 in Caracas, Venezuela, hundreds of student demonstrators attacked Vice President Nixon's automobile, throwing tomatoes and eggs at the limousine, shouting expletives at him and generally scaring his pants off.

No one was chasing the Yankees.

By the end of June the lead was still nine games, and by the end of July it had stretched to a full fifteen games! The rest of the league, the Sorry Seven, rolled over and conceded. In 1957, when the Yankees were 52–26, they only led by three and a half games. This year at 51–26, their lead was twelve games. The great Cleveland pitching staff had collapsed when Herb Score was injured. Chicago, after trading Larry Doby and Minny Minoso to Cleveland, was a very ordinary team. Boston had no pitching, and Detroit no depth. ''In this league there are no pennant contenders,'' said Cleveland manager Joe Gordon. ''There is just the Yankees and no one to challenge them.''

On August 2 the lead grew to seventeen games. No team in the history of baseball ever had a lead that large so early. The depth of the Yankee team seemed unmatched in the history of baseball.

Whitey Ford (13–4) pitched three consecutive shutouts in July, and on August first Bob Turley (16–4) shut out the White Sox. The next day Art Ditmar (7–2) beat the Sox, allowing them only one run to raise his two-year Yankee record to 15–5. Bobby Shantz (7–3) continued to pitch excellently. Don Larsen (7–5) was the hard-luck pitcher on the staff, and when a starter would occasionally falter manager Stengel would bring in from the bullpen the Gargantua, Ryne Duren.

Duren, a 30-year-old rookie, had been obtained by Weiss in the Billy Martin trade, and in 1957 he spent the year at Denver where he was 13–2 including a no-hitter in his first start under manager Ralph Houk. Duren was as fast as Bob Feller and Herb Score, but he had a legendary lack of control both on and off the field. Duren became a minor league folk legend, a Paul Bunyan in flannel. It is said that Duren was so wild that once he hit the on-deck batter with a warm-up pitch! It is also said that in a Louisville bar Duren got drunk, picked a fight with five men, and was beaten unconscious, landing in the local jail for the night with teammate Norm Siebern, a quiet man trying to help protect Ryne.

At Denver Duren's chronic eyesight problems were finally diagnosed properly, and with new glasses, his pitching control improved. In the spring training of 1958 Stengel, at the urging of Houk, made Duren a Yankee reliefer. At first Stengel thought Houk was crazy to suggest such a thing, but Houk, elevated to Yankee coach, showed excellent judgment, and Duren was superb for the Yankees in relief. Ryne's seventeen saves and 1.38 earned run average was leading the league when on July 24 he was beaned by a pitch thrown by Paul Foytack of the Tigers. The ball struck the Yankee pitcher with a sickening thud, his glasses and helmet flying awry. Duren slumped to the ground, blood flowing from his left cheek, and was carried off the field on a stretcher and taken to Detroit's Memorial Hospital. Duren missed a week, but in the first few days of August he pitched three innings of no-hit ball against Baltimore, and seemed none the worse for wear.

Stengel platooned his regulars with impunity, and whomever he played, played well. Mickey Mantle, troubled by an ailing right shoulder, booed mercilessly by the Stadium fans after only hitting two home runs in June, began a resurgence in July when he hit eight home runs in nine games. In August he hit fourteen more home runs to raise his season total to twenty-eight, tying Kansas City's Bob Cerv and trailing only Jackie Jensen of the Red Sox. The three sluggers had been named to start the all-star game, an oddity because in 1952 all three were Yankees trying to replace Joe DiMaggio.

When Mickey was injured and had to miss a few games after an August collision with shortstop Kubek, rookie Norm Siebern was inserted in center. Siebern responded with game-winning home runs against the Tigers, and with a streak that shot his average close to .300, the *Journal-American* called Norm the hottest hitter in the league. Hank Bauer in right was hitting close to .300, and when Hank needed a rest Stengel played Enos Slaughter. Slaughter, also a pinch hitter, was batting .351. Ellie Howard played left and caught when Berra needed a rest. Howard was batting .348. In the infield, second-baseman Gil McDougald and shortstop Tony Kubek developed into the best double-play combination in the league. "They kill you both ways," said White Sox manager Al Lopez, who himself had an excellent DP combination in Nellie Fox and Luis Aparicio, "both in the field and at bat. Especially that McDougald. I've always said he was one of the best." Both McDougald and Kubek were hitting in the .280's. If one of them needed a rest, Stengel had the slick-fielding Bobby Richardson in reserve. At first base Bill Skowron was an RBI machine when he was able to play, and when he wasn't Marv Throneberry batted a respectable .270 and did an adequate job at first. Andy Carey and Jerry Lumpe platooned at third base, though Stengel was becoming more and more perturbed by Carey's adamant refusal to play any position other than third. "I always had a lot of three-way men around here," Stengel often said. "Lumpe, he's a three-way man. McDougald. Richardson. Martin. Coleman. They can all play second, short, and third. Only Carey. He's not a three-way man, he's not even a two-way man. Some day I'll find me a third-baseman who wants to play another position, and they'll back the van up and take that guy away."

In one July game Carey hit two home runs and drove in five runs against Herb Score of the Indians and the next day went four for four including a double and triple against Billy Pierce, another lefty. In the final game of the series against right-handed Ray Moore, Stengel started Lumpe at third, and the youngster drove in the winning run in the tenth inning. A couple days later Lumpe hit a three-run home run to beat the A's. Carey and Lumpe were both hitting in the .280's. Catcher Yogi Berra, who suffered through a 1–42 slump in July, had the *lowest* average on the team at .259. On August 2 the Yankee team batting average was .278. Detroit, second to the Yankees, was eleven points lower.

To add to this wealth general manager Weiss continued his Kansas City-Yankee good-neighbor policy, sending Bob Grim, expendable with the emergence of Duren, and Harry Simpson, the black outfielder Stengel never used, to the A's for Virgil Trucks and Duke Maas, two veteran pitchers.

Cries of "Break Up the Yankees" were louder and more vociferous than ever before because so many of the Yankee regulars were young, and the dynasty looked like it would continue indefinitely. Richardson was only 22, Kubek 22, Lumpe 25, Throneberry 25, Siebern 25, and of the veterans, Mantle was 27, Carey 27, Skowron 28, and Howard 29. The Yankees were booed unmercifully around the league and continually blasted in the press. Stengel, sensitive to every criticism of the Yankees, couldn't understand why everyone so resented the Yankees' success. "Why is everyone mad at us?" he said. "What do they expect us to do, roll over and play dead? Draw up a chair and sit by the roadside until the rest catch up? Sure it's tough on the other seven clubs, but why take it out on us? If you ran a delicatessen store, you would want it to be the best delicatessen store, wouldn't you?" Stengel's logic only served to make the others more angry.

As the lead grew Stengel became more grouchy and more demanding with his players. In 1953 he was insufferable during the team's eighteen-game winning streak. This year he was insufferable the entire season. The further in front the Yankees were, the more uneasy Stengel was. To insure that the players didn't blow the pennant and make him look bad, Stengel drove them without mercy. He rode them, chewed them out on the field and in clubhouse meetings, and blasted them in the press. After one rare Yankee loss Stengel complained, "How can you guys be so lousy and still have a lead like that?" His tongue, always barbed, became poisonous, especially toward the younger players. Stengel had the reputation of being a lovable old clowner who spoke indecipherable Stengelese. Only the players saw his other side. Once in the late thirties when Stengel was managing the hapless Boston Braves, Max West, a Braves outfielder crashed into a wall chasing a fly ball as several runs scored on the play. Stengel rushed out to West, and when he crouched over the groggy, prostrate outfielder, said, "Great pair of hands you got there, Max." Another time his third-baseman, Sibbi Sisti, booted a ground ball for a two-base error. After the inning Stengel, fuming, said to Sisti, "Next time the ball is hit to you, don't touch it. Let the left fielder handle it. He'll hold it to a single."

When Stengel was hired by the Yankees in 1949, he enjoyed instructing the youngsters. He was an observant, patient mentor who liked developing kids on the way up. Stengel was now 68 years old. Nine years and eight pennants later, his patience with the rookies and youngsters had run out.

Stengel just couldn't stand to have the young players making mistakes. If a young infielder made an error, Stengel would yell at him when he came back into the dugout, "Goddamn it. How the hell can you miss a goddamn ball like that? What the hell is the matter with you?" and the sensitive youngster would think, "God, I can't boot another one because that ole son of a buck is going to get on me again." He would tighten, and more errors would often follow. Stengel kept the young pitchers edgy by constantly second-guessing them every time they gave up a base hit. A batter would hit a curve and Stengel would yell, "How the hell can you throw that guy a curve?" If a batter hit a fast ball, it was, "How the hell can you throw that guy a fast ball?" The young pitchers didn't get much support from pitching coach Jim Turner, either. If you were a star pitcher like Bob Turley, and you walked into the clubhouse in the morning, Turner would say, "How are you this fine morning, Bob baby?" If you were one of the other starters, Turner would say, "Hello. How's everything?" If you were a reliefer, it was, "Hi," and if you weren't doing too well, it was, "Hrmph." If you were a Zack Monroe you were invisible. The Zack Monroes never felt too wanted.

It almost seemed that the Yankee manager went out of his way to haze the youngsters, and some of them, including Richardson and Kubek, were able to survive this trying and difficult period in their careers, always being criticized, always being platooned. But for others like Norm Siebern and Jerry Lumpe, minor league stars of immense potential, their ordeal under Stengel's whip made them unbearably tense, nervous, and ill at ease both on and off the field.

Stengel was continually harping at the left-handed Siebern to pull the ball to take advantage of the inviting right-field Stadium seats—despite the introverted outfielder's .300 batting average in 1958. Also Stengel was forever yelling at him to be a more aggressive outfielder. Siebern, always fearful of running hard toward center field and colliding with Mantle and injuring the Yankee star, did win the Golden Glove award. Years before it had been Mantle who was afraid to run hard into center lest he collide and injure Joe DiMaggio. Yet despite the positive aspects of Siebern's game, Stengel was always critical, and never subtly. Bob Turley was pitching a no-hitter late in one spring game in '58 when a batter hit a fly ball that fell between shortstop Tony Kubek and the hard-charging Siebern in left. After the game the writers went to Stengel to ask him whether he thought the ball should have been caught by Siebern. "What do you think?" Stengel said sarcastically. "Sometimes," Stengel once mused aloud, "I wonder how he won all them medals at Denver."

Infielder Jerry Lumpe was another youngster who never felt loved. Stengel once told a reporter, "Lumpe looks like the best hitter in the world until you put him in the lineup." In 1957 Lumpe was a utility player, 24 years old, living with his family in New York City and making a measily $6,000 salary. Unable to make ends meet, on September 1 he met with the Yankee front office to discuss the situation. George Weiss agreed to raise his salary to $6,600 for the year. But Lumpe discovered that the raise was not retroactive over the entire season. Weiss was actually giving him less than $100 more! And then, in 1958, the front office tried to bargain with Lumpe on the basis of a $6,600 contract from the year before! "They don't make you feel too wanted around here," Lumpe said.

Though both Siebern and Lumpe played well the rest of their careers, the psychological scars from playing under Stengel may well have inhibited them from fully reaching their once-great potentials.

In early August the Yankees maintained a seventeen-game lead for about a week, but unexpectedly they began to lose more than they won. An epidemic of sore arms and other injuries decimated the pitching staff. Whitey Ford didn't win a game after August 8. On that day Ford shut out the Red Sox, his seventh shutout of the year and his fourteenth win against five losses. Two days later he was called in to relieve, and warming up too quickly, he injured his elbow, and for the entire month of August and into September, Ford was unable to pitch without pain. In mid-September Whitey returned to the rotation but did not win another game, though he finished the season leading the league with a 2.01 ERA.

Tom Sturdivant, who had won sixteen games in 1956 and 1957, returned from his arm miseries to pitch well against the Orioles on August 12, his third win of the season. But a week later, playing tag with Shantz in the outfield, he was inadvertently spiked on the heel. The wound required seven stitches to close. Sturdivant was placed on the disabled list, fined $250 for "horsing around"—for the remainder of the season he was virtually useless.

Only Turley, Ditmar, and Kucks remained from Stengel's original staff. Turley pitched excellently all year long, but as soon as the Yankees won the pennant, Stengel stopped pitching him, ostensibly resting him for the world series but quite possibly also holding down his 1959 salary. After Turley's twentieth win on September 12, the big right-hander only started three more games. Kucks and Ditmar pitched poorly, Kucks 1–5 and Ditmar 2–6 the last two months.

Saving the Yankee staff from total decimation were Duke Maas and Virgil Trucks, Weiss's most recent Kansas City acquisitions. Maas, a low-ball, control pitcher, finished the last two months 5–1 as a starter, and Trucks, the 39-year-old veteran who in 1952 pitched two no-hitters, became the Yankees' top relief man.

The final two months ailments struck the regulars, too. Tony Kubek suffered from an impacted wisdom tooth, lost twenty pounds and was weak, and then pulled a thigh muscle. He hit .240 the last two months. Gil McDougald, in the running for Most Valuable Player in August, suffered from spasms in his back, a problem which he kept secret, and by September a 14–101, .138 stretch eliminated him from MVP contention. He hit .207 the last two months, nevertheless finishing the year with a respectable .270 season average. Bill Skowron, perpetually hampered by back woes, hit only .223 the final two months, dropping his .295 average twenty points. "The way he's hitting," Stengel growled, "he'd be better off if he was hurt." Hank Bauer, at age 37, was giving indications of slowing down as he hit only .203 in August and September.

Only Mantle and Berra continued to play well. Mickey finished the year with forty-two home runs to lead the league, and showed his base-running skills by stealing fourteen bases in seventeen attempts. The fans at the Stadium continued to boo him because he was no longer a triple crown threat, but the excitement he created, whether hitting home runs, stealing bases, or striking out, something he did with alarming regularity, made him the top gate attraction in baseball. Over the last two months Mickey hit .331, finishing the '58 season with a .304 average and ninety-seven runs batted in. Berra, the Old Pro, also finished strongly, batting .280 the final two months, and ending the year with twenty-two home runs and ninety RBI's. Two of Stengel's platooned players, Andy Carey and Norm Siebern, also fielded and batted well.

Essentially, though, it was the decline of the Yankee pitching staff that caused New York's precipitous 25–28 end-of-season slump. The poor play combined with Stengel's lambasting served to fray the nerves of the Yankee athletes by the end of the year. On one late-season off-day, Stengel called a rare practice session. "If you don't think I can do this," he growled, "read your contracts. You fellers are so bad you need extra practice."

Tony Kubek yelled back, "You're not going so hot yourself lately."

On September 14 the Yankees finally clinched their runaway pennant. That night they held their pennant-clinching party in Kansas City at the Muhlenberg Hotel after a doubleheader win over the A's. After the party the team boarded the train where the players continued imbibing champagne and liquor into the wee hours as the train sped toward Detroit. Pitcher Ryne Duren, inebriated and bellicose, decided that he was going to challenge Yankee first-base coach Ralph Houk to a fight. "I hear you've never lost a fight," Duren said to Houk, a burly ex-Marine and Duren's manager at Denver the year before. "I hear you're a real tough guy. You know what I think I'll do," Duren said. "I think I'll push that cigar you're smoking right down your throat." Houk, wishing to avoid a scene, tried to humor his big pitcher, but Duren continued his menacing behavior. When he began to push at Houk's lit cigar, Houk swatted Duren away with the back of his hand, accidentally scratching Duren above the right eye with his world series ring. Duren took a wild swing at Houk, and after much difficulty several of the players subdued the powerful Duren, who kept repeating, "After all I've done for this team, after all I've done for this team." Duren, who was so drunk that he could not remember the incident the next morning, was finally put to bed, but not before he kicked Don Larsen in the face, cutting the inside of his mouth. The incident caused no animosity or any lasting consequences except to bring the Yankees some adverse publicity. "Duren shouldn't drink," Houk said. "When he does, he's a Jekyll and Hyde."

The Duren-Houk cigar-stuffing incident was only a day old when the Yankees became involved in another headline-provoking situation. General manager George Weiss was so disturbed by the lackluster performance of his team that he was convinced that the players' night life must have had something to do with it. When the team arrived in Detroit, Weiss hired private detectives and ordered them to follow the players and submit reports of their evening activities. Mickey Mantle and Whitey Ford especially were to be closely watched.

The detectives were spotted almost immediately. A number of the Yankees, including Mantle and Ford, were lounging in the lobby of Detroit's Statler-Hilton Hotel when they noticed two suspicious characters at the far end of the lobby, one wearing a white Panama hat and red shoes, the other wearing a London Fog raincoat. Both were peering over the tops of newspapers.

"Watch this," Ford said to the others. "This should be funny." Ford, Mantle, and Darrell Johnson slowly walked out the front door of the hotel. The two suspicious men followed them. Mantle, Ford, and Johnson raced into a cab. As the other Yankees looked on, the two men jumped in a car waiting outside and followed. The players' cab raced off. The detectives' car pulled out after them, swerving to avoid running over a woman who was crossing the street, and almost slamming into several parked cars. The chase was on.

Several minutes later Ford, Mantle, and Johnson's cab pulled up to the front door of the hotel. It had made one complete circle around the block and returned. Seconds later the squealing tires of the detectives' car were heard down the block behind them. The players waved to the frenzied detectives and walked back into the hotel.

Later Mantle, Ford, and Johnson played hopscotch on the sidewalks of Detroit to give the detectives something to tell Weiss, and after the players became tired of the masquerade, they ditched their pursuers by going in the front door of a Catholic church and slipping out the back.

Other detectives followed Bobby Richardson, Tony Kubek, Bobby Shantz, and Johnny Kucks to the Detroit YMCA where the four men spent the evening playing Ping-Pong. These players also noticed that they were being followed, so after the Ping-Pong, they went into a movie theater to buy popcorn. The detectives thought the players were going to see the movie and bought tickets so they could keep watch on their quarry. As soon as the players saw the detectives buy the tickets, they walked out of the theater, leaving the cursing private eyes with wasted stubs. When the reports of the Keystone Kops comedy appeared in the New York papers the next day, Weiss called a halt to the surveillance.

It was not the first time a general manager or a manager had trailed the players with private eyes. Yankee general manager Larry MacPhail had had Joe Page, John Lindell, Frank Shea, and company trailed during the mid-1940s. Back in the 1920s New York Giant manager John McGraw put detectives on a couple of his players. On one road trip McGraw had two of his outfielders, Irish Meusal and Casey Stengel, followed. When Stengel discovered he was being followed, he went running to McGraw. "I don't deserve this kind of treatment, you putting detectives on Irish and me," Casey bellowed.

"How should you be treated?" McGraw asked his fun-loving outfielder.

"I got a right to have a whole detective to myself," Stengel said. "I don't believe in no sharing!"

When it was revealed to all the Yankees that they had been spied on by Weiss, most of them were both insulted and angered. "I'm going to ask for a raise next year," Tony Kubek said, "and tell them to give me what they paid the cops to follow us."

The last two weeks were uneventful and at the end the Yankees won the pennant by ten games over the White Sox. In the National League Milwaukee, as the Braves' players had predicted, won the pennant easily, wresting first place from the Pittsburgh Pirates in July and coasting home in front. The so-called experts were favoring the Yankees to win the series, perhaps reflecting their respect for the Yankee tradition of series success. It certainly did not reflect objectivity. After the Yankee lead grew to seventeen games in early August, their record the last two months was 25–28, not even five hundred ball.

The Yankees did not start this series any better than they had finished the last one. Opening in Milwaukee Warren Spahn, who had won twenty-two games during the season, started for the Braves against Whitey Ford, who hadn't won since early August. The Yankees did all they could to hand Spahn the ball game. In the first inning Hank Bauer singled and was picked off first. In the second inning Yogi Berra singled, and when Bill Skowron singled to left field, Berra tested left fielder Wes Covington's arm by continuing to third, and Covington threw him out to end the threat. Skowron, whom Stengel blamed for losing the '57 series because of his absence, scored the first run of the game in the fourth with a home run just inside the left-field foul line, but the Braves retaliated with two runs when Hank Aaron walked, went to second on a passed ball, and with two outs, Crandall, Pafko, and Spahn singled on consecutive pitches. In the fifth the Yankees took the lead, 3–2, when Ford walked and Bauer picked out a Spahn screw ball that failed to break and sent it hurtling high and far into the left-field bleachers of County Stadium. Into the eighth inning Whitey held the lead, striking out eight Braves and pitching masterfully. In the eighth, though, Ford walked Eddie Mathews, the slugging third-baseman, and when Hank Aaron doubled against the right-field wire fence just over Bauer's desperate leap, the Braves had men on second and third and nobody out. Stengel slowly walked to the mound and waved in Ryne Duren, who lived up to his audience's expectations by firing the first warm-up pitch far over catcher Berra's head and high against the backstop screen. An audible "Ooooooooooooooooooh" rose from the awe-filled spectators. Adcock struck out on four pitches for the first out, but Covington hit a drive to center field that Mantle raced a long distance into left center before hauling down. Mathews tagged at third to tie the score at 3–3. Crandall then became Duren's second strikeout victim to end the inning.

In the ninth Duren shut out the Braves, striking out pinch hitter Frank Torre and Mathews. While Spahn held the Yankees scoreless, Duren opened the bottom of the tenth by smoking the ball past Aaron, his fifth strikeout in seven outs. Adcock broke the spell with a single to center, but Covington hit a towering fly to left field that Howard caught with his back to the wall for the second out. Duren seemed safe, and the restless Milwaukee fans sat on their hands waiting for the eleventh inning. Duren then sent Crandall sprawling to the ground with his "purpose pitch," but the Braves catcher returned to the box and hit another single to move Adcock to second. The crowd began to come alive. Milwaukee manager Fred Haney had unsuccessfully sent left-hander Billy Bruton to bat for right-hander Pafko in the ninth, but in Bruton's second at-bat, the Braves outfielder, out the entire '57 series with knee injuries, sent everyone home as he lined a drive between center fielder Mantle and right fielder Bauer that the swearing Yankee outfielders took one look at and ignored, as the ball rolled to the fence to give the Braves a 4–3 opening win.

In the second game Yankee frustrations mounted when in the first inning they loaded the bases with nobody out and only scored one run against Lew Burdette, the Yankee-killer of 1957, who during the '58 season won nine of his last ten starts to finish with a 20–10 record. Bob Turley, rested for the series by Stengel, had nothing on his fast ball and couldn't control his curve, and it was like batting practice for the Braves in the first inning. The inning was capped by pitcher Burdette who homered over the left-field fence for the fifth, sixth, and seventh runs of the inning. The rest of the game was played solely to determine the Braves' margin of victory, which was 13–5. Two long home runs by Mantle, and a three-run shot by Bauer scored the Yankee runs. Burdette allowed seven hits in all and won his fourth-straight against the New Yorkers.

The next day was a travel day, and back at the Stadium there was a brief indication of Stengel's black mood when TV commentator Howard Cosell asked Stengel whether he thought the Yankees had "choked up" in the first two games. Stengel first looked at Cosell as though he couldn't believe that anyone would have the audacity to ask such a question, and then he brought his face close to Cosell's and virtually shouted, "I haven't choked up and none of my players choked up. Ball players don't choke up. But if anybody's gonna be choked up it's gonna be somebody holding a microphone."

In the third game, against burly Bob Buhl, acquired by the Braves from the Cubs at the end of the '57 season, and his reliefer, Don McMahon, the Yankees managed only four hits. But Hank Bauer, hitting in his seventeenth consecutive world series game—a record—connected for three of them, drove in four runs, and the Yankees won 4–0. Larsen allowed six Braves singles in the first seven innings, throwing off the timing of the Milwaukee batters by switching back and forth from his no-windup to a windup motion, striking out eight. Duren allowed no hits in the final two innings, though he kept everyone on edge by walking two Braves and making a wild pitch before retiring the side in the eighth without damage. After the game Stengel uncharacteristically hugged Bauer. "You had a big day. You did a big job," Stengel said. Inside the Yankee clubhouse there were smiles of relief and audible sighs as the great tension of being on the brink of disaster faded slightly. Four Yankee hits wasn't anything special, but a win was a win.

In the fourth game the Yankees were able to get but two hits against the crafty Spahn: a single by Skowron in the fourth, and a 400-foot triple by Mantle in the seventh; but neither of the hits produced runs. Nothing else did either, and the Braves won 3–0. Ford, for his second consecutive start, pitched well enough to win, but didn't. Ford and Spahn were scoreless into the sixth inning when rookie left fielder Siebern lost Red Schoendienst's fly ball in Yankee Stadium's brutal sun field. Siebern saw the ball leave the bat and made his initial move to left center. Mantle, seeing Siebern running under it, stopped short, but as the ball rose above the first-base stands and began to descend, Siebern stopped, too. The sun was right atop the stands, and he lost sight of the ball. The ball hit the ground between the two outfielders and rolled to the deep bleacher wall for a triple. A ground ball then rolled through shortstop Tony Kubek's legs as Schoendienst scored to give the Braves a 1–0 lead. Then in the seventh Crandall walked and with one out Pafko looped a double just in front of Mantle in center to send Crandall to third. With Spahn, a lefty batter, up, Stengel motioned Siebern to come in closer. Siebern moved in a little, but Stengel frantically kept motioning him to come in even farther. As Ford pitched the ball, Stengel was still motioning when Spahn looped the ball just over the infield and in front of the Yankee left fielder, scoring Crandall with the second run.

In the eighth the Braves scored their third and final run when Logan lofted a fly ball into left field, another ball that Siebern lost in the sun. The ball bounced right beside him and into the seats for a ground-rule double. An Eddie Mathews' double scored Logan, and Ford was taken out of the game, a victim of the bright October sun on a hazy New York day. After the game Siebern patiently answered questions with tear-filled eyes, and in the Milwaukee dressing room the Braves, leading three games to one, were exultant about their upcoming series triumph. "I wish the Yankees were in the National League," said Burdette, repeating what Spahn had said the year before. "They'd be lucky if they finished fifth." Logan said the Yankees were "over the hill" and Spahn predicted that "the last two games at County Stadium would be unnecessary."

Stengel chose Turley to start the fifth game. Fred Haney chose Burdette in another battle of twenty game winners. In the Yankee clubhouse there was an air of impending doom and clenched-teeth anger at the Braves' arrogance. Into this grim scene Mickey Mantle entered, an Indian arrow sticking into one side of his head and seeming to protrude from the other side. The grinning Mantle walked to the middle of the locker room and said, "Now I know how Custer felt." Immediately the atmosphere changed, and once more there was laughter and kidding.

It was a very cold day in New York, and for this game Turley was the overpowering pitcher he had been during the season, striking out ten Braves and only allowing five hits, beating the Braves 7–0.

Spahn had been wrong. It was necessary to return to County Stadium, for the sixth game as the Yankees figured Milwaukee manager Haney would rest Spahn in case a seventh game was needed and pitch a fresh Bob Buhl or Bob Rush. Instead Haney decided to gamble and pitch Spahn with two days rest. Then if a seventh game was necessary he'd go with Burdette with two days rest. The strategy cost the Braves the series.

Ford volunteered for the sixth game assignment, himself only having two days rest. On this damp and dreary day Hank Bauer led off the game with a home run into the left-field bleachers, but Ford was not sharp. After one and one-third innings, two runs, and the bases loaded with Braves, Ford was gone, replaced by the forgotten Art Ditmar who threw shutout ball until the top of the sixth when Stengel pinch hit for him. After the Yankees tied the score 2–2 with a run in the top of the sixth, Duren came in to pitch. He and Spahn engaged in a scoreless duel that stretched through the seventh, eighth, ninth, and finally the tenth inning. In the tenth Gil McDougald homered, and the Yankees scored another run for a 4–2 lead.

In the bottom of the tenth Duren induced Schoendienst to ground to second-baseman McDougald, who fumbled the ball and just barely threw the Braves' batter out. Logan then walked on 3–2, a pitch that appeared to both Duren and Berra to be a perfect strike. Duren ran off the mound toward plate umpire Charlie Berry, and after arguing to no avail, he walked back to the mound. Before pitching to the next batter, Duren put his hand to his neck, the traditional sign for "choke," probably the most sensitive word in an athlete or umpire's dictionary. Berry didn't see Duren's insult because catcher Berra was blocking his view, but commissioner Ford Frick was watching the game on TV and clearly saw it. Frick fined Duren $250. Duren denied he gave the choke sign. "I was fixing my tie," he said. With Logan on first Duren then struck out Mathews for the second out. It was Duren's eighth strikeout in four and two-thirds innings of series relief pitching. The strikeout was Mathews eleventh of the series, a record. With two outs and Logan still on first, the unpredictable Duren then unexplainedly went into a full windup, forgetting about Logan, who raced for second and then scored easily when Aaron singled to left field. The Yankee lead was cut to 4–3. Adcock's single then sent Aaron to third. Stengel called time, and in a surprise move called in Turley, the complete-game winner of the day before. The Braves' manager Haney countered by pinch hitting the left-handed Frank Torre for the right-handed Crandall. With two outs and men on first and third, the tension had mounted, as the local Braves fans rooted for a base hit that might result in a Milwaukee series victory.

Turley completed his warm-ups. Torre stepped in. The players of both teams edged toward the front of their dugouts. Turley threw a rising fast ball, and Torre swung, hitting the ball on the handle of the bat. The Braves crowd roared when it looked like the ball was going on a line over the head of McDougald, the Yankee second-baseman, but the soft line drive died in midair, and McDougald back-pedaled and caught the ball easily near the outfield grass to end the game and tie the series at three games apiece.

Stengel did not announce his seventh-game starter, and an hour before the game he gave the assignment to Don Larsen. Burdette was pitching for the Braves. For the fourth series in a row, the Yankees were playing a seventh game. Only once, in 1925, when the Pittsburgh Pirates defeated the Washington Senators, had a team trailed three games to one and emerged victorious.

The Braves scored a run in the first inning, and the Yankees countered with two in the second, but when Larsen faltered in the third, Stengel once again brought in Bob Turley—the third day in a row Turley pitched. Turley shut out the Braves until the sixth, when Del Crandall tied the game 2–2 with a home run.

Burdette had given the Yankees nothing since the second, and the two pitching stars fought intensely for the championship of the world. In the eighth inning the Yankees broke the game open. Burdette retired McDougald and Mantle, but Yogi Berra lined a double against the right-field fence, and Ellie Howard singled to score him for a 3–2 lead. Andy Carey singled, sending Howard to second, and when Burdette tried to throw a high slider past Bill Skowron, the Moose lost the ball into the left-field bleachers for a 6–2 lead. Almost on cue, the 46,367 Milwaukee faithful rose en masse and began streaming for the exits while Skowron rounded the bases amidst total silence.

Turley raced through the eighth in style, but he prolonged everyone's agony by walking Mathews to start the ninth. Crandall flied out, and Logan lined out, but Joe Adcock pinch hit for reliever Jack McMahon and singled to left field. Mathews pulled into second. Mathews, who had hit 4–25 for a .160 average in the series looked over to Yankee shortstop Tony Kubek who had hit 1–21 (.048). "Hey Tony, we're really horseshit, aren't we?" Mathews said. Both men smiled. With two out and two men on, Red Schoendienst hit a routine fly bàll to Mantle to end the game and the series. Turley had completed six and two-thirds innings of brilliant relief work, allowing only two hits.

On the bus from the stadium to the airport, the players hijacked the bus's air horn, and all the way to the terminal boomed their Bronx-cheer razz to the fans of Milwaukee.

Back in New York the usually staid Yankee fans were more vocal and exuberant after this series triumph. New York City bars were packed two and three deep for the game, and after the finale ended, cars on the streets tooted their horns and some confetti was thrown in a mini-demonstration of civic pride.

The four games had been won by Turley, Larsen, and Duren, all refugees from the extinct St. Louis Browns franchise. On the way home, Larsen commented, "We needed Satchel Paige. That's all we needed." On the plane ride home players drank champagne and jeered the Braves. Just before the plane landed at Idlewild, Whitey Ford burned the corks of the champagne bottles and painted designs on the players' faces. When it was Stengel's turn, he sat patiently in his seat as Whitey applied the artwork, etching large dollar signs on his cheeks. Late in the evening the team arrived in New York City, and the Yankee contingent was met by reporters and fans at the airport. Stengel, sporting his dollar-signed face, greeted the reporters. "I guess," said Stengel, "we could play in the National League after all."

1959

Great expectations . . . The nonpareil Ryne Duren—
and his personal tragedy . . . Fierce booing for Mantle
. . . Injuries . . . Dashed hopes

Spring arrived in 1959, and millions of Americans threw their backs out of
whack spinning hula hoops. President Eisenhower continued to ignore all
Russian pleas for trade agreements and peace talks, and rebel leader Fidel
Castro, with Eisenhower's blessing, began his final campaign against Batista
with a New Year's Day raid against Havana. In France, Charles de Gaulle was
enthroned.

There was dissension among the members of the Yankee front office before
spring training opened for 1959. Owner Dan Topping decided to eliminate the
instructional school, much to Casey Stengel's displeasure, and Topping instructed George Weiss to get even tougher with regard to the players' salary
demands. When camp opened, several of the stars including Ford and Mantle
were unsigned, and a number of the others, in a poorer bargaining position,
signed but were resentful.

Casey Stengel, now 68 years old, almost didn't come back. Usually Casey
would sign a new contract in the fall of the year, but this time after his contract
had expired, he waited until the start of spring training to sign another two-year
deal. The lure of winning a tenth pennant and tying mentor John McGraw's
record became too great. He returned despite a sub-par physical condition
which during the second half of the '58 season tired him easily, causing him to
sometimes doze off during second games of doubleheaders. It bothered him
that he did not have his usual strength. The internal changes in the organization
were also agitating him, and he was getting third-person reports that Topping
was losing confidence in him. Off the field Casey was loud and boistrous, and
his drinking increased to the point that Topping and Weiss called his wife,
Edna, in California and asked her to come to St. Pete. After she arrived
Casey's excesses lessened, and his spirits were buoyed.

When camp opened Casey surveyed his domain and found it to be solid and
unshakable. "As to what I think of our prospects this year," Casey said, "I'll
tell you what I think of our prospects. I think we've got the world by the ears,
and we're not letting go." The Yankees had just won their fourth pennant in a
row, and though the team had not played well the last two months of the '58

season, it did come back to beat the Braves in the series. Casey was optimistic. So was George Weiss. The Yankee general manager refused to trade. His nucleus of players was strong, and in addition minor league star Clete Boyer was promoted from Richmond. Weiss felt the Yankees had a pat hand. So did everyone else.

The Yankees were starting with Bill Skowron, Gil McDougald, Tony Kubek, Andy Carey, Jerry Lumpe, Bobby Richardson, and rookie Clete Boyer in the infield, and in the outfield there were Mantle, Hank Bauer, Norm Siebern, Enos Slaughter, and Ellie Howard. Howard would assist Yogi Berra with the catching. "I can get any player in the league for Howard," Stengel said, "but I'm not going to do it." The pitching staff was as talented and deep as ever with Whitey Ford, twenty-one-game winner Bob Turley, Don Larsen, Tom Sturdivant, Art Ditmar, John Kucks, Bobby Shantz, Virgil Trucks, Duke Maas, and all-star reliefer Ryne Duren.

As the season began the Yankees were struck by an epidemic of injuries, beginning with Larsen and Sturdivant, who started the year with sore arms. Boston pitcher Bill Monboquette hit McDougald on both hands with a pitch, and Gil was out two weeks. Mickey Mantle made an off-balance throw from the outfield and reinjured his throwing shoulder, the one Schoendienst had injured in the '57 series, and then in batting practice Mantle suffered a fracture of his right index finger when he was hit by a pitch thrown by Maas. Andy Carey suffered from an infected hand and barely hit .200. Tony Kubek played center in Mantle's place. Bobby Richardson replaced McDougald. Jerry Lumpe played short and third. None of the young replacements hit, and under Stengel's intense prodding, all were pressing. Unexpectedly neither Hank Bauer nor McDougald, when he returned, were hitting over .230 in mid-May.

On May 7 in Los Angeles the Yankees played a benefit for Roy Campanella before 93,000 in the Coliseum, and Yankee first-baseman Bill Skowron, wearing a corset to protect his injury-prone back, tore a hamstring muscle behind his right thigh running out an infield single. "What have I done that this should keep happening to me?" asked the injured Skowron. Even Weiss was sympathetic. "You don't give us any trouble, Moose. You mind your own business," said Weiss. "Why does it always happen to you?"

With so many regulars injured, the team was losing. Then the Asian flu bug struck Mantle, Marv Throneberry, Clete Boyer, Tom Sturdivant, and Ryne Duren, and on May 20 the Yankees sank into the American League cellar. It was the first time since May 1940 that the Yankees were in last. Yankee haters all over the league were gleeful, and newspapers were calling the team the Basement Bombers. A headline, "The Day the Yankees Hit the Bottom," was accompanied by a picture of a downcast Mickey Mantle with his head bowed. Yankee fans, the poorest losers in America, booed their fallen heroes more than anyone. Mantle, in particular, playing in pain, absorbed one of the fiercest booings in the history of professional sports.

The day the Yankees plunged into the cellar Mantle hit a two-run home run off Frank Lary during the 13–6 defeat, and the Stadium denizens booed him with each mincing step he took around the bases. His right shoulder and right index finger pained him terribly, but he nevertheless insisted on playing. Batting left-handed, he was unable to hold his bat properly and was striking out a lot. His average was low, and as his frustrations mounted, he again began punching walls and kicking the drinking fountain. Several times after fans threw things at him, he would raise his middle finger high in the air to tell them off. The boos cascaded from the Stadium. In one game after he struck out twice, the third time up he took three straight pitches as though he didn't care any more, incurring the vengeful wrath of the crowd and the extreme displeasure of manager Stengel. Mantle later apologized to his teammates for his behavior.

The Yankees were dead last, eight and a half games behind the league-leading Cleveland Indians, and the fans were taking it out on Mantle. "We're having a bit of trouble with everything," said the bewildered Stengel. "You got nine guys not hitting, and the pitching isn't so hot either, and what are you going to do?"

If you're George Weiss, you're going to make a trade, most likely with Kansas City, and in the final week of May, Weiss sent Tom Sturdivant and John Kucks, star pitchers who suddenly fizzled, and Jerry Lumpe, the young reserve infielder, to the A's. In return he got Hector Lopez, a hard-hitting, excellent third-baseman, and Ralph Terry, the young pitcher Weiss had sent to the A's in the Billy Martin deal. Terry had undergone his apprenticeship and now Weiss, needing him, got him back. After the trade was announced, there were howls of anguish heard throughout the offices of the other American League teams. "Nobody else will trade with us," Weiss smugly answered.

Lopez was acquired on May 26, and immediately Stengel started him at third, benching Andy Carey, the gadfly with the low batting average. Since Carey had joined the team in '54, Stengel had used him as one of his prize scapegoats. Rather than berate a more sensitive player, he instead screamed at Carey a great deal, knowing Carey reacted positively to it. Carey would get angry, not sulk. It had been a continual battle between Stengel and his stubborn third-baseman. By '59, however, Stengel's patience with Carey had completely run out. Stengel was still yelling "Butcher boy, butcher boy" at Carey, who preferred swinging for the fences. Before one spring game Carey was in the batting cage playing Home Run Derby. From the dugout Stengel limped out to the cage. "Hey Carey," yelled the Yankee manager, "I understand you got some kind of record for hitting the ball in the bleachers during batting practice. That right?"

"Yes, sir, that's right," Carey said.

"Did you get that bonus for hitting the ball in the bleachers?" Stengel asked.

"No, sir," Carey said.

"That's right," Stengel virtually screamed. "You didn't get that bonus for that. But you might get a bonus if you get forty hits." Stengel stomped back to the dugout.

The Carey-Stengel battle was not all one-sided. Carey knew just how to agitate his crusty manager. When Carey was playing third he had the habit of holding his glove by the side of his face, and when Stengel would scream, "Play in for the bunt, Carey," Andy would hide his face and pretend not to have heard. Stengel would start yelling, "Move in, move in," but Carey wouldn't budge as Stengel writhed in frustration.

On the bench, especially during the second games of doubleheaders, when Stengel dozed off Carey would wait for a Yankee batter to get a hit or make an exciting defensive play, and then cheer right into the ear of the napping manager. Stengel would jump up, startled, and pace up and down the dugout yelling, "Way to go." Then he'd return to his seat, and when he dozed off again, Carey would be waiting.

Now with the acquisition of Lopez and with young Boyer waiting in the wings, Carey's future with the Yankees was uncertain.

Led by Lopez, the Yankees began a slow June climb back up the American League ladder. Skowron, returning after a week's absence, resumed his slugging, and Richardson, given a real chance, raised his average close to .300 and fielded like no Yankee second-baseman since the early form of Jerry Coleman. Lopez continued his professional hitting, driving in more runs (eight) in his first week of playing than Carey and Lumpe together had driven in all season long. Mantle, taking personal responsibility for the Yankees' poor showing, responded to the criticisms of both the fans and the management by raising his average in the eleven days following the Yankees' drop into the cellar almost fifty points. He was connecting for base hits, stealing bases with blinding speed, and creating excitement throughout the league. Whenever Mickey reached first base, the entreating chants of "go, go, go, go," reverberated. Yogi Berra, a slow starter, also began to hit, and with this new-found support, Whitey Ford, Art Ditmar, Don Larsen, and Duke Maas began winning. From the bullpen, peerless reliefer Ryne Duren, the bespectacled, massive Rhino, created an excitement all his own whenever he strode from the bullpen into a game to throw his invisible whooshes of sound which exploded into the catcher's mitt, perplexing and frightening those who faced him. On June 26 against the White Sox, Duren relieved in the seventh inning and struck out Earl Torgeson, Harry Simpson, and Sherm Lollar. In the eighth he struck out Billy Goodman and Johnny Callison, and in the ninth he fanned Luis Aparicio, Nellie Fox, and Earl Torgeson again. "He's the most exciting thing in baseball," said Stengel. "If the people won't come out to see him, they won't come out to see anybody. When he hops over that bullpen gate, the folks stop eating their peanuts."

Between April 30 and July 16 Duren pitched thirty-six consecutive innings of scoreless baseball, a span of eighteen games, getting credit for seven saves, a win, and more impressively, striking out fifteen of the last nineteen batters he faced during that stretch. His ERA was 0.96. By mid-June, less than two weeks after dropping into the cellar, the Yankees were only two and a half games out of first place, trailing the Indians who were running scared, looking behind them, fearful of Mantle's big bat and Duren's lightning fast ball.

The arrival of Ryne Duren into a ball game was as exciting as his actual performance. There was a ritual pageantry to his entrance. The gate of the pen would open, and Duren, husky and imposing, would slowly amble in, peering from behind thick, dark glasses. Upon his arrival at the mound, he would shed his jacket, throwing it to the bat boy without looking at him, and then carefully wipe off his thick, black lenses while scratching at the dirt with his feet to locate the rubber, suggesting less than subtly that this vision was poor. His glasses sufficiently wiped, he would nonchalantly fire his first warm-up pitch in the general direction of the plate. Invariably that first pitch would sail ten feet over the catcher's head and crash into the safety screen, bringing a roar of delight from the crowd. The Stadium would come alive, regardless of the situation or the score. Duren could throw a baseball more than 100 miles an hour and there were few human beings willing to take a toehold against Rhino, what with his reputation for poor eyesight and his legendary renown for erratic behavior. Against those foolish enough to brazenly defend the batter's right to stand up to the plate, Duren was never shy about throwing his "purpose pitch," a head-high fast ball that sent many a fear-stricken batter hurtling to the ground.

Duren became Yankee property in 1957 in one of the many Yankee-Kansas City deals, George Weiss getting him in the Billy Martin trade in mid-June. Duren was acquired only a month after he had pitched against New York. Gil McDougald was one of those who wanted no part of Duren. Ryne knocked Gil on his ass, threw a strike, knocked him down, threw a strike, knocked him down, and so forth. The knockdown pitches were blazing only inches above his skull, balls Gil could barely see. McDougald, cowed, struck out three times. "Who wants to kill himself because some idiot can't see?" McDougald said. Hank Bauer, another normally tough and gutsy player, but also a realist, stood three feet from the plate and docilely took three strikes. Bauer wasn't about to get killed. Neither was anyone else. After the game Bauer requested that Stengel try buying Duren. It's not every team that can get a player it covets for the asking.

In 1957 Duren was a 28-year-old prospect who had been pitching in the minors for nine years. That year, just before the Yankees acquired him, for the first time an eye specialist properly diagnosed why Duren did not see well. When Duren was twenty, he had suffered from rheumatic fever, and for six months he lay helpless, the illness ultimately affecting the muscular balance of his eyes. After the proper corrective lenses were prescribed, once again Duren could see the outline of home plate. During the remainder of the 1957 season Duren started for Denver under Ralph Houk, compiling a 13–3 record, over-powering the International League, and was on the verge of stardom.

In 1958 Duren joined the Yankees, and for two years he was the most respected and feared pitcher in baseball. He was a relief pitcher in the grand style of Joe Page, a reliever who did not rely on a trick pitch like Hoyt Wilhelm's knuckle ball or Roy Face's fork ball. Ryne relied on pure speed. "I would not admire hitting against Duren because if he ever hit you in the head you might be in the past tense," said manager Stengel. Duren was in a class by himself. In 1958 he won six and saved twenty, striking out eighty-seven batters in seventy-five innings, and had a 2.02 ERA, leading the team to a pennant. In 1959 he was even better, though the Yankees lost the pennant. Duren won three, saved fourteen, struck out ninety-six in seventy-six innings and had a 1.88 ERA. At the peak of his career, for two or three innings Ryne Duren came as close to being invincible as any pitcher who ever lived.

For all Duren's success, though, he seemed to be having a great deal of difficulty getting a solid grip on himself. Ryne was subject to abnormally peaked highs and lows. When he won, he would be so elated he would be literally drunk with success, feeling like Superman, cape or no cape. When he'd lose or not pitch well, his confidence would be severely shaken, and often he would go into deep depression. When Stengel would use another reliefer Ryne would become almost uncontrollable with fear. "He doesn't like me any more. He isn't going to use me any more," Ryne would say. "You've got to be kidding," the other players would respond, not understanding the magnitude of his insecurity. When he felt down, he would drink. When sober, Duren was a loner, but after a few drinks he would undergo a personality change, becoming overly friendly, usually with somebody's wife or girl friend, and then when the guy would voice his objections, Ryne would take offense. "What are you getting so upset about?" he would ask. "I'm just trying to be friendly." Then Duren would become hostile, taking off his thick glasses to engage in fights, a mistake for someone with as poor eyesight as he had. Throughout his career Duren manifested his personality problems by drinking one too many and becoming violent. "Rhino shouldn't drink," said anyone who knew him well.

Everyone in the Yankee organization knew that Duren's problems centered around his drinking. Yet no one suggested he see a psychiatrist or go to Alcoholics Anonymous to get help. As long as he performed on the field, what he did off it was irrelevant. Yet not too many years after his flash of success, Duren found himself in a mental institution, practically a basket case, his marriage destroyed, his career at an end, his life approaching ruination because of alcoholism. On New Year's night 1965 in San Antonio, Texas, Ryne, alone and despondent, drank a dozen beers and drove his automobile onto the tracks of the local railroad, turned off the ignition and waited to die. The police beat the train to Duren's car.

Duren was committed to San Antonio State Hospital, and then in May he was transferred to the DePaul Rehabilitation Hospital in Milwaukee where he began training as an alcoholics' counselor. After a year of working with delinquent boys, the Stoughton, Wisconsin, Community Hospital hired him to run the alcoholics' rehabilitation program in the town, a small community about fifteen miles south of Madison, the state capital. Stoughton is a quiet, suburban community, rich farm country in America's heartland. Off the main street a couple of blocks to the left is the Stoughton Hospital, and in a small clapboard two-story frame house is the Alcoholic Rehabilitation Center. It is a simple, no-frills building, and inside the furnishings are sparse, with sofas and chairs for people to come in and sit and talk. In the downstairs living room a broad-shouldered, bespectacled man in a work shirt and blue jeans talks softly and intently with one of the locals. The man with the glasses is Ryne Duren. The other man is talking about his drinking problem. Duren, sober for six years, now a community leader successful in his work, nods, showing understanding and compassion. "When you feel like a drink, I want you to call me, you understand?" Duren says, firmly but still softly. "You understand? Call me." The man nods. A few minutes later, the man leaves.

"There was a man," Ryne said to me, "who had been the town drunk. He's been sober for quite some time now." It was said matter-of-factly, casually, almost in a whisper. "That made a strong impact on the community here."

Duren, a big man at 6 foot, 200 pounds, exuded a placid, almost religious peace of mind. In a previous lifetime he had been a magnetic, aggressive Yankee sports hero, but there was none of the boistrousness or swagger that he had once displayed strolling in from the bullpen. Instead he was sedate, thoughtful, very much a searcher for truth behind his wire-rimmed glasses. In an upstairs conference room, on the wall behind him, were several Yankee team portraits and a few pictures of him pitching or with his teammates. "People change attitudes by being in contact with people," Ryne said, still surprising me by the softness of his voice. "All of these pictures were put away for a number of years, four or five years. Finally I stopped hating myself and I took them out again."

I asked Ryne if he was willing to discuss the changes in his life over the past fifteen years.

"I don't mind," he said, "if it's pertinent to your book. I was a certain person when I was playing ball, and I can look at that in retrospect, and it was pretty meaningless as to what was actually going on then. I can see things that kept me from ticking a lot better, things that brought me in thirty-nine years to that hospital. As far as the rehabilitation goes, the personal recovery of an alcoholic, that's kind of a separate life for me, though I am the same person. I can talk about it, though. I don't have any intention of hiding what happened."

"Where did the problems start?" I asked.

"Oh," Ryne said, "I was from Cazanovia, Wisconsin, and a lot of it had to do with my cultural background, plus a masculine identification very early in life, plus what some of my relations were, and what the peer pressure was at that time. It was all part of it. There was a group of about ten of us who were hell-raising roughneck guys who pursued a lot of it through drinking. And naturally when I got into baseball, I wanted to fit into the team style. I think on every team I played on, 75 to 80 percent of the guys drank, and about 50 percent of those guys drank heavier than most.

"I probably belonged to the 20 or 30 percent of the heavy drinkers, and of course through the process of alcoholic addiction I stayed pretty much with the other players who were addicted to alcohol—either psychologically or culturally addicted, whichever way you want to put it. Finally some of us passed into a phase of alcoholism where we couldn't ever return to social drinking. And this was costing us possibly fifteen or twenty years off our lives. Do you see the team picture of the Yankees there?" Ryne said. "There were several full-blown alcoholics on that team, and there were three or four more who came pretty close." When Duren talked, his soft voice sounded sad, regretful. For his teammates? For himself? I wasn't sure.

"I think," he said, "any time you're talking about alcoholism, you're talking about the quality of living, and the quality under which I was living for years was terrible. When I was a Yankee, I was a mess. I was a sick guy. There was that feeling inside, the feeling of isolation, put-downs by other people, the lack of self-image, the relationship within my marriage. You talk about an alcoholic being lonely in a crowd. I was a sick guy for a long, long time. All my life."

"The other players didn't relieve your loneliness?" I asked.

"They did," he said, "to a certain extent, but when you go through life with a pessimistic attitude, it's pretty hard to tell someone, at least for me, to explain what I was feeling, to explain that I always felt that I would be a failure. There I was, an outstanding relief pitcher in the big leagues for the Yankees, and though I always felt that something terrible was going to happen, something terrible never did happen. And I lived with that fear. And I didn't have anything to compare it to, so I naturally thought everybody lived like that. Only after I had stopped drinking for a couple of years, was I able to talk in depth about things that had been going on in my head. I remember one day I was riding into Milwaukee, and I had been sober for eighteen months, two years, this was the summer of 1970, and I'm driving into Milwaukee, I don't remember what for. But I remember that I let my mind just wander, and I couldn't think of anything that scared me. Anything about life or dying or anything. For the first time in my life. Finally, here I was, free from this fear that had been over me all my life, and it was a great feeling. And today, that's the way I live. But for the first thirty-nine years of my life, I was running scared.''

"And there was no opportunity to talk to the other players about your feelings?'' I asked.

"Oh, I don't know," he said. "Remember you can only be as honest about your feelings as you are aware of them. And you cannot be honest if you are defensive, and with the male chauvinist background that I came from, you had to be pretty defensive all the time. You were always concerned with the way you came across to others." Ryne paused. "I think the only measure of honesty that I ever had came from Hank Bauer,'' he said. "We were playing the Braves in the '58 world series, and there was a guy who had been in the Marines and had stormed some beachheads, and he was honest enough to say before that first game that he was just scared to death. Oh, I'm sure there were other moments. Whitey Ford was a tremendously honest person. Mantle was an honest person.'' Again he paused, and it was a long pause.

"Do you remember the 36 innings of shutout ball you threw in 1959?''

"Yeah," Ryne said, "it was kind of a fun thing because through that time I gave up no runs, but what wasn't fun was that through that same stretch the Yankees didn't score many runs either, and I wasn't getting much credit for it.''

"The Yankees weren't so great in '59,'' I said.

"When I was going into September my earned run average up to that point was below one. It was fantastic. That was the year that George Weiss sent me the contract. After '58 I made $15,000; after the '59 season, he sent me a contract with a $2,000 cut! I got it in the mail on Christmas Eve. I remember. It was Christmas Eve. I was never more disgusted with myself in my whole life. That was a tough situation for me.''

" '59 was your last great year,'' I said.

"You have to remember something," Ryne said. "In 1960 I was 32 years old, and my arm didn't bounce back like it once did. And I think, too, that I was becoming a sicker and sicker person. I was having more and more problems. If you are a baseball player, your marriage has to be solid to last, and my marriage was falling apart, and I was solving more and more problems with alcohol.''

"Was your alcoholism the reason the Yankees traded you in 1961?'' I asked.

"I think that was part of it," he said. "Certainly. Also my record wasn't outstanding. In 1960 Luis Arroyo came to the team, and in 1961 he had an outstanding season and Casey went to him. I had good speed four out of five pitches, but four out of five isn't good enough, and little by little I was slipping farther and farther.''

Duren wandered from the Yankees to the California Angels, Philadelphia, Cincinnati, Philadelphia again, and finally Washington—all the while trying to handle his drinking, sometimes succeeding for a few months, but never free of his addiction completely.

"In August of '65 Washington released me, and the procrastination when I got home! I kept putting off thinking about what I was going to do. I'd get drunk, and I'd stay drunk for a week. You know, not falling-down drunk, but just beer drinking, staying away from my family, not wanting to face reality. Along in November I was home drunk, and I went to sleep with a lit cigarette in my hand, burned out the house, and then my wife moved and filed for divorce. I was practically broke, jobless, and I felt like I was crazy, wanting to crack up. I knew some people in San Antonio, one of them being a doctor who got me admitted to a state hospital down there, but when I was admitted, I was admitted as an anxiety reactionary, not as an alcoholic. You have to understand, even though 1965 wasn't that long ago, a lot of places were not dealing with alcohol problems the way they deal with them today. We've made a lot of strides since then. So I was dealt with more as a psychiatric patient under the care of a psychiatrist. There were AA meetings, but AA meetings weren't really enough. There were a lot of other things that I needed, testing, counseling, my wife needed counseling to understand alcoholism for our marriage to survive. I needed more help than the hospital down there had to offer. So I stayed there eighty-two days, came out, and I got into a service station business in San Antonio. Then that collapsed, and ten or eleven months after my hospitalization, I was drunk again. I had gotten back into my household, and when I got drunk again, my wife left me again. Then I got a job with an insurance company, and I stayed sober for another ten or eleven months, but the business wasn't working out, and this time I decided to take the geographical escape. I moved to Milwaukee—I'm from Wisconsin—and I got a job selling heavy trucks, and my wife got a divorce without me in San Antonio, and again I started back drinking, the snowballing process again, and I was getting into really bad trouble, and well, I finally collapsed in May of 1968. I became a basket case.'' There was very little emotion in Ryne's voice. It was almost as though he was giving the chronology of someone else's life. "At this point I was admitted into the DePaul Rehabilitation Hospital in Milwaukee.''

"Through all those years of self-defeating behavior, nobody recognized your problem?" I asked.

"No,'' Ryne said, shaking his head, "I was just drunk. You have to understand that drunken behavior has always been seen as drunken behavior and not as alcoholism, not something treatable, but something to laugh at, something that everybody grew up with—that it's the norm. You know. So everything is quite understandable as far as I'm concerned. See, I'm not blaming anyone. But I'm trying to explain the nature of human beings without pointing a guilty finger. Anyway, I got back in Wisconsin, at the DePaul hospital, and for the first time I was getting help that I had never had before, psychological testing, some other things. Of course, I didn't have a family any more to counsel, but the hospital gave me a new family. I was given a job, just given it, in an institution for delinquent boys, the Norris Foundation, and there I had a lot of protection, a lot of my needs were met for the first time, not the needs I thought I required, like being a big-shot truck salesman, not that, but the need to recognize a lot of the characteristics of human beings, including and especially myself. Then I got into school at the University of Wisconsin, taking psychology courses, necessary for the work I'm doing, but also damn good insight into the growth of my development. I worked at the school a couple of years, and I grew to a point where I started threatening some of the other people there, and I outgrew my thing there. The fact that I was an alcoholic and had this background then allowed me to go into alcoholic rehabilitation, which is what I'm doing now."

"If people could only see what happened to me and my family and a lot of people I know because of alcohol," Ryne said. "Losing my wife, being denied the beauty of seeing my son grow up. It was so degrading. For me the jury's in. If somebody you know is an alcoholic, for them the jury will never come in, and believe me, it's an act of love to give somebody a kick in the ass to get them into treatment. The quality of their lives, the decency of their lives, the beauty, it all depends on it. Help is available, and the knowledge is there. Not to take advantage of it is almost criminal." Ryne smiled. "It must sound like I'm preaching," he said, "but it isn't easy to understand what it is to be an alcoholic unless you've been to hell and back yourself."

During the final eventful week of June, Ingemar Johansson, smashing his "Thunder of Thor" into the face and body of Floyd Patterson again and again, knocked Patterson to the canvas seven times in the third round to win the heavyweight boxing championship. In Little Rock, Arkansas, 200 seniors graduated from T. J. Raney High School, the biggest of the "private" schools established in Little Rock after Governor Faubus declared the public schools closed to prevent integration. The 200 seniors wore confederate-gray gowns. The school flag was the confederate flag.

Fidel Castro, who had fled to Mexico in May of 1955, and then had returned to Cuba in 1956 began his revolution against President Batista, won his fight against Batista after three years of guerilla warfare. Castro, whom the United States indirectly backed by imposing an arms embargo against Batista, was upsetting President Eisenhower by nationalizing all Cuban landholdings over 1,000 acres. When Castro began denouncing American imperialists, Eisenhower was beginning to have second thoughts about whether he had supported the right side in the Cuban struggle.

The Golden Age of television had passed. New shows included "Night Court," "Divorce Court," and "Small Claims Court," and on Sunday afternoons millions watched "College Bowl," with teams from two colleges vying for scholarships by answering esoteric questions. There were a great many reruns of old shows on TV. The Yankees were planning a rerun of their 1958 season. It never got on the air.

With the Yankees only a game and a half out of first place after Ryne Duren's spectacular June 26 performance (eight strikeouts in three innings) they went to Chicago and proceeded to lose three out of four to the White Sox in 100-degree heat. Bill Veeck, the new White Sox owner, gave the fans circus entertainment between games of the June 28 doubleheader. The biggest clowns, though, were the Yankees. In one game Bob Turley was leading 2–1 in the eighth inning on two home runs by Hector Lopez who now had twenty-six RBI's in thirty-two games, but in the bottom of the eighth Suitcase Simpson, never given much of a chance with the Yankees before he came to the Sox, rocketed a grand slam home run into the Comiskey Park bleachers to win the game for the Sox. The doubleheader the next day was a disaster, too, with Earl Battey winning both games with home runs against Ford and Larsen.

On the final day of June Mickey Mantle severely injured his right ankle, and with Mickey hobbled, the month of July was calamitous. The sequence of catastrophic mishaps coalescing with mediocre pitching ended the Yankee pennant hopes early. If only one or two pitchers had been sub-par, Stengel could have substituted, but with Turley, Larsen, Shantz, and rookies Jim Coates, Jim Bronstad, and Eli Grba *all* ineffective, Stengel wore out the turf between the dugout and the mound.

Larsen didn't win another game after June 13. Turley, 21–7 the year before, finished '59 8–11, his blazing fast ball on vacation. "Last year he pitched like Cy Young," wrote New York *Daily News* columnist Dick Young. "This year he pitches like Dick Young." Shantz was suffering with arm miseries. The team still had Duren, but rarely were the Yankees in the lead when he entered the ball game, and when he did get in, rarely did they score any runs for him. Between July 9 and July 13 in six consecutive games against the Boston Red Sox in Fenway Park, the Yankee starting pitcher was shelled from the mound, and in five of those six games, all ending in defeats, the relief pitching held no salvation. When the reeling Yankees left Fenway, they were in fifth place, seven and a half games out of first place.

Then the injuries began to mount. Bill Skowron suffered a stabbing, incapacitating pain in his lower back reaching down for a ground ball. The other dependable, Hector Lopez, was struck on the elbow by a pitched ball and was out. Mantle reinjured his right leg, and though he played, was virtually ineffective. In July Mantle was at bat with fifty-seven men on base. He drove in four of them.

It got worse. Gil McDougald and Tony Kubek collided chasing a pop fly, McDougald losing the ball, Kubek losing consciousness. Kubek suffered from a concussion, neck pain, and shoulder aches, and McDougald suffered from dizzy spells. That week Andy Carey came down with hepatitis and was lost for the season.

The final blow occurred on July 25 in Detroit. Skowron, out two weeks, finally returned, and on his first play in the field Coot Veal, a slender Detroit Tiger infielder, slapped a ground ball to third-baseman Lopez who had already made two throwing errors in the game. Lopez, unsure of himself and losing confidence with each game, fumbled the ball then hastily recovered and threw just inside first base. Skowron, in the baseline, reached to stop the ball from sailing into the stands, and Veal smashed into the lunging first-baseman. His glove went flying and Skowron dropped to the ground, groaning in agony, his left arm broken in two places. Skowron, with fifty-nine RBI's, second only to Harmon Killebrew of Washington, was batting .298 with fifteen home runs. He was finished for the season, too.

With Mantle clearly limping and playing poorly, outfielder Hank Bauer showing his age, and Norm Siebern not hitting for average or fielding well, by August the Yankees were twelve distant games from first place. Only the play of Ellie Howard, who split his time between catching and the outfield, Yogi Berra, who hit .395 for the month, and Bobby Richardson, the only regular hitting over .300, kept the Yankees respectable. In the wake of a disastrous July, the Yankee season was over. Everything else to follow was just playing out the string.

The Yankee fans, whose team had won nine pennants in the last ten years, and won 104 games in 1954, the year they lost the pennant, were not used to such a dismal showing by their team. Through the summer the booing in Yankee Stadium that greeted the players was unprecedented, and Mantle, who drove in exactly two runs in August, was the focus of much of it. It made one wonder whether Mickey's days as a Yankee were numbered, and as the booing increased in intensity, the tension the moody center fielder normally felt increased. His elbow-bending and lack of sleep made his temper even more volatile, especially with the fans and the press. More than once after a poor game Mantle retired to the trainer's room, refusing to talk to reporters, sulking in there like Achilles in his tent. Even Stengel, normally more patient with Mickey than others, derided Mantle in the press, calling him his "greatest disappointment."

Stengel, riding his players especially hard, showed no mercy, especially to the youngsters. He was fast to criticize and quick to second-guess, frequently berating an individual in front of all the others and causing his men uncomfortable sieges of anxiety. His critiques in the papers became more vitriolic. After one game that Ralph Terry lost in the last innings on a home run, Stengel growled, "The only thing wrong with that fella is he ain't smart enough to cross the street." The players tried to avoid Casey whenever possible.

Stengel himself came under increased criticism. Topping, who wanted Casey out, would not fire him because his contract ran for two years and he didn't want to pay Casey for not managing as the Dodgers once did. But the dissatisfied Topping was not above second-guessing his manager as his manager did his men. After one loss Topping criticized Stengel's platooning. "And here I have been winning with it all these years," Casey said. "The owners have gotten too much like fans." In *Newsweek* magazine one unnamed Yankee executive was quoted as saying, "If Stengel were to quit tomorrow, and coach Ralph Houk were named manager, our team would win the pennant. But he's not going to quit, and we're not going to win." Casey, too, was beginning to drink more than previously, and his relations with Weiss were becoming strained, as was Weiss's relationship with Dan Topping. In August Roy Hamey, the assistant general manager, flew to Richmond to confer with Jack White, the Richmond farm club general manager. "Weiss is going to be retired soon,'' Hamey said, ''and I'm going to take over. I'd like you to come back to New York to assist me.'' White agreed, though no change immediately resulted. Several months later Topping told White, ''I want you to stay at Richmond one more season. At the end of next year I'm going to make a move.''

In September, it looked like the team was beginning to turn around. Whitey Ford was pitching well again, and bullpen man Art Ditmar, given an opportunity to start, won some games, finishing 13–9 with a 2.90 ERA. Duke Maas, despite an earned run average of 4.50, won fourteen games on the year. Rookie Jim Coates, long and lean and nasty, was 6–1 and appeared to be the best new pitching blood around, and youngster Ralph Terry, while allowing too many home runs in crucial situations, showed too much potential to be dismissed.

And for the second year in a row, Ryne Duren was sensational, the one focus of excitement for the fans. But at the end of September even Duren was lost to the team when in Boston, running from the bullpen to the dugout after the final out of a game, he was tripped up by a couple of fans running from the stands to the mound. Duren didn't see them, tangled his feet, and fell heavily and awkwardly. When the dazed Ryne reached the dugout, he confided to Ralph Terry that he thought his wrist was broken. It was, in two places, and Ryne was out the final ten days of the season. Duren's unsurpassed fast ball, his bread and butter pitch, left him forever. He was never a star again.

The Yankees finished the year 79–75, in third place thirteen games behind the White Sox. It was a dismal finish, bereft of any excitement or interest, except in visiting ball parks where fans of the other teams flocked to see the lordly Yankees get their asses whipped. Yankee road attendance lacked only a few thousand of the all-time record set in 1949.

At the end of the season George Weiss, who blamed the lack of success on the various outside financial interests of the players, received a poem in the mail which he pointedly thumbtacked to the Yankee clubhouse bulletin board the next spring training. It read:

> *To an ex-American League pennant winner*
>
> *Although you were defeated, Yanks,*
> *You shouldn't feel too blue;*
> *Just think of all your bars and banks*
> *And bowling alleys too.*
> *As businessmen you guys are tops,*
> *It really seems a shame*
> *That you should leave your shops*
> *Just for a lousy game.*

Later, on the poem someone added in marking pen, ''Fuck you.''

1960

Weiss's last great trade via the Kansas City shuffle—Maris becomes a Yankee and an MVP . . . The "Glass" Moose . . . A surprise pennant and a stunning world series loss to the Bucs . . . Bobby Richardson . . . Casey "retires"—bitterly

It was a bitter winter of discontent for Yankee officials, as Dan Topping, Del Webb, George Weiss, and Casey Stengel decided who was to blame for the 1959 debacle. George Weiss, now 65 years old, was considering retirement, but he had been talking about retirement since 1954 and no one was taking his quitting talk seriously any more. Casey Stengel, 70 years old, had a year left on his two-year contract, and because Dan Topping didn't feel that Stengel was as sharp mentally in '59 as he had previously been, Topping directed his personal attorney, Arthur Friedlund, to ask Chicago White Sox manager Al Lopez if he would consider managing the Yankees in 1960. Lopez, a close and loyal friend of Stengel, declined the offer. After Lopez said no, Topping decided to allow Stengel to finish out his contract and then retire. Topping made pitching coach Jim Turner the scapegoat and fired him. Eddie Lopat replaced Turner.

Weiss smarted from the Yankees' unaccustomed poor finish. Through the winter he talked trade, and when he finally completed one, it was a blockbuster, another swap with his bosom brothers in Kansas City, the fifth consecutive major deal with the A's management. Weiss sent the A's Norm Siebern, the young outfielder with a world of potential whose talents Stengel did not fully appreciate; Marv Throneberry, who under Stengel had lost whatever confidence he had, striking out too much and dropping balls at first; Hank Bauer, the 37-year-old veteran who had hit only .238 in '59; and sore-armed Don Larsen, in Stengel's doghouse, a pitcher who did not win a game after June in '59. In exchange the Yankees received Joe DeMaestri, a veteran defensive shortstop; Kent Hadley, an ex-Yankee first-baseman; and Roger Maris, a young outfielder of immense potential.

Roger Maris. The name *sounded* like a baseball player's. He had started his career in the Cleveland organization, signing for $5,000, and after an excellent four-year apprenticeship, Maris was hailed as "Cleveland's future Mickey Mantle." Now the two were playing together. In 1957 with the Indians, Maris was leading the competition for Rookie of the Year in late May when he broke two ribs in a vicious slide, and the rest of the year, playing in pain, he hit about .200, making some people wonder. In 1958 manager Bobby Bragan platooned

Maris with another youngster of potential, Rocky Colavito, and after Maris became extremely unhappy with his situation in Cleveland, Indian general manager Frank Lane shipped him in June of '58 to Kansas City. There he played under manager Harry Craft, a man he admired and respected. Maris finished the season with twenty-eight home runs and eighty RBI's. In 1959 he continued his slugging, and was leading the league in batting at the end of July with a .344 average, but a mysterious slump, during which Maris batted .165 the last three months of the season, dropped his average to .272.

Based on Maris's flashes of brilliance and his ability to pull a baseball with power from the left-handed side of the plate, a dearly sought talent for a man playing in Yankee Stadium (a talent Siebern, for one, did not possess), Weiss decided to "take his chances" with the hot-and-cold Maris. Parke Carroll, the A's general manager, also knew of Maris's potential, but he liked Siebern's consistency, and Siebern was a much friendlier chap. The trade was viewed in the press as a coup for the Yankees, who gave up nobody they had planned on using in 1960 for a slugging right fielder who would play every day and field with speed and fluency.

Still, there were questions. Would Moose Skowron recover from his broken arm, and if he did, could he keep from injuring himself once more? Should Tony Kubek play shortstop or the outfield? Who would play third base from among Andy Carey, out last year with hepatitis, Hector Lopez, Clete Boyer, and Gil McDougald, the ten-year veteran who had announced that this would be his final year? Would Yogi Berra, at age 37, still be able to play regularly? Would Mantle's weak underpinnings take him through another season? Were the injured arms of Whitey Ford and Bob Turley healthy again? Were any of the young pitchers ready to step into the rotation and win?

At the Yankee spring training camp in St. Petersburg, the Yankees were compounding their 1959 miseries. Off the field Mantle, his morale hurt by the demonic booing he had received in '59, received another blow when Weiss demanded he take a $17,000 salary cut. For two weeks of spring training Mickey held out, and then when he finally signed, taking a $7,000 cut to $65,000, he tried to do everything too quickly, and his weak right knee became inflamed and ballooned. His right shoulder, the one he injured in the 1957 series, continued to impede his batting, and the combination of his injuries and salary cut made the veteran Yankee slugger a very bitter man. Stengel, too, held it against Weiss that he had forced such a large salary cut on Mantle, and Weiss and Stengel, for so long working partners, now had few friendly or even polite words for each other.

While Mickey was holding out, he didn't endear himself to Weiss when he and Whitey Ford and several of the other players were picked up in the middle of St. Petersburg Bay by the harbor patrol, naked and treading water, when the boat on which they were being entertained caught fire and sank.

In spring training as usual, the team lost more than it was winning, its 11–21 record the worst of all American League teams, but Stengel was more interested in looking at his prospects than in winning. While Stengel wasn't concerned, Topping, Webb, and Weiss were unhappy. Most experts picked the White Sox, the '59 champions, to repeat.

Stengel, craggy-faced and wrinkled, seemed older than his 70 years, and his monologues seemed to be getting even more disjointed and hilarious than ever. Before one exhibition game against Chicago, a team led by three diminutive men—Luis Aparicio, Nellie Fox, and Jim Rivera—Stengel went into a discussion of the White Sox players. "Remember men," he was saying in the clubhouse meeting, "these guys are no bigger than Coke machines. They can run, and they're gonna beat you if you don't beat them. Remember, they're no bigger than Coke machines." Veteran Gil McDougald looked at newcomer Joe DeMaestri, and each bit hard on their tongues not to laugh. Casey was becoming as indecipherable as the Sphinx. He continued to keep late hours, drinking with the newspapermen, telling stories until four in the morning, and the combination of the lack of sleep and the hot Florida sun was causing him to doze off on the bench more than ever.

The season opened ambivalently. Stengel started Whitey Ford and Bob Turley, his veterans, and alternated his young arms, Coates, Terry, John Gabler, and Bill Short, looking for consistency. Everybody won more games than they lost, not always because the pitching was good but rather that the hitting was so potent. Jim Coates, in winning his first five decisions, was backed by anywhere from eight to sixteen runs.

With Maris in the lineup, a modern Murderer's Row of Mantle, Maris, Skowron, and Berra was emerging—no one team in the majors had this kind of home-run potential. By the end of May the Yankee firepower was becoming an awesome force to reckon with despite Mantle's average dropping below .250 because of his bad legs.

Maris was the catalyst. The entire spring he hit with authority, and by the end of May he was leading the league in home runs with nine. Asked one whimsical reporter, "Do you think you can break Babe Ruth's record?" Maris looked at the man and said, "Now that's damn silly. I haven't made this club yet, and here you're talking about that Babe Ruth bullshit." Off the field Maris, a quiet man who showed little sense of humor to the public, kept to himself and preferred to let his baseball ability speak for him. Strangers saw him to be aloof and hostile. On the field he was the added spark the Yankees had lacked the year before. Maris played his right-field position with unmatched skill, displaying speed and a disregard for his personal safety. On base he was a daring and aggressive base runner whose streamrolling blocks were dumping infielders throughout the league.

Casey Stengel, suffering from a virus and a high fever, suddenly was hospitalized on May 28, and coach Ralph Houk was named acting manager. Houk, given the reins, shook up the lineup, playing Hector Lopez in left field, starting Clete Boyer at third for the first time, and giving John Blanchard a chance to catch a few games. Houk also returned Art Ditmar to the starting rotation. Under Houk the team wasn't any more successful than before (7–6)

dropping three straight to Baltimore to fall six games behind the league-leading
Orioles, but morale under Houk was high and no one was very discouraged.

In early June, with Stengel in the hospital, the Yankees played the defending
champs, the White Sox, four games. After a disastrous game that Whitey Ford
lost when Gil McDougald misplayed a couple of balls at third, the Yankees
began their turnaround with three tightly played victories. Coates pitched a
four-hitter, Turley a three-hit shutout, and Ralph Terry, Johnny James, and
Bobby Shantz combined excellently in the third win. Mantle hit four tremendous home runs during the three wins, Skowron was hitting well, and Hector
Lopez, playing again, went on a 16–31 tear. Stengel returned from the hospital
on June 8. "You look good," Dick Young said to Casey, welcoming him back.
"I'll tell ya something," Casey croaked hoarsely. "They examined all my
organs. Some of them are quite remarkable, and others are not so good. A lot of
museums are bidding for them." But when Casey returned, suddenly the
Yankee team, moribund since August of 1958, came to life. They reeled off
eight wins in a row, losing one game when Dick Williams of the A's homered
off Whitey Ford, and then winning six more in a row including a four-game
sweep of the White Sox in Comiskey Park to regain first place.

The White Sox sweep was most satisfying. Not only did the Yankees grab
first place, but the normally humorless Yankee front office thumbed their noses
at arch-rival Bill Veeck, the maverick owner of the Sox. Veeck, one of the
great showmen in baseball history, hated George Weiss with a passion and
never missed an opportunity to criticize Weiss and the Yankees. His 1959
pennant victory was made even sweeter because it was Weiss who was defeated.

When the Yankees arrived for their series in Comiskey Park, Veeck had just
installed a brand-new $300,000 scoreboard, a prototype of scoreboards for
years to come which exploded and whistled and sent rockets into the air when a
Chicago player hit a home run. When an opposing player hit a home run, the
gargantuan scoreboard remained annoyingly silent.

Bob Fishel, the Yankees' public-relations director, had worked for Veeck
when the latter owned the St. Louis Browns, and the men were close friends.
Fishel, himself an unemotional man in public, revealed the humorous side of
his character when he handed Stengel Fourth-of-July sparklers before the first
White Sox game. That night Clete Boyer, who was now playing regularly at
third, hit a home run. As usual the giant scoreboard remained silent and unlit in
the darkness, but as Boyer was circling the bases, in the Yankee dugout there
were Stengel and Mantle and all the Yankees parading up and down, holding
their lit sparklers aloft. In the Yankee bullpen the relief pitchers wandered
around the pen, the sparklers emitting a nose-thumbing electricity to
everyone's amusement but Veeck's. Later in the game when Mantle homered,
again the sparklers were lit, and all the Yankees danced around. "That's typical
of Weiss," Veeck said. "He probably got them at a discount, too." Veeck was
even less pleased when the Yankees won the second game on home runs by
Maris, Mantle, and Skowron, and also the final two games, behind Coates,
who had raised his record to a perfect 8–0, and reliefer Johnny James, a little
guy who was 3–0 in relief.

Jim Coates was called the Mummy by the other Yankees because he slept with his eyes open. On one bus trip during training in '59 when Casey was accompanied by his wife, Edna, Coates fell asleep a couple of rows behind where the Stengels were sitting. Edna, looking down the aisle, noticed Coates, his head tilted at an odd angle, his eyes open and his body motionless. She turned to Casey and whispered, "Dear, I think one of your players is dead!"

Coates also had violent nightmares and awakened roommates related that in his sleep Jim would scream the words of "Swanee River."

Mostly what the tall and skinny Coates was, was mean. On the mound he threw toward the plate with a sidearm delivery, turning his head away from the batter at the last second, thus upsetting the hitter tremendously, because his rock-hard fast ball often was thrown too far inside for safety. The scowling Coates delighted in throwing at the hitters. He enjoyed seeing the panicked batter crash to the ground, despite the protestations of his teammates, who inevitably were the targets of retaliation. Coates would throw at a batter for several reasons: if he was good, if Jim didn't like him, or if he was Latin or black. That didn't leave too many batters he left alone.

Casey liked Coates for his vile nature, and Coates, 8–0, was keeping the Yankees in first place while the rest of the staff was straightening itself out. For some reason, whenever he pitched the Yankees scored a lot of runs for him. He'd pitch well, and the Yankees would win 9–1, and his teammates would kid that he was the luckiest man ever to put on spikes. Two outs, the bases loaded, and the batter would hit a screaming line drive—but always at someone. It was uncanny.

Also helping to keep the Yankees in first place was Bill Skowron, the powerful first-baseman with the brittle body. Injured severely almost every year he played, Bill became known as the Glass Moose, but in 1960 through June he was playing regularly, without the usual string of muscle pulls and back injuries. He was batting over .300 with forty-three RBI's, third in the league behind Maris with forty-eight and Baltimore's rookie shortstop, Ron Hansen, with forty-four. Skowron, a free-swinging guess hitter, always had been a .300 hitter. But this year he was playing every day. With Maris and Skowron hitting, some of the load was taken from the backs of both Mantle and Berra. No longer did Mickey have to feel that he was carrying the offense on his broad shoulders as he had in '59. Mantle was playing better, and this inspired the others. By mid-June the old Yankee enthusiasm had returned full-blown, and everyone was reinforcing each other. "We're hungry again," Skowron said. "We want to prove that we aren't a third-place club. Also, we sure missed that world series check."

Bill Skowron, 6 feet tall and 200 pounds of brute strength, was a powerful hitter who could reach the distant Stadium bleachers hitting the ball with one hand on the bat. His teammates called him Popeye, a tribute to his muscularity, yet Skowron was not a fighter. He was a big, likeable, gentle guy, and though he always had a black scowl on his face, it was a mask, for he was an extraordinarily good-natured person.

Teammates often made Moose the focus of their practical jokes, treating him the way Phil Rizzuto used to be treated. Moose one time brought a new pair of sporty, green-checked dress slacks to the ball game. After the game he put the slacks back on, only to discover to his anguish that one of the legs had been scissored at the knee. Often he found his sweatshirts, underwear, and socks tied in combinations of undecipherable knots, and there were times when he put his foot into his spikes and discovered caked deposits of dried mud stuffed into the baseball shoe.

He was kidded mercilessly. Skowron had attended Purdue University where he had played football, and always his teammates made fun of his college attendance. "How the hell did you ever get into college, Moose?" they would say. "With your IQ you probably can't even spell Purdue!" Moose would feign anger, growl, and chase his tormenters around the locker room, but he loved the attention and always came back for more. They'd tease him and he'd respond, "Aw c'mon, fellas." Above all Bill wanted very much to be liked. Skowron was a conscientious, sincere, and hard-working man. If any teammate asked Moose to come out to the park at any time to practice—an infielder needing a first-baseman, a pitcher who wanted to work on his pick-off move, another first-baseman who needed instruction—Moose would be there to help in any way he could. He was a tremendous asset to the Yankee ball club, both for his ability and his attitude.

But in baseball there are problems inherent with being conscientious and hard-working. Moose suffered the same way Mickey Mantle suffered, feeling that *every* time he batted he should get a base hit—and when he didn't, it would anger him. When Moose found himself in a prolonged slump, he would brood and become sullen, making his slump even worse. Skowron would walk around the clubhouse like a puppy with its tail between its legs, telling everyone how worried he was. His teammates called him the "most dedicated worrier" they ever saw, and when Moose worried, the entire team became his psychiatrist. Moose would wander around the clubhouse asking anyone and everyone, "What am I doing wrong? What am I doing wrong?" His teammates would talk to Moose to try to give him confidence, buoy his spirits, and eventually Moose would break out of his slump and surge on a hitting streak of tremendous productivity. His streaks were as high as his slumps were low, and in Skowron's seven years under Casey Stengel, beginning in 1954, he batted .340, .319, .308, .304, .273, .298, and in 1960 .309 with twenty-six home runs and ninety-one runs batted in. He was an American League All-Star from 1957 to 1961, kept from greatness only by an incredibly ill-fortuned, debilitating string of injuries which impeded his mobility and caused him mental and physical anguish. Every time Skowron went to the plate to swing a bat or whenever he bent over to field a grounder, he feared that that bending movement would cause yet another injury. Moose was accused by some of being a hypochondriac, but few knew just how badly he suffered. At night because of his painful back, he was unable to lie down on soft beds, and would often sleep sitting up in bed or in a chair, his head propped on his hand. In June of 1959 when Moose broke his wrist and was out the last half of the year, Jimmy Cannon summed up Moose's ill fortune. "You're Bill Skowron," Cannon wrote, "and all your games have been played this season. Your summer's over. . . . You never knew that there were this many doctors in the world until you became a Yankee. Your luck never changes.''

For all of his sensitivity and good nature, Moose Skowron for many years had unbelievably bad luck. He was a man injured more than he was healthy, and during the final five years of his major league career he had to contend with a marital situation which often brought him to the edge of insanity. Moose bestowed upon his wife more clothes, jewelry, and creature comforts than any one person had any right to expect. He was a dutiful husband and father, but like all baseball players, he had to be away from his family when the team was on the road. After eight years of Moose's absence during these trips, his wife without prior warning, began calling him in his hotel room at odd hours of the night, checking to see if he was there, accusing him of infidelity, while at the same time, tired of sitting around the house waiting for him to return, she decided to do some entertaining of her own.

Loyalty was very important to Moose, and when he lost hers, he could not accept what was happening to his marriage. ''Why me?'' he kept asking. ''What have I done to deserve this?'' Skowron was beyond consolation, though the other players tried to comfort him as best they could. The split between him and his wife became wider and her hostility intensified. Moose finally resorted to putting detectives on her trail; he was beside himself when the detectives sent him their reports on her activities. It was a situation which he could not understand or handle rationally. In the middle of a game Moose would approach a teammate. ''Do you know who she was out with last night?'' he would ask. ''That contractor again.'' Then Moose, his eyes reddened, would ask, ''What should I do?'' There wasn't much he could do except sue for divorce, a divorce he was granted in 1964 after he had left the Yankees.

In June of '60 the Yankees were virtually unbeatable, yet despite their excellence they were unable to advance their lead over the Baltimore Orioles by more than a game. Baltimore had the youngest team in the league with pitchers Chuck Estrada, Milt Pappas, Jack Fisher, and Steve Barber all under 23 years of age, and in the infield 22-year-old shortstop Ron Hansen and 23-year-old Brooks Robinson were all-stars. At first base Jim Gentile and at second base Marv Breeding, both age 26, were playing their first seasons. Ex-Yankees Gene Woodling and Gus Triandos were the veterans who were holding the Baby Birds together. Through the entire summer the Orioles were expected to slip, but gamely they clung to the lead in July.

The Yankee hitting continued to be consistently awesome. The cannonading was filling American League ball parks at a dizzying rate as the Yankees set attendance records wherever they played. Only the pitching caused manager Stengel to lose sleep. Coates, 9–0 at the end of June, won only four more games the rest of the year, and neither Ford nor Terry were consistent. Ford suffered arm miseries all season long, so one game he would throw a shutout when his arm felt all right, and the next time out he would be unable to throw a curve ball, and would get shelled. Youngster Terry had the enraging habit of throwing two blazing fast balls to a batter and then experimenting to see if the batter could hit his slow curve. More often than not he could, and out of exasperation Stengel told pitching coach Lopat to hide the kid in the bullpen where he would never have to see his face again. "I'm not gonna look at some of these guys all summer," said Stengel. "I have never seen such horrible pitching, especially from the bullpen. It won't continue much longer." Only Art Ditmar was pitching with consistency, and though Ditmar certainly was not a flashy athlete, he was a fierce competitor who did not cringe at throwing a fast ball in the direction of a batter's head to keep him honest. Ditmar won seven midsummer games in a row, becoming the stopper on the staff. Quietly, unobtrusively Ditmar had come from Kansas City, and Stengel had intended to use him primarily in relief, but in '59 he became a starter when so many others went bad, finishing at 13–9 with a 2.90 ERA to lead the Yankees. Then in '60 after Stengel returned him to the bullpen, for the second year in a row Ditmar ended up in the rotation and was the best pitcher on the Yankee staff.

On August 14 in the course of losing a doubleheader to the lowly Washington Senators, Stengel blew up at Mantle. With Maris on first, Mantle, plagued by ligament damage in his right knee, hit a ground ball to the infield which in frustration he refused to run out. Mantle stood at the plate, disgusted, as Washington completed a double play that Mantle might have prevented. To make Mickey look even worse, Maris badly injured his ribs when he barreled into the knees of the second-baseman. Maris didn't play again until September. Stengel never had been so angry with Mantle. "It don't look very good us trying to win when the man hits the ball to second or third and doesn't run it out," Stengel shouted at the newspapermen after the game. "That's not the first time he's done that. If he can't run, he should tell me. If he wants to come out, all he has to do is tell me. Who the hell does he think he is, Superman?" After Mantle had grounded out, Mickey waited by first base for someone to bring out his glove. Instead Stengel sent Bob Cerv to play center field. It was a humiliating experience for Mantle, standing there while the fans at the Stadium booed and booed some more.

Later a more subdued Stengel said, "He doesn't stop running because he's lazy. He gets mad at himself because he isn't hitting the ball good. And then he goes into the dugout and kicks things around. It's a bad habit. And he's got to get rid of it, for the good of the club and for the good of himself."

After the two losses to Washington, Baltimore and Chicago both led the Yankees by half a game. The Yankees' next opponents were the Orioles, winners of eight straight and thirteen out of their last fourteen.

Against Baltimore in the first inning when Mantle's name was announced, the Stadium crowd accorded Mantle the loudest crescendo of catcalls ever heard at the park. Loud, venomous boos rolled in from the bleachers, mingling with shouts of "You're a bum" and "You stink" to form a cacophony of derision. Mantle grounded out weakly and as he ran into the dugout the booing continued, loud and strong. Throughout his career all the fans ever read about was Mantle's insolence, his contempt for the fans, his lack of visible emotion, and now that he was down, the people really lit into him. "In all my years of baseball," said Stengel, "I never saw a city that booed a man so much before he went to work."

Ron Hansen hit a two-run homer to put the Orioles ahead, and in the fourth inning Mantle came to bat after a single by Hector Lopez. Once again the boos and catcalls descended. Mantle swung, and powered a long drive that arched over the right center-field fence into the Yankee bullpen to tie the score. The booing became mingled with cheers, and when Mantle crossed the plate he made a rare gesture to the crowd, tipping his bat as he trotted back toward the dugout. Ditmar continued pitching excellently into the eighth when he gave up only his fifth hit, a home run by Jackie Brandt for a 3–2 Oriole lead. In the Yankee eighth knuckle-ball reliefer Hoyt Wilhelm was on the mound for Baltimore. Lopez walked, and with Mantle up, Wilhelm induced Mantle to pop up to the catcher, Clint Courtney, who was wearing an oversize catcher's glove to enable him to better catch the knuckler. This oversized glove had been an innovation of manager Paul Richards, but though the glove helped catch Wilhelm's knuckle ball, it made catching high pops more difficult. Courtney dropped the ball. Then on the two-strike pitch Mantle swung and hit Wilhelm's pitch on a line into the seats in right field, scoring Lopez ahead of him, winning the game, and putting the Yankees back in the American League lead. The fans in Yankee Stadium stood and clapped and shouted and cheered, unashamed in their exuberance for this moody, extraordinary athlete. "I wanted to be good tonight more than I ever wanted to be good in my life," Mantle said. "I don't know what I would have done if I had had another bad day like yesterday." Mantle and Stengel never said another word about the incident of the day before, but after Mantle learned that Stengel had been dismissed at the end of the season, Mickey approached the Old Man, and in a low, halting voice said, "About the other thing, Case. I'm sorry."

In the papers the next day the writers all wrote about Mantle's injuries, his courage, his deep commitment to perfection, and his human qualities, instead of about his faults. Never again was Mantle booed at Yankee Stadium. The fans had finally gotten their wish, an indication from Mantle that he was indeed human and not above them.

In the excitement few noticed that Art Ditmar had won his fifth straight game in a row, a neat five-hitter. During his entire career with the Yankees, despite his important contributions, very few ever noticed Art Ditmar.

The Yankee pitching was beginning to come around. Earlier in the year general manager George Weiss, wary of his staff, bolstered it by bringing up from the minors right-handed youngster Bill Stafford and trading for minor league reliefer Luis Arroyo.

The pot-bellied, cigar-smoking Arroyo proved to be an instant cure for Stengel's bullpen ills, saving a half a dozen games in July and early August. "Who'd ever think a guy like that would be lying around dead somewhere?" Stengel said of his new bullpen savior. When Stafford joined the Yankees in August, he immediately jumped into the starting rotation with Ford, Ditmar, and either Turley or Eli Grba. Terry and Coates were long-relief men in the bullpen.

Tall, military-straight, and cocky, Bill Stafford looked to be the best rookie pitcher to come up to the Yankees since Whitey Ford in 1950. He had a live arm and a mature head for a 20-year-old kid. With three consecutive doubleheaders at the end of August, the Yankees needed all the pitching help they could muster. They got it, winning five of the six games, and going into September led the league by two and a half games, a lead they lost and then regained by .002 percentage points. The Yankees had fifteen games left in the season and the smallest of leads.

They won all fifteen—ending the suspense and the American League season.

It was one of the most awesome pennant drives in the history of professional baseball. The Yankee bullpen earned seven of the final eleven wins, allowing one earned run in the twenty-six and a third innings it pitched. Whitey Ford recovered fully from his shoulder woes and won his final three starts. Terry only allowed two runs in twenty-two and two-thirds innings. After Terry beat the Red Sox 4–3 to clinch the pennant on September 25, Stengel, niggardly with his praise, said to him, "You looked like Walter Johnson in the stretch. You were one of the best I've ever seen." Rookie Bill Stafford didn't win any of his last three starts, but it certainly wasn't his fault as he only allowed three runs in the nineteen and a third innings he pitched. Turley, making a comeback from his disastrous '59 season, finished with a 9–3 record and a low ERA. From famine to feast, the spotty Yankee pitching corps suddenly became a remarkably strong one. The foundation to continue the dynasty of the 1950s was in the offing. The Yankee inner defense had become the strongest in the league. As Clete Boyer gained confidence at third, he began catching anything and everything hit in his direction, diving for balls, throwing from his knees, and demonstrating amazing reflexes. At second Bobby Richardson was quick, rangy and steady, and at short Tony Kubek was excellent and getting better. At first Bill Skowron was an above-average fielder who swung a potent bat.

Berra and Howard were the two best catchers in baseball, and the outfielding trio of Mantle, Maris, and Lopez carried unmatched authority at the plate. Mantle hit forty home runs in '60 to lead the American League, and Maris finished second with thirty-nine, as the Yankees set a new league season record for homers with 193. Though Lopez occasionally made glaring errors in the field, it was only his first year of playing the outfield, and by the end of the year he had improved considerably. At bat he was a professional hitter who could hit to either field and hit in the clutch.

On the bench there was DeMaestri, for seven years the starting shortstop at Kansas City before he was traded along with Maris, and for reserve strength in the outfield there was Bob Cerv, who in his last two seasons with the A's had hit fifty-eight home runs and batted in 191 runs. George Weiss also acquired home run slugger Dale Long from the San Francisco Giants, and backing up Berra and Howard behind the plate was Johnny Blanchard, the most sought-after young catcher in either league. George Weiss had done a magnificent job of rebuilding.

When the season finally ended, the Yankees in front by eight full games over the deflated Orioles, Stengel pointedly praised Mantle, the man he had openly chastised earlier. "I believe," said Stengel, "the most powerful factor has been Mickey Mantle, who hit forty home runs and drove in ninety runs and played fifty hours through three doubleheaders on a bad knee without asking for relief or flinching. He has worked hard and hustled and in my mind he is my most valuable player.'' What was remarkable was the tenderness in the voice of the crusty old manager, a tenderness there in part because Stengel had been told that this pennant would be his last. Del Webb had called Stengel up to his hotel suite just before the end of the season and told Casey that he wanted to work out a suitable retirement plan. Casey said he didn't want to retire, but Webb was adamant. Webb had been the president of the Denver club when Houk had been the manager, and neither Webb nor Dan Topping wished to lose Ralph Houk as a manager. Webb told Stengel that this was to be his last year. ''You guys run the ball club,'' Stengel said. ''A lot of times I managed for you and I never had a contract. I don't want to be around if I'm not wanted. Whatever you do I'll agree to.'' Casey, though unhappy with the arrangement, agreed with Webb and Topping that he would tell the press that everyone was parting on friendly terms and that he had decided to retire. The press didn't make the situation any easier when thirty-five members of the New York Baseball Writers Association circulated a petition and gave it to Stengel, asking him not to retire.

''It was wonderful of them,'' said Casey. ''But I've been here twelve years, and when a feller stays so long in one place he gets a lot of people mad at him and he gets mad at a lot of people when they blame him for blowing the tight games.''

In the National League the Pittsburgh Pirates won their first pennant since 1927 (the year Babe Ruth, Lou Gehrig, and Co. crushed them in four straight). Manager Stengel had played right field for the Pirates in 1918 and 1919, before any of his ball players were born.

The 1960 world series opened in a carnival atmosphere at Forbes Field in Pittsburgh, a town covered by ''Beat 'Em Bucs'' signs and posters. The field itself was a league antique, opened in 1909, but it was intimate and colorful, with dimensions very close to those of Yankee Stadium: a short right-field fence and a 457 distance in straightaway center. Stengel was faced with several problems going into this world series. He was unsure who to pitch in the opening game, and he was mistrustful of his ''green peas'' like Richardson, Boyer, Lopez, and Stafford who had had little or no series experience. All the coaches—Ed Lopat, Ralph Houk, and Frank Crosetti—agreed to withhold Ford until the teams returned to New York for the third game because of Ford's unbeatable record in the Stadium, but the disagreement then arose as to who should start the first one. Lopat, the pitching coach, pushed hard for Stengel to start the rookie Stafford. ''This kid is the closest thing I've seen to Whitey Ford,'' said Lopat over and over. ''He doesn't care who he's pitching against or what the situation is. He justs wants the ball and he knows what he's doing all the time.'' Stengel agreed, but Houk and Crosetti were adamantly opposed to starting a rookie in the first game of a world series. They felt Ditmar should start. He got it, against Pirate ace Vernon Law, a Mormon deacon with a 20–9 record in '60. Ditmar didn't get through the first inning.

In the top of the first Roger Maris hit his first home run since September 16 to give the Yankees a 1–0 lead, but in the bottom of the inning Pirate center fielder Bill Virdon opened with a walk. With Dick Groat, a crafty hit-and-run man at bat, second-baseman Richardson and shortstop Kubek were communicating with each pitch as to who would cover second base in the event of a steal or a hit-and-run attempt. On the second pitch to Groat, there was a breakdown in communications, for when Virdon broke for second, neither of the infielders covered, and when Yogi Berra fired the ball to second, it flew into center field, allowing Virdon to streak to third. Groat then lined a run-scoring double down the right-field line and scored when Bob Skinner bounced a fieldable ground ball past Richardson, through the right side of the rock-hard Pittsburgh infield, that the ground crew had tailored to be like macadam. It was not easy for a newcomer to play the infield in Forbes Field. Not only was the grass area very hard, but when a player ran on the dirt surface, the ground didn't hold together, and holes would appear, four and five inches deep. When the Yankees held their first infield practice there, it was ten minutes before anyone caught a ground ball, and everyone was getting gun-shy.

This was not the end of Ditmar's string of mishaps. After Dick Stuart lined out, with Roberto Clemente up, Skinner tried to steal second and Berra threw the ball over Richardson's head. Kubek, backing up, stopped Skinner from going to third, but the stolen base was crucial because Clemente then bounced one of his patented high-hopping singles through the fast infield to score Skinner with the third run of the inning. Jim Coates relieved Ditmar, and the Yankees were effectively finished for the day. In the fourth Bill Mazerowski hit a two-run home run, and after Bill Virdon doubled in a run in the sixth, the Pirates led 6–2. Ellie Howard's pinch-hit home run in the ninth made it closer, but not close enough.

Virdon, the Pirate center fielder, had gone to the St. Louis Cardinals from the Yankee farm system for Enos Slaughter in 1954, and after winning the Rookie of the Year award in '55, he was traded to Pittsburgh. In the fourth inning with Mantle and Maris on base, Yogi Berra lifted a high, powerful drive that was headed for the right center-field wall, a triple at the least, but the catlike Virdon raced to the wall, catching the ball at the top of a bounding leap, holding it in his glove despite a collision with right fielder Clemente, also pursuing. Virdon's catch was the game.

To add to the trauma for the Yankees, in the second inning after Berra and Moose Skowron singled to open the inning, as Clete Boyer strode to the plate to hit, Stengel called him back to the dugout. Boyer walked back, wondering what advice Casey was going to give him. There was no advice. Only a pinch hitter, Dale Long, who skied out to right. The Yankees did not score, and the humiliated Boyer, in his first world series, retreated to the clubhouse where he was inconsolable. He sat in his locker for a half hour and cried. "If the world had ended the next minute I wouldn't have cared," Clete said. Criticism was heaped upon Stengel for his cruelty. Stengel defended himself, saying he was trying for the big inning, trying to break open the game early. The other players, as concerned with Clete's self-confidence and feelings as with the outcome of the game, flocked around the youngster to buoy his spirits. Boyer didn't get into the series again until the sixth game.

In the second game it was manager Danny Murtaugh who erred in his strategy. With the Yankees leading 3–1 in the fourth inning, Murtaugh pinch hit for Bob Friend, the other Pirate pitching star, and after Friend left, the Yankees pounded Fred Green, Clem Labine, George Witt, Joe Gibbon, and Tom Cheney for thirteen more runs, seven in the sixth inning. Mantle hit two gargantuan home runs batting right-handed, a two-run shot in the fifth off Green and a three-run two-iron liner that whizzed above pitcher Gibbon's head and kept rising until it landed over the dead center-field fence 457 feet from the plate. Mantle was the first right-hander in the history of Forbes Field to hit a ball over the wall at that point. The Yankees won the game 16–3 behind Bulletless Bob Turley, now primarily a curve ball pitcher, who lasted for eight and two-thirds innings in the only game in his major league career in which he didn't strike out at least one batter. Throughout the game the gleeful Stengel marched up and down the bench shouting, "Pour it on. Don't let 'em up," desperate in his quest for this series victory which would give him a total of nine, one above Joe McCarthy with whom he was tied. Perhaps Stengel also hoped that a series victory might sway public opinion and save his job.

The third game was much like the second. Whitey Ford was given his chance to pitch in the Stadium, and Whitey did not disappoint, allowing the Pirates four harmless hits and no runs. Left-hander Vinegar Bend Mizell started for the Pirates. He didn't get past the first inning. Neither did his reliefer, Fred Green, as the Yankees scored six runs, the final four coming on a grand slam home run by diminutive second-baseman Bobby Richardson. With two runs in and the bases loaded, twice Stengel ordered Richardson to bunt, and twice Bobby fouled the pitches. Now with two strikes on him and Crosetti at third yelling, "Hit the ball to right side, stay out of the double play," Richardson pulled a high inside fast ball that just cleared left fielder Gino Cimoli's head and landed in the seats for a grand slam home run. During the entire 1960 season, Richardson had hit only one home run.

In the four-run sixth, Richardson again batted with the bases loaded, and this time singled to drive in two runs for a total of six, a series record for one game. The other two runs in the fourth came on Mantle's third home run of the series. The Yankees won 10–0. The series was becoming an embarrassment to Pirate fans. The left-handed pitchers of the Pirates were taking a fearful pounding.

Right-hander Vern Law evened the series in the fourth game, allowing two runs, a homer by Bill Skowron in the fourth, and another in the seventh when Skowron doubled, went to third on McDougald's single, and scored when Richardson hit into a force play. With Bobby on first, Blanchard pinch hit a single, and Elroy Face relieved Law. Face threw a fork ball, but against left fielder Bob Cerv his ball didn't break, and Cerv launched a rocket toward the right-field bullpen. Virdon got on his horse, and the feisty Pirate center fielder leaped and as he crashed into the barrier, caught the ball just before it cleared the fence. Again Virdon saved a game as the Pirates won 3–2 after scoring three runs in the fifth off Ralph Terry, the last two runs driven in by a blooping dying quail over Richardson's head by Virdon.

For game five Stengel again had to choose between Stafford and Ditmar, and again he chose wrong, and again Ditmar received no support. When Stengel finally came in with Stafford, the kid the rest of the coaches had wanted to start, the Yankees were too far behind to catch up. Stafford pitched from the third inning through the eighth, giving up only three hits and no runs. Lefty Harvey

Haddix won 5–2, allowing only a cheap run in the second and a home run by Maris in the third. For the rest of the game the Yankees were only able to get two singles against Haddix and Elroy Face, whose fork ball was darting sharply over the final two and two-thirds innings. The Pirates took a one-game lead heading back to cozy Forbes Field.

Game six was another Yankee massacre as Whitey Ford threw his second-straight shutout, a seven-hitter, and the Yankees won 12–0. The Yankees scored one run in the second off Friend, and then five in the third to finish him, the final two runs scoring when little Richardson again showed his muscle by tripling off the left-field scoreboard. In the seventh Richardson tripled again for another run batted in, finishing the series with twelve, a record. Blanchard hit two doubles and a single. It was Ford's seventh series win, tying him with Vic Raschi and Allie Reynolds. It was his first series win away from Yankee Stadium, and after an unusually mediocre 12–9 record over the 1960 season, Whitey Ford may very well have saved himself from being traded.

The night before the seventh and deciding game, Casey Stengel told Bill Stafford that he was going to be the starting pitcher. Stafford thanked him and told Casey not to worry. Though only twenty years old, Stafford slept soundly, supremely confident in his ability. The next day when the Yankees arrived at the ball park, Stengel informed Stafford that he had changed his mind, that Bob Turley was going to start against Vern Law, the winner of the first and fourth games.

Turley lasted one inning. In the bottom of the first inning left-handed first-baseman Rocky Nelson hit a two-run home run, and with Stafford and Terry warming up in the bullpen, Smokey Burgess singled sharply to open the second inning. Stengel removed Turley and brought in Stafford who quickly loaded the bases with nobody out, recovering nicely when he induced pitcher Law to hit into a pitcher-to-catcher-to-first double play. Virdon, a constant thorn in the side of the Yankees, then singled to right, his bat shattering on impact, as two runs scored and the Pirates took a 4–0 lead.

Shantz entered the game for the Yankees in the third and pitched brilliantly until the eighth inning. A Moose Skowron home run in the fifth inning cut into the lead, and then in the sixth the Yankees finally got to Law and drove him to cover. Richardson singled, Kubek walked, and again Danny Murtaugh relieved with Elroy Face, a pitcher who had been taunting the Yankees to the press. All during the game Yogi Berra had been predicting, "If we can get Law out and Face in, we'll win." After Face came in, Mantle singled up the middle to score a second Yankee run and move Kubek to third, and then Berra, the prophet, pulled a three-run home run into the upper deck close to the right-field foul line for a 5–4 Yankee lead.

In the eighth the Yankees added two more runs to the lead. With two outs Berra walked, Skowron beat out a high chopper, and Blanchard singled for a run. Young Boyer doubled for the second run of the inning. The Yankees were ahead 7–4 with only two innings to go.

As the Yankees took the field for the bottom of the eighth Tony Kubek started to run out to left field, because in the late innings of most of the previous series games, Stengel had been inserting Joe DeMaestri at shortstop and moving Kubek from short to left field as a defensive replacement for Yogi Berra. Berra, however, had been scheduled to bat in the ninth, so the Yankee manager decided to stay with Kubek at short and Berra in left. Shantz, who had not pitched five innings in one game all season long, was still in the game, now pitching his fifth inning, and that he didn't retire a batter in the Pirate eighth was through little fault of his own. Gino Cimoli pinch hit for Face and singled to right center. Virdon then hard-hit a three-hop double-play ball at shortstop Kubek, but the ball hit a clod of dirt that had been dislodged by an earlier base runner and angled sharply, striking Kubek squarely in the Adam's apple. The ball lay a few feet from the prone infielder as Cimoli raced safely into second and Virdon was safe at first. Second-baseman Richardson hastily called time-out, and from the dugout 70-year-old Stengel ran out to check on Kubek. "Give him room! Give him room!" Stengel started yelling. "He'll be all right. He'll play. Give him room!" Kubek lay there gasping for breath. Mutely Tony also insisted he was all right, but trainer Gus Mauch knew better, and after Kubek gagged advice to Stengel that he should leave Shantz in the game because it was a bunt situation and Shantz was the best fielding pitcher the Yankees had, he was rushed to the local hospital. Joe DeMaestri replaced him. Shantz did stay in, but Dick Groat, the National League's Most Valuable Player in 1960, singled past Boyer at third for a run. The Yankees still led 7–5. Stengel brought Jim Coates into the game. Bob Skinner bunted to move Virdon to third and Groat to second, and when Nelson flied to Maris in right field, Virdon declined to challenge Maris's excellent arm, and Coates was one out from extricating the Yankees from their most serious trouble.

Coates pitched carefully to Roberto Clemente, who chopped a ground ball to the right of first-baseman Bill Skowron. Skowron moved quickly to his right, caught the ball, and turned to throw to Coates covering first, but Coates had stopped midway to the base thinking that Skowron would make the play. Skowron ate the ball as Virdon scored to cut the Yankee lead to 7–6. With Groat on third and Clemente on first, Coates pitched to defensive replacement Hal Smith, a catcher who started in the Yankee organization and was traded to Baltimore in the Turley-Larsen trade in 1954. On 3–2 Coates threw a letter-high fast ball that Smith lined over the left-field wall for three runs and a 9–7 Pirate lead. In disgust Coates threw his glove ten feet in the air, and before it landed Stengel was on his way to the mound to replace him with Ralph Terry, who had been warming up practically all game long. He had warmed up for Turley, Stafford, Shantz, Coates, and finally for himself. Don Hoak flied out to end the inning, but Terry didn't have much left.

Three more outs and the Pirates would be world champs. Bob Friend, ineffective all series through, started the ninth and again was a bad selection. Richardson singled to left to open the inning, and Dale Long, pinch hitting for DeMaestri, singled to right, Richardson racing into third. Murtaugh relieved Friend with Harvey Haddix, who induced Maris to pop out to catcher Smith, but Mantle then singled to right center to score Richardson and move Long to third. The Yankees trailed 9–8. Stengel sent Gil McDougald to run for Long at third. Yogi Berra then hit a scorching one-hopper down to first-baseman Nelson, who stepped on first to retire Yogi for the second out. Mantle, off first but leaning toward the bag, dove back under Nelson's glove, avoiding the tag as McDougald scored the ninth and tying run.

The game had been seesawing violently all afternoon, and as Terry went out to the mound to pitch the bottom of the ninth, there was a low murmuring through the Pirate crowd. Ditmar was warming up in the bullpen when Pirate second-baseman Bill Mazerowski stepped into the batter's box. Terry's first pitch was a high slider. Catcher Blanchard called time and walked out to talk with his pitcher. Terry had been having trouble adjusting himself to the mound. "Come on," said Blanchard. "Get it down." Terry nodded his head, and on the next pitch he held on to the ball a little longer to bring it down, but he only got it as low as Maz's waist and Mazerowski hammered the ball over the vines covering the left-field wall. Left fielder Berra stood motionless, helplessly staring as the ball carried over the ivy-covered wall. After seeing it descend till it dropped out of sight, he tucked his glove under his arm and trudged toward the dugout as a frenetic, uncontrollable crowd followed Mazerowski's every footstep around the bases, the elated Pirate whirling his right arm as he rounded third and headed for home. He had to force his way to home plate past joyous teammates and insane spectators. When Terry saw the ball headed out he quietly said "Shit," and walked off. In the dugout Terry walked over to Stengel and said, "Casey, I hate to have it end this way." "How were you operatin'?" asked the Yankee manager. "What were you trying to throw him?" "I was trying to keep it low," Terry said. "As long as you were trying to pitch him the right way," Casey said, "I'm going to sleep easy at night."

When Terry sat dejectedly in his locker stall Coates came over and said, "I sure hate to see it happen to you, but you sure took me off the hook." Terry glared at his teammate, but didn't answer.

The Yankees were in a state of shock, wandering aimlessly in their locker room. Mutterings of "I can't believe it, I can't believe it," softly echoed in the quiet room. Mantle hid in the trainer's room and broke down sobbing uncontrollably, fearful that this might be his final year with the Yankees after hitting only .275 during the season. It was also a bitter disappointment for Stengel who had thus lost his final appeal to Topping and Webb before his enforced retirement. New York City Mayor Robert Wagner telegrammed Stengel, "Our city is solidly behind you and hope that you will stay with the Yankees and win the series next year."

The 1960 world series against the Pirates was an anomaly. The Yankees outscored the Pirates fifty-five runs to twenty-seven, outhit them ninety-one to sixty, hit ten home runs to four for the Pirates—and lost. Mantle, Maris, Skowron, and Berra had been expected to hit well, and they had, but the surprise performer was stocky Bobby Richardson, the smooth, solid, reliable second-baseman. In the series Richardson, with eleven hits, drove in twelve runs, a series record, hitting two doubles, two triples, and a grand slam home run, a most remarkable showing for a little guy who had only hit one home run and drove in twenty-six runs all season long.

Though Bobby had hit .301 in 1959, his achievement went little noted because the Yankees didn't win the pennant that year, so it was in the 1960 world series that Richardson's excellence first became apparent to the public.

Bobby was an important member of the Yankees, catlike and quick at second, and his great range enabled him to overcompensate for Moose Skowron's relative inability to catch high pop-ups. Any pop within Bobby's reach, Bobby caught, saving Moose many opportunities for embarrassment. He was also the spiritual leader of the Yankees, a religious man who was highly respected for his morality and clean living. Around him his teammates tried as best they could to control the urge to speak in the athlete's more earthy patois of four-letter words. Though Bobby himself never objected, they knew he felt uncomfortable when people took the name of his Lord in vain, or swore. Often a group of Yankees would be standing around the clubhouse, one of them telling an off-color joke, and Richardson would innocently come up to the group, and all of a sudden silence would descend, destroying the whole joke.

One afternoon in New York, Moose Skowron struck out for the third time in a game, returned to the dugout and slammed his helmet down, slammed his bat down, and cussing up a storm, walked toward the far end of the dugout by the drinking fountain. In the midst of this stream of obscenities, Moose passed Richardson and blurted, "Excuse me, Bobby," and kept walking by, resuming his stream of curse words. Stengel and the rest of the bench went into hysterics.

Sumter, South Carolina, where the Richardsons live, is about ten miles west of Interstate 95 as it wends its way from New England through South Carolina south toward sunny Florida. This is Bible Country, and on the local AM radio stations religious programs are frequent and popular. Sumter is a small, quiet town, where strangers are most welcome, treated with the utmost courtesy, and told, "Come back soon, y'hear?" as long as they don't dress funny, talk funny, or look like troublemakers.

The Richardson house sits on the corner of Adams Avenue. It is simple, unpretentious, and warm and hospitable inside, reflecting the personalities of the owners. Most everyone in town knows the Richardsons and their children.

Bobby Richardson is not the type of person you *become* friendly with. Rather he's one who is your friend as you shake hands for the first time. When he drawls, "Welcome to our home," you want to throw off your shoes and unloosen your tie. Betsy Richardson is the same way. They are an adoring couple with five warm and loving children, a true-to-life Ozzie and Harriet family.

Bobby Richardson is a devoutly religious Christian. He has a strength and confidence in himself that he attributes to his belief in Jesus Christ. He is not an aggressive proselytizer, less comfortable speaking one-to-one than before groups at banquets, dinners, and testimonials. Bobby does not volunteer much about his beliefs unless you ask him. He prefers to show his Christianity by practicing rather than preaching.

After dinner Richardson and I played some Ping-Pong in the playroom. While we played I understood perfectly how Moose and the other Yankees must have felt about swearing in front of Bobby. After I would make a weak return that Bobby, twice the runner-up in the South Carolina state Ping-Pong championships, invariably slammed back on my side of the table, out of my reach, my immediate reaction was to bang my paddle against the edge of the table and through clenched teeth blurt, "Jesus Christ." This is not in especially good taste, particularly when your opponent is Bobby Richardson, so during the match I found myself continually saying, "Jesus Christ. Excuse me, Bobby. Jesus Christ. Excuse me, Bobby. Jesus Christ. Excuse me, Bobby." I was embarrassed though Bobby never said a word.

After Richardson soundly throttled me, I was soaked through to the skin with perspiration. Bobby, in complete control throughout the game, had not a hair out of place. This is characteristic of the way he looked playing baseball, too.

"How'd you and Stengel get along?" I asked him while I toweled off.

"With Casey it just seemed that he was getting on Kubek and me all the time. We were always together, we roomed together, and he picked on us together. I remember when we each made an error one day, and the next day in the papers he called us Little Rock and Big Rock. Stengel never really came right out and talked to you. You'd read it in the papers." To the press Stengel once said of Richardson, "He don't smoke, he don't drink, and he still can't hit .250." "But still," Richardson said, "in '57 he put me on the All-Star team. Even though before and after the All-Star game I was sitting on the bench."

In '57 Richardson played in ninety-seven games. In '58 he only played in seventy-three. He became so upset from the frustration that he would break into tears while sitting on the bench in the middle of a game. He was ready to quit baseball and return to college.

"I was on a great ball club, but I really wasn't satisfied," Richardson said. "I wasn't playing regular, and I couldn't help but think that I should be doing something else. I guess my confidant had been Ralph Houk, who was my manager during my two years at Denver, and I'd go to Ralph and say, 'Here I am traveling around the country, not playing, and I just think I'd be more satisfied doing something else,' and Ralph very wisely said to me, 'I know that you enjoy speaking to youth groups. You stick with baseball, because baseball will be an avenue that will open doors to you that you won't believe. Don't be discouraged. Give it all you've got, and you won't be discouraged.' And I really appreciated his advice. I had a lot of confidence in him. He's the one who kind of kept me in baseball. And then in '59 Bill Dickey kind of took me as a project, and he made me realize that I had been a defensive hitter, and that it was necessary for me to hit the ball through the infield with authority. He got me to crouch a little bit, use a heavier bat because the ball takes off faster with those heavier bats, and I became a better hitter." Bobby jumped from a .247 average in '58 to a .301 record in '59.

"The thing I remember about that," Richardson said, "is I didn't hit .300 all year long. It was the last day of the season, and Stengel came over and told me I needed two hits to hit .300. We were playing the Orioles, and we were in third place, and it was almost comical. Billy O'Dell is pitching. He's a good friend. We hunt together. He says, 'Whatever you want me to throw, I'll throw.' And Brooks Robinson at third said to me, 'I'll be playing deep. Just lay one down any time you want.' And Ed Hurley, the umpire at first, said, 'Just make it close. You'll be safe.' And I remember getting up there the first time, and O'Dell threw and the catcher, Gus Triandos, said, 'Fast ball.' And I didn't swing. I was startled. Should I believe him or not? You know. And then I hit the beatingest line drive you've ever seen and Albie Pearson in center field made a good catch on it. Anyway, I later got my two hits, and Casey took me out of the lineup. I finished at .301.

"I still see Case," Richardson said. "When he sees me, he'll say, 'I ran into a guy the other day who thinks like you do.' I've never sat down with Casey and discussed my beliefs with him. I'm not that type of person. The only thing I've ever done, I gave him a little book, "The Four Spiritual Laws," a kind of detailed outline of God's plan. I said, 'Casey, you have a long plane ride back to California. Sit and read this on the plane.' Well, the next time I saw him, he didn't say anything about it. I really don't know whether he read it or not."

"Was it a good move retiring Stengel?" I asked.

"I'm a Ralph Houk man," Richardson said. "I hated it for Stengel's sake, but I was glad for Ralph. I just don't know of a better man. When Ralph Houk took over after '60, all my apprehensions died down. Ralph always was in my corner. When things would go bad, he was always there. So when he took over as manager, that was the greatest day in my life. And he just said, 'I don't care if you hit .170, you're going to be my second-baseman.' "

Bobby's career peaked under Ralph Houk. He won the Golden Glove Award as the best defensive second-baseman from 1961 through 1965, and with Tony Kubek at shortstop and Clete Boyer at third, Bobby was a cornerstone of one of the tightest infields ever aligned. In his last six years with the Yankees he averaged more than 175 hits a year, in 1962 finishing second to Mickey Mantle for MVP honors after batting .302 with 209 hits, the most in the league. He was a complete ball player on the field, and off the field he was an inspiration, admired for his ability and for his ethics. When baseball stopped being enjoyable, he retired in 1966, a twelve-year veteran at age 31. Bobby was religious, but he was not a holier-than-thou stuffed shirt. He abided by his rules, and the religious services that he held on Sundays were well-attended by the Yankee players.

"Did you know that when Mickey wrote his book, *The Quality of Courage,* that he chose my son, Ron, to be on the cover of the book with him? He always liked my boys, took a special interest in them, watched them grow up. Mickey and I have a little place together near Grandfather Mountain in North Carolina. We're close in a strange kind of way. We really are good friends.

"I remember one time we had a party in Fort Lauderdale, and Mickey and Clete, all the guys came down, and we just had the best time in the world. We had a basketball game, and played some games that were just so silly. We had one where you lay down and put a dime on your nose and try to pass it to the next person. And I remember Mickey turned to his wife, and said, 'You're right. I guess we can have fun without drinking.' I think that was one reason Mickey and I were such good friends, because in a way I think he looked at something Betsy and I had, our faith in the Lord, and though he never really said it, I think he was longing, looking for something.

"We must have a purpose in life, and that purpose should be to please God," Bobby said softly. "I simply realize that it is God who has given me the ability, the opportunity, and certainly any earthly glory that I might have received during my baseball career." Richardson's faith is unshakeable, giving him an inner peace in the knowledge that his God is watching over him and his family.

Two days after the 1960 world series ended, Dan Topping conducted a press conference in Le Salon Bleu of the Savoy Hotel in New York City. Stengel agreed to show up and let Topping announce his retirement. Instead of stressing that the Yankees were making this move to keep Ralph Houk in the organization, Topping said that they were letting Stengel go because of his advanced age. It sounded heartless and cruel.

Arthur Friedlund, Topping's attorney, prepared a speech that Stengel was to read, which further infuriated the proud old war-horse. After Stengel read the carefully worded statement, Joe Reichler, the baseball editor of the Associated Press, said, "Casey, tell us the truth. Were you fired?" Stengel said, "You're goddamn right I was fired." That turned the whole press conference around. Stengel proceeded to talk about what changes he would have demanded had he been offered another contract. Casey charged that Topping forced him to play Tony Kubek at shortstop when he wanted to play Clete Boyer there, he complained that he never had been allowed to pick his own coaches except for Jim Turner, who was fired after the Yankees lost the pennant in '59. "When Weiss was the boss," Stengel said, "and I wanted a player, he would get him for me." Was Casey implying that Weiss was on his way out, also?

"I couldn't be a yes-man," Stengel said, dabbing his moist cheeks with a handkerchief. "I never was and I never will be."

In papers across the country writers blasted Topping and Webb for firing Stengel, for as one writer put it, "Two millionaires' inhumanity to a fellow millionaire." New York *Post* columnist Max Lerner ridiculed Topping's pretext of age as the reason for firing Stengel. "Justice Holmes could still outthink the youngsters at age 90, and Robert Frost is more of a poet than most bearded young men reciting in cafés. This isn't a job where Casey has to go out and hit a ball or pitch it or outrun it." Webb defended the change in managers months later, far too late to combat the adverse publicity of the Yankees' coldness. "We couldn't hold Houk any longer," Webb said. "And if anything had happened to Stengel after we lost Houk, we'd have been out of luck." Said Casey bitterly, "I'll never make the mistake of being 70 again."

Topping, actually a charming and gracious man, took the brunt of the criticism. "Twelve years ago," he said, "we were ridiculed when we hired Casey Stengel. Today when Casey is leaving, we are ridiculed again."

Unfortunately for Topping and Webb, Casey would surface again, with the neophyte New York Mets, and proceed to attract more fans to the ball park than all the stars he left behind.

The Disorganization Before the Fall

The Czar, George Weiss, retires . . . The roots of the decline

On November 2, 1960, the other shoe dropped. Like Stengel before him, George Weiss, too, was put out to pasture, but unlike Stengel before him, Weiss took Topping's and Webb's hint that it was time to retire, and he "retired" gracefully.

Again a conference was held in Le Salon Bleu of the Savoy Hilton, and Weiss handed out a one-sentence statement. "After forty-two years of operating clubs in organized baseball, twenty-nine with the Yankees, I have decided to avail myself of a clause in my contract, entered into in 1958, which will relieve me of full-time duty as general manager of the Yankees as of December 31, continuing in an advisory or consulting capacity through 1965."

Weiss, a man who was terrified to make a speech, handed out the statement, and then said, "I want to thank you fellows. It's certainly been swell. See you around." The cold fish, the arrogant and remote czar of the Yankees then started to cry.

Later, at a private party for the press, Weiss said, "I want to apologize to you for never getting close enough to know you or you to know me. I am sure it has been a great loss to me, but time just didn't permit. Running an operation as big as the Yankees have become was too time-consuming. I regret this is the way it had to be." Again there were some tears, but privately the more cynical reporters saw the tears as an ironic hypocrisy, remembering how cold-heartedly Weiss had sold Vic Raschi after Raschi held out in '54, how he had released Phil Rizzuto on Old-Timers' Day of '56, how Weiss fought his players tooth and nail for every penny of salary, and how he sent a traded player a Western Union telegram without even a spoken word of thanks. If ever there was a dramatic example of the Protestant Ethic, the Yankee tradition as practiced by George Michael Weiss was it.

George Weiss was a Yalie from New Haven who possessed a brilliant business mind and had a flair for promoting. As a collegian at the turn of the century, he fielded a team of outstanding semi-pro players who had played for his high school. Joe Dugan, later a Yankee, and Chick Bowen, later a Giant, were on the team, and Weiss scheduled major league and ex-professional opponents, his team drawing more fans than the established New Haven team in the Eastern League.

Before he was to graduate from Yale, Weiss quit school to run the family grocery store when his father died, supporting his mother, brother, and sister and also continuing to manage his semi-pro team. In 1920 the Eastern League team offered to let Weiss buy it, and Weiss sold the store and bought the franchise, shrewdly signing his own players and selling them for large profits to the major league teams. That year Weiss conducted his first business with Yankee general manager Ed Barrow, booking the Yankees to play his team in an exhibition game. But when newly acquired attraction Babe Ruth did not show, Weiss refused to pay Barrow his guarantee. Barrow went running to Judge Landis, who backed Weiss. Barrow was outraged.

In 1929 the brilliant young executive was hired to be the general manager of the Baltimore franchise in the prestigious International League, the top minor league. At Baltimore he continued to build his reputation as a shrewd manipulator who, it was said, could squeeze a nickel so tightly that the ass of the buffalo had a permanent crease in it. It was this quality that the frugal Ed Barrow particularly admired in him.

In 1932 Barrow brought Weiss into the Yankee organization. Yankee owner Jacob Ruppert had successfully spent more than a half-million dollars to rape the Red Sox in the 1920s, but in the '30s, during the depths of the Depression, the outright purchase of ball players was becoming an uneconomical manner of doing business. Ruppert had spent $135,000 for minor leaguers Lyn Lary and Jimmy Reese, neither one a sensation; he spent $35,000 for Jim Weaver, who never made it; and spent $150,000 for infielders Frank Crosetti and Jack Saltzgaver, the former a solid Yankee regular for ten years, the latter another failure. Ruppert needed a cheaper way of obtaining talent. Branch Rickey, the general manager of the St. Louis Cardinals, had begun a farm system where a major league team bought several minor league teams to form a chain, and then scouted the country for talent to stock these teams, paying prospects seventy-five to ninety dollars a month to play during those Depression times. Ruppert wanted Barrow to hire someone to do the same for the Yankees. Barrow chose Weiss, aware of his splendid reputation as a businessman and also conscious of the cunning with which he had refused to pay his guarantee when the Yankees played his New Haven team. Two hardheaded, clever Germans were Barrow and Weiss.

Ruppert purchased the Newark, New Jersey, and Kansas City, Kansas, ball clubs, and at Weiss's direction later added such franchises as Butler, Pennsylvania; Easton, Pennsylvania; Akron, Ohio; Amsterdam, New York; Springfield, Massachusetts; Beaumont, Texas; Augusta, Georgia; Portland, Oregon; Bassett, Virginia; Binghamton, New York; Norfolk, Virginia; and several others as Weiss and his four-man scouting staff signed thousands of Yankee prospects to Yankee contracts. For every player who reached the Yankees, there were twenty-five who did not, but jobs during the Depression were scarce, and at that time professional baseball was an avenue away from poverty.

Weiss's farm system was a marvel of organization. The Yankees were spending less money on talent than any other team except the Cardinals, but between 1932, when Weiss started his farm system, and 1943, when the war interrupted, the Yankees won the American League pennant eight times. During all those years the Yankees purchased only five players, two of whom were Joe DiMaggio and Tommy Henrich. The five players cost the Yankees a total of $100,000. The players whom he signed and sold to other organizations netted the Yankees over $2,000,000. Weiss's ability to evaluate player talent was sheer genius and hard work, and before he made a deal (after thorough investigation), he always knew more about the opposing talent than the management of the opposition. Weiss, in making a trade, would say casually, "What's the name of that little fellow who plays third base for your New Orleans team? Oh yes, Jones. If you throw him in, we'll call it a deal." And then Weiss would take economic advantage of the throw-in. A series of transactions beginning in 1937 is an example of the way he operated. His scouts signed catcher Willard Hershberger to a contract, and later Weiss sold him to the Cincinnati Reds for $40,000 and throw-ins Eddie Miller and Les Scarsella. Weiss then sent Miller to his own farm team in Kansas City, where Miller excelled, and the next year Weiss sold him to the Boston Braves for $40,000 and five throw-ins: Vince DiMaggio, Johnny Riddle, Tom Reis, John Babich, and Gil English. DiMaggio was then sent down to Kansas City where he led the International League in home runs. Because his fielding was not up to Weiss's standards, Weiss sold him to the Cincinnati Reds for $40,000 and Frenchy Bordagaray. Later, after selling Scarsella, Reis, Riddle, Babich, English, and Bordagaray to other major league clubs, Weiss had parlayed his original $500 investment in Hershberger into over $200,000. After more than one such Weiss coup, Barrow would say to him, "George, doesn't your conscience bother you?" It never did.

Weiss had been the genius who had built the Yankee dynasty, but few shed tears for him when he said good-bye, and though he had been with the Yankees for thirty-five years, the day after he cleared his effects from his desk, when he was gone, nobody said a word.

According to his closest acquaintances George Weiss was the shyest of men. At Lou Gehrig's funeral and at other public functions he would instruct his wife not to leave his side lest he have to engage a stranger in conversation. Once Weiss was asked to make a speech, and for several days before it was scheduled he walked his bedroom floor through the night muttering, "Oh my God. I can't do it. I can't." Yet when he did speak, his talk was short and perfect. Weiss was so reticent that when he played golf, if strangers were standing around the first tee, he would insist on walking to the second tee and starting the round there. George Weiss was so formal that he did not speak in the first person, even among friends.

By the press, the players, and many of his employees Weiss was seen to be humorless, impersonal, close-mouthed, secretive, dictatorial, and cheap. He seemed about as lovable as a rattlesnake, a reputation he rather enjoyed because it was a barrier that effectively kept him from others. Whenever possible Weiss sought to keep his distance from all but his closest friends. He refused to become personally involved with the players. Roy Hamey, his assistant, talked contract with all but the highest-paid players. He sent telegrams to players he released. Never did he enter the dugout or clubhouse where the players congregated. Weiss only granted the press interviews after careful investigation of the reporter. Then if Weiss did grant the interview, he would first establish the line of conversation and stick to it. His answers would be prepared even before the questions were asked. If the reporter asked a question about which he was not prepared, he would refuse to answer. Over the years hostility between Weiss and the press grew with the rise of sports journalism, and Weiss bore much of the brunt of the blame for the arrogant, bigoted, and cold reputation of the Yankees.

First and foremost, George Weiss, the architect of the Yankee dynasty, was a businessman, and baseball was his business. He had two measures of success, making money and winning pennants, and he was brilliant at doing both. Short, paunchy, somber, and aristocratic in dark flannel, Weiss was slavishly devoted to his work. He was a work fanatic, a perfectionist who was meticulous, shrewd, farsighted, practical, and unusually successful. Weiss was a prideful man who hated to lose. Once his charming wife, Hazel, embroidered throw pillows for a charity contest. There were thousands of entries of beautifully embroidered pillows, and hers were awarded second prize, a noted accomplishment as far as she was concerned. When she told her husband, Weiss said, "There is no such thing as second place. Either you're first or you're nothing."

Weiss had been a disciple of predecessor Ed Barrow, himself a working dervish and a tyrant, and like Barrow, Weiss made running the Yankees a twenty-four-hour-a-day, seven-day-a-week task. Occasionally Weiss would spend a day on the golf course or a day at the race track, but other than going out for dinner, he had no interest whatsoever except the Yankees. Weiss worked every day, including Saturdays and Sundays, and often he worked into the night. Often he would stay in town, renting a hotel room in order not to waste time commuting to and from his home in Greenwich. He was the general manager, he ran the stadium operation, plus he was the head of the farm system. He was perpetually checking with his minor league managers, keeping current with the progress of every player in baseball—major league and minor, not just the Yankee farm players, but *every* farm player—checking ticket sales, overseeing stadium repairs or new construction, comparing notes with Casey Stengel on the status of the Yankee players, checking with the doctor concerning the medical condition of the Yankee players, communicating long distance with his scouts to see how they were progressing, checking, always checking every detail of the operation. Weiss was on top of everything, every purchase order, every minute detail, down to the brand of toilet paper used in the locker room. Everything germane to the Yankee organization crossed his desk.

A dedicated, loyal man, Weiss made certain that the other Yankee employees followed his lead. If a worker didn't like baseball, that worker didn't last long in the organization. When Jerry Coleman retired as a player, he accepted a job in the front office as Weiss's assistant. Coleman's hours were nine-thirty to five-thirty, and invariably Weiss would call Coleman into his office at five-twenty-nine for a conference. Coleman would say, "George, why couldn't this meeting have started at four-twenty-nine? Why always five-twenty-nine?'' Weiss would ignore the question, growl a little, and proceed with the meeting. Rarely did Coleman arrive home in time for his six o'clock dinner. Working under Weiss required a religious dedication.

Working long hours by itself rarely insures success, but Weiss's combination of dedication and thoroughness accounted for much of his genius. He was a man of great attention to detail, a perfectionist to the extreme who insisted upon receiving total value from his employees and from his investments. He kept a ubiquitous envelope in his white shirt pocket, and whenever he wished to follow up on a matter, he would write himself a note on the back of the envelope. No detail was too small to avoid his scrutiny: the absence of candy in a candy machine, a vendor spilling mustard on a customer during a game, a car parked improperly in the team parking lot. Weiss's note eventually became a memo sent to the offending party, and Weiss would keep checking until he was certain he had rectified the situation.

Weiss prided himself in *not making mistakes,* in being an extremely cautious, bankishly conservative person. When he sought to purchase a player from another team, he would call anyone and everyone who could give him information about the player's ability and about his character, contacting even the clubhouse boy of the team to ask about the player. Weiss would check every conceivable angle to obtain as much information as possible before making a move, and rarely did he act hastily. Weiss was a great believer in the policy of delay. "Time will usually tell you which way to go," he would say. A salesman could never enter his office and sell him on a computer or a new type of phone or on an idea without a thorough investigation first being made. When Yankee owner Dan Topping told Weiss that he was installing a modern scoreboard, Weiss spent months studying scoreboards before finally deciding on the one he wanted.

Weiss's thoroughness was well-known by his employees, and when Weiss periodically toured his minor league facilities, for weeks before his arrival the minor league executives would clean and scrub and primp. Once when Weiss visited the Norfolk farm team during an afternoon practice, Weiss called over Norfolk manager Mayo Smith. Weiss was pointing to one of the outfielders shagging flies in left field. Weiss had noticed that the player had a hole in his outer sock about the size of a half-dollar. "Never," Weiss told Smith, "do I again want to see one of your players with a hole in his uniform." When a batter hit a grounder down third into the outfield a few minutes later and no one bothered to run over and pick it up, Weiss gave Smith a stern lecture on the cost of baseballs, and for the rest of Smith's managerial career, even during batting practice, Smith hollered at his players to retrieve any baseballs left lying around.

Weiss's inspections of the minor league ball parks were agonizingly thorough, and the minor league heads played hard at trying to satisfy Weiss. Once when Weiss traveled to inspect his Kansas City facility, Blues' general manager, Frank Lane, told Mrs. Weiss, "I've got him this time. He won't find a single thing wrong." "Betcha ten dollars," Hazel Weiss said. Lane took the bet. After Weiss inspected the grass, the dugouts, the stands, and the bathrooms, he had not said a word, and Lane was gloating. "Pay up," he whispered to Mrs. Weiss. As the three returned to the main office and Weiss opened the door to go inside, he noticed a row of six telephone booths. "How many years ago were the windows of those telephone booths washed last?" Weiss barked. Mrs. Weiss smiled at Lane. "Gimme my ten dollars," she said.

Hazel Weiss enjoyed teasing her dour husband. "George," she'd say, "did you find the toilet paper all right?" Weiss would only glare or tell her to hush up. Weiss operated his minor league clubs on a shoestring, eliminating all frills. He was trained to operate in the black. Also he felt that the primary purpose of a minor league team was to develop ball players, and George Weiss's farm system developed ball players better than anyone else's farm system in baseball history.

Weiss was resented by nearly all of the Yankee players. Topping and Weiss had set up a generous profit-sharing plan for their employees, and Weiss, the highest-paid employee and the biggest beneficiary of the plan, kept the salary expenses as low as possible, thus maximizing profits and earning extra money for himself. His hard-nosed contract bargaining kept their salaries down, and few of them could successfully argue against his mass of statistics which inevitably proved that the player was not really worth as much as he thought he was. Sometimes Weiss's scheming reached such depths of skulduggery that one had to admire his audacity. For example, after Phil Rizzuto was named the league's Most Valuable Player in 1950, Weiss sent Rizzuto a contract calling for a $35,000 salary. Rizzuto sent it back, telling Weiss he wanted $50,000, not an unreasonable salary for the MVP of the league. After a great deal of haggling, Weiss called Rizzuto into his office and finally agreed to pay Rizzuto the $50,000. Weiss asked his secretary, Miss King, if she had a blank contract handy. She said she didn't, so Weiss told Rizzuto that if Phil would sign the contract for $35,000 which was sitting on the desk, Weiss would write Phil a personal check for $15,000 to make up the difference, which he did. At the end of 1951 when Rizzuto again came before Weiss to negotiate his 1952 salary, Weiss took the signed $35,000 contract from his files and tried to begin negotiations from there instead of from $50,000, Phil's actual salary from the year before!

Weiss had no scruples about cheating the players, and if a player was a poor businessman, Weiss welcomed him into his office with open arms. Bill Skowron, an all-star for a number of years, signed for $21,500 after the 1956 season. Three seasons later Skowron was only making $1,500 a year more: Weiss always impressed on Skowron how injury-prone he was, how his injuries were always costing the Yankees. Skowron, a home-run hitter and important RBI producer, accepted Weiss's monetary appraisal of his worth. Skowron, a player who never realized his own value, who would have played for nothing, always signed quickly and without argument. In '60 after he hit .309 to lead the Yankees in batting, ex-teammates Gil McDougald and Hank Bauer, money-wise friends who could no longer sit by and watch Moose be treated so unfairly, went to the naive and gullible Skowron and explained to him just how valuable a man he was. "You deserve much more money, Moose," McDougald told him. "I do?" Skowron said. The properly oriented

Skowron threatened to hold out and after five seasons he finally received a decent raise.

Weiss and his assistant, Roy Hamey, worked a ploy on the players that was particularly effective in keeping the salaries low. It was an adaptation of the good cop–bad cop game the police often use when trying to pry confessions from suspects. The first cop who enters the cell to interrogate the prisoner treats him like dirt, swearing at him, threatening to beat him, scaring him to death. Then he leaves, and a second cop takes his place. The second cop, sweet, sincere, and friendly, offers all the help he can give to keep the prisoner from the clutches of the first cop. Very often the suspect is only too happy to tell his new friend whatever he wants to know. Hamey and Weiss worked the same way. On the Yankees Hamey first negotiated contract with all but the top stars, and always Hamey was as ornery, insulting, and hard-nosed as he could be, offering the player far less than he was worth. After hours of fighting Hamey, the player would then ask Hamey if he could talk with Weiss, and when Weiss offered the player a couple of thousand dollars more than Hamey—but still far less than the player was worth—the player often would accept Weiss's offer, thinking he was getting the best of Hamey, when in reality Weiss and Hamey were getting the best of him. "The boys have to be hungry for that world series money," Weiss often said.

Rather than pay higher salaries to players and employees, Weiss ran the Yankee operation on the paternity system. If the wife or child of a player or executive became ill, Weiss made certain that the best doctors were in attendance. If a loan was needed, Weiss arranged for it. That way, while keeping the payroll down, he was making others beholden to him for his generosity. Weiss ran the Yankees the same way the Godfather controlled his "family."

Not long after Weiss was retired by the Yankees in November of 1960, he developed ulcers and became ill. He moped around his house, enjoying no hobby or interest. Then in the winter of 1961 he was asked to run the expansion New York Mets. Weiss drove from his Connecticut home down to Florida for the winter meetings. His ulcers, aches, and pains immediately left him. He was back in business. When Weiss retired as Mets general manager in December of 1966, the Amazin' Mets were higher in the standings than the not-so-amazing Yankees, and the Mets were drawing thousands more fans at the gate. Most of the players on the 1969 Mets world championship team had been developed under Weiss. Weiss had signed and developed Tom Seaver, Jerry Koosman, Nolan Ryan, Tug McGraw, Cleon Jones, Ed Kranepool, and Bud Harrelson among others. At Weiss's resignation party from the Mets, he couldn't resist one final subtle jab at his old Yankee employers. "I do want to thank the Mets," Weiss said, "because they send you out of the game you love with the right kind of taste in your mouth."

In May of 1971 Weiss suffered a paralyzing stroke, and on August 14, 1972, he died. Only Branch Rickey rivalled Weiss as an influence in professional baseball, and his far-reaching influence remains behind in the persons of the many front office executive assistants whom he had trained before they moved on to top posts of their own. Under Weiss at one time or another were Parke

Carroll, Kansas City general Manager; Ray Kennedy, Pittsburgh GM; Roy Hamey, Philadelphia Phillies and Pirates GM; Lee MacPhail, Baltimore and Yankee GM; Bill DeWitt, Cincinnati Reds GM; Frank Lane, GM of several teams; and Bob Howsam, St. Louis Cardinal GM. Another Weiss assistant, Jack White, is presently the general manager of the San Francisco Forty-Niner football team. It's remarkable the number of general managers who walk around with blank envelopes stuck in their shirt pockets taking notes.

The enforced retirement of George Weiss in November of 1960 was in retrospect the beginning of the end of the Yankee dynasty. Though owner Dan Topping was energetic and benevolent, he had neither Weiss's administrative ability nor Weiss's cold-hearted, totally impersonal approach to the job of general manager, nor did he have the experience to replace Weiss. Topping's appointed general manager after Weiss's departure, Roy Hamey, had worked under Weiss for twenty-nine years, but Hamey did not have Weiss's genius for signing personnel or for running the farm system, and Hamey's mistrust of trades hurt the Yankees.

Hamey remained Yankee general manager between 1961 and 1963, and while he was general manager Ralph Houk was field manager. Houk, a loyal, hard-working man who had toiled in bullpen obscurity behind catcher Yogi Berra for many years, was a man who knew baseball and knew men, and in 1961, '62, and '63, Houk managed the Yankees to three straight pennants. Houk was considered to be a great manager, one who was loved by all the players, one who treated his high-salaried athletes as if they were something special. His stars, especially Mantle, Ford, and Maris, responded to his gentle prodding and to his running commentary of praise.

During 1962 Hamey contracted hepatitis, and at the end of the 1963 season he decided to retire as general manager. Topping, a great admirer of Ralph Houk, felt that Ralph would be the perfect man to replace Hamey. Topping didn't consider whether the qualities that made Houk an excellent manager —his refusal to make a hasty decision, his refusal to criticize—would also make him suited for the job of general manager. Houk had had no front-office experience, and furthermore, after three years of Houk's telling his players how great they were, now as general manager it was his job to tell the players why they were *not* so great and why they didn't deserve as much money as they might ask. When Houk did become the cold-hearted general manager, the enormous respect he had built and his unquestioned credibility suffered greatly. Players like Roger Maris, Ralph Terry, John Blanchard, Clete Boyer, and Jim Bouton, men who played under him and then had to haggle salary with him, and suffer trade or release under him, became bitter and angry with Houk.

Another man who has harbored resentment against Houk is Yogi Berra. At the end of 1963 when Houk became general manager, he was given the job with the understanding that Yogi would be the manager in 1964. Dan Topping had always respected Berra, and when he needed a manager to combat the press of Casey Stengel and the Mets, Topping chose Berra. Houk accepted his general manager's job with Yogi prepicked. Berra, never even a minor league manager, was lacking in experience.

Yogi, struggling in the beginning, made numerous mistakes. Toward the end of the season his managing improved, as did the team, and in 1964 he won the American League pennant, much to the chagrin of Houk who had decided to fire Yogi in July regardless of where the team finished. As in 1948 when the Yankees fired the popular Bucky Harris and in 1960 when they fired the legendary Casey Stengel, when Yogi was dismissed, the public abuse and outrage was loud and vituperative.

In 1965 Houk's man, John Keane, took over as manager, a change that became the one that completely broke the organization's back. Keane from the start completely alienated the Yankee players, causing dissension unmatched on a Yankee team. Keane treated the players inhumanely, forcing them to play injured, causing clubhouse backbiting, debilitating antimanager cliques, and dissension in general which Ralph Houk, returning as manager in 1966, entering the fray like the cavalry trying to save the fort, failed to stem. Under Houk in '66, the Yankees finished dead last, and in an effort to shake up the team there followed a series of trades which completely demoralized the team, the Yankees never again returning to their former glory.

Administrative deficiencies on the major league level after George Weiss's retirement thus were one of the prongs of a two-pronged pitchfork that combined to bring the Yankee dynasty to its end. The other prong was the decline of the Yankees on the minor league level, a decline in the farm system, the foundation of the Yankee empire that Weiss had built. Weiss had been accused of not spending money for bonus players during his last few years as general manager, an unsubstantiated charge. Between 1958 and 1960 Weiss signed Joe Pepitone, Horace Clarke, Tommy Tresh, Pete Mikkelsen, Jack Cullen, Jim Bouton, Rollie Sheldon, Alan Hall, Jerry Heintz, Bill McClain, Danny Eoff, and Tom Dukes, all bonus players, most of them in the $20,000 range. What Weiss refused to do was spend $100,000 on an untried prospect. During his tenure he had signed pitcher Ed Cereghino for $70,000, Marv Throneberry for $50,000, Bobby Brown for $60,000, Tommy Carroll for $40,000, Frank Leja for $50,000, and Andy Carey for $65,000, and after most of these high-priced men took his money and never became productive on the Yankees, Weiss in the final years decided that it did not pay to dole out huge bonuses to one player, when he could spend the same money and sign five less-ballyhooed players. When Weiss went to the Mets in 1962, he continued this policy, and he built the team into world champions by 1968.

After Weiss left the Yankees in 1960, owner Dan Topping spent large sums of money on prospects for only one more year. In 1961 Topping and Webb spent a half a million dollars, signing Howard Kitt for $80,000, Jake Gibbs for $105,000, and offering Rick Reichart more than $100,000, money he turned down to sign with the Los Angeles Angels for double that and a pair of Gene Autry's cowboy boots. None of these men gave equal value for money received. On the other hand, Al Downing, who received a meagre $16,000, and Mel Stottlemyre, who was paid a small bonus, did become successful.

Dan Topping's health began to decline in 1962. He developed emphysema and a heart condition, and had to be operated on for the partial removal of his stomach. Then there was a rectal operation, and subsequently he suffered through several heart attacks. Sick and weak, Topping approached partner Del

Webb, offering Webb his share of the team. Webb, who was so busy running his multitentacled construction business, had no time to run the Yankees, and the two owners decided to sell the team. When they decided to sell, they realized that future expenditures on players would not benefit them by the time those players reached the majors, so rather than purchase players, they decided to accumulate the profits to make the balance sheet look as attractive as possible to future owners. The Yankees signed Roy White and Curt Blefary in 1962, Fritz Peterson in 1963, and Bobby Murcer and Jerry Kenney in 1964, but the amount of money spent on new players was only a fraction of that spent in the past. While Topping and Webb were seeking new ownership, the other teams were signing the best prospects. Then as Yankee stars Tony Kubek, Bobby Richardson, Ellie Howard, Tom Tresh, Jim Bouton, and Roger Maris became injured or old or were traded because they had become disenchanted, it became time to replace them and there was a void. There were no quality replacements, and the fortunes of the team waned.

When CBS bought the Yankees in August of 1964, the farm system was virtually barren. As purchaser Mike Burke characterized it, "CBS bought a pig in a poke." The combination of no farm players, an inordinate number of injuries to Yankee regulars, and disastrous management by general manager Ralph Houk and manager Johnny Keane brought the Yankee dynasty to its knees by 1965.

When George Weiss was given his walking papers in November of 1960, he told reporters, "The Yankees have five more years at the most under the new management." Weiss, the master builder, knew his business. "Five more years at the most," he had said. At the end of the predicted five-year period the Yankees finished a dismal sixth.

The Final Years: 1961–1964

1961

The greatest team ever? . . . Houk takes over . . .
Sixty-one in sixty-one . . . The M & M boys chase the
Babe . . . "Red-Assed" Roger . . . Another pennant
. . . Awesome power and an easy series victory

When the 42-year-old Ralph Houk arrived in spring training at St. Petersburg, it was readily apparent that there was a new, exuberant spirit among the players. Under Houk the players immediately felt a greater sense of security. Houk did not believe in shuffling the players around from position to position. He did not believe in platooning extensively. He did not believe in holding out pitchers to face certain teams. In his first week Houk announced that Richardson and Kubek would be his second base and shortstop combination, as they had been at Denver, that Boyer would be his third-baseman, and that Ellie Howard would be his first-string catcher, with Berra and Hector Lopez to play in the outfield. Houk announced that his pitchers would pitch every fourth day, and he announced that the Yankees would win the pennant.

The players loved him. Stengel had always told them how much room for improvement there was. Houk told them how great they were. Playing baseball was fun again.

This was a man they respected and liked. When Houk was at Denver, he had a wicked temper, usually displayed in the defense of his players. Only one time did one of his players, pitcher Ed Donnelly, try to cross him. Houk lost his head and decked him. At Denver he had been forbidden by the league commissioner from abusing the umpires because of several previous brushes with the men in blue. During this probationary period, Houk, feeling that his team had been wronged in a close game, rushed up to an umpire and said, "I'm not allowed to cuss you out, but I thought you might like to know I passed a kennel on my way to the park, and your mother is all right."

Houk had risen to the rank of major in the Marines in World War II, winning medals for bravery and valor. He was part of the Omaha Beach invasion on D-Day with the Ninth Light Armored Division. Never a subtle man, Houk had expert aim with a chaw of tobacco, and he certainly could be gruff, but rarely with his players—only with the press. More often he was quick to smile, and always a man who could find the brightest side to any unpleasantness. "If there is a cholera epidemic somewhere," New York *Post* writer Vic Zeigel once wrote, "Houk would think it to be a great experience for young doctors."

Houk knew how to motivate his men, and quickly he instigated his own course in self-confidence. Mantle was his primary target, because Ralph knew how much Stengel's criticism had pained Mickey. Under Casey, no matter how well Mickey did, it was not good enough. In 1960 Mantle batted .275, hit forty home runs, drove in ninety-four runs, finishing second to Maris in the MVP balloting. "All I read and heard," Mickey said, "is, 'When are you going to do what you're supposed to do?' Dammit, I try. From what you'd hear, you'd think I wasn't trying." Under Houk the criticism was stilled. Houk rather set out to convince Mickey that he was going to be the team leader and unofficial captain. "He's one player all the players like," Houk said. "They look up to him, and I don't think he realizes how much. Just think how much they'll like him if he goes out and shows them the way." Indeed.

Expansion finally came to baseball because Branch Rickey threatened to form a third baseball league, the Continental League. As a result of the player pool to stock the new Washington and Los Angeles franchises, the Yankees lost much of their bench and second-line pitching, as Bobby Shantz, Eli Grba, Duke Maas, Bob Cerv, and Dale Long were lost to the new teams. Another player, veteran Gil McDougald, a Yankee since 1951, had also been tapped in the draft and offered a bundle of money to play, but instead he retired. Pitching coach Eddie Lopat was also gone, having been fired along with Stengel and Weiss. Ex-Yankee pitcher Johnny Sain, strong-minded, independent, able, and admired, had been picked by Houk to be in charge of the pitching staff. Wally Moses had also been added as a batting coach.

When the season began the Yankees gave little indication that this team would be special. By mid-May Whitey Ford, pitching every fourth day, was leading the staff with a 6–1 record and showing no signs of arm trouble, but Bob Turley and Art Ditmar were erratic, and Ryne Duren was ineffective and drinking even more than earlier. On May 8 Hamey traded the troublesome Duren along with Johnny James and Lee Thomas to the expansion Los Angeles Angels for relief pitcher Tex Clevenger and outfielder Bob Cerv. It was Cerv's third tour of duty with the Yankees.

Mickey Mantle, chronically pained by an ailing right knee, but in an excellent frame of mind under Houk, started the season with a brace of home runs, and by the end of May he and Baltimore's Jim Gentile led the American League with thirteen each. Yankee catcher Elston Howard was hitting over .400, left fielder Yogi Berra and shortstop Tony Kubek were both over .300 and first-baseman Bill Skowron was close to it. Roger Maris, voted Most Valuable Player in the league in 1960, perhaps the finest fielding right fielder since Tommy Henrich in his prime, started slowly, hitting only .240 with seven home runs despite spring predictions that Maris had an excellent shot at breaking Babe Ruth's single-season home-run record of sixty. In February Casey Stengel was asked if Roger could break the record. "Why shouldn't he break it?" Stengel said. "He's got more power than Staleen."

On Memorial Day the Yankees gave a sneak preview of their forthcoming summer slugging. Against the Red Sox in Fenway Park in *one game*, Maris hit his tenth and eleventh home runs, Mantle hit his twelfth and thirteenth, Bill

Skowron hit his sixth and seventh, and Yogi Berra added a home run, only the fifth time that three batters on one team hit two homers each in a game. The next day Maris hit a three-run home run deep into the Fenway bleachers and Mantle added a two-run blast for another Yankee win. An awesome Yankee team was stirring.

In early June the Detroit Tigers were leading the league by three and a half games. Pitchers Frank Lary, the Yankee-killer, Jim Bunning, and Don Mossi were keeping the Tigers on top, but the team had little depth and needed to remain injury-free throughout the season to stay in the lead. What was hurting the Yankees, Ralph Houk realized, was pitching, especially Turley and Ditmar. Houk relegated Turley to the bullpen, and in mid-June offered Ditmar and either Hector Lopez or Deron Johnson to Kansas City for A's pitching star Bud Daley, who in 1960 had won sixteen games. Frank Lane, the A's general manager, picked Johnson to accompany Ditmar to KC, and the deal was closed. The Yankees and A's had new general managers, but their incestuous relationship continued.

To replace Turley and Ditmar in the rotation, Houk was forced to rely on his unproven pitchers, 25-year-old Ralph Terry, 22-year-old Bill Stafford, and 25-year-old Rollie Sheldon, a poised, talented rookie from Class D. Also available was Jim Coates, 12–3 in 1960, but better as a long relief man than as a starter. Aided by the coaching and the encouragement of Johnny Sain, these pitchers joined Whitey Ford, who won eight games himself in June, to form a powerful rotation. In June the team won twenty-two games and climbed to within one game of the tenacious Tigers. Consecutive complete games by Terry, Sheldon, and Stafford sent shudders of apprehension through the league.

In June Tony Kubek hit in nineteen straight games, Mickey Mantle continued to hit home runs and spark the team, and Roger Maris, displaying a sweet Yankee Stadium swing, exploded for fourteen June home runs to increase his league-leading total to twenty-seven.

For the first time during the season a reporter, Joe Trimble of the *Daily News,* asked Roger the magic question. "Roger," Trimble asked, "do you think you can break Babe Ruth's record?" Maris shrugged his shoulders. "How the fuck do I know?" he said. Despite Maris's excellence on the field, he continued to mystify the front office and the news media with his antagonism toward them. Roger the Red-Assed Yankee, reporters called him. "He doesn't take surly pills," Trimble wrote, "he only acts that way." Responded Maris facetiously, "Anybody can be nice when they're going good."

The home-run slugging continued into July. On July 1 against the new Washington Senators at the Stadium, Mantle hit his twenty-sixth and twenty-seventh home runs, but the Yankees still trailed 6–5 in the ninth inning when Tony Kubek singled and Maris unloaded his twenty-eighth home run to win the game 7–6. The next day, in another brutal demonstration of power, Mantle hit his twenty-eighth home run, Maris his twenty-ninth and thirtieth home runs, Bill Skowron hit an incredible one-handed blast into the left center-field bleachers, the ball sailing into the stands to the left of the 461-foot sign, Ellie Howard hit a 400-foot home run into the left-field stands, and Bob Cerv hit a double that bounced off the wall at the 457-foot mark in left-center field as the Yankees scored thirteen runs!

The next day 74,246 people crushed into Yankee Stadium to watch the fireworks, the largest Stadium crowd to see baseball in fourteen years. Yankee victories and home runs, an unbeatable draw, were attracting the curious to see the Yankees in ball parks across the country as the Yankee batters continued to suggest that this group had the potential to rival the Murderer's Row of the 1930s when Babe Ruth, Lou Gehrig, Tony Lazzeri, and Bill Dickey roughed up the league.

As Maris's home-run total was growing, the usual group of New York writers was being complemented by additional curious scribes seeking a story. Where earlier Maris was able to avoid reporters by arriving early, now the reporters were arriving even earlier, and there were too many for him to avoid. By mid-July there began a daily ritual for Maris of talking to reporters, a task he never enjoyed but nevertheless resigned himself to, and he was usually gracious and cooperative, spending hours of his time answering oft-asked questions. Though he was not eloquent or quotable, Maris usually kept his wits and his temper, and rarely did a reporter who sought Maris out leave without a story. Only on occasion did Maris lose his temper, usually when a writer asked what Maris thought to be a stupid question. "If you were a pitcher," Maris was asked, "how would you pitch to yourself?" Roger bristled. "You nuts or something?" he said. "Whaddya think I am?"

Maris and Mantle were making headlines with their home-run hitting, the pitchers were excellent with Ford (17–2) on an eleven-game winning streak, Stafford (8–4), Terry (5–1), Sheldon (6–3), and Daley (4–1), aided by the superb relief of chubby left-hander Luis Arroyo (5–3) who had twenty saves. The Yankees inner defense was the best in both leagues. Only the Baltimore infield of Jerry Adair, Ron Hansen, and Brooks Robinson came remotely close to the Yankee infield. "We have the finest infield in baseball," Ralph Houk often boasted. "It's the best Yankee infield since I've been around, and that's since 1947." The Richardson, Kubek, Boyer infield was as renowned as any in baseball history. Only the trio of Tinkers to Evers to Chance, three Hall-of-Famers immortalized in poetry, rated above them in recognition. In 1910 in their best year the Tinkers, Evers, Chance, Steinfeldt Cub infield completed 110 double plays. In 1961 the Yankee infield completed 180.

Bobby Richardson at second base was established as a steady, durable operator, stopping everything in his territory, and at third Clete Boyer was gaining confidence with each game and was rivalling his brother, Ken, as the top third-baseman in the majors. The more Houk told Clete how spectacular he was at third, the more spectacularly he played, displaying lightning reflexes, racing to his right and to his left to stop sure doubles down the line and into the shortstop hole, and throwing batters out from his knees. After a slow start Boyer was also helping the team with his bat, hitting around .250. "The Old Man always tried to hide me in the bottom of the lineup," Boyer said. "Ralph has confidence in me."

The quarterback of the infield was shortstop Tony Kubek, a boyish, awkward-looking, tall string bean with a flattop crewcut a Corsair could land on. Kubek, like his close friend and companion Richardson was tight-lipped and difficult to approach off the field. "Here's a boy," Stengel once said, "who sits on the bench without opening his mouth so you don't know which side he's on. But," Casey continued, "when he goes out on the field, you know." Only 25, but already a five-year veteran, Kubek had the maturity of a man ten years older. He was always serious, determined, and quietly aggressive. He was religious, didn't drink, didn't smoke, didn't chase women even before he was married, and didn't play poker with the other guys. Fun, for Tony, was going to church and lighting a candle. At night he and Richardson would stay at home. Bobby would read the Bible and Tony would read self-improvement books to expand his vocabulary and his intellectual horizons. Kubek shunned publicity and for years even refused to appear on the Red Barber postgame shows. Though Kubek was the heart of the Yankee infield for half a dozen seasons, his reticence made him almost invisible in the media, and his complete absence of flair or color prevented him from attaining the recognition of some of his equally talented teammates. More than once when the writers were grilling Maris about his home runs and his personal life during Roger's chase of Ruth's record, Maris would snap, "Write about someone else for a change. Write about Kubek. He plays great every day, and he *never* gets his name in the paper."

Kubek was a player everyone took for granted, and his true value was ascertained only after he retired in 1965. Ten years later the Yankees are still trying to find an adequate replacement for him. Kubek was second in the batting order, ahead of Mantle, Maris, and the other sluggers, and his job was to get on base and score runs. He did this with regularity. In 1961 Tony scored eighty-four runs, third on the team behind Roger and Mickey.

On July 14 the Yankees temporarily regained first place from the Tigers with a 6–2 win over the Chicago White Sox. Maris hit his thirty-fourth home run, and Mantle his thirtieth, but it was a play by Kubek that saved the ball game. Luis Aparicio, the fleet White Sox shortstop, was on first when Sox second-baseman Nellie Fox hit a hard ground ball between third and shortstop. Third-baseman Clete Boyer raced toward short to try to cut it off, but the ball was by him, and shortstop Kubek had to race behind Boyer deep into the hole, where he fielded the ball and fired the long throw over to first for the out. Aparicio continued past second base, saw that Boyer was far to the left of third and sprinted for third. Kubek quickly anticipated the situation, beat Luis to the base, and Aparicio was stunned when Kubek took the return throw and slapped the ball on him to end the White Sox threat. "He's a very good shortstop," Aparicio said later. "They talk about Zorro Versailles and Dick Howser. Forget it. Kubek's the best." Two days later in a 9–8 ten-inning win over the White Sox, Chicago was leading 8–7 in the ninth inning. Richardson led off the ninth for the Yankees with a walk, and Kubek deftly sacrificed Bobby to second. Maris doubled him home to tie the score. In the tenth Boyer doubled, and Kubek drove Clete in with a single to win the game. The next day against the Orioles with the score 1–1 in the ninth Kubek doubled to left center, and Mantle drove him home with a single to win. When the Yankees needed the intricate, important play, the hit-and-run, the sacrifice, the lead-off single, the clutch play, Kubek was there to deliver.

When Tony Kubek became a Yankee in 1957, the 20-year-old string bean created excitement not seen in the Yankee instructional camp since Mantle burst on the scene in 1951. Kubek was predicted to be the next Yankee super-star, as good an infielder as the best Yankee infielder, as good an outfielder as the best Yankee outfielder. Tony could play second, shortstop, third, and all three outfield positions with skill and intelligence. At bat his measured, calculated swing sprayed line drives to all sectors of the ball park. Through Casey Stengel's final few years of managing the Yankees, whenever Mantle in center was injured or needed a rest, or Bauer in right, or Howard in left, or Carey at third, or McDougald at short, or Coleman at second, he would substitute Kubek, and wherever Tony played, he was outstanding. In 1957 Kubek was chosen as the American League Rookie of the Year, and through the next few years his value increased as he improved with experience. "He is," said Stengel, "a remarkable young man." When Ralph Houk became manager in 1961, one of his first changes was to permanently move Kubek to shortstop and Richardson to second, the combination that had performed so brilliantly for him at Denver in 1956. Houk felt permanence would bring security and improve the defense. In 1961 on a team best known for its slugging prowess, the Yankees won as many games with their superior infield play as they did with their powerful hitting. Against the Pierces, Donovans, and Bunnings, pitchers often involved in 1–0, 2–1 games, the Yankees didn't usually beat them with home runs. They beat them with pitching and defense.

In 1962 Kubek was drafted into the Army when his reserve unit was activated, and a neck injury which he suffered playing touch football during his tour of duty shortened his baseball career. Like infielders Jerry Coleman and Billy Martin, when Tony returned from military service he was not playing at 100 percent, and because of his final few years of relative ineptitude caused by his back and neck miseries, his .280 pre-service lifetime batting average dropped more than eleven points. After the 1965 season doctors told him he had to quit or chance paralysis, and by that time the excellence of his earlier years was unfortunately tarnished. He was never flashy, never as smooth as some shortstops, but in his prime Kubek was as good as any of his contemporaries. He was quick, and his strong and accurate arm saved many a critical situation for the Yankees. Years after Casey Stengel had left the Yankees he said of Kubek, "Who could be more valuable in fifty years of my life?"

July was another spectacular twenty-victory month for the Yankees. Whitey Ford's winning streak reached thirteen games as he raised his 1961 record to a stunning 19–2. What the starters didn't finish, Luis Arroyo and Jim Coates did.

At the end of July Roger Maris had forty home runs and Mantle thirty-eight. As the home runs continued, the talk of the sports world was their chase of Ruth's hallowed record of sixty home runs in one season. Baseball commissioner Ford Frick, once the personal friend and ghost-writer of the Babe, a great admirer of both Ruth the man and Ruth the legend, tried everything he could think of to keep Maris and Mantle from dimming the memory of the Bambino. Frick declared that if either Yankee slugger did not hit the sixty-one home runs within 154 games the record would have an asterisk placed beside it in the record books. Frick also did not discourage remarks which suggested that there was a lively ball being used, an advantage that Ruth in his day did not have. Frick defended and protected the Babe, like Ron Ziegler defending Richard Nixon. The controversy raged as the chase continued.

There were other Yankee heroes. Ellie Howard, an American League all-star for the sixth year in a row, was batting .350 and leading the league in hitting. First-baseman Bill Skowron injured his back again and returned wearing a corset to hit towering home runs. Yogi Berra also was hitting home runs, belying his 37 years.

The Yankees most unlikely hero was their third-string catcher, John Blanchard, a 29-year-old bench warmer who kept the Yankees even with the Tigers by winning games with a string of four home runs in consecutive times at bat, two of them crucial pinch hits. Blanchard, who had only hit six home runs in his entire career, began his streak July 21 in Fenway Park against the Red Sox. Boston was leading 8–7 in the ninth inning, and with two outs and the bases loaded, the 6-foot-1-inch, 200-pound reserve pinch hit for Clete Boyer and slugged a line shot deep into the Red Sox bullpen in right field for a grand slam and an 11–8 Yankee victory. The next night Boston was again leading in the ninth with two outs, 9–8, and again Blanchard pinch hit for Boyer, and again lined a home run to tie the game 9–9. The Yankees won it when Red Sox pitcher, Gene Conley, allowed light-hitting Luis Arroyo to double, and Richardson drove him home with a single.

The Yankees returned home to play the White Sox, and with Blanchard back on the bench, the Yankees swept a doubleheader in which Mantle hit his thirty-seventh home run and Maris struck numbers thirty-seven, thirty-eight, thirty-nine, and forty. The next day manager Houk rested Howard and started Blanchard. In the first inning Mantle blasted his thirty-eighth homer and Blanchard, batting fifth behind the Mick, followed with another long home run, John's third in a row. The next time up in the fourth inning Blanchard again teed off, a home run into the right-field stands, his fourth in a row! In the seventh Blanchard's long fly ball to deep right field was hauled down by White Sox outfielder Floyd Robinson, who caught the ball with his back to the fence as Blanchard continued running down the first-base line into the outfield to give the ball body English. To no avail. The fans gave Blanchard a standing ovation as he trotted back to the dugout.

After the game Blanchard said "Who am I to break records?" He looked over at Mantle and Maris. "Record breaking is for others."

August began as July ended, with home runs and victories. Ralph Houk sat out a five-day suspension for shoving umpire Ed Hurley after two adverse calls by the umpire cost the Yankees a ball game. Frank Crosetti managed the team while Houk was cooling his heels. Crosetti won six of seven. Mantle hit his fortieth home run against the A's on August 2; Maris hit his forty-first home run against the Twins August 4. In that game, with the score 5–5 in the tenth inning, two outs and two Yankee runners on base, the irrepressible Blanchard homered to win the game 8–5. Two days later on a day when Mantle hit home runs number forty-one, forty-two, and forty-three, Blanchard batted in the tenth inning with the Twins ahead 6–5 and homered to tie the game as the

Yankees went on to win in the fifteenth inning. Of John's first fifteen home runs, five tied games the Yankees went on to win, and two won them outright.

The sore-armed pitchers were returning to form. Terry, fully recovered, won five games in a row in August before losing to raise his record to 11–2. Stafford, pitching well and losing some close ball games, was 12–7, and rookie Sheldon was 9–3. Whitey Ford, completing a fourteen-game winning streak, finally lost 2–1 to the White Sox. At the end of August Ford was 22–3, burying speculation that he was over the hill. Under pitching coach John Sain, Ford had learned a fast curve, a "slurve," to complement his other pitches, and his sinker ball was forcing the batters to ground out, often into double plays. In 1961 Whitey Ford was by far the best pitcher in baseball.

Manager Ralph Houk continued to heap praise on his men, and the players, loose, carefree, and successful, were having the summer of their lives. The pitchers had so much confidence in their fielders and hitters, and the hitters had so much confidence in their pitchers, that the Yankee clubhouse seemed to be one large mutual admiration society. "Just keep us in the ball game until the seventh inning," the hitters would tell the pitchers. "As soon as we get our second or third look at their pitcher, we'll get him."

In three early August days against the expansion Washington Senators, Mantle hit his forty-fourth and forty-fifth home runs, and Maris hit numbers forty-three, forty-four, and forty-five, and on August 13, with forty-six games remaining before the magic game number 154, both Mantle and Maris were sixteen games ahead of Babe Ruth's pace of 1927. Four days later Maris hit home runs number forty-seven and forty-eight off Billy Pierce of the White Sox. On the floor of the U.S. Senate, Milton Young, a senator from Maris's home state of North Dakota, interrupted Senate debate to announce the news. Maris hit seven home runs in six days to set an American League record. At the end of August Mantle, in a mini-slump, had forty-eight home runs. Maris had fifty-one. On the final day of the month Bill Skowron hit his twenty-second home run, the team's 194th, breaking the American League team record for home runs in a season. Later in the game Hector Lopez hit home run number 195. Yankee home-run hitting was the most discussed topic in the sports world, with the race between Mantle and Maris usually the focus.

Because of the Mantle-Maris tandem, the fans and the press were beginning to take sides. Mantle had been the Yankee glamor boy since 1951, and Maris was a newcomer. Because Maris was perceived to be a surly, unfriendly individual and because Yankee fans were beginning to feel that Maris was taking away some of Mantle's thunder, most were aligning themselves on the side of Mantle, who only one year before had been booed so unmercifully no matter how well he did. Mantle, because of Maris, was becoming a New York City hero of unparalleled proportions, while Maris was beginning to hear the boos previously reserved for Mickey. Maris also was receiving less and less complimentary press. Untrue reports were being circulated that Maris was jealous of Mantle. Reporter Lenny Shecter of the New York *Post* wrote that Maris was only playing because of the money. Maris was outraged. "I love baseball," Roger said. "If I didn't, I'd quit right now." Other reporters were beginning to get on his nerves, and he on theirs, as the number of correspondents increased and his time became less and less his own. Certain annoying questions kept reappearing. "Roger," he would be asked, "are you hitting more home runs because the ball is more lively?" "That's a lot of shit," Roger would bristle in self-defense. "More home runs are being hit because more people are swinging for home runs. The old-timers swung for singles. I swing for home runs."

There was one question which made Maris's neck redder than any other, and that was the question he must have been asked a thousand or more times. "Roger, do you think you can break Ruth's record?" was the query. First there would be an icy stare from Maris. Then a reply, "Don't ask me about that fucking record. I don't want to talk about the record. All I'm interested in is winning the pennant." It was the truth, but most people could not accept Maris's answer that he was more interested in the common good than his own.

Because Maris was getting most of the attention from the press, Mickey Mantle was enjoying the summer immensely. Mickey learned to relax, and his droll sense of humor gradually became more public.

"You can't have a private life," Mickey often said. "Wherever you go people think they know you." But Mickey was learning to control his emotions in public situations, and nobody talked about *his* churlishness any more.

In the clubhouse after a game one of the band of free-lance reporters who were covering the Maris-Mantle home-run chase naively asked Mickey where he lived, a secret Mickey guarded with tenacity. Mickey, within earshot of Ellie Howard, told the reporter, "I've just moved to Teaneck, New Jersey." With a straight face, Mickey said, "Would you like to know the address?" The reporter, drooling, naturally said yes, and Mantle gave him a Teaneck address. Howard, half-listening to the conversation, awakened. "Hey," Ellie said to the reporter, "what address did he give you?" The reporter told him. It was Ellie's home address.

Mickey most enjoyed kidding his friend Maris. Of all the players, Mantle most appreciated what Maris was going through, because in 1956 when he won the triple crown, he had been subjected to much the same pressures, so when the rumors of the jealousy between the two men surfaced, rumors which were totally false, Mickey enjoyed ribbing Maris about their "feud." He also enjoyed putting on the reporters. "After Roger hits a home run," Mickey told one writer, "I tell him how lucky he is." He told another reporter with a straight face, "On the last day of the season, I can see it. Roger and I are tied for the home run lead. Roger's on first, and I hit a home run, and Roger gets halfway to second and runs back to first. I can just see the headlines," Mickey said, "Maris Fucks Mantle!"

That the Tigers had managed to remain so close for so long was remarkable, even to Detroit manager Bob Scheffing. "If someone had told me early this spring," Schiffing said, "that Maris would have fifty home runs, Mantle close to fifty, and Ford would have twenty wins, I would have bet you that the Yankees would be leading the league by twenty-five games."

During the first three days of September, the Yankees and Tigers battled for the pennant. With thirty games still left in the season, the Yankees had eighty-seven wins, the Tigers eighty-six. The Yankees had home-run sluggers Mantle and Maris. The Tigers had home-run sluggers Rocky Colavito and Norm Cash. The Yankees had pitchers Ford, Terry, Stafford, Daley, and Sheldon. The Tigers had Mossi, Bunning, and Lary who already had forty wins among them with twenty complete games. In the bullpen there was Paul Foytack and Hank Aguirre.

In the first game, before 65,000 sweltering fans at the Stadium, Whitey Ford, then Bud Daley, and finally Luis Arroyo held the Tigers scoreless for nine innings while Mossi, throwing slow curves and change-ups, also was pitching shutout ball into the ninth. "You hold 'em here," Bill Skowron told Arroyo in the ninth, "and I'll win the game for you when we get up." Arroyo retired the Tigers without a run, and in the bottom of the ninth Ellie Howard singled, Yogi Berra singled, and with runners on first and third and nobody out, Skowron made good on his promise, pulling a hard bounding ball through the narrow passage between shortstop Chico Fernandez and third-baseman Reno Bertoia as Howard scored to win 1–0. Tiger manager Scheffing, an admirer of the Yankees, admitted that the Tigers were not in the Yankees' class. "A tip-off on this Yankee club," Scheffing said, "is that a strong hitter like Bill Skowron bats seventh, and that seems to be the proper place for him." Richardson was batting first, then Kubek, followed by Mantle, Maris, Yogi Berra, Ellie Howard, hitting .360, and then Skowron, who batting seventh finished the season with twenty-eight home runs and eighty-nine runs batted in! The win gave relief star Luis Arroyo his tenth win in a row.

The second game, on a sweltering, sticky afternoon, pitted Ralph Terry against Frank Lary, a nineteen-game winner, a crafty veteran with an illustrious history of defeating the Yankees. This year, as last, Lary was facing an added obstacle whom he could not overcome—Maris. In the first inning Tiger outfielder Rocky Colavito hit his fortieth home run to give Detroit a 2–0 lead, the only runs Terry allowed. With the score 2–1 Maris doubled, went to third on a wild pitch, and scored on a bunt by Mantle. In the sixth, the score still tied, Maris who was suffering through a 6–50 slump, overanxious because the pitchers were refusing to throw him strikes, lined his fifty-second home run into the lower right-field seats to give the Yankees a 3–2 lead as the 54,000 sweltering Stadium fans roared their approval. Later in the game Kubek drove in two runs with a sharp single, and then Maris again unloaded a home run, his fifty-third as the Yankees won 7–2. Arroyo relieved winner Terry (12–2), recording his twenty-sixth save of a remarkable season. Only a muscle pull in Mantle's left arm spoiled an otherwise glorious afternoon.

For the third Detroit game manager Houk was planning on benching Mantle, but Mickey arrived at the Stadium several hours before the game, took a whirlpool, taped his arm, and after swinging some bats in the clubhouse, told Houk that he wanted to play. Reluctantly Houk wrote Mantle's name in his usual fourth spot on the lineup card. In the first inning Mantle batted against Jim Bunning, the top right-hander on the Tiger staff, and grimacing in pain on the swing, pulled his forty-ninth home run into the right-field stands. His teammates were astounded by his grit and heart. Then in the fifth Bunning himself hit a long drive headed for Death Valley in left-center field that Mantle after a long run speared with a spectacular over-the-shoulder catch. Despite Mantle's heroics, the Tigers were still winning by a run in the ninth inning.

The first Yankee batter to face Tiger reliefer Gerry Staley was Mantle, and to the ecstatic delirium of the packed house, he pulled his fiftieth home run of the season into the right-field bleachers. A thunderous wallop hit by a man with a painfully pulled muscle in his left arm, it traveled 450 feet and tied the score 5–5. Following the home run, the rest of the Yankees finished off Detroit. Yogi Berra, who had followed Mantle's first-inning home run with a home run of his own, singled. Bill Skowron walked, and against reliefer Ron Kline, Ellie Howard, batting .359, smashed his fifteenth home run into the left-field seats for three runs to win the game 8–5.

The Tigers departed the Stadium four and a half games behind the Yankees, completely demoralized, awed, and buried. At the end of the next nine days the pennant race was over, as the Yankees won their next ten games in a row while the Tigers lost nine of their next ten. A one-and-a-half-game lead on September 1 ballooned to a twelve-and-a-half game lead by September 12. It was a thrilling year to be a Yankee fan. It was Christmas almost every afternoon.

With the pennant race virtually over, everyone concentrated on the Mantle-Maris home-run derby. In every park where the Yankees played, attendance records were set as people flocked to see whether Mantle and/or Maris would break Babe Ruth's single-season home-run record.

At Yankee Stadium the booing of Mantle had ceased. It was as though the Yankee faithful were apologizing to him for the harsh treatment he had been receiving all those years, and to make up for any past hurts, the Stadium fans were making a concerted effort to understand his temperament, overlook his imperfections, and shower him with huzza's of love. In one game in which Houk had kept Mickey on the bench because of his sore arm, he went into the game for defensive purposes and received a standing ovation. A few nights later when he hit his fifty-second home run, the Stadium crowd rose as one and applauded and stomped wildly as he trotted slowly around the bases. Mantle was deeply moved. The applause did not stop until after he had crossed home plate and returned to the dugout.

On September 10 Mickey hit his fifty-third home run. It was a long home run in the first inning against Jim Perry. His arm was aching and his legs pained him chronically—but still he played. The home-run derby had caught him up in something which didn't permit rest.

Then a head cold further deteriorated his physical condition, and on September 11, just before the Yankees left for a long road trip, Yankee announcer Mel Allen, worried about Mantle, took him to his personal physician for a penicillin shot. For the next week Mantle's physical condition did not improve, but Mickey kept playing. His home-run total stayed at fifty-three while Maris hit his fifty-seventh home run against Frank Lary of the Tigers on September 16. On September 17 Bill Skowron made an error to send a game into extra innings, thus giving Maris two extra at-bats. In the twelfth Maris hit his fifty-eighth home run off Terry Fox to win the game.

The next day Mantle arrived at the ball park drawn and sweating badly. He had a temperature of 103 degrees and was developing an infection and rash where he had been given the penicillin shot. There were only three games remaining before the Yankees played their 154th ball game of the season, commissioner Frick's Midnight Hour to break Ruth's record. Mantle could not play any more. He was too weak. His challenge to the Babe was over.

Now only Maris remained, and the mounting pressure on the young right fielder was choking him in a vise-like stranglehold. The publicity was increasing in quantum jumps. Reporters hounded his every footstep, recording what he was eating at every meal and following him to the movies. "The only time I'm by myself is when I'm taking a crap," Maris said. Life was becoming increasingly more unpleasant for the man in the goldfish bowl.

Before and after every game the reporters and cameramen were lined up three deep in front of Maris's cubicle. One afternoon Maris listened to and answered a series of questions cabled to New York from a wire service in Tokyo. From halfway around the globe they were asking the same questions he had been answering for the last two months. "No wonder I'm going nuts," Maris said when he was finished. Writers who never covered sports before were covering Maris, and some of their questions bordered on the absurd. He was getting questions like "How does it feel to be hitting so many home runs?" and "Does all of this make you excited?" and "Do you still sleep well at night?" There were also questions like, "What's a .260 hitter like you doing hitting so many home runs?"—to which Maris answered "You've got to be a fucking idiot." That Roger was hitting .260 was discussed often. "Would you rather hit 60 home runs or bat .300?" he was asked. "No comment," Roger said. Obviously if it meant more to him to hit .300, he would have cut down on his swing and tried to hit .300. The reporter persisted. "Well, which would you?" he was asked. "What would you rather do?" Roger asked him. "I'd rather hit .300," the reporter said. Maris exhaled. "You do what you want, and I'll do what I want."

Away from the ball park anyone who saw Maris on the street or in a restaurant wanted his autograph. He was not afforded five minutes of peace and quiet. "Some people want autographs on demand no matter what you're doing," Maris said. "They think they have a right to order me around. It's just a matter of courtesy." Maris shook his head. Too often there was no courtesy.

Only on the field was he afforded refuge from reporters, photographers, and autograph seekers. On the diamond, however, some of the fans, seeing that Roger was a man with a temper who reacted adversely to criticism, constantly reminded him that they thought Mickey Mantle should be the one breaking Ruth's record. Others reminded him that they thought that Ruth's record never should be broken at all. At the Stadium he took a frightful booing, and though the people applauding far outnumbered those booing, the ferocity of the minority made a strong impact on Maris. He was not used to being booed, but it was especially weird since he was being booed for doing something extraordinary. "Give me the Kansas City fans any time," Maris said. "There's no place that can compare with the people there." While at Kansas City Roger during one streak was 6–110. Never once was he booed. But Roger's criticism of the New York fans didn't make him any more popular.

On the road Maris was the target of vicious verbal abuse and bottle throwing. After a doubleheader in Detroit during which Roger spent the entire day dodging garbage thrown at him from the right-field stands, he was so upset that he hid from reporters in the trainer's room for forty minutes after the game. "It's pretty tough to have to listen to it all through two games and then come in and have to answer a lot of questions I've answered a hundred times." Most of the reporters were not very sympathetic. Maris was causing them to miss their deadlines. The next day in the New York papers Maris was labeled a boor, a cry baby, and worse.

On September 19 the Yankees flew to Baltimore for a series with the Orioles. Maris needed three home runs in three games to break the record within Frick's deadline. Baltimore was the hardest park in the league in which to hit a home run. The day before hurricane Esther had skirted the city and a powerful wind was still blowing in from right field as the Yankees and Orioles prepared to play a Sunday doubleheader. Before the games Maris as usual was surrounded by reporters. "My daughter, Susan," Maris said, "is four, and she's getting to an age where she wants her daddy home. She can't understand why the other kids her age have their daddys home and hers isn't. That's what I'm thinking about. Everybody thinks all I have on my mind are home runs." One reporter wanted to know if it was true the Yankees were having him trailed by private detectives. He denied it. The rumor was not allowed to die, though. In gossip columns Maris's name was appearing alongside names of renowned starlets making him even less receptive to writers of the press. "How can they write shit like that?" he kept asking.

The Yankees split the doubleheader. Maris did not hit a home run. Steve Barber, a left-hander, was sharp in the first game. Skinny Brown and Hoyt Wilhelm, two knuckle-ball pitchers, stopped him in the second.

One more game to go. The 154th of the season. Maris needed two home runs to tie the record, three to break it. The pressure was causing Maris excruciating inner pain. Maris was a stoic individual, but he was human, though few accepted his frailties. Before the game Roger was sitting silently in front of his locker. It was very early. Most of the reporters had not yet arrived to stampede him. Maris's face was haggard, his eyes were red. Shaking, Maris walked from his locker. He went into manager Ralph Houk's office. Tears began streaming down his face. The shakes became worse. "I need help," Roger said to Houk. "I need help. I can't stand it any more. All those goddamn questions. I'm at the end of my rope. I just can't take it any more." He buried his head in his hands. Houk was surprised at the intensity of Maris's distress, but the Yankee manager was able to convince his hitting star that with just a little more patience the season would be over. When the two men finished talking, Maris was once more in complete control and before the game answered the questions of reporters with outward calm. Only the constant tapping on the floor with his spiked shoes indicated this game was any more important than any other.

Baltimore manager Paul Richards didn't want Maris to break the record against his club. To stop Maris he pitched another of his fast, young arms, 22-year-old right-handed flame-thrower Milt Pappas. Pappas had a further advantage. With Mantle still out, he could pitch around Maris.

Maris, batting in the first inning, hit a long fly ball to right field. There was a gasp, then a groan. Maris had gotten a little too far under it and flied out to Oriole right fielder Earl Robinson. In the third when Maris batted again, he said to Oriole catcher Gus Triandos, "If you don't think my ass is tight, you're crazy." Pappas threw, and Maris hit a rising line drive far above the outstretched glove of the second-baseman that quickly rose until it landed out of reach in the Baltimore bleachers. It was Maris's fifty-ninth home run, tying Ruth for the second most ever hit in a 154-game season. Hank Greenberg and Jimmy Foxx each had hit fifty-eight home runs in a season.

In the ninth inning, with the Yankees safely ahead and one inning from winning another pennant, Maris again batted. There were two outs. Facing him was Hoyt Wilhelm, the toughest relief pitcher in the history of baseball, a knuckle-ball pitcher with more wins, more saves, more innings pitched, more strikeouts, and the lowest earned run average of any reliever ever. It was said that trying to hit Wilhelm's knuckler was like trying to swat a fly in midair with a pencil. The ball darted so erratically that neither Wilhelm nor the catcher ever knew where or how it would break, one reason catcher Gus Triandos led the league in passed balls year after year. In the 112 innings Wilhelm had pitched this year to this game, he had allowed but five home runs.

Wilhelm, a quiet man, was more than willing to throw Maris a fast ball or two to give him a chance, but Richards, the crusty manager told Wilhelm, "If you throw him anything but knuckle balls, it will cost you $5,000." Obviously too dear a price to pay for being a nice guy. On Maris's final chance for immortality, Wilhelm threw Maris knuckle balls. The first one hit his bat and glanced off foul. It was deadly silent in the Baltimore ball park. In homes across the country all activity ceased while Maris batted. The second pitch was again a flutter ball, and again Maris took a half-swing at the elusive, darting pitch. This time, however, the ball hit the bat, and while Roger stood in the batter's box, the ball bounded ten feet down the first-base line, in fair territory. Wilhelm ran over to field the ball, and it was easy for him to tag Maris, who had barely left the plate. The chase to catch the Babe as defined by Ford Frick was over.

There was a noisy Yankee clubhouse after the game. The Yankees had won the game 4–2, clinching the pennant. The players were celebrating with champagne. Everyone was drenched with the bubbly—except Maris. The players knew that he did not engage in that sort of hijinks. They respected him for it and left him alone. Reporters surrounded him admiringly. His eyes were strange, wild and crazy. He was breathing strenuously, trying to catch his breath. "I tried," he said. He took several more swallows of air. "I tried." Everyone could feel the deep respect for Maris in that clubhouse. The other players shook his hand and congratulated him for his effort. They gazed at him in awe. "I felt," one reporter said, "like I was in church."

Despite Frick's ruling, there were still nine games left in the season for Maris to hit more home runs, nine more games of answering endless questions, nine more games of pressure. When Maris talked, his right leg jiggled nervously. In the fourth game of the Baltimore series he went oh for four and after the game discovered his blond hair was falling out in clumps. Bald spots were appearing on the back of his head. He was frightened, and he ran to Doctor Gaynor, the team physician, to find out why. It was the result of nervous tension.

With five games left in the season on September 26 the Yankees returned to the Stadium for two games against Baltimore and three against the Red Sox. Everyone was still interested in Maris, but the tension had lifted perceptibly after the 154th game. In game 158 versus Baltimore against 22-year-old Jack Fisher, another Baby Bird with great promise, Maris swung at a curve ball that Fisher threw a little too high. After Maris swung, he remained at the plate, leaning on his bat, watching the flight of the ball. The vocal crowd of less than twenty thousand people, many of whom were packed into the lower right-field stands where Maris hit most of his home runs, rose, baseball gloves ready to retrieve the souvenir, and when the ball fell into the upper-deck stands, the crowd sent up a deafening roar. Maris nonchalantly tossed the bat away and circled the bases in a jog, savoring the moment. The Oriole right fielder retrieved the ball after it bounced back onto the field and tossed it back in as the Yankees waited for Maris to return to the dugout. When Maris crossed the plate and disappeared into the dugout every Yankee walked over to him to shake his hand. The crowd continued to cheer, and it would not stop until Maris reappeared to take a bow, something he was extremely reluctant to do. "I didn't know what to do," Roger said, "I never was in a spot like that." His teammates knew what to do. They pushed him back out onto the field where Maris doffed his cap and waved to the appreciative fans. Maris was even with the Babe. Fisher, who had given up Ted Williams' final home run the day Ted retired, was philosophical. "I'm out there to win," Fisher said. "It doesn't matter to me whether it's Maris's sixtieth or someone else's first. I don't care who hits home runs as long as I win." Fisher lost 3–2.

The next day exhausted and harried Maris took the day off. He sat on the bench and watched the game. Mantle, his infection worse, stayed home.

Maris played in games 160 and 161 and was shutout. Again most of the fans who came sat in the three decks of right-field box seats, trying to capitalize on a five-thousand dollar reward offered for home run number 61. It was like "Let's Make a Deal" where Monte Hall innocently asks, "Who wants to win some money?" and everyone in the audience shouts, "Me, me, me, me, me."

That left game 162. There was tension, because it was Maris's final opportunity, but at this game much of the attraction was of instant riches for the person who caught the ball.

Only one run was scored in the ball game. The Boston pitcher, 24-year-old Tracy Stallard, a fast-ball pitching rookie, threw his finest game of the year, a slick five-hitter. One of those hits came in the fourth inning. Maris, waiting patiently in the batter's box, took an outside fast ball and a curve inside as the fans booed Stallard loudly. Maris banged his spikes with the end of his bat, and set himself again. The pitchers in the Yankee bullpen were all peering in from their right-field vantage point, hoping Maris would hit the ball to them. Before the game Maris had told them, "If you catch it, don't give it to me. Take the $5,000." With the count 2–0, Stallard threw a fast ball out over the plate. Roger swung smoothly, and a joyous roar followed the crack of the ball on bat as the ball rose high and carried over the head of right fielder Lu Clinton, backed against the stands. It fell into the lower right-field stands for a home run, the sixty-first home run of the season for Maris. When the ball descended, the rush of fans to catch it was frenzied. "Holy cow!" yelled Yankee announcer Phil Rizzuto. "Look at the fight for that ball!" Even when the lucky fan caught it, others punched him and tried to take it away from him. He was ultimately rescued by the Stadium police.

Maris circled the bases as usual not showing any emotion, but in the stands, apart from the fighting for the ball, the rest of the fans were screaming in absolute ecstasy, so pleased that Maris had overcome the forbidding odds against him over the excruciatingly drawn-out season. As Maris rounded third, a young fan jumped out of the lower stands and raced to shake his hand. Maris shook it, as he did the hand of third-base coach Frank Crosetti. After Maris crossed the plate, the entire Yankee team was waiting for him. When they returned to the dugout, Maris's teammates would not let him in. While the crowd continued its wild, spontaneous cheering, the players kept pushing Maris back on the field where he sheepishly waved his cap. Four times he tried to reenter the dugout. Four times he was rebuffed. Even when he was finally allowed back in the cheering continued. It was a magic moment in baseball history.

Stallard, who each time he batted received an ovation for having the guts to pitch to Maris when he could have more safely walked him, was not upset by the home run. "I have nothing to be ashamed of," Stallard said. "He hit sixty others, didn't he?" Maris's home run was the Yankees' 240th of the season, a new record. Previously the record was 221 set by the 1947 Giants and 1956 Reds. The home run also gave Maris the RBI crown as he finished the year with 142, one more than Baltimore first-baseman Jim Gentile.

The Yankees won the pennant by eight games over a strong Detroit team. Whitey Ford finished the year with a remarkable 25–4. Ralph Terry finished second in winning percentage to Ford with a 16–3 record. Bill Stafford, losing many close games and not getting credit for a number of other excellent performances, finished 14–9, and Jim Coates and rookie Rollie Sheldon both finished 11–5. Luis Arroyo completed one of the finest relief performances in baseball history with a 15–5 record and twenty-nine saves.

At the bat there was never a team with as much power throughout the entire batting order. Richardson and Kubek were not power hitters, but they were adept at getting on base to be driven in by the others. Behind them were Maris, who finished with sixty-one home runs and 142 runs batted in, Mantle with fifty-four home runs and 128 RBI's, first-baseman Bill Skowron, injury-free for most of the season, finishing with twenty-eight home runs and eighty-nine RBI's. Yogi Berra hit twenty-two home runs, Ellie Howard hit twenty-one, and the third-string catcher, John Blanchard, also hit twenty-one. Clete Boyer, the third-baseman, had eleven. It was a year for home runs as opposing players were hitting them, too. Gentile hit forty-six. Harmon Killebrew hit forty-six. Rocky Colavito hit forty-five, and Norm Cash forty-one. It was an exciting year, a year in which Roger Maris, complete with asterisk, became the Home-Run King of baseball.

Before the advent of television and of the "new journalism," an athlete to be idolized needed only to be proficient on the field. The guy could have been the meanest, nastiest son of a bitch since Simon Legree, but if he could hit consistently with men on base or pitch with lightning speed, he was a hero, and how he treated his fellow man was quite irrelevant.

By 1961, however, television made Roger Maris visible and instantly recognizable even to those people who didn't know a stolen base from a stolen car. To the fan, the personality of the athlete had become as important as his statistics, and Maris's isolationist philosophy served to make him look both belligerent and nasty. In truth, toward most people he was neither of these. To most he was an honest, outspoken, unsophisticated man who was kind and considerate to his friends and warm and loving to his family. To those who infringed upon his privacy, especially to newspaper reporters who dogged his every step during his home-run chase, he was irritable, unfriendly, and distant. As a result the reporters wrote what they observed: that Maris was irritable, unfriendly, and distant. Thus the fans who read the papers saw Maris in this light, and when they came to the ball park, they believed that to boo Maris was to boo a Snidely Whiplash in pinstripes, a man who would tie Little Nell to the railroad tracks and watch the train run over her. This image of Maris in comparison made the equally closed-mouthed Mickey Mantle look like Dudley Dooright, the man who would ride in and save Little Nell. Neither characterization was accurate, but the fans saw these two men this way, and to this day their respective images have remained.

Maris's problems with the press and the fans really began the day in December of 1959 when it was announced that George Weiss had obtained him from the Kansas City Athletics. To most players, going to the Yankees was an honor and a privilege. It was a chance for world series loot. To Maris, a devout family man, it meant being separated from his wife and children, since he didn't want to uproot them from their Kansas City home.

When the trade was announced, the New York reporters immediately called Maris for a comment. They expected to hear how thrilled he was to be coming to New York. Instead Maris said that he liked it in Kansas City and didn't want to leave. "I know that financially I can do much better in New York," he said. "Therefore I will go." It was not a diplomatic answer, but it was honest, consistent with his basic philosophies of life: "To thine own self be true," and "Don't bullshit me." It was his strict adherence to his own principles that caused Maris to be labeled a malcontent and a troublemaker.

In 1953, when Roger signed with the Cleveland Indians, the club wanted him to start at Daytona Beach, Florida, in Class D. Maris insisted on playing for Fargo, a Class-C team in his home town where he could play in front of friends and be with his girl. The Indians said no. Roger refused to accept no for an answer, and said that he wouldn't play. He'd go out and work for a living. Roger got his way, played at Fargo, and hit .325. This stubbornness nevertheless began his reputation as a troublemaker. Maris, however, felt he knew what was best for Maris and figured that what was best for him was also going to be best for whoever was paying his salary.

In 1954 Cleveland wanted Maris to spend another year at Fargo. This time

Roger demanded to be promoted. He was, to Keokuk in Class B, where he hit .315 with thirty-two home runs and twenty-five stolen bases. In '55 he was promoted to Tulsa in Class AA. Early in the season after Maris overthrew third base from right-field and cost the team a game, the Tulsa manager, Dutch Meyer, ordered a special practice for Maris. Meyer hit fly balls to right field and the embarrassed and enraged youngster practiced his throwing to third. After a number of long throws Maris, steaming at what he felt to be an unjust humiliation, tucked his glove under his arm and walked off the field while Meyer stood at home plate with his fungo bat, screaming, "Get back out there." Maris resolutely continued to the dugout and into the locker room.

"I'll never take abuse from anybody, big or small, important or unimportant if I think it's undeserved," Maris said. "You've got to have enough pride to stand up for yourself." Maris was immediately demoted to Reading. Meyer was fired shortly thereafter.

In 1956 Maris starred for Reading, where Yankee general manager George Weiss first noticed the youngster, and in 1957 he starred at Indianapolis, the top minor league team in the Cleveland organization. Weiss followed Maris's progress.

In 1957 he finally was brought up to the Indians. Weiss told Kansas City A's owner Arnold Johnson that if he could trade for Maris, the Yankees would trade the A's for him, and then make an offer Johnson would not be able to refuse. Weiss knew that Cleveland general manager Frank Lane would never trade Maris to the Yankees. Injuries and another Maris feud made it possible for Johnson to acquire Maris in mid-1958. Weiss, true to his word, acquired Maris from the A's in the winter of 1959. It is said that when Weiss acquired Bob Turley and Don Larsen in the winter of 1954, he set the rest of the American League back five years. When he acquired Maris in the winter of 1959, he set it back another five years.

The Yankees in 1959 had finished a dismal third. In 1960 Maris helped return the franchise to its winning tradition. In 1960 he hit thirty-nine home runs, in '61 he hit sixty-one to break Babe Ruth's record, in '62 he hit thirty-three, and in '63, though he was out half the season with injuries, he still managed to hit twenty-three home runs. In 1964 Maris hit twenty-six home runs, and then in '65 he broke his hand and played sparingly as the Yankees plummeted. For five years Roger Maris was one of the great home run hitters in the game, and teamed with Mantle, they were the most fearsome one-two punch since Ruth and Gehrig.

Casey Stengel, who managed him in 1960, didn't completely understand the closed-mouthed Maris. "That Maris," Casey said. "You tell him something, and he'll stare at you for a week before answering," but Casey nevertheless appreciated his excellence as a complete ball player. "I give the man a point for speed," Casey said. "I do this," he said with unassailable logic, "because Maris can run fast. Then I can give him a point because he can slide fast. I give him another point because he can bunt. I also give him a point because he can field. He is very good around the fences—sometimes on top of the fences. Next I give him a point because he can throw. A right fielder has to be a thrower or he's not a right fielder. So I add up my points,'' Casey concluded, ''and I've got five for him before I even come to his hitting. I would say this is a good man.''

Maris was far better than a good man. Back-to-back in 1960 and 1961 he won the Most Valuable Player award in the American League. In '61 he won the Hickok Belt for the best professional athlete of the year. He was named the Top Catholic Athlete of the Year. He won the Sultan of Swat award, the Bill Corum award from the New York City B'nai B'rith. What he never won was a sympathetic press. At banquets he was criticized for mumbling "thanks" and sitting down. The Yankees kept getting letters complaining that he didn't speak. It was reported that the Yankees tried to explain to Maris the value of public speaking and that they even wrote a speech for him. "I'm no speaker," Maris protested.

When spring training of 1962 began, Maris figured that the pressures the media placed on him would cease. He was wrong. From the start of spring training, there was a new set of standard questions, the most prevalent one being, "Will you hit sixty-two home runs in 1962?" Maris became angry whenever someone asked him that. "This was the first time in thirty-four years that someone hit sixty home runs. Anybody who expects me to do it again must have rocks in his head," he replied.

In March his worst public-relations problems began when a reporter from the Fort Lauderdale *News* wrote that when one youngster asked Maris for an autograph, Maris wrote an X on the ball. It was a malicious, false accusation, making Maris appear cruel to children. Maris was livid. He had made an X, but Maris who liked kids, was only making a joke and afterwards signed a personal inscription and his signature. Maris vowed not to talk to any reporters from the local Florida papers. The next day a Miami reporter asked Maris, "How do you think you'll do this season?" "No comment," growled Maris. "How much do you weigh?" "No comment," Maris answered. "Do you think we should sign a nuclear-disarmament treaty with the Russians?" "No fucking comment," Maris growled. Maris then explained that his new policy was not to give interviews. "Let 'em write what they want," said Roger. "Ted Williams was right. Go your way and let the writers go theirs."

A few days later, the day after St. Patrick's Day, Oscar Fraley, the author of "The Untouchables," the TV show starring Robert Stack as Eliot Ness, wrote an article for UPI about Maris which was prominently displayed at the top of the Fort Lauderdale sports page. Fraley had never met Maris or even talked to him, but he knew he didn't like him anyway. Fraley criticized Maris for his refusal to be courteous with newspapermen and submit to interviews. "If either of my two sons has a hero," Fraley concluded in his article, "I hope it's a modest fellow named John Glenn who went for the circuit when it really counted. Because guys like Maris bat a round zero with me."

When the fighting mad Maris finally caught up with Fraley, Roger called him every name in the book, publicly, to his face. "If you weren't so old," Maris told him, "I'd knock you right on your ass." He stormed into the clubhouse. Following behind him was Jimmy Cannon, the highly respected journalist from the New York *Journal-American*. "Can I talk to you?" Cannon asked the shaken Maris. "Not now," Maris said. "Later." Cannon shot back, "Go fuck yourself."

Two days later Cannon began a two-part series. The headlines of the two columns read: "Maris—'The Whiner'—a Threat to Yank Pennant" and "Maris Envies Mantle's Prestige Among Yankees." It was another distorted piece by an irate journalist who should have controlled his temper and been more objective. "The community of baseball feels Mantle is a great player," Cannon wrote. "They consider Maris a thrilling freak who batted .269 . . . but his reputation is demolished when they compare him to Mantle. This apparently irritates Maris, who gives the impression that he inhabits a league filled with enemies. Obviously Maris considers Mantle a competitor instead of a partner on a team."

By this time Maris was ready to pack his bag and go home. His character had suffered such assassination that if he had discovered a cure for cancer he still would have been thought of as an arrogant and aloof scientist. "Rude Roger" some writers were calling him in the papers. Cannon continued to call him the Whiner.

There was yet another ugly scene. A photographer asked Maris to pose with New York Mets coach Rogers Hornsby, one of the game's great hitters. Maris, still seething at the beating he was taking, did not want to pose. During the 1961 season Hornsby had said that there was only one thing Maris could do as well as Babe Ruth, and that was run. In his agitated state, Maris saw Hornsby as another critic who had been taking potshots at him. The headlines in the papers the next day read, "Hornsby Calls Maris 'Little Punk Ball Player!' " "I've posed with some real major leaguers, not bush leaguers like he is," Hornsby said.

Before the end of spring training, Roger was so agitated that he didn't know his friends from his enemies. He even offended the elderly Dan Daniel of the *World-Telegram,* one of Maris's strongest supporters. "Maris will have to learn to laugh, even while bleeding internally," Daniel wrote. "If he continues to be the Angry Man, may the Lord have mercy on him. The customers won't."

And the customers didn't. When Roger did not hit sixty-two home runs in 1962, he was booed. When he responded to the booing by giving the finger to the fans, the booing increased. By the end of 1962, Maris had hit thirty-three home runs, an excellent total for anyone else, but unsatisfactory to the fans. The booing upset the Yankee management. If manager Houk had not insisted that Maris remain with the Yankees, general manager Roy Hamey would have traded him at the end of '62. The booing continued. He was a marked man. "Some kids feel they're big shots if they boo me," Maris said. "I don't have to explain why I don't like certain fans. Would you like it if someone threw a beer can at you? How 'bout if someone threw a bottle at you?

"What the hell," Maris said philosophically, "as long as I stay in New York, it's going to keep on. They're on my back, and they're never going to get off. There's no use letting it bug me." Maris was right. They never did get off his back, even after he helped lead the Yankees to five straight pennants. The booing did, however, bug him.

The writers never got off his back, either. It was never written that Maris was surly because he was bitter. "Charm is not his strong suit," wrote writer Charles McCabe. "He is said to feel he should be paid to smile. And maybe even breathe. It is believed that in his sleep he intones the stirring shibboleth of the professional athlete, 'What's in it for me?' He is a red-neck. He ain't bright. He's about as lovable as a tarantula. And he ain't even hitting .300 these days." "What would the New York writers say," said Maris, "if they knew my uncle was Adolph Eichmann?"

His teammates, traveling with him every day, felt that Maris was a straight-forward, no nonsense person. They admired him for his courage, marveled at his sixty-one home runs in the face of intense pressure and respected him for what he was: the best right fielder in the American League. Around his teammates Maris did not have to pick and choose every word. He had a cutting, Billy Martin type of humor, so that when Ellie Howard got on the bus, Martin would say, "Ellie, get in the back," and everyone would laugh. "Hey Mick," Maris would say, "I'm not talking to you today. I'm jealous of you." Roger, contrary to what McCabe wrote, was not a dumb guy. He was, in fact, quite articulate around his friends—only around his friends. He had been burned too often to trust any strangers.

In 1964 Maris's hitting was the key factor in the Yankees' winning the pennant, his last great Yankee hurrah. In June of 1965 Maris, playing despite a pulled hamstring muscle, tried to score from second base on a base hit. When he slid home he dislocated two fingers on his right hand when they caught on the spikes of umpire Bill Haller who had been standing too close to the plate. Several days later, batting against Washington, he felt something pop in the palm of his right hand while swinging the bat. There was no official diagnosis of what had happened to him, but throughout the season the Yankee bulletins kept saying Maris was almost ready to play. When the season ended Maris had not played one inning after the June injury. The hand was so badly injured he was unable to turn a doorknob with it. It was broken. Maris played again in 1966, but was only a shadow of his old self. The fans still booed him, the press still picked on him, and his performance suffered terribly. He hit .233 with thirteen home runs and only drove in forty-three runs. The Yankees finished last. In December of 1966 Yankee general manager Lee MacPhail traded Maris to the St. Louis Cardinals for Cardinal third-baseman Charlie Smith, the ex-Met, White Sox, Phillie, and Dodger who never hit too well and wasn't much of a fielder, either. It was the final insult from the Yankees. Roger Maris for Charlie Smith. When Maris led the Cardinals to pennants in 1967 and 1968 it was Maris who had the last laugh. In his first time at bat in a Cardinal unifom Maris hit a double and went flying into second. The Cardinal fans gave him a standing ovation. He was made. He was promised a beer distributorship by Gussie Busch, the Budweiser beer baron who owns the Cardinals. In 1968 he retired to his Gainesville, Florida, home to run that beer distributorship.

I was aware of Maris' antipathy toward the media when I wrote him a letter asking him if I could talk to him. When he didn't write back, I assumed that he wished to continue his anonymity. Then while driving through the Southeast, on a hunch I detoured through Gainesville, Florida, hoping to find him working at his beer distributorship, located near the Gainesville airport. When I arrived he wasn't there, and I waited two hours for him. All the employees, including his brother, said that they did not know where he was or how he could be reached. The only evidence that Roger Maris was associated with the operation was a Sultan of Swat trophy, awarded for his home-run hitting, and a Most Valuable Player award, tarnished mementos which sat alone, unexplained, on the bottom shelf of a drab brown, glass-enclosed case, the silver bowls uncared-for symbols of an uncherished past.

After waiting fruitlessly, I went to visit with Bill Skowron in Dunnellon, Florida, about seventy-five miles south of Gainesville. Skowron and Maris were close friends, and Bill generously offered to call Roger and ask him if he would have breakfast with us. "I'd love to see you, Moose," Maris said, "but leave the other guy home." After writing Maris another letter, I gave up.

Months later when I was arranging to see Clete Boyer in Atlanta, I called Clete to tell him when I was coming. Clete said, "I got a buddy of mine down here with me. Roger Maris."

"Will he talk with me?" I asked.

"I don't know," Clete said. "You'll have to see."

We met at Boyer's nightclub, the Golden Glove, where a live band was playing very loud rock music in the darkly lit, low-ceilinged bar. Boyer, Maris, and I sat down at a table, ordered drinks and made small talk for a minute or two. Clete then excused himself to go to the bar and talk business. I was left alone at the table with Maris, who hasn't changed much since his playing days. He still looked like the son of Odin, a sandy-haired Viking with piercing eyes and broad shoulders. I told him about some of his Yankee teammates I had seen, but I didn't come right out and ask him if he would talk. I didn't want to ask, because if he said no, it would have spoiled everyone's evening. Maris and I sat over our drinks, minutes of deadly silence hanging heavily while the blaring of the raw rock music was drowning out coherent thought. I was groping for a comfortable topic when Roger looked up from his drink. "This noise is really brutal," he said. "Let's go out into the parking lot. We can talk there." He got up to go. I followed.

The air outside was fresh, and though the music was still audible, it was no longer piercing. I sat on one of the parked autos while Maris stood alongside, sipping his drink. Seeing my tape recorder, Roger nodded toward the music. "You'll get some good background music." He smiled. Already I was saying to myself, "Is this the Roger Maris who kicks dogs and hates children?"

"I guess," I said, choosing my words carefully, "the thing I want to ask you about most is that after 1961 when you hit all those home runs, your relationship with the Yankees deteriorated. You had problems with newspapermen, the fans were really lousy, and it was just a bad thing." Now I had to phrase the question properly. "What are your feelings today about all the things that happened to you in New York?" I asked.

Maris sipped his drink. "Actually," he said, "I don't really feel that bad about it. It's something that happened, something that I had no control over. It was the writers' control. Sure, things could have been handled a lot differently by the Yankees. But they weren't. And it was just something that . . ." He paused and shrugged his shoulders. "Who knows how they happened or why they happened? It's stuff that's gone behind me, and really, it hasn't bothered me a lick." He paused again. "It would have been a lot nicer had it been the other way around, but . . ." A shrug.

"It almost seemed that everyone was holding this tremendous feat that you had performed against you," I said.

"Well," Maris said. "You might call it that. I guess I came along and did something that evidently was sacred, something that nobody was supposed to do. Especially me."

"Did this feeling against you affect your play?" I asked.

"There's no question about it," Maris said. "You don't go out there and play 162 ball games and have people on your back continuously day in and day out and not have it affect your play. It took a lot away from the game as far as I personally was concerned. Naturally you're trying to do your best, but when all the elements are somewhat against you, I don't really feel that I got the best out of me."

"You were under a great deal of pressure," I said.

"Well, like I said before, and I'll say again, as far as playing the ball game, there was no pressure. Playing was probably the easiest part of it. Well, mentally it got pretty strong, the press before and after the ball games, the continuous questions, continuously trying to be on your guard because there were a certain few looking for you to maybe make a slip. I'm not trying to knock anybody, you understand, but when you're trying to answer one question, someone else butts in with another thing, and another guy comes in on half of what you said, and they misinterpret, and through all the continuous questions being fired at you, the pressure was quite strong. Mentally it was tough. I needed time off, and in the last week I took a day off."

"In the spring of the next year, the spring of '62, it was one incident after another."

"Yeah," Roger said. "There were a lot of things I didn't understand. There are a lot of things I won't ever understand. But," he said, again shrugging, "these things happen. They have happened to other ball players before me, a certain few. But like I say, unfortunately I was one of those few who had that type of publicity, and you just somewhat have to live with it. The Fraley article, for instance," he said. "After I read that I was burning, and I just didn't want to talk with anyone. And Jimmy Cannon came over and asked me if he could talk to me, and I said, 'Jimmy, not right now. I'm not in the mood to talk with anyone.' And we were close friends, I thought. Every morning we had breakfast together. And Jimmy said to me, 'If that's the way you feel, the hell with you.' And that was the end of our friendship." There was a look of hurt and disappointment on Roger's face. "I really thought our friendship was worth more than that," Roger said. "To me it's all over and done with, what happened with the Yankees, and the people I got to know, I let them judge me for themselves. I just let it go at that."

"Any number of your teammates," I said, "told me that there was one season when you had a broken wrist, and the doctor didn't even tell you it was broken."

"It was a broken hand," Roger said. "Someone was told not to tell me; I can't say it was the doctor."

"Ralph Houk certainly must have known that the X rays showed it to be broken," I said.

"Well, I'm sure Ralph knew about it," Maris said. "It's sort of a peculiar thing. I didn't feel that I was just the ordinary, run-of-the-mill ball player, and to break a hand in May and not find out about it until a week before the season was over in September . . . you know? And it just sort of seems strange, because the whole time they kept saying it was a day-to-day proposition. I felt personally that there were a few people who made me look like I didn't *want* to play, that I was just there to draw a salary. And I really didn't think that was too right, either.

"Once I broke the hand in '65, though," he said, "really, it was all over for me, because even today I don't have the gripping strength in two fingers of my right hand. I would swing the bat and have that hand slip right out there.

"It was sort of a disappointing thing," he continued, "because the ball club had taken X rays. We took X rays in Washington. We took them in Minneapolis. We took them in New York, and there was never any mention of a break. At first it started out I could go out in the field and take infield, throw the baseball. Then the ball club every four or five days asked me to take batting practice, so I'd go ahead and try a few swings, and it didn't work, and it got to the point where I couldn't even throw a baseball, 'cause I couldn't hold the baseball in my hand. And yet they were asking me to continuously take the batting practice. Now I'm not going to knock Mr. Houk. I'm not going to knock anybody. Everybody's going to draw their own conclusions. There are just a lot of things that I don't understand, and I never will. A lot of things. I just don't want to get into knocking Ralph. I've got my own personal feelings. I feel that a lot of things could have been handled a lot differently than they were, and naturally I was quite disappointed in the way they were handled. I can turn around and say something in my defense, and that means nothing. So you end up sitting back and saying, 'Let it quiet down.' I was more interested in just having things quiet down than continuously bringing up things from the past."

"There reached a point," I said, "near the end of your Yankee career you told Lee MacPhail you weren't going to play in New York any more."

"No," Roger said. "I really didn't say it that way. I said that I was not going to play any more. Anywhere. I had plans to retire after the '66 season, and I told Ralph Houk that. I told Ralph that in July of '66, and when I came to the end of the season, rather than announce I was not going to play the following year, Ralph told me to wait till spring training before I announced it to make sure of what I was doing. So I said okay, and I went home after the season ended. Lee MacPhail called me up one day and asked me if I had changed my mind. I said, 'No, I haven't.' But just detecting the way he was talking, I thought he had something in mind, and I said, 'Lee, if you have any intentions of trading me, let me know now, and I'll announce my retirement.' He said, 'No, we have no intentions of trading you.' I said, 'Then let's just do it the way Ralph wanted to do it, wait till spring training, but I'm still not going to play.' And he said, 'Okay.' And a few days later I was traded. So I personally thought that they could have respected me a little bit by letting me retire if I wanted to retire instead of doing things the way they did them. If I wanted to retire, I think I should have had that much courtesy from the ball club. But when this came up the way it did, I had voiced to only a couple of people that I was retiring, and the writers would have made me look bad again. They'd say, 'Well, he's not going to play because he was traded away from the Yankees.' They would have jumped on me like it was a big news story. So I finally agreed to go ahead and play the year.'' Roger ultimately played two more years, an integral member of the 1967 and '68 pennant-winning Cardinals.

"Will you ever come back to New York?" I asked. "You never come back to the Old-Timers' games."

"Oh," Maris said, "one day I'll come back. When, I don't know. Right now I just don't have the desire to do a lot of those things. Like this year I had many people writing letters to me, asking me to come back to the Old-Timers' games in New York, and from what I understand, the ball club put out the word through the announcers that the reason I'm not coming back to New York for the Old-Timers' game is because I'm afraid the people are going to boo me." Roger smiled and shook his head. "I've been booed by the best of them for many years," he said. "The ball club is trying to push off, 'Well, bad ole Roger again, he's not going to come out because the poor boy is afraid of boos.' That's not the case. I have had other reasons why I have not wanted to go up there. The ball club knows what they are. Ralph Houk knows what they are. Lee MacPhail knows what they are."

"But aren't Ralph and Lee gone?" I asked.

Roger grimaced slightly and nodded, but his silent response indicated that though the two men were not Yankee executives any longer, the wounds they caused him still remained. There was something heroic in Maris's stoicism, in his insistence in not verbally retaliating against the men who helped sully his image.

"You've got to understand me," Maris said. "I've never believed in knocking people. Never. It's not my nature. I really don't even care to get into those kinds of things, 'cause all you do is reopen wounds. Right now Roger Maris is in Podunk. Nobody knows he's around. You know? Half of us haven't heard of him in the last five years, and it's beautiful. I really hate to reopen old wounds. No news is good news. This is basically what it amounts to."

Clete Boyer joined us in the parking lot, and following him was an older woman, tottering slightly, and in her hand was a Polaroid camera. "Can I take your picture?" she asked Boyer, a home-town Atlanta favorite. "Why sure you can," Clete said graciously. "Roger Maris is here, too. You can get both of us together." The lady didn't register any surprise or delight that Clete's friend Maris was there, too. "You know who Roger is, don't you?" Clete asked the woman.

"No, ah don't," she said.

Roger, posing with Boyer, smiled. "That's just the way I like it."

The Berlin crisis worsened. The communists razed the land around the massive, sinister wall, barbed-wired it and patrolled it with soldiers. President Kennedy sent 40,000 additional soldiers to European bases, and 50,000 Russian troops moved into East Berlin.

In October of 1961, as the world series was beginning, both the U. S. and Russia were aggressively testing their nuclear weapons, as rumors of World War III intensified. Families were building fallout shelters in secret to prevent neighbors from trying to use them.

The Yankees themselves were facing a crisis: the state of Mickey Mantle's deteriorated health. In late September he had to be hospitalized as the abscess in his thigh became more infected and ultimately bored down to the bone. Though now out of the hospital, he was weak, listless, and underweight. Mickey couldn't see how he could play in the series, though Houk, aware of Mantle's high threshold of pain, thought he would play some. A flesh-colored bandage covered the raw wound which was about a foot square and packed tightly with gauze. Mantle walked gingerly to limit the bleeding and pain.

The series opponents for the Yankees were the Cincinnati Reds, a surprise winner over several teams which on paper seemed to be stronger. The Reds last were a pennant winner in 1940 when they beat the Tigers, and were winners before that in 1919 when they won the series that the notorious Black Sox threw. This year many experts said the Reds would be lucky to finish, never mind finish first, but under their fiery manager Freddie Hutchinson, the Reds parlayed some excellent pitching with the hitting talents of outfielders Frank Robinson and Vada Pinson and infielders Gordie Coleman and Gene Freese and emerged on top, four games ahead of the Koufax, Drysdale, Podres Dodgers.

The series opened with two games in Yankee Stadium. In the opener on a dark, overcast fall afternoon, two Irish left-handers pitched: Whitey Ford of the Yankees and Cincinnati's stubble-bearded Jim O'Toole, a 19–9 pitcher this year. Mantle, still too weak to play, was not in the lineup, but thanks primarily to his buddy Ford, the Yankees didn't need him. Whitey pitched a crisp, methodical shutout, allowing two well-spaced singles, and with Ellie Howard and Moose Skowron hitting home runs off O'Toole, the Yankees won routinely, 2–0. Clete Boyer provided the dazzle in an otherwise dull game with a display of defensive excellence at third base. In the second inning Boyer brought the Stadium crowd to its feet with a lightning-fast, sprawling back-handed grab of a hard grounder close to the bag hit by Gene Freese, whom Clete threw out while on his knees. In the eighth, on a sharply hit grounder to his left, Boyer again amazed, diving on his stomach while his chin scooped an indentation into the infield, somehow coming up with the ball in his glove, recovering to his knees quickly, and throwing Dick Gernert out as the crowd went absolutely crazy.

Ford, pitching his third consecutive world series complete-game shutout, won his eighth series game, a record. His twenty-seven innings of scoreless series pitching was only two and two-thirds innings short of the series record set by Boston pitcher Babe Ruth in 1916 and '18, an achievement Ruth always said he cherished far more than his record sixty home runs in one season.

In the second game Yogi Berra, playing left field, hit a two-run home run against twenty-one game winner Joey Jay, the ace of the Reds staff. Gordie Coleman hit a two-run homer off Ralph Terry, tying the game. With two outs in the fifth inning, Terry, the two-pitch loser to Bill Mazerowski and the Pirates in the fateful seventh game of the year before, allowed a single by Elio Chacon, an unknown second-string second-baseman of the Reds. Chacon was playing only because Don Blasingame, the veteran starter, had jammed a finger. Shortstop Eddie Kasko singled Chacon to third, and with Vada Pinson up, Terry threw an inside slider that brushed Pinson back. The ball tipped off the glove of the lunging Ellie Howard and rolled only fifteen feet behind the plate. Because Howard in retrieving the ball instinctively looked to first to be certain Kasko wasn't going to try for second, he failed to see the daring Chacon break for the plate. Belatedly Howard rushed back with the ball, diving to tag the speedy Cincinnati infielder as he swept across the plate. In a cloud of bodies Chacon was safe, and the Reds led 3–2. Johnny Edwards, a weak-hitting, second-string catcher singled home runs in the sixth and eighth innings. Jay allowed only four hits, and the Reds won 6–2, angering the Yankee players who were not impressed by either Jay or the Reds. "How the hell did we let that stiff beat us?" they said. "Just wait till the next time he pitches. He won't get through the first inning."

The teams traveled to balmy Cincinnati for the next three games, playing in antiquated Crosley Field, a 1912 ball park, where the outfield in left sloped uphill, and whose cozy dimensions offered power hitters a bonanza. For seven innings under midsummer skies Bill Stafford and Bob Purkey (16–12), the ex-Pirate knuckle-baller, battled with the Reds ahead 2–1. The first two Yankees were retired in the top of the eighth when manager Houk waved John Blanchard in from the bullpen to pinch hit. Before Blanchard went up to hit, he first asked Mantle, who had been playing for the first time in the series, "What's this guy doing? What's he getting us out with?" "Here's what he does," Mantle said. "The first pitch he throws you is a slider to get ahead of you. After that it's all knuckle balls, so jump on the first pitch." As Blanchard left the dugout, he was so intent on hitting that first pitch that had Purkey thrown it over the backstop, he would have swung. On the first pitch, as predicted by Mantle, Purkey threw a slider, breaking in toward the left-handed Blanchard, who hit the ball deep into the left-field bleachers to tie the game 2–2. When Blanchard came back to the bench, there was Mickey, grinning.

Luis Arroyo retired the Reds in the eighth without a score. In the top of the ninth with the score still 2–2, Roger Maris, 0–10 in the series, was first up. There were the usual boos, catcalls, and taunts. With a one-two count Purkey tried his slider, and Maris cracked it twenty rows deep into the right-field stands for a 3–2 Yankee lead. Arroyo, enjoying one of the finest seasons in the history of relief pitching, had been sent down by Reds manager Freddie Hutchinson when Hutch took over in 1959. After Arroyo pitched for Havana, a team that moved to Jersey City, the Yankees bought and revived him. Arroyo shut off the Reds for a most satisfying Yankee win, one from which the undermanned Reds were unable to recover.

With the Yankees leading two games to one, on a clear 80 degree shirt-sleeve afternoon Whitey Ford once again displayed his mastery. Ford and Jim O'Toole matched scoreless innings three times, but in the fourth O'Toole broke. After Roger Maris walked, Mantle, playing for the second straight game with his thigh swathed in bandages, lashed a drive into left center off the distant scoreboard, an easy double for him normally. But after he hit the ball, he limped into first, standing on the bag on one leg like a flamingo, sweat running down his face, his teeth tightly clenched. Houk sent Hector Lopez to run for him, and as Mickey limped back into the dugout, his teammates spontaneously stood and joined the throng applauding him. Mantle could not hold back the tears in his eyes, not so much from the pain but from the knowledge that as in 1951 against the Giants, in '55 against the Dodgers, and in '57 against the Braves, this would be another world series when he would be letting his teammates down because he could not play. It was a bitter disappointment, especially in bandbox Crosley Field, where he had fervently wished to play since the park's dimensions were tailored to his power-alley drives. When Mantle sat down on the bench his teammates were horrified to see crimson oozing steadily from the gaping hole in his thigh as his uniform soaked red through the bandages. The players who accompanied him as he limped to the clubhouse saw the medics pull yards and yards of bloody gauze from where the wound had been packed. Later in the game Bobby Richardson was spiked at second completing a double play, and blood was soaking through his stocking. He stayed in the game. "I'd be ashamed to come out after Mickey's been playing with what he's got," Bobby said.

After Mantle's hit in the fourth, Maris went to third and then on to score the first run of the game on a double play. It was all the Yankees needed to win. Ford pitched five innings of shutout ball, increasing his shutout skein to thirty-two, breaking Babe Ruth's hallowed pitching record. "This sure wasn't a very good year for the Babe," Ford said after the game. In the sixth Ford batted, and then joined Mantle on the trainer's table when he foul tipped a ball onto his right foot batting against O'Toole. Jim Coates completed the shutout, allowing only one hit in the final four innings while the Yankees were bombing O'Toole and reliefer, turned best-selling author, Jim Brosnan, for six more runs. Clete Boyer and sub Hector Lopez each drove in two, and Kubek and Skowron drove in the others as the Yankees won 7–0—an impressive, methodical victory.

The fifth and final game was another rout, more impressive still since it was accomplished without stars Mantle and Yogi Berra whose shoulder was paining him after a tumble onto the left-field slope. Joey Jay, the second-game winner, did not finish the first inning. Bobby Richardson opened with a single, and after two outs, John Blanchard, playing for Berra, homered into the right-field bleachers for the first two runs. Ellie Howard followed with a powerful drive that soared directly into one of the inning slots of the left center-field scoreboard for two bases, and Bill Skowron then lined a ball off the center-field wall, scoring Howard but losing a double when Moose, never a gazelle, tripped and fell flat on his face rounding first. Jay was removed, but 21-year-old Jim Maloney wasn't any more successful. Hector Lopez, playing for Mantle, drove in the fourth run with a long triple, and Clete Boyer sent Lopez home with a ringing double. Before the first inning carnage was over, the Yankees had banged out two singles, two doubles, a triple, and a home run for five runs. Maris doubled in a run in the second to drive out Maloney. Nevertheless, Ralph Terry, ahead 6–0, failed to get his first series win, allowing a three-run home run by Frank Robinson in the second inning and getting the hook too soon to be credited with the win. With the Reds trailing 6–3 Bill Skowron, finishing one of his finest seasons, singled two runs home with the bases loaded, and Lopez, tremendously underrated, hit a three-run home run over the 383-foot sign in left-center field for an 11–3 Yankee lead. Lopez batted only nine times in the series and led the Yankees with seven RBI's, squeezing home still another run in the two-run Yankee sixth. Bud Daley, another underrated Yankee, allowed a two-run homer by Wally Post, but they were the only runs he allowed in six and two-thirds innings of strong relief, and the Yankees were winners 13–5, the world series theirs four games to one. It is doubtful that any team in baseball history, with perhaps the 1927 Yankees the exception, could have beaten them in this world series, the quality of Yankee play from both regulars and substitutes was so incredibly good. The 1961 team was a most awesome machine.

1962

*Tommy Tresh . . . The Amarillo Gang—Pepi, Linz,
Bulldog . . . Ralph Terry and his super season . . .
Another pennant . . . A series victory over the Giants—
by inches*

In February of 1962 Colonel John Glenn became the first U. S. astronaut,
orbiting the earth three times and giving the country a sorely needed morale
boost. In the spring the specter of nuclear war continued to hang threateningly
over the world. While Khrushchev boasted of one hundred megaton bombs and
harangued the U. S. to get out of West Berlin, President Kennedy further
bolstered American troops by activating two new divisions, promising that they
would be combat-ready by the end of 1962. He warned Khrushchev that Russia
had better not start anything, because the U. S. also had nuclear bombs at the
ready.

For the Yankees, President Kennedy's announcement of the added divisions
was welcome because it meant that the two national guard units which had been
temporarily activated in October would be released in August. Tony Kubek,
the Yankee shortstop, would be one of the men released.

In spring training Kubek's absence caused manager Houk the greatest
concern. His pitching staff was solid with Whitey Ford, Ralph Terry, Bill
Stafford, and Jim Coates to start with Luis Arroyo and newcomer Marshall
Bridges in the bullpen. Ellie Howard was the catcher, with Bill Skowron at first
base, Bobby Richardson at second, Clete Boyer at third, and Roger Maris,
Mickey Mantle, Yogi Berra, and Hector Lopez in the outfield. John Blanchard
and veteran Dale Long would provide the bench. The only question was who
would start the season at shortstop. Joe DeMaestri had retired, leaving the
position to one of two outstanding rookie prospects, Tom Tresh or Phil Linz.
Tresh, who had been the only minor leaguer called up by the Yankees at the end
of the '61 season, seemed to have the inside track. In the spring of '61 both
athletes had competed for the Richmond shortstop job. Tresh won the Virginia
job and hit .315, second highest in the International League and was named
Rookie of the Year. Linz was sent to Amarillo where he led the Texas League
in hitting. Tresh, a switch-hitter, looked to be the best prospect in camp, a
"can't-miss" who impressed Ralph Houk strongly. Tresh displayed good
power and the maturity and serious nature befitting a young businessman on the
way up. His first spring training Tresh, a Michigan boy, went downstairs for

breakfast and ordered grits, thinking they were griddle cakes, with a side order of bacon. The waitress looked at Tresh funny and said, "Grits and bacon?" Tresh, though discerning something was wrong, said, "Yeah, grits and bacon."

After the waitress left, while he talked with his teammates, he looked around the coffee shop. For some of the other guys she had brought back a plate of eggs and this white stuff that looked like mashed potatoes or rice. Tresh watched carefully as the others put butter and salt and pepper on this stuff. He kept his mouth shut and didn't say a word. Fifteen minutes later, when his order finally came—a big bowl of sticky grits and a side order of bacon—Tresh grabbed for the butter, salt, and pepper, picked up a spoon and went to town on the grits, hating every bite of it. When the bowl was empty, the waitress came over and said, "You must really love grits." "Oh, I love them," Tresh said. "I don't get much of a chance to eat them up North." And from time to time Tresh would order another bowl of grits just to maintain his reputation. "I didn't want to seem like a hunky-dunky from Detroit," Tresh said.

There were two other rookies who seemed good bets to make the Yankees, Joe Pepitone, a young talented first-baseman, and Jim Bouton, a strong-armed right-handed pitcher. Pepitone and Bouton, along with Linz—the Amarillo Gang—had played together in Class-AA ball in the Texas League, and all showed outstanding talent. Because expansion had drained the Yankee farm system, it was expedient that Hamey and Houk bring them up. At Amarillo the three had set the league afire while giving their manager ulcers. They were certainly not typical overawed, reticent rookies. The three made every day with the Yankees an adventure.

Joe Pepitone, tall and skinny with a large nose, was the ballsiest, brashest youngster the Yankee veterans had ever seen. Pepitone as a kid had been shot in the stomach at school, and his reputation for being irresponsible and carefree preceded him to camp, a reputation he added to by taking his $20,000 bonus and buying a fancy car, a motorboat, and some expensive duds. At spring training Pepitone derived great joy squealing the tires of his souped-up Bonneville as he dragged out of the parking lot or raced around Fort Lauderdale. He was fun. He loved craziness and good times, and even veterans Mantle and Ford enjoyed being with Pepi and his sidekick, Linz, another fun-loving individual who never wore a wristwatch. At Amarillo, Pepi and Linz collected women friends like some people collect stamps or coins. Neither one of them spoke out against alcohol, either. They were ball players, but to them having a good time was just as important. Bouton, outspoken like Pepitone and Linz, hid his eccentricities better than the other two, keeping to himself during training camp. Houk had told Tresh and Linz that they had made the team, and Pepitone seemed certain to stay. Bouton, though, still had veteran Robin Roberts and another rookie, Hal Stowe, to beat out for a spot on the roster. He kept his mouth shut and worked maniacally, running in the outfield, hustling, pitching any time he was asked.

Manager Ralph Houk, in order to keep an eye on the unpredictable Pepitone, roomed him with a muscular babysitter—Moose Skowron. Spring training was only a few days old when Pepitone told Moose that he and Billy Gardner, a utility infielder, were going out on the town. Moose told Gardner, "You get him home by ten o'clock, because if he ain't home by ten, I'm putting the chain on the door, and he ain't getting into the room." That night Gardner and Pepitone were out until two in the morning, and when Pepi tried the door, it was bolted just as Skowron had promised. Pepitone rapped on the door. "Moose, Moose, it's Joe. Let me in," Pepitone said. "Sleep in the hall," Skowron replied. "Why, Moose?" asked Joe. "Because I told you to be in by ten o'clock," said Skowron. "You're not coming in. Sleep in the hall." Pepitone stood back and gave the door several violent kicks with his left leg, knocking the chain in and tearing wood from the walls. When Joe finally got in the room, he snarled, "Moose, don't you ever lock me out again. You hear me?" Skowron, himself enraged, ripped off the covers and got out of bed. Pepitone, never having seen the Tarzan-like Skowron without his shirt, was immediately terrified. Inching toward the doorway, Pepitone said to Skowron, "I'm not sleeping here tonight. No way. I'm going to another room." Skowron stood by his bed glowering as Pepitone fled to find another empty bed.

The next day Pepitone went back to discuss the situation with Skowron. "Moose," Pepi said, "you have to let me in at night. You have to." Skowron remained adamant. "You come in at ten o'clock," Moose said, "and I'll let you in." For the rest of spring training, Pepitone was in by ten o'clock. Most of the time, anyway.

The Yankees were spending their first spring training at their Fort Lauderdale training complex. Though owner Dan Topping's creation, he did not attend opening game ceremonies because he was having lunch with President Kennedy aboard the presidential yacht. The exhibition season was smooth-running and successful.

Tresh, though not as proficient at the double play as Kubek, filled in adequately and hit well. Linz batted .348 and Tresh .302, the only two to hit over .300. Tresh was named the outstanding rookie prospect in camp. Only Rollie Sheldon, last year's rookie sensation, was not performing up to expectations. With rookies Tresh, Linz, Pepitone, and Bouton added to the team along with reliever Marshall Bridges, many, including manager Houk, felt that this team had the potential to be even greater than last year's.

For the first time the country of Vietnam was being mentioned in discussions of U. S. military strategy. In early April the South Vietnam government forces, aided by spies, crushed an attack of 1,200 Vietcong, the communist forces. Said one American military advisor, "A few more wins like that and the backs of the Vietcong will be broken in the area." A day later two American GI's were killed by communist guerillas, the first American soldiers to die in Vietnam.

When the season began the Yankees displayed a perfect balance of hitting, pitching, defense, and bench strength that suggested that this team would be one of the outstanding clubs in baseball history. By mid-May a Yankee loss was a rarity, and though the surprising Cleveland Indians stayed close, it was generally conceded by July that the Yankees would clinch the pennant. There wasn't another team in the Yankees' class. Whitey Ford, Ralph Terry, and Bill

Stafford were outstanding on the mound, and Mantle and Maris were hitting as prodigiously as they had the year before. Slugging along with the two outfield stars were Moose Skowron, John Blanchard, Hector Lopez, Ellie Howard, and a surprising Clete Boyer who was batting close to .400 and was developing into an exciting and spectacular third-baseman. Rookie Tresh was hitting close to .300, and he and second-baseman Bobby Richardson, also hitting over .300, were a competent keystone combination. Rookies Joe Pepitone and Phil Linz, while not playing much, were valuable reserves who always provided the team with a laugh or at worst, a smile. Early in the season in Detroit, for instance, Mickey Mantle and Whitey Ford were having a few drinks at the bar of one of the better Motown restaurants when they noticed Pepitone and Linz, who were there eating. "Come on over guys," Mantle said to them. "Have a drink with us." It was about ten o'clock in the evening. "You know," Mickey said, "you two are the best rookies who ever came up. You say your piece, say what you want to say, and I really like you for that." The two youngsters were awestricken. Ford said, "Joe, Phil, later on this evening we're going to the Flame Lounge for a few drinks. We're going to have dinner here, and as soon as we finish eating, we'll meet you over there." Whitey gave them the address. "Grab a cab," Whitey said. "It should only be a couple of bucks. We'll be right there." Pepitone and Linz, on cloud nine, left the restaurant and hailed a cab. "The Flame Lounge," Pepitone ordered the cab driver.

The cab took off through the heart of Detroit, but the "short" trip became longer and longer and the money on the meter accumulated alarmingly. An hour later with the bill close to fifteen dollars, the cab finally stopped, and the cabbie said, "This is the joint." Pepitone and Linz looked out the cab window and couldn't believe their eyes. They were in the heart of the slum district of Detroit, an ominous neighborhood. The Flame Lounge had big round windows with strippers dancing in them and was the one night spot on the block. Phil and Joe paid the cab driver and walked inside. Drunks were spread out on the bar, and behind the bar a large, black bartender curiously asked Pepitone and Linz, "Can I help you?" Joe said, "Yeah. Mickey Mantle's table." The bartender said, "You mean the ball player? You kiddin'? Mickey Mantle sure don't come in here!" It cost the two rookies another fifteen dollars to ride back to their hotel on the other side of town. On the way, Joe said to Phil, "We'll say we didn't go. Right? We'll tell 'em that I came back to the hotel and called my mother and didn't feel like going."

On the team bus the next day Mantle and Ford, smiling broadly, came sauntering up the steps, looking for Pepitone and Linz. Pepitone, trying to look serious, said to Mantle, "Hey, Mick, I'm sorry about last night. I just couldn't meet you guys." Mickey, not believing Joe for a second, said, "You went, didn't you?" Pepitone, trying to look innocent, said, "No. Why? Didn't you go?" Mickey said, "Oh yes, we were there." Pepitone, unable to keep a straight face any longer, was forced to 'fess up. All Joe could say was, "Why, you no good son of a bitch." Mantle roared.

The only Yankee not enjoying himself was Maris. After a series of spring incidents with reporters in which the Yankee slugger was pictured to be a man who would pull wings off butterflies and sell his children for money, the fans in the ball parks began booing him fervently and unmercifully. In Detroit during the second game of the season, a fan in the right-field third deck hurled an empty liquor bottle down at Maris which grazed his arm and barely missed his head. Maris quickly called time and angrily ran into the dugout demanding police protection. After a five-minute delay, he returned to the field, greeting the fans with a classic one-fingered gesture, emphasizing his displeasure by slapping his left palm across the crook of his right arm. The booing crescendoed. Even at Yankee Stadium he was treated disdainfully. On Easter Sunday the fans threw Easter eggs at him. When he batted, the booing was fearful. He became an unhappy, ultra-introverted person. "Sometimes," Maris said, "I wish I never hit those sixty-one home runs. All I want is to be treated like any other player." But that was no longer possible. Public opinion had turned irrevocably against him. In mid-May Roger was hitting over .300 as his critics had wished; he was driving in runs, winning ball games, playing excellently in the field, and still the booing continued unabated. He was a professional playing in the face of massive disapproval by the home fans. The ill treatment was making him bitter. "You got to take it," he said, "but you don't have to like it. You stop trusting people, and I was never that way. I liked people. I did."

Never did the booing stop. When Maris met with general manager Roy Hamey, after the 1962 season, he told Hamey, "If it was up to me, I'd like to build a house on the top of a mountain, and if I never saw another person, that would be okay with me." It was a sad and unfortunate situation. A man with his talent, could have been the king of New York City. And all he ever wanted was to be left alone.

Where Maris was booed, Mantle was cheered lovingly. A Mantle home run was greeted with an emotional outpouring of cheers and adulation. Mantle, his human weaknesses accepted and forgiven, had become the most popular player in Yankee history and perhaps in baseball history. One Mickey Mantle card was worth ten Willie Mayses or ten Stan Musials, or twenty-five of anybody else. Clever traders could even get an entire set of the Boston Red Sox for one Mickey Mantle card.

On May 18, Mantle, batting close to .400, hitting home runs, stealing bases, playing excellently in center field, was the final batter in a game against the Minnesota Twins. He grounded to the infield and raced down the first-base line where ten feet short of the base he collapsed in a heap. Mantle lay still on the ground, his face contorted in pain. A muscle high on the inside of his right thigh had been severely torn. He refused a stretcher, and with the aid of John Blanchard and coach Wally Moses, Mickey limped uncertainly into the clubhouse where he had to shower on crutches. From then until June 22 Mantle was unable to play. Without Mickey in the lineup, opposing pitchers much more willingly walked Maris or forced him to fish for bad pitches, and the impatient Maris with Mickey out batted 21–110, his average dropping below .250 while the Yankee offense suffered doubly.

Two days after Mantle was hurt, relief star Luis Arroyo was placed on the disabled list, his arm aching, his screw ball not breaking, his career finished. One day after Arroyo's demise Whitey Ford, after pitching seven innings of no-hit ball against the Los Angeles Angels, suffered muscle strain in his pitching arm and had to leave the game. Ford was out from May 22 until June 21, and without Mantle, Ford, and Arroyo, the complexion of the Yankee team changed radically. The pennant no longer was guaranteed, though it was fortunate for Yankee fans that the second-best team, the Detroit Tigers, were similarly decimated, with Al Kaline, Bill Bruton, and Frank Lary, three of their stars, all out for long periods of time with injuries. Only the relative weakness of the league kept the Yankees in contention. After the Yankees lost seven out of eight games to Baltimore and Cleveland at the end of June, they were in fourth place, four games behind league-leading Cleveland, who were ahead of the Minnesota Twins and the surprising expansion Los Angeles Angels. In the span in which Mantle missed thirty games and Ford pitched only one inning, the Yankee record sagged to 15–15. To add to manager Houk's woes, Roger Maris, Bill Skowron, Ellie Howard, and Yogi Berra were all in slumps, with only Bobby Richardson, rookie shortstop Tom Tresh, and left fielder Hector Lopez getting on base consistently. Houk, ever the optimist, was not alarmed. "When Mickey and Whitey return," he said calmly, "we will win."

And when Mantle and Ford returned, the Yankees did win. Ford in his first game back pitched a three-hitter against the Orioles. In his next two starts he allowed two hits and four hits, and through the summer of 1962 Ford won nine of his ten starts, complementing Ralph Terry, a certain twenty-game winner, and Bill Stafford.

When Mantle returned the Yankee slugger rejuvenated the offense. In a four-day span in early July Mantle hit six home runs in four games and batted .458, and with his return opposing pitchers no longer could afford to walk Maris who began to see better pitches to hit. Maris also hit six home runs in a four-game span. Cleveland, its lack of pitching strength laid bare, folded, and the Yankees quickly regained the American League lead. In the second week in July the Yankees won ten straight games, expanding their lead to three games over the Angels. By the end of the month Jim Bouton, who had defeated the Tigers in a twenty-two inning game by pitching seven final innings of shutout ball, replaced Rollie Sheldon in the rotation and gave the Yankees a fourth powerful starter. The Yankees had not clinched the pennant, but there was now little doubt that it was theirs. With the Yankees continuing to bring up young prospects like Stafford and Tresh, it looked like the Yankee dominance would continue indefinitely.

In Bill Stafford and Tom Tresh the Yankees owned two fine young prospects. Stafford, only 22 years old, was swaybacked and compensated by strutting like a ramrod-straight Prussian soldier. In high school in Athens, New York, Stafford once pitched a seventeen-inning game, striking out thirty-one batters. Stafford was fast, with an excellent slider and professional poise, and the Yankees outbid fourteen other clubs to get him. In 1961, his first year in the Yankee rotation, Stafford was 14–9, with a 2.68 ERA, second in the American League. In 1962 again he was 14–9, but both years there were numerous games when he pitched well enough to win but didn't. With more luck Stafford would have won twenty in each of those years. He was a million-dollar pitching prospect with a golden arm and a brilliant future, a tough, hard-headed kid with such desire and determination to succeed that only serious arm injury could bar him from ranking with the top right-handed Yankee pitchers.

Tom Tresh, a 24-year-old rookie, was a player in the old Yankee tradition of Gene Woodling, Hank Bauer, and Gil McDougald, a gutsy youngster who kept his mouth shut and his ears open, absorbing the wisdom and experience of his elders as he developed. Tresh was the closest to a Yankee Jack Armstrong—the All-American boy—since Bobby Brown, another collegiate Yankee infielder. "I want to have the Yankees in first place by the time Tony [Kubek] gets out of the service," Tresh said. "If that's where we are, I'll feel I've done my job. If we're in first with me at short, that's exactly what Tony would have done." When Kubek returned in August, the Yankees were in first and rookie Tresh had been chosen as the all-star shortstop. After Kubek returned, manager Houk, wishing to return Kubek to shortstop where he had excelled for so many years, moved Tresh to the outfield, a position Tom had never played professionally. It was not long before Tresh was being compared to former Yankee left-field stars Bob Meusal and Charlie Keller. Tresh became the first regular, nonplatooned left fielder for the Yankees since Gene Woodling was traded at the end of 1954.

Like so many young Yankee outfielders, Tresh was being touted as the "next Mickey Mantle." Like so many Yankee outfielders, Tresh found it impossible to live up to Mickey's standards. Like Mantle, Tresh was a switch-hitter, but where Mickey was a natural, Tom had to slave at his trade. When Tom would slump, there were times at four o'clock in the morning when he would be standing in front of the hotel-room mirror swinging a coat hanger, *whish, whish, whish, whish,* practicing his swing, experimenting with his stance, working, practicing, worrying, until he once again found the batting groove. His intensity was genuine, and there was nothing false about his desire to exceed. After his outstanding 1962 season, in '63 he again was chosen for the All-Star team, this time as an outfielder. His .269 average with twenty-five home runs and seventy-one RBI's swelled the sentiment that he would become the next great Yankee. With the Yankee team falling apart around him in 1964, Tresh led the team in most batting categories, hitting .279 with twenty-six home runs and seventy-four RBI's and winning the Golden Glove Award as the best-fielding left fielder in the American League. It was his last year of competence. In the second spring training game of 1966 Tresh tore the cartilage of his right knee, and manager Ralph Houk, seeing the team falling into disarray and ultimately into the cellar, asked Tom to continue despite the weak underpinning. Had Tresh undergone an operation at the time of the injury, his career might have been saved, but because Tresh played hurt, his performance suffered dramatically. Though he hit twenty-seven home runs in '66 his average dropped to .233, and then when the leg became worse and the home runs ceased, he was booed unmercifully for his incompetence. Tresh's confidence waned, and during his final three years Tresh had trouble hitting .200. It was a pathetic end to such a bright, promising career. In June of 1969 Tom was traded to the Detroit Tigers, his value to Houk reduced to zero, and when the Tigers released Tresh during the spring of 1970, he retired.

On the Yankees there was success, and craziness. Bill Stafford bought a pair of $85 alligator shoes which Mantle and Ford nailed to the floor with large railroad spikes the very first time he wore them into the clubhouse. Marshall Bridges, an erratic but successful relief pitcher obtained by general manager Roy Hamey from Cincinnati, was deathly afraid of snakes and mice. Mantle and Ford refrigerated a slimy rubber snake, put it in Bridges' pants leg, and the entire team watched as Bridges tore the pants off his body to get away from the creature. Another time Bridges left the Stadium in paper shower-shoes after finding a few dead field mice laid to rest in his expensive shoes.

In early August Tony Kubek returned from the Army, and Ralph Houk, faced with an overabundance of talent, had to decide where to play him and who to bench. Tresh at shortstop was hitting close to .400 during the last couple weeks, and had been voted onto the all-star team behind Chicago shortstop Luis Aparicio. Hector Lopez was playing in left field, the other position Kubek played with proficiency. Lopez, a steady hitter, had raised his batting average over .300, driving in runs with regularity, but he had occasional fielding lapses which prompted his nickname: "What-a-Pair-of-Hands Hector."

When Kubek reported, Houk had to make room for him on the roster, and he decided the Yankees would be stronger if he reestablished his all-star double-play combination of Richardson and Kubek, shifting Tresh to left field and using Lopez as a substitute and pinch hitter. Houk also returned crazy Joe Pepitone to Richmond the day after catching the young bon vivant standing outside the hotel elevator, dressed to kill and ready to go out at three o'clock in the morning.

In Tony Kubek's first game back on August 7 against the second-place Minnesota Twins, he made two spectacular plays and hit a three-run home run on his first at-bat, soliciting a nice hand from the Minnesota fans and a surprise handshake from home-plate umpire Ed Hurley. When Kubek returned to the bench, every Yankee came over to shake his hand. Tresh, in left, was a revelation for a kid who hadn't played the position since junior high school. Tom hit two long home runs against the Twins in a 14–1 rout, and proved to be a smooth, classy outfielder who with Mantle and Maris formed the top outfield in the majors.

The Twins never got any closer than three games. On September 10 Ralph Terry won his twenty-first game of the season and Mantle hit his 400th career home run to tie the game as the Yankees won in the ninth on a single by pinch hitter Hector Lopez. The Twins lost and fell back. The next day Yogi Berra hit his 350th career home run in the tenth inning to win the game for rookie Bouton, pitching in relief. Again the Twins lost, falling four and a half games behind, their threat over, as the Yankees waltzed to the pennant.

The weaknesses of the expansion-stripped competition were evident. It was difficult to find weaknesses on the Yankees. At first base Bill Skowron, worried and depressed over his publicized marital troubles, still hit twenty-three home runs and drove in eighty runs. Bobby Richardson, the second most valuable player in the league next to Mantle, became the eighth player in Yankee history to produce 200 hits in a season, the first player to accomplish the feat since Phil Rizzuto in 1950. Tresh completed an outstanding rookie season with twenty home runs and ninety-three runs batted in. Kubek, after he returned, batted .314; his shaky fielding was attributed to the long lay off. At third base Clete Boyer was consistently spectacular, the league leader at third in putouts, assists, double plays, and throwing runners out from his knees. His .272 batting average was a surprising plus. Catcher Ellie Howard hit twenty-one home runs with ninety-one RBI's and was the best in the league. Hector Lopez and Yogi Berra split outfield chores before Kubek's return and between them drove in ninety runs. Mantle, in center, was the Most Valuable Player in the league for the third time, hitting thirty home runs with eighty-nine runs batted in despite missing six weeks, and his .321 batting average was second only to Boston's Pete Runnels' .326. In right field Roger Maris, voted the Flop of the Year by the UPI, hit thirty-three home runs, drove in one hundred runs, and was the top run producer on the team. On the bench John Blanchard, Phil Linz, and Joe Pepitone, who finished the year with the Yankees, gave the team excellent reserve strength.

On the mound the Yankee pitching was strong, though a little thin. Whitey Ford, at 33, finished 17–8 and again was excellent. His 2.90 ERA was the third best in the league behind Hank Aguirre, and Baltimore's Robin Roberts, whom the Yankees had cut during spring training. Bill Stafford, 14–9 for the second straight season, was skillful and poised, and the third member of the Yankees' Big Three, Ralph Terry, was the outstanding pitcher in the league, finishing 23–12. In the bullpen Marshall Bridges, replacing Arroyo as the lefty specialist, won eight games and saved eighteen. Of the other pitchers, rookie Jim Bouton showed promise, and Bud Daley in relief pitched thirty-five consecutive shutout innings in one fourteen-game stretch and had a very effective season throughout. Only Sheldon and Jim Coates were disappointing.

The strong arm of the staff belonged to Terry. "Where would we be if Terry had had a mediocre year?" asked manager Houk. Terry, who finished the second half of the season 16–5, pitched a league-leading 299 innings, and his twenty-three wins also led the league. When Terry was at his peak, he worked with such efficiency that, like Ford, the fast-paced, effortless ease with which he pitched made the game of baseball dull. Ralph walked fewer than two men per nine innings of pitching, and his 176 strikeouts were third in the league behind fast-ball pitchers Camilo Pascual of Minnesota and Jim Bunning of Detroit. Terry himself had a live fast ball, and his intelligent use and excellent control of a slider and change-up curve made him overpowering when he was right. In 1962 Terry allowed opposing batters forty home runs, a staggering total, but most of those home runs were hit with no one on base and with the Yankees far in the lead. Everyone seemed concerned with his gopher pitching except Terry. Terry was only interested in the *W* after his name in the box score. Not since 1928 had a Yankee right-hander recorded so many *W*'s.

Ralph Terry's headline-making career with the Yankees was a bittersweet one. It started in 1954 when at age 18 Terry signed a contract with the Yankees. The problem was that he had also signed a contract with the St. Louis Cardinals, creating a legal mess that commissioner Ford Frick ultimately resolved in favor of New York. After two years of shuttling between Binghamton and Denver, Terry was brought up to the Yankees in 1956 as a 20-year-old phenom, a pitcher who was supposed to follow in the footsteps of 1954 sensation Bob Grim and 1955 rookie star John Kucks. Unfortunately, Terry did not pitch much or well in 1956, and he became a rookie flop. After a mediocre season in 1957, despite his tremendous potential, the Yankees traded him to Kansas City. Then two years later George Weiss, evidently deciding that he should not have parted with Terry in the first place, told A's owner Arnold Johnson that he would like to have Terry back, and in May of 1959 Terry and Hector Lopez became Yankees for Kucks, Tom Sturdivant, and Jerry Lumpe. During the next year and a half under Casey Stengel, Terry again showed that his potential was there but that the ability to win consistently was not. He demonstrated an infuriating tendency to experiment with his off-speed pitches in crucial situations, experiments which were often unsuccessful and resulted in opposition home runs. "He always does two or three things that boggle him up," Stengel said about Terry, "and he don't win." Terry had a superior fast ball, a blazing, rising pitch that was overpowering, and a rinky-dink lollypop curve which he, and the batters, both favored. Against a hitter like Rocky Colavito, for instance, Terry would throw two fast balls by him, and on 0–2 try to fool the husky slugger with his little slow curve which Rocky would gratefully hit out of the ball park. Stengel and the pitching coaches would scream at him, but the stubborn Terry believed he needed an off-speed pitch to complement his fast ball and continued to experiment—and continued to lose games he could have been winning. Terry's most famous loss under Stengel came in the seventh game of the 1960 world series against Pittsburgh when he threw the pitch that Bill Mazerowski hit for a home run in the bottom of the ninth inning to win the game and the series for the Pirates.

After the 1960 series defeat, the Yankees fired Stengel and hired Houk, who in turn hired the innovative Johnny Sain as pitching coach. It was Sain who provided Terry with an alternative to his lollypop curve, substituting a quick-darting slider which broke about six inches just as it approached the plate. It became Terry's "out" pitch, and in 1961 Terry was a brilliant 16–3, and in '62 he was even better, developing into the top pitcher in the league. In the '62 world series against the San Francisco Giants, Terry won two games including the classic seventh game, a 1–0 victory for the championship. He was the star of the series and at the pinnacle of his career. Though in '63 his record slipped to 17–15, he still led the league in complete games with eighteen and lost nine one-run games. In '64 Yankee manager Yogi Berra felt that Terry's fast ball had deserted him, and Terry felt that Yogi had deserted him. Terry was one of the "players to be named later" in an August trade with Cleveland for Pedro Ramos as he finished 7–11 for the season. With the Indians in 1965 Terry was 11–6 in mid-August, but then manager Birdie Tebbetts mysteriously stopped pitching him, and he wasted on the bench the remainder of the season while the Indians floundered. In April of '66 he was shipped back to Kansas City, and by August he and the A's desired a divorce. Terry became a New York Met, pitching poorly the rest of the year in relief for the Mets. He was released in the spring of 1967 and retired. For a young pitcher who had been so brilliant, his career quickly screeched to a halt.

The Roxiticus Country Club in Mendham, New Jersey, looks like a golfing establishment Jay Gatsby would have enjoyed. Nestled in the two-hundred-acre privacy of what was once the palatial estate of a railroad tycoon robber baron, in late April the golf course was elegantly beautiful, green and lush, with bubbling brooks running through the wooded rough. I drove up the narrow dirt drive which winds up a gentle hill to the estate house at the top, and when I arrived Ralph Terry, the teaching pro, was in the final minutes of a putting lesson. After the lesson Ralph suggested we adjourn to the private dining quarters for lunch where we could talk in relative quiet. We entered the door of the dining room through stately white-fluted columns, and we sat in an isolated alcove near a large picture window overlooking the course. Terry, part-owner of the club, was enjoying his life as the club pro immensely, and as the members strolled by us and waved or smiled it was clear that they thought highly of him. Ralph talked golf talk with one of the members, chattering about the dogleg on one of the holes and the slant of the green on one of the others, and after the man left, we talked about Ralph's baseball career. Ralph, tall and still thin, with a movie-star charisma, was serious, speaking only after careful thought, but speaking his mind. Like so many of the players, he demonstrated an exterior toughness, especially when we talked about subjects which touched raw nerves.

"After the Yankees went to great lengths to sign you in '53, it wasn't too long before they traded you to Kansas City," I said. "Weren't you a little annoyed?"

"Yeah," said Terry, remembering the June 1957 trade where he went to the A's with Billy Martin. "Darn right. I never thought I'd be traded. I was 1–1, shut out Baltimore in '57, and we were in Kansas City. I was pitching batting practice real hard that evening, and Casey Stengel called me into his office. It's real funny. They don't want to trade you one day and have you come back the next day and beat them, so they wear your ass out just before they trade you. Especially when they send you from one side of the field to the other. So Casey called me in and said, 'We just made a little trade. You're going to Kansas City.' I was just a nondescript rinky-dink at the time. So I said, 'Who all is involved?' He said, 'We're giving you and Billy Martin and Woody Held and Bob Martyn for Suitcase Simpson, Ryne Duren, and a player to be named later,' who was Clete Boyer. I said, 'Casey, it seems like you gave up a hell of a lot.' And Casey, he had tears in his eyes, said, 'Yeah. That Martin is one hell of a ball player!' " Terry made a derisive laugh. "Ha, ha. So Casey says, 'You go over there, and you'll have a chance to pitch.' Casey was a very wise man. And I said, 'Casey, I just want you to know, the next time I face you I'm going to be out there to beat your ass.' And he kind of sat back there in his chair. And the first time I faced the Yankees in New York, I had a no-hitter going with two outs in the eighth. Sturdivant pitched against us, and we got twelve hits, we left guys on, two or three guys got thrown out at the plate, and it was really a frustrating game. And I was tired and I gassed at the end. The guy who beat me was Suitcase Simpson, the guy I was traded for."

"But then the Yankees got you back in May of 1959 in the Hector Lopez trade," I said.

"Yes," Terry said. "Casey told me personally that he got rid of me and that he got me back."

"When I really put things together was when Johnny Sain became the pitching coach in '61, and he taught me the hard slider," Terry said. "You put your fingers off to the side of the ball and throw it like a fast ball, and it comes up to the batter looking like a fast ball and breaks. I was 16–3 in '61, and I would have won twenty games if I hadn't hurt my arm during the middle of the summer. And I knew '62 would be a good year, and it was. I pitched 299 1/3 innings, gave up forty home runs, but hell, one game I won 8–4, another 21–7, and in that game they hit four solo home runs. You're pitching with big leads. And I had twenty-three wins, the most for a Yankee right-hander since 1928 when George Pipgras won twenty-four and Waite Hoyt won twenty-three. And I win two more in the classic, and for one year that's the most wins a right-hander in Yankee history ever won. Nobody ever knows about that. The hitters got all the publicity. But I'm real proud of that. And the last couple weeks of the season I didn't pitch much because we had a pretty good lead. I could have pitched over 300 innings which would have been the most in a long, long time. Early in the year I lost some close games, but after June I finished 16–5." It was Terry's year to be proud. Without him the Yankees could never have won. The rest of our discussion would not be about his successes.

"You were 17–15 in '63," I said. "Did you lose something that year?"

"Yeah," Terry said harshly. "I lost seven out of nine games in the first half of the season where I gave up two earned runs or less after pitching at least seven innings in each game. That's what I lost. 'Cause I was rolling out there every fourth day, and the club wasn't going too good, and that was the difference in winning twenty games or not. We didn't win those games when I gave up only two runs or less. Nine times! And at the end of the year I was tied with Camilo Pascual for the most complete games, eighteen, and Whitey just beat me out for the most innings pitched. Ain't pitching too bad, and at the end of the year Houk calls me and Sain in and says, 'I'm going to pitch Al Downing in the series. If he's right, he's going to shut the Dodgers out.' It was a shocker. What the hell! I was right against the Giants, a pretty good club the year before. And I was healthy and throwing the ball pretty good. Everybody said to Houk, 'You're going to use the Big Guy, aren't you?' meaning me, and he said, 'Oh yeah. He's big in my plans.' And I pitched three innings in relief in the 1963 series. Gad! And that kind of pissed me off.

"But I never said anything. I tried to do my job. But I was hurt by it—I was disgusted. I thought he'd played a hunch, he was strictly a hunch manager, and you don't manage that way. I thought that was a bad move on his part. I thought it was a move of desperation. I think he was overawed by Maury Wills and the Dodger running game. And it turned out the kid was nervous, and he didn't have it at all. He didn't have shit. And in '64 the kid was shoved in there again, and Ken Boyer grand-slammed a change, and again they didn't use me." Terry was biting off his words. "You're getting into a sensitive area," he said, taking a deep breath. "Then I ended up going to Cleveland. Houk didn't like my attitude, I guess." Terry chuckled sarcastically.

"What was your reaction when the Yankees made Houk the general manager in 1964?" I asked.

"I think that was a case similar to what Vince Lombardi did," Terry said.

"Ralph wanted to be an executive. Houk really should have been a field manager. He's not a front-office man. Can you picture putting this guy in with Gabe Paul or Bill Veeck? Making deals? They'd skin him alive. When you're general manager you have to be sophisticated about a lot of things. I think Houk's limitations were that he thought he was an evaluator of talent, that he was all everything. When he became general manager, he surrounded himself with a lot of Houk-men, yes-men. There was no value to it. A lot of good people left the organization. Johnny Sain left. Wally Moses left, these are the guys who did it, the men who can teach. There are a lot of coaches and back slappers and rah-rah guys, but they aren't teachers. They can't teach you a new pitch or how to pull the ball. Ask Blanchard what he thinks. Ask Boyer. Ask 'em. They'll tell you probably the same things I'll tell you. That Houk hogged all the credit. Houk would say, 'I told this guy to stand up more at the plate' or 'I told this guy to use the curve more.' But it wasn't Houk. It was Sain and Moses. But they weren't political or controversial. They just wanted to coach and teach and get paid a little, and they weren't interested in hogging the glory. They always tried to give the credit to the player, to the boy, and they were wonderful men. They didn't want to be managers. And Houk was afraid that somebody's success in the wings was going to sneak them in and take his job. People like Jack White left the organization. After the '63 season Sain asked for a raise to see how he stood with Houk, the general manager, and Houk gave him the 'you're not indispensable' routine. And all Sain wanted was a pat on the back. He just wanted a little congratulations.

"Houk was a great field manager," Terry said. "But he's a bullshitter and a smoke-blower, and he's lied to a lot of players and come up short. They say he's a players' manager. Bullshit. Nobody's a players' manager. The players are too wise for that now. The best thing about Houk is he has a burning desire to win, and the players like him for this. Also, he'll tolerate a lot of their mistakes.

"He just overstepped his boundaries," Terry continued. "He thought he was good at everything. And when CBS bought the Yankees, he got into bed with Mike Burke right away, and Burke is a nice guy and has since learned a great deal, but originally he didn't know, he wasn't a professional baseball man, and Burke needed somebody to show him the ropes so he could go to CBS, let them know what was going on. Houk sews up a three-year contract, and he's smoking cigars, and Yankee attendance went to zero—why were they smiling and giving him big contracts and not producing? And after he hired Johnny Keane, and Keane couldn't have been worse, then Houk comes back to manage like the Messiah." Terry clenched his fists and gritted his teeth. He continued. "I just know Houk very well," he said, speaking slowly, carefully. "He's a climber and a bullshitter, and I remember when he was still a coach, and he would say, 'Boy, I wish I were back there with you guys playing hearts.' I got to listen to this bullshit. Meanwhile he's carrying drinks to Topping and Webb, brown-nosing to beat hell, cause he knows Casey is going to retire. He's a Sammy Glick, see. What makes Sammy run?"

"When he was manager the first few years the players loved him," I said.

"Yeah," Terry said, "they dug it. Houk knew that he had to come in and take care of the stars and treat them good. The way management is nowadays, you got to get along with the players. Houk was wise in this respect, and he would battle the guys who were low-rated. Mantle, he loved Houk as a manager. Mickey's chink in his armor was that he was 4-F. Mickey saw his buddies sign up and get killed in the Korean War, and he wanted to join, too, but he couldn't. Mickey was a red-blooded American. And Houk, he was a silver-star man, and he dropped a couple war stories on Mantle and treated Mantle like he was great, and Mantle loved it, especially on the heels of how Stengel treated him. Then when the Yankees started to decline, the owners felt that Houk was the salvation. The looked to him for leadership, and he didn't quite have it. They needed him where he belonged. As field manager.''

Houk dealt Terry to Cleveland where he won eleven games the first half of the season and rarely pitched during the second half. Terry contends that he was offered and signed an illegal incentive contract calling for a $1,500 bonus for every game above ten he won. With Cleveland safely out of contention, after Terry won his eleventh game, there arose a sudden "youth movement." Terry sat the rest of the year.

"I said, 'Fuck Cleveland. I ain't never throwing another pitch for you. You just lost a ball player,' '' Terry continued. "So that was that. I walked out of there, and was traded to Kansas City, and Finley and I didn't get along, and I finished out with the Mets. What the hell! By that time all I wanted to do was play golf, anyway.'' Terry laughed, but it was not a very happy laugh. He really couldn't understand why the various managers and general managers had submarined his baseball career. The managers felt, or said they felt, he had lost something. Ralph will never accept that.

In one respect Terry is one of the lucky ones. After baseball he is doing something he really loves, playing and teaching golf. He is content, happy with his new career, his new life.

We had been talking for several hours, and it was time for his next lesson. In the shop, Terry and a couple of the members were talking golf talk again. ". . . and then I chipped out of the trap,'' the member said, "laid it up three feet from the green, and I three-putted.'' Terry was laughing. His baseball career had been in a different time and a different place—a long time ago.

In 1962 in the National League, with seven games remaining in the season, the Los Angeles Dodgers boasted a four-game lead over the rival San Francisco Giants, but the Dodgers ceased winning and the Giants won a game more than they lost, as both teams finished the year with identical 101–61 records, necessitating a three-game playoff. The first two games the teams split, and in the finale the Dodgers, led by Maury Wills who stole 104 bases including three in this game, were ahead 4–2 in the ninth inning. The Giants tied the score and then strolled to the pennant when Dodger pitcher Stan Williams walked Jim Davenport with the bases loaded to let in the winning run. All of Brooklyn was laughing at the Dodger defeat.

When the well-rested Yankees arrived in San Francisco for the first two games, everyone was in a gay mood. Flying cross-country, each of the Yankees had tried to guess the exact minute when the plane would touch down on the

Coast, the winner to receive free use of a rental car for three days. "There's no use even entering," Whitey Ford said. "Yogi, the lucky bastard, will win it." Berra guessed the plane would land at 6:15. The plane landed at 6:15.

Manager Houk chose Ford to open the series, and Giant manager Al Dark chose his most rested pitcher, Billy O'Dell, the ex-Oriole Baby Bird. O'Dell found himself in trouble from the start. With two outs Richardson and Tresh singled and Maris drove them home with a double, a wind-aided fly that carried against the chain-link outfield fence. Ford allowed runs in the second and third innings, his world series-consecutive-shutout-inning skein ended at thirty-three and two-thirds, but these were the only runs he allowed. With the score 2–2 in the seventh inning Clete Boyer, a standout in the '61 series, led off against O'Dell with a line drive home run over the left-field fence to win the game. The Yankees added three insurance runs, and Ford won his fifth-straight series game 6–2.

Ralph Terry, 23–12, was matched against Jack Sanford, 24–7, in the second game. Sanford, signed originally by the Philadelphia Phils, had been dealt to the Giants for Ruben Gomez and Valmy Thomas, a disastrous deal for the Phils engineered by their general manager, Roy Hamey, now the Yankee general manager. Sanford and Terry pitched very much alike. Sanford had a tailing fast ball, a fast curve, and an off-speed looping curve which he used as a change-up, and he had excellent control of his pitches. Against the Yankees in the second game Sanford allowed three hits and no runs. Terry only allowed two hits, but both resulted in scores. One was by Willie McCovey—batting in the seventh the mammoth Giant launched a titanic home run that sailed far over the right-field fence for the second Giant run. The 2–0 San Francisco win tied the series at one each.

The teams returned to New York and took a day off to recover from jet lag. Houk chose Bill Stafford to pitch against Billy Pierce, and for seven innings Pierce, the ex-White Sox star, battled Stafford to a scoreless tie. In the seventh Tresh and Mantle singled, and when Maris singled to McCovey in right and McCovey bobbled the ball, both runners scored and Maris slid safely into second. Ellie Howard then hit a deep fly ball to Willie Mays playing center field, and Maris alertly tagged and raced to third, later scoring on a ground out. With the Yankees ahead 3–0 in the eighth inning, Felipe Alou ripped a fast ball back through the box. The ball crashed sickeningly against Stafford's right shinbone, causing a lump the size of a grapefruit. Stafford painfully struggled through the final two innings, retiring the Giants in the eighth but allowing a double by Mays in the ninth and a two-run home run by Ed Bailey that blooped tantalizingly down the right-field Stadium line, landing just out of the reach of Maris in right. At the end of the 3–2 victory Stafford could barely walk off the mound, and he did not pitch in another game in this series. Again the Yankees led.

And again the Giants bounced back. In the fourth game, with the score 2–2 in the seventh inning and both starters Ford and Juan Marichal out of the game, the Giants rallied. When Yankee reliefer Jim Coates walked Jim Davenport and allowed a double by Matty Alou, manager Houk went out to the mound and replaced Coates with Marshall Bridges, his bullpen ace. Houk ordered pinch hitter Bob Nieman walked to load the bases. Bridges retired Harvey Kuenn, in 1959 the American League batting champion, but Chuck Hiller, a low-average slap-hitter who had hit only three home runs all year, pulled a fly ball toward the Stadium short right-field porch, and with Maris backed as far as he could against the wall, the ball just cleared the reach of the Yankee outfielder for a grand slam homer and the ball game. Don Larsen received credit for the 7–3 win, and the series was tied at two apiece.

The fifth game, postponed a day because of rain, matched Terry and Sanford again. Both pitched well, and in the eighth with the score tied 2–2, Sanford tired and allowed singles by Kubek and Richardson. Facing Tom Tresh, Sanford threw a fast ball a little too good, and Tresh pulled the ball into the right-field stands for a three-run home run, the winning margin in the 5–3 game. Before Tresh's home run, in sixteen innings against the Yankees Sanford had allowed six hits and no runs. After the game in the clubhouse Yankee publicity director Bob Fishel kidded Tresh. "How do you like Corvettes?" he asked the Yankee rookie, referring to the prize given to the outstanding series performer. Five games into the series Tresh was leading both teams in hitting.

Also in the clubhouse was Casey Stengel, now the manager of the fledgling New York Mets. Stengel made a point of congratulating Ralph Terry, finally a series winner after two losses against the Pirates in 1960, a loss to Cincinnati in '61, and a loss to Sanford and the Giants in game number two of this series. "I'm glad you finally did it," Stengel said to Terry. The Old Man warmly shook hands with the young pitcher. Terry was moved. "I'm only sorry," he said, "I couldn't have done it for you."

Typhoon Frieda was pelting the San Francisco Bay area when the series shifted back to the Coast for the final two games, and for four interminable days everybody sat around waiting for the rain to cease. When it finally did stop, more than six inches of water had been deposited on the peninsula, and to help dry out Candlestick Park, the Giants hired helicopters to hover inches over the field. While it had poured outside, inside the elegant Town House the Yankees played poker all night for high stakes to break the monotony. On another floor general manager Roy Hamey, also with time on his hands, called manager Houk to his room to present him with an idea that he and owner Dan Topping were considering. Houk, finishing the second year of a two-year contract, assumed Hamey was going to extend his contract. That was not why Hamey had called Houk, and to open the conversation Hamey began rather obtusely. "Have you ever thought about the good side of the game?" Hamey asked. Houk had no idea what in the world he was talking about.

"I'm going to retire at the end of next year," Hamey said, "and I'd like you to take my job." Houk looked at his boss like Hamey was crazy. The idea of becoming general manager rather overwhelmed him.

"Think about it," Hamey said. "We'll talk about it later."

On October 15, five days after game number five, the soggy field was finally playable. Candlestick Park was filled to capacity, and the Giant fans enjoyed watching Billy Pierce three-hit the Yankees 5–2. With no score after three innings, Whitey Ford lost the game in the fourth when, with Mays on first and Felipe Alou on second, he tried to pick Alou off and threw the ball twenty feet to the right of second base, where it bounced into the outfield and rolled dead in the high, wet grass. Before Maris could retrieve the ball, Alou scored, the first of three Giant runs that inning. Maris, playing with a bad shoulder, homered against Pierce in the fifth, but the Giants scored two more runs in the bottom of the inning and went on to win 5–2. The other Yankee run came in the eighth on a double by Boyer followed by a Richardson single. Ford lost his first series game after five straight wins.

The evening before the final game Mantle, Ford, Berra, Terry, and Boyer continued their high-stakes poker game in Mickey's hotel room. Toward the end of the evening, battling for several hundred dollars in the kitty were Yogi and Ralph Terry, the scheduled starting pitcher for the seventh game. Yogi, reputed among the Yankees to be the luckiest man alive, had been dealt a king-high flush and, certain of victory, was plowing chips into the middle of the table trying to force Terry to fold or foolishly challenge. Terry had four spades and was hoping to buy a fifth for a spade flush, and perhaps recklessly, he stayed in. Berra stood pat. Terry bought one card, and again Yogi plowed chips into the kitty, and again Terry stayed with him. When showdown time came, Yogi triumphantly laid down his king-high club flush. One at a time Terry showed his spades: three, five, ten, jack, and ace. As Terry gleefully raked in the chips, Berra across from him was mumbling swear words. Terry was saying, "I beat Yogi. I beat Yogi. Man. It's an omen." Ralph collected $300 and went to bed.

Only because of the three-day rain delay was Terry able to pitch the seventh game. He had pitched game five a full six days earlier, and now he was rested. With Stafford injured, had it not rained Houk would have been forced to start rookie Jim Bouton.

At Candlestick Park for the seventh game, the Yankees were primarily interested in getting the game over with and going home. They were restless, and though it was a world series, the long wait for the last two games to be played removed much of the tension normally present. It was more like an exhibition series. When the game finally began, it moved along quickly, Terry matching goose eggs with Jack Sanford until the fifth inning when the Yankees loaded the bases with nobody out. Manager Al Dark, willing to trade a run for a double play, kept his infield back, and Tony Kubek obligingly grounded into a double play as Bill Skowron scored.

The Giants, meanwhile, could do nothing with Terry. They didn't get their first hit until the sixth, a cheap single by pitcher Sanford, and Terry, unusually fast and sharp, helped himself by not pitching two balls in a row through the first eight innings.

Both pitchers were aided by a forty-mile-an-hour gale blowing in from left field, but especially Terry as the Giant long-ball hitters lofted sixteen fly balls into the gloves of Yankee outfielders. Tresh in left caught six of them, a series record, and with the wind playing havoc with fly balls, he was hot having an easy time of it. On one fly Tresh loudly called for a ball that the gale wind started blowing back toward the infield. The young outfielder had to race to the edge of the infield dirt, passing shortstop Tony Kubek, to catch the ball. In the seventh inning, with two Giants out, Tresh made a spectacular catch of a Willie Mays line drive that was heading for the left-field corner, a certain double. Tresh raced thirty yards to the line and caught the ball in the webbing of his glove just before crashing into the extreme left-field corner wall of the ball park, out of sight of the Yankee dugout. When Tresh emerged with the ball, the Yankees rejoiced, and when Willie McCovey then launched a triple into the wind far over Mantle's head in center field, the catch by Tresh took on even greater significance.

With the Yankees still leading 1–0, Matty Alou, a clever bat manipulator and .300 hitter, led off the ninth for the Giants. He bunted for a base hit. The next two batters, Chuck Hiller and Felipe Alou also tried to bunt, but they were unsuccessful and Terry struck them out. Man on first, two outs in the bottom of the ninth. Willie Mays stepped into the batter's box.

Twice Terry threw the Giant immortal inside fast balls, trying to jam him, and twice they were called balls. On the next pitch Terry threw an excellent pitch, a low and away fast ball, but Mays opened his stance and lined an opposite-field hit into the right-field corner of the ball park. Roger Maris in right, running hard to his left on wet and treacherous underfooting, completed a desperate race for the ball as Alou on first rounded second and headed for third and perhaps home. Maris, who had suffered with a dead throwing arm for the past couple of months, sought out second-baseman Richardson, who had been keeping the secret by racing far into right field to take the relays. Maris hit Richardson on a short throw, and Bobby, aware of Alou's speed, wheeled and fired home a perfect peg. Matty Alou, playing safe and smart, rounded third and held up. Terry, backing up the play behind home, slipped in the mud and fell down, and while he was brushing himself off, manager Ralph Houk called time out and walked to the mound to discuss the situation with his pitcher. Willie McCovey, who had homered against Terry in the second game and had hit that long triple in the seventh inning of this one, was the batter, with Orlando Cepeda following him. Cepeda in 1962 hit thirty-five home runs, drove in 114 runs and hit .306. At the mound Houk really didn't know whether Terry should pitch to McCovey or walk McCovey and pitch to Cepeda. With men on second and third, a base hit would score both runners. Pitching to either Giant batting star seemed equally odious.

"I really don't know what the hell I'm doing out here," Houk grinned at Terry, "but I thought I'd better come out and talk with you anyway." Terry smiled at his manager's levity in the face of the situation. "What I'm getting at is," Houk continued, "do you want to pitch to this guy or walk him?"

"I'd rather pitch to him in good spots than walk him," Terry said. "If I walk him I'd be losing my advantage, 'cause I'd have to be much more careful pitching with the bases loaded." Terry had remembered that Dodger pitcher Stan Williams had walked in the winning Giant run with the bases loaded to lose the pennant to the Giants. "Let's give McCovey good stuff just outside the strike zone and hope he'll fish for it." Houk agreed and left the mound for the dugout.

Around second base Bobby Richardson and Tony Kubek were talking things over. "I hope McCovey doesn't hit the ball to you," Kubek said. Richardson wanted to know why. " 'Cause you've already made a couple of errors, and if you blow this one, we're in real trouble.'' Tony smiled, and both Richardson and Willie Mays, standing on second, laughed. The second-base umpire joined the Yankee infielders. "Can I have your cap if this guy makes out?'' the ump asked Bobby. "I have a little nephew who would like to have it.'' Bobby agreed to give it to him.

On the mound Ralph Terry, watched by 40,000 in Candlestick Park and 40,000,000 on television, was sweating profusely from under his cap, wishing the game was over already. McCovey, at 6 feet 5 inches and 200 pounds, stood in his size-seventeen shoes at the plate, slowly swishing his big bat back and forth. Kubek at shortstop was mumbling to himself that he was sure glad that McCovey was left-handed. Tresh in left field was telling himself that he was sure glad he wasn't still playing shortstop. Richardson at second stood his ground grimly.

Terry's first pitch to Big Stretch McCovey was a slow curve, low and outside. Swinging off-stride, McCovey hit it off the end of his bat, the ball lofting lazily down the right field line. Maris thought he had a chance to catch it, but the gusting crosswinds caught the ball and drifted it deep into the seats, foul. Not wishing to throw the same pitch twice in a row, Terry fired an inside fast ball, putting all the strength he could muster behind the pitch. McCovey swung and sent a screaming line drive on a blur toward Richardson at second. Without moving a step, Richardson caught the ball chest-high for the third out, going down to one knee to be certain the ball did not get past him. It was a relatively easy play, but because of the ball's tremendous speed, had it been hit two feet to either side of him both runners would have scored and the Giants would have won the game and the series. Ten years later McCovey confided to Richardson that it was the hardest ball he ever hit. Richardson as promised flipped his cap to the umpire, while on the mound Terry triumphantly tossed his cap and glove high in the air.

The series victory, Terry's second of the series, was a final vindication for a man still haunted by the spectre of Bill Mazerowski's 1960 home run. Said Terry in the clubhouse after the game, "I want to thank God for a second opportunity. You don't often get a second chance to prove yourself, in baseball or in life.''

1963

The Man with the Golden Glove, Clete Boyer . . . Great pitching . . . Super Sub John Blanchard . . . Another pennant . . . A Koufax, Drysdale world series

After the events of the previous fall and winter, it was most fortunate that in 1963 there was a spring to have training in. In late October 1962 President Kennedy, alarmed that the Russians were setting up missile bases on the U.S. doorstep in Cuba, ordered a quarantine of Cuban waters, U. S. Navy warships blockading the area. Any Russian ship carrying missiles was to be stopped and searched, and if such a ship refused, it was to be blown out of the waters. It was like the shoot-out at the OK Corral, except that instead of six-guns, each side would be exchanging fifty-megaton atomic bombs.

Fortunately for the world the Russians decided that having missiles in Cuba wasn't worth having the world destroyed, and Premier Khrushchev turned the convoy of ships around to avoid a confrontation. Castro called Khrushchev a coward.

At the Yankee spring training camp in Fort Lauderdale Ralph Houk optimistically predicted that the Yankees would again win the pennant. "Why not?" he reasoned. "We're better than we were last year." No one disagreed with him. This would be Houk's last season as Yankee manager, because he finally accepted Hamey's offer to become general manager in '64 during a meeting held on Dan Topping's yacht, away from reporters. It was their little year-long secret—shared by Yogi Berra, 38 years old, this year a player-coach, next year Houk's replacement as Yankee manager. It would be a year of instruction and learning for Yogi while Houk was to "learn him all his experience," as catcher Bill Dickey once had done. Berra seemed to be just what management needed to fight the fledgling Mets and Casey Stengel for newspaper space. On the road in 1962 the Yankees had drawn over 2,000,000 fans. At Yankee Stadium New Yorkers, still reacting negatively to Stengel's discharge as manager, began flocking to the Polo Grounds to watch the Old Man orchestrate his Amazin' Mets.

The 1963 pennant seemed a shoo-in. General manager Roy Hamey had made one trade over the winter, and it seemed to be the icing on an already overly frosted cake. Hamey traded Moose Skowron, for nine years the Yankee first-baseman, to the L. A. Dodgers for starting pitcher Stan Williams, a strong right-hander, 15–12 in 1961, 14–12 in '62, a hard-working operator with a live fast ball and vast potential. To replace Moose at first, there was Joe Pepitone, the free-wheeling, skinny kid who was excellent defensively and had a quick, powerful bat. Pepitone started quickly and his nine home runs led the team in the spring.

The team figured to be stronger than in '62 because Tony Kubek would be at shortstop for the entire season, and Tom Tresh, in left field, would have both experience and security. The rest of the team was set. In the infield with Pepitone and Kubek was second-baseman Bobby Richardson and third-baseman Clete Boyer, the two best at their positions in the league, and at catcher was all-star Ellie Howard. With Tresh in the outfield were Mantle and Maris, the heart of the Yankee attack, Maris the MVP of the league in 1960 and '61, Mantle the MVP in 1956, '57, and '62.

On the mound in addition to Williams was Whitey Ford, 17–8 in 1962, looking forward to a twenty-game season this year; Ralph Terry, 23–12 last year; and Bill Stafford, 14–9 the last two years but still hoping for a twenty-game season if the batters would get him just a few more runs. Also there was second-year man Jim Bouton, a fearless competitor in the mold of raging Vic Raschi who impressed the coaching staff more with every outing. On the mound Bouton was a terror, as on every overhand pitch he threw his right arm forward and launched his body toward the plate with every ounce of strength and determination within him. Mantle had labeled him a bulldog, and now everyone was calling him Bulldog. Pitching coach John Sain had taught Bouton to throw the hard curve (slerve), the pitch that had made Terry so successful, and the critics were predicting that if Bouton could break into the starting rotation, he could be the star of the staff for years to come. In the bullpen the Yankees would be strong if their relievers stayed healthy. Marshall Bridges, the '62 bullpen star, had to miss the first month of training while recovering from a gunshot wound he suffered in mid-February in Fort Lauderdale. Bridges was trying to pick up a girl in a bar down there when she took out a pistol and shot him in the knee, breaking a bone. Marshall was now called Lead Leg and Bang Bang by his teammates. In the bullpen along with Bridges was another re-cuperating star, Luis Arroyo, who after missing most of '62 with arm miseries, was in camp hoping to make a comeback. Bud Daley and Jim Coates were available, and rookie Hal Reniff was a possibility. On the bench the Yankees boasted Hector Lopez, the best fourth outfielder in the league, a consistent hitter and an improved outfielder—with a gentle disposition and great patience—a perfect substitute both physically and mentally. John Blanchard, catcher-outfielder-first-baseman, home-run-hitting pinch hitter, was also a valuable sub as was infielder Phil Linz, who would have been a starter on almost any other club. Another infield sub, rookie Pedro Gonzalez, batted .325 in the spring and showed potential. On paper, before the first regular season game was played, the pennant was a TKO for the Yankees.

An injury to Whitey Ford's pitching arm was the only disquieting note of the training period. He felt pain when he threw his curve ball. There also were some less serious injuries. Tony Kubek bent over to field a ground ball, and suddenly felt great pain in his neck and shoulders. He couldn't straighten up. He was better after a rest and the problem was diagnosed as a spasm.

The Yankees completed spring training 12–19—a meaningless record. When the season started, they would be ready.

. When the season did start, almost everyone performed as expected, and though the Yankees trailed Chicago and Baltimore by a game or two in May, there was little concern. By the end of the month Ellie Howard was being touted for MVP along with Tommy Tresh. Howard hit a half-dozen home runs and drove in the winning run in late innings five times, in addition to being superlative behind the plate. Tresh, hitting home runs and establishing himself as an integral force in the Yankee offense, was playing left field like he had been playing there all his life. The untested Joe Pepitone was hitting well and often, and his fielding prompted Dan Daniel, a chronicler of ancient baseball greats, to compare Pepitone to Frank Chance of the 1900 Chicago Cubs, hitherto accepted as the greatest fielding first-baseman in the game. Pepitone had great range, much more than Bill Skowron, and as a result Bobby Richardson, at the peak of his career at second base, was able to play closer to second, allowing shortstop Tony Kubek to play deeper in the hole at short, and giving third-baseman Clete Boyer the leeway to hug the third-base line. On opening day Pepitone hit two home runs, and by the end of May he was hitting .310, in the top ten of American League batters along with Mantle, who, though playing excellently, had painfully swollen and abused legs. The incomparable third-baseman, Clete Boyer, was a pleasant surprise at bat, hitting .336, fourth in the league. Roger Maris, bothered by muscle pulls and a bad back, was still receiving a bad press, and his efforts remained largely unnoticed and unappreciated. During one game, obeying Ralph Houk's orders not to exert himself racing to first when he hit routine ground balls, Maris jogged down the line on a grounder to short. The shortstop, who fumbled the ball, thus had time to throw Maris out, and the fans, unaware of the extent of his injuries, booed him and threw garbage at him, causing Roger to lose his cool and once again give them all the finger—this time on TV. "I'll only satisfy people when I get out of baseball," Maris said bitterly. "Everything will be all right with them when I'm gone."

The biggest disappointment was Kubek. He was fielding as well as ever, but his quick bat was gone, and he looked pathetic during a 1–35 streak which sunk his average far below .200. Kubek, in a panic, feared the premature end of his career.

Another career which seemed at an early end was that of Bill Stafford. Determined to finally win twenty games in 1963, Stafford had pitched a strong-man forty innings during the exhibition season. He had been sharp and fast and in control. But during his first regular season start, a night game in Kansas City played in 30-degree weather, Stafford, who had been rolling along on a three-hitter for almost seven innings, threw an extra hard fast ball, and from within his arm there emitted a snapping sound like the cracking of a twig. He took himself out of the game and then rested for ten days. In his next outing he lasted less than three innings. He rested again, this time for two weeks, and in the next game he lasted less than four innings. By the end of May Stafford had an ERA of 5.30, and the reality of his failure was leaving him nervous and heartsick. In the same Kansas City game that finished Stafford, Bud Daley, excellent all spring, pitched one inning in relief. The raw, freezing weather caused Daley's arm to ache when he was finished. Three days later he awoke with a lump on his elbow the size of a grapefruit. It was the only inning Daley pitched all year.

Stan Williams, uninjured, wasn't pitching particularly well. One start he would be excellent, the next unacceptable. Neither Houk nor pitching coach John Sain nor anyone else could figure out what was keeping Williams from becoming an outstanding pitcher, and frustrations grew as Williams continued to flounder. On the bright side Whitey Ford, though losing a few tough games, was 5–3, and Ralph Terry, pitching as well as the year before, wasn't compiling an impressive record only because he wasn't getting support in 2–1, 3–2, 2–0, and 2–0 losses. His earned run average was low, and he knew that his record soon would come around.

The biggest surprise was Bouton. When Stafford was suffering from a sore arm, Houk inserted Bouton into the rotation, and in his first start on May 13 the cocky kid pitched a two-hit shutout over the Orioles. After the game the reporters gathered around him for some quotable sayings. Jim didn't want to talk. "I'm just a second-year man," he said. "I have no intention of being controversial. I'm a company man." The writers were impressed by his class. By the end of May Bouton was 6–1, the savior of the staff, and his energetic and effective pitching was the talk of the town. Mickey Mantle likened him to Camilo Pascual. "He has that big curve like Pascual," Mickey bragged, "and I think his fast ball is even better." There was only one reservation about Bouton. He enjoyed reading intellectual books, and while the others played cards, he read.

In June there was an epidemic of injuries. Tom Tresh raced after a pop fly in shallow left field in Fenway Park as shortstop Tony Kubek was angling back toward it, each set of eyes glued on the descending ball, and just after Kubek settled under it, Tresh rammed into him with his shoulder, and they both tumbled dazed to the ground. Kubek, his left leg paining him and his neck jarred, was unable to continue, and he left the game, returning two weeks later. A few days later, on June 5, the Yankees were in Baltimore playing the Orioles. Brooks Robinson, the O's star third-baseman lined a Whitey Ford breaking pitch toward the right center-field fence as Mickey Mantle raced after it in pursuit. Mantle was closing fast, but before he could reach the descending ball, his flight was intercepted by the chain-link outfield fence, and at top speed he pancaked into it. His left spike caught in the wire mesh, and he fell awkwardly. Roger Maris and Bobby Richardson raced to Mantle. He was in tears. "It's broken," he said. "It's broken. I know it's broken." Mickey was right. His left foot was broken, and if Mantle played again before August he would be doing well. Not a week later Maris, too, was injured, slamming a foul tip off his left ankle, missing several games. Phil Linz, Kubek's replacement at shortstop, tried to steal third and ripped ligaments in his right knee, killing the best opportunity he had to prove himself. Until Kubek returned in mid-June, manager Houk shifted Boyer to shortstop and played a recent acquisition, Harry Bright, a third.

With all these players injured, the Yankees proceeded to laugh in the face of adversity, winning ten of eleven games. Maris returned and hit over .300

despite the opposition pitching one left-hander after another against the Yankees, especially in the Stadium. Usually a home-run powerhouse, this year the Yankees were winning with pitching and defense. Houk, dissatisfied with Stan Williams and fearful that Stafford's arm had lost some of its strength, called up Al Downing from Richmond on June 10, and with Downing and Jim Bouton joining Whitey Ford and Ralph Terry in the rotation, no team could match starting foursomes with New York.

Bouton, winning, completing games, losing his cap with every frenetic pitch, was 10–2 before the all-star break, and quickly was becoming one of the most popular Yankees with both fans and newspapermen. There were clubhouse jokes that he was perhaps a little too friendly, though the comments were never made with malice. Jim was a little eccentric, but most important he was winning, and winning often. Whitey Ford, at his peak, had won ten of eleven starts after losing his first two decisions of the season using the fast curve he and John Sain were developing, plus a screwball, a spitball, a mud ball and a diamond-ring ball. Ralph Terry, 8–8, continued to pitch complete games, yet lose the close ones, and his record did not indicate his effectiveness.

The catalyst was Downing. A soft-spoken, well-mannered gentleman in the Yankee tradition and the first black ever to start for the team, Downing got his first start against the Washington Senators on June 11. In 95-degree muggy heat in Washington, D.C., the little left-hander allowed two hits, no runs, struck out nine, and had the crowd oohing at the blinding speed of his fast ball. His fast curve, also taught to him by Johnny Sain, crackled and dropped sharply as it reached the plate. A black Sandy Koufax was the ballyhoo. He looked overpoweringly good.

These four men: Ford, Terry, Bouton, and Downing, represented both the excellence of the present, and the future continuation of Yankee dominance. Plus the Yankees were still counting on Bill Stafford to return to his earlier form. Stafford, pitching in spots, at times looked good, but his arm hurt and too often his fast ball would fail to explode, and base hits would shell him from the mound.

Behind these men the Yankees boasted their nonpareil inner defense, and this combination was enough for the Yankees to pass both Chicago and Baltimore and take over first place by mid-June. Almost anything a batter hit on the ground was converted into an out. Joe Pepitone at first base played sixty games in a row without making an error. He made six all season. Bobby Richardson and Tony Kubek were the best DP combination in the majors, and at third was cat-like, daring Clete Boyer with a howitzer for an arm. It was an infield that made defense fashionable, and in 1963 it compiled the best fielding percentage in Yankee history.

Playing Boyer at third permanently was one of Ralph Houk's first changes when he became manager in 1961. Casey Stengel, never impressed with Clete's bat, preferred others. Houk, seeing something special in the way Boyer operated around third, gave the youngster the opportunity to play, told him he would be great, told the press he would be great, and Boyer proceeded to fulfill Houk's expectations.

Through mid-June of 1963 Boyer, in addition to saving many games with his extraordinary fielding, was winning them with his bat. He was fifth in the league in hitting, at .316 with ten home runs going into the summer months, and though he was usually the number-eight batter in the Yankee lineup, Houk did switch him around, at times even batting him fourth. Off the field he enjoyed liquor and good times, but on it, Boyer was serious and spectacular. During the three years Houk managed, Boyer led the league in putouts, assists, and double plays, over even the celebrated Brooks Robinson, though it was Robinson, not Boyer, who inexplicably kept winning the Golden Glove award. In 1962 Boyer came within nine assists of the record 405 set by Harland Clift of the 1937 St. Louis Browns. But Robinson won the Golden Glove that year. Robinson never had Boyer's range or arm, but what Brooks could do better than Boyer was hit.

Boyer electrified viewers of the 1961 world series with his defense, throwing out runners from his knees after desperate, diving stops of bullet-hard ground balls. He was the best defensive third-baseman the Yankees ever had. Only when the Yankees stopped winning, when the power hitters stopped hitting, did Boyer and his magic glove become expendable. In 1965 Clete, drunk, punched out a man in a Fort Lauderdale bar, and during the '66 season, after eight years as a Yankee, he was traded to the Atlanta Braves for Bill Robinson, Minor League Player of the Year, an outstanding prospect and a Yankee bomb. General Manager Lee MacPhail said that Boyer was traded because he drank too much. His teammates said it was not his drinking, but his independence and his outspoken, biting nature that hastened his departure.

It was warm in Atlanta in January, unseasonably warm and everyone was walking around in shirt sleeves, enjoying the Georgian sunshine. On Stewart Avenue, near the municipal airport, sits the Golden Glove Lounge, a one-story brown brick building set at the end of a large parking lot. Entering and closing the door behind me, everything suddenly went pitch-black, and I had to stand still for several seconds, fearful of tripping on an unseen step or piece of furniture or walking into a wall. My eyes slowly adjusted to the light—long, mysterious, purple florescents overhead—and in the darkness I perceived a massive glass-and-metal jukebox and two large dance floors. Iron fencing separated them on either side of the central four-cornered bar. On the jukebox Charlie Pride, the black country-and-western singer, was sadly crooning, "Did you happen to see the most beautiful girl in the woooooorld." Once Pride had been in the lounge as a guest of one of the Atlanta Braves, who often drink here. Hank Aaron had been invited to come here. Aaron chose not to go. In Atlanta, where many things are either black or white, this part of Atlanta is white, and the Golden Glove's clientele is white only—though by choice, I was told. The musty smell of stale spilled beer permeated the air, and around the bar there was a handful of people taking their late-afternoon drinks. Two of the men, with large stomachs protruding, were softly talking football, arguing the merits of the local Falcons.

Benny, who is an ex-football player friend of Clete Boyer (owner of the Golden Glove), bought another drink and tried to explain his personal frustrations since his shoulder was separated, ending his pro aspirations. An aura of sadness and lost hopes hung heavy. "We have good people come in here," Benny said. "Every afternoon almost I come here to drink, to pass the time, and to visit with my people. If you're lonely, you can't beat it, you know. Drinking, I mean. Best thing in the world for the blues." He laughed sadly.

I was supposed to meet Boyer at the bar of the Golden Glove Lounge at six in the evening, but he didn't arrive until nine. He had spent the day drinking and he had forgotten, but he was contrite and apologetic. Tomorrow he was going to Japan to start the baseball season there. Today he was reveling. He didn't really want to go to Japan, but the pay was too good to pass up, and if he didn't play in Japan he would have to give up the game entirely. So on the last day before his Asian exile, Boyer was downing a few, enjoying himself. By nine o'clock the live band had arrived, rocking above all conversation, and it was necessary to take our drinks into the parking lot to be heard. We picked a late model Oldsmobile, placed ourselves on the hood of the sedan, and had a liquid picnic. Clete, while not drunk, wasn't close to cold sober either.

Clete Boyer grew up in Alba, Missouri, in a family of thirteen kids. All of the Boyer brothers played professional baseball, with Ken, Clete, and Cloyd reaching the big leagues. "What do you remember about the Boyer family when you were a kid?" I asked him. Clete smiled broadly. "It's like when I went to Japan," he said, "the first thing everybody asked was, 'What did you notice about Japan?' A lot of fucking Japs over there. And it's like that about the Boyer family. There's a lot of fucking Boyers."

"When you came to the Yankees, Casey Stengel was the manager," I said.

"Casey, I'll tell you," Boyer said, "he always bragged about me playing third base. We had that little spat there in the 1960 world series when he took me out for a pinch hitter in the second inning of the first game, but with Casey it was nothing personal. It was like whipping one of your kids. The next day you still love him. I'll tell you, one thing Casey always said, 'That boy can drink, but he'll go out the next day and throw the ball all the way across the diamond on his knees.' He always bragged about me." Clete's reddened eyes were glistening, mostly from drink, partially from reflection.

"I don't know," Boyer said softly. "A lot of people, to them he was supposed to be some kind of a god, and I think all rookies just looked up to him, and he couldn't do anything wrong. And I remember him sending Deron Johnson out one year, and you know, the Yankees had so many great young ball players that you had to send someone out because you only have room for twenty-five guys, and Casey told Deron to go down to the minors to learn how to bunt! Ha! I mean guys believe stuff like that, and he'd tell guys to go down and learn how to slide or something like that, and the young ball players believed that bullshit of his. Actually I don't think Casey liked young ball players. I think he liked that Old Pro that was developed. He gave me the greatest disappointment I ever had in my life, because in 1960 I started playing regularly when Casey got sick, went to the hospital, and Ralph Houk took over and put me, John Blanchard, and Hector Lopez in the lineup. I started playing, and from then on I played 124 games, and then I started in the world series, and the first time up in the first game the old bastard took me out for a pinch hitter." Clete laughed the final few embarrassing words. "And there was no reason for it. It was one of the biggest thrills in my life, starting in a world series, and in the bottom of the second inning the son of a bitch took me out for a pinch hitter. I wanted to hit him over the head with the fucking bat. And then I got mad at some of the writers. You know the writers in New York, how sharp they are. And they wrote some things I didn't actually say, but they said I did, and so then I didn't start until the sixth and seventh games of the series. It was probably my biggest thrill and biggest disappointment on the same day. He didn't have to take me out in the second inning and knock my confidence. But I'll tell you, I'm glad I played under Casey. Really. He'll go down in history. Everybody knows Casey Stengel. So it's one thing I can always remember. I played under Casey Stengel."

"Did you prefer the way Ralph Houk treated his players?" I asked.

"Ralph Houk," Clete said. "I loved him. I thought he was the greatest son of a bitch who ever wore a pair of spikes. For three years he was the greatest son of a bitch who ever lived. I ain't kidding you. At one time I thought he walked on water. That was when I was young. I just wanted an opportunity to play, and he let me play and never bothered me, and he really stuck with me, and although I was supposed to be a horseshit hitter, he didn't take me out much for a pinch hitter." Clete chuckled. "Of course he didn't have to because the Yankees were always ahead, and I was noted for my glove, but I didn't think I was that bad of a hitter. I thought I did a pretty good job in the clutch. It's just that we had so many super-stars on our team, where in the hell am I going to hit?" Clete cracked up. "I mean I was lucky even to be in the lineup. I'm not shitting anybody. I looked at those monuments in center field every day, and I took my hat off. And I appreciated it every day that I played, boy, and I'll never forget that. I still can't believe that I played for the New York Yankees for eight years. You know?" He smiled.

"It seemed that you were always suffering little injuries that affected your average," I said.

"That doesn't cause me to be a horseshit hitter," Clete said. Again he laughed. "Cause I knew what I was, knew what I was supposed to be doing. That's the one thing that the Yankees taught you. To learn what you *can* do, and to try to do that. And I knew that my fielding was my number-one asset, and I appreciated it and loved it, and the New York writers wrote good about me, and I took a lot more pride in it. You know, I didn't know I was supposed to be so good, but every time I'd read where I'd make a pretty good play, Christ, pretty soon I thought that I was the greatest third-baseman in the world. And then I *really* started making some good plays. And if they had written bad about me, I probably would have become self-conscious. So I know how important confidence is in baseball. When I was on the Braves I could tell Darrell Evans that he's a good third-baseman, and I'll be a son of a bitch, he'll be a good third-baseman. Piss on this other bullshit, stand this way or that way. Tell a guy he's good, and he's going to be good. You know, this is really what the game's all about, confidence. And in 1964 I just never could get started under Yogi. Yogi Berra never built any confidence in anybody. I don't think he was the type of man to build your confidence. You know? And I wouldn't play, and I wouldn't play, and I couldn't do nothing for him, and then pretty soon you get to looking at yourself, and you don't have any confidence at all, and you can't do nothing. And then you wonder why they even keep you, why they don't release you. I guess it really wasn't Yogi's fault, but I guess I tried to take it out on him. He just wasn't my type of manager, although Yogi must be a good manager."

"Why did they fire him?" I asked.

"I don't know," Clete said, "but my personal opinion was that Houk hated him. I don't think Ralph liked Yogi."

"So Houk hired Johnny Keane to replace him," I said.

"Yeah, Keane," Boyer said, "and Jesus this was a shame, cause he was a great person, you know, really religious and such a super person, the guy you want as your neighbor, but he doesn't belong in a uniform. And that's a shame. He was like a Jekyll and Hyde. That man was sick when he got a baseball uniform on. He didn't know how to handle men. He used to say, 'You guys make the plays, play your regular game, and I'll figure out a way to beat this team,' silly statements that you didn't understand. You know what I mean? And he thought everybody was supposed to play when they were hurt and that everybody playing baseball was a machine. And you're not. You're just not. It's just the opposite. Everybody is kind of like babies. You have to baby 'em. Well not everybody, but 90 percent of the people I know want to be babied instead of treated like a machine. And Keane wasn't a Yankee-type manager. Keane thought we were just machines, and we're not. We're just human beings, really. Just down-to-earth human beings." Keane lasted through 1965 and two weeks into '66 when he was fired, and Houk returned as manager. At the end of 1966 Boyer was traded, his golden glove no longer outweighing his .240 batting average. Furthermore, his drinking was becoming public, an idiosyncrasy not appreciated by the image-conscious CBS Yankee management.

"What was your reaction to being traded?" I asked.

"What was it?" Clete said. "It pissed me off. I knew I only had to play two or three more years, and I would have been the number-one third-baseman in games played for the Yankees. And I was young when I was traded. Thirty years old. I loved that organization so much. And then when they traded me, and I came to Atlanta, I forgot about the Yankees. All of a sudden I woke up. I didn't deserve to be traded. And you say, 'What kind of an organization is this?' And it really hurt me with the Yankee organization. I had tried to put out for them and play all the time. Richardson and Kubek quit, and Christ, I was the best infielder they had. I was really the only one. And then they trade me. I didn't deserve to be traded." Clete clearly was hurt, his pride pierced. His bitterness still strong.

With the Atlanta Braves in 1967 Boyer was outstanding, hitting twenty-six home runs and driving in ninety-six runs and fielding spectacularly at third where he starred for the Braves until mid-1971 when he was released after a bitter feud with general manager Paul Richards. Boyer complained publicly that the organization didn't teach the players the proper fundamentals. Richards complained that Boyer was a troublemaker.

"For a month Richards and I were making headlines every day," Boyer said. "He's ripping me and I'm ripping the Braves organization, and now I've got him where he's got to release me. For three days when I'm on waivers, when nobody is supposed to talk with me, Charley Finley calls me three times, offers me a two-year contract plus a new car and $1,000 worth of clothes and all this bullshit, and I'm going for it. And now since I've ripped that organization so much, Bowie Kuhn's man Fitzgibbon, who to me is really a piece of shit, calls me in and says, 'I want to talk to you.' And I didn't know what the hell he wanted to talk to me about. He says, 'Have you ever bet on football or basketball?' And I said, 'Well, hell, yes I have.' I was stupid there, because I should have said, 'Are you accusing me of something?' and I should have called Marvin Miller, which they have to do now. But now they've got me because I've bet on football.

"So I went up to see the commissioner to see what he was going to do, and he charged me with exactly what I told Fitzgibbon. He didn't even investigate the goddamn thing. He just said, 'This is what you've done.' And I said, 'Sure it is, because I told him that I did that.' So then he fined me $1,000, and for some reason he told all the owners, and now nobody would talk to me. Charlie Finley wouldn't accept a call. Nobody. Boston, who was in the pennant race. San Francisco was up there, and Alan Gallagher was making errors at third base every day. Nobody would even talk to me. And I feel that I was blackballed in the States for saying what I really thought." Again Clete looked hurt. Others might have become angry and sued, charging their rights were violated under the due process clause of the Constitution. Clete didn't sue. He picked up his bat and his glove and his spikes and signed to play in Japan.

"I don't want this to sound like I'm knocking baseball," Boyer said. "Baseball is a suuuuuuuuuuuper, suuuuuuuuuuuuuper game. I've met some suuuuuuuuuper athletes in my day." Tomorrow Boyer would be returning to Japan for another season of baseball. He has been successful there, where few Americans actually make it. Now 38 years old, he still wows ball park fans with his brilliant stops and long, hard, accurate throws. A fighter, a drinker, a rebel, he was too hot to handle for American owners. To Boyer it was their loss even more than it was his, though he longs to return to the States to play ball as age erodes his once unparalleled skills, his athletic career ebbing in a foreign land.

"And it's a shame," Boyer said. "Like old ball players—like myself. I should quit now. But shit, I have to go back to Japan for the money. I hate to be embarrassed like that, to just hang on, hang on for the money."

In the hot summer of 1963 there was a continuance of the revolutionary racial equality movement. In Birmingham, Alabama, four hundred marchers, including Dr. Martin Luther King, were arrested for demonstrating in the streets, and in Jackson, Mississippi, Medgar Evers, the field secretary of the NAACP, was killed in front of his home by a sniper. President Kennedy, responding to the unrest, urged Congress to pass civil-rights legislation giving equal access to public facilities to everyone, white or black. Kennedy was on the verge of a nuclear test ban treaty with the Russians. It was Camelot in Washington, D.C.

It was also Camelot for Yankee fans. Almost every day was a holiday. If pitching is 70 percent of the game, as many experts proclaim, then the Yankees had the advantage from the first pitch of the game regardless of who they played. Whitey Ford, the Chairman of the Board, winner of twelve games in a row before finally losing in the final days of July, raised his record to 19–6 after a mediocre August, his excellence, poise, control, and leadership a marvel to the opposition and fans around the league. Ralph Terry, a winner seven times in a row at the Stadium, was using more off-speed pitches than before, but he was usually effective, and his 15–13 record could have been much better had he been more fortunate during the earlier months. Jim Bouton was 19–6, selected for the all-star team his first year as a regular. He was a winner, a crowd-pleaser, and a showman. Al Downing, the rookie, was more devastating than anyone, his potential unlimited. In July he pitched a one-hit shutout, a two-hit shutout, and a four-hit shutout; in another game he struck out fourteen batters in seven innings. In August he was 5–1, winning a two-hitter, two three-hitters, and a six-hitter, all complete games, his record 11–4 before September in only two and a half months of pitching. Had Downing not sat on the Yankee bench for two months during the 1961 season and hence been ineligible, he would have been the rookie of the year. "It's good to see some good, young players coming into the league," said Jimmy Dykes, an American League manager for many years, "but why do they always have to be wearing that Yankee uniform?" In one stretch in early August, Yankee starters completed eleven of thirteen games. On consecutive days Stan Williams, excellent all summer, pitched a one-hit shutout, Downing pitched a three-hit, one-run game, Terry a six-hit, one-run game, Bouton a five-hit shutout, and Ford a five-hit, one unearned-run game! In another six-game period at the end of the month, Ford pitched a six-hit shutout, Downing a two-hit shutout, Williams allowed nine hits and two runs in eleven and one-third innings, losing, Bouton pitched a two-hit shutout, Terry a five-hit shutout, and Ford a five-hit one-run game, a total of three earned runs in almost sixty innings of pitching!

The bullpen of Steve Hamilton, acquired from Washington for Jim Coates, rookie Hal Reniff, and Bill Stafford wasn't particularly strong, but with that starting strength, who needed a bullpen?

Bill Stafford, his arm paining him and his temper peaking, was in decline. He started a game against the lowly A's and walked the first five batters he faced. Houk yanked him. Two days later Houk pitched Stafford in the bottom of the twelfth inning in a tie game with the A's. Bill walked the first three batters he faced for eight in a row, and after getting one out, walked yet another batter, allowing the winning run to cross the plate and losing still another game. In the clubhouse after the game, New York *Post* columnist Lenny Shecter asked Stafford whether he was having trouble with his control. Stafford jumped off his little round stool and cocked his fist. Had Clete Boyer not intervened he would have separated Shecter's head from his portly body.

The Yankees were tearing the American League apart. On the first of July their lead over the White Sox was two and a half games. On the first day of

August, the lead swelled to eight games, and on the first of September it was eleven games, a lead built in large part without the services of Mantle, recuperating from his broken foot and torn ankle tendons. After the June 5 injury Mantle missed sixty-one games and didn't return until August 4 in the second game of a doubleheader against the Baltimore Orioles at the Stadium. It had been rumored that Mickey might be ready to pinch hit, and all week long in pinch-hit situations, the Yankee fans began chanting "We want Mickey, we want Mickey." With the Yankees trailing 10–9 in the bottom of the seventh inning against left-hander George Brunet, the fans again sensed that this was an opportunity for Mantle to pinch hit. With 38,000 people in the ball park, and all eyes glued on the Yankee dugout, the chant for Mantle began again. The fans seated on the third base side saw number 7 across the diamond in the dugout grab a bat and adjust his batting helmet, and the word quickly spread throughout the entire Stadium. As Mantle took his first step from the dugout on to the green field, a roar of adulation reverberated and enveloped the Stadium, an outpouring of love for Mantle in an emotionally electrifying moment.

Brunet threw a fast ball, low and outside, that the crowd booed. Mantle, batting right-handed, swept his arms in practice swings, stopping his bat at the top of the swing just before Brunet threw the second pitch, an inside slider that he pulled high and deep toward the left-field stands. At first it looked like left fielder Boog Powell was going to catch it, but the ball continued to carry and landed far over his head into the left-field stands for a home run. As Mantle circled the bases slowly, the cheering, stomping, whistling, clapping and shouting burst into a love-in for Mickey Mantle. As Bobby Richardson, sitting on the bench, waited for Mantle to return to the dugout, large tears rolled down his face. As Mantle crossed home plate, he touched the brim of his cap, and the swell of noise made a quantum leap. Gut feelings were being expressed from somewhere deep inside the ecstatic fans. Mantle would always be something extra special to them. The Yankees went on to win the game in the tenth inning on a single by Tony Kubek, a hit-and-run single by Bobby Richardson, and a sacrifice fly by pinch hitter Yogi Berra. Mickey for the next month exclusively pinch hit, not starting a game until September, and during the month in pinch-hit situations, the fans, both home and away, continually called for Houk to put Mantle in the game.

With Mantle out most of the time, Roger Maris became the team leader. Roger was batting close to .300, driving in crucial runs, playing an outstanding right field, and then on July 11, he too was hospitalized for rectal surgery required to close a fissure. When he returned, he was plagued by backaches which made it difficult for him to play during August. For a short while Tom Tresh was injured, and the Yankees played with their entire starting outfield on the bench. The Yankees kept winning nevertheless. "Mantle-less, Maris-less, merciless," wrote Dick Young of the *Daily News*. Taking up the slack were Ellie Howard, Joe Pepitone, the only Yankee starter on the all-star team, plus Hector Lopez, a regular since Mantle's injury, and John Blanchard, the Super Sub, always ready in the wings to provide the Yankees with instant offense. Between July 22, when Maris left the lineup, and August 24, Blanchard became a powerful force in the Yankee lineup, hitting ten home runs including grand slams against Boston and Cleveland and contributing forty RBI's in thirty-five at-bats! During that period his bating average was .220! "But he's certainly the best .220 hitter anywhere in baseball," said Ralph Houk.

John Blanchard was an easygoing guy, the captain of the Scrubbinies, a catcher outfielder first baseman pinch hitter, pinch anything, a man who would have been batboy to stay with the Yankees. Blanchard had been an all-star minor leaguer with a bright future, an excellent catcher with a booming bat, but when he came to the Yankees to stay in 1959 he played behind Yogi Berra and Elston Howard, and in his seven years on the team the most games he ever caught was forty-eight in 1961, and many of those were only late inning appearances. Arndt Jorgens for eleven years sat on the bench behind Bill Dickey and never played much, but collected share after world series share. Charlie Silvera for nine years sat on the bench behind Yogi Berra collecting series checks. Blanchard did the same, happy in his role of bullpen catcher and pinch hitter. "I'd never want to be traded," Johnny once said. "I'd rather sit on the bench with the Yankees till the bench rots. Besides, being a bullpen catcher with the Yankees isn't so bad." He could have been a star with anyone else.

Blanchard was the perfect bench warmer, a guy whose ego didn't prompt him to complain about not playing. He was happy. When Maris was hospitalized Blanchard became the regular right fielder, and during the month of July, John drove in sixteen runs in fifteen games, hit six home runs, and pushed the Yankees to their insurmountable eight-and-a-half-game lead. When Maris returned, Blanchard returned to the bench. Others would have stewed. Blanchard didn't mind at all. "I'm tickled to death that I've been able to do the job, but I'm no Maris. I'm still Roger's caddy."

John Blanchard was at his desk at the Brooklyn, Minnesota, showroom of American Motors cars where he is a salesman, when I called and told him I was in town. Within a half-hour there was a knock at the door of the Sheraton where I was staying in nearby Minneapolis, and a large, smiling man with a ready laugh and a friendly demeanor was standing outside, eager to relive his years with his beloved Yankees and anxious to hear about how his teammates were doing. We took the elevator down to the dining room of the hotel and talked while we ate. He joked a lot and enjoyed having a good time, yet when we were finished my impression was one of lost youth and opportunity, of unfulfilled promise—disguised with genial laughter.

"Stengel never gave you much of a chance to play," I said.

"There wasn't any room for me to play," John said. "Let's face it. We had Yogi Berra and Elston Howard, and both of them could play the outfield."

"When they made you a catcher, weren't you aware of these guys?" I asked.

"No, not really," he said. "I didn't think about that at all. I was getting down, having to play behind Yogi and Ellie, but I wasn't griping. I was just worried that someone would come to me one day and say, 'John, we don't have room for ya. We're going to trade ya.' So I was getting down. But I wasn't griping. That's one thing I never did. I never griped, never said play me or trade me or bitched about things like that. I had a home with the Yankees. I was very proud just to be a part of the ball club. Let's face it. I wasn't a youngster at the time when I was a rookie. Hell, I was 26 years old, and the biggest thing I thought about to myself was that all my minor league days and all my time I had spent in sacrifice for the game of baseball would have been shot had I not gotten the pension. What I wanted to do was get my five years in toward the pension regardless. I just shut my mouth. Do your job, don't complain, get your five years in so all those years in the minors aren't in vain. That's what I wanted to do. If I had to sit, fine. And it worked out fine—I got my time plus, and then later on, I did get a chance to play, and when I got a chance to play, I had to do better than the average regular to excel, because for me there was no tomorrow. When I was put in, if I goofed up too much, it was 'I'll see you later. You had your chance. You blew it. See ya.' That's how I felt. So whenever I did play I tried to really bear down and come through. Because that was it. And every time I did come through, that may have kept me around for a couple more days, for another month, and if they had ideas of getting rid of me, this may have kept me around for a while longer."

I couldn't understand how he could have felt that way. "But by 1961 you were the best pinch hitter in the whole league!" I said. "You hit four home runs in a row."

"There was so much happening," John said. "We were in the process of putting together the best year that a baseball team could possibly have. I don't think that even back in Ruth's time they were that good. That 1961 Yankee team, everybody from the bench to the pitchers put it all together in one. Guys were having good years that . . . well, myself for one. They didn't expect the year out of me that I had." John hit twenty-one home runs, drove in fifty-four runs and batted .305 in a part-time role. "I didn't expect it myself. Everybody put everything together in one season, and that to me was the greatest baseball team ever assembled. We had six guys who hit twenty-one or more home runs. We hit 240 home runs in a season as a team. This is unheard of! Especially in that orchard in New York. You're playing the Big Orchard. I'll bet you if we played in any other park in baseball, I don't care what park it is, we would have hit 300 home runs as a team. But you know Yankee Stadium. Death Valley. Mickey Mantle would hit shots that . . . well, Mickey hit fifty-four home runs and I'd venture to say that if Mickey was playing in any other park in the United States, including Yellowstone, they caught balls on him on the track, shots that would have been out of airports. That was a fantastic year. I enjoyed it. And by George, one of the biggest thrills I ever had was when I hit the four home runs in a row. And I just missed the fifth by two inches!" John laughed. "That was such a fun year."

"The second half of '63 you were a star there for a while, too," I said. "You hit a whole bunch of home runs."

"Every time I got the opportunity. I really had to work hard," Blanchard said. "And it just so happened, as fate would have it, I did come through. I was going for the downs, swinging for the long ball. I'm not up there to punch the ball around. No, I didn't need that. And the situations were such that when I did it, I used to come through. Let's face it," he said. "It was luck."

"Luck!" I said. "How could it have been luck? For crying out loud, you were in the minors ten years. Why was it luck?" His humility and self-doubt were killing me.

"Well, you've got to be lucky to a degree," he said. "You really do. Everything fell into line for me. I hit home runs at the right time. That was it, see. If we had been winning eight to nothing, they wouldn't mean anything, but I hit a lot of them in the clutch, and this would carry me. Hell, I was hanging by a thread. I didn't feel like I was a Yankee until about my fifth year there." His fifth year there was 1963.

"You mean you didn't feel part of the team even after that great '61 season you had?" I asked.

"Naw," he said. "I still didn't have that feeling really. Not until '63, I'd say. Up until that time I didn't feel secure. Ralph, he would have said that I was secure, but no, I didn't feel that way. Then when I finally did, Father Time caught up with me, and I was swinging the bat just as hard as ever, but it was taking a little longer to get around."

"In '64 the Yankees made Yogi the manager," I said. "I read where you said that he had been placed in a position that was too big for him."

"Well, I could see Yogi as a player and a coach, yes. But to take a man like that and to put him into a brand-new position such as manager, there's so much responsibility there, and 95 percent of managing is to keep the horses happy. If you have the horses, you're going to win. Well, Yogi, they threw him right to the dogs. Yogi didn't have a good rapport with his team. I don't know how to say it. I'm certainly not criticizing him. It's something he had to learn, and I know that Yogi today has learned it, but in '64 he'd blow off the handle out loud in the dugout with an individual, and well, you don't do this. If you have something to say to a player, take him in your office and close the door and explain it to him. But don't yell at him in front of everybody."

"He never yelled at Mickey and Whitey and his close friends," I said.

"No," Blanchard said, laughing, "it was me or Pepitone or Phil Linz or any pitcher. His timing was wrong. I remember it as plain as day. He was wrong for chewing out an individual in front of everyone, and I knew right then this causes problems. I said, 'This is not right. Yogi is making a mistake.' Which he did. Houk knew it, the front office knew it. If I have it coming, I don't care, I'd let my boy yell at me. But if I'm right, and they yell at me, no, it's a different ball game. And whenever I went to Yogi to ask him what I was doing wrong when I was in a slump, Yogi would always say, 'You're thinking too much' and walk away." John paused. "I didn't play much in '64. Maybe the way the season went there was no need to use me. I don't know if Yogi knew how to manipulate, who to pull, when to hit, see. He just threw the nine horses out there, and I know that there were many situations where I thought I would play. But I don't think it was a personal thing. Yogi didn't think that far ahead or didn't think about it. That was the situation. Nothing personal. And God knows, we won the pennant, so we must have put out for him. So you can't look back and say, 'He should have done this.' What the hell. He won."

"It was the last year the Yankees won," I said.

John for an instant looked disgusted. "CBS shouldn't have bought the

Yankees,'' he said. ''How the hell can you go from first place to tenth place? Only Jackie Gleason could have made some of those trades. Or Imogene Coca. Art Carney maybe was in on some of those trades.'' The air of fond memories was gone. ''For Christ's sake, my kid could make better trades than what they made. How can you give Roger Maris to St. Louis for Charlie Smith even-up? Come on, who's kidding who? How can you trade Clete Boyer to the Braves for Bill Robinson? How can you do this? Myself and Rollie Sheldon to Kansas City for Doc Edwards? Awww, buckets. I'll never figure that trade out as long as I live. For Christ's sake, I've never figured out why they got rid of Mel Allen. At the end of the '65 season I'm playing in Milwaukee with the Braves when Mel Allen comes in the clubhouse. Last game of the season. I hadn't seen Mel all year. I shook his hand, and I said, 'Jesus, Mel. I know what happened to me, but I can't understand you. Seventeen years. You were as much a part of the ball club as anybody, practically.' He did a hell of a job. A hell of an announcer. He looked at me and he damn near had tears in his eyes. He said, 'I don't know, John.' I said, 'Oh bullshit, Mel. They don't dump you after all these years and not give you a reason.' He said, 'This is God's truth, John. I don't know what happened.' Hell, it's water over the dam now, but I thought that was pretty lousy. This is not the Yankee management that I used to know.''

''You remember May 3, 1965?'' I asked.

''You mean the night I was traded,'' Blanchard said.

''Yeah.''

''Christ, yes,'' John said. ''I'll say. That was a shock. That was a blow. I'll tell you one thing, usually when there's something in the wind, and I don't care what ball club it is, there ain't no way it's kept a secret. The rumor gets around the clubhouse, and all the guys start talking about it. The rumor gets out, and even if its a partial rumor, I don't give a shit, 'cause somebody somehow lets the cat out of the bag. Well this was just a complete blank. This was after an exhibition game with the Mets for the youth of New York, and the game is over, and we're in the clubhouse, and up until that point there was not even a rumor. So the manager, Johnny Keane, he called me and Sheldon in and told us, and it hit me like a ton of bricks. Just like a ton of bricks. And I just went to pieces.'' After Keane told him of the trade, he cried like a baby, tears running down his cheeks, choking behind the tears, taking loud gulps of air. ''God, good God,'' he cried. ''It makes you sick. I hate to leave these guys, my friends. They couldn't hurt a guy more. I'll never have a sadder day in my life.'' Bobby Richardson came over to comfort Blanchard. ''I'm going to Kansas City, Bobby,'' John said. ''Great,'' Bobby said, ''you'll get a chance to play every day.'' ''I don't want to play every day,'' John said. ''I want to stay here.''

''It wasn't that I thought my job was secure,'' John said, ''but for Christ's sake, it was the first of May, gimme till June first and then dump me, see. My pride was hurt. It really was. I felt sorry for myself. I didn't want to leave the ball club. There's no goddamn way I wanted to leave that ball club. I didn't care about any other team in baseball, and I had to leave. Packing my bag and leaving, that was too much for me. I couldn't stand it. Also, this was in May of 1965. In spring training of '65 I was having contract troubles. Ralph Houk was the general manager. I went over to Ralph's apartment and he said, 'John, if you sign for the same money you made last year, I promise you that you'll be with the Yankees as long as I'm the general manager.' Well, I said to Ralph, 'Where do I sign?' Three months later I was gone. And then after I was traded, Ralph said that he was going to come down and talk to me, but he never showed up. After Keane talked to me, I felt really bad, and I was told Ralph would come down and talk with me. But he never did.'' It was almost ten years later, and as we talked John's eyes were shining. ''What's the difference?'' he said. ''You know the old saying: Time heals all wounds. We were just a bunch of numbers to them, and it was none of our business, the trades. If they want to push the buttons, pull the strings, it's none of our business.'' But the trade clearly killed Blanchard's spirit. After several desultory months with the A's, he was traded to the Milwaukee Braves where he finished out the year and called it a career. His months with the A's made his decision to quit that much easier.

''I got nothing against Charlie Finley,'' Blanchard said. ''I think Charlie's good for the game. He's brought a lot of color into the game, white shoes and uniforms, asses. Donkeys, I should say. When Charlie traded for me he was looking for another ass. He had a twenty-mule team and he was looking for another ass. And he pulled things in Kansas City that I wasn't used to. I think the first night I got there, I put the shin guards on, my chest protector, got my mitt, turned my hat around my head, the pitcher's all warmed up, ready to go. Eight o'clock you run on the field, and goddamn, it's eight o'clock, and we don't take the field. Haywood Sullivan is the manager, he was one of Finley's puppets, and Finley whispered something into the dugout to him, so Sully says, 'Wait a minute.' And I said, 'Shit. Let's get going. Let's get the show on the road.' He says, 'No, wait a minute.' And all of a sudden the center-field fence opens up and here come these flunky guys with these shoes turned up on the ends, these elf shoes, and trumpeteers, long trumpets, in green and gold uniforms blowing these fucking trumpets, and I thought, 'Wait a minute. What's going on here?' And here comes a mule, see, walking from center field to home plate. And these two jokers are carrying this birthday cake, the biggest-assed cake you ever saw! And I said, 'For Christ's sake, Sully, what the hell is going on?' Sully says, 'Hey Blanch, I don't know. I don't know.' I say, 'Don't give me that bullshit. I've been around too long. Come on.' And Sully just laughed. He said, 'Here's the deal,' and by this time the mule has got all the way to home plate and these trumpeteers are blowing these bugles. He said, 'We all have to go out to the mound and sing happy birthday to Charlie O, the mule.' I said, 'Sullivan. I'm going to tell you something right now. There's no goddamn way that I'm going out to that mound and sing happy birthday to that fuckin' mule. And there ain't nothing in my contract that says I got to. I can't do it, buddy. See ya.' I went up to the clubhouse and listened to them sing happy birthday on the radio. For Christ's sake! They were going to fine me $100 for that. I said, 'Jesus, take a grand. I could care less.'

''Now this is a long way from the Yankees,'' he said. ''Come on! I love baseball, but this is ridiculous. So what happens, a few days later Finley sent down the word, 'I'll give each guy $25 if we go into ninth place.' We were a half-game out of ninth. The Red Sox were in ninth place, and we were playing the Red Sox at home that night. 'The money'll be in a brown envelope

344 *The Final Years: 1961–1964*

in your locker if you win. It'll be called a celler-bration.' Okay, so I'm out there catching, and everything is going smooth, we're whipping them, get to the ninth inning, and we're ahead 2–1. Fred Talbott's pitching, and Freddie gets tired. Sully comes out, and I go to the mound. It's a hot night in Kansas City. Sully says, 'I think the cork is out.' Freddie says, 'Yeah, I'm a little tired.' So Sully waves to the bullpen. Talbott leaves the mound, goes to the dugout, and me and Sully are standing on the mound, and he waves to the bullpen for Catfish Hunter to come in and pitch to two men in the ninth inning. So Sully waves him in, and Catfish just stands there looking dead-ass at us. He didn't move. So I whistled, 'Come on.' And he stood there. And I said, 'For Christ's sake, Sully, is he blind?' And all of a sudden the goddamn center-field fence opened up, and here comes that fucking mule again. A 2–1 ball game, we're in the ninth inning, and the mule goes from center field around the track to the bullpen, and Catfish had to jump on the son of a bitch bareback and ride him to the mound! I said to Sully, 'Is this your idea? For Christ's sake, we're trying to win a ball game.' And here comes Catfish, and that fuckin' mule starts for the stands, see, and Catfish is riding him bareback, and pulling on his mane so that mule's eyeballs were sticking out of his head! I'll tell you, that mule started for the stands, just wandering along, and when Catfish got finished pulling on him, that mule couldn't swallow for a month. Finally he gets out to the mound, slips and damn nears breaks his neck getting off the mule at the mound, and I told Sully right there, 'This ain't the name of the game. Come on!' So we've completely lost our concentration. One man on, a two-one pitch, home run, we get beat, 3–2, and we're back in tenth place.

"I can't wait for Old-Timers' Day," Blanch said, changing the subject back to the Yankees. "Jesus Christ, I make every one of them. When they contact me at home, I'm like a kid with a toy. Honest. Just can't wait for the day to get there. I fly to Pittsburgh, Kansas City, New York, wherever the game is, put the jock on and go out just to shoot the crap with those guys. The biggest thrill I have today. The Old-Timers' games. I just live for the letter to come in the mail. I enjoy that no end. The line drives are getting linier, the long balls are getting longer, the catches, today they are unbelievable! Jesus, it's like in Minnesota here. I hunt and fish, see. Well, I get a couple of brew in me and my fish stories are all of a sudden magnified. I started off, caught an eight-pound northern pike, and in the last three years that fish is twenty-two pounds and climbing!

"You know," he said, "I sure enjoy reminiscing about those Yankee days. I sure do." John smiled. "It sure was fun."

During the last weekend in August 1963, Dr. Martin Luther King led the largest demonstration ever held in Washington, D.C. Two hundred thousand peaceful marchers, most of them black, were demonstrating for equality in civil rights. "I have a dream," Dr. King said, "that one day in the red hills of Georgia the sons of former slaves and the sons of former slaveholders will be able to sit down together at the table of brotherhood." Also in Washington, President Kennedy, wary of the cauldron in Southeast Asia, said that the United States was prepared to assist the South Vietnamese in their war against communism. "But," Kennedy said, "I do not think that the war can be won unless the South Vietnamese people support the effort, and in my opinion the government has gotten out of touch with the people.''

September provided the Yankees an opportunity to assert their clear-cut superiority over the rest of the league, their lead bulging to fourteen games. No Yankee regular hit thirty home runs or hit .300 or drove in one hundred RBI's, and the bullpen was rather weak, but no team in baseball—with the possible exception of the Los Angeles Dodgers, whom the Yankees were to meet in the world series—had a trio of starting pitchers like the Yankees had. Whitey Ford, his ERA 0.92 in his last eleven starts, compiled a 24–7 record and had his finest season. In 1961, when Whitey was 25–4, he had dependable Luis Arroyo to bail him out. This year, with a weaker bullpen, Whitey had to hold more leads himself, and he completed thirteen games and had 2.74 ERA. Ford was preparing for the Koufax-Ford opener against the Dodgers. ''We'll have a good Jewish-Irish crowd for that one,'' he joked.

Jim Bouton was 21–7 with a 2.53 ERA. Jim won his nineteenth game on September 1 and then came down with a twenty-four hour virus. ''I was so sick I thought I was going to die,'' Bouton said later, ''but how can you die with nineteen wins?'' He didn't die. His twentieth win, a six-hit shutout over Minnesota September 15, clinched the pennant, further enchancing his popularity with the fans. Wrote Lenny Shecter of the *Post,* ''One of these days he'll forget to let go of the ball, and he'll whiz by the batter bodily—hand, arm, shoulder, chest—everything but his shoes. Those will still be on the mound, smoke rising from within.''

The third star of the trio, Al Downing, was a threat to throw a no-hitter every time he took the mound. Al finished with a 13–5 record, ten complete games in twenty-two starts, four shutouts, and an ERA of 2.56. He struck out 171 batters in 175 innings.

Ralph Terry, finishing 17–14, completed eighteen games, best in the league with Camilo Pascual. But for some reason toward the end of the season he had lost his slider, his out pitch, and when the batters, choosing between his fast ball and his change-up curve, guessed correctly, Ralph found himself in trouble. Houk, unhappy with Terry, replaced him in the rotation with Stan Williams in the final week of the season. Terry, the star of the 1962 world series against the Giants and now shunted to the bullpen, had fallen a long way—fast. For 24-year-old Bill Stafford, his bright future behind him, it was even worse. Stafford, his arm aching, pitched only twice in September, both in relief, and his season's ERA was 6.02, his future with the Yankees in question. The rest of the bullpen—Hal Reniff, 4–3, eighteen saves, a 2.62 ERA, and Steve Hamilton, 5–1, five saves, ERA 2.60—didn't get much work either. On June 9, the ERA of the Yankee starting pitchers was 3.56. Then, with Downing in the rotation, in the next 111 games Yankee pitching allowed only 2.90 runs per game! Even with Mantle and Maris out most of the season, all the team had to do was score an average of three runs a game to win!

Mantle, his ankle still weak, continued solely as a pinch hitter. On September 1 in Baltimore, with the Yankees trailing 4–1 in the eighth inning, Clete Boyer, in a deep slump, singled, and with relief pitcher Tom Metcalf due up, the fans were peering into the Yankee dugout to see if Mantle would pinch hit. Mickey, not expecting to play, was hung over from the night before, bleary-eyed and in a foul mood. When Ralph Houk asked him to grab a bat and hit, Mantle swore softly to himself, but picked out a bat and went out into the batter's circle. He waited his turn to the roar of the Baltimore crowd, the same crowd that had cheered in June because he had broken his foot. Baltimore's pitcher, Mike McCormick, a left-hander, tried to throw the first pitch by Mantle, a mistake which he pulled into the left-field stands for a long home run. Gleefully Mantle trotted around the bases, and when he crossed the plate and sauntered into the dugout he said, "They don't have any idea how hard that really was." Everyone laughed uproariously at their boisterous, human team-mate. The Yankee players loved him as much as the fans did. McCormick, shaken, gave up a single to Bobby Richardson, and after Oriole manager Billy Hitchcock replaced him with Dick Hall, Tom Tresh promptly homered into the right-field grandstands to win the game 5-4. That's the kind of year it was.

Maris, when he was able to play, contributed, too. Though he was only in ninety games, Roger nevertheless managed twenty-three home runs and fifty-three RBI's, and despite his prolonged absences, was still a very valuable man. On September 4, for example, Washington was leading 4-3 when Maris batted in the bottom of the ninth with a man on. Claude Osteen, the Washington pitcher, threw a fast ball which Maris pulled for a two-run home run and a 5-4 Yankee win.

Mantle and Maris finally got in a game together the next day, though Tom Tresh, the third outfielder, could not play because of strained ligaments in his right hand. A couple of days later Tresh returned, but Maris had to go into the hospital for treatment of his ailing back. Then on September 24, four days before the end of the season, all three Yankee outfielders, Mantle, Maris, and Tresh, started a game together. It was the first time all eight regulars had started a game since June 1, the day Tresh and Tony Kubek collided, sending Kubek to the hospital.

With Mantle and Maris out so much, Ellie Howard, the next in line for team leadership, assumed command. Howard had not become a regular until 1961, and by '63, finally established, he became more outgoing, assertive, and confident, a confidence he transferred to his pitchers. There would be a runner on base and an 0-2 count. Ellie would say to the pitcher, "Throw a curve in the dirt. Make him fish for it." The pitcher would say, "But I'm afraid of throwing a wild pitch." "Don't worry about anything," Howard would say. "I'll get it." He hit .287, with a career high twenty-eight home runs and eighty-five RBI's. At the end of the year Howard was voted the league's Most Valuable Player. Jackie Robinson, Roy Campanella, Willie Mays, Hank Aaron, Ernie Banks, Frank Robinson, and Maury Wills, all black, previously had won the MVP in the National League. Elston Howard was the first black to win in the American League.

The two promising youngsters, roommates Joe Pepitone and Tom Tresh, had productive seasons. The irreverent and cocky Pepitone, perhaps at times too careless and frivolous but always the life of the party, hit .271 with twenty-seven home runs and eighty-nine RBI's. The serious Tresh, a manager's dream, hit .269 with twenty-five home runs and seventy-one RBI's. Richardson, Kubek, and Boyer, the inner defense, each drove in fifty runs. All were outstanding in the field. Ralph Houk drew the rest of his offensive support from the bench.

Hector Lopez, called "one of the best hitters ever to come out of Panama" by Yogi Berra, was best with men on base and became a key factor in the Yankee runaway. His single up the middle with a man on second could kill you. His solo home run would be the game winner. When Lopez was on the bench, Houk would call over, "Hey, Hector, do you think you can get a single off this guy?" "Sure," Lopez would say, "if you want a single, I'll give you a single." Subbing for Mantle, Lopez drove in the winning run more than a dozen times, and though much improved in the field, his "What-a-Pair-of-Hands" Hector reputation still haunted him. Lopez threw out many a base runner trying to stretch a single into a double, and in the field he caught everything hit in his direction, except for maybe a couple. He was underpublicized, underpaid, and overlooked, but by his teammates he was admired both for his ability and his friendly nature. He was a regular guy, riding the subway from his apartment in Brooklyn to the Stadium, and with Phil Linz, the infield sub, the two men formed the Yankees' L-and-L duo, battling the more renowned M and M for headlines. Linz, who played twenty-two games at shortstop, thirteen at third, twelve at second, and two in the outfield, was good enough to star for another team. Like John Blanchard, on the Yankee bench his skills eroded and his confidence suffered. Linz never was the player he should have been. "Baseball is a fun game," Linz once said. "It beats working for a living."

John Blanchard finished the year with sixteen home runs and fifty-five runs batted in and personally won about a dozen games for the team. Player-coach Yogi Berra, catching part-time and pinch-hitting, at the age of 38 batted .293 and hit eight home runs. In his final active season, Yogi passed Babe Ruth for number of games played in a Yankee uniform and was only forty-eight games shy of Lou Gehrig's record 2,164. The Yankee bench was stronger than the starting lineup of some teams, and combined with excellent pitching, the Yankee machine rolled to another convincing pennant.

In early October Robert McNamara, the Secretary of Defense, and General Maxwell Taylor, in Vietnam on a factfinding mission, advised President Kennedy that the war in Vietnam might be won as early as 1966. There was only one *if:* if the political crisis there did not adversely affect the military effort. Kennedy shortly thereafter, skeptical of Diem and his fascists, ordered a withdrawal of 1,000 military personnel from South Vietnam before the end of the year. The President was unsympathetic to a government that was persecuting Buddhists, and he promised, "I will never send draftees over there to fight." He told Walter Cronkite in an interview, "It is their war."

The Los Angeles Dodgers, a team that blew the pennant to the Giants the year before, was the Yankee opponent in the 1963 world series. The Dodgers were led by Sandy Koufax, the Jewish kid from Brooklyn, the best pitcher in baseball in the 1960s, five years in a row the league leader in ERA, three years a winner of twenty-five games or more, four years the strikeout leader, setting a major league record in 1965 by striking out 382 batters. This was a man to be feared in a short series. The Dodgers also had Don Drysdale, a tall, hulking sidearm right-hander, a Hollywood type who himself was a strikeout pitcher, three times leading his league, consistently striking out 200 batters a year. The third starter was Johnny Podres, the 23-year-old hero of the 1955 world series, now 31 and balding but still an effective, winning pitcher. Maury Wills, who stole 104 bases in 1962 and 40 this year, and Tommy Davis, a .325 hitter with a team-leading eighty-eight RBI's, led the pitty-pat Dodger attack. Behind Koufax, 25–5 with eleven shutouts and a 1.88 ERA, the Dodgers didn't have to score many runs.

The first two games of the 1963 series were played at Yankee Stadium, and the Yankees went into the series confident about the outcome. In the opener, Whitey Ford, magnificent all year, opposed Koufax. "He doesn't throw that hard," the Yankees were saying about Koufax before the game. "He's only human." They were wrong. The first five Yankees Koufax faced—Kubek, Richardson, Tresh, Mantle, and Maris—struck out, and before the day was over Sandy had struck out a record fifteen batters including Richardson and Mantle three times each. The Yankees never were in the game. Koufax's fast ball shot upward as it approached the plate like nothing the Yankees had seen before, and his curve dropped as if off a table. On this day Richardson, who in 630 regular season at-bats struck out 22 times and normally was an aggressive swinger, had to choke up on the bat and try vainly to just to get his bat on the ball. After Bobby struck out for the third time, he passed Mantle, coming to the plate to face the executioner. "There's no use me even going up there," Mickey said.

In the ninth inning with two outs and the Yankees losing 5–2, many in the Stadium were rooting for Yankee pinch hitter Harry Bright to strike out so the personable Koufax could break Carl Erskine's record of fourteen strikeouts in one series game. When Bright swung for strike three, Sandy was throwing as hard as he had been in the first inning. The Yankees seemed something less than invincible against him. The two runs the Yankees scored came on a two-run home run by Tommy Tresh, but it came in the eighth inning when the Yankees trailed 5–0.

Before the game Ford asked Stan Williams, last year a Dodger, how to pitch to behemoth Frank Howard. "Throw him high fast balls," Williams said. In the second inning Ford threw Howard a high fast fall, and Howard hit a ball that shortstop Kubek leaped for and just missed. Then as it continued to rise, center fielder Mantle leaped for it, and he too missed. The ball continued 461 feet from the plate, striking the loudspeaker standard in center field and bouncing halfway back to second. The ponderous Howard rambled safely into second. Bill Skowron, traded for Williams but having a poor year with the Dodgers, singled Howard home. A few innings later Moose also drove in another run. After Moose's first hit in the second, Dick Tracewski singled, and then John Roseboro, the successor to Roy Campanella, hit a hanging curve ball Ford served up for a three-run home run. It was Whitey's one bad pitch, but against Koufax he could not afford that mistake. After the game no one was saying that Sandy wasn't very fast.

In the second game the Dodgers again took an early lead, and again the Yankees were unable to catch up. Rain fell briefly just before game time, too briefly for the Yankees. In the top of the first inning, against Al Downing, Dodger speedster Maury Wills singled up the middle. Junior Gilliam singled to right, scoring Wills who had stolen second and on a double by Willie Davis, Gilliam scored. The Dodgers had all the runs they needed. Bill Skowron, continuing to torment his old teammates, homered in the fourth for a 3–0 Dodger lead, and two hits by the Davises scored a fourth run before the Yankees finally pried a run loose in the ninth from Podres and his reliefer Ron Perranoski. The Dodgers easily won 4–1, and the Yankees' hopes were further dimmed when Roger Maris, chasing a ball into the right-field corner, smashed violently into the low fence, his left arm losing all feeling after the impact. The swollen and discolored arm was crisscrossed with contusions, the fence pattern discernible. Maris would probably miss the remainder of the series, an injurious finish to an injury-prone year for the Rajah.

In Los Angeles, the night before the third game, Jim Bouton, the third-game pitcher against Don Drysdale, and Phil Linz, Bouton's flaky, irrepressible buddy, were roaming the theatrical district of Los Angeles, searching for a little fun, when they noticed a costume and makeup shop on the strip. In the window was a display of lifelike horror masks, masks designed by studio artists to fit snugly over the head. For $20 Bouton and Linz bought a mask of a person whose face had been hideously and pathetically burned, scar tissue covering most of the face. The two Yankees then wandered over to Grauman's Chinese Theater, one of Hollywood's best known tourist attractions. While groups of tourists were looking down at the footprints set in concrete, Bouton, wearing the mask, would kneel beside someone, strike up a conversation, and after a few sentences look up at the unsuspecting victim. Inevitably the person would gasp but at the same time try to keep cool so that the hideously deformed man wouldn't think they were embarrassed by his appearance. The people, chagrined at their fright, then would continue their discussion as though they hadn't noticed anything. For a couple of hours Bouton and Linz traded off, scaring the wits out of people downtown. Then they returned to the hotel. Linz, Tony Kubek's roommate, got into bed. Tony, after taking a sleeping pill to counter his nervousness, was half-asleep around midnight when there was a knock at the door. Linz feigned sleep. "You get it, Phil," Kubek said. "I can't," Linz said. Tony got up, unlatched the chain, opened the door, and standing in front of him was the most godawfully deformed person he had ever seen. Tony was too scared to scream. Instead he tried to run into the bathroom with the frightening creature in pursuit. Kubek was hysterically whispering, "Phil, Phil, Phil," when he noticed Phil and the deformed man laughing at his discomfort. Tony wasn't too upset when he discovered Bouton under the mask, but the next day the coaches, particularly Frank Crosetti, not understanding how these stunts could go on the night before a series game, expressed great displeasure.

Then on the bus going to the ball park Bouton again upset the coaches, exhibiting a newspaper with a mock headline, "Bouton No-Hits Dodgers," that he had had made up the night before. Such jinxes were not normally tolerated. It was like mentioning that a pitcher had a no-hitter in the middle of a game. The coaches could not understand how these players, behind 2–0 in the series, could act so frivolous, so carefree, so unserious, right before a game. They had never seen people like Bouton or Linz or Joe Pepitone, a bus-ride entertainer who crooned better than Billy Eckstine himself.

After the third game, though, no one could blame Bouton that the Yankees had not won. At his bulldoggy best, he allowed just four singles and one cheap run in the first inning, on a walk, a wild pitch, and a ground ball that took a bad hop off the pitcher's mound, and then took a bad hop off Bobby Richardson's shin for the hit that drove in the run. Bouton's opposing pitcher, Don Drysdale, however, allowed three hits, two by Tony Kubek, and no runs. "We're not hitting," Ralph Houk observed. The Dodgers were threatening a sweep.

Against Koufax in the fourth game, Whitey Ford pitched a two-hitter—and lost. Stan Williams, again advising Ford how to pitch to gargantuan Frank Howard, said, "If you can't get your fast ball by him, try a slow curve." In the fifth inning Ford threw Howard a slow curve, and Frank hit the ball into the upper deck in Chavez Ravine, one of the very few times a ball has been hit there. Mickey Mantle tied the game in the seventh with a home run against Koufax, Mickey's fifteenth world series home run, tying Babe Ruth. It was thus 1–1 in the bottom of the seventh inning when Junior Gilliam, a relic from the Ebbets Field era, opened the inning with a high, trickily bounding ball down the third-base line which would have been a double had Clete Boyer not backhanded it. Boyer, setting himself, threw quickly and on a line to first, but against the white-shirted background, Joe Pepitone lost sight of the ball as it sped across the diamond. The ball hit off his arm, grazed his chest, and continued uninterrupted toward the first-base box-seat railing where it hit and bounded off into right field with Pepitone in pursuit. When Joe finally caught up with it, Gilliam was on third, and when Willie Davis hit a long fly ball to center, Gilliam tagged and scored easily far ahead of Mickey Mantle's perfect one-bounce throw to the plate. The Yankees trailed 2–1.

It was still 2–1 in the ninth when with two outs and a man on first, Ellie Howard grounded routinely to shortstop Wills, who flipped casually to Dick Tracewski, who just as casually dropped the ball. The joyful Koufax, his arms raised in triumph, ran toward the dugout when he saw the ball bound toward Wills. He couldn't figure out why no one rushed to congratulate him until the dejected Tracewski brought him the ball. Koufax returned to his chores against Hector Lopez, who tried to check his swing on an inside pitch, accidentally rolling the ball to Wills, who threw Hector out to end the game. The Dodgers mobbed Koufax.

In the Yankee clubhouse afterward the players were feeling bad, their egos squashed by a four-straight beating. Joe Pepitone, sitting on his stool in tears, was feeling especially blue, apologizing to anyone who would listen. Whitey Ford, the losing pitcher, strolled over to Pepitone, and with a straight face said, "You really blew that son of a bitch, didn't you, kid?" And Pepitone, wise to Whitey's humor, cracked up. Ford then laughed, and Mantle too, and with one sentence Ford had dispelled the gloom. Ralph Houk shouted, "Okay, let's get the hell out of here," and the Yankees went home. "I don't care if the Dodg-

'ers had beat us ten games in a row,'' Mickey Mantle said on the way out, ''I know we still have a better team.''

A week later, back in New York City, the Yankees announced a shift in management personnel. General manager Roy Hamey retired, and Yankee owner Dan Topping had hired Houk to take Hamey's place with Yogi Berra prepicked to be the Yankee manager for 1964. Berra, approached by Boston and Washington to manage in 1962, had not wanted to manage a second-division team. ''You only have the job for two years,'' he reasoned. ''Then you get fired.'' In the summer of 1963 powerful Baltimore had approached him to manage, but by then he already was secure in the knowledge that he was going to be the Yankee manager in 1964. Houk, an excellent field manager, had not attracted enough fans into the Stadium, and he did not have the charisma or personality to compete with lovable Casey Stengel of the Amazin' Mets, who were hurting the Yankees at the box office. Dan Topping, who felt Yogi would be good copy in the papers, wanted Berra to be the manager. Del Webb, aware that Yogi was not the most articulate of men, was against Berra becoming manager. Topping and Houk, however, talked Del into the move. ''Mr. Webb,'' Houk said to Webb, ''Yogi is well-liked by the press, and also, he's the type of guy I can keep my arm around.'' Webb, not buying what Houk was trying to sell, said, ''Houk, you know goddamn well, suppose somebody said that about you? What kind of manager would he be? You're not kidding me—I don't think it'll work.'' Eventually though, Webb, against his will, gave in. Yogi, aware of Webb's displeasure, flew out to the Coast to speak to Del before the announcement was made. ''I understand you're not for me being manager,'' Yogi said to Webb. ''You're wrong on that score,'' Webb said. ''I'm for you more than anyone in the world. The decision has been made. But I'll tell you what I think. I think a manager has to go down to the minor leagues and manage some like Houk did. Also I don't think a fella can play on a team one year and manage the same club the next. This is wrong. How can you handle these guys you've known so long when you have to discipline them?'' Yogi told Webb he would have no trouble with discipline. Mickey and Whitey had always gone their own way, and it was inconceivable that ex-teammates like Tony Kubek and Bobby Richardson or Clete Boyer and Ellie Howard would do anything to jeopardize Yogi's job. Also Yogi had Ralph Houk to back him up.

When the announcement of his appointment as Yankee manager was made, Yogi, in a $300 suit, was neither as comical-looking nor as humorous as his reputation had suggested. At the press conference, he was, in fact, quite defensive about that reputation. ''I was surprised they offered me the job,'' Yogi said, ''but this is not a joke.'' The newspapermen listened respectfully. Yogi's eldest son, Larry, was less respectful. Yogi came home with the news, and Larry said, ''You? The Yankee manager?''

''I've been with the Yankees seventeen years,'' Berra told reporters, ''watching games and learning. You can see a lot by observing.''

1964

Yogi takes over . . . Pepi . . . The Bulldog—Jim Bou-
ton . . . The Harmonica Incident . . . The final flag
. . . A loss to the Cardinals . . . Goodbye to Mel and
Red . . . Houk and Keane . . . The end of the Dy-
nasty

By the spring of 1964 the outlook of the country had been violently altered by events of the past few months. Lee Harvey Oswald became a household word, and because of his shooting accuracy in Dallas, there was a new President named Lyndon Johnson, a man who drawled "My fellow Amuricans" at the start of every speech, a dour Texan who was replacing a murdered leader now buried beneath an eternal flame at Arlington Cemetery.

With Berra at the helm, there was a new image of humanity brought to the Yankees, and though Yogi certainly was not in Casey Stengel's class as a performer and entertainer, he nevertheless appeared to be much more personable than Houk. Houk, though an excellent manager, had a cold and efficient image, one which helped cause Yankee attendance to decline by more than 400,000 people during his three-year reign, while at the same time Casey Stengel and his Mets were attracting fans in amazin' numbers.

Unfortunately for Yogi, though, right from the start the players found him to be neither personable nor humorous, and they seemed to resent his presence as manager, preferring Houk instead.

More crucial to the performance of the team, neither Mantle nor Maris were completely healthy, and shortstop Tony Kubek seemed unable to either field or bat. During the spring the Yankees' batting average was only a handful of points above .200. On the mound the team still was strong, with Whitey Ford doubling as pitching coach, and only Jim Bouton, last year's twenty-one-game winner, not up to par after missing two weeks of spring training following a violent contract squabble with GM Houk. New faces included Pete Mikkelsen, a sinker-ball pitcher Berra liked, pitcher Tom Metcalf, infielder Pedro Gonzalez, and two expensive rookies, Archie Moore and Chet Trail, remained on the roster for the season as demanded by the new bonus rule.

The Yankees lost their first three games of the season in extra innings, and though the season was barely under way, the players were already criticizing Yogi behind his back for leaving his starting pitchers in too long. This backbiting continued throughout the season, and many of the players were complaining privately to Houk about Yogi's leadership, his strategy, and his faults, expressing their fervent wishes that Houk come back and be their manager again. The general manager listened patiently—too patiently—to what they had to say, but there was little he could do, for a while.

During the early weeks of the season both Mantle and Maris pulled hamstring muscles, and when Tresh pulled one also, the Yankees were forced to start an outfield of Hector Lopez, Pedro Gonzalez, and John Blanchard. Shortstop Kubek continued to recuperate from his neck miseries in the hospital while Phil Linz filled in adequately. Only a spate of rain-outs saved the team from total disaster, with regular Clete Boyer hitting less than his weight and first-baseman Joe Pepitone hitting less than his wife's weight. Nevertheless the team remained close to leaders Chicago and Cleveland, with Ford, Bouton, and Downing pitching excellently and reliefer Mikkelsen taking on the brunt of the relief chores and doing well.

Then in mid-May Downing strained his back and Bouton developed a painful muscle pull in his pitching arm. The inexperienced Berra, while using Mikkelsen extensively, had inadvertently ignored his other reliefers, and now when he needed to use Bill Stafford, Bud Daley, Stan Williams, Ralph Terry, and Hal Reniff, they were either injured or ineffective. Compounding his difficulties, Berra often caused his relief men to warm up several times during a game, thus tiring them needlessly. The relief pitchers had a saying, "We're going to win this pennant despite Yogi." There developed a steady stream of complainers to Houk's office, and on one occasion in July, Houk asked the benched Tony Kubek whether the team was getting away from Yogi. Kubek said that he thought that it had. Houk thought so, too, and when Topping and Webb, who didn't want Yogi in the first place, concurred, it was decided that day in July that at the end of the season regardless of what the Yankees did the remainder of the year, Berra would be fired. If Yogi during the year felt deserted by the management, he had every right to feel that way.

After falling so far behind, however, the Yankees swept five games from the White Sox in mid-June to reenter the race, with Yogi starting reliefer Steve Hamilton and receiving excellent pitching from his beanpole lefty. Ford, Stafford, Daley, and Williams pitched well. Mantle returned and raised his average above .300, and in the sweep against the Sox he hit a cluster of home runs and sparked the team. A week later the Yankees pushed back into first place, again sweeping the White Sox. Ford raised his record to ten and one, and Downing and Bouton pitched well despite mediocre support behind them. The Yankees were in front for one day, June 24, and for the team in general and manager Berra in particular, the next day was a disaster.

Before a game against the second-place Orioles, Kubek reported to manager Berra that a pulled groin muscle would prevent him from playing, and with Boyer at third only hitting .200, Berra decided that he would rather have a weak bat at shortstop and a better bat at third, so he moved Boyer to short and started Phil Linz, who was hitting close to .300, at third base. It was the same move Houk had made the year before when he shifted Boyer to short and played Harry Bright at third. The players grumbled about Berra's strategy.

"If I was manager," offered Joe Pepitone, "I'd rather see Boyer at third."

"Where would you like to see Linz?" a reporter asked Pepi.

"Amarillo," Pepitone said.

The Yankees raced out to a 7–2 lead over the Orioles, and in the seventh inning manager Berra decided to pinch hit for starter Rollie Sheldon, who had been doing well. The pinch hitter grounded out, and in the eighth Berra called in Mikkelsen to the mound. Mikkelsen forced the Orioles to hit the ball on the ground, but most of the ground balls were hits through the infield, including two just inside the third-base line that Linz either misplayed or failed to intercept, ground balls that the other players felt that Boyer, had be been playing there, would have stopped. Baltimore scored seven runs to win the ball game, and for the rest of the season the players talked about how Yogi was going to divorce his wife and marry Mikkelsen and how Yogi was playing both Linz and Boyer out of position. The bullpen members were bitching the loudest, though few noticed that the statistics showed the bullpen to have a 20–7 record with fifteen saves to this point.

The Yankees trailed the Orioles throughout the summer, with a superb starting cast of Ford, Downing, and Bouton getting occasional support from little-used Terry and Sheldon. In the team's roller coaster manner, it took over first place again on August 6, but when Whitey Ford was unable to pitch against the White Sox and Orioles during the subsequent fifteen-game series against the two contenders, the strain on the rest of the staff was almost fatal. The in-and-out Mantle was also debilitated during this period, having jammed his sore left knee into first base diving back on a pick-off play. On August 20, after losing ten of the fifteen games, including four straight to Chicago, the Yankees found themselves four and a half games back. The criticism of Berra was now a torrent of behind-the-back abuse, the players unaccustomed to being behind so late in the season and in need of a scapegoat for their own uninspired play. They continued to run to general manager Houk, and Houk continued to listen to them, knowing Yogi was gone at the end of the year but at the same time expressing his complete confidence in the rookie manager. Added to everyone's insecurity was the announcement that the team had been sold to the Columbia Broadcasting Company by Topping and Webb. When the Yankees lost a game to the Red Sox, a large Fenway Park banner was unfurled reading, "CBS can't beat Boston." "All we gotta do is start hitting," insisted Berra. "Remember, I went through this back in '49. Didn't we win on the last day that year?" Few took the doughty round man seriously, though.

The smoldering acrimony finally surfaced while the team was riding on the bus from Comiskey Park to O'Hare Airport, a silent entourage after having just lost their fourth straight to Chicago. The bus was caught in the postgame traffic, and as it sat in the noisy congestion, boredom was beginning to set in and there was a feeling of impatience added to the frustration of having to maintain a grim silence after such a string of devastating defeats.

Berra and his coaches were sitting in the front seats of the passenger bus, and in the last two rows on either side of the aisle were most of the regulars, including Pepitone, Kubek, Ford, Maris, Mantle, Richardson, and Linz, the bespectacled infielder with the impish sense of humor. Amidst the gloom and dreariness, Linz pulled a small piece of sheet music from his pocket and placed it against the back of Ellie Howard's head right in front of him. Joe Pepitone, sitting next to Linz, whispered, "What's that for?" "I'm learning how to play the harmonica," Linz said, pulling a Marine Band Horner harmonica from his pocket. "Heeeeey, man," whispered Pepitone. "What are you going to do with that thing?" "I'm going to play it," Linz said. "You gotta be shitting me," Pepitone said, a little louder. "Fuck it," said Linz, and began a musically inept attempt at "Mary Had a Little Lamb." Up front Berra heard the amateurish tootling, stood up and said, "Whoever's playing that thing, shove it up your ass." Berra then sat down. "Hey Phil," said Pepitone, "come on. Put it away." "Bullshit, man," said Linz. "I can play if I want to." A week before Yogi had inadvertently posted Linz's name on the dugout lineup card while at the same time writing Kubek's name on the one handed to the umpires, so just before the game started, Linz had taken infield practice, and was ready for the contest to begin, when Kubek sheepishly raced onto the field to inform Linz that he was not starting. Linz had not appreciated Berra's talents from the start, but this incident had strained their relationship even more. He did not respect Berra as manager, and because Phil had been playing well despite the string of defeats, he felt no obligation to keep the deathly morgue silence. Once more "Mary Had a Little Lamb" screechily filled the air, and once more Berra rose from his seat, but this time with fire in his eyes. Lumbering down the center aisle of the bus, Yogi growled at Linz, "I thought I told you to shove that thing up your ass?" Linz yelled back, "If you want it shoved up my ass, why don't you shove it there?"

Linz then flipped the instrument at Berra, who slapped at it with his hand and knocked it in Pepitone's direction. It cut through Pepi's trousers and sliced his leg. A great commotion ensued. Maris yelled at Pepitone, "Sue him, sue him," and Pepitone, rolling on the floor of the bus, holding his nicked leg, started screaming "Mayday, mayday, I need a medic. Get a Band-Aid, my leg, my leg." Yogi and Linz continued to exchange words. "For Christ's sake," Linz yelled, "why don't you leave the ball game on the field?" And Berra shouted back at him, "You son of a bitch. I'll talk to you later," and as a few players mockingly called, "Ooooooooooh," he marched up to the front.

After Yogi returned to his seat, Mantle retrieved the harmonica from the floor, and yelled over to Whitey, who was sitting across the aisle, "It looks like I'm going to be managing this club pretty soon. You can be my third-base coach. And here's what we'll do. One toot," Mantle said, pretending to play the harmonica, "that's a bunt. Two toots," and he pretended to blow twice into the instrument, "that's hit and run." Those players in the back who were listening to Mickey began to giggle and relax and the ugliness abated. Berra ultimately fined Linz $200 for his insubordination, a small penalty in light of the $20,000 contract Linz signed with the Horner Harmonica Company. The incident proved to have little or no subsequent effect on the team except to publicize the existing squabbles. The next day in the Yankee dressing room up in Boston, Mantle and Ford set off a cherry bomb that rocked the clubhouse. That *really* shook up the team.

Criticism of Berra and the team continued internally and externally as the Yankees lost the next two games to Boston to fall a full six games out of first place. The players were accused of not having the hunger in their guts any more, of being too complacent after so many years of winning. Only Berra refused to concede that his team was out of it. ''We still have a long way to go,'' he would say. ''If Chicago and Baltimore can knock each other off, we have a good chance,'' and every day when he announced the team was not out of it, the reporters had a good laugh on ole Yogi.

Baltimore and Chicago then split their eight games and both started to lose to lowly clubs like Washington and Cleveland, and with the coming of September the Yankees rarely lost. Ford returned to his brilliant early-season form; Bouton, who had nursed a tired arm the first half of the season, regained his strength and won thirteen games the second half of the year; Downing looked like a black Sandy Koufax, striking out eight or nine batters every game; and Mel Stottlemyre, a rookie brought up from Richmond, won nine games in the final seven weeks. Over Houk's objections, Dan Topping traded for hard-throwing Pedro Ramos, who day after day came into a game in the last inning or two when the shadows had descended and threw his blazing fast ball past the frustrated hitters who could not see the ball when it skipped from the sun into the shadows. Houk didn't think Ramos would be of much help. ''We're not close enough for him to make a difference,'' the general manager told Topping. On offense Mantle, playing on one leg, batted .424 righty to finish the season at .303 with thirty-five home runs and 111 runs batted in. Ellie Howard hit close to .400 the final few weeks. Roger Maris was an inspiration in the field and at bat, and Joe Pepitone, the toupeed, slope-nosed playboy, hit twelve home runs and batted in thirty runs in September to finish with twenty-eight homers and an even one hundred RBI's.

The surging Yankees recaptured first place on September 17, while both Chicago and Baltimore played win-one, lose-one baseball. Manager Berra was beginning to look very, very smart, and everyone who had lost faith in him very, very dumb. The clubhouse regained its lost gaiety, as Pepitone once more offered renditions of Billy Eckstine that out-Eckstined Eckstine. Mantle and Ford would grab his ski-slope nose and twist it while yelling ''honk honk,'' and the players would tease Pepitone about his penchant for teenyboppers.

Tall, swarthy, and handsome in a sinister way, Pepitone was a Yankee matinee idol, dressing in tight-fitting pegged pants and see-through shirts. The women—young, old, tall, short, fat, and thin—flocked to Yankee Stadium to watch him play, and it was not uncommon that Joe would conspire with the Stadium grounds crew to meet some adoring female fan under the stands during a ball game to engage in some intimate public relations. Joe loved to live and lived to love, and he was not shy about getting his loving wherever and whenever he could get it.

For five decades the Yankees had signed players who not only were great ball players, but who were also staid and conservative in the Yankee tradition, subordinating their personalities to the image of the faceless team. In the past, with the notable exception of Babe Ruth, there had been no room for flakes. The Yankees had always had a non-flake just as good, another man who lived in the honored ''Yankee tradition.''

No longer. When the Yankees traded Moose Skowron at the end of the 1962 season, Pepitone was the best first-baseman in the organization, and he played and starred, his individuality and his idiosyncrasies notwithstanding.

As a teenager, Pepitone had been a $100,000 prospect at Manual Training, now John Jay High School in Brooklyn, where he was the coach, the captain, and the star of his baseball team. During his senior year he was shot just below the heart by a friend who was showing off his .38 and quickly became a $20,000 prospect as most of the interested teams questioned his sense of responsibility and his maturity. He recovered quickly, though, and the Yankees bravely gave him $20,000 to sign, which he immediately squandered on a souped-up Bonneville and a fiber glass speedboat. Now only the Yankees questioned his sense of responsibility and his maturity. When Pepitone arrived at his first spring training, the veterans invariably introduced themselves with, "Aren't you the kid who got shot?" or "Aren't you the kid who bought the boat?"

At the training camp, Pepi was given uniform number 69. That high a number was rarely seen on a baseball uniform. Even then they knew. He was stovepipe skinny, with kinky hair, a big nose, and ears that stuck way out. He sported a greasy D.A. and his cap sat squarely atop his head like a jet sitting on the deck of an aircraft carrier. The first time he appeared in uniform, one fan shouted out, "That uniform suits you, 69." Before anyone knew his name, Joe Pepitone was a man who was noticed.

New York City has not had a baseball player with his personal magnetism since Pepitone was traded from the Yankees at the end of 1969, when the Yankee management finally tired of his eccentricities. When he visited the Stadium last summer to see a ball game during a short visit to New York, in the middle of the game the management requested that he leave his box seat because his presence was creating an unruly commotion.

Pepitone shuffled from the Yankees to the Houston Astros to the Chicago Cubs to the Atlanta Braves in three years of controversies with managers and owners marked by suspensions and fines. After quitting the Braves in 1972, one of the pro teams in the Japanese major leagues made him a three-year offer he couldn't refuse. In that foreign land, he wasn't playing well, but the fans were as adoring as ever.

When I met Joe, he was visiting his mother in the Rockaway section of Brooklyn, a quiet, immaculate street lined by identical two- and three-story red brick apartment houses with identical sidewalks flanked by little plots of grass. An Italian Civil Rights League decal was pasted on the window of the front door. Pepi was visiting with his newest wife-to-be, Stephanie, and his friend Sam, a member of the Chicago Cubs ground crew. We sat in the living room, a picture of the Virgin Mary on the wall behind Joe.

"I'll tell ya about my first year in professional baseball," Pepitone said. "I went down to play for Auburn, New York, Class D, the last month of the 1958 season. I had just signed, and they needed an outfielder. That's when I first met Phil Linz. When I got there, I looked around, and I said to myself, 'Who can I get to be friends with?' and I saw this guy with glasses, skinny as hell, and I said, 'Yeah, him.' And little did I know that I was getting involved with a maniac! Worse than me! My first week on the team we were on a road trip, staying in an old hotel in some little hick town. Phil and I were rooming together, and it's night, and we're laying on our beds, and all of a sudden a water balloon comes through the transom above the door and splatters on Phil's bed. So Phil turns to me and says, 'Hey, Joe, the shit's on tonight—a water fight. You want to get in on it?' I said, 'Okay, as long as the other guys don't mind.' So Phil goes to his dresser drawer and takes out about fifty balloons, and starts filling them up with water. Fifty. I don't believe it! And I can hear the other guys running down the hall. We go out of our room, and these guys are throwing water balloons through the door transoms, kicking open doors and throwing balloons at other guys, and Phil says to me, 'Joe, grab the fire extinguisher. Someone's coming down the hall.' So I grabbed it off the wall and stood around the corner, and when the guy gets near me, I turn the extinguisher over, and *pssssssssssssssssssss*. I cover him with foam. Cover him. And he's standing there, and I'm squirting, laughing my ass off, and then I see he's wearing a suit. It's Tommy Gott, my manager.

"I said, 'I'm sorry, Mr. Gott.' And I turn the extinguisher back over, but it ain't stopping. *Shhhhhhhhhhhhhhhhhhhhhh*—all over the place. All the wallpaper was ruined. And the next day Gott called me over and he said, 'Joe, I have to send in a report to the Yankees about this. I'm not going to fine you, but this report will stick with you for the rest of your career.' And for the rest of my career I did nothing but get in trouble."

"I heard that once you hijacked an elevator," I said.

"That was in Amarillo," Pepitone said. "I got back to the hotel about two o'clock in the morning—curfew was at twelve—and it was another one of those old hotels with a hand elevator. The operator was sleeping in front, and we knew he was a stool pigeon for our manager, Sheriff Robinson. We knew he snitched on everyone who came in late, see. So me and my roomie, Joe Miller, he was our catcher, we took off our shoes and we snuck by him and closed the elevator door real quick. But we must have woke him up, because right after we closed the elevator door, he started banging. 'Let me in, let me in.' And I was running the elevator, and that son of a bitch elevator, I couldn't get it to stop at the floor. I almost drove it through the ceiling. And the only place I could get it to stop was between floors, so we forced open the door, climbed on top of the car, and forced open the outside door at our floor. And now they couldn't find the elevator because it was between floors. They just can't find it, so they call up Sheriff Robinson and they tell him that they think one of his players stole the elevator. So Sheriff calls my room. The first guy he calls is me! Miller answers the phone, and Sheriff says, 'Is Pepi in?' Joe says, 'You don't want me to wake him, do you?' So Sheriff says, 'Yeah, wake him.' So I grab the phone and say, 'Is something wrong? What's going on? Is anybody sick? What are you waking me up for?' He says, 'Don't give me that. Did you steal the elevator?' I said, 'Man, what are you talking about? Steal an elevator? You got to be kidding—I've been asleep since nine o'clock. I'm trying to sleep, and you're telling me that I stole an elevator! Are you drunk?' I said. So Sheriff says, 'Now listen, Joe. Tell me the truth. Did you steal it?' I said, 'Oh no, Sheriff. That's stupid. How can you call me up and ask me a stupid question like that?' "

When Robinson hung up in disgust, Pepitone and Miller were rolling on the floor in gales of laughter. The next day the hotel found its elevator. "To this day," said Pepitone, "every time I see Sheriff, he says, 'Hey Joe, I talked to Joe Miller the other day, and he told me you stole the elevator.' Since 1961 he still asks me if I stole that elevator. That was a funny night. He called up, and he said, 'Okay, Joe. Where the fuck is the elevator?' We had fun. We just had a lot of fun.

"I remember the first year I came up with the Yankees in 1962. We were in Detroit early in the season, and I had a date with a stripper for three in the morning. We're on the road, and it's about one, so I get up and get dressed, put on a suit and tie and shaving lotion all over my body. Linz is in the other bed sleeping, and I'm dressed and ready to go. I tiptoe out of the room and press the elevator button, and the elevator comes up, the door opens, and as I go to step into it, who's coming out but Ralph Houk. So Ralph looks at me, and he says, 'Where the hell are you going?' And I didn't know what to say—here I am all dressed up, smelling like a prince, and I said the first thing that came into my mind. 'Phil hasn't come in yet, and I'm going out to look for him.' 'You're what?' Ralph said. I said, 'I'm worried about Phil. I'm going out to look for him.' And Ralph says, 'Get back in your room or you're going to find your ass back in Richmond.' I said, 'Okay, Ralph. I'll go back to my room.' And Ralph follows me into the room, and there's Phil in bed, of course, and I look at Phil and say, 'Hey, man, how did you get here? Where the hell were you?' And Phil says, 'What do you mean, where was I? What the hell are you talking about?' And the next day I was back in Richmond. I swear to God. Ralph sent my ass out."

Yet despite Pepitone's antics, the skinny first-baseman with the quick bat had the potential to be a super-star, so when Hamey and Houk were offered L. A. Dodger pitcher Stan Williams for veteran Bill (Moose) Skowron during the winter of 1962, they made the deal confident that Pepitone would be ready to replace Skowron in 1963.

"I told him in '62, too," Pepitone said. "I said, 'Moose. This is your last year.' He says, 'In another five years you can have the job.' I says, 'No, Moose, in '63 I'll be the first-baseman.' He says, 'Another five years. I've got to teach you everything first.' I said, 'You don't have to teach me nothing. What can you teach me about first base, you clumsy ox, you?' Mickey used to laugh at what I said to Moose. Mickey used to tease Moose, he'd say, 'What do you know about first base? Every time you stretch you hurt yourself.' But I tell you, Jesus Christ, Moose used to get mad at me. One day he said something to me, and I said, 'Yeah, yeah. Now I know why they call you Moose. Not because you're big and strong, but because you look like one.' I would say, 'Next year and you're gone.' And that was '62, and they won the world series. I only played half the season and wasn't eligible for the world series, so I'm watching TV, and a picture of me comes on, and they say, 'Bill Skowron traded to the Los Angeles Dodgers.' I'm sitting in a chair in my living room, and I got chills. I said, 'Oh gee, I hate to see Bill go, but,' Pepi looked crestfallen and then brightened, 'but fuck him.' "

During the spring training of '63 Pepitone hit twelve home runs and clearly demonstrated his professional ability.

"It's the last day of spring training before cut-down day," Pepitone said. "I was scared. I didn't want to come to the ball park. And I'm sitting in my locker stall, and I'm watching for Pete Sheehey, because he's the guy who tells you Ralph wants to see you to send you down, and sure enough, here he comes. He walks over to me and says, 'Ralph wants to see you.' My face started wrinkling up, and I was going to cry. I went into Ralph's office, and Ralph says, 'What the hell do you want?' I said, 'Pete told me you wanted to see me.' He said, 'Get the hell out of here. You're going with us to New York.' " Sitting in his mother's living room, Pepitone let out a banshee scream that probably was heard in Staten Island. *"Yeeeeeeeeeeeeeeeeeeah.* And I ran out, and everybody came over and shook my hand. Beautiful." Joe hit .271 his rookie season with twenty-seven home runs and eighty-nine RBI's. "It was beautiful," said Pepitone. "When you're winning, everything is good. You put on that uniform, and what a feeling! Because you're the best. At the time we were the greatest. I would put my uniform on, and my number was 25, and as soon as I put it on, I felt like I was 6 foot 10 and weighed 280 pounds, and I was the strongest son of a bitch in the whole world. That was the feeling you got when you put it on. And man, you broke your ass for the Yankees. You really worked hard, because if everybody else was hitting, you *had* to hit too. But we had fun. We had so much fun. And that's what you don't see in baseball any more—the kidding around. You had a bad day, and you didn't feel too bad about it because you were having fun. But now everything is so serious, if you have a bad day you worry about it. It's bad news. And I'm tired of traveling, man. It's about time for me to pack it in." Joe was dour. Then he brightened. "Did they ever tell you about the time I put washing-machine soap in Mantle's whirlpool? You can't see the soap. And he's in the thing, and it's like 130 degrees in there, and he sits down and turns it on, and instantly, *whoooooooooooosh,* he's drowning in bubbles! And he came running out of there, and I'm hiding in my locker, and all I can hear is this, 'Where is that son of a bitch? Where is he?' I said, 'Uh oh!' And he really took off after me.

"I loved Mickey Mantle," Pepitone said. "He treated me so nice, and I showed him ten times as much respect. Listen, Mickey took care of me. I was separated from my second wife, I didn't have much money, and I was living day to day on paychecks, and Mickey says, 'You come stay with me at the St. Moritz.' And I stayed with him in his suite for a month. He took me everywhere he went. He wouldn't let me take a penny out of my pocket. And he just got involved with me, told me everything. He'd come home at night, and he'd cry. He'd cry about how he thought he was going to die soon. About how his father died so young. He was actually crying. Sitting there, crying. And I'd grab him and hug him. I'd say, 'Mick, come on, man. Hey, idol.' He was just a beautiful person, and the last few years he played I never saw him leave his hotel room. He'd never go out on the street. He couldn't. If Mickey Mantle would walk down the street, you'd have 10,000 people after him. He'd go to a restaurant, and he couldn't finish a meal, 'cause every ten seconds there was someone at the table. I remember one time we went to the Tower East. I was dressed in a black suit, wore dark glasses, and we went in and sat down, and whenever someone came over to the table, I would look at them and growl, 'Hey you, get away. He don't want to be bothered. Understand?' And they left. They thought I was his bodyguard. I swear it.

"One time I wanted to pick up the check in the worst way while I was staying with him at the St. Moritz, and I had heard him on the phone ordering something from downstairs, and he said, 'Joe, I'll be right out. I'm taking a shower.' And I said to myself, 'When the stuff gets here, I'm going to pick up the check.' So the goddamn tray comes in, and it has a white tablecloth over it, and the food is piled two feet high, and I say to the waiter, 'Give me the check for this.' And he said, 'It's for Mr. Mantle.' I said, 'That's all right, I'll pay for it.' And what I didn't know was that he was having people over, and I looked at the check and it was for $230! I said to the waiter, 'Uh, just one second. Mr. Mantle is in the shower. He'll be right out.'

"And then he came out of the shower and ordered a hamburger. I picked up the hamburger, and I was barely able to afford that.

"He was the nicest guy in the world. Just fantastic," said Joe. "A man of many moods. He really would get depressed a lot. He had a lot to worry about. He worried about his health, his family having a history of death at young ages, and even though he was so healthy, those are the people it happens to, and it was really on his mind. He would play with injuries, and if he didn't play good, he'd cry. I couldn't believe it. One time he was really in a bad slump, this was 1965, and I think he was something like oh for twenty. The club was in second or third, and he knew the club wasn't going anywhere without him hitting. During the game I went down to the dugout toilet, which is right down the dugout stairs and he was in the bathroom. Crying. Sobbing. And I was shocked, and I went up and told Ralph Houk, and Ralph said, 'Joe, he'll be all right. He'll be all right.' And I went down and said, 'Hey, come on, Mick.' And I started crying, too. Here's a man who was so dedicated, who loved the game so much, a guy who did so well for so many years, and he didn't want to start losing now. I gained so much respect for him. There were times when I'd say, 'I don't feel like playing. I'm tired,' and I'd look out in center field, and here's this man, and I'd say, 'Jesus Christ. If he can play, I got to play, too.'

"Mantle," said Pepitone, "has been an idol for so many years to people my age and your age, and they grow up idolizing him, and then Jim Bouton goes and says those things about him in *Ball Four* about him closing bus windows on the kids' fingers and stuff like that. Listen, if you had 4,000 kids sticking pens through the window, hitting you in the eye, in the chest, you'd try to get away from them, too. Mickey would sign autographs, but you can sign just so many, and then when you try to close the window, push their hands away, maybe you are going to catch somebody's hand. Jim made it sound like the worst thing in the world.

"Kids grew up with a lot of good images about Mickey Mantle," he said. "They felt good just thinking about him, and the next thing you know they're depressed because of what Jim wrote. Why should Jim give a shit? He's not going to see the kids' faces, see the way they feel. And then Jim Bouton puts in the book, 'If he didn't drink so much, and if he didn't do this so much and if he didn't do that so much.' How can you make a statement like that? Who the hell are you to make a statement like that? This is the greatest player in the world. If Jim didn't talk so much, maybe he might have been the greatest player in the world. You know? He still might be around. But I can't cast opinions on anybody. I don't have a degree on casting opinions, man."

"Were you friendly with Jim?" I asked.

"I had mixed feelings about Jim," Pepitone said. "At times I couldn't stand him. Things I've seen him do all through the minors when we played together. Him pitching a game, and I'd miss a ball at first, and he'd turn around and scream and holler, and then in the papers he'd say something like, 'If Pepitone didn't miss that ball, I would have won.' You just don't do that. Jim Bouton was for Jim Bouton. He really was. And that's cool, that's fantastic. But keep it to yourself; don't let everybody know about it. I think that today most ball players, whether they admit it or not, are for themselves. But they won't show it. They'll go out and hit behind the runner to show what a team player they are, but still they think about themselves. Jim showed it. And he also put down other players to the writers. And then his book made a lot of enemies. There were just things that he wrote that he could have been more discreet about. But that isn't going to sell books. If you're going to sell a book, you're going to have to write exactly the way it is. Jim didn't care who he hurt. You can't write about Mickey Mantle beaver shooting. I remember one time they told me to come up on the roof of the Shoreham Hotel in Washington, and they said, 'Look.' And in one window we could see a girl with a bra and panties on. I said, 'Wow, big deal.' I had just come up there from my room where I was in bed with a girl who was naked. Big deal. The way Jimmy explained it, though, we were up there every night.

"I'd get mad at Jim Bouton. I got in a couple of fights with him. But we had a funny kind of relationship. I don't dig him, and then I do. I like him and I don't. You know. You think about what Jim has to say, about what he thinks about the baseball owners, and I respect him. How they were, how they wheel and deal. Hell, if they can, they'll take whatever money is coming to you and take it right out of your pockets. They kick you around, treat you like cattle, sell you here, sell you there, and you have nothing to say about it, and that's bullshit. You can't believe how these people can become so involved in your life. That's what baseball can do. I don't give a shit how much you're making. They can't pay you enough.

"I've come to the conclusion that I can play another five years. I know my potential. I know I can go out, swing a bat and hit, and I can play better than 75 percent of the guys playing today. But I have to love the game to play it, and I can't do it any more. It's tough to play baseball and have fun. The older managers don't understand what's going on, don't understand the kids today. The players' attitudes aren't what they used to be. It's not that gung-ho shit. They want to have some fun, they want to laugh, they want to be friends with the other players. But these managers who have been managing for twenty years, they give you that ole Gashouse Gang shit, and they treat the ball players their way—kick 'em in the ass, yell at 'em, fine 'em. Bullshit like that. They tell me, 'Don't talk to the other ball players because they're your enemy.' Bullshit. They're my friends. I got to know everybody in both leagues, and I'm really going to miss the guys themselves, and I'm going to miss the fans. I really enjoyed getting on the field before the game and feeling the respect they had for me. But as far as the owners and the managers are concerned, they can go shit in their hats. Today you've got a lot of ball players who don't want to play any more, some great players who could draw people into the park. Shit, I'm not saying I'm the greatest ball player in the world, but I draw more people to the park than most of the guys who are playing today. Because the fans like to see the players kidding around. They like to see color and charisma. The guys can't fight any more. You can't yell at the umpire, kick dirt. Man, they love that. That's what they come to the ball park for. Not to watch some goddamn boring ball game. You take such shit when you're a player."

"Did Yogi give you a hard time?" I asked.

"No. I liked Yogi as a manager," Pepitone said. "Yogi got me to play in 160 ball games. I used to come up to him and say, 'I don't feel good today.' He'd say, 'You're playing.' I'd say, 'Yogi, I'm sick.' He'd say, 'You're playing.' And he'd turn around and walk away. I played 160 ball games. And I had my hundred-RBI season that year. Twenty-eight home runs. He made me play and I admired him. Left-handers, right-handers, I played. And I remember at the end of the 1964 world series against the Cardinals, and he said to me, 'Listen, I've got a meeting today. I'm going to sign a new contract today. Make sure you come down to spring training light. Don't get heavy now.' And then I found out he was released. I was shocked. It was hard to believe. And I think that was the start of the downfall right there. He was good. I enjoyed him. There were a couple guys who used to make fun of him when he used to pronounce the lineup. He'd go over the lineup, and when he went to say Yastrzemski, he'd say, 'Yastreski,' you know. But what the hell. The man knew his baseball. I don't care if he can't pronounce a name. It means nothing. The man's a millionaire, and that shows me some smarts right there. There are plenty of guys who know how to read and are poor. I admired the guy. He made me play. And he's Italian, and that made me like him even more. He just really understood me. He knew when I was bullshitting him or not. I'd say, 'I'm all upset today, Yogi.' He'd say, 'Yeah, I know you are, Joe. But you won't be upset, because you're going to get two hits today.' You look in the book. That's the most games I ever played in a season.

"You remember Johnny Keane, may he rest in peace," Pepitone said. "He was the start of my problems on the Yankees. Right off the bat he and I didn't hit it off. He had something against me. One time I was taking my time dressing, and everybody was out taking batting practice, and my turn for hitting hadn't come up yet, but he wanted me to get out there and field some ground balls. So he came in the locker room and he said, 'Get your backside up and get dressed and let's hurry out there.' And I said, 'I'm getting dressed. Don't worry about it.' He said, 'Right now.' I said, 'Johnny, please leave me alone. I'll get dressed. I'll be right out.' He said, 'Right now. I'm going to stand here until you leave.' So I ripped off my uniform, my buttons, ripped my pants off, and I threw them at him. I said, 'You take this uniform and shove it up your ass.' And I got dressed and walked out of the ball park. When he came, that was it for the Yankees.

"After I got traded to Houston, I once walked out on the field during batting practice without a hat, and Harry Walker, the manager, yells at me, 'Goddamn it, Pepitone. Put your hat on. You're a ball player.' Pull my pecker. You know what I mean? I'm also me. When I was traded to Houston, Walker gave us a paper with twenty-five rules and regulations on it. He said to me, 'If you don't like some things, just cross them off and hand the paper back to me.' So on the top of the paper it said, 'Rules and Regulations.' I crossed that out. I said, 'I don't want to read the rest of it. Leave me alone and just let me play my game.' He said, 'Those rules are going to help us win ball games.' I said, 'Ain't nothing going to help you win ball games except us players. You're not going to win them.' Here's a manager making $20,000 yelling at $100,000 ball players. I just couldn't stand it. I gave up. I need the money? You can take the salary and shove it up your ass. My own head and my own being mean more to me than the money. I can go down to Coney Island and buy four Nathan's hot dogs and lie on the beach all day. A lot of people say, 'Who are you going to live off of?' I'll live off my mother. She'll take good care of me.

"It got so bad," said Pepitone, "that I didn't even like to touch a baseball. I was right down the street here walking my dogs, and kids were playing, and someone hit the ball to the outfield, and the ball rolls near me, and one kid yells, 'Hey mister, get the ball.' I said, 'Fuck you. Get the ball yourself.' I wouldn't even go after it. You know? That's how much they made me dislike the game. The 'I own you' type of attitude. Ain't nobody owns me. You know? It took the fun right out of the game. And I'll only do something if I can have fun, 'cause if I'm having fun, I don't give a shit if I'm making $100 a week. Enjoying myself, making me happy that I'm doing a job—that's what's important. Take Richie Allen of the Chicago White Sox. Chuck Tanner, the manager, lets Richie do whatever he has to do. If Richie wants to work out, Richie works out. If he doesn't, he doesn't. But Richie goes out there and does his job. 'Cause he's left alone. You tell him what to do, yell at him, and he'll either punch you in your face or he'll walk out on you. And without him, the White Sox are nothing. And that's the way you have to treat kids today. Kids today have their own minds. So together. College educated. And if they don't have baseball, they're going to do something else. That's their attitude.

"Hey man," he said. "I got a thousand problems. But you'll never notice them. What's the worst that can happen? Are they going to electrocute me? Are they going to hang me? If it came to that, then I'd start worrying. But they can't do that to me. I just believe in laughing, having good friends, and making my friends laugh and have fun with me. That's it. Just having a ball, man."

On September 17 the Yankees regained first place after they defeated the Los Angeles Angels the last two out of three games. Chicago and Baltimore were only one game behind. But in the next week the Yankees won nine more games in a row from lowly Kansas City, Cleveland, and Washington for eleven straight, and with only eight games left in the season took a three-game lead. Once more the team played like a well-oiled machine. Roger Maris retained his home-run touch, striking his 1,000th career hit and 236th home run to defeat the Angels, and Ford rejoined Stottlemyre, Bouton, and Downing, to form the best starting staff in the majors. Mantle, Howard, and Pepitone hit with vigor. Among the starters, only Tony Kubek was having difficulty. Hampered by a back condition which did not allow him to raise his right arm properly, Kubek, hitting less than .230, two weeks before the end of the season became so frustrated after striking out, he stormed from the dugout to the clubhouse, and on the way out violently punched the dugout door which he thought was plywood but which was actually metal sheeting. Kubek suffered a severely sprained wrist, and he was out for the rest of the year. Phil Linz replaced him at shortstop.

Pete Ramos continued to be a bullpen stopper, performing with perfection his first eight appearances, and entertaining his teammates with his cowboy outfits, fine cigars, and passion for night life. Pepitone confounded the Yankee trainer by placing a piece of popcorn under his foreskin, claiming he had contracted a new strain of venereal disease.

With three days left in the season Ford threw a four-hitter to clinch a tie for the pennant, and the next day the Yankees won their fifth in a row as Mikkelsen rewarded Berra's faith in him with a relief win. Ramos pitched a 1, 2, 3 ninth inning. Despite the seemingly insurmountable obstacles, Berra's patience and outer calm were being vigorously applauded by season's end. Yogi never panicked, even in the face of his players' preference for Ralph Houk as manager. With the inexperience of his rookie season behind him, Berra understandably felt he had a very bright future as the Yankee manager.

Over in the National League the Philadelphia Phillies under manager Gene Mauch were leading the league by six and a half games in mid-September and seemed a shoo-in, but Mauch, unlike Berra, panicked when his team began to lose, and the Phillie pitching staff became so fouled up that the team crashed in one of the worst collapses in baseball history. While the Cincinnati Reds were winning nine in a row, the Phillies were losing ten in a row, and when the St. Louis Cardinals then won eight in a row, both the Reds and the Cards passed the Phillies with only days remaining in the season. It was a season of turmoil for National League managers. Pirate manager Danny Murtaugh was ill and stepping down, and Cincinnati manager Freddie Hutchinson was dying of cancer. Johnny Keane, the St. Louis Cardinal manager, became so incensed at owner Gussie Busch's lack of faith in him before his team began its run for the pennant that Keane tendered his resignation, declaring that he would not be Cardinal manager in '65 even if the team won the pennant—which they did on the final day of the season with a win over the Mets while the Phils knocked the Reds out of contention.

It was an embarrassing situation for Gussie Busch when the season ended with the Cardinals in first place. Busch pleaded with Keane to return, but it was even more embarrassing to Keane and to Ralph Houk and the Yankee management, because Houk had sent Mayo Smith to speak to Keane in early September to see if Keane wanted to manage the Yankees in '65, and John had said yes. Thus when Busch was offering Keane his old job back with a new contract and a whopping raise plus a belated apology, Keane, a religious man, had to lie to Busch that he "didn't know" if he wanted to return. Keane could not tell Busch that he had already agreed to manage the Yankees the next year. Thus when the Cardinals and the Yankees both unexpectedly won their pennants, Johnny Keane was managing against the team he knew he would be leading the following year!

While Ralph Houk and Johnny Keane were carrying out their embarrassing charade, in Washington, D.C., President Johnson, running for reelection after finishing John Kennedy's term, was leading an unsuspecting American public into a devastating war with a charade of his own. In late September it was reported by the State Department that two American destroyers, the *Richard Edward* and the *Morton,* were fired upon by four attacking North Vietnamese gunboats, seemingly all poor shots as no damage to the American ships was reported. The Republican presidential nominee, Barry Goldwater, proclaimed, "As sure as the sun sets, we are at war." The North Vietnamese swore that none of their ships attacked anyone. Johnson, firm, told the American people that the Vietnamese were lying. The Pentagon had some doubts as to whether the attacks ever did take place, and there was censorship of letters from American seamen on the two ships who tried to write home that they had not been attacked. One sailor, whose letter got through the censorship, wrote that North Vietnamese ships were sighted. "We shot at them," the sailor wrote home. "They didn't shoot at us." Johnson, gearing the country for war, coerced Congress, citing the attack on our ships, into backing his escalation of the fighting in Vietnam. Before the Tonkin Gulf incident, only 190 U.S. soldiers had been killed. "Before I send American G.I.'s into war," Johnson said, "I must consider every facet very carefully." After Johnson's term, 25,000 American soldiers lay dead in the hostile rice paddies of a devastated country.

At home the 1964 world series was billed as the corporate championship of baseball, the CBS Yankees against the Anheiser-Busch Cardinals. The Cards, having won the pennant in the last few days, were a strong, balanced ball club with excellent pitching and consistent, strong hitting. Bob Gibson, 19–12, was the ace of the Cardinals' staff, the money pitcher on the team, and two left-handers, Ray Sadecki, a 24-year-old, and Curt Simmons, ten years his senior, won twenty and eighteen games respectively during the season. The Cards had two hitters with 200 hits for the season—Curt Flood, the introspective, moody center fielder, and Lou Brock, catalyst of the Card pennant, a .345 hitter after he was traded from the Chicago Cubs to the Cards in mid-June. Both Flood and Brock were exceptionally fast, scoring consistently in front of Ken Boyer, Clete's older brother, a fine third-baseman whose 119 RBI's led the majors. Bill White, the smooth, intellectual first-baseman, hit .303 with 102 RBI's, and starring for the Cards at shortstop was Dick Groat, the shortstop for the Pirates for almost ten years, a .292 batter this year with seventy RBI's. Tim McCarver, the catcher, in his second year as a regular, and Mike Shannon, the third outfielder, were hitters who were home run threats. This was a strong Cardinal team, and the Yankees, no longer considered the supremely invincible team of the past, were at even a greater disadvantage, having to play at less than full strength because of the loss of the hot-tempered Tony Kubek, and the ineligibility of Pedro Ramos, the only effective reliefer in the Yankee bullpen the last two weeks. Ramos had arrived too late in the season to play in the series.

The first two games were played at Busch Stadium, once called Sportsman's Park, the home of the Cardinals since 1920, a homey arena with a country-fair atmosphere, and a right-field wall only 310 feet from the plate. Ray Sadecki, the Cards' starter, was in the fourth grade when Ford pitched in his first world series as a rookie in 1950, winning the final game against the Philadelphia Whiz Kids. Since that year Ford had pitched world series games in the Polo Grounds, Ebbets Field, County Stadium in Milwaukee, Forbes Field in Pittsburgh, Crosley Field in Cincinnati, Candlestick Park in San Francisco, Chavez Ravine in Los Angeles, and now Busch Stadium in St. Louis. Whitey had won and lost more series games than any other pitcher, and recorded the most innings pitched, strikeouts, and walks in series play. He was a walking series record book.

Ford, hiding the pain he felt when he had to throw a curve, was not sharp in the first game. The Cards singled home runs in the first and second innings, but Tom Tresh overcame the deficit with a three-run home run deep to left center to temporarily give the Yankees a 3–2 lead in the fourth. Tresh, performing excellently in his third-straight series, also singled home a run in the fifth as the Yankees went ahead 4–2, but an inning later Ford stopped retiring batters. Ken Boyer singled, and Mike Shannon, born and bred in St. Louis, platooned most of the season, tied the score with a towering 500-foot home run that sailed over the left center-field wall at the 358-foot mark, over thirty rows of bleachers, higher than the scoreboard atop the bleachers, and hit against the *B* of the Budweiser sign crowning the scoreboard. When McCarver followed with a double to right-center, Yogi removed Ford. New York lost the game when Cardinal pinch hitter Carl Warwick singled against reliefer Al Downing and drove in McCarver. Four more runs against Downing and Rollie Sheldon, a pitcher largely forgotten by manager Berra all year long, sealed a 9–5 Cardinal win. In this loss the Yankees had scored more runs than they had in the entire 1963 series against the Dodgers. Ford, 10–8 in series competition, lost his fourth straight postseason game.

In the second game Cardinal pitcher Bob Gibson started out like a Sandy Koufax. After walking a batter to open the game, he struck out Richardson, Maris, Mantle, and Howard in succession. Nevertheless, going into the seventh he had given up a couple of runs and trailed 2–1 against Mel Stottlemyre, the poised sinker-ball-throwing rookie. The Cards fell farther behind in the seventh when Phil Linz singled, went to second on a wild pitch, and scored on a Richardson single. A Maris single and a Mantle ground-out scored another run, and with Gibson lifted and Barney Schultz in, the 37-year-old hero of the Cards' pennant drive, the Yankees scored three more runs. Linz opened the ninth with a home run, Maris singled, and against left-hander Gordon Richardson, Mantle doubled sharply over the third-base line, scoring Maris. A walk and a Pepitone single scored Mantle. Returning to the bench, Mantle sat down next to Ralph Terry. "You know my double," Mantle said to Terry, softly, matter-of-factly. "I wish it had gone foul. I would have hit one out of here."

Stottlemyre, the savior of the staff, was pitching a three-hitter into the eighth when he tired and gave the Cards four more hits and two more runs in an 8–3 victory. Mel, in top form, induced twenty-one of the twenty-seven Cardinals who were retired to ground out. He seemed a man destined to prolong the Yankee dynasty.

The series shifted to the Stadium for the next three games. Two eighteen-game winners, Jim Bouton and Curt Simmons, an original Whiz Kid, faced each other. Simmons had signed with the Phillies in 1947 as an 18-year-old school-boy, and three years later he, Robin Roberts, and Jim Konstanty led the Phils to a pennant. However, two weeks before the series against the Yankees, Curt had the honor of becoming the first major leaguer to be drafted in the Korean War, and he was deprived of his opportunity to pitch in the series. When he returned, the Phils wouldn't win a pennant again. Now, after sixteen seasons, Simmons was getting his chance. Throwing mostly change-ups and off-speed breaking balls, he battled young Bouton to a 1–1 tie through the eighth inning. Clete Boyer had driven in a run in the second inning for the Yankees, and Simmons himself drove in the Cardinal run in the fifth, but despite his RBI, when the Cards batted in the top of the ninth Simmons was removed for a pinch hitter by manager Keane. When the Yankees batted in the bottom of the ninth, Keane had to use another pitcher, and again he went with Schultz.

In the ninth the first Yankee batter was Mickey Mantle, who was standing with Ellie Howard in the on-deck circle as Schultz completed his warm-ups. "If he throws the first ball over," Mickey said, "I'm going to hit it out." When Schultz was ready, Mantle, batting left-handed, stepped in. Schultz threw one pitch across the plate, knee-high, a knuckle ball which didn't flutter, and from Mantle's bat there was a loud, sharp crack that reverberated like a gunshot. As 67,000 people stood to watch and marvel, the ball left the bat and rose until it hit the copper facade above the distant third deck in the right-field stands. It was still rising when it hit. Yankee rooters hollered, clapped, and carried on as Mantle slowly toured the bases and was greeted at home plate by his team-mates. Young fans were jumping over the fences to romp in the outfield, and as Mantle rounded third, Frank Crosetti, rarely demonstrative, slapped Mickey on the back and followed him, footstep by footstep to home plate where the Mick was mobbed in celebration. The home run, Mantle's sixteenth in world series competition, broke Babe Ruth's record. Bouton, pitching brilliantly, was the winner of the 2–1 Yankee victory.

Whitey Ford was the scheduled pitcher for the fourth game, but Al Downing took the mound instead, and those who knew Whitey feared that his arm was injured far more seriously than anyone was telling. Ford, dependable for so many years, didn't miss a series start unless there was something very wrong.

Downing was almost good enough. The Yankees scored three runs in the first inning on five hits, driving out Ray Sadecki. Roger Craig, the ex-Dodger and Met, relieved. Downing held his 3–0 lead for five innings, pitching one-hit ball and finally showing his potential in a series game after two years of lackluster postseason pitching. What happened to Downing in the sixth was not entirely his fault. Carl Warwick, again pinch hitting, singled, and Curt Flood singled, sending Warwick to second. After an out, Dick Groat then hit what should have been an inning-ending double-play ball to Bobby Richardson at second. Richardson, no more than fifteen feet from the bag, went for the ball as Linz, the shortstop, raced over to take the relay to start the double play. Bobby had trouble getting the ball out of his webbing, and Linz, who held his ground over the bag, was dumped by the hard-charging Flood, causing him to drop the ball. All three Cardinal runners were safe. With the bases loaded, the Cards' top RBI man, Ken Boyer, was the batter. Downing threw Boyer a low fast ball, ball one, and Yankee catcher Ellie Howard, feeling the shirts in the background were making it difficult for the batters to see Downing's lightning pitches, called for another fast ball. Downing shook him off, insisting on a change-up. Howard capitulated, Downing threw his change-up, and Boyer hit a long fly ball down the third-base line, deep enough to be a home run, but close enough to the line that none of the runners started until they saw the left-field umpire making a circular motion with his upraised right hand. Boyer had a grand slam and the Cardinals led 4–3. The Yankees were shut out the rest of the way. The series was tied at two apiece.

In the fifth game Stottlemyre and Gibson matched shutout innings until the fifth when the Cards scored two runs. Shortstop Linz, stumbling in pursuit of a pop-up hit by Gibson, thus was unable to reach the ball, so Tom Tresh had to race in desperation after it, and after a long run the ball hit his glove and bounced to the ground. With Gibson on first, Curt Flood then hit an easy double-play grounder to Richardson at second, who uncharacteristically fumbled the ball for an error. Lou Brock then singled in one run, and with one out Bill White grounded again to Richardson, who fielded this one cleanly and threw to Linz for the force. But Linz, hurrying his throw, bounced the ball in the dirt to first-baseman Pepitone who made a nice scoop to complete what should have been an inning-ending double play. First-base umpire Al Smith, though, called White safe, and another run scored as manager Berra and first-baseman Pepitone screamed in futility.

Gibson, leading 2–0, was pitching a four-hit shutout going into the ninth when Mantle hit a ground ball to sure-handed, experienced shortstop Dick Groat, the anchor of the Cardinal infield. Groat booted the ball. After an out, Joe Pepitone quick-wristed a Gibson fast ball right back at the tall pitcher, striking him on the hip. The ball rolled toward the third-base line. Gibson, catlike, pounced on the ball, and with a fluid underhand motion whiplashed it to first base after Pepitone had crossed the bag. Umpire Smith, again costing the Yankees, called Pepitone out, and this time Joe, first-base coach Jim Gleeson, and manager Berra were beside themselves. Now there was one man on and two outs in the ninth.

But young Tresh, surprising and delighting the Stadium crowd, hit a Gibson fast ball into the right-field bleacher seats, a two-run home run that tied the score 2–2. Had Pepitone properly been called safe, the game would have been over, the Yankees 3–2 victors. As Tresh circled the bases, the Yankee players were both elated not to have lost and frustrated not to have won. Bobby Richardson, whose error had allowed one of the Cardinal runs, was so excited he jumped up from the bench, striking his head on the concrete dugout roof and almost knocking himself out cold.

The elation lasted just five minutes. Rookie Pete Mikkelsen, 7–4 with 12 saves during the season, a rookie sinker-ball pitcher with control, pitched the Cardinal tenth. Mikkelsen walked Bill White, and manager Keane ordered Ken Boyer, his best power-hitter, to sacrifice bunt. Boyer complied, laying down a bunt to the first-base side of the mound as both Mikkelsen and Pepitone ran to cover first. No one ran to field the ball, and Boyer was credited with a single. Keane, still playing for the one run, ordered Dick Groat to bunt, and Mikkelsen threw a sinker ball that Groat missed. White, running from second to third on the pitch, should have been dead, but the surprised Ellie Howard threw the ball to third in the dirt, and White was safe. Groat grounded out, White holding third, and with men at first and third and one out, the Yankees needed a double play. Mikkelsen, pitching carefully to Tim McCarver, ran the count to 3–2 and then threw a not-so-fast ball that McCarver drilled into the lower left-field box seats for a three-run homer and a 5–2 Cardinal lead. Gibson, who struck out thirteen, retired the Yankees in the tenth as the Stadium ticket holders solemnly made for the exits. It was a loss the Yankees just could not accept. The two calls at first had cost them the game—and perhaps the series, unless they could win the final two games.

Back at Busch Stadium for the finish, the Yankees behind Jim Bouton won the sixth game, Jim's second series win, giving him twenty wins for 1964. Two singles and a double play gave the Cards a run in the first inning, but Bouton in the fifth singled home Tresh, who had doubled, to tie the score. In the sixth Curt Simmons, who allowed only two runs in thirteen innings of gutsy pitching and had nothing to show for it, threw Roger Maris a slow curve, and Maris pulled a long home run into the right-field pavilion, the ball caroming off the foul pole. Mickey Mantle followed Maris's home run with one of his own, hitting a slow outside curve to the opposite field to right, high off the screen in front of the right-field pavilion. The Yankees led 3–1, and in the eighth they scored five more runs against Schultz and Richardson, the unsuccessful Cardinal relievers. In the eighth with the bases loaded Keane brought in Richardson, a left-hander to pitch to the left-handed Pepitone. Pepitone swung at the first pitch, a darting slider, up and in, and popped it up behind the plate. McCarver raced back for the ball and unceremoniously dropped it. Richardson threw Pepi another slider, and Joe hit the ball completely over the roof in right field onto Grand Boulevard for a grand-slam home run. The Yankees ended the game with an 8–3 victory, forcing a seventh game.

It should have been Whitey Ford's game to pitch and win, but the circulation in his pitching arm was restricted and the blood to the main artery of his left shoulder was shut off completely, causing the entire area to ache like a tooth cavity. The pulse in his left wrist was imperceptible, his left hand was eerily cold, and he didn't sweat under his left armpit. "I'm the only guy," Whitey quipped, "who can get ten days out of a five-day deodorant pad." But the pain wasn't funny. Only a few nights before, Ford had been eating dinner in a St. Louis restaurant and couldn't raise his arm high enough to cut his tenderloin.

Without Ford, manager Berra didn't have a fresh pitcher he trusted. Bouton had pitched the day before, Stottlemyre two days before, and Yogi was not satisfied with Downing or with the others he had given up on months before: Bill Stafford, Ralph Terry, and Rollie Sheldon, all either sore-armed or ineffective, yet pitchers who only three years earlier were supposed to have kept the Yankees on top for the next decade. Berra decided to start Stottlemyre with only two days of rest. Keane did the same thing with Gibson.

For the third time in a series, the Yankees kicked the game away. With no score in the bottom of the fourth, the Yankee infield again submarined its pitcher. Ken Boyer singled, and after Groat walked, Tim McCarver bounced a grounder wide of first on which Pepitone made a nice stop in the hole to his right. Pepitone threw to Linz at second for the force-out, but Linz, inadequate at short throughout the series, threw a bouncer wide of first, allowing McCarver to be safe. Ken Boyer scored from second on the play. When Mike Shannon singled, McCarver went to third, and ahead 1–0 Cardinal manager Keane ordered a double steal which surprised catcher Ellie Howard who doubled-pumped waiting for someone to cover at second and then threw in haste, high and wide of the base. Second-baseman Richardson's throw back home to McCarver bounced in the dirt past Howard, and another Cardinal run scored. After Dal Maxvil singled, Shannon tried to score from second, and he was safe when Mantle's throw from center field was way wide of home. The Cards led 3–0.

In the fifth inning Berra relieved Stottlemyre with Downing, who threw four pitches: home run, single, double. Rollie Sheldon came in, and two more runs scored on a ground out and a sacrifice fly as St. Louis roared to a 6–0 lead.

Gibson, tired and perhaps letting up a little with a big lead, allowed sixth-inning singles by Richardson and Maris. Mickey Mantle, still heroic at age 33, with legs feeling twice that, pulled a home run into the left center-field bleachers for three runs, giving Mantle eighteen world series home runs, a record; forty RBI's, a record (one more than his manager, Berra); forty-two runs scored, a record; and fifty-nine hits, second only to Berra's 71.

In the seventh Ken Boyer homered off Steve Hamilton to make the score 7–3, and Gibson, fighting to the end, struck out Tresh in the ninth before allowing a home run by Clete Boyer, struck out Blanchard before allowing a home run by Phil Linz, and when Bobby Richardson, 13 for 32 with nine of those hits against Gibby, popped out to Maxvil at second, Gibson was mobbed by his teammates, his teammates were mobbed by the fans, and all of St. Louis exploded. For the Yankees the ending was fast, furious, and futile.

In the locker room there were only expressions of frustration. Stottlemyre, the loser, a kid pitching under the most difficult of circumstances with only two days' rest, told a reporter that he felt he had let down the entire team. Whitey Ford, overhearing, refused to allow Mel to disparage himself. "He did a tremendous job," Whitey said. Ellie Howard, protective of his young pitchers like a mother hen, put his arm around Stottlemyre and said softly, "You did a hell of a job." The general feeling was that the Yankees should have won the series with ease. That was always the feeling when the Yankees lost.

"We'll get 'em next year," Yogi Berra said in the clubhouse afterward, and there were valid reasons for Yogi's optimism. Yogi had come within one game of winning the world series during a year when Pepitone at first showed only flashes of his promise, both Richardson and Kubek were sub-par, Boyer didn't hit, Tresh was inconsistent, Mantle missed games with injuries, and Maris was cold until a team-leading September. In addition Berra was undercut by the gripes of some of his players, and his general manager had deserted him. With a pennant now under his belt, managing would be an easier task next year.

Berra, furthermore, would be coming to camp with the best group of starting pitchers in the league. His buddy Whitey Ford, 17–6 with a 2.03 ERA, would not have to double as pitching coach. There was Al Downing, 13–8, only 23 years old, fast and talented; Mel Stottlemyre, 9–3 with a 2.06 ERA after only two months' work, was a rookie; and there was the team's top winner, Jim Bouton, the Bulldog, 18–13 with a 3.02 ERA, only 25 years old, the Yankee workhorse who had also added two wins during the world series against the Cardinals, his second straight twenty-win season.

During the first half of 1964 it was Bouton who had held the Yankees back, pitching ineffectively with a sore arm, but after his arm recovered, he won thirteen games during the second half of the year, many of them key games down the stretch. Jim appeared to have the talent and ability to be a Yankee pitching star for many years to come.

But he wasn't. In spring training of 1965 his sore arm returned, plaguing him the entire season, and he finished 4–15. He was no longer the open, down-to-earth, opinionated, flaky guy who told jokes, cut your tie in half, and imitated Frankie Fontaine doing Crazy Guggenheim. When he stopped winning he became the commie, pinko, big-mouthed malcontent who talked to enemy reporters and who signed autographs for kids in order to show up the other guys. When he was traded to the Seattle Pilots in 1968 it was good riddance.

In 1969 Bouton wrote *Ball Four*, an irreverent—to say the least—look at his baseball world, a book he wrote with sportswriter Lenny Shecter, the players' most-hated New York writer. When Bouton's book was published, exposing some of his teammates as human beings who liked to have fun in human ways, some of those teammates regarded Bouton as Judas reincarnate. Part of the athlete's code has always been, "In this clubhouse what you hear here and see here, stays here." Bouton broke the code. He has suffered for it ever since. He has never been invited to a Yankee Old-Timers' Day game. Mickey Mantle and Ellie Howard, men who were close to him when they were teammates, refuse to have anything to do with him, and the baseball establishment has branded him a traitor.

For several years Bouton was a New York City sportscaster, a maverick who lends an irreverent and often humorous eye to the world of sports. Viewers love him and they hate him. Ignoring him is not easy. When Bouton visited Spain, he sent back a piece on bullfighting. He entered a ring and fought a mangy baby bull to show viewers what it would be like to face a snorting, raging beast in an arena. Bouton escaped intact. When he returned home, he received a letter from a fan. "Dear Jim," it said, "Too bad the bull didn't have better aim." In 1973 Bouton put on a disguise, a beard and moustache, to try out incognito as a 20-year-old kid pitcher with the Yankees. After his first few pitches, the Yankee scouts recognized his familiar overhand motion. They kept him at the tryout to have the satisfaction of telling him that he had flunked out.

Jim and his family live in suburban Englewood, just across the George Washington Bridge on the Jersey side. I visited him one Sunday morning. It's not a good idea to arrive before noon. He looks like hell.

After Bouton's freshman year at Western Michigan University, he was pitching for a top Chicago semi-pro team when major league scouts first took notice of him at the National Amateur Baseball Congress tournament at Battle

Creek, Michigan. Scouts from more than ten teams spoke to him, but after that summer tourney he only received a few tryouts, and those he failed. The scouts thought he was too small at 5 foot 10 and about 160 pounds. By that November young Jim sensed that nobody was really interested in him, and he was keenly disappointed. His dad, a clever guy, decided to write to the pro teams who had shown prior interest. He sent out a letter that read, "Dear———————, My son, Jim, is prepared to sign a major league contract by Thanksgiving. If you are interested, please have your bids in or else you won't get a chance to sign him. Sincerely, George Bouton." The Yankees sent in the only bid and signed Bouton. The George Bouton fake-letter gambit was a success.

He signed in the winter of '58, and after spending two years in the minors, like Pepitone and Phil Linz, Bouton found himself at Amarillo in 1961. "Pepi and Linz and I were considered brash and audacious by Yankee standards," said Bouton with a gleam in his eye, "but on the Amarillo team we were just three normal guys. This was one of the wildest minor league teams in baseball history.

"We had a guy by the name of Don Brummer, our second-baseman," he said. "He was probably one of the classic all-time movers with the ladies. We had songs for everybody on the club, and we would sing them while we were riding on the long bus trips. Brummer's was 'I Cover the Waterfront.' At two in the morning he could be seen pounding the pavement searching for stuff. Four in the morning! Brummer was like a ghost. We could be in a cab driving forty miles from town, and there would be Brummer standing on the corner, hustling. And then we'd drive back to the hotel, and there would be Brummer chasing stuff down in the lobby. Or down on the docks, Brummer would be there. Wherever we looked, Brummer was always there. I always wondered if there weren't three or four of Brummer.

"And there were Dick Berardino and Mike Mathieson, a roommate combination, and their style was to pull their car up to a girl in the next lane, roll down the window and say, 'Come up to our apartment now or forget about it.' Before Bobbi and I were married, she came down to see me, and half the ball club propositioned her before she got to see me. They knew she was my girl, but the way we felt about it, anybody was fair game including each others' girls and mothers. And we were a pretty persistent group. I remember we would pull into a town like Victoria, Texas, and the waitress would come over to us, and we would be, say, her fourth table, and one of the guys at our table would say, 'What are you going to be doing when you get off work?' And she would say, 'Are all you guys like this?' She had just been propositioned at the other three tables before she came to our table.

"And then there was Joe Miller from Linden, New Jersey. Joe Millah. Millah. He had a funny way of talking. Like he was from New Joisey. Miller was Joisey. He was Pepitone's roommate. I remember we were driving in our bus, and the distances we used to travel, if you transpose the map of Texas up north, some our trips would be as long as going from New York to Cleveland, so we took all the seats out of the bus and we had metal-frame, double-deck beds in there so we could sleep on the bus as we traveled from town to town. We were just constantly on that goddamn bus. One night it was about four in the morning, and we were driving to the next town, and everyone was asleep. Miller was sleeping in the front of the bus, and he had to go to the bathroom. He had one of the uppers, and so instead of getting out of bed, he just opened his window and went out the window. And Mathieson, who was sleeping in the back, was riding along with his window open, and all of a sudden he yells out, 'Holy shit. It's raining.' And it wasn't really raining at all. It was just Joe Millah.

"Amarillo was in the Texas League, and during the season we spent a couple weeks playing against teams from the Mexican League in Mexico. So here we are, a bunch of wild-ass sons of bitches, traveling through Mexico, and it's not the Mexico that the tourists know. Small towns. Poserica. Puebla. Vera Cruz, a very tough coast town, and I remember our manager, Sheriff Robinson, told us we should be very careful. 'Remember,' he said, 'the girls are going to say dos pesos. Dos pesos! Be careful, because if you guys don't watch out, they'll get the pesos, and you'll get the dose!'

"And I remember while we were playing in Mexico the whole team got Montezuma's revenge from drinking the water, and at times we didn't have hardly nine guys to put on the field. One game I had to play third base and a couple of the other pitchers had to play the outfield. And one game, I was pitching, and Mathieson, the third-baseman, he comes over and says to me, 'Don't let 'em bunt, because I'm not moving one inch for the ball.' And he stood there at third with his legs locked, as though they were cemented together. And when the inning was over, he walked off very, very slowly without making any sudden movements. We had a terrific ball club, a tremendous ball club, and we were winning all the time. We won the league in a runaway, but halfway through the season Sheriff got ulcers. And the Yankee management couldn't figure out why."

Bouton finished 13-7 at Amarillo with a 2.97 ERA in '61, and the next year he impressed manager Ralph Houk and made the Yankee varsity, pitching mostly in relief. In '63 he was inserted into the regular rotation in May. Bouton would put every ounce of his strength into each pitch, scraping his right leg against the ground on the follow-through and often knocking the cap off his head by the sheer force of his forward momentum. Mantle nicknamed him a "bulldog with stuff," and Bulldog Bouton won twenty-one and only lost seven that year, endearing himself to both management and the fans. He was touted as the best right-handed pitcher to come out of the Yankee farm system since Vic Raschi, and others compared him to Dodger star Carl Erskine and to Camilo Pascual, the excellent pitcher from the Washington Senators.

"What do you remember about the 1963 season?" I asked.

"I remember thinking," Jim said, "I didn't think it would be this easy. I remember thinking that I would be able to do this for years and years and years and years and that I would probably be in the Hall of Fame and it would be no sweat. That ball would just fly out of my hand, and it would do exactly what I wanted it to do, and it was fantastic. It took a lot of energy to throw it, but I had never had a sore arm. For my size I used to throw very, very hard. I thought, Jesus Christ, I would be able to throw forever. You know. That I have the right combination of guts, that I make the best pitches when the chips are down, that in the big ball games I usually did better. That I had all the ingredients for greatness. I thought it would be just a matter of showing up for spring training. No problem, year after year. That I could keep winning forever, and in '64 when Mel Stottlemyre came up, I figured with Stottlemyre, myself, and Al Downing, that we were just never going to get beat, that we were going to go on forever.''

"And then?" I said.

"And then," Bouton said, "about twelve guys got old one day. And it was the following morning when Tresh's legs got heavy and my arm started hurting me. And there were other reasons. The basic downfall, of course, was one that none of us were aware of. We were able to see it later upon reflection. It was that Dan Topping and Del Webb, knowing they were going to sell the ball club, did not invest in the foundation as they had always done in the past. Why shell out a lot of money for a Rick Monday when they would be long gone by the time Rick Monday bore fruit? So there was no investment in the basic guts of the team, the raw materials. So when the twelve guys got old, there was really nobody there to replace them. CBS bought a shell—a name and good will. They didn't realize that our minor leagues were empty. All those years we had been giving away two young guys for Dale Long. They had to stick with us as long as they could because they didn't have anybody else. We were allowed to hang on and do badly and continue struggling because there was nobody to replace us. Why did they stick with Pepitone all those years? Because Buddy Barker wasn't any better than Pepitone was.

"And there was one other thing," Bouton said. "The morale of the club disintegrated all at once when Houk became general manager in 1964. 1964 was his first year as general manager, and he had financial reasons for being tough on contracts, and I also think he wanted to set a precedent for being a tough guy. But he made me hold out. I had won twenty-one games, and I was asking for $20,000, a $10,000 raise for winning twenty-one games, which I didn't think was so outrageous. But he wouldn't give it to me, and I had to hold out until a week before the end of spring training. Outrageous. He threatened to fine me $100 a day if I didn't accept his offer of $18,500, and I was young and scared and didn't think I had any choice, so I signed. But after that I came to hate the guy. I came to realize that Houk had two faces, that he would do whatever he thought he had to do, whatever his job was, and I came to realize, and so did a lot of the other guys, that he never really had liked us when he was the manager. He only liked us because by being nice to us he was getting something out of us. But he never really cared for us as people. Otherwise why treat us that way when it came to paying us? But what can you do? So I lost a tremendous amount of respect for Ralph, and a lot of the other players did, too. They lost that deep feeling they had had for Ralph. We were just meat on the block. We all realized the reason he treated us the way he did in 1961, '62, and '63 was because he realized that that was the way to get the most out of us. It was calculated friendliness. It had nothing to do with the fact that he really respected us as people. We found out what he really thought of us when it came time to pay us money.

"And then in '64 there had been some grumbling about Yogi," Bouton said.

"This I couldn't understand, really, why the players didn't like Yogi. See, the players had liked Houk so much as a manager that they weren't able to accept anybody else, and we were never able to accept Yogi. Guys were constantly talking behind Yogi's back. It was really terrible. They'd say, 'Yogi has no tact.' 'Did you hear what Yogi said at the meeting the other day?' 'Yogi never gives you a pat on the back.' 'Yogi's not cracking down.' It was a universal thing. Richardson, Kubek, practically the whole ball club. And Yogi is a good manager. He knows strategy. He learned when to take his pitcher out of the ball game. The thing he's not good at is holding a team meeting. He would say things, and sometimes guys would laugh, giving the guys the opportunity not to respect him. He was not a commanding figure like Freddie Hutchinson or Ralph Houk, and he was not the type of guy to walk into the clubhouse and psychologically blow smoke up your ass like Houk was able to do. Houk knew just what to say to each guy. He had it all figured out, and he was a master psychologist. Yogi wasn't. Yogi was very blunt, but a good man nevertheless and a good manager. The Yankees won the pennant under Yogi. How bad could he have been, for Christ's sake? But Houk didn't think that Yogi was a good manager. Houk never backed Yogi up. Also Yogi had not been Houk's choice. Houk was given the general manager's job at the same time Yogi was given the manager's job. Houk considered it a big promotion, and he didn't want to rock the boat by saying, 'Hey, I don't think he ought to be manager.' And so Houk wanted to get rid of Yogi so he could get his own man in there. All the time the players would come in to Houk's office and complain that Yogi did this or did that, and 'Why can't you come back?' Houk never kicked those guys out of his office. He never said, 'Mind your own business and get the hell out of here.' He never did. He listened to all of them. He never backed Yogi up. Any time the players had a complaint about Yogi, he would listen, never sympathizing with Yogi. In June Yogi was gone. In June. Houk was looking for somebody already."

"Did you get along with Yogi?" I asked.

"Oh yes. I always got along good with Yogi," he said. "I've gotten along good with him all the way, even after *Ball Four* came out. I always have liked Yogi. In fact I got along with Ellie Howard, too. I got along good with everybody in '63 and '64 because in baseball your popularity seems to be in direct ratio to your won-lost record. Guys who have difficulty getting along with managers and coaches and other players usually are going bad and having trouble. On the Yankees we had very little animosity while the team was winning. It's so much easier to sit on the bench when the team is winning and it looks like you're going to get a world series share, so you want to stay around. But when the Yankees started losing, we started having the same internal problems as the other clubs. Listen, in '64 during the first half of the season I had a sore arm, and while I wasn't going so well, Yogi didn't pester you, didn't bug you. He didn't tell you to do this and do that. He knew my arm was bothering me and we just hoped that it would get better. He'd say, 'You'll be all right.' And then he'd leave me alone. And he kept me in the rotation, and after the all-star break I pitched two shutouts in a row, and I won thirteen games in the second half of '64. I finished 18–13, and then I won two more in the world series. In '65 that sore arm was there for the entire season, a dull toothache in my bicep. A tired arm. I must have strained a muscle next to the bone. But it never went away." Bouton finished 4–15 in '65 and was on his way out. In the next five years Bouton won a total of eleven games before he retired in 1970.

"And because you had rebounded in '64," I said, "that's why you continued to pitch in '65?"

"Right. But in '65 the soreness never went away. And that was it."

"What do you remember about '65?" I asked.

"In '65," Bouton said, "Houk finally got to pick his own man, and he picked Johnny Keane. Keane had won the pennant over at St. Louis, the players had really played for him over there, he sort of had the class-guy look about him, and he had been part of a winning organization for a long, long time with a reputation of building from the ground up, and so Ralph picked him. And he was absolutely the wrong guy. The players hadn't respected Yogi, but at least they liked him. Keane they didn't like or respect. Johnny was too old for us and too much of a traditionalist, and he never could get used to our outrageous habits and life style."

"Like what?" I asked.

"Like running around on the roof of the Shoreham Hotel, absolutely never coming in on curfew. Christ. During that spring training we hardly ever slept at all. I remember Keane's first meeting in spring training. He said, 'I'm Johnny Keane. We have a great ball club. I'm proud to be the manager of the Yankees. I've always considered this to be the greatest job in baseball. I want you to know that, and I will let you guys play ball, and I'm going to let you do things your way because you have been successful. I'm not going to try to tell you how to play ball. You're men, and I'm going to let you be on your own. In all my years of managing you're not going to show me anything that I haven't seen before.'

"Okay, fine," Bouton said. "About two weeks of spring training goes by, and in spring training we're losing, we're about one and eight, and Keane started hanging around the hotel, and nobody was coming in. Guys were drunk in bars, staggering around the hotel, guys were overweight, and we would come to practice in the morning with alcohol coming out of every pore of our bodies, and I want to emphasize the *our*. Include me in on this so we don't have any doubts. So John held another meeting. He said, 'Fellas, I told you the first day that I had seen just about everything in all my years of baseball. But men, I was wrong. There are about five of you who have gotten into some careless habits. You are acting very carelessly. And I would like to see a stop to that.' And I remember sitting in a bar with the guys, and I would say, 'Should we have another round?' And they would say, 'I don't know. It's awfully careless of us. Should we be doing something so careless? Yeah, let's.' And we still didn't keep any hours at all. And a couple weeks later we had another meeting, and he told us that there were about fifteen of us who were getting careless.

"Christ. We had never needed spring training before. Spring training was just so they knew we were going to show up for the first regular-season game. So maybe we would practice plane rides and bus rides a little before the season started. We really didn't need spring training. We had never kept hours in the past. We figured that Bobby Richardson was getting in early for all of us.

"But Keane couldn't tolerate this," he said, "and he wanted us to win in spring training, which had never been important to us in the past. If we won in spring training, big deal. If we didn't, so what? It didn't matter. We would start winning on opening day. So it was getting near the end of spring training and Keane called another meeting, and at this meeting the number of guys who had gotten careless had increased to twenty-three. And by that last meeting we were all sitting there snickering, grinning, with our hands over our mouths, and Bobby Richardson and Tony Kubek knew that they were the only ones on the club who weren't careless.

"But then Keane began to turn and become angry," Bouton said. "And where before they were only complaining once in a while about Yogi, they were complaining every single day to Houk about Keane, and it was terrible. And John didn't have the good humor to laugh it off. John didn't have any past good associations like Yogi did. We might laugh at Yogi, but we really couldn't get pissed off at him. Keane you could get pissed off at right away. John also was a very religious man, and our behavior was upsetting his moral values. Yogi didn't like it only because he thought we could play better with some rest. But Keane, this was an affront to his sensibilities as well. And John didn't have the patience and flexibility to deal with this. He was an older man, and he was convinced we were playing tricks on him. And I guess we were. We were always talking about what 'Squeaky' said today, always talking behind his back. I remember one time there was a group of us standing in the lobby, and John walked by and nodded his head, and we said, 'Good afternoon, John,' and he said, 'Good afternoon, gentlemen of the jury.' He knew he was on trial and that we did not care for him.

"And we had a lot of injuries that year. Mantle and Maris were playing tunes on their hamstrings every other week, and Keane thought the players were babying themselves too much, so then he started making guys play with injuries. He would always try to get Mickey to play in a game. That's in *Ball Four*. I used to make up this conversation where I was Keane and Mantle, and Mickey used to get a big kick out of it. I'd say, 'How's your leg, Mick?' And I'd say, 'Not too good, Skip. It's broken in four places.' 'But Mick, can you set the bones in time for the game? We sure could use you.' 'If I can set the bone, I can play, Skip.' 'Good. How's your back?' 'Skip, my back fell clean off.' 'Can you get another back, Mick? We can probably find one for you before the game starts.' 'That will be fine, Skip. If you find me another back, I guess I can play. Shit. I can play, Skip.' 'Good, Mick. I knew you could.' And he played Maris when he was injured and he shouldn't have been playing, and of course Houk backed Keane on that when he should have backed Maris, and Ellie played when he shouldn't have, and I pitched when I shouldn't have been pitching. The year was a disaster." The Yankees finished sixth that year, and in '66 when the team opened 4–16 under Keane, Houk finally agreed to return as manager. In '66 the Yankees finished last, and Keane passed away shortly thereafter.

"It was an extremely unhappy clubhouse that year," Jim said, "and everybody was in a bad mood. I can't remember laughing and smiling and joking like we used to. Everybody was rubbing each other the wrong way, and it was just an incredibly difficult period. My losing affected my personality. From being a pitcher who had it so easy, suddenly I had a sore arm and I wasn't contributing at all. It made me very difficult to get along with. Plus when you're not contributing, the other guys are not willing to go that extra step and tolerate what they otherwise might have. And these are very powerful people—Yogi, Whitey, Mickey, Maris, Boyer, myself—used to having control of destinies, controlling all situations, but when you put us all together in a losing situation, it's like taking rats and putting them in a tight situation where they can't get out and turning up the electricity. You can imagine what they would do to each other. And this is what was happening at the end.

"You see losing clubs bicker, and you think maybe if they pulled together they would win. No. That's not it. If they won, they would pull together."

In October of '68 Bouton was sold to the Seattle Pilots of the Pacific Coast League and remained with the Pilots in '69 when the team joined the American League. In mid-69 he was traded to the Houston Astros where he finished out the season. In *Ball Four* he described the 1969 season. The next year he quit baseball when he was sent to the minors.

"I had spent the last part of '68 in the minors," said Bouton, "so this was to be a book about a minor league team. This was no planned vendetta in my last year of major league ball. I didn't even know if I'd be in the majors in '69. I had wanted to write a book about baseball ever since my first spring training. A true book, because all the other baseball books had been such bullshit. But baseball is such fun, it's so exciting, and there are so many great tales and crazy stories. I remember my first day of spring training, with Auburn at Columbia, South Carolina. I pulled into town late at night, and there was a line of guys outside my hotel room. There was some local talent there entertaining the ball club one at a time. I said, 'Geez, I'm going to like this.' But I had grown up on Chip Hilton stories, the all-American boy who worked in the soda shop to support his widowed mother. Bobby Richardson is the only Chip Hilton I've ever met in baseball. So in the meantime Lenny Shecter, who had just done a story on the adoption of our son, David, who at the time was Kyong Jo, a Korean orphan, said, 'Why don't you keep a diary of the '69 season and talk it into a tape recorder at night? Maybe there'll be a book in it.' And that's what I did."

"Some of your teammates are pretty pissed off," I said, "especially that story you told about Mickey Mantle and the other guys on the roof of the Shoreham Hotel in Washington.

"You know," Jim said, "I never would have thought that people would get upset over that. In the book *I* was taking Hovley and Pagliaroni up on the roof to show them what *we* had done once with the Yankees. And I wasn't trying to tell it like it was something perverted, but what I was trying to say was, 'Gee, what an adventure. Can you imagine me, a nobody only a year or two ago, being up here with Mantle and the other guys on the Yankees? What fun this is.' In that vein. I never even considered that we were doing anything wrong. Christ. Much worse things have been committed. I'm sure, though, that Mickey has heard only the very worst of what I wrote, and it was probably exaggerated and told in the wrong context. For instance my feelings about why we were on the roof of the Shoreham Hotel. He probably was told that I accused him of some kind of perverted behavior, slinking around at night, when I didn't mean it that way at all.

"This is the thing," he said, "that I have felt worse about than anything—Mickey's reaction to the book. Because in many ways I always felt the same way that the other guys felt about Mantle. I loved him. When I was a player, I too loved him. He was winning games for me. He was great around the clubhouse, telling great stories. He was just fun to be around. When I was a rookie he was nice to me. There were so many reasons to love the guy. Shit. My first world series win, 2–1 over the Cardinals, Mickey hit a home run in the ninth off Barney Schultz to win. I think I jumped on Mickey's back. After my first shutout in the big leagues, Mickey laid a path of white towels from the clubhouse door to my locker. And I told about those things, but no one will ever tell him about them. He'll never read about them or listen to them, so he'll never know how I feel and how much I love him, too.

"But I was also a reporter, and there were some things I couldn't close my eyes to. The problems Mickey would have with the press, or when he would say 'Beat it' to a kid asking for an autograph. The reporter in me says I did the right thing, and then the ball player in me is saying, 'What happened to the great relationship you used to have with Mickey?' I remember he once told me in a bar one night that I reminded him of Whitey Ford, that I had the same kind of guts that Whitey had, that in the clutch I threw my best curve, and that's what he liked. These are things I will never forget as long as I live. So the ball player in me feels very, very unhappy about what happened since *Ball Four*." There was a deep sadness in Bouton's face, for as much as he enjoyed writing his book and enjoys producing his sportscast, like most ex-baseball players, he is an athlete first, and anything else second.

Jim's wife, Bobbi, who was sitting with us during the latter part of our discussion, had been silent until now when it seemed to be at an end. "Did Jim tell you," she asked, "how fast he'd drop everything to be able to pitch again?"

"He didn't have to tell me," I said.

The day after the final game of the 1964 world series manager Yogi Berra was spending the morning playing golf with Eddie Lopat and Joe Collins at the Ridgewood Golf Course in New Jersey when he received word that the Yankee management wished to speak with him. Yogi left the course and answered the clubhouse phone, fully expecting that Topping or Webb was calling to congratulate him and perhaps also discuss his contract for next year. Instead he was told that he had been fired as manager of the Yankees.

Firing Berra was a terrible stroke of public relations, one that became immediately worse when Berra was hired by the cross-town Mets to be a coach assisting Casey Stengel.

The next day both the Cardinals and the Yankees called major press conferences. The reporters arrived blasé and bored, assuming that both teams were going to announce the rehiring of their pennant-winning managers. They were wrong. That morning in St. Louis Johnny Keane announced that he was *not* returning to the Cardinals, and submitted his letter of resignation, shocking

Gussie Busch. At the news conference Keane was asked, "Do you have any future plans?" "To do a little fishing," Keane said, his plane ticket for New York City in his vest pocket.

At the afternoon press conference in New York, Ralph Houk, the Yankee general manager, announced that Yogi Berra had been dismissed by the Yankees because he could not communicate with his players and because he wasn't a good manager. Ralph never did explain that he hadn't ever wanted Yogi in the first place.

"Who's going to replace him?" Houk was asked.

"We have two or three men under consideration," Houk said.

"Is Keane one of them?" he was asked.

Houk acted surprised. "He's not available, is he?" Houk asked. Ralph was told by the reporters that Keane had resigned as Cardinal manager a few hours earlier.

"I didn't know that," Houk said, hoping the news conference wouldn't run too late and cause him to miss Keane's plane at LaGuardia airport. "In that case," Ralph said, "I would add him to the list."

Stan Isaacs, a friend and admirer of Berra's, fully understood Houk's role in these machinations, and shortly after Yogi was fired, in his *Newsday* column he presented Houk with an award. "It is for the number-one charlatan, mountebank, boob, quack, fop, fraud, and ass of the sporting panorama."

Several days later it was officially announced that Johnny Keane would become the new Yankee manager. Keane's reign as manager was disastrous. Yogi Berra looked like a great manager considering how poorly the Yankees played after he was fired. In 1965 the team started losing, and Keane, who was respected by few on the team, was constantly at loggerheads with his men. Clete Boyer entered everyone's doghouse by getting drunk and punching out a man in a Fort Lauderdale bar during spring training. Maris broke his hand during the season and became enraged and disenchanted when the management deliberately kept the extent of the injury from him. Ellie Howard injured his arm and Keane played him anyway. Tony Kubek's back pained him so badly he was barely able to bend over, and after a .218 season, he retired at age 29. Bobby Richardson hit .247, and he quit the next year at age 32 to be with his family. Joe Pepitone hated Keane and refused to play for him, and Mantle on one leg hit .255. In 1965 Mel Stottlemyre won twenty games and Ford won sixteen in his last productive season, but the rest of the staff foundered and the team finished a dismal sixth. In 1966 the Yankees opened with a 4–16 record, and Houk returned as manager. Lee MacPhail became the general manager. The move, however, failed to improve matters because the deep respect the players once felt for Houk had disappeared after his general managership and because by then the talent he had inherited had declined dramatically. In 1966 the Yankees finished dead last.

Then came the housecleaning. Roger Maris was traded to St. Louis for Charlie Smith; Clete Boyer went to Atlanta for Bill Robinson, who was supposed to be the next Yankee super-star; Phil Linz was traded to Philadelphia for Ruben Amaro, a no-hit, good field shortstop who injured his knee and retired. Bouton, after several years of ineffectiveness, was finally sold to the Seattle Pilots; Al Downing was traded to the Oakland A's for Danny Cater; and Joe Pepitone, a shadow of his potential self, was traded to Houston for Curt Blefary.

The Yankees made another break with their tradition by firing both Mel Allen and Red Barber, their famed announcers. Allen, hired by Larry Mac-Phail during World War II when both were stationed in Washington, D.C., had become a sports personality in his own right, a popular idol with an easy southern drawl who endeared himself to Yankee fans by becoming the most rabid Yankee fan of all. Allen, who became enthusiastic about a hard-hit ground ball, had indelibly nicknamed many of the Yankee ball players, including Old Reliable, the Yankee Clipper, the Springfield Rifle, and the Super-chief, and when he said, "Going, going, gone," he created an added feeling of excitement about a Yankee home run.

Over the years, though, Mel had become too independent for the Ballantine sponsors as he often rambled on the air about nonbaseball subjects and became more temperamental in his relations with the front office. Mel demanded special arrangements as he flew from one commitment to another, doing newsreels, sports specials, year in, year out, running, running, running, until he reached near-physical collapse on occasion. What further angered Yankee officials was that he would retire late at night and arise late in the morning, leaving a "Do Not Disturb" order with the switchboard of his hotel so that no one could ever reach him away from the ball park. At the end of 1964 Dan Topping and Ballantine public-relations man Ed Fisher decided that Allen should be eased out. For the 1964 world series, announcer Phil Rizzuto replaced Allen, a move that infuriated Allen to the extent that he went to the commissioner to demand a reinstatement. After the series Allen was dismissed, a grievous public-relations mistake considering Allen's unique contribution to the Yankee tradition. When Allen's traditional opening, his slightly slurred, southern-style, "Hello there, everybody," disappeared from the scene, so did many Yankee listeners. Additional Yankee listeners followed when Red Barber was fired. The Ole Redhead, soft-voiced, witty, and observant, also a southerner, was the first to call Yankee Stadium "the house that Ruth built." But Barber, too, had become too independent for management. During one home game during 1965 when the Yankees were sinking and there was an especially sparse crowd under leaden skies, Barber demanded that the camera-man pan to the rows and rows of empty seats. When Jack Murphy, the director, refused, Barber insisted that Yankee president Mike Burke be called. The answer back from Burke was, "Definitely not." And it was Mike Burke who informed Red on the final day of the 1965 season that he was fired. Phil Rizzuto, Jerry Coleman, and Joe Garagiola became the broadcast team, an excellent trio of professionals, but for many it just was not the same without Allen and Barber calling the game. Again the Yankee management was criti-cized for its callousness and its arrogance, and when the fans stopped listening, attendance began to fall, too, as many disgruntled and disillusioned Yankee supporters started rooting for the more human Mets.

By 1967 only a heroic, one-legged Mantle, a shadow of his former self, remained to symbolize the glory days. The Yankees were starting an infield of Mantle, Horace Clarke, Ruben Amaro, and Charlie Smith, with Steve Whittaker, an unhappy Joe Pepitone, and a crippled Tom Tresh in the outfield. Jake Gibbs caught, and on the mound were Stottlemyre, Downing, Fritz Peterson, Fred Talbot, and Steve Barber. Before thousands of empty seats these men finished ninth. The management began screaming that people were not coming to see the Yankees because the neighborhood was bad, when in fact it was the Yankees who were bad.

The dynasty was over, the tradition of success and greatness at an end. The million-dollar infield of the early sixties was gone, and the young, strong-armed pitchers were over the hill. The legend of Yankee invincibility had been cracked. Wrote Jerry Izenberg of the Long Island *Press:*

> *Where is the magic that was Mantle?*
> *Kubek to Moose, a double play.*
> *I don't recall growing older.*
> *When did they?*

A HEARTFELT ACKNOWLEDGMENT

When during the summer of 1971 I first approached Yankee publicist Marty Appel for assistance in researching a book on the Yankees, a book that had no format, no title, and no publisher, Marty promised me that if and when I found a publisher the voluminous files of newspaper clippings and publicity photos would be at my disposal. A year later, after I finally found a house willing to take a chance on a pushy, unpublished author, I called Marty once again and asked him if I could do a couple of weeks' research in his office.

Over a year later, I was still sitting in his office, painstakingly poring over thousands and thousands of newspaper clippings digested and sorted as a basis for the interviews in this book. Until I finally hit the road Marty and Bob Fishel, formerly the Yankee publicist and vice-president, and their secretary, Annie Mileo, the indispensable Annie, made me feel a part of the Yankee family during my stay. For their assistance, and especially for their kindness, I shall always be grateful. I tell them that without them this book could not have been written, and though they do not believe me, it is true. To Marty, Bob, and Annie, again I thank you.

There are a number of other Yankee employees who assisted me both in body and soul whom I feel I must acknowledge: Jo Anne Berry, Margaret Murphy, and Fred Bachman, Pearline Davis, Dave Weidler, Kathy Bennett, and Vince Natrella, Mike Burke, Howard Burke, and Gabe Paul. Also Vic Rallis, Tony Morante, Barbara Dresch, Barbara Quinn, Jeannie Collins, Mary Collins, Perry Green, Pat Kelly, and Mike Rendine.

There are over 300 hours of tape-recorded interviews sitting in my file drawers, the guts of this book, and in this space I wish to express my appreciation to those who gave their precious time to bare their souls and share their memories, the players interviewed within these covers, and in addition Bobby Brown, Andy Carey, Bob Cerv, Jerry Coleman, Joe Collins, Bud Daley, Joe DeMaestri, Art Ditmar, Al Downing, Billy Hunter, Billy Johnson, Charlie Keller, Jim Konstanty, Tony Kubek, John Kucks, Bob Kuzava, Don Larsen, John Lindell, Hector Lopez, Jerry Lumpe, Cliff Mapes, Tom Morgan, Irv Noren, Joe Page, Eddie Robinson, Bobby Shantz, Norm Siebern, Charlie Silvera, Bill Skowron, Enos Slaughter, Bill Stafford, Tommy Tresh, and Gene Woodling. Your anecdotes and memories were indispensable, and my gratitude to you is limitless, as it is to Larry MacPhail, Lee MacPhail, Mike Burke, the late Del Webb, Marse Joe McCarthy, Mrs. Red Rolfe, Mrs. Hazel Weiss, Betty King, Jack White, Jackie Farrell, Mayo Smith, Red Paterson, Ralph Houk, Frank Lane, John Drebinger, Ralph Hubbell, Roger Kahn, Bill Kane, Jimmy Conte, Luis Morales, Jimmy Esposito, Frankie Albano, Nick

Priori, Danny Coletta, and Bobby Napolitano. This chronicle is a compilation of your deeds and your memories. It is your story.

I would be remiss if I were not to thank the people at Prentice-Hall, particularly Nick D'Incecco and Dick Petrella, who saw something in me to push for the publication of this book, and Frank Coffey, an extraordinarily talented, patient, and understanding editor. And finally my thanks to the Sohn family, Viv, Leon, Nanalushka, and the boys for your hospitality, love, and companionship.

INDEX